D0214744

The Political Systems of Empires

S. N. Eisenstadt · THE

POLITICAL

SYSTEMS of

EMPIRES

The Free Press of Glencoe

COLLIER-MACMILLAN LTD., LONDON

Copyright © 1963 by The Free Press of Glencoe
A Division of The Macmillan Company

Printed in the United States of America

All rights in this book are reserved. No part of this book
may be used or reproduced in any manner whatsoever
without written permission except in the case of brief
quotations embodied in critical articles and reviews.

For information, address:
The Free Press of Glencoe
A Division of The Macmillan Company,
The Crowell-Collier Publishing Company
60 Fifth Avenue, New York 11

Library of Congress Catalog Card Number: 63-7656

Collier-Macmillan Canada, Ltd., Galt, Ontario

321.03
E36p

155630

To Martin Buber
and to the memory of
Richard Koebner

Mills College Library
Withdrawn

MILLS COLLEGE
LIBRARY

Preface

The material presented here is the first fruit of a work that has occupied my research interest since the period of my studies in sociology and history at the Hebrew University in the early 1940's, when I became fascinated by the problems and possibilities of applying sociological tools and concepts to the analysis of historical societies. I made some very tentative efforts, in a seminar essay on the "Sociological Bases of Absolutist States" and in my Master's thesis on the "Social Background of the Rise of the English Labour Party."

This interest has been continued, while I was engaged in other research projects and problems, through the courses and seminars on comparative sociological analysis of political systems that I conducted at the Hebrew University from 1948 to 1962.

During 1955–56, I was a Fellow at the Center for Advanced Studies in the Behavioral Sciences in California. That year was crucial in the development of this interest and in planning the present work. It was during my stay at the Center, and in my visits that year to Harvard, Michigan, Minnesota, Chicago, and Princeton, that I became convinced of the potential importance of such an approach; and it was there that the first outline of this book was drawn.

The purpose of this book is to apply sociological concepts to the analysis of historical societies, through the comparative analysis of a special type of political system. This analysis does not purport to be a historical analysis or description, that is to say, a description of the unfolding of a given society or polity in time, nor an application of sociological tools to the analysis of such a history of any single, concrete society. Its main objective is the comparative analysis of a certain common type of political system that can be found in different societies, and it seeks to find some patterns or laws in the structure and development of such political systems. Our analysis does not focus on the description and analysis of the total social systems; it is mainly concerned with those aspects which are relevant for the analysis of this specific type of political system. It may, perhaps, disappoint the historian, whose major interest is the description of the emergence and development of a concrete historical entity; but I hope that he may find here some hypotheses worth exploring independently, and some evidence of the utility both of the explication of various assumptions about social and political systems found in any historical work and of comparative analysis. On the other hand, I hope that this work may show sociologists and political scientists some of the possibilities for sociological analysis inherent in comparative studies, based on historical materials.

Any such comparative work poses a series of problems. The first is due to the fact that no single worker can master all the primary sources of all the societies on which the comparative analysis must be based. Hence, he must rely largely on secondary sources. He must be fully acquainted with historical research in these fields and know the different controversies among historians, so that he can evaluate them, can beware of too facile use of any data or view, and can explore the extent to which such data can be analyzed according to the problems he analyzes and the categories he uses.

There are also several difficult problems of presentation. The author is torn between the desire to give as full an exposition of the gathered material as possible and the awareness not only that such an exposition can but rarely be an original contribution to the analysis of any society but also that too lengthy and detailed an exposition may prove a burden on the reader. Thus, the necessity always arises for making some type of condensed presentation.

In writing this book, I have taken into account some of the criticisms made of the mode of presentation I used in my former book dealing with comparative analysis, *From Generation to Generation* (Free Press, 1956). Accordingly, I have inserted the analyses of several case studies, chosen carefully according to some explicit criteria of central importance to our argument, throughout the various chapters of the book. All the data from other societies that were analyzed here have been condensed and are presented in the tables. Such tabular presentation necessarily entails many difficulties. Many think that a table cannot do justice to the variety and complexity of the historical reality it represents. It seems to me, however, that when a table is carefully used—when the criteria are carefully established and applied to well-defined and limited phenomena and when the table obviously does not serve for complicated mathematical manipulations—it may be a very good way of presenting varied and numerous materials. Tabular presentation may well serve to bring some order into what might otherwise easily become an impressionistic evaluation.

An additional aspect of the problem of presentation is, in a way, a great disappointment to the author—namely, the necessity, imposed by space and continuity of argument, to omit many of the materials gathered for this work. Among these necessary omissions, I should mention those related to the analysis of bureaucracy itself. It was impossible to include a systematic analysis of the structural aspects of bureaucracy—the internal division of labor, patterns of decision-making, and administrative behavior that develop within it. To keep the thread of the analysis and argument intact, we had to limit the presentation to the analysis of the political orientations and activities of the bureaucracy.

Finally, the analysis here includes several societies (the Ahmenid, the Carolingian, the Mongol Empire, feudal Europe, and the Greek city-states) that, because they shared some, but only some, characteristics of the bureaucratic societies, served as control groups with regard to the hypothesis about the conditions of institutionalization of the political systems of the historical bureaucratic societies. When materials were available, most societies of the latter type were included in our analysis. Some cases—for example, the Southeast Asian states and the Aztecs, and some of the Arabic and Islamic states—were necessarily excluded because of the paucity and inadequacy of the available materials or because it seemed that the particular "cultural" type had already been represented. It is quite possible, of course, that several omissions have nevertheless been made inadvertently. I would be grateful to have these pointed out to me, and grateful if the analysis attempted here is applied to other societies.

In the course of preparing this work, I have become indebted to people and institutions who have helped me in a variety of ways. My primary debt—and one that can never be fully expressed—is to my teachers who inspired me to explore the possibilities of applying sociological analysis to historical phenomena: I have dedicated this book to Professor Martin Buber and the late Professor Richard Koebner, but this is an inadequate expression of my gratitude and indebtedness to them.

Much of this work—as of all my work—owes a great deal to Professor Edward Shils, whose help, encouragement, and guidance have been invaluable during the fifteen years we have been acquainted.

Another great debt is the one to my students, who have participated in my courses and seminars on this subject at the Hebrew University and have helped me with their suggestions and criticisms.

I have already mentioned the Center for Advanced Study in the Behavioral Sciences as the place where my ideas for this book first took shape. I owe much to the inspiring and relaxed atmosphere of the Center, created there under the guidance of its Director, Dr. Ralph Tyler, and his staff, headed by Preston Cutler and Jane Kielsmeier. Anyone who has been privileged to spend a year at the Center knows that a year's stay there is a unique experience in the rather crowded contemporary academic life. There, during my discussions with several colleagues, many problems of comparative sociological studies were thrashed out. I should like to mention especially D. Aberle (Brandeis), R. Bauer (Harvard), U. Bronfenbrenner (Cornell), J. S. Coleman (Johns Hopkins), R. Dahl (Yale), H. Goldhamer (The RAND Corporation), B. F. Hoselitz (Chicago), A. Inkeles (Harvard), M. A. Kaplan (Chicago), J. March (Carnegie Institute of Technology), K. Knorr (Princeton), S. M. Lipset (Berkeley), D. R. Miller (Michigan), and D. M. Schneider (Chicago). My conversations with them and others stimulated me to outline some of the basic problems of this book. Also, the generous help of the Center enabled me to gather many materials vital for the continuation of this work.

The research on which this volume is based has been greatly facilitated by research assistance provided by the Eliezer Kaplan School of Economics and Social Sciences, the Hebrew University; by a free "grant-in-aid" made by the Behavioral Sciences Division of the Ford Foundation; and by two research grants from the Committee on Comparative Politics of the Social Science Research Council, under the chairmanship of Professor Gabriel Almond.

My sincere gratitude goes to my colleagues at the Hebrew University—Dr. J. Arieli, Dr. J. Ben-David, Professor J. Katz, and Mr. D. Weintraub—and to Professors Alex Inkeles and Talcott Parsons of Harvard, who have carefully read one or more drafts of the manuscript and have made detailed comments which have been invaluable in revising it.

I would like to thank especially Professor M. A. Kaplan of the University of Chicago. He helped me, at a very crucial stage in the preparation and revision of the manuscript, by reading it thoroughly and making valuable comments and criticisms.

I would also like to thank the following, who have read parts or the whole of the manuscript and have commented on it in its various stages: Professors R. Aron, B. Barber, P. M. Blau, W. Eberhard, J. K. Fairbank, C. Friedrich, B. F. Hoselitz, Dr. Y. Garber-Talmon, M. Gluckman, L. Guttman, M. Janowitz, J. G. March, J. J. Spengler, and S. Thrupp.

The following have also helped me with problems relating to different historical materials: Professor J. Prawer, on Byzantine history; Professors W. Eberhard, A. Wright, E. Balázs, and Dr. D. Twitchett, on Chinese history; and Professor W. Boorah, on Spanish-American history.

I would also like to express my sincere gratitude to those who have helped in gathering and preparing the materials on which the analysis is based—especially to Mr. O. Shapiro, who prepared the material on England; Mrs. R. Bar-Yossef, who prepared the material on T'ang China; Dr. Z. Schiffrin who prepared the tabulation of the Chinese materials; and Mrs. J. Miller, who prepared the material on France. I would like to thank especially Mr. Eric Cohen, who organized and supervised the preparation and analysis of the historical materials presented in the tables, himself analyzed the materials on Indian Empires, and worked most assiduously on the preparation and organization of the tables, and also made valuable comments on themes; Mr. S. Deshen, who worked on Islamic societies, and helped greatly in the preparation of the tables in general and was instrumental in the preparation of the bibliography; Miss Z. Stoup, who worked on Byzantine and European societies; Mrs. Y. Levi, who worked on Russia; Mr. U. Rappaport, who worked on the Roman and Hellenistic empires; and Mrs. H. Adoni, Mrs. R. Shaco, and Miss Z. Cohen, who helped in this work. I wish to thank Mrs. Z. Porat and Mrs. M. Magen for their help in polishing the English and especially Miss S. B. Abelson for her wonderful editorial work on the book, Mrs. H. Bursztyn for typing the manuscript, and my secretary, Miss Z. Tam, for her invaluable help throughout this project, and to Mrs. K. Purcell, Miss M. Mandel, and the staff of The Free Press for preparing the book for print. For help in reading the proofs I would like to thank Mrs. R. Shaco, Mrs. C. Harkness, and Miss E. Heed.

I have also been greatly helped by several libraries—namely, the National and University Library in Jerusalem; the University libraries at Stanford, Berkeley, and Harvard; and the British Library of Economics and Political Science, at the London School of Economics, where I stayed as a Visiting Member in the summer of 1958 and where I was able to gather important materials for this work.

I have also lectured on some of the topics of this book at the Universities of Chicago, Harvard, Michigan, Oslo, and Copenhagen, and at the Christian Michelsen Institute at Bergen. I have profited from the discussions at these places.

I would like also to thank Professor B. Lewis and the editors of *Studia Islamica* for permission to quote from his article "Some Reflections on the Decline of the Ottoman Empire," Vol. IX, 1958.

S. N. EISENSTADT

The Eliezer Kaplan School of Economics and Social Sciences
The Hebrew University of Jerusalem

Contents

TWO

*Conditions of Perpetuation of the
Political Systems of the Historical
Bureaucratic Empires*

10] The Place of the Bureaucracy in the Political Process   273

ONE

Conditions of Development

of the Political Systems of the

Historical Bureaucratic Empires

1

The Historical Bureaucratic Polities

The Setting and the Problem

[1] *Introduction*

This book is devoted to a sociological analysis of the political systems of the historical bureaucratic empires. It attempts to describe the nature of the basic characteristics of these systems, and to analyze the social conditions under which these characteristics develop and function and the social and political processes conducive to their maintenance and continuity or causing their change.

This analysis is based on two closely connected assumptions. One is that the political system is a basic part of any society's organization, and an examination of its place within the social structure and its relation to other parts of this structure is the most profitable method of analyzing its functioning. The second assumption is that different types of political systems develop and function under specific social conditions, and the continuity of any political system is also related to such specific conditions. On the basis of these assumptions, we shall attempt to analyze the political systems of the historical bureaucratic polities.

Historically, these empires represent stages in the development of the most important civilizations of mankind. They have developed in the Near Eastern civilizations; in Egypt; in the ancient American civilization (among the Incas and Aztecs); in the Hellenistic, Roman, and Byzantine worlds, in Persia and India; among the most important Far Eastern civilizations, especially in China and India; in the Moslem world, as in the Abbaside, Fatimite, and Ottoman empires; and in modern Europe, in the Age of Absolutism.

At one stage or another in each of these civilizations, political systems and organizations have developed that belong, as we shall see, to the broad type designated as "historical" (i.e., non-modern) centralized bureaucratic empires or polities.

Each of these empires or polities has played a great and important role in the history and culture of mankind, and has left its imprint on many cultural traditions and on many aspects of modern society and civilization. In many ways, it is impossible to understand the features and problems of the modern political system without analyzing their historical derivation from these empires.

These political systems are also of great importance from the comparative, or typological, point of view. Historically and analytically, they stand between what may be called the "traditional" and the "modern" political systems and regimes.

Most of these empires were ruled and governed by monarchs with claims to traditional-sacred legitimacy. Similarly, they closely resembled more traditional political systems in the relatively great political passivity of the many parts of the population and in the lack of any general franchise and political rights. On the other hand, within them several basic characteristics developed that were akin to some characteristics of modern polities. Among these, the most important were a relatively unified centralized polity; organs of bureaucratic administration and of political struggle; and a relatively intensive political struggle connected with attempts by those who participated actively in this struggle —the rulers and various active elites—to mobilize the political support of many groups in the society.

Thus these political systems combined, in varying degrees, elements both of the less developed, traditional, and of the more developed, differentiated, political systems; and within them, political problems characteristic of both these types arose. Moreover, they had to combine, within the framework of a single political organization, these different elements. In this, some of their problems may be akin, to some degree, to those of various "new states" now undergoing processes of modernization.

Hence the analysis of these historical political systems is interesting in many ways: for understanding the dynamics of complex political systems and the processes of modernizing such systems, and as previewing modern political systems.

[2] *Some Basic Characteristics of Political Systems*

Let us briefly examine the assumptions stated above.

Recent developments in sociological, anthropological, and political science literature make it possible now to present a common preliminary approach to the *sociological* analysis of political systems—even though many analytical problems in this area need further clarification ([A]* *Almond, 1960; Apter, 1958; Beer, 1958; Easton, 1957, 1959; Eisenstadt, 1954, 1959; M. Levy, 1952; Parsons, 1960; Parsons and Smelser, 1956; Roberts and Almond, 1957; Sutton, 1955*).

We shall not enter into a detailed examination of the differences· among the sociological, anthropological, and political approaches and all their analytical implications. At this point, it is sufficient to list those attributes which are more or less accepted as the basic characteristic of the political system.

These attributes are as follows:

1. The political system is the organization of a territorial society having the legitimate monopoly over the authorized use and regulation of force in the society

2. It has defined responsibilities for maintaining the system of which it is a part

3. Therefore, its organization imposes severe secular sanctions in order to implement the society's main collective goals, maintain its internal order, and regulate its foreign relations (*adapted from* [A] *Apter, 1958*). All social roles or groups fulfilling these distinct functions in a society, regardless of what other tasks they may perform, constitute the society's political system

This definition presupposes that every society necessarily features a political system—i.e., that no society exists that implements its collective goals and maintains internal and external order, without having a legitimate pattern of interaction by means of which these goals are implemented or this order is maintained. Specific political roles, as such, may, in some societies, not be clearly distinguishable. But to deny their existence would be to argue that the fulfilment of political functions is random. Accordingly:

---

* Capital letters in brackets refer to the various sections of the Bibliography at the end of this book.

Intermittent action on the part of the oldest male of a band, in response to specific situations, or informally formulated consensus on the part of a group dealing with some serious threat to internal order, or some problem of foreign relations, implies a special type of political structure, not its absence ([A] *Roberts and Almond, 1957*).

In other words, it is now usually accepted that the traditional distinction between primitive societies constituting states and those not constituting a state (the so-called "segmentary" tribes) should be reformulated as a distinction based on the extent to which the several political activities and organizations in these societies can be discerned and differentiated ([A] *Eisenstadt, 1959*).

This analysis of the major characteristics of all political systems enables us to understand the basic types of activity within them. It indicates that the major types of political activities existing in every political system are as follows (*adapted, with modifications, from* [A] *Roberts and Almond, 1957*):

1. The "legislative decision-making" or the "ultimate ruling" activity, i.e., the determination of the society's primary goals and formulation of general rules for maintaining (or changing) the existing order in the society

2. The administrative activity, dealing with the execution of these basic rules in different social spheres and with the organization of technical activities necessary for their efficient execution. The main purpose of the administrative activity is to provide various services to various groups in the society, and to regulate and assure the provision of resources to the political system (e.g., revenue) by different strata and groups

3. "Party-political" activity—i.e., activity mobilizing support for different political measures and rules, and for the holders of different political positions

4. The juridical activity, concerned with testing and authorizing the validity of applying the basic rules to particular, concrete cases arising in the society

In discussing the main types of political activity, we must distinguish between the parts played by the "rulers" and the "ruled." The rulers are those who play the active part in the political process, i.e., those who define the goals, formulate and execute the rules, adjudicate, and contend for political support. The ruled are those who are subject to the rules, who demand adjudications, and who wish to influence the legislators. In many societies, the same person may be a "ruler" at one time or in one respect, and "ruled" another time and in another respect, and the rulers may be also subject to the different rules promulgated by themselves; however, the broad distinction between rulers and ruled is inherent in the very nature of political activity.

[3] *The Relations between the Political System and the Other Institutions in Society*

These different types of political activities are analytically distinct, but they necessarily supplement each other. The continuous interaction between them constitutes the political process in a society. True, the degree to which each of these types of political activity is differentiated varies greatly from one society to another and constitutes, as we shall see, an important problem for comparative study. But all are inherent in any political system, and they indicate and specify the nature of the interrelations between the political institutions and other parts of the institutional structure of a given society. They point out the kinds of inputs (i.e., the types of support and resources) the political system needs in order to fulfil its functions, and the nature of the system's major contributions or outputs to the society as a whole.

What, briefly, are these interrelations between the political and other institutions in the society? (*On input-output analysis in sociology, see* [A] *Easton, 1957; Parsons, 1960; Parsons and Smelser, 1956.*)

The polity's specific output to other institutional spheres consists of various authoritative decisions concerning the following:

1. Definition of the major collective goals that can be implemented, and determination of their order of priority

2. Allocation of prestige, influence, and authorized use of power and facilities to various groups in the society

3. Distribution of various facilities, benefits, and rights to such groups and individuals

Through these decisions, the political institutions can perform their major functions in the society—to articulate their specific characteristics in relation to other parts of the society. However, these activities cannot, of course, be performed without help from other social spheres and institutions—from those very spheres toward which its decisions are oriented.

The polity is dependent on other institutional spheres for the continuous inflow of resources, services, and support needed for implementation of the various collective goals, for maintenance of the polity's position in the society, and for fulfilment of its regulative and integrative functions. From the economic sphere, the polity must receive various manpower, labor, material, and monetary resources. It depends on the cultural institutions for basic support of the regime, identification with its symbols, the legitimation of the rulers, and motivation for the performance of political roles. The sphere of social stratification and organization provide it with necessary support of different policies, and the ability and willingness of different groups and people to engage in various political activities.

However, the interactions between the polity and other institutional systems of the society are not limited to the mutual contributions just outlined. These *contributions* are articulated through the *demands* that the political institutions make on different groups and strata in the society, and through the transmission of political decisions from the rulers to the ruled.

The amount or extent of the resources and support available to the polity is never given or fixed; those in political roles must always make *continuous* demands on other institutional spheres for them. These demands are, of course, closely connected with and largely contingent on the demands made on the polity, by these different groups, to implement various types of decisions. Like the resources accruing to the polity, the decisions of the polity are neither given nor fixed. The demands of the various groups are transmitted to the polity through the political orientations and activities of these groups—mainly, through the articulation of their interests in political terms and the aggregation of these interests in frameworks of some political organizations. This continuous interaction between the polity and other institutional spheres, in terms of their specific contributions and demands, constitutes the dynamics of political process in any society.

[4] *Major Criteria for Comparative Analysis of Political Systems*

In the preceding section, we outlined various characteristics of the political system and process that are common to all political systems. They indicate the basic characteristics or elements of *any* political system. However, our main interest is one particular type of political system. It is, therefore, important to see in what ways, and according to what criteria, different types of political systems can be construed.

We feel that such criteria can be construed on the basis of the above considerations concerning the place of the political system in the social structure and the major interrelations between the polity and other subsystems or spheres of the society. The following seem to be main areas, or criteria, of comparison between political systems or of construction of different types of such systems. (*For some approaches to comparative analysis, see* [A] *Almond, 1960; Apter, 1958; Easton, 1957; Eisenstadt, 1954, 1959; M. Levy, 1952, ch. x.*)

1. The first area of comparison is the extent to which the major political activities are organized in special roles and differentiated both

from other roles and/or groups in the society, and from each other.

2. Closely related is the extent to which the different political activities are organized in specific collectivities or groups, or, conversely, the extent to which they are embedded in other (especially ascriptive, kinship, territorial, and status) collectivities. Thus, we may ask, about any society, whether it features special organization of the legislative, administrative, juridical, and party political activities.

3. Another area of comparison refers to the goals of the polity, for whose implementation the rulers use their power monopoly and the resources available to them. These goals may be classified according to: (a) their content, which we may at this stage of our discussion broadly distinguish according to the main institutional sphere—e.g., cultural, economic, political (expansion)—that they represent; (b) the extent to which they are considered as the goals of any other group or institutional sphere in the society (e.g., kinship, territorial, or economic groups, or religious institution) and the extent to which they are determined by such groups, or, conversely, the extent to which they are defined and implemented as autonomous goals specific to the political sphere; (c) the criteria governing the definition of these goals, especially the extent to which they are determined by political or non-political values, interests, and orientations; and (d) in so far as these goals are considered distinctly political, the extent to which members of different groups in the society may participate in or compete over their definition.

4. The final area of comparison is the type of legitimation sanctioning a given political system and its rulers. By "legitimacy," we mean the appraisal of the rulers and their activities in terms of some common values of the society and the designation of the proper rulers ([A] *Parsons, 1960*). Such appraisal can be made on a variety of grounds, according to different values or orientations. We shall not now undertake a detailed analysis of the different possible types of legitimation; we will mention here only the distinction between traditional, charismatic, and legal-rational legitimacy proposed by Max Weber ([A] *Weber, 1920–21, pp. 122–76, 642–49;* [A] *Parsons, 1960*). Later, we shall see how adequate this typology is for our purposes.

Every system of legitimation includes some patterns of accountability of the rulers, e.g., "reference groups" for decision-makers, sufficiently significant that they will make decisions with such groups in mind. Such groups will either modify decisions of the government or refuse formal approval before a final decision is made ([A] *M. Levy, 1952, ch. x; Apter, 1958*). Of course, in different societies the nature of such groups, and their power and the extent of the articulation of their demands for consent, are different.

We believe that the variables just discussed are the most important for the comparative analysis of political systems. Obviously, each can be elaborated to different degrees of detail, according to the requirements of each specific analysis and problem. But it seems—at least at this stage of our analysis—that when the variables are taken together, they constitute an adequate framework for a preliminary systematic approach to the comparative analysis of political systems. These variables refer to the extent of articulation of the polity as a subsystem of the society, the main direction of its political activities, and its main points of interdependence with other institutional spheres. They thus make explicit the main problems confronting one who tries to examine the political system as a subsystem of society.

These variables are closely interconnected. At the same time, however, each can vary somewhat, independent of the others. Nevertheless, they do not vary entirely at random; and the degrees of their respective variations are related in different degrees. Accordingly, one primary task of a comparative analysis is to investigate the extent of their independence and interdependence, or the extent to which they can vary independently of one another.

[5] Principal Types of Political Systems. The Major Instances of Historical Bureaucratic Empires

Theoretically, the possible interrelations between these variables are manifold; however, several major types stand out in the history of the development of human society. Most of these types have not as yet been subjected to a systematic sociological or political analysis, and their classification has hitherto been largely descriptive. Even so, they represent the most common forms of political systems encountered in the history of human societies. These main types are as follows:

1. Primitive political systems

2. Patrimonial empires (e.g., the Carolingian and the Ahmenid or Parthian empires)

3. Nomad or conquest empires (e.g., those of the Mongols, and the Arab kingdom under the first caliphs)

4. City-states (e.g., ancient Athens, Republican Rome)

5. Feudal systems (as in Europe, Japan, the Middle East, and possibly also in other places)

6. Centralized historical bureaucratic empires, or, in short, historical bureaucratic societies

7. Modern societies of various types (democratic, autocratic, totalitarian, "underdeveloped")

The list is necessarily provisory and far from exhaustive. Moreover, each of these types of political system can be divided into several distinct subsystems; and probably there are many marginal and overlapping cases. As we have said, this classification is mainly descriptive, even though each of the listed types may be distinguished by some specific characterization according to our comparative criteria. Only further analysis will show the extent to which each historical type is analytically distinct, or the extent to which different types of political systems cutting across those listed would have to be distinguished.

As stated, this work will be concerned with one major type of political system, namely, with the centralized historical bureaucratic empires or states. The most important examples of these are the following:*

1. The ancient empires—especially the Egyptian, Babylonian, and, possibly, the Inca and Aztec as well

2. The Chinese Empire, from the Han period to the Ch'ing

3. The various Persian empires, especially the Sassanid, and, to a lesser extent, the Parthian and Ahmenid

4. The Roman and the Hellenistic empires

5. The Byzantine Empire

6. Several ancient Hindu states, especially Gupta, Maurya, and the Mogul Empire

7. The Arab Caliphate, especially from the reign of the Abbasides and Fatimites, the Arab Moslem states in the Mediterranean, Iran, and finally the Ottoman Empire

8. The West, Central, and East European states, from the fall of the feudal systems through the Age of Absolutism

9. Conquest empires (i.e., the various political systems established in non-European countries as a result of European expansion, colonization, and conquest—especially the Spanish-American and French empires, and the British colonial empire in India)

The majority of historical centralized bureaucratic systems developed from (1) patrimonial empires, like Egypt or the Sassanid Empire; (2) dualistic nomad-sedentary empires (necessarily sharing many characteristics in common with the patrimonial ones); (3) feudal societies, like the European, probably the Chinese, and, to some extent, the Japanese; or (4) city-states (the Roman and Hellenistic empires). Known instances of bureaucratic systems developing directly from primitive polities are rare. Perhaps only the ancient Inca and Aztec empires, and, to a smaller extent, the ancient Egyptian empire, have developed thus.

---

* Bibliographic information is supplied about all these societies both in the following chapters and in the Bibliography. Full descriptions of their historical emergence are also indicated.

Are we justified in grouping these various historically and geographically separate and distinct, societies under one heading, and claiming that they constitute or belong to one type? Obviously, many differences must exist between these different societies—differences in historical and geographical backgrounds and in cultural traditions. And yet, from the point of view of comparative sociological analysis, they seem to belong to one type evincing some basic common characteristics. These common characteristics do not, of course, eliminate the cultural and historical differences between them—but at least some of these differences can most profitably be regarded as variations of these common qualities, or as factors which influence such variations; and they can be most fruitfully analyzed as such.

It is, obviously, not enough to claim the existence of one common type encompassing so many distinct societies. To some extent, this whole work will continuously have to substantiate this claim. At this stage of our analysis, we must confine ourselves to a rather formal and descriptive listing of the major characteristics. On the basis of this listing, we shall try to point out the main problems in the sociological analysis of these political systems. In order to be able to understand the major characteristics of these political systems, we shall start with a brief description of the patterns of their development.

2

The Fundamental Characteristics

of the Political Systems and the Social Conditions

of Their Development ⸻ Basic Hypotheses

[1] *The Patterns of Development of Centralized Polities*

Despite the great variety of the historical and cultural settings of these polities, they had some common features in the patterns of their establishment. The initiative for establishing these polities came, in all cases, from the rulers—emperors, kings, or some members of a patrician ruling elite (e.g., the more active and dynamic element of the patrician elite in Republican Rome). In most cases, these rulers were either from established patrician, patrimonial, tribal, or feudal families, or usurpers from lower-class families, who attempted to establish new dynasties or to conquer new territories. Sometimes, they were conquerors, attempting to subdue and establish rule over various territories.

Usually, such a ruler arose during a period of unrest, turmoil, or dissolution of the existing political system (whether a patrician city-state, a tribe, a patrimonial empire, or a feudal system) or of acute strife within it. Usually, his objective was to re-establish peace and order. Such a ruler did not, however, attempt to restore the old order *in toto*—although, for propagandist and opportunistic reasons, he would sometimes uphold the restoration of, e.g., a political ideology or slogan. He always had some vision of distinctly political goals of a unified polity. He aimed to establish a more centralized, unified polity, in which he could monopolize political decisions and the setting of political goals, without being bound by various traditional aristocratic, tribal, or patrician groups. Even when these rulers were conquerors—as in the cases of the Roman, Islamic, and Spanish-American empires—they also had such a vision and attempted to transmit it to at least parts of the conquered populations.*

Their aims were very often oriented against, and opposed by, various social and political groups. However great the turmoil, unrest, and internal strife may have been in the previous political regime, there have always been some groups that either had benefited from it, or had hoped to do so, or planned to re-establish the old order in which they had held positions of power and influence. These groups—generally consisting of some aristocratic groups, patrician, or some more traditional urban groups, and traditional cultural elites—usually felt menaced by the new objectives and activities of the ruler. In many cases, they considered the ruler as a renegade, upstart, or barbarian. But, beyond these purely "social" reasons, they felt that their positions were threatened by the trend to political centralization; and they were not willing to help to implement this trend. Therefore, they frequently attempted to deny the rulers resources and support, and plotted and worked against them either in open political warfare or by sleight of hand, infiltration, and intrigues.†

The rulers had to find allies, whether passive or active, who could enable them to achieve their goals in spite of these various aristocratic or patrician forces. They had to forge various instruments of power and policy with which to mobilize the various resources they needed —whether economic resources, manpower, or political support. They naturally tried to find their allies among the groups and strata whose interests were opposed to those of the more traditional and aristocratic groups, and who could benefit from their weakening and from the establishment of a more unified polity. These potential allies were,

* On the historical circumstance of the development of these empires, see the Bibliography.
† Full description of the oppositions to the attempts of these rulers can be found in the historical works cited in the relevant section of the Bibliography.

basically, of two kinds. Some were from the more active (mostly urban) economic, cultural, and professional groups, who, by origin and/or by their social interests and orientations, were opposed to the aristocratic-traditional groups. The second kind were from the wider, politically and socially more passive strata—especially peasants, and, to a smaller extent, some lower urban groups who could benefit, even if indirectly, from the weakening of the aristocratic forces and from the rulers' establishment of peace and order.

In order to utilize these potential allies to mobilize necessary resources and to implement their policies, the rulers had to forge some reliable instruments of political and administrative action that they could use to provide various services to the strata from which they got their potential allies or supporters.

[2] *The Political Activities Undertaken by the Rulers to Insure the Development of Centralized Polities*

Usually the rulers could draw on some existing administrative and political organs and personnel which, at least during the preliminary stages, would serve in organizing the necessary political and administrative activities. But even in such a case, the rulers had to alter the personnel and organs of administration to adapt them to their own purposes.*

When the existing personnel were related to the aristocratic forces, the ruler often had to change the personnel in so far as they were so related. But changes of personnel were not enough. He had to assure the new personnel's remaining faithful to him and dependent on him, and that they would not be "reconquered" by the opposing forces.

Moreover, the rulers had to make sure that the administrative organs and personnel were so organized that they could perform various functions both for them and for their supporters among the major strata in the society. Hence, they would always try to reorganize them in several directions which would insure their ability to perform the tasks for which they were created and their loyalty to the rulers. To this end, the rulers attempted to monopolize the making of nominations to these positions, and tried so far as possible to appoint persons loyal to them and having the necessary qualifications for the execution of their tasks; and the rulers would always stress the point that these

---

* The ways in which administrations have been changed or shaped by the rulers are described in basic historical works on these societies, especially those cited in the relevant section of the Bibliography.

officials were either their personal servants or the servants of the polity that they wanted to establish, but were not representatives of any groups or strata in the society. The rulers would try to control the budget of these organs and to have enough resources at their disposal to enable them to provide for the necessary expenses and to pay the officials' salaries—thus emphasizing again their dependence on the rulers.

Such rulers attempted to make these organs as independent as possible of the more traditional and aristocratic strata and groups, and to give them some power and prestige vis-à-vis these strata. Here the rulers had necessarily to allow them some measure of autonomy and independence. This tendency toward their having a degree of autonomy was enhanced as the scope of their activities grew and as the execution of these activities became more dependent on experience and "know-how." (The administration's tendency to autonomy and some service orientation is documented in most of the historical literature. *For general treatment, see* [A] *Borch, 1954;* [A] *Weber, 1922;* [X] *Hintze, 1907.*)

Of course, in many cases the rulers wanted to use these organs only, or mainly, for the purpose of exploiting the population and its resources. But, even in a conquest empire, if the ruler wanted to perpetuate his rule, he had to allow these services to take into account some needs of some of the social groups—even if only to provide them with peace, security, and some basic services. This can best be shown by a brief analysis of the chief patterns of activities of these administrations. (The structures of the major administrations considered here are described in detail in the relevant works cited in the Bibliography. The particularly important ones are as follows: *for Egypt,* [F] *Kees, 1933[a], 1933[b]; Drioton and Vandier, 1952. For Sassanid Persia,* [G] *Christensen, 1936, 1939; Altheim and Stiehl, 1954. For the Roman Empire,* [Q] *Burn, 1952; Boak, 1955[a], ch. xix, xxiii, and chapter bibliographies. For the Byzantine Empire,* [L] *Bréhier, 1949[b]; Diehl, 1927; Stein, 1954. For China,* [I] *Des Rotours, 1932, 1947–48; Y. C. Wang, 1949; Hucker, 1950; Kracke, 1953. For the Spanish-American Empire,* [R] *Haring, 1947; Gongora, 1951; Fisher, 1926, 1936. For European countries in general,* [S] *Beloff, 1954; Lindsay, 1957[a];* [Y] *Zeller, 1948; and* [X] *Rosenberg, 1958. For additional data, see ch. 6.*)

[3] *The Development and Structure of Administrative Organs*

In the administration of the societies we shall study here, several types of what we may call "departments" or "groupings" of specialized activities tended to evolve. In general, these were concerned mainly with four major kinds of activities: financial, political and military, administrative, and internal-supervisory.

The treasury or financial organization was always a central department. It mobilized, primarily through taxation, the financial resources necessary for the government, and distributed them to other departments. Other departments, closely connected with the financial organization, dealt with what may be termed the various technical and regulatory aspects of public and economic life—e.g., the maintenance of the irrigation systems in Ancient Egypt, China, and some of the Central American empires, the regulation of the economic activities of manual workers, merchants, etc.; and the maintenance of services for the adequate supply of food, especially in the cities. The departments concerned with communication and postal services, and those dealing with maintaining peace and order in the society, were also of special importance. There were, too, special administrative organs concerned with (to use a broad term) cultural and educational matters. The latter were often closely connected with police activities.

Activities or departments existed which were concerned with drafting laws and organizing supervision of the judiciary, or with administrating jural activities. There were departments dealing mainly with the "external political" problem—i.e., with military and diplomatic affairs.

In most of these administrations, activities and departments developed to cope with the internal problems of the bureaucracy itself. These included departments devoted to supervising other departments and, especially, the provincial governors; and departments or activities for the selection, training, and advancement of persons for posts within the framework of bureaucratic administration. In some societies—especially in China and, to a smaller extent, in the Ottoman Empire—there were special agencies engaged with these problems. However, these special agencies did not exist in many societies, where these problems were solved by various rule-of-thumb methods, traditions, personal relations, and different exigencies of political pressures.

Finally, there were different archives where the "collective memory" of the administration was stored.

[4] *The Development of a Structure of Organs of Political Struggle*

The preceding discussion indicates some of the basic problems which developed in the relations of the rulers to these administrative organs.

From the outset of his rule, such a ruler was torn between his wish to use these organs for his own (mostly exploitative) purposes and the necessity of using them to provide for various needs and demands of the active social groups. He was also torn between the necessity of granting these organs some measure of autonomy and independence, a necessity which became inevitable in almost every case, while still protecting them from the various aristocratic and traditional strata and maintaining his own control over them.

This kind of ruler faced rather similar problems with regard to his various councils and representative institutions serving as organs of political struggle. He would attempt to wrest the monopoly of their memberships from traditional and/or aristocratic groups, to make membership in them contingent on his own will or to vest it in politically more "reliable" groups, and to make these organs into avenues in which he could utilize conflicting interests for his own benefit. However, he could do so only if he allowed some measure of autonomy to these organs and permitted some free political struggle within them—even while attempting to control them and those who participated in them.

Accordingly, in most of these countries, the various organs and channels of political struggle—be they court cliques, royal councils, or representative institutions—developed several distinct patterns of activities, although the degree of their institutionalization varied greatly from society to society. The most important of these activities were: regulating conflicts among the various groups, and between them and the ruler on the question of their place and influence in the councils; attempting to influence the ruler's political decisions, through bargaining with him and/or by controlling him through potential allocation of resources to him or through monopolizing central political and administrative positions; and trying to establish various legal rights of the groups vis-à-vis the ruler.

[5] *The Major Characteristics of the Political Systems.*
The Development of Autonomous Goals

It was out of the interaction between these different forces—the rulers, the major social groups, and the political and administrative organs—that the major characteristics of these parties tended to develop.

What, then, are the basic characteristics of the political systems of the historical bureaucratic empires?

The major feature of centralized bureaucratic polities is the *limited autonomy* of the political sphere. This is manifested by:

1. The development of autonomous political goals by the rulers and, to some extent, by those who participate in the political struggle

2. The development of a limited differentiation of political activities and roles

3. Attempts to organize the political community into a centralized unit

4. The development of specific organizations of administration and political struggle

The first major characteristic of the historical bureaucratic polities was the development of specifically political goals, both by the rulers and by some of the groups participating in the political struggle—and especially by the former. Those who implemented these goals—i.e., mainly the rulers—perceived them as different from other types of goals or from goals of other (than the political) spheres or groups of the society. Their formulation, pursuit, and implementation became largely independent of other groups, and were governed mostly by political criteria and by considerations of political exigency, even though they were necessarily influenced by the value-orientations and interests of the rulers and of other groups in the society. In other words, the rulers of these societies favored the development of a certain level of generalized power—i.e., of power not embedded in the structure of ascriptive groups, and usable, in a generalized way, to implement different goals.

The autonomy of political goals and their specifically political implementation was limited by several factors, however. The most important was the pattern of legitimation and accountability of the rulers.

The legitimation of the rulers in historical bureaucratic societies was mainly religio-traditional; and the criteria governing their appraisal usually combined political and religious values and orientations. The designated rulers of these societies were either members of hereditary traditional groups, or charismatic persons embodying the society's *"sacred" values* and symbols and expected to establish new hereditary dynasties.

At the same time, however, several *secondary* patterns of legitimation evolved in these societies, chiefly in respect to the administrative bodies. The criteria for judging these bodies were more legal-rational than traditional, focusing mainly on their efficiency and adherence to fixed rules. However, these legal-rational patterns of legitimation were greatly limited by the preponderance of the traditional legitimation of the rulers.

In close relation to the patterns of legitimation in these societies, a relatively complex pattern of the rulers' accountability also tended to develop. Although the rulers had a monopoly in formulating the polity's goals and were not *formally* accountable to anyone, in fact many groups—like religious and intellectual elites, the bureaucracy and aristocracy—developed claims that the rulers were responsible to them and attempted, in varying degrees, to institutionalize these claims. However, such claims were never fully institutionalized in these political systems. The rulers retained not only their monopoly of political decision-making and of formulating political goals, but also of representing the (mostly traditional) central values of the society.

[6] *The Limited Differentiation of Political Roles*

The second major characteristic of these political systems was the development of a *limited level of differentiation of political roles and activities*. It was manifested in the following ways:

1. Most of the political activities of the rulers were differentiated to varying degrees from other, non-political activities; and their embeddedness in basic ascriptive—especially kinship, clan, territorial, and religious—groups was relatively small.

2. The rulers' various political activities were themselves somewhat differentiated from one another. The greatest differentiation was between the "middle" administrative and judiciary activities and the ultimate ruling and party-political activities. The two former types of activity were usually organized in specific groups; the other two were usually less differentiated from one another.

3. Although the political roles and activities of the ruled—i.e., those to whom the major political rules and decisions were applied—were far less differentiated than those of the rulers, they were not entirely embedded in various ascriptive units. The basic role of the "ruled"— of the subject—occasionally became to some extent distinct from other basic (e.g., kinship, or community-membership) roles, and the subjects may have had direct relations with the rulers that were not entirely mediated by their kinship, territorial, or status groups. True, in most of these societies, the subjects had no real, direct political rights, i.e., rights to participate in the legislative or decision-making processes. Nevertheless, they were often able to influence these indirectly, through the rulers' political-party activities; also, different usages often developed making some influence possible, in the administrative and judiciary spheres, beyond the more traditional representation and petitioning on behalf of kinship or territorial groups.

[7] *The Development of Centralized Polity*

One major corollary of the rulers' objectives of implementing autonomous goals was demonstrated in attempts to organize a relatively centralized political community, as in the following:

1. Attempts to establish a unified, relatively homogeneous rule over a given territory, and a more or less clear definition of the frontiers of this territory

2. The definition of the total political unit in terms of political allegiance to the central authorities as subordinating allegiance to any intermediary authorities

3. The gradual establishment of centralized administration

[8] *The Development of Organs of Political Struggle and Bureaucratic Administration*

In close connection with the differentiation of political roles and with the drive toward specific, autonomous political goals, several special organizations of political activity developed in these societies. The most important were: (1) bureaucratic administrative organs and (2) special channels of political struggle.

In the historical bureaucratic societies, administrative organizations developed into distinct and separate organs devoted specifically to fulfilling various administrative and governmental functions. Although these organs often grew out of the administrative organs of feudal or patrimonial systems in the framework of the centralized empires, they tended to acquire some distinctive characteristics. Their distinctiveness from other groups was based on the following attributes:

1. The organization of specifically administrative, as distinct from other political, activities

2. A system of recruitment usually not requiring membership in any kinship, local-territorial groups, but based to a greater extent on criteria of skill, wealth, achievement, or political loyalty to the rulers

3. The development of an internal organizational autonomy tending to develop in a bureaucratic direction (i.e., toward internal centralization and specialization of tasks, establishment of a relatively unified hierarchy of authority, and a system of abstract rules regulating the work of these organs)

4. Growing professionalization of the staff, with the officials becoming gradually a type of *salaried* personnel, recruited on the basis of some of the above-mentioned criteria

5. The development of a professional or semi-professional ideology, stressing that the incumbents of the various administrative offices were usually not considered as only or mainly personal servants of the rulers, but rather as public officials serving the polity of which the ruler was the head

The most important specific channels of political struggle that developed in these societies were:

1. Various court offices, cliques, and royal councils
2. The higher echelons and councils of the bureaucracy
3. Representative institutions, like the Byzantine Senate, and the European parliaments and assemblies of estates

In many cases, these channels evolved from similar ones found in feudal and patrimonial societies. In these pre-bureaucratic polities, representation in such institutions was largely limited to the members of various particularistic kinship, territorial, and hereditary status groups; but in the centralized bureaucratic empires, it was extended to include representatives of other wider, more differentiated, and flexible groups. And representation in these institutions was frequently based on wider and more flexible criteria.

[9] *The Political Systems of the Historical Bureaucratic Empires as Distinguished from Patrimonial, Feudal, and Modern Political Systems*

The political systems of the historical bureaucratic empires were characterized by the development of some autonomy, albeit limited, of the political subsystem, indicated by the tendency toward centralization and development of autonomous political goals, and then by the relatively high organizational autonomy of certain political activities. These contributed to the development of certain levels of generalized power in these societies. Nevertheless, the differentiation of these political activities, organizations, and goals, and the scope of generalized power, was still limited by several factors. The first limitation was the basically traditional legitimation of the rulers. The second limitation was imposed by the fact that the subject's basic political role was not fully distinguished from other basic societal roles (membership in local communities); it was often embedded in these roles, and the citizen or subject did not exercise direct political rights through a system of voting or franchise. Third, many traditional-ascriptive units —e.g., lineages, and territorial communities—performed many political roles and served as units of political representation. The scope of political activity and consequential participation was far more narrow than it is in most modern and contemporary bureaucratic societies.

Thus, in these political systems—*within the framework of the same political institution*—traditional, undifferentiated types of political activities and organizations coexisted with more differentiated and autonomous ones, all closely interwoven in the major aspects of political activity. From this point of view, historical bureaucratic societies differ from feudal and patrimonial political systems (from which they frequently evolve, and into which some of them may develop) and from modern bureaucratic societies (into which some of them may develop); as it were, they stand between them.

Patrimonial, feudal, and historical bureaucratic societies might resemble each other in the *content* of their political goals and in the patterns of legitimation of their rulers. However, they vary greatly in the extents to which their political activities and organizations are differentiated, and to which their goals are articulated as specifically political ones. As contrasted with bureaucratic historical societies, patrimonial and feudal systems are characterized by:

1. The absence of clear territorial centralization

2. The existence of closely parallel, if not identical, social, political, and economic hierarchies

3. Relatively small articulation of the political sphere as organizationally distinct and as featuring autonomous goals

In both patrimonial and feudal societies, the administrative officers are usually considered as private officers of the monarch or of some lords or clans. The officers' great dependence on them and their resources precluded them from achieving autonomous organization. Similarly, although the rulers of feudal and patrimonial societies might have attempted to formulate and pursue autonomous goals, they were not too likely to succeed for any length of time. They were often denied the support of many groups who found that these goals represented the special interests of the royal clan, family, or estate, and not of the whole community, and that the goals might well have been in conflict with those of other kin and traditional groups. (*On feudal systems, see* [D] *Bloch, 1939–40; Coulborn, 1956; Ganshof, 1947; Hintze, 1929;* [A] *Weber, 1922, pp. 724–32; on patrimonial systems, see* [A] *Weber, 1922, pp. 173ff., 679–723.*) Only where the entire country was actually, and not merely symbolically, considered to be the patrimony of the monarch—as in Egypt (but not, e.g., in the Carolingian or Ahmenid empires, where there were strong, traditional groups of local nobility)—was the difference between the patrimonial and bureaucratic systems quantitative rather than qualitative.

The major differences between historical bureaucratic political systems and modern ones (*on modern political systems as a distinct sociological type, see* [S] *Heller, 1934;* [A] *McIver, 1926; Friedrich, 1950; Finer, 1949*) consist in the following features of the *latter*:

1. A far greater differentiation of political activities, of the roles of the "ruled," and the development of "division of power" between the major aspects of the ruling institutions

2. The distribution of political rights—as manifested in systems of voting—among the ruled, and consequently a much broader scope of political activity in the society

3. Potentially active participation by various groups in determining political goals

4. Extensive development of specifically political and administrative organizations and, particularly, of special party-political organizations

5. The weakening of traditional hereditary patterns of legitimation of the rulers, and the growing institutionalization of formal accountability of the rulers to the holders of political rights and to their representatives; and

6. Some formal or actual institutionalization of competition over power and attainment of ruling positions

[10] *The Problem of the Social Conditions of the Development of the Political Systems*

The coexistence of the different types of political characteristics we have already described in the centralized historical empires distinguished these empires from other types of political systems and created their specific contours and problems. Within the framework of unified political institutions, there coexisted here traditional undifferentiated and autonomous differentiated political activities and orientations. Their coexistence was the root of the central problem of the empires' political systems. The combination of these different elements led to a complex interrelation between political institutions and the other parts of the social structure. The complexity of this interrelationship was manifest both in the types of groups engaging in the political struggle, and in the nature of the resources needed by and available to the rulers.

In the political sphere, the rulers needed traditional political support, and more complex, differentiated political support; and they were dependent on both. The political sphere's traditional relation to other parts of the social structure was evinced by the fact that many political activities were still conducted by politically non-specialized collectivities, i.e., by kinship, territorial, and economc groups. All these groups constituted centers of potential power and providers of resources to the political sphere. Naturally, they often made demands, on the political sphere, oriented to maintaining their traditional settings. On the other hand, the very autonomy of the political sphere made the rulers dependent on a *type* of resources not available through various ascriptive-traditional commitments and relations. The political institution was in need of more flexible support and resources, not embedded in fixed, ascriptive relations and groups, which they could use to implement their varied goals according to autonomous political consideration. In order to assure the continuous supply of these non-traditional, differentiated resources, specifically organized groups and channels—such as cliques, special propagandists, and party-political organizations—had to be created and maintained.

Similarly, the political demands made on the rulers by various groups in the society were of the traditional, ascriptive type—i.e., they consisted of demands to uphold different groups' fixed traditional rights and benefits; and also, they were demands of more complex and differentiated types—i.e., demands for participation in formulating the rulers' political goals, or in changing the effective balance of power between different groups in the society, or even in determining the legitimation and accountability of the rulers. Because all these factors were operative in these societies, even the traditional legitimation of the rulers was no longer *based* on "automatic," fixed support; it had to be mobilized continuously.

These different political activities and orientations did not coexist in separate "compartments," combined only loosely and unstably. They were bound together within the same institutions; and the continuity of each type of political activity and organization was dependent *also* on the existence of both types of political orientation. The rulers' activities were, therefore—paradoxically—oriented to maintaining basic *traditional* legitimation through manipulating both traditional and non-traditional support, and to mobilizing traditional resources for politically autonomous goals through non-traditional channels. Hence the political systems of a historical bureaucratic society could subsist only in so far as its rulers could maintain, within the framework of the same political institutions, simultaneously and continuously, both levels of legitimation, support, and political organization. It is, therefore, a major concern of this work to analyze the ways in which these different levels of political activity were organized by the rulers, how different groups participated in them, and the conditions under which these processes developed and functioned.

These systems were confronted with endemic problems with which they had to deal. In order to be able to understand these problems in a fuller way we must necessarily consider the conditions under which these political systems developed and could maintain themselves.

We have already presented the hypothesis that every type of political system developed is maintained under specific local conditions. We must, therefore, analyze the conditions necessary for the development and maintenance of the political systems of the historical bureaucratic empires, with their specific characteristics.

To do so, we must first indicate the ways in which the different characteristics of these systems were combined or interrelated in their concrete historical settings. In this frame of reference, the first two characteristics—autonomous political goals and limited differentiation of political activities—differ from the last two. The tendency to autonomy of political goals created the first impetus toward and possibilities for the creation and development of these polities. The second two characteristics—the development of a centralized polity, and organs of political struggle and administration—constituted the specific organizational and institutional ways through which the institutional implications of the first two characteristics could be fully established. Hence we must analyze the necessary conditions of the full realization of these implications.

The problem of the social conditions of the historical bureaucratic empires may be divided into two parts. The first is related to internal conditions in the political sphere, i.e., the types of political activities and organizations facilitating the continuty of these centralized polities.

The second part of the problem relates to the specification of the external conditions. That is, the major aspects of institutional structure of these societies—of their economic or religious institutions, or of their system of stratification—that facilitated the institutionalization of the internal conditions and the continuity of these systems.

In the following section, we shall present a series of hypotheses about the types of conditions which made the institutionalization of these political systems possible. Later, we shall attempt to verify them, and then see what additional problems can be derived from these analyses and from the verification of the hypotheses.

[11] *The Internal and External Conditions of the Development of the Political Sysems. The Development of Aspirations to Autonomous Political Goals and of Limited Differentiation of the Social Structure*

We have just discussed the problem of the conditions under which the political systems of the centralized bureaucratic empires develop, become institutionalized, and are maintained; and we have pointed out the necessity to present specific hypotheses about the nature of these conditions.

Our main hypothesis about these conditions follows:

First, those "internal" conditions in the political sphere—are the rulers' development of articulated political aspirations and activities which promote the development of autonomous political goals.

Second, the "external" conditions—are certain developments in the non-political institutions, in the fields of economic and cultural activity or social organization and stratification. The major such external condition is the development, within *all* the institutional spheres of a society (albeit in differing measures), of certain limited levels of differentiation, together with what we shall call "free-floating" resources. This limited differentiation is manifest in:

1. The development of many types of groups, especially among the middle and higher strata of society, that are either functionally specific or ascriptive solidary groups, but not embedded in the structure of basic, ascriptive territorial or kinship groups

2. The development, within the society's major institutional system, of certain roles—especially of what may be termed the roles of "producers," as distinct from the roles of "consumers"—differentiated from those of other institutional spheres and from each other

3. The decrease of the extent to which these roles are allocated, especially among the middle and higher groups and strata, according to criteria of membership in basic ascriptive, kinship, and territorial groups, and, conversely, the increase of the extent to which they are allocated according to criteria of achievement or of membership in wider and more flexible groups (e.g., occupational, educational, or political)

4. The development of a definition of the total community that is wider than the definition of any basic ascriptive group

5. The development, within the value system prevalent in the society, of group orientations wider than any basic ascriptive group, and possibly also containing some universalistic elements

The development of such limited differentiation created, first, "free-floating" resources, i.e., resources—manpower, economic resources, political support, and cultural identifications—not embedded within or committed beforehand to any primary ascriptive-particularistic groups. It also created a reservoir of generalized power, in the society, not embedded in such groups, that could be used by different groups for varying goals. These free-floating resources and the generalized power were both necessary, as we shall see, for the rulers to establish autonomous political institutions and to pursue some autonomous and differentiated political goals and activities; and they created the potential for the institutionalization of differentiated political roles and organizations.

[12] *The Inadequacy of the Internal Conditions. Two Cases of Unsuccessful Attempts to Establish Centralized Polities*

In order to be able to have a first glimpse at the interaction between the internal and the external conditions, we shall first present a brief preliminary analysis of two cases of unsuccessful attempts to establish centralized polities.

We have seen the concrete ways in which, in most cases, the different specific characteristics of the political systems of the centralized historical empires became interconnected. The development of the rulers' political goals usually provided the initial impetus for the evolving of these political systems. To implement their aims and to withstand the opposition of the traditional-aristocratic forces, the rulers had to secure both material manpower resources and political support. For these purposes, they tried to find or coerce allies who could provide such resources and to create or foster various organs for mobilizing resources and implementing their policies. The specific organizations and activities of these organs evolved from the interaction between the needs and objectives of the rulers and the needs and demands of the strata from which the necessary resources were mobilized. (*On the development of these organs, see the descriptions in the chief relevant works cited. The problem is treated generally, in a way that has special pertinence for European developments, in* [D] *McIlwain, 1932;* [S] *Hintze, 1930; and, more generally,* [S] *Hintze, 1931.*) In Europe, the transition from the medieval, ascriptive-traditional type of representation to the more differentiated kind was especially important. (*On this, see* [S] *Hintze, 1930, 1931;* [D] *Cam, 1954. For a somewhat more problematic view, see* [S] *Lousse, 1937, 1943;* [Y] *Zeller, 1948; Pagès, 1928, 1932[b];* [Z] *Pares, 1957; Namier, 1952. Some wider considerations, which have reference also to Roman and Byzantine experiences, are in* [L] *Bratianu, 1938, 1948[a], 1948[b].*)

But the rulers did not always succeed in establishing centralized polities and in developing these specific political organs. A closer analysis of the unsuccessful attempts may contribute to our understanding of the nature of the centralized bureaucratic empires. We have selected two examples of failure for analysis—the Carolingian ([E] *Halphen, 1947)* and the Mongol empires ([C] *Spuler, 1950;*

Vladimitsov, 1948, 1950; Schram, 1954; Krader, 1955; Haenisch, 1933, 1941, 1943; Lattimore, 1947, 1951, ch. iv; Vernadskii, 1938, 1939; Pelliot, 1951; Bacon, 1954).

In each case, the rulers tried valiantly to establish new centralized polities. They had a vision of a unified polity, of an empire or realm in which the rulers would be free from the fetters of traditional groups in setting and implementing political aims—although the rulers claimed religious and traditional legitimation for their positions. They tried to establish new patterns of centralized administration; to wrest the monopoly of political and administrative positions from the representatives of hereditary aristocratic clans and groups; to recruit new personnel for these positions, so the rulers could supervise them and utilize them to implement their political goals.

However, the rulers considered here did not succeed for any long period of time. In the Carolingian Empire, the whole structure created by Charlemagne crumbled after his death; while in the Mongol Empire —even at its zenith—Genghis Khan was not able to establish a unitary polity. The rulers could not control their officials for any length of time or provide them with adequate resources and remuneration. These officials very quickly became semi-independent lords, or were absorbed into the older aristocracy. Neither could the rulers find strong enough allies against the various traditional-aristocratic forces—whether clans or feudal lineages—and these traditional groups soon regained their predominance. The new administrative organs created by the rulers speedily dwindled away, resuming their older, traditional form. Any incipient differentiated political activities emerging among some groups or strata were stifled while still incipient.

Thus we see that even when the ruler evinced a marked orientation to autonomous political goals and to establishing new administrative and political organs, existing conditions were not necessarily always appropriate for the continuous development of such organs. In cases like this, these organs did not develop beyond the embryonic stage—in other words, they did not become fully institutionalized. And their noninstitutionalization undermined, in a relatively short period of time, the ruler's attempts to establish a centralized polity. Polities of this kind generally "regressed," so to speak, into types of "precentralized" polities—patrimonial empires, dual-conquest empires, or feudal states.

[13] *The Inadequacy of the Internal Conditions.*
The Problem of the "External" Conditions.
The Development of Limited Differentiation
in the Social Structure as the Main External Condition.
The Historical Data to Be Used in Analysis
and Illustrations

Clearly, the institutionalization of the channels of political struggle and administration was not determined only by the internal conditions, i.e., on the ruler's activities and aims. The ruler's success was greatly dependent on some external conditions—i.e., those beyond the political sphere proper—in other parts of the social structure of the societies. Through the development of such conditions, the resources needed by the ruler could be provided; and they could have facilitated the crystallization of different patterns of differentiated political activities among the more active groups in the society.

Our hypothesis stated that these external conditions consisted mainly in the development of a certain limited level of differentiation of the social structure. To explain this, we must first describe the social structure of the major institutional spheres of these societies and the ways in which such differentiation was manifest in them. Then, we must explain the exact ways that the development of the limited differentiation of these institutional spheres, and of the free-floating resources within them, facilitated the institutionalization of the political systems of the centralized bureaucratic empires. Finally, we must test these explanations by applying them to the available historical materials. We will attempt to do all this in the following chapters.

We shall not be able to deal here with the problem of "what" created the external conditions of this type of social structure, just as we did not ask what the specific conditions under which there arose rulers with autonomic political orientation were. Such an analysis could be attempted—e.g., one could attempt to specify the antecedent conditions within the structure of the societies from which the societies studied here have developed, under which either rulers with autonomous political orientations and/or a certain level of social differentiation emerged. However, such an analysis is beyond the scope of our concern here.

Any comparative analysis must stop somewhere and treat certain conditions as given *for the sake of this analysis.* For this reason, we shall not deal here also with a detailed analysis of the different types of societies from which the historical bureaucratic societies have evolved, nor with the possible impact that these differences of historical antecedents had on the development of these societies. Such impact will be considered, later, only indirectly in so far as it effects the major variables of the societies studied here.

We shall, throughout our discussions, draw on materials from "pre-bureaucratic" and historical bureaucratic societies. The data for most of these societies are summarized in the various tables. Each table deals with a different problem discussed in a specific chapter; the discussion and analysis in each chapter will be based on the material contained in the relevant table.

In order to make our discussion and analysis more concrete, we shall also describe the developments in the social and political structures of several historical bureaucratic empires. One will be the Sassanid Empire, which provides an example of the least developed and differentiated type of such empires. The Chinese Empire (especially from the Han [206 B.C.–A.D. 221] to the T'ang [A.D. 618–905]) will be used to illustrate the predominantly agrarian-bureaucratic, Oriental societies with strong "cultural" orientation. The Byzantine Empire is an example of a society in which the level of over-all social and economic differentiation was high, and the political goals of the rulers were highly articulated. We shall utilize material about the Spanish-American Empire to illustrate the historical bureaucratic empire which developed through conquest. Data about West European countries (especially England and France) during the Age of Absolutism (the seventeenth and eighteenth centuries) provide information about the most differentiated types of historical bureaucratic societies; in some cases, we shall also utilize Prussia and Russia as examples. When we discuss the problems of the spread of "universalistic" religion through conquest, we shall use materials from additional societies—especially the various Islamic (particularly the Abbaside Caliphate [A.D. 749–1258]) and the Ottoman empires. All these cases serve, however, only as illustrative material; for full and systematic presentation of the data, reference should be made to the tables. (*On the Sassanid Empire* [A.D. 226–641], *see especially* [G] *Christensen, 1933, 1936, 1939; Ghirshman, 1954; Delaporto and Huart, 1943; Massé, 1939, 1952, ch. v; Altheim, 1955[a], 1955[b]; Altheim and Stiehl, 1954, 1957; Fry, 1956; Widengren, 1956. On the Chinese Empire, see* [I] *Franke, 1930–52; Van der Sprenkel, 1956; Balázs, 1950, 1959[a], 1959[b], 1960; Aspects de la Chine, 1959; Bodde, 1956; Des Rotours, 1932, 1947–48; Eberhard, 1948[a], 1952; Fairbank, 1957, 1958; Wittfogel, 1935, 1938, 1957; Nivison and Wright, 1959, Lattimore, 1951; Pulleyblank, 1954; 1955; Stange, 1950. On the Byzantine Empire, the basic works are* [L] *Diehl and Marçais, 1936; Diehl, 1943; Diehl et al., 1945 Bréhier, 1947, 1949[b], 1950; Ostrogorsky, 1956[a], 1929[a], 1941, 1956[b]; Baynes, 1926, 1955; Baynes and Moss, 1948; Bury, 1889; Hussey, 1957; Runciman, 1933; Stein, 1919, 1928[a], 1928[b], 1949, 1954. On the Spanish-American Empire, see [R] Haring, 1947; Gongora, 1951; Konetzke, 1951[a], 1953; Ots Capdequi, 1941; Parry, 1957; Vida Viceus, 1957; Zavala, 1943. For differentiated historical bureaucatic societies, see [Z] Ashley, 1952; Plumb, 1950; [S] Beloff, 1954; [Z] Davies, 1937, 1955; Namier, 1952; Pares, 1957; Trevelyan, 1944; on France, see [Y] Sagnac, 1945, 1946; Cobban, 1957[b]; Lough, 1954, 1960; Pagès, 1928, 1932[b]; Zeller, 1948. On Prussia, see [X] Carsten, 1954, 1955; Bruford, 1935; [S] Beloff, 1954; [X] Hintze, 1915, 1943[c]; Rosenberg, 1943-44, 1958; Schmoller, 1898, 1921. On Russia, see [S] Beloff, 1954; [W] Pares, 1958; Nolde, 1948, 1952–53; Sumner, 1947, 1949. Concerning the Islamic empires, see [M] Hodgson, 1960; Lewis, 1950; Grunebaum, 1946, 1954, 1955[a], 1955[b]; [N] Cahen, 1955[a], 1955[b], 1957[a], 1957[b]. On the Ottoman Empire, see [O] Stavrianos, 1957[a], 1957[b]; Gibb and Bowen, 1950, 1957; Wittek, 1938.)*

3

The Economic Structure

of the Historical Bureaucratic Societies

[1] *The Development of the Economic Organization*

We shall begin with an analysis of the economic organization in the historical bureaucratic societies, attempting to indicate how various types of free resources have developed in this field.

From the outset, we must emphasize that, in all the societies studied here, the economy was not based entirely on such free resources—although the degrees to which they were so based varied. In these societies, many parts of the economy were still organized in relatively self-contained, traditional units. But in all the societies examined, the major types of economic resources—labor, capital, commodities, and means of exchange—became disembedded from these self-contained units to an extent that permitted the flow of free resources to influence the functioning of all the parts and sectors of the economic structure.

The economic and social structures of these societies were characterized by a transition from a relatively closed, agricultural economy, centered in closed units, to a more differentiated economic system.

Usually, the relative self-sufficiency of wide economic and social units broke down and gave way to more differentiated and specialized economic units. In turn, these became dependent, at least to some extent, on external resources of the necessary capital and labor; they thus had to produce largely for "external" markets.

[2] The Basic Characteristics of the Agricultural Sectors

Consequently, in most of these societies, the village community or districts gave way either to more differentiated villages, composed largely of independent peasants or tenants, or to large-scale latifundia.

The major types of agricultural producers in these societies here were (1) the aristocracy and gentry; (2) independent peasants; and (3) various types of tenants and semi-servile, dependent rural classes controlled by the lords and the gentry. Both the independent and the dependent peasant groups were sometimes organized in large or small family holdings; the dependent ones sometimes were attached to various larger agricultural units owned by the aristocracy and gentry. In some cases, the difference between the dependent and the independent peasants could be merely one of degree. Most often, however, the difference was striking in regard to personal freedom and freedom of movement—the free peasants were not usually tied to the land.

Whatever the extent of peasant dependency, on the one hand, and of embeddedment of peasant economic activities within village and kinship communities, on the other hand, in most of these societies several tendencies developed which undermined or limited these traditional-ascriptive economic frameworks. The most important of these tendencies to differentiation in agriculture was manifested by the developments of independent private peasant property, and then of some measure of mobility of manpower and labor. In most cases, there were a relatively widespread weakening of ascriptive community rights in land and a growing of some measure of individual (or small family) property rights—although these rights were often still severely limited either by the traditional fetters of various kinship and community rights or by obligations to agricultural overlords or to the state.

[3] The Structure of the Agricultural Sectors

A. SASSANID PERSIA

Only in the least developed societies, like Sassanid Persia (in general, on Sassanid Persia see [G] Christensen, 1933, 1936, 1939; Delaporte and Huart, 1943; Ghirshman, 1954; Massé, 1939, 1952; Altheim,

1955[a], 1955[b]; Altheim and Stiehl, 1954, 1957; Adoniz, 1937), did the traditional village communities, dominated by overlords, retain a large measure of self-sufficiency. Even there, in various periods, more independent peasant-proprietors emerged.

The lot of the peasant in Sassanid Persia was not, on the whole, very good. The enlightened attitude from which he had benefited during the Hellenistic period was a thing of the past. He was downtrodden, dependent, and uneducated; he was attached to the soil; he was the property of the state, a great noble, or a temple, except, occasionally, when he preserved a precarious independence. As the great landed proprietor became increasingly powerful, the small land-owner was driven, by fear of economic crisis and state encroachment, to seek his protection. The proprietor's responsibility for levying taxes on behalf of the state further increased the number of people under his control. Although the collection of taxes and dues was thereby facilitated, the state became dependent on the feudal or military lords, and its attempts to limit their influence were abortive. Finally, the power of the nobles became so great that the king was financially and militarily dependent on them; the great estate developed into a closed enterprise.

B. THE BYZANTINE EMPIRE

In the Byzantine Empire (*on the economic structure, see* [L] *Ostrogorsky, 1956[a], passim; Baynes and Moss, 1948, ch. ii, iii; Bratianu, 1938; Ostrogorsky, 1929[a]; Charanis, 1944-45, 1951[a], 1951[b], 1953[a], 1953[b]*), the characteristic feature of post-sixth-century society was the free village community. (*Ostrogorsky, 1929[a], 1941, 1949, 1959; Charanis, 1944-45, 1951[a], 1951[b]; Bréhier, 1917. For the texts of the famous "Farmer's Laws," see Ashburner, 1910–12; Bach, 1942; Malafosse, 1949; Ostrogorsky, 1947. The interpretations of* [L] *Lemerle [1958] and Karayanopulus [1956] differ from Ostrogorsky's.*) Each peasant owned the land individually and cultivated it himself, but if for some reason he could not cultivate it himself, he could let it to another member of the community either on a share basis or for money payment. For taxation purposes, each such community formed a fiscal unit; if one farmer failed to meet his treasury obligations, his neighbors were held responsible for them unless measures were taken to relieve them of this responsibility. On the whole, these villages, at least in the eighth and ninth centuries, were prosperous: of course, many of their members were poor; but a considerable number were well-to-do peasants, while a few had become extremely wealthy ([L] *Charanis, 1944–45; Rouillard, 1953, 1940; Lemerle, 1958*).

MILLS COLLEGE
LIBRARY

During this period, freedom of movement for the non-servile elements of the population was another feature of the rural society of the Empire ([L] *Bréhier, 1924, 1917; Diehl, 1906–08, 1929; Rouillard, 1953*). But this mobility was probably not very extensive. The vast majority of the people, unless moved by the government or driven from their homes by some foreign incursion, grew and died in the community where they had been born.

In Byzantine society, a continuous struggle was waged between the free peasants and the aristocratic landlords who wanted to encroach upon the peasants' property. Throughout the Empire's periods of greatest strength, the free peasants were able, with the help of the Emperors, to maintain themselves; but after about the eleventh century, the power of the aristocracy grew, and the free villages began to disappear ([L] *Andréadès, 1935; Dölger, 1933; Stein, 1923–25, 1954; Lemerle, 1958; Charanis, 1951[a], 1951[b], 1957; Guilland, 1947–48; Xanalatos, 1937; Ostrogorsky, 1954, 1956[b]*).

C. THE T'ANG EMPIRE

The Chinese economic structure was, from very early times, based on agriculture. The valleys of the big rivers and the hillsides were the cultivated areas. Water control became the central problem of the agriculture, which was afflicted heavily by the frequent floods and droughts. The combination of agriculture with irrigation created at once specific social needs and patterns of power relationships.

The control of canals was an important issue in the struggle between the emperor and the feudal lords. Maintaining and repairing canals and dikes were the main duty of the central administration and became symbolic of a well-organized and efficient administration ([I] *Lattimore, 1951; Eberhard, 1948[a]*, passim; *Wittfogel*, [A] *1932*, [I] *1935, 1957*). The organizational unit of the agriculture was the peasant village, which evinced an extreme stability of organization and characteristics irrespective of changes in laws of tenure and ownership.

In the village, the concept of "property" was largely synonymous with the concept of "collective property," the only question being which was the owner unit. The traditional property unit was the family, but, when the Confucian system emphasized the ideological integration of the family and the state, the latter was easily accepted as the supreme owner of the land. Thus, instead of ownership of land, in reality there were only different types of tenure.

In the first T'ang period, the tenure system ([I] *Balázs, 1953[b], 1954[a]; Eberhard, 1932; Maspero, 1938, 1950[a]; Gernet, 1958*) was the equal-field system taken over from the Sui. According to this,

equal land allotments were made for each married couple. This simplified taxation, since the register of the number of family units was
a sufficient basis for taxation. The tenure was strictly bound to demographic structure; and changes in the household (death, birth, marriage,
disability) caused redistribution. According to the data of the Household Registers, the redistribution occurred annually ([I] *Pulleyblank,
1955; Balázs, 1931–33, 1953[a], 1953[b], 1954[a]; K. Wang, 1956*).

The property rights of the gentry and the officials were less restricted than the peasantry's. The former acquired their property
either as a gift from an emperor—then it was hereditary and tax-
free—or as benefice, tax-free as well given together with the office (*see
also* [I] *Schurmann, 1956[a]*).

However, despite all attempts to maintain a relatively rigid type
of agricultural organization, reforms of the property system were the
recurrent pattern of Chinese agrarian policy. Each new dynasty tried
to tackle anew the land problem. The major systems of holdings—equal
allotments or other systems—usually broke down, because of the faults
of the administration and because of the rapacity of the officials, who
wanted to extend their own ownership and privileges and thus were
not overly willing to enforce laws limiting their own privileges (*see
also* [I] *Eberhard, 1945, 1948[a]* passim; *Lattimore, 1951; Frankè,
1953[a]; Twitchett, 1956[a]; Liang, 1956[a], 1956[b]*). Thus, for
instance, during the early T'ang period it had already become clear
that the chun-t'ien (equal-land) system was fictive, as was the tax
system. The situation became untenable after the An Lu-shan rebellion, when the whole registration system broke down, and when (in
the eighth century) a mass movement developed of peasants leaving
their lands and migrating from province to province (*Pulleyblank,
1955; Balázs, 1931–33, 1953[b], 1954[a]*).

This grave situation led to a new policy of making exemptions,
grants, and amnesties to refugees willing to settle and thus to return to
fulfilling the expected duties of a Chinese peasant, as expressed in the
sacred books. The policy of the later T'ang was directed to full utilization of potential resources: any available agricultural land had to
be cultivated; the manpower had to be turned into a well-organized
labor force; and evasion of taxpaying had to be reduced to the minimum. The most important means toward realizing these aims were
the state colonies, the transfer of population to the frontier areas,
planned incentives to motivate people to settle there, and various reforms intended to increase the efficiency of the tax registers ([I] *Pulleyblank, 1955; Balázs, 1931–33, 1953[a], 1953[b], 1954[a], 1948, Introduction. For later periods of Chinese history see* [I] *Franke, 1953[a];
Twitchett, 1956[a], 1957[c]; Maspero, 1938, 1954[a]; Rieger, 1937;
Liang, 1956[a], 1956[b]*).

D. THE SPANISH-AMERICAN EMPIRE

In the Spanish-American Empire, a large part of the native Indian population was subjugated by the conquerors to the policies of the Crown, directed against the "feudal" tendencies of the Spanish conquistadores. This subjugation gave rise to a somewhat differentiated and flexible type of land-ownership and system of cultivation. ([R] *Haring, 1947, chaps. ii, iii, ix, xiii. On the development of the economic system in the Spanish-American Empire in general, and of the agricultural system and policy in particular, see* [R] *Bagu, 1949; Cardos, 1955; Chaunu, 1956; Gibson, 1955; Chevalier, 1952; Hernández y Sanchez-Barba, 1954, 1955; Konetzke, 1953; Kerns Barber, 1932; Miranda, 1941-42, 1951; Ots Capdequi, 1946[b], 1951. On the laws dealing with Indian labor, see* [R] *Gallo, 1951[a]; Gongora, 1951; Konetzke, 1953; Simpson, 1934, 1938, 1940, 1950; Service, 1951; Phelan, 1959; Zavala, 1935[a], 1935[b], 1943; 1949; Vida Viceus, 1957.*)

Land-ownership was officially vested in the Spanish Crown, which, however, delegated title to its deserving subjects in reward for services rendered. Essentially, there were three types of land holdings:

1. THE INDIAN VILLAGE. The land of the village was held in common under the tutelage of a native nobility. Its inhabitants were subject to a form of *corvée*, due both to their own chiefs (who also owned slaves) and to the imperial administration. The latter frequently delegated its rights to private individuals, holders of *encomienda*, mine owners, and others.

2. SMALL LANDHOLDINGS. Spanish settlers were granted individual titles to relatively small tracts of land, which theoretically were to be worked by themselves and their families, and with hired and slave labor. However, the limitations placed on enslaving Indians and the high price of Negro slaves were an obstacle to the free development of this type of landholding. The serious shortage of labor for hire (caused by the overriding competition of the privileged holders of *encomienda*) and the large demand of the various sectors of the economy were responsible for the ultimate shrinking supply of Indian labor.

3. THE LARGE PLANTATIONS. These were fostered both by large land-ownership and *encomienda*. The latter was an institution entitling its holder to receive tribute from the natives of a certain area; the tribute could be collected in the form of work upon the land of the *encomiendero*. The *encomienda* involved also certain obligations on the part of the *encomiendero*, of a civilizing and Christianizing nature. The institution became a source of friction between the government, which strove to abolish it, and the plantation owners, who were dependent upon it.

Similarly, the mobilization of labor was not always assured, and it reflected in itself some more flexible developments. After the abolition of Indian slavery, various more flexible ways of recruiting Indian labor for the latifundia and the mines developed. However, these were also based on force—although the laborers were rewarded with wages (*see especially Gibson, 1955; Hernández y Sanchez-Barba, 1954; Konetzke, 1946*).

In addition, the estates had begun to attract Indians to leave their own villages and reside permanently there; the estates managed to hold the Indians by forcing them into debt and peonage. The autarchy of the native villages was finally broken by draining off their populations and leaving the burdens of tax, tribute, and labor service on those remaining.

The growing demands for specialized skilled and semi-skilled labor finally caused increased wages to be offered. This eventually brought about the existence of a permanent proletariat, depending on wages for a livelihood.

E . ABSOLUTIST EUROPE

In the majority of the European (especially Western European) countries in the sixteenth century, most of the old "feudal" fetters on agriculture were cast off; and, although many taxes and feudal taxes remained, in most Western European countries the peasants became legally free. Various types of individual property or tenantship prevailed, and agricultural activities were oriented to markets and to procuring monetary resources; and a large degree of labor mobility developed. It was only in the Eastern European countries, like Prussia and Russia, that, after the initial period of colonization by free peasants, the state combined with the landed aristocracy to close in on the peasants, limiting their personal liberty and developing many prescriptive policies directed to minimize their mobility and to tie them to the land. Personal liberty, private property, and agricultural labor mobility became predominant in most Western European countries. The traditional communal and feudal or patrimonial ties were relegated entirely to secondary importance. In all other countries, these ties subsisted to some extent. Even when they were important, however, the self-sufficiency of the agricultural units and sectors became greatly weakened, and most of their activities became oriented to the market. (*There are general surveys in* [S] *Wilson, 1957; Lindsay, 1957[a]; Clark, 1929–59, 1957; Meuvret, 1955; Slicker van Bath, 1955.*)

[4] The Basic Characteristics of Mercantile and Industrial Activities

The development of specific units of production was much more prominent in the non-agricultural sectors of production and in the fields of exchange, where different types of organization of production could be found. Several of these were largely specialized and needed considerable fluid capital and manpower to function.

In all these societies, cities became centers, not only of administrative and cultural activities, but also of some commercial and industrial activities. These were not so diversified, specialized, and organized as a modern industrial market system; and the scope of their organizational activities, and the range of their operation and relations, were relatively limited—although the limitations necessarily varied in different societies.

The simplest type of specialized organization was represented by the workshop owned by an individual or a family, employing but few workers (quite often, members of the family) and requiring only minimal capital, and usually producing for a very restricted traditional local market. More complicated types of organization were represented by the larger workshop or factory which employed a staff of skilled and semi-skilled labor and specialized in a specific type of commodity destined for a wider and specialized market. A workshop like this may have belonged to one family, its owner may have been a member of a guild, and some of its workers may have had "inherited" their callings from their fathers. But obviously, this already provided some place and demand for more mobile labor.

The most complicated type of organization were the great industrial or semi-industrial enterprises. Usually, these workshops and factories were operating with larger capital and were naturally much more oriented to the local markets and to various wider specialized markets. The various mining enterprises (mining of metals, salt, etc.) were of special interest among the industrial or semi-industrial enterprises. They developed in most of the societies we examine, and were frequently owned and managed by the state, by state contractors, or by guilds. Similarly, many of the large enterprises were either owned by the state or worked as contractors for the state and the army; and farming out state contracts was an important aspect of economic activity in most historical bureaucratic societies.

Along with these various units of production, specific units of exchange developed. In addition to the simplest activities of itinerant and local merchants of the "traditional" or primitive type, there were much more specialized kinds of merchants and bankers, or trading associations and organizations. Some were of purely local scope; others had wider national or international interests. Some of these associations were permanent and engaged in continuous economic activities. Others developed for the purpose of mobilizing capital for only one or for a limited series of trading or industrial enterprises, or for farming out contracts from the state ([A] *Weber, 1924[a], 1924[b]*).

[5] *The Structure of Mercantile and Industrial Activities*

A. SASSANID PERSIA

Even in Sassanid Persia, the least differentiated of the societies studied here, a rather marked commercial, manufacturing and "industrial" activity developed.

In commerce, Sassanid coinage of silver, copper, and—more rarely —gold circulated widely. The bill of exchange appeared during this period; Jewish banking circles in Babylonia, and analogous Persian institutions, played a leading part in its circulation.

More money was in circulation in the towns, as shown by the great number of silver *dirhems* found in Iran and neighboring countries. In the rural districts, however, the wages of the peasant, soldier, and official, and even the taxes, were paid in kind—a custom that persisted, in certain countries, to modern times.

Foreign trade was already conducted entirely on a monetary basis. It continued to expand. The chief commodities it handled were valuable merchandise and luxury goods demanded by the Court and wealthy aristocracy. Levying dues and taxes in kind enabled the government to build up large stocks of essential goods, from which its agents supplied the market; the reserves could also be used, in time of famine, to alleviate distress.

In internal commerce, apparently the merchants and the country pedlars who depended on the traders in the great centers became more specialized. Banking activity was confined almost entirely to commerce; banks came into play only in the event of a bad harvest or at the time of tax payment. However, the limited bank activity did not prevent the state from taking an increasing interest in the working of credit institutions, and the government imposed controls that were so well organized that they remained unchanged for many centuries.

Production improved and expanded—particularly in the silk and glass industries—and it also was marked by a greater degree of specialization. As a result of its monopolies, the state became a producer and ran its own workshops. It also intervened in certain private industries, notably those that directly concerned the Court, army, and administration; it supervised the prices of raw materials, and the wages and organization of the workers. New tendencies thus arose, and finally crystallized as types of medieval-like guilds ([G] *Ghirshman, 1954; Christensen, 1933, 1939; Altheim and Stiehl, 1954, 1957; ch. i–iii*).

B. THE BYZANTINE EMPIRE

In the Byzantine Empire, industry and trade were much more developed and differentiated; they produced both for everyday use and for luxury, and dealt with international and internal trade ([L] *Baynes and Moss, 1948, ch. iii; Runciman, 1952; Bratianu, 1934[a], 1934[b], 1938; Segrè, 1942–43, 1945; Mickwitz, 1936[a], 1936[b]*).

On the whole, Constantinople appeared to medieval eyes as a great industrial city; and this impression was only enhanced by its great importance as a center of international trade. Its geographical position was inestimably beneficial, for it automatically made Byzantium such a center.

Despite occasional interruptions caused by wars, Byzantine foreign trade increased in volume until the international convulsions of the eleventh century. It received very little encouragement from the imperial authorities, whose interest in it was confined to questions of revenue and of acquiring the raw materials needed by the imperial factories. The emperors were often ready to sacrifice foreign trade in the interests of diplomacy and of maintaining order in Constantinople.

Internal trade consisted primarily in supplying Constantinople with the necessities of life and with a growing number of luxuries. Thus both trade and industry constituted important elements of Byzantine economy and society, although they were not the most powerful element. But they formed a basic and dynamic part of Byzantine social structure.

Every branch of industry formed a corporation, and some of the corporations (e.g., those concerned with the silk industry) were subdivided into several guilds. Each guild enjoyed a real monopoly. On the other hand, the guild was subject to rigorous state control, which fixed the profits, the conditions of admitting new members, the restrictions on the exportation of goods, and a number of other points. In certain cases, the state even determined the localities where booths and workshops could be established. The prefect of Constantinople also exercised a close surveillance over the members of corporations and had the right to inspect their workshops. (*See* [L] *Andréadès, 1934; Bratianu, 1934[a], 1934[b], 1938; Stöckle, 1911; Lopez, 1945. On the book of the prefect, see* [L] *Boak, 1929; Freshfield, 1932.*)

Byzantine industry was mostly concentrated in the hands of the emperor, some private individuals, and the guilds. It was largely governed by the guilds with their officials, and supervised and controlled by state officials.

C. THE CHINESE EMPIRE

In China, the scope of urban commercial and industrial development was more limited, but the range of commercial activities was wide. During the Han and T'ang dynasties, the cities were primarily administrative and cultural centers. Only relatively small-scale commercial, transport, and manufacturing enterprises—beyond the state monopolies and enterprises—developed there ([I] *Fairbank, 1958, p. ix; Balázs, 1954[b], 1960; Murphey, 1954; Eberhard, 1956; Gernet, 1956, 1958*). The non-state activities were rather severely limited by two additional factors—the low status of the merchant, and the officials' continuous supervision. But even then, many types of commercial banking activities (albeit restricted) developed, ranging from pawnshops to credit associations and intercity commercial enterprises.

Under the Sung (A.D. 960–1293) there was expansion of both internal and international commercial and manufacturing activities. The urban groups involved in these developed a more intensive autonomous social and economic life, exerting strong influence on the officialdom—although formally they were still of inferior status ([I] *Kracke, 1953, 1955; Balázs, 1954[b], 1960; Gernet, 1956, 1958; Eberhard, 1948[a]* passim). This development subsided again under the Ming (A.D. 1368–1644) and Ch'ing (A.D. 1644–1911) dynasties (*see also* [I] *W. Franke, 1956; Twitchett, 1957[b], 1957[c]*). Throughout Chinese history, the merchant has been considered by the official as a minor ally whose activities could be used in the interest of the official class or of the state. Commercial transactions were always subject to superintendence and taxation by officials. Government monopolies of staple articles—like salt and iron, in ancient times, or tea, silk, opium, tobacco, and salt, later—were one expression of the overriding economic prerogatives of the state. No merchant class was allowed to rise independently and encroach on these prerogatives ([I] *Balázs, 1954[a], 1960; Fairbank, 1958, ch. iii; Lattimore, 1951*).

However, it was always possible to work out a close community of interest between the merchant and the official, since official patronage and support were necessary for any big commercial undertaking. Merchants, bankers, brokers, and traders of all kinds therefore constituted a class attached as subordinates to the bureaucracy ([I] *Fairbank, 1958, ch. iii; Maspero, 1950[a]; Eberhard, 1948[a]* passim; *Pulleyblank, 1954, 1955*).

Merchants could move, with some ease, into the gentry class, through purchasing land and/or intermarrying. The fact that the farmer was free to sell his land gave the merchant an opportunity to invest in land and thus gain both a steady income and social prestige ([I] *Kracke, 1953, 1955; Balázs, 1960; Chang, 1955*). Unlike Europe, China in her formative period was involved in little foreign trade in which a merchant could invest. Land remained the great object of his investment. As a result, the merchant class produced landlords more readily than an independent class of commercial capitalists would have. (*See* [I] *Balázs, 1960; Schurmann, 1956[a]; Kracke, 1953, 1955.*)

Another sign of the prominence of agriculture in the Chinese economy was the restricted use of money. Creation of credit among the villages was retarded by the relative self-sufficiency of the peasant household and its dependence on short-term purchases from sources close at hand. Similarly, the government relied heavily on taxation in kind and on payments of stipends in grain. The capital at Peking, for example, was fed by grain shipped from the provinces via the Grand Canal. In addition, the government had at its command resources of *corvée* labor to which no money wages were paid ([I] *Swann, 1950; Fairbank, 1958; Schurmann, 1956[a], 1956[b]*).

D. THE SPANISH-AMERICAN EMPIRE

In the Spanish-American Empire, manufacturing was widely distributed among small entrepreneurs and artisans. It consisted largely only of an extension of the universal handicrafts of the Indians, who operated both as independent entrepreneurs in their villages and as hired laborers in the colonial towns. A textile industry flourished, based primarily on cotton and wool and carried out under the ancient Indian methods. There was a brief interlude of extensive silk cultivation, declining after the colonization of the Philippine Islands. There was a great deal of metalworking, but it was almost exclusively devoted to ornaments. Shipbuilding, carriage-making, furniture-making, and leather industry were also widespread ([R] *Haring, 1947, ch. xiii; Bagu, 1949; Borah, 1943; Chaunu, 1956; Dusenberry, 1947; Miranda, 1944; Palm, 1951; Guthrie, 1939; Sayous, 1934*).

The legal trade was monopolized by privileged Spanish merchants (Peninsulars), while the native Americans (Creoles) had to be content with retail establishments and smuggling. During the entire colonial period, the Spaniards struggled constantly to enforce trade restrictions and to keep out rival interlopers, particularly the French and the British. Trade and industry were strictly regulated and subject to taxation and licensing. However, illicit trade was almost ubiquitous;

and rigid enforcement of all the rules was all but impossible. The state monopolies on commodities like mercury and salt, and taxes on amusements, tobacco, and the like, were major sources of income for the treasury. The regulation of trade sometimes included a form of price control; and, during bad crop years, a system of rationing went into effect, that included the establishment of state granaries and the forced deliveries of agricultural produce at fixed prices, as well as strict interdiction of illicit trade with the Indian population, who had to deliver their produce to officially licensed markets ([R] *Haring, 1927, 1947, ch. ii; Christelow, 1942, 1947; Miranda, 1944; Guthrie, 1939; Ots Capdequi, 1934[a]; Pares, 1936*).

There was a merchant guild (*consulados*) whose purpose was to regulate domestic trade, and to act as court of dispute—handling bankruptcies, and setting rules and precedents. It represented the interests of the merchant class in Spain.

There was also a miners' guild, created in 1783, that gained important privileges for the mine-owners and operators. It permitted them a great deal of self-regulatory autonomy, set standards, and established a mining school. It got the price of mercury reduced, and caused the revival of the mining industry, which had lagged for some time ([R] *Haring, 1947, ch. xxiii; Howe, 1949*).

E. ABSOLUTIST EUROPE

Only in Absolutist Europe—where the commercial manufacturing and industrial activities of the urban middle class gradually developed beyond local confines—the scope of these enterprises, the range of their activities, and the extent of their specialization became very great; and a more infused mercantile and monetary system developed. But even there, till the end of the eighteenth century, this system was mostly commercial; it was not yet industrial or *fully* organized around a market. (*For a general survey, see* [S] *Wilson, 1957; Nef,* [Z] *1940,* [A] *1958;* [S] *Clark, 1929-59, 1957;* [Z] *Ashton, 1955[a], 1955[b];* [S] *Braudel and Spooner, 1955; Leuillot, 1955; Vidalene, 1955.*)

[6] *The Major Types of Exchange Mechanisms*

All the developments described above attest to the weakening of self-sufficient economic units and to the growing interdependence of the various economic units and sectors in the society—of ecological units, on one hand; and of the different economic sectors, agriculture, industry, and trade, on the other hand. These various units and sectors became increasingly dependent on more fluid resources of manpower and capital, and fluctuations in one unit or sector necessarily affected others.

This growing interdependence led to a concomitant increase in the importance of various exchange mechanisms in the economic structure of these societies. In these societies, there did not develop uniform or homogeneous mechanisms of exchange; and, in each society, different levels or types of such mechanisms developed and operated.

The first type of exchange mechanism was composed of the traditional ascriptive-reciprocal arrangements within any village, groups of villages, or kinship groups—e.g., various traditional arrangements for mutual help and distribution of goods.

The second type was local barter for local or city markets, based on barter or intermittent, non-regular individual trade.

The third level of mechanism consisted of exchanges between different social classes (or, to some extent, also between the subjects and the ruler, acting as representatives or head of such classes), wherein different classes received certain services and goods according to their ascriptive status positions. Most important in this respect were the several kinds of tribute, to rulers or to higher strata; and arrangements of fixed prices that regulated and assured the supply of various goods to different groups in the society (e.g., of food to the populations of urban centers) irrespective of market fluctuations.

Smelser has called the fourth type of exchange the "mobilizatory" one. It was characterized by the intensive mobilization of various economic resources for implementing the goals of the ruler or of the state. Its most important instrument was taxation. Also, in this connection there developed accumulation and conservation of resources by the rulers, and the regulation for political purposes, of movement of trade and of prices. Frequently, the resources accumulated were used by the rulers for foreign exchange and trade. However, such trade was usually of a distinctly political nature, i.e., it was mainly an instrument of political expansion, of maintaining political relations, or of mobilizing resources for political purposes ([A] *Smelser, 1959*).

The next level of exchange mechanism operating in these societies was that of local, national, or international market exchange. This consisted either of specialized markets for various products (as was, to some extent, the case in Iran, Byzantium, China, and the Spanish American Empire), or of more general, economically more autonomous, self-regulating market exchange mechanisms.

[7] *The Scope and Operation*
of Market and Monetary Mechanisms

Thus there developed, in the economic systems of the societies we have examined, side-by-side, different types of mechanisms of exchange. These types were necessarily closely related to the extents of differentiation of economic activities, and of these activities embeddedness in non-economic social groups and mechanisms.

The first three levels were the most embedded, and were not specific to the societies investigated here. The mobilizatory mechanism generally developed with the growth of the autonomy of the political sphere, and emphasized the predominance of political over purely economic mechanisms. The mechanism of market exchange, was the least embedded and economically the most autonomous. The relative co-dominance of the last two mechanisms is characteristic of the economic structure of the historical bureaucratic societies.

The respective extents to which the purely economic mechanisms were operative necessarily varied among the different societies; and in each society, large sectors of the economic system were still embedded in other, non-economic groups. However, in each society, the relatively autonomous mechanism of the economic system was not isolated or marginal; it permeated, though in different degrees, all parts of the economic system. This is demonstrated by the importance monetary mechanisms had in all the societies studied here—each had developed some monetary means and policies.

The Sassanid monarchs instituted various kinds of coinage as one means of unifying the Empire and controlling some of its economic activities ([G] *Altheim, 1955[a], 1955[b]; Altheim and Stiehl, 1954, 1957; Ghirshman, 1954*).

In China, many monetary systems, both private and public, developed; manipulating currency was one of the government's major concerns. Currency manipulation acquired special importance after the T'ang tax reforms, which required payments to be partly monetary. However, the Chinese monetary system was rather backward. The old currency system was extremely complex and inefficient. The unit of account (under the Manchus, the ounce or tael) varied locally and also between trades and government agencies. Twenty different units of account might simultaneously be in common use in one city. It was impossible to maintain a minted currency of fixed value. It was necessary to adopt the clumsy expedient of circulating pure silver, each ingot of which had to be weighed and assayed for its purity. Few governments could refrain from debasing the copper coinage. The resulting confusion of currency units and of the exchange arrangements among them was a serious handicap to any merchant ([I] *Swann, 1950 [here adapted from Fairbank, 1958, ch. iii]; Lattimore, 1951; Franke, 1949; Balázs, 1931–33, 1960; L. S. Yang, 1952; Gernet, 1956, 1958*).

In the Byzantine Empire, most of the rulers' policies and the activities of the administration demanded large expenditures of money. Thus a large proportion of the rulers' endeavors was oriented to having a continuous supply of monetary resources and maintaining of a balanced budget [L] *Segrè, 1945; Lopez, 1951[a], 1951[b]; Andréadès, 1911, 1921[b], 1924; Bratianu, 1938*). To do so, the rulers developed a great variety of monetary policies which continuously affected all the sectors of the economy—although, in the later periods of Byzantine history, growing taxation and inflation facilitated the evolution of more closed semi-feudal estates.

The economy of the Spanish-American Empire was a mixture of "natural" barter economy and economies of market trade with a market economy. The Spaniards superimposed the market economy, based largely on monetary units and transactions, on the various local strata and units. A monetary system did not develop in the Spanish-American Empire immediately after the conquest. During the first stage of the conquest—the stage when private enterprises were relatively preponderant, though directed by the state—direct tribute and booty of precious metals and wares were strongly emphasized. Only after the Empire had begun to be bureaucratized, and more limitations were imposed on the private conquerors, did a unitary monetary system gradually develop. (*See* [A] *Haring, 1918, 1947; Borah, 1951; Hamilton, 1934; Konetzke, 1951[a], 1951[b]; Ots Capdequi, 1934[a], 1932; Sayous, 1930, 1934; Zavala, 1943.*)

Among the societies we are examining here, monetary mechanisms and policies penetrated most widely in the various European countries during the Age of Absolutism. In these countries, the whole economy gradually became geared around the monetary system. (*For a general survey of the development of monetary systems in Europe, see* [S] *Wilson, 1957; Clark, 1947; Braudel and Spooner, 1955; Heaton, 1937;* [Y] *Zeller, 1952.*)

In all the societies considered here, monetary units, systems, transactions, and policies became important means of regulating the interrelationships between various economic groups. This was especially true when the society's scope of trade and exchange extended beyond local levels and was not conducted only according to purely political considerations.

Of course, monetary mechanisms did not penetrate all sectors of the economy to the same extent. They had less influence on some sectors, particularly the agricultural—but even these were touched by monetary mechanisms, through problems of taxation, exchange, and trade. Thus even the relatively self-sufficient economic units and sectors became, in some measure, sensitized to monetary problems and developments.

In the economic systems of the societies studied here, the traditional-ascriptive, the political (mobilizatory), and the purely economic exchange mechanisms interacted together. The degree to which these different mechanisms were operative was determined by the specific society and sector of society. But whatever importance they had relative to each other, the "economic" (i.e., exchange or monetary) principles became extremely important, and greatly influenced and penetrated the other types of exchange mechanisms.

Through the pervasive (though sometimes limited) operations of these economic (and, to a lesser degree, the mobilizatory) mechanisms, changes in one part or sector of the economic system affected other parts or sectors. All the parts thus became very sensitive to fluctuations in monetary resources and prices. Moreover, the very coexistence of "economic" and non-economic regulative mechanisms, and of self-sufficient non-differentiated and differentiated economic units and sectors, made possible both continuous fluctuations between them, and changes in their relative powers—even up to the dwindling of the "free" resources and sectors. The extent to which, and the conditions under which, this occurred will be considered in some later chapters of this volume.

[8] *Differences among the Economic Systems of the Empires*

The general characteristics of the economic systems of these societies are common to all of them. However, each society's economic system differed from the others' systems, as both the discussion above and the material presented in the tables attest.

The most important differences were in the following areas:

1. The extent to which specific economic roles were differentiated

2. The degree of development of specific units of production, exchange, and consumption, in the major sectors of the economy

3. The relative importance of different types of exchange mechanisms—especially the prominence of the "purely" economic, market, and monetary mechanisms

4

Religious and Cultural

Organization and Orientation

[1] Introduction

We shall now analyze the religious and cultural structure in the societies we are examining. In each of these societies, complex religious organizations and specialized religious roles developed, although the religious life of the "common" people was still largely confined by kinship and territorial groupings.

Except for the Inca and the Ancient Egyptian empires, these societies formed the arenas in which the major historical religions developed and became, in different degrees, institutionalized. Their main value systems were grounded in religious values, symbols, and traditions; and their populations' outlooks on life were colored by these. In some of these societies, various secular anti-religious movements emerged. However, these were usually reactions against the religious institutions and atmosphere and not, as yet, autonomous developments undermining the predominance of religion in the spheres of values and culture. But the identification of the total (political) community

with the religious sphere that is found in most primitive and patrimonial societies no longer existed.

[2] *Religious Organization*

A. SASSANID PERSIA

In Sassanid Persia, the Mazdaist church evolved from the Zoroastrian cult groups ([G] *Nyberg, 1938; Benveniste, 1938; Christensen, 1936; Ghirshman, 1954. On the Mazdekite movement, see* [G]
Christensen, 1925; Klima, 1957). From the beginning of the Sassanid
Dynasty, the regime was strongly allied with the Zoroastrian magi and
church. The Church was a very important part of the state, and
performed many functions, like the religious, educational, or juridical
ones, within it. However strong its position, the Zoroastrian church
was never fully secure. Throughout Sassanid history, the Zoroastrian
clergy had to compete with many other religions. These religious conflicts were very significant in the social and political history of the state.

There were several foreign religious communities in the Sassanid
Empire. Jews were numerous, especially in the cities of Mesopotamia
and of Babylonia—particularly at Seleucia-Ctesiphon, where the Jews'
civil and religious head, the *Resh Galuta,* lived. His election had to
be confirmed by the Great King.

Christianity first began to spread in western Persia toward the end
of the Arsacid Era, thanks to the zeal of the missionaries of Edessa.
In the eastern regions of the Empire, Buddhism claimed many fol-
lowers.

The Mazdaist clergy were somewhat disdainful in their relations
with, and to a certain extent intolerant of, non-Mazdaists—particularly
dangerous innovators like the Manichaeans. But the adherents of
foreign religions could live in peace, and their organizations and their
religious laws were respected, as long as they did not set themselves up
against the authority of the state or conspire with its enemies. Political
reasons, more than religious intolerance, caused the first great persecution of the Christians under Shapur II.

The Zoroastrian clergy developed into a minute hierarchical organization (*following* [G] *Christensen, 1939*). The magi (*maguan*)
constituted the lower stratum of the clergy. The head of each of the
various temples bore, apparently, the title *moaguan magu.* The whole
state was divided into ecclesiastical districts, each headed by a *mobadh.*
The chief of all the *mobadhs* was the *mobadhan mobadh*—the head of
the Church and the main ecclesiastical dignitary of the state. He di-

rected all ecclesiastical matters and appointed the *mobadhs;* it seems that he himself was nominated by the king, to whom he was the primary religious advisor.

Another group of ecclesiastical officials were the *herbadhs,* who conducted the rites in the temples. Their chief, the *herbadhan herbadh,* was an important official; at certain periods of Sassanid history, the *herbadhan herbadh* was second only to the *mobadhan mobadh.* There were a few other special priests, about whose functions we know little or nothing, and the *dastuar*—the theological scholar.

During the Sassanid regime, the Zoroastrian religion became fully organized, with many new important doctrinal and theological ramifications. The main internal religious developments were, first, the full formalization and canonization of the most crucial theological writings and symbols, second, the emergence of wider and universalistic orientations, within the religion, and, third, the formation of sectarian movements, closely associated with the first two developments or in reaction against them ([G] *Christensen, 1936, 1939; de Menasce, 1955; Mole, 1953; Coulborn, 1958–59*).

The evolution of some universalistic elements, some claim to universalistic applicability, and some—albeit weak—missionary attempts and orientation, was closely related to the general intense religious development then occurring in that part of the world. The wider orientations, combined with prompting and encouragement from the kings, also gave impetus to attempts at codification, whose objective was to work out a generally valid tradition which could be presented, as it were, to the world, and which could serve as a basis for cultural and missionary activities. The growth of sectarian activities and the rise of sectarian movements—social-religious movements, predominantly the Mazdakite one—were probably also connected with these activities and orientations.

B. THE BYZANTINE EMPIRE

The Byzantine (Orthodox) church played a very important part in the social, political, and cultural life of the Byzantine Empire. Throughout the duration of the medieval Orthodox church, the secular and ecclesiastical authorities worked together, one supplementing the other. (*See* [L] *Barker, 1957, pp. 26-54, 86-89; Bréhier, 1947, 1949[b], 1950; Berkhof, 1947; Grégoire, 1948; Hussey, 1937, 1957, pp. 85–100; Gelzer, 1907, pp. 571 ff.; Baynes, 1955, ch. iii, iv.*)

THE HIERARCHY. The Patriarch was at the apex of the complex, bureaucratic hierarchy of the Byzantine church. Below the Patriarch were the metropolitans, who were appointed to rule the ecclesiastical provinces. These were divided into bishoprics. Within his diocese, the bishop was responsible for all ecclesiastical matters, like the discipline of his clergy or of the monasteries, and for the spiritual well-being and instruction of the laity. He had certain rights of jurisdiction when clerics were involved in a case, and the laity could call him in to arbitrate.

The Orthodox church allowed the great majority of the secular clergy—that is, those whose places in the hierarchy were below that of bishop—to remain married if they had been married before being ordained sub-deacons. They also engaged in all kinds of trade, until it was prohibited by canon law. Their status was often low, and many worked as agricultural laborers in the fields, like the present-day *papas* in the Greek countryside. When an estate was sold, they went with it—just as did the *paroikoi,* or dependent tenants, in the village, with village property.

The Church was not poor, and imperial legislation abounded with regulations controlling the administration of its property.

Since the Emperor was the representative of God, he naturally had a special relationship to the Church. After the middle of the fifth century, it became customary for each emperor to be crowned by the Patriarch of Constantinople, the highest ecclesiastical authority in the Byzantine church. To some extent, this did differentiate the Emperor from the ordinary layman. Everywhere, and on all occasions, the Emperor's unique—indeed, his sacred—position was emphasized ([L] *Barker, 1957; Gelzer, 1907; Bréhier, 1948[b]; Hussey, 1957, pp. 100– 114; Baynes, 1955, ch. ii, iii).*

The very conception of a single Christian empire implied that the Church was part of the polity and was in all respects under the general care of the Emperor—even though there were certain specific functions which he himself could not perform. The dichotomy between what was Caesar's and what was God's was not so obvious in the *imperium christianum* of East Rome as in Western Christendom; it came to the surface only when the Emperor was a heretic. The Emperor's special responsibility for maintaining law and order among his subjects, ecclesiastical as well as lay, was recognized—the imperial novels contain many references to regulations concerning this responsibility.

Above all, the Emperor had had, from the beginning, a vital place in the most important organ of church government, the General Council. Though generally accepted as normal, the imperial concern for all aspects of the Church did not go unchallenged; but protests were rare. In the East, after a period of readjustment, certain limitations on imperial control in the Church were accepted—but never to the same extent as in the West. In general, the relation of the Emperor to the Patriarch, of the secular to the ecclesiastical, in Byzantium is best expressed, not by the misleading word "caesaropapism," but as one of "interdependence." (*On the major disputes between Church and state in the Byzantine Empire, see* [L] *Bréhier, 1899, 1904, 1938; Ostrogorsky, 1929[a], 1930[b]; Grégoire, 1927–28[a]; Lander, 1940.*)

MONASTICISM. Monasteries constituted a basic aspect of Byzantine religion. (*[L] Hussey, 1937, 1957, pp. 114-31; Oeconomos, 1918; Barker, 1957, pp. 25-56; Delahaye, 1948 [adapted here mainly from Hussey, 1957, and Barker, 1957].*) Throughout the Middle Ages, monasticism remained an integral part of Byzantine life. From its inception, all Byzantines, great and small, were fervently attached to the institutions. In addition to their spiritual attractions, monasteries offered other benefits of primary importance to the Byzantines. For example, monasteries were also peaceful asylums.

Monasticism served the Byzantine polity in many ways. It did not have to provide education to the extent that Latin monasticism did in the early Middle Ages, but it was a useful ally in the field of social services. Chronicles abound with instances of defeated politicians, deposed Emperors, and unpopular queen mothers who entered monastic houses—sometimes, only to leave them again at the earliest opportunity; more often, to disappear forever from the world.

Monasticism had its abuses; its very popularity meant that it had to fight to maintain its standards within monasteries. The immeasurable growth of monasteries, their acquisition of vast stretches of land, and manpower's flight to them—all contributed not a little to the social and economic, and hence political, disintegration of the Byzantine Empire ([L] *Charanis, 1948, 1951[a], 1951[b]; Ostrogorsky, 1954*).

The monasteries were a very important political factor, as was demonstrated during and after the iconoclastic wars. The fact that monastic intervention in politico-religious disputes was so often successful is due, not merely to the influence of a few outstanding personalities, but also to the wide popularity of the monastic body as a whole.

Nevertheless, monastic life, as it evolved in the Eastern Empire, was not specifically organized toward the pastoral ministry—monks, for the most part were laymen—nor even with a view to charitable work or "social service" (*adapted from* [L] *Barker, 1957, pp. 26–54*). The aspirant's intention, on entering the monastery, was to serve God by working for his own perfection and salvation; he was moved by no burning zeal to contribute to the welfare of others. Eastern monasticism had nothing parallel to the Western variety of orders and religious congregations. Greek monasticism never found its place within a powerful organization; it was never subjected to rigorous discipline or controlled by a permanent and unquestioned authority.

Herein lies the contrast between monasticism in the Byzantine Empire and in Western Europe. Byzantine monasteries were intimately interwoven with the secular world. The East had no central ecclesiastical authority comparable to the Papacy, for the Patriarch was, in matters of administration, subordinate to the Emperor—who was a secular ruler and could not be exclusively, or even primarily, concerned with ecclesiastical organization or monastic reform. Byzantine monasticism seemed to be used almost as a part of secular existence, and it had none of the force and vigor which monks of the West derived from the consciousness of their definite place in a well-ordered church hierarchy; there was no lack of monasteries, but they were isolated and rarely outlived their founders. In general, they produced neither statesmen nor ecclesiastics, neither scholars nor schools; they produced monks concerned with the orthodox performance of their monastic vows.

Byzantine monasticism shared one very significant quality with the Byzantine church. Despite its close relations with the state and the secular world, it survived the downfall of the state and continued to thrive thereafter.

C. CHINA

In China, religion in the dynastic era (from the Han, and especially T'ang, periods on) was already a complex cultural and organizational structure, the outgrowth of merging four distinct religions:

1. *The "primitive" Chinese religion*—more precisely, a conglomeration of several belief trends and ritual systems, like ancestor worship, the yang-yin belief system, the belief in certain deities, the wind-water rituals, etc. ([I] *Des Rotours, 1955; Maspero, 1950[b]; Hodous, 1951.*)

2. *Confucianism* ([I] *O. Franke, 1930-52; Balázs, 1959[b]; Kaltenmark, 1959[a]; Nivison and Wright, 1959; Wright, 1955; De Bary, 1955; Levenson, 1958, p. 1; Shryock, 1951; Chan, 1951*).

3. *Buddhism*—especially Mahayana Buddhism, though several other forms had important impacts ([I] *Gernet, 1956; Wright, 1959; C. K. Yang, 1957; Demiéville, 1959[a], 1959[b]; Nicolas-Vandier, 1959[a], 1959[b]; Liebenthal, 1952*).

4. *Taoism* ([I] *Kaltenmark, 1959[b]; Maspero, 1950[c]; Dubs, 1951*).

CONFUCIANISM. In so far as Confucianism was a religion, it was the religion of the state and not a personal belief system. It did not develop specialized religious roles or organizations; but it permeated the state organization, turning the Chinese state into a special type of church-state.

The Confucian scholars started their activities at the dawn of the Confucian era as experts of rituals. Although they later became politicians, statesmen, and men of letters, they did not abandon their original role. The exclusive political status of Confucianism only strengthened their position as the rightful representatives of the accepted state ritual.

Emperor Wu of the Han first established the Confucian monopoly, by issuing, in 141 B.C., an imperial edict ordering the dismissal of non-Confucian scholars from the supreme Board of Scholars. In 136 B.C., the Confucian doctrine was officially proclaimed as a state dogma.

The Confucian scholars who took over the teaching of the state dogma started to organize their institutions. The Board of Scholars was divided into five faculties, each specializing in one of the five Confucian classics. These were: *Shi-Ching*, the *Book of History*; *Shi-Ching*, the *Book of Odes* (the classic of poetry); *I-Ching*, the *Book of Changes*; *Li-Chi*, the *Record of Rites*; and *Ch'un Ch'iu*, the *Spring and Autumn Annuals*.

In 129 B.C., the Confucians founded the first state university at Ch'ang-an. The stated purpose of the university expresses clearly the religious and the political aspects of the new Confucianism. The purpose is described as being "to transmit the sacred ways of the ancient rulers and to achieve the moral and intellectual advancement of the empire." After this university had been established, many other schools were founded in the provinces to teach the Confucian doctrine.

The Confucianism which became the basis of the state dogma comprised a synthesis of the early Confucian doctrine and several popular Chinese beliefs. It was codified in a series of books and rituals ([I] *Dubs, 1938[b]; Kaltenmark, 1959[a]*).

The canonization and codification of the Confucian writings were followed by the apotheosis of Confucius. In A.D. 59 Emperor Ming ordered sacrifices to be made to Confucius and to his disciples in all cities and government schools. The home of Confucius became a center of pilgrimage, and many Confucian temples were erected. The growth of Taoism and Buddhism only accelerated the process of deification—under their influence, Confucianism absorbed some of the cult elements so well developed in them. At his temples, the image of Confucius replaced the name tablets; and by the T'ang Dynasty, a Confucian cult, complete with an officially sanctioned sacrificial ritual, coexisted with the other cults ([I] *Eiichi, 1960*).

BUDDHISM. In China, Buddhism reached its apogee under the T'ang, especially during and after the reign of the Empress Wei (A.D.

705–712). (*In addition to the literature already cited, see* [I] *Pulley-blank, 1955; Wright, 1957[b]; Hu Shih, 1932; Tsukamoto, 1960.*)

In the fourth century, during the period of the first division of China, political disaster prepared men for the acceptance of new ideas. Confucianism had failed: its promise of security and stability had not been realized, and the belief in the superiority of the scholar was shattered. Taoism was intellectually stimulating and had a soothing effect, but it had little to offer as a social orientation.

The golden era of Buddhism started while renewed attempts were being made to unify the Empire under the Sui and then under the T'ang emperors, who were ready to accept Buddhism as a state religion and to use it as the cultural and religious integrating force of the Empire.

The organizational foci of the new faith were the monasteries established in all the parts of the Empire. The monks and the nuns were the most important missionaries of Buddhism—its true representatives and its devout servants. An intermonastic hierarchy existed. At its apex were the Archbishops (*Seng-lu*), who controlled the monasteries of the whole country. Immediately below were the bishops, who "are only for the area of jurisdiction of a single Government General." The actual authority of these officials was not well defined and it changed according to imperial policy, the connections between the state and the monastic orders, the readiness of the monasteries to submit themselves to a central authority, or even the respective personalities of the dignitaries.

The monasteries held a very strong position, because they were semi-supported, being subordinate to the Board of Sacrifices. Their monks and nuns were not registered with the laity, but on separate census lists (called *Seng-chi*); it is possible that their property was also registered separately.

The state's relation to the monasteries followed a clear-cut division of functions. The authority and the political control remained vested in the state. In the metropolitan districts, monasteries were controlled by the Commissioners of Good Works (*Kung-te-shile*); while in the provinces, the local civil officials had the actual authority ([I] *Gernet, 1956; Wright, 1959; Twitchett, 1956[c], 1957[b]*).

In China, Buddhism attained its greatest heights during the early T'ang period, and its heyday ended after the rebellion of An Lu-shan and the gradual decline of the T'ang ([I] *Pulleyblank, 1955; Wright, 1959, 1951; Ch'en, 1952; Chia, 1956*). Since then—especially since the revival of neo-Confucianism under the Sung—Buddhism has played only a very secondary part in Chinese religious, cultural, and political scene ([I] *Wright, 1959*).

TAOISM. According to its official history, Taoism was founded by Lao-tzu in the sixth century B.C. Under the Han, the importance of Taoism varied in inverse relation to the importance of Confucianism ([I] *Maspero, 1950[b]; Kaltenmark, 1959[b]*).

Taoism, in its popular form, spread quickly during the mid-Han period. Taoists organized secret societies which became deeply rooted in village life; the Taoists' secret societies and semi-monastic communities offered some relief in the period of unrest following Wang Mang's death. One important outcome of this popular movement was Chang Tao-ling's founding of the Taoist state in Szechuan. This was a well-organized church-state headed by Taoist priests. As unrest and disorder grew in the Empire, the Taoist state became a sort of spiritual center for rebellious movements. The Yellow Turban Rebellion was apparently inspired and directed from Szechuan. Although the Yellow Turbans were defeated, Taoism did not lose its hold on the masses.

Taoism was a salvationist religion, promising immortality to its adherents. Immortality could be attained by good deeds and the purification of body and soul. The Taoist moral attitude was based on an individualistic ethic, and not on the existing social structure and its groups—in fact, it negated the basic rewards given by the society: official power, wealth, and prestige. According to Taoism, the most exalted act the individual could perform was voluntarily relinquishing his wealth and office. The paradoxical aspect of this ideology was the evaluation of the act of withdrawal as against outside status. The poor man never had so much merit as the rich man who gave away his fortune, the member of the low class was not so esteemed as the member of the uppermost class who resigned his offices. Thus, to be an ideal Taoist, the individual had first of all to strive to achieve those things which he then would have to abandon.

Perhaps these characteristics of Taoism explain why, even after it had declined as a "semi-official" religion, it persisted in various popular forms—especially among the higher classes, whose religious outlook it continuously influenced.

[3] *Major Characteristics of Chinese Religious Organizations as Crystallized during the T'ang Regime*

During the T'ang Dynasty, the major characteristics of the Chinese religious system, especially in relation to the social system, were fully established. These characteristics were as follows:

1. Chinese "traditional" society was not an outstandingly religious society, since its supreme values were not religious ones. The primary

ideological emphasis was on the stability of the existing social organization; and this was expressed in religious terms through the theory of social and celestial harmony.

2. At the same time, however, paradoxical as it may be, Chinese society was not a secular society: no important activity or sphere of life was free from religious involvement.

3. In spite of the existence of different religions and their interpretations from time to time, a certain degree of religious continuity and homogeneity was preserved. The basic features of this continuity were: (a) the perseverance of several religious ideas of the ancient Chinese belief system—filial piety, ancestor worship, the theory of yang-yin and the tao, and the magical-religious role of the emperor; (b) the dominance of Confucian ethics, which formed a sort of framework within which all the changes occurred; (c) the mutual influence of the four religions—each new trend emerged against the background of the complete religious pattern of the society, and new ideas introduced by one trend somehow influenced the whole pattern; (d) the dominance of Confucianism was not a monopolistic religious rule—Confucianism did not try to answer many of the "eternal" questions of religion, and so secondary, and mostly salvationist, religions could develop; and (e) each of the great religions had at least a dual theological and ideological system—an abstract system, with a marked philosophic flavor, and a popular system that emphasized the magical aspect. The cleavage between the nobility and the commoners, and the tradition of the literary education of the nobility, seem to have been closely associated to the development of such dual ideologies.

4. There was no organized church in China. The Buddhist monasteries of the T'ang Dynasty most closely approximated a central church system; but they were still nothing like the Catholic Church of Europe. None of the Chinese religions became a properly organized autonomous unit; the concept of church or parish was foreign to the Chinese mind. Exclusive groups of believers hardly emerged. The usual religious orientation was eclectic and extremely tolerant, especially in the spiritual (ideological) sphere, of contradictory beliefs. Religious antagonism or intolerance was formulated in terms of non-conformist acts rather than of dissenting beliefs. The religious persecution which often developed in China was usually predominantly a political phenomenon, and much less a cultural-spiritual one. In China, persecution and intolerance usually developed when the state or power groups within the ruling stratum grew apprehensive about the political or economic power accumulated by another group, which happened to belong to a certain religious denomination ([I] *C. K. Yang, 1957; Groot, 1903; Pulleyblank, 1955; Wright, 1959*).

[4] *Religious Organization in the Islamic States, the Spanish-American Empire, and Europe*

In the Islamic states, and especially in the early *Caliphate,* the relation between state and religion was much more complicated. These states were created by conquest—a new universal religion emerged in and was diffused by conquering tribes. In the initial stage of the conquest, the identification between tribe and religion was very great. In later stages, it became weakened, when the more centralized bureaucratic empires (the Abbasides and the Fatimites) developed ethnically heterogeneous elements were welded together by a common religion and a new political framework.

In theory, the caliph continued to be subject to the rules of the *Sharia* (the holy law of Islam). As most of the later caliphs (Abbasides and Fatimites) rode to power on the crests of religious movements, each sought to retain popular support by stressing the religious aspect of his authority and by courting the religious leaders. But the religious leadership was not organized as a separate church and did not constitute a closely organized body; it was, therefore, itself greatly dependent on the rulers ([M] *Lewis, 1950,* [N] *1953,* [M] *1954; Brockelmann, 1943; Grunebaum, 1946, 1955[a], 1955[b];* [N] *Cahen, 1955[a]; Dennet, 1939, 1950*).

Hence, the religious check on the political authority was not effective. There was no machinery except revolt for its enforcement, and indeed, various religious sects and movements continuously developed in these states and very often contributed to their downfall ([N] *Cahen, 1957[a], 1957[b]; Lewis, 1953;* [M] *Hodgson, 1960*).

In the Spanish-American Empire ([R] *Desdevises du Dezert, 1914, 1917; Haring, 1947, ch. x; Hanke, 1937, 1951; Mörner, 1953; Vida Viceus, 1957*) and most European countries, religious organization was dominated by the Catholic church and its different, most highly developed autonomous religious organizations (the "official Church" and the monastic orders). The Church's strong universalistic orientation transcended any given political community. As an organization, it has always constituted an autonomous and independent political force.

In some European countries during this period, the Church's monopoly was broken by the Protestant dissension. This gave rise to specifically intensive religious sects (whose organization varied from country to country) with very intensive, autonomous political orientations. (*For a general survey, see* [S] *Cobban, 1957; Greaves, 1957; Clark, 1929–59, 1957; Sykes, 1934; Jedin, 1955; Leonard, 1955; Orcibal, 1955.*)

[5] *The Development of the Autonomy of the Religious System*

As the preceding descriptions show, the religions which developed in the respective societies studied here were very different. Nevertheless, they had some common features, when considered in terms of the social differentiation of the religious field. In these societies, this differentiation was manifested in the development of (1) the religious field or sphere as distinct and autonomous from other institutional spheres in the society; (2) specific religious organizations and roles; and (3) several types of religious orientations emphasizing the autonomy of religious values and activities vis-à-vis other institutional spheres of the society.

In the societies we are examining, the identity between the entire community and the religious sphere, found in many primitive and even patrimonial societies, was largely absent. In most of the societies studied here, one religious organization or several competing organizations encompassed all the society's members. Yet these organizations—even when one included all members of a society—were separate, distinct units and had their own distinct identity and organizational hierarchical structures: In only a few of them—probably, only in the ancient Egyptian and Inca empires—was there a complete fusion of some major political and religious roles (for instance, in the role of the "King-God"). Even when the monarch performed some role in the religious hierarchy, this hierarchy was distinct from the political one.

The autonomy of the religious sphere was clear also in the multiplicity of religious organizations and in the competition between them. In most of the societies concerning us here, several major religious groups or organizations developed and often competed with each other. Their competition was usually connected with the fact that they all had wider, sometimes universalistic, orientations.

However, in the historical bureaucratic societies, the religious sphere's autonomy did not entail its total separation or distinctiveness from other institutional spheres, or the development of secular value orientation. Religious values and symbols were prominent in the cultural orientations of all strata. The legitimation of the rulers was usually couched in religious terms, and the cultural life of most strata was organized around religious symbols and institutions. These institutions were the main centers of cultural creativity and of transmitting the cultural traditions of these societies.

The limited distinctiveness of the religious sphere was manifested, to an even larger degree, in the extent to which specific religious roles and organizations developed. Many specialized religious organizations —temples, religious "foundations," priestly associations, sects, churches, and monastic orders—evolved, and many of them were organized bureaucratically. Closely linked with them was the development of many specialized religious roles—priests, preachers, and/or monks—holders of different positions in ecclesiastical organizations and hierarchies.

On the other hand, the religious worshipping community was, to a great extent, either identical with or closely related to local groups. A special type of religious *community* developed only in sects and monastic orders. Thus, in some crucial aspects of the organization of the religious sphere—in the roles of religious leaders and devotees, in the structure of religious associations and their goals, and in the relations between these associations and the political sphere—this sphere evolved with a marked autonomy and distinctiveness. To a much smaller degree, the extent of this distinctiveness was evinced by the structure of the over-all religious community, where most religious activities, participation, and roles were embedded in other (generally kinship and territorial) groups, and closely associated with familial roles and community participation.

[6] *Characteristics of Religious Value Orientations*

We may now examine several aspects of religious orientations and values that are important for our analysis.

The first such aspect is what we shall call the "group referent" of these religions. The second comprises some components of the religious belief systems significant in the relation between religious attitudes and political activities and organizations. The third is the development, in these religious and value systems, of relatively strong autonomous ideological orientations.

The primary feature of the group referent of most of the religions examined here is that it was wider than that of any ascriptive and territorial groups composing one of these societies. The basic group referents of most of these religions were (1) the total society, as symbolized by religious values and as a bearer of such cultural and religious values; and/or (2) the specific religious community; or (3) wider, i.e., "potential," religious collectivities, like "all believers" or "all mankind." The more particularistic orientations focused on a given polity occur mostly in the less differentiated and more traditional societies, like Egypt, Persia, and to some extent, China. ([F] *Otto, 1953; Wilson, 1951; Frankfort, 1948. On Persia, see* [G] *Ghirshman, 1954; Christensen, 1939; 1936 pp. 110 ff.* et passim; *Mole, 1953; de Menasce, 1955; Klima, 1957; Coulborn, 1958–59.*) In the last, there already existed a more general cultural orientation to systems of rites and ethics that were presumably applicable to all Chinese at all times—and that possibly had an even more universal application. The Roman Empire made many attempts to give a wider, almost universal meaning to various aspects of Roman culture and of the "Pax Romana." In Byzantium, in European countries during the Age of Absolutism, in the Arab Caliphate, and in the Spanish-American Empire, there were full-fledged universal religious or cultural orientations.

These "wider," often universalistic, orientations enhanced in several ways the autonomy and distinctiveness of the religious sphere. First, they undermined the legitimation of any purely particularistic group; and, to some extent, they emphasized some common allegiances, norms, and symbols that cut across any given territorial group or status hierarchy. Also, the very structure of these value orientations necessarily emphasized some autonomy of the cultural-religious sphere, in terms of its organization in specific groups and its direct appeal to various population groups. Third, the legitimation which these religions provided for the rulers and ruling elites was not unconditional and "given." It was often conditional on the rulers' accepting approved patterns of behavior and values, and on their finding some *modus vivendi* with the religious organizations. Tension and competition easily arose between the rulers and the religious organizations. The religious institutions could become independent forces and foci of power in the society, not only because of their separate organizational identities, but also by virtue of the components of their value systems.

The second major aspect of value orientation of the religions studied here relevant to our analysis is the emphasis on individual moral-religious responsibility and what we may call individual religious "activism." The emphasis on the right moral and religious attitudes, and on the fulfilment of moral obligations implied by the individual's religious attitudes, constituted an important facet of most of these religions. The prevalent and predominant religions were characterized by some such activist trend, which emphasized the devotee's commitment to certain religiously prescribed tenets and lines of action, to the endeavor to implement them in social life, and to influence and judge at least some aspects of his life according to the criteria inherent in his religious commitments. The ways of expressing this emphasis varied greatly from one society to another, as did the emphasis on performance aspects in general. But several important ingredients of this emphasis existed in all the religions studied and usually had important repercussions in the structure of social and political activities.

The *activist* trend and emphasis on individual responsibility and performance, combined with the wider group referent, provided the religious activities with an autonomous dynamism of their own, with an impetus toward organizing various social activities and groups, and with a set of autonomous criteria for judging various aspects of secular reality. These criteria could vary in kind and content. In some cases—such as Buddhism, Mazdaism, and, to a smaller extent, Eastern Christianity—their orientation was "other-worldly," entailing a rather passive attitude to political life. ([L] *Barker, 1957; Hussey, 1937, 1957;* [G] *Christensen, 1936, pp. 11 ff., 1939; Ghirshman, 1954; Klima, 1957.*) In others—like Confucianism, Catholicism, and, especially, Protestantism—the criteria were mostly oriented to activity within the social and political realities of their respective societies. Whatever their particular content, they often tended to engender the creation of special types of activity and organization, such as sects and religious orders that could easily become independent foci of social orientations and political loyalties.

[7] The Development of Autonomous Ideological Orientations in the Religious System

The remaining aspect of these religious and value systems relevant for our analysis is their internal development of relatively independent ideological systems—i.e., systems of ideals and activities that attempted to organize and evaluate, according to ultimate values, the social reality in which they develop, and that endeavored to shape the world according to a given set of values and purposes and to convert others to this endeavor.

Ideological elements can, of course, be found in all religions and value systems. Each contains some reference to, and evaluation of, the social reality in terms of basic religious values and symbols. However, these references and orientations are often embedded in the prevalent religious and mythical thought. In many of the religious and value systems of the societies investigated here—particularly in the more universalistic ones—there was a tendency, on the contrary, to develop some autonomous ideological orientations and systems, which committed their members to evaluate social reality and then propel it in the "proper" direction. The commitments imposed by these systems were not simply embedded in ritual and religious acts; they implied more specific social or political activities.

The ideological elements were intimately related to the activist trends in those value systems. Many conservative ideologies, directed toward justifying the status quo, have, of course, appeared, and have often become predominant in the value systems of these religions. However, the very existence of autonomous ideological systems could serve as a potential focus for various dynamic and autonomous activities.

Each of these aspects of the distinctiveness of the religious sphere could also be found in other types of societies. However, the combination of all of them seems much more prominent in the historical bureaucratic societies than in others.

All these aspects of the religions' value orientations emphasized, from different points of view, the relative autonomy of the religious sphere and its "disembeddedment" from the total community and from the other institutional spheres. However, as indicated above, in the societies examined here, this distinctness of the religious sphere was rather limited. Throughout the history of their religious elites tried to maintain dominance in the cultures of these societies. Their attempts are best illustrated by several patterns of activity which they developed or promoted.

The first such pattern of activity by religious elites and organizations is the great formalization and codification of religious traditions by the manifold elites and priestly groups. This formalization was manifested in (1) the codification of sacred books; (2) the development of schools devoted to interpreting the texts; (3) the growth of special educational organizations to spread religious knowledge; and (4) the elaboration of total world-views and ideologies.

The second major pattern of activity was intimately related to the "spread" of religious knowledge. It consisted of attempts to integrate-love, to use Redfield's nomenclature, the "Little Traditions" of various localities into the "Great Tradition" of the cultural centers.

[8] *The Structure of the Educational Systems*

The analysis of the cultural-religious sphere in the historical bureaucratic societies would not be complete without a consideration of the development of education within them.

For our discussion, the first important characteristic of the process of education in the higher, more active strata of these societies is that it was no longer entirely embedded in fixed ascriptive family or territorial groups. Special formalized educational institutions, schools and universities of various kinds, developed. Several rudiments of such educational institutions existed in Sassanid Persia. They were fully developed in the school, academy, and university system of the Byzantine Empire ([L] *Hussey, 1937, pp. 22–116; Bréhier, 1927–27; Fuchs, 1926; Grégoire, 1927–28[b]; Buckler, 1929; Dietrich, 1918*), and in the system of Confucian schools and preparatory schools for the civil service examinations in the Chinese Empire. Such schools developed to an even greater extent in the Spanish-American Empire, and, of course, in France and England ([Y] *Sagnac, 1945, 1946;* [Z] *Ashley, 1947;* [R] *Haring, 1947, ch. xi, xii; Priestley, 1918*).

It is in these institutions that most of the training both for governmental posts and for the professions and elites was centered. The schools served as major channels of mobility within the society. However, the training they provided, especially in the upper and middle grades, was not usually specialized; and they were not envisaged as places where only technical knowledge and know-how were transmitted. (*For instance,* [L] *Andréadès, 1926; Baynes, 1955, chaps. i, ii; Barker, 1957;* [R] *Haring, 1947, chap. x.*)

These institutions were concerned to a great extent both with the transmission of knowledge and with the inculcation of wider, more diffuse cultural orientations and values, which were more encompassing than the culture and traditions of any local group and which incorporated many elements of different "Great Traditions." Sassanid Persia ([G] *Christensen, 1936; Altheim, 1955[a], 1955[b]; Massé, 1952; Mole, 1953; de Menasce, 1955;* [I] *Galt, 1951 passim; Hucker, 1950, 1951; Balázs, 1950; Kaltenmark, 1959[a]*) sponsored identification with the new state, the dynasty, and the formalized Mazdaist religion ([G] *Christensen, 1936, 1939; Altheim, 1955[a], 1955[b]*); in Byzantium, many schools (both private and public), academies, and universities developed, that fostered the identification with the Hellenistic culture, while the Byzantine society and polity perceived themselves as the principal progenitors of this culture ([L] *Baynes, 1955, ch. i–iii; Diehl, 1943; Barker, 1957, pp. 1–26, 50–56; Bréhier, 1950; Jenkins, 1953*). In China, many schools and academies arose; most of them were oriented to preparation for the state (Confucian) examinations, or constituted centers of Confucian (and, in some cases, also of Buddhist and Taoist) learning ([I] *Galt, 1951; Maspero, 1950[b], 1950[c]; Eberhard, 1948[a]; Strange, 1950; Franke, 1930–52*). In the Spanish-American Empire, many schools and universities evolved which fostered identification with Christian-European culture. In France and England, the schools and institutions were permeated with orientation to the wider Christian culture, to its various local subcultures, and, gradually, to a broader European culture as well. At a later stage, these European institutions, as well as various cultural groups and associations (discussed below), became part of the new secular-rational trend that developed in Europe.

It is important to note that, in most countries, these institutions and groups were developed and maintained both by the state (as part of its bureaucratic organization) and also by various private groups and individuals. The most important of these groups were, of course, the various cultural elites. (These will be described in greater detail subsequently.) For example, in Byzantium the academies were supported not only by the state but also by private donors and the Church, while the schools were almost entirely privately supported ([L] *Hussey, 1937, 1957, pp. 145–56; Barker, 1957, pp. 26–54*). The importance of various social groups and "private resources" in the establishment, development, and maintenance of schools and universities was even more pronounced in the European countries and in the Spanish-American Empire.

In China, many Confucian academies were established and maintained by gentry and scholar families. Many local schools were established by various religious sects and by local groups and families.

A similar pattern evolved even in some of the conquest empires, once they had passed from the primary conquest stage to a measure of stability. The example of the Spanish-American Empire is highly instructive. There, many institutions of learning were established by political, religious, and social groups—usually, groups of conquerors. These institutions served as foci of common values and wider orientations—and to some (even if limited) extent, they bridged the gap between the different racial groups.

These institutions were not entirely confined to the upper and uppermiddle strata, although they were most prominent among them. When we discuss the patterns of communication among the lower strata, we shall see that among them also there existed some educational and cultural organizations whose function was to propagate such wider values and orientations. In several cases—for example, in Sassanid Persia and in the Byzantine Empire ([L] *Diehl, 1957, 1943; Bréhier, 1948[a], pp. 334–430; Jerkins, 1953*)—the army was a very important agent in developing, spreading, and maintaining these wider orientations, especially among the lower-class peasant and urban groups ([L] *Diehl, 1943, 1957, pp. 40–53; Stein, 1920*).

[9] *Summary*

In the fields of education, culture, and religion, certain orientations and attitudes that can be seen as "free-floating" developed. Cultural and religious activities and orientations became largely disconnected from primary ascriptive kinship and territorital groups and roles. A potential of such activities and orientations developed, that tended to be organized in specific groups and roles and could serve as a reservoir for the creation of such groups and roles. These orientations and ideologies could innovate centers of power and activity that would have to be regulated by mechanisms differing from those of the basic ascriptive kinship and territorial groups. The differentiated or separate ideological systems increased the extent of autonomous orientation to the social and political spheres. By virtue of all these factors, the religious groups and organizations could themselves become centers of this free-floating power—and could attempt to organize it according to their own orientations and interests.

The various characteristics of the religions we have outlined were, in a general way, common to all the societies studied here: however, many differences existed between the different religions, as we have already illustrated above to some extent. These differences are often crucially important for our analysis. The most consequential differences were in the following factors:

1. The extent of the basic differentiation of the religious sphere from other social spheres and institutions

2. The scope of the religion's organizational distinctiveness, autonomy, and cohesiveness

3. The degree to which the religion identified with the political regime

4. The importance and strength of universalistic orientations in the major orientations of the religion

5. The strength of activist orientations and of autonomous ideological elements in the religion's value orientations

5

Social Organization and Stratification

[1] Introduction

The next institutional field whose development will be examined is that of social organization and stratification. In this as in other institutional fields, we can see that the societies studied here developed from feudal or patrimonial systems in which there existed a relatively undifferentiated, ascriptive, and rather rigid systems of status and social organization. These evolved, in spite of the fact that there still prevailed many ascriptive criteria, into much more flexible and differentiated patterns of social organization and stratification.

[2] Social Organization and Stratification

A. SASSANID PERSIA

The least flexible and differentiated kind of social organization and stratification was the kind in Sassanid Persia. (*Here following* [G] *Christensen, 1939; Benveniste, 1932. For more detailed analysis, see* [G] *Christensen, 1936 passim; Altheim and Stiehl, 1954; Altheim, 1955[a], 1955[b].*)

At its apex was the head of the state, the King of Kings. There were four groups below him; their sizes varied progressively from small to large, with the largest at the base. The first class comprised the vassals —the great and petty princes who, for recognizing and being loyal to Persian overlordship, were allowed to retain possession of their thrones. This class also included princes of the royal blood, who were entrusted with the government of the great provinces and of conquered and annexed territories.

Below them on the social scale were the heads of the seven great families—this number had persisted, through the centuries, from the Ahamenid period. They had inherited their feudal system directly from the Parthians, under whom the power of the nobles had deprived the kingdom of political stability. Although they had taken over the system, the Sassanids endeavored to curtail its power. In fact, their power diminished during the early years of Sassanid rule, until the death of Shapur II; but it increased again during the 125-year period of trouble and weakness that lasted until the accession of Khosrou I. It was curbed once more by the last two Great Kings.

The seven families certainly exercised authority over entire provinces where the peasants were obliged to pay taxes to them in addition to the taxes demanded by the royal treasury. In return, the families provided the Crown with military support and were obligated to levy troops, if necessity arose. Some of these families held hereditary offices, both civil and military, that must have undergone certain changes during four centuries of Sassanid history.

The class whose members were designated as "the grandees and nobles" had the function, in effect, of checking the power of the great families from encroaching. This class included the high state officers, ministers, heads of the administration, and royal officials. Its growth and development introduced a new element into society; and by relying on this class and on the army, the Sassanid monarchy was able to reorganize the state and endow it with a strength that had been unknown under the Arsacids.

At the bottom of the hierarchy were the freemen, the small landed nobility or headmen of villages (Dekhans), the link between the peasant and the official representative of the central government. They were responsible to the administration for the collection of taxes levied on the peasants, who formed the great mass of the population. Though free *de jure,* the peasants were *de facto* reduced to the condition of serfs attached to the soil, and were sold along with the land and villages.

In Sassanid times, there apparently was also a relatively strong and wealthy bourgeois class composed of merchants, heads of industrial workshops, etc. It was concentrated primarily in the cities, especially in the capital. ([G] *Ghirshman, 1954; Christensen, 1936, ch. i.*)

In addition to the ecclesiastical groups, some groups of what we may call "cultural elites" or "specialists" existed. Among these, the astrologers and the various types of medical specialists were especially important. They were not usually fully organized but formed loose groups of individual specialists.

As far as is known, Sassanid social structure was relatively rigid and formalized. Officially, at least, clear distinctions were made between different social classes—especially between the higher and the lower ones—and there was seemingly little social mobility between them. It is, however, possible that the structure was not so rigid, in practice. Many cases of an individual's rising from one class to another (especially in the higher and middle groups) are known; and the kings themselves seem to have encouraged these individuals, through the system of honors they distributed.

B. THE BYZANTINE EMPIRE

The structure of Byzantine society was much more flexible than that of the Sassanid Empire, although in Byzantium also several "traditional" undifferentiated areas and groups persisted. (*On some of the general aspects of Byzantine society, see* [L] *Charanis, 1944–45, 1951[a]; Hussey, 1957, ch. viii, ix; Diehl, 1906–08, 1929, 1943, ch. ix; Runciman, 1933, ch. viii, ix; Bréhier, 1949[b], ch. i, ii, iv, v.*) At the top were the aristocracy and bureaucracy, composed mostly of the big landowners—many of whom came from long-established families. Many members of this top group, however, were relative newcomers who owed their memberships to frequent political upheavals. Since there was no formal legal definition of aristocratic status, the aristocracy for the most part constituted a group of those having landed property. Members were often recruited from the higher echelons of the civil bureaucracy. Military leaders and the great magnates of the provinces could join the aristocratic ranks. The aristocracy was characterized by its members' similarity of interests and ways of life, but it was fairly accessible to newcomers. (*On Byzantine aristocracy, see* [L] *Ostrogorsky, 1956[a] passim, 1954 passim; Jenkins, 1953; Lemerle, 1958; Runciman, 1929, pp. 109 ff.; Charanis, 1951[b]; Guilland, 1947–48, 1954; Beck, 1956.*)

There is no doubt that the bureaucracy was one of the most powerful groups in Byzantine society and that, until about the twelfth century, talent was one means of entering it. The bureaucracy was a main channel of social mobility; and many of its members were recruited from the different rural and urban strata that entered imperial service. (*On the bureaucracy, see Bréhier, 1949[b], pp. 39–166; Stein, 1924, 1954; Dendias, 1939; Kolias, 1939; Andréadès, 1926. On the aristocratization of the bureaucracy in the later periods of Byzantine history, see Guilland, 1953–55; Ostrogorsky, 1929[a], 1956[a], ch. v–vii, ix; Lemerle, 1958; Stein, 1924.*)

The merchants and the artisans were, as indicated, the second most important elements in the urban population of the Empire— especially of the capital. Thus, between the landed aristocracy and the vast majority of the city populace, there was a class of people which may be described as the bourgeoisie. The bourgeoisie were probably of popular origin. As they rose in wealth and influence, their sympathies seem to have favored landed aristocracy ([L] *Bratianu, 1938; Bréhier, 1949[b], ch. vi, vii, 1950, ch. iii, iv*). In the great popular uprisings which shook Thessalonica in 1342 and again in 1345, the bourgeoisie did not co-operate with the rebels against the aristocracy—and, for that reason, they were destroyed.

In addition to the various groups of merchants and artisans, and the court, aristocracy, and bureaucracy, Byzantine urban society comprised several other strata. The most important were, undoubtedly, the various religious, cultural and professional groups. At this point, we must note that these groups were not restricted to the urban sectors of the society; they spread also to the rural society—as did also, to a certain extent, other cultural groups.

The members of the various semi-professional groups—especially the jurists and the doctors—were more urban in character. These groups were of fair importance in the urban centers; the jurists, in particular, were also strongly aligned in special organizations. Similar organizations seem to have existed among the doctors ([L] *Runciman, 1933; Hussey, 1957, ch. vii; Bréhier, 1949[b]; Baynes, 1955, ch. iv*).

These semi-professional organizations were very close to the main centers of learning—the academies and universities ([L] *Hussey, 1937, 1957*), and the imperial court—and served as important centers of political and cultural activities. Though closely supervised by the emperors, they were autonomous bodies with a great deal of internal solidarity and common outlook and values.

Lowest on the social scale of the Empire's urban centers were, of course, the masses ([L] *Ostrogorsky, 1956[a], especially ch. ii; Bratianu, 1938; Manojlovic, 1936; Janssens, 1936. See also Hadjinicolaou-Marava, 1950; Lopes, 1933*). Though the emperors' bureaucracy—and, later, the aristocracy—actually ruled the Empire, their positions were not entirely uninfluenced by the city masses. For the city populace, especially in the capital, played a part in the political life of the Empire that was not insignificant. The different sectors of the urban population belonged to different political organizations and institutions. The upper groups, the aristocracy and bureaucracy, in which urban and non-urban elements intermingled, were represented in the Senate ([L] *Diehl, 1924,*

1929, 1943, ch. iv.; Stein, 1940). The lower urban groups were organized in the demes or "circus parties"—the famous factions of Blues and Greens—organizations with political purposes and not merely for sports. The popular parties of the Blues and Greens, whose leaders were appointed by the government, had important public functions: they served as the city guard, and participated in repairing the city walls. The Blues and the Greens played a very important part in all the big cities of the Empire, since the people voiced political opinions through them. ([L] *Maricq, 1949; Dvornik, 1946; Bury, 1910, pp. 105 ff., Bratianu, 1937, 1948[a]*.)

The demes apparently were effectual only during the fifth through seventh centuries. Subsequently, their political value greatly diminished; gradually, they became merely recreational groups, dwindling entirely in importance. But even by the thirteenth century, the force of the city populace in the political life of the Empire had not been destroyed. Surpressed for a while during the glorious days of the Macedonian Dynasty, the masses re-emerged in the eleventh century; and it was to them that the last representative of the Macedonian Dynasty owed the recovery of his throne from Michael V.

The peasantry constituted a crucial part of the Byzantine social structure, and the emperors were always concerned to maintain a free peasantry, independent of the aristocracy. The free peasantry, concentrated in these village communities, provided an important source of recruits for the army, bureaucracy, and even the profession. ([L] *Rouillard, 1953; Iorga, 1940[a], 1940[b]; Diehl, 1943, ch. iv, ix, x; Bréhier, 1924; Jenkins, 1953; Ostrogorsky, 1956[a], ch. ii, v; Charanis, 1944–45, 1951[a]*.) It was only after the eleventh century that the free peasantry began to decline, as a result of the aristocracy's continuous encroachments and of the weakening of the central power.

C. T'ANG CHINA

During the T'ang Dynasty, many characteristics of the "Confucian" Chinese system of social organization became crystallized. At the same time, however, several remnants of earlier times—as evidenced especially in the relative prominence of aristocratic groups—were still discernible.

The major characteristics of the new social organization that began to take definite form then were as follows:

1. The relative predominance of political-literary criteria in the definition of status—i.e., the official prominence of the literati and officials

2. The growing importance of Confucian ideology in the definitions of the criteria of stratification

3. The relative weakening of the aristocracy, and the growing social and economic predominance of the gentry

4. The development of the court as an important focus of the system of stratification

5. The evolution of several secondary patterns—like the actual rather than the official importance of merchants, the special place of the military, and the development of many local variations. (*On the general characteristics of Chinese social structure, as it developed from pre-Han times and crystallized in the T'ang period, to persist throughout the imperial system, see* [I] *Eberhard, 1948[a], 1952, 1958; Wittfogel, 1935, 1938, 1950, 1957; Stange, 1951; Pulleyblank, 1958; Eisenstadt, 1958; Bodde, 1956; Lattimore, 1951, Balázs, 1952, 1959[a]. For the post-Han period, see* [I] *Balázs, 1948, 1950; H. Franke, 1951.*)

These major qualities of Chinese society were greatly influenced by the Confucian ideology ([I] *O. Franke, 1930-52, 1945; Fairbank, 1958*), which regards society as a hierarchical order of four groups: scholars, farmers, artisans, and merchants. Each group is evaluated on the basis of its productive contribution to the existence of the ideal society. Scholars have the highest prestige, because only they know and perpetuate the right living. The farmer's duty is to provide the livelihood of the scholar. Merchants have no prestige, because commerce is "nonessential" and "frivolous." (*See* [I] *Chu, 1957;* [I] *Fairbank, 1958, ch. ii, iv; H. Franke, 1951; Pulleyblank, 1954.*)

The actual structure of the society was much more complex, and the hierarchy less clear, than the Confucian image. The framework consisted of a fairly stable dichotomous class system, and each class contained subdivisions ([[I] *Pulleyblank, 1954, 1955; Balázs, 1952, 1959[a], 1960*).

Officially, the dichotomy was made basically according to an occupational criterion—the differentiation between mental labor and physical labor. Mental labor (governmental and scholastic) was the duty and the privilege of the upper class, which was accorded undisputed prestige. Physical labor was the function of the lower class. Legal privileges and the right to political power were enjoyed exclusively by the upper class.

Neither class was homogeneous. In the upper class, subgroups were differentiated according to birth, scholarship, and political power; in the lower class, according to occupation and wealth.

In the upper group, the criteria of subdivision created three partially overlapping groups—the aristocracy, the (literary) gentry, and the officials.

The prestige of the aristocracy in relation to the prestige of the literati changed from time to time, until the end of the T'ang Dynasty, when the aristocracy became less important ([I] *Pulleyblank, 1955; Twitchett, 1956[b]; Eberhard, 1952; Balázs, 1948, 1950; Des Rotours, 1926, 1932, Introduction*). The periodic strengthenings of Confucian ideals were usually followed by an enhancement of the gentry's prestige.

Within this social structure, the gentry class was of special importance. It had comprised the stratum of families, based on landed property, that came between the earth-bound masses of the peasantry, and the officials and merchants who formed a fluid matrix of over-all administrative and commercial activity. (*On the different definitions of "gentry," see* [I] *Eberhard, 1945, 1948[a], 1951, 1952; Wittfogel, 1957; Pulleyblank, 1958;* [I] *Chang, 1955; Bodde, 1956. On the relations between gentry and literati, see* [I] *Chang, 1955; Eberhard, 1945, 1948[a], 1951, 1952; Pulleyblank, 1955, 1958;* [I] *Balázs, 1952, 1959[a], 1960; Ho, 1959; Kracke, 1957.*)

The gentry were not a "feudal" class in any proper sense of the term (a term too readily applied today). The Chinese peasant, both in law and in fact, had been free to sell and, when possible, to purchase, land. He was earth-bound as a result of many circumstances, but not by any institution similar to European feudalism.

The gentry lived chiefly in the walled towns instead of in the villages. They were the local elite, conducting certain functions connected with the peasantry below, and certain others connected with the officials above. The peasant community regarded them as the land-owners, the lowest rung of the great ruling class; and the gentry managed the system of customary and legal rights to the use of the land ([I] *Lattimore, 1951; Fairbank, 1958*). Within the Chinese social structure, the extended family performed a crucial role and constituted the focus of social organization ([I] *M. Levy, 1955; Liu, 1957, 1959[b]*).

In the lower class, each occupational group had its own prestige hierarchy. Wealth accentuated the internal differentiation of the occupational group, and influenced the status of each occupation ([I] *Balázs, 1954[a], 1960*).

"Classical" (Confucian) education was the legitimate channel of mobility from the lower to the upper class ([I] *Dubs, 1938[b]; Martin, 1893; O. Franke, 1945, 1930–52; Ho, 1959; Des Rotours, 1932, 1947–48; Chang, 1955*). This path was legally closed to merchants, but the wealthy ones managed to direct their most gifted sons to scholarship.

Merchants had two other means of moving, with some ease, into the gentry class—purchase of land, and intermarriage. Since farmers were free to sell their land, merchants had an opportunity to invest in land and thereby gain both steady income and social prestige. Unlike Europe, China in her formative period engaged in little foreign trade in which a merchant could invest. Land remained the great object of commercial investment; and the merchant class produced more land-lords than independent commercial capitalists ([I] *Fairbank, 1958; Chang, 1955; Eberhard, 1952; Ho, 1959*).

The legitimate entrance to the bureaucracy was through examinations. However offices could be also acquired either by purchase or through direct bestowal of titles (mostly to military leaders) by the emperors. These means varied in importance in different periods; but in most times, they constituted an important channel of mobility ([I] *Des Rotours, 1947–48, Introduction; Chang, 1955; Pulleyblank, 1955*).

In addition to the two classes defined as the integral and necessary parts of society, there was a third, caste-like group. This comprised the outcasts, "mean" people—slaves, prostitutes, entertainers, government runners, servants, beggars—whose occupations were branded as socially useless ([I] *Wilbur, 1943; Chu, 1957; C. I. Yang, 1956[a], 1956[b]*). Since they were barred from contact or intermarriage with the lower class, and excluded from competing in the examination system, they had no chance to change their menial status.

D. THE SPANISH-AMERICAN EMPIRE

The society that developed in the Spanish Indies comprised several different elements. The two basic ones were the Spanish and the Indian communities. But gradually, there developed many differences within these groups as well as some—albeit very small—mobility and intercourse between them. Within the Spanish society, a great difference evolved between the Insular Spaniards, sent over for different periods of time from Spain, to serve as officials, etc., and the "native" Spaniards, the Creoles. Among the Creoles, many different groups emerged—the landed aristocracy, the merchants (although these two groups were often closely interrelated), and the lower groups (the small land-owners, small traders, marginal professionals, etc). (See [R] *Bagu, 1949; Konetzke, 1949[b], 1951[a], 1951[b], 1952, 1953; Vida Viceus, 1957; Miranda, 1951; Hernandez y Sanchez-Barba, 1954, 1955; Ots Capdequi, 1934[b], 1941, 1951; Durand, 1953; Villabolos, 1951; Zavala, 1943, 1949.*) Within the Indian community, several differentiations also grew. ([R] *Vida Viceus, 1957; Gallo, 1951[a], 1951[b]; Gibson, 1955; Garcia, 1900; Gongora, 1951; Konetzke, 1949[a], 1949[b]; 1953; Miranda, 1952[b]; Hanke, 1936[b]; Simpson, 1934, 1938, 1940, 1950; Zavala, 1943.*)

THE SPANISH COMMUNITY. The few descendants of the conquistadores, settlers related to distinguished families in Spain, higher civil officials, and wealthy Creoles with a title or decoration or who had acquired some perpetual office, combined to form a colonial aristocracy based chiefly on wealth (mostly, but not entirely, landed wealth). They

virtually monopolized access to the legal profession, to militia com-
mands, and to the higher clergy. They were the *gente decente,* distinguished from other subjects by finer apparel. But this aristocracy's
feudal tendencies were curbed very early by the Crown, and their
political—and, to some extent, also economic—powers were curtailed.

The fundamental unit of local political organization among the
Spaniards in America was the town. It had been the dominant form in
medieval Spain, and it served as the means of reorganizing and His-
panicizing the conquered lands.

Many of the towns rapidly developed elective and consultative features that insured firm control by the townfolk—even though the first
council, in almost every town, had been appointed by the governor of
the district or by the head of the conquering expedition. Under a decree issued in 1523 and incorporated in the Laws of the Indies in 1680,
the burghers were settled to elect their councilors unless the royal contract with the leader of the conquest had provided otherwise. Even
where the council was appointed, its members had to be burghers—
and usually there were so few burghers that it was difficult to find
enough to serve. In the early towns, which were composed of fighting
men, no council could hope to function unless it had the approval of
the burghers ([R] *Moore, 1954; Haring, 1947, ch. ix; Ots Capdequi,
1934[a], 1941; Palm, 1951; Vida Viceus, 1957; Borah, 1956; Durand,
1953; Gongora, 1951; Castañeda, 1929*).

During the seventeenth century, however, a progressively larger
number of posts in local administrative bodies were offered for sale or
made hereditary. The authority of governors and *corregidores* increased
at the expense of the elected *cabildos.*

THE INDIAN COMMUNITY. Since the whole economic and social
structure of the Empire rested, to a large extent, on the labors of the
Indian community it was obviously a very important—albeit the lowest
—part of the social structure of the Spanish-American Empire.

The Spanish conquest inevitably caused several changes in the structure of the Indian community, and many of the community's older
social differences were necessarily obliterated. Spanish policy did recog-
nize a colonial Indian nobility, whose members were granted tribute
exemptions and a number of special privileges—e.g., permission to ride
horses, to wear Spanish clothing, to carry swords, and to use Spanish
honorific titles. Occasionally, caciques were awarded royal coats of
arms and other insignia. Some of them were wealthy ranchers; a few
owned Negro slaves; nearly all seem to have held municipal offices. But
by the mid- and late sixteenth century, the native nobility had already
acquired a fixed colonial status. Its members were located almost exclusively in the towns and cities; their privileges were hereditary; they

included both males and females; and its members had been accorded by the rank of the hidalgo class of Spain.

The municipal governments in Indian towns were formally organized, in most instances, during the mid-sixteenth century. They consisted of local hierarchies, of offices and institutions, to which both Spanish and Indian traditions contributed.

The situation of the Indian communities deteriorated considerably during the seventeenth and eighteenth centuries. One of the most important agents of this deterioration was the development of the large farms, the haciendas, by the Spanish colonists. Another important agent was the internal pressure of the strong Indian people exploiting the local groups. These pressures, from both within and without the pueblos, resulted in further dislocation of Indian populations. Many fugitives from the oppression of the local nobility found anonymity and sanctuary in the centers of Spanish life, particularly in Mexico City. There the fluid intermittent migration of Indians from surrounding towns became one of the foremost problems confronting native and Spanish authorities.

E. EUROPEAN COUNTRIES IN THE AGE OF ABSOLUTISM

During the Age of Absolutism, the social system of European countries was continually changing under the impact of developing economic and social differentiation. Eighteenth-century European society was, from the social point of view, still predominantly aristocratic—even though the respective positions of the aristocrat might vary a great deal for the politically powerful nobles of Poland, Sweden, and Hungary, and (in an entirely different way) England, and the politically impotent nobles of France, Denmark, or Spain. In Prussia, aristocrats had to serve the state, either in the army or in the civil service; and attempts were made to secure similar service in Russia and in parts of the Hapsburg Empire.

The peasantry still formed the bulk of the population of Europe. Their conditions varied greatly—from the free villagers of England, Sweden, and some parts of France, to the serfs of many areas of central eastern, and southern Europe. (*For a general survey, see* [S] *Lindsay, 1957[a]; Beloff, 1954. On France and England, see especially* [S] *Labrousse, 1955;* [Z] *Ashley, 1952; Mathew, 1948;* [Y] *Lough, 1954, 1960. On Prussia, see* [X] *Carsten, 1954, 1955, 1959; Bruford, 1957; Hintze, 1900, 1914, 1915, 1943[a],* passim; *Rosenberg, 1943-44, 1958;* [S] *Beloff, 1954, ch. v. On Russia, see* [W] *Brunner, 1953; Eck, 1959; Nolde, 1952-53; Sacke, 1938[a], 1938[b]; Young, 1957; Beloff, 1953,* [S] *1954, ch. vi. On Austria, see* [T] *Blum, 1948; Jelusic, 1936; Macartney, 1957; Schenk, 1953;* [S] *Beloff, 1954, ch. v.*)

One trend was evident throughout the seventeenth and eighteenth centuries: the growth in the numbers and influence of the urban middle class. As overseas trade expanded, the merchants, especially in England and France, increased numerically and in wealth. In central and eastern Europe, the ranks of the middle class were swelled by the appointment of more and more civil servants, particularly during the latter part of the eighteenth century.

[3] *The Structure of Associations and Communities*

The preceding data may provide a good foundation for analyzing the system of stratification and social organization in the societies studied here. Our analysis will focus primarily on the development of differentiation and various types of free-floating resources. Accordingly, the aspects of the system of social organization and stratification that will concern us here will be the following:

1. The structures of the major groups and associations in the society

2. The nature of the definition of the "total" society or cultural community

3. The extent to which traditional ascriptive criteria were prevalent in the status system—i.e., the extent to which criteria of status were based on kinship and territorial principles, and status groups were embedded in kinship and territorial groups

4. The uniformity and rigidity of the hierarchy of status

We shall begin by analyzing the structures of major groups and collectivities in these historical bureaucratic societies.

Our discussion has already shown that a great multiplicity and variety of groups and associations can be found in most of these societies. Within these societies, and particularly in the economic and cultural fields, various groups existed who had some functionally specific orientation. In most of these societies, there were artisan and merchant guilds, merchant associations, and cultural and religious groups and associations, in one form or another. There were also several types of "social" and cultural-social groups, oriented to performing specific functions and tasks, and to their members' participating in somewhat broader areas of social and cultural life as well. Social clubs, the cult societies, and various associations in China, and the numerous cultural, social, and recreational associations that arose in the towns of the Spanish-American Empire and in Europe, may serve as illustrations. These associations were formed in all societies studied, although, of course, there are many differences among them. The associations may have differed from each other in the scope of their activities, in their ideological frameworks, and in their contacts with other groups. They may have been purely local, bound to one city or locality; or countrywide, or at least having many contacts with various groups in other places ([L] *Bréhier, 1950, ch. ii, iii;* [Y] *Sagnac, 1945, 1946; Barber, 1955;* [U] *Desdevises du Dezert, 1925, 1927;* [R] *Haring, 1947; Vida Viceus, 1957;* [I] *Balázs, 1954[a]; Fairbank, 1958; M. Levy, 1955*).

Although the exact structures of the respective associational activities in the various societies studied here were diverse, they all had some discernible common characteristics. The most important of these common characteristics was the development, especially among the higher and middle strata, of (1) some tendency toward dissociation of kinship, territorial, ecological, and tribal units from the major types of associations—both various "specialized" associations and broad ascriptive-solidary groups; and (2) a rather limited differentiation between functionally specific and more solidary or culturally oriented associations.

In most of the historical bureaucratic societies, many of both the functionally specific and the solidary-integrative types of associations developed. All these groups were dissociated, though to different degrees, from territorial or kinship groups. Usually, membership in the associations was not based on criteria of kinship or of belonging to a specific cohesive territorial unit—although many associations were actually confined to certain localities. On the whole, their activities were relatively broad in scope, cutting across both kinship and limited "traditional" territorial units.

Obviously, the degree of their dissociation from kinship and territorial limits varied, both according to societies and according to various strata of any given society. Usually, such dissociation was of smallest extent in the lower strata (peasantry, urban lower classes); limited in the upper hereditary classes (especially the landed aristocracy); and greatest in the urban and rural middle classes, and in religious elites and organizations. However, even in the upper and lower classes, some measure of dissociation tended to develop. In many of these societies, members of the aristocracy were active in various economic, cultural, and religious organizations. And the peasantry often formed solidary associations—of different types, such as secret cult groups and mutual aid associations.

Similarly, in these societies the rigidly defined territorial and kinship groups became dissociated from the major ascriptive solidarities. In most primitive and feudal societies, the major ascriptive solidarities, like status groups and total cultural collectivities, were almost entirely embedded in territorial, kinship, and hierarchical groups. In the societies we are examining, such ascriptive solidarities became distinct from traditional kinship, territorial, and tribal groups, and became more fluid and flexible. Mutual solidarity, or at least some similarity, was recognized among urban and even rural groups—even though their primary identifications were mostly local. Members of orders (e.g., the orders in Rome), of culturally active groups, of educational, cultural, and legal elites, literati (in China), and sometimes even free peasants and soldiers, became aware of a community of interest and outlook, and of partial social and cultural similarity, without being organized in one group or collectivity. Although such consciousness of similarity or of loyalty was often limited to a locality or town, in many cases it trenscended such boundaries.

A similar trend emerged in the definition of the total cultural unit and its major symbols. As discussed, the main symbols of common identification and cultural heritage were no longer chiefly mythical, as were the symbols of primitive tribes. Several more general and more comprehensive symbols appeared—some of which even exhibited a degree of historical consciousness. Although the newer symbols too usually had distinct territorial referents, these references were much broader than those in many primitive, patrimonial, and feudal societies. The reference included far more subgroups of various kinds; at times, it contained several universalistic ideological elements as well.

Generally, in connection with the new definition of the common cultural unit, many strata evolved some measure of *differentiated, and not rigidly ascribed,* identification with common cultural symbols. These symbols were neither entirely limited to any one territorial or kinship unit nor mediated by such a unit. They fostered feelings of over-all participation in the cultural heritage ([U] *Sarrailh, 1951;* [Y] *Cobban, 1957[a];* [L] *Bréhier, 1949[b], 1950; Barker, 1957;* [R] *Haring, 1947; Vida Viceus, 1957;* [I] *Balázs, 1952; Fairbank, 1957, 1958; Nivison and Wright, 1959; O. Franke, 1945; W. Franke, 1956; Pulleyblank, 1954*).

Such dissociation between various associations and ascriptive kinship and territorial units tended to develop; and yet, the functionally specific and the solidary-integrative associations and groups frequently tended to coalesce and to merge. Many functionally specific groups developed various symbols of common solidarity and dealt with a very wide range of problems confronting their members. They regulated many aspects of their members' private lives and represented them in various legal and political affairs. In these ways, they performed integrative functions of wider scope than inherent in their purely specialized explicit objectives. Moreover, these integrative activities had the property of limiting and regulating the more specific and instrumental operations of these groups.

These developments in the associational structure of the historical bureaucratic societies cannot be equated with the growth of associational activity and national consciousness in modern societies. Though varying from society to society, participation in most of the historical associations was still limited to relatively select urban or aristocratic groups, and by many traditional orientations and patterns of organization. Moreover, the extents to which such associations became oriented toward central values and symbols were greatly different; and many of them were limited to small localities. The same applies to their participation in the common cultural life and their identification with common collective and cultural symbols. Nevertheless, each of these associations, whatever the scope of its membership or orientation, brought a distinct element of differentiation to its society.

[4] The Basic Characteristics of the Systems of Stratification

To facilitate our fuller understanding of the various implications of the associational structures of the historical bureaucratic societies, we shall turn now to analyzing the systems of stratification in them.

For our analysis, two related characteristics of the status systems of these societies are most important. The first is the fact that, in almost none of them (except in some borderline patrimonial-bureaucratic societies, or in declining bureaucratic polities), did there exist a completely traditional-ascriptive system. The other characteristic is that no completely rigid system of stratification developed that petrified, as it were, all property, power, and status relations within rigidly ascriptive groups.

In most of these societies the system of stratification may, on superficial examination, seem to belie the above statement. Ostensibly, the system appears both simple and rigid. At its apex are the king, the aristocracy, and the upper (and, possibly, also the middle) echelons of the bureaucracy. Next—but far lower and without much political power —are various urban groups, usually much more developed than in feudal or patrimonial societies, and cultural elites. Lowest of all come the peasantry and the urban lowest classes. It is often assumed that, in the majority of these societies, the king had a total monopoly of power, and that there was an unbridgeable gulf separating the political elite from other groups of the society. This conception may be somewhat applicable, but it is oversimplified and does not take into account the flexibility of the status system—a flexibility which existed and was of great importance in these societies.

This flexibility and relative "openness" of the status system derived mainly from the growth of some measure of differentiation among the three major criteria of stratification—wealth, power, and prestige—and the consequent emergence of somewhat different and relatively non-rigid status hierarchies, and of distinct groups with much greater prominence in one field than in another.

Thus various economic groups emerged in these societies. Their predominance in the economic field did not necessarily imply that they ranked high in the scale of prestige and legitimate power. The merchant and artisan groups in ancient Egypt, Persia, and especially in China, provide good illustrations. In China, the official prestige of the merchants was even lower than that of the peasants. Even in societies like Byzantium and Absolutist France, where the merchants enjoyed relatively high prestige and influence, these were not proportionate to their economic ranking. On the other hand, other groups arose—like the religious, cultural, and intellectual elites—that, although they had considerable symbolical prestige, did not necessarily have equivalent political or economic rank.

Such divergence between status criteria in individual cases is, of course, also found in less developed societies. But only in the societies we are examining was there some growing structural and organizational differentiation between these criteria. In these societies, the fact that the same group could (and did, often) have different status rankings according to the various scales of evaluation applied to it was not an indication of accidental deviances; it was a sign of basic structural characteristics of the system.

Another extremely significant manifestation of the existence of different status hierarchies is the development of special elite positions and activities. In most of the societies studied here, there developed special categories, of groups or of people, whose members engaged in leadership and communication in various institutional spheres, while these categories were not rooted in any ascriptive status groups, roles, or positions. In the religious and cultural organizations, there arose several such positions, whose incumbents were recruited from many, though not necessarily all, status groups, and whose activities cut across these groups. In this respect, the members of special religious groups and organizations, like monks, preachers of various kinds, and members of different religious orders, were particularly important.

In the political field, in the monarch's entourage or in the upper echelons of the administration, a relatively new type of position and activity developed, i.e., specific "party-political" activities. Persons emerged whose main functions—even if they held specific administrative positions—were to be the monarch's special political agents, emissaries, and bearers of his propaganda and entreaties; and to mobilize support and resources, for various policies, among different strata of the population. These party-political positions became important avenues of mobility for ambitious individuals from various groups and strata. Their activities were usually not confined to any given stratum, but intersected several. Occasionally, particularly in Rome and Byzantium, even emperors sometimes attained power through such channels ([L] *Bréhier, 1924, 1949[b], ch. i; Ostrogorsky, 1956[a]* passim; *Runciman, 1933; Diehl, 1943*).

In the economic field, some specific elite functions also evolved, mostly in the various economic associations, like workshops, guilds, merchant groups, and banks. The elite functions either dealt with the internal problems of the associations, or mediated between them and the cultural and, especially, the political spheres.

These distinctive elite functions did not arise only on the higher levels of political and cultural activity. They also developed, albeit in a somewhat different way and to a smaller degree, on the lower levels. Political and cultural leadership in rural settings and in the lower urban strata was no longer entirely a matter of traditional hereditary position. These new types of elite were not so prominent locally or in the countryside as they were in the central institutions and in the cities. Among the peasant masses and, to some extent, in the more traditional cities or urban quarters, the old, traditional pattern of leadership might persist and dominate. But even here, new types of leadership frequently developed. These often differed from the traditional ones, and were connected to the great extent of differentiation and to the party politics and political manipulation that developed in these societies. (*See* [L] *Iorga, 1939, 1940[a], 1940[b]; Bréhier, 1924; Rouillard, 1953;* [G] *Altheim and Stiehl, 1954; Fry, 1956; Christensen, 1936;* [Y] *Königsberger, 1955; Sagnac, 1945, 1946;* [R] *Haring, 1947; Vida Viceus, 1957;* [I] *Chang, 1955; Michael, 1955–56; Eberhard, 1948[a]* passim.)

[5] The Scope of Flexibility of the Systems of Stratification

The relative flexibility of the hierarchies of status in the historical bureaucratic societies is evinced by several aspects of their systems of stratification. The most important of these aspects were: (1) the narrowing of the scope of *legal* definition of the status of different groups, and the weakening of the importance of those legal definitions persisting in various groups and strata; (2) the relatively small extent of legally non-free strata; (3) the relatively high mobility between strata; (4) The great importance of "free" urban groups; and (5) the development, especially within these urban centers, of various strata with flexible orientations and symbols of identification.

The rigidity of the legal definition of status groups, and the range encompassing legally free groups, varied greatly from one society to another; but most of the societies exhibited a tendency toward weakening such definitions or their importance.

Thus, for instance, in Persia—one of the least differentiated countries in our sample—discernible attempts were made to define all social positions by law, although these definitions were often vague; and some mobility between the strata existed. However, the peasants were still largely bound, in one way or another, to the soil ([G] *Ghirshman, 1954; Christensen, 1936, 1939; Altheim and Stiehl, 1954*).

In the Roman Empire, conditions varied greatly in different periods. It is significant that a rigid ascription developed during the Empire's decline. However, some legal distinction among the various orders (senatorial, equestrian, etc.) existed prior to the decline ([Q] *Boak, 1955[a]*, passim; *Momigliano, 1934; Burns, 1952; Charlesworth, 1936; Pflaum, 1950*).

In the Byzantine Empire, ostensibly several official status positions, like those in the bureaucracy, were defined by law; and titles proliferated. However, closer examination reveals that many official positions were not legally defined as personal status positions, and that vast strata of free citizens were not legally prescribed to any group or category. Moreover, some of the major legal reforms of the sixth and seventh centuries were directed at the establishment of a "free peasantry" and at the abolition of the former period's legal restrictions. Following the decline of this peasantry in subsequent periods, many legal restrictions on personal freedom developed; but even then, these restrictions were not so fully articulated legally as in the first period ([L] *Diehl, 1927; Bréhier, 1949[b], 1950; Ostrogorsky, 1929[a], 1956[b]; Lemerle, 1958*).

In China, the positions of the literati were defined by law, but they were officially open to all. Moreover, there were no legal restrictions on the personal freedom of most of the lower-class population (peasants, artisans, etc.) except vagabonds. ([I] *Balázs, 1950, 1959[a]; Pulleyblank, 1954; Eberhard, 1948[a], 1952; Bodde, 1953, 1956; Chang, 1955; Michael, 1955–56; O. Franke, 1930–52.*)

In the Spanish-American Empire, the conquistadors' attempts to establish a rigid feudal system of titles and stratification did not succeed. Although different social strata (especially a strong landed aristocracy) developed, they were not fully defined by law. Officially, even the Indians were free, although they were bound by many obligations to the state and to their own communities. *(See* [R] *Konetzke, 1951[a], 1951[b], 1952, 1953; Haring, 1947; Zavala, 1943. On the legislation with regard to the Indians, see* [R] *Miranda, 1951; Simpson, 1934, 1938; Gallo, 1951[b]; Gongora, 1951.)*

In the European states during the Age of Absolutism, the situation was somewhat more complicated. There existed many legal definitions, privileges, and symbols of various status groups, especially the higher ones, like the aristocracy and the *noblesse de robe,* as well as professional groups, like the notaries. Some legal restrictions were imposed on the lower strata of the peasantry, although outright serfdom was almost entirely extinct in Western Europe. On the other hand, there was a great deal of mobility between strata, mostly resulting from intermarriage and from titles bestowed by the king. Moreover, the more active and powerful social groups, especially the rising bourgeoisie, tended to "explode" most legal restrictions and establish centers of power and of new status groups beyond these legal frameworks.

The most flexible system of stratification arose in England. There, the legal definition of status (through patents of nobility) was not the only determinant of the place of even the highest social groups in the stratification system (especially as a title descended through the firstborn son of a peer). In the England of that time, there were hardly any legal personal restraints, and a great degree of mobility between strata developed. *(For a general survey, see* [S] *Lindsay, 1957[a];* [Y] *Barber, 1955; Sagnac, 1945, 1946; Lough, 1954, 1960.)* Other, far less flexible European status systems existed in Russia and (to a smaller degree) in Prussia, where the major strata (aristocracy, merchants, and peasants) were still largely defined in legal terms—their legal privileges and rights, or the lack of them.

[6] The Place of the Urban Classes in the Social Organization

In the societies we are examining, one major manifestation of the relative flexibility of the system of stratification was the great social, political, and cultural importance of cities and free urban strata.*

---

* The literature on cities is given in most of the works cited above. For a more general survey, see [A] *Recueils de la Société Jean Bodin,* VI, VII, VIII (1954, 1955, 1957); for an analytical approach that is relevant to some of the problems with which we are concerned, see [A] Redfield and Singer, 1954.

The respective numerical volumes of urban population varied greatly among these societies, but in none of them was the urban population very large. Most of these societies were predominantly agricultural. Nevertheless, in each one the cities played a very important role in its economic, social, and political structure; and the cities were the centers of its administrative and political power, and usually the sites of its main cultural institutions as well.

The social composition of the cities was as varied as its components' functions. The urban population comprised both specifically urban elements, like merchants, artisans, and manufacturers, and also many aristocrats with town residences; it also included numerous transient elements. The several types of differentiated social organizations—guilds, merchant associations, cultural associations, and various types of self-government—arose mostly in the cities. It was also mostly—if not entirely—in the cities that the cultural, religious, and professional elites often cut across any fixed status groups. There, too, the majority of cultural and educational institutions developed and were concentrated. Although these groups might have been active rurally as well as urbanly, their activities were usually centered in the cities, whether capital or provincial.

In most of the societies concerning us, therefore, the cities served as centers of intensive economic and social activities, of cultural activity and creativity, and of cultural diffusion and communication to the countryside.

The fact that these vital functions were performed by the cities explains why the influence wielded by urban groups was out of proportion to their numerical strength in the population, and why purely economic urban groups—artisans, merchants, and manufacturers—were sometimes influential in fields which apparently did not directly concern them. Through their relations with various elites and professions, these groups could be organized in wider social strata, with wider consciousness and sometimes with special activities of their own. Moreover, it was in the cities that there developed, around the activities of various elites and associations, those wider, more flexible orientations and symbols of status and cultural identification analyzed above, that cut across any fixed and rigid status groups.

The importance of urban strata and groups, the importance of cities as social and cultural centers, were usually very closely related to a fairly high mobility between different strata—especially, mobility to the higher and middle-upper echelons of status hierarchies and to the various elite positions. Although there are no exact data about the rates of mobility in these countries, all the available information seems to indicate the presence of a relatively high mobility in all of them. This mobility constituted an important manifestation of the flexibility of the social system. Moreover, it was a very significant link between different strata, between the more passive groups or outlying provinces and the central political and cultural institutions.

[7] *The Extent and Limits of Criteria of Universalism and Achievement in the Systems of Stratification*

We may now summarize our analysis of stratification systems by examining the criteria governing the composition of the main groups and strata.

In the status hierarchies of these societies, we have noted some weakening of fixed, ascriptive, and particularistic criteria. Within several sectors of social organization, criteria of achievement developed. Roles were allocated according to such standards of achievement, as indicated by the fact that positions and membership in bureaucratic, economic, military, and religious groups could be attained by means besides inheritance. Such attainments were not exceptions, but instances of a more or less general rule. In some of these societies, membership in even the highest echelons was, at least to some extent, accessible by achievement and could be attained through the various channels of mobility.

Along with these developments, partial specialization appeared, as indicated by various professional activities and the emergence of economic activities and organizations. Similarly, some universalistic criteria of status and somewhat specialized definitions of various positions and roles were evolved. The most important examples of this occur in the religious field, where many positions were, in some measure, open to anyone with the basic qualifications of devotion and learning, and in the military field, where military prowess was an important criterion for advancement. Such criteria of qualification also developed in the legal field and, to a smaller extent, in the economic one.

However, the fact that ascriptive and particularistic criteria of status, and diffuse definitions of various positions, were weakened did not mean that they were abolished, or even that they were no longer dominant in the social and cultural systems of these societies. The ascriptive and particularistic criteria for allocating roles were still more or less preponderant in all the societies studied. This predominance manifested itself in several ways.

In most of these societies, the more ascriptive strata were paramount, both quantitatively and in their importance in the status and power hierarchy. Their ascendancy was, of course, closely connected with the relatively low degree of social and economic differentiation and the predominantly agrarian bases of these societies. With the partial exception of China, each of these societies had some sort of landed or bureaucratic aristocracy. The lowest classes, as well, were composed mainly of factually hereditary peasant families and of a rather unstable urban proletariat. The middle-class and professional groups also tended to acquire as much more diffuse and ascribed symbols of status as possible, and, to some extent, to "aristocratize" themselves. Moreover, although recruits for various groups were often selected largely according to criteria of achievement, their symbols of status and ideology greatly emphasized diffuse, ascriptive-traditional values. In many cases, these groups were inclined toward hereditary transmission of positions within them. The same inclination prevailed in most of the urban strata and groups. It was especially true of the urban associations (e.g., guilds and cultural associations), most of which emphasized the particularistic and somewhat ascriptive nature of their membership and stressed the traditional and diffuse nature of their status symbols.

As already noted, participation in the political field was also influenced by traditional orientations. The "belongingness" to the total political community was usually defined ascriptively. In addition, the citizen usually had no universalistic-political rights, and the relations between the population and the monarch were defined largely in traditional ascriptive symbols. Only in the relations between the population and the administration was there a tendency for some universalistic rules and criteria to develop.

This combination of diffuse-particularistic contents of activities with some mobility and recruitment according to criteria of achievement was, perhaps, best exemplified by the Chinese gentry and literati. The Chinese system of examinations provided a major avenue of mobility through achievement. At the same time, the contents of the examinations, and the symbols learned, were markedly diffuse and non-specialized; they consisted of the entire Confucian tradition, and not of any specialized activity or knowledge.

Only in European countries (France and England), and to a smaller extent in the Spanish-American Empire, were some of these limitations broken. More truly universalistic and achievement oriented groups arose in some parts of the social structure, and the definitions of roles included somewhat greater emphasis on specialization.

Thus, although the criteria of achievement and universalism greatly affected the processes of mobility and the composition and internal structure of various groups in the historical bureaucratic societies, their importance in the value orientations, basic composition, and way of life of these groups was relatively smaller. However, even the lowest strata were often affected by the process of differentiation; although they could not change their low economic and social position, they strove, at least, to some extent, to attain higher status in several spheres and thus to ameliorate their condition in general. The most important examples of this are provided by the attempts made to establish and maintain a free peasantry and soldiery.

The relative predominance of ascriptive and particularistic criteria in the stratification systems of the societies studied here is also discernible in the structure and composition of the major elite groups. Although elevation to these elites was largely "open" and based on achievement, the elites' internal organization values, style of life, and criteria and processes of selection were markedly ascriptive, diffuse, and even traditional. For all these reasons, the degree to which the elites were accessible to non-elites, and the elites direct dependence on non-elite groups, were limited.

Thus, although the particularistic and hierarchical-ascriptive social system of these societies was weakened by the development of many areas in which criteria of achievement and universalism prevailed, these criteria did not become dominant. Rather, they were more or less adapted to the ascriptive elements of the system, and assumed crucial but *secondary importance* within it. Consequently, these areas in which the criteria of universalism, achievement, and specificity prevailed made inroads which engendered significant repercussions in the structures of the strata of these societies. These areas were not predominant; but neither were they marginal to the structure of the societies, and they were very closely linked with the growing differentiation between hierarchies of status and with the absence of a uniform, rigid system of stratification.

The differentiation of the social structure, and the development of strategic social spheres dominated by criteria of achievement (specifically universalism), refute the simplified assumption that in these societies, the social structure was rigid, and all power and prestige were monopolized by the political elite ([I] *Wittfogel, 1957; Eisenstadt, 1958; Eberhard, 1958; Pulleyblank, 1958*). The ruler held a paramount position in each of the societies studied; and in some (Sassanid Persia, Byzantium, and, to some extent, China) the political sphere and the state were the strongest social factors. Yet in no case did they have a complete monopoly of status and power. In all these societies, they were sufficient free exchange, market relations, and differentiation between types of social relations to effect continuous change in property, status, and power relations. Such changes were effected among various individual and family groups, and also among structural, economically specific, and more general and diffuse status groups. Each of these societies witnessed, in the course of its history, many such fluctuations and many instances of various groups' attempting to change their social position and to increase their political influence and social standing. In these societies, most important of these struggles were those between the aristocracy and the small peasants, between the former and the Church, and between all these groups and the ruling elite. In a subsequent chapter, we shall systematically analyze the various aspects of these struggles. Here it will suffice to note only that they all indicate that no group had a complete monopoly of power and status, nor was there a strict correspondence among the positions of any (except, perhaps, the lowest) group on the scales of wealth, power, and prestige.

[8] *Summary of the Main Characteristics of the Systems of Stratification and Social Organization*

In the fields of stratification and social organization, "free" resources developed—i.e., activities and orientations, not embedded in the structure of ascriptive groups, which could serve as a potential reservoir for flexible types of groups and organizations.

The existence of such free-floating resources was not unchallenged. Many traditional, aristocratic groups continuously attempted to limit the scope of such resources and to extend the scope of more traditional types of regulation. Further, in many cases the rulers themselves tried to limit free-floating resources by excessive regimentation, and to establish rigid hierarchies of status as a means to control the various strata. All these attempts were made, however, on the basis of the existence of such free-floating resources; and they could not entirely obliterate these resources without undermining the entire social and political system of these societies. But the continuous fluctuations in the system of stratification and the struggles between various groups (especially between the more traditional groups and the more differentiated, flexible ones) for predominance in this field could, under certain conditions, have resulted in diminishing the more flexible strata and in the development of a much less differentiated status system.

Like all the other spheres which have been analyzed, the respective spheres of status and social organization differ for each of the societies we are studying. Their differences can be estimated mostly according to the following criteria:

1. The relative importance of criteria of achievement and universalism in the status system

2. The extent of mobility between major strata

3. The scope of different associational activities and the extent of differentiation between types of associations

4. The degree of rigidity of the status system

The preceding description and analysis and the tabular material indicate the way each of these societies evolved from a relatively non-differentiated social structure to a more differentiated one, even if the differentiation was still limited.

The developments of limited but pervasive differentiation within the major institutional fields of these societies, and of the different types of free resources affected the degree of self-sufficiency of most groups and strata in each society. They all became greatly dependent on external resources and had to organize their own activities in ways enabling them to mobilize external resources and to compete for them with other groups. This was true even of many of the more ascriptive and traditional groups, like the village communities, and especially of those highest in the status hierarchy—the aristocratic families, lineages, and organizations. Hence they developed a tendency to emphasize achievement of different goals, and geared many of their internal activities to this purpose. That is, they evolved, within their organization, many special activities—e.g., those of representing the groups in economic and political relations, of technical communication—mainly oriented to providing such varied resources.

Another feature of the growing differentiation was the emergence of a great *variety* of groups. Not only did many "parallel" groups develop; in addition, there developed, within most institutional spheres and ecological units, many *different* groups, with different structures and compositions of membership, and pursing different goals. This growing variety was a constant facet of the social structure of these societies, although it was much more pronounced in the higher and middle strata than in the lower.

The social structure of these societies depicts pervasive but limited differentiation and variety. The differentiation was pervasive in that it occurred, though in different degrees, in *all* the institutional spheres. This pervasiveness illustrates one main difference between these and other types of societies (e.g., feudal or patrimonial ones, or some city-states).

The differentiation was, however, also limited. It was confined mostly to middle and higher strata; it was more marked in the development of special groups than of special roles; and, in so far as it did develop in various roles, it did so more markedly in "producers'" (as distinct from "consumers'") roles—although within these societies, many starting points for further differentiation developed. This differentiation created, in these societies, a certain *limited* potential of generalized power, i.e., power not committed to fixed, ascriptive groups and goals that could be used by different groups to implement different objectives.

In the social structure of these societies, there coexisted continuously, in common frameworks, two levels of social organization—the traditional and relatively non-differentiated level and the non-traditional, more differentiated one. However, the continuous shifts in the relative strength of the different groups in the society could result in the weakening and dwindling of each of these sectors, and in the undermining of the basic characteristics of the social structure of these societies.

[9] *General Summary of the "External" Conditions and the Problems of Perpetuation of the Political Systems of Centralized Empires*

From the point of view of our hypothesis, it is of great interest to observe the extent to which this process of differentiation was independent of the rulers and their activities. We shall consider this in detail in a later chapter, but some preliminary remarks are pertinent here.

The rulers' relations to this process of differentiation were complicated. In many cases, the rulers initiated and greatly promoted these processes of differentiation. They could, however, do so successfully only in so far as there already existed, within the various strata and groups, some facilitating preconditions or predispositions. On the other hand, very often the rulers attempted, because it was to their interest to maintain their traditional legitimation, to restrict such differentiation, or tried to "freeze" it through maintaining rigid control over it for the sake of their own political aims. The ways that these different tendencies of the rulers have worked out in concrete situations will be discussed in some forthcoming chapters. Their very complexity of the relations attests to the fact that the rulers' political tendencies and the extent of societal differentiation are, in the societies studied here, two analytically distinct and independent variables.

6

The Social Conditions

and the Institutionalization

of the Political Systems

[1] Recapitulation of the Hypothesis

In the preceding chapters we described and analyzed the development of autonomous political orientations and of limited differentiation in the major institutional spheres of the societies studied here—in the economic and the cultural-religious spheres and in the system of stratification. Such differentiation was manifested by a relatively high degree of development, in the major institutional fields of the society, of varied specific organizations, of "producer" roles, and, to a much smaller extent, of "consumer" roles. In all these spheres, this differentiation created different types of free-floating resources.

This limited but pervasive differentiation constituted those "external" conditions which, according to our hypothesis, were necessary for the institutionalization of the major features of the political systems of the societies examined here—i.e., a centralized polity of bureaucratic administration, channels of political struggle, and differentiated political activities.

Our argument is, then, that it is the convergence of the tendency toward autonomy of political sphere, as evinced by the development of autonomous political goals and aims of the rulers, and of the "external" conditions—i.e., the development of the pervasive but limited differentiation analyzed above—that facilitates the full institutionalization of the main organizational features of the political system of the centralized bureaucratic empires, and the establishment of a unified polity. Before testing this hypothesis, we must attempt to explain it. Therefore, we have to investigate and determine what, in the simultaneous development of these two sets of conditions, is the quality that facilitates such institutionalization.

[2] Explanation of the Hypothesis.
The Regulative Problems Arising from the Autonomy of the Political Sphere and the Differentiation in the Social Structure

The starting point of our explanation is that the development of the differentiation and of various free-floating resources created certain problems of allocation, regulation, and integration in the societies within which it occurred.

The first such problem was related to internal arrangements of the major groups and institutional spheres in these societies. It was also related to the fact, already discussed, that these groups could no longer be assured of manpower and resources for implementing their goals and for their self-maintenance, so they necessarily competed or struggled to acquire various free-floating resources.

The second problem is closely connected with the first. It was that of regulating the relations and conflicts between different groups and their integration within the total society.

Let us explain these two problems in some detail.

As the major social spheres and groups became increasingly autonomous and differentiated from other institutional systems and groups, as they became less embedded in one another, their interaction could no longer be regulated only or mainly by their internal, common, or complementary mechanisms. Although the greater differentiation of spheres and groups made them highly interdependent, their direct and immediate contact with each other did not necessarily continue. Thus, they could be certain neither of smooth allocation and flow of facilities and resources, nor of smooth and semi-automatic regulation of potential conflicts, among them. Their internal mechanisms, as well as the pre-existing norms and arrangements, were not so adequate for dealing with their problems of interrelation as with those of less differentiated societies.

Moreover, integrating various groups within the wider society posed many new problems. Each group's place in any hierarchy—of status, wealth, or power—was not entirely fixed; and a continuous struggle went on among various groups over their relative places and positions in the society. Hence, the integration of any group into the total society. and its loyalty to the society, were not so self-evident as in less differentiated societies. In addition, the growing *differentiation* in the social structure was also connected, as we have seen, with a growing *variety* of different groups—i.e., with the emergence of different types of groups, each with different structure and problems, which precluded uniform regulation of their interrelations.

These general problems gave rise to certain specific needs in the evolving social structures of these societies.

The need developed for mechanisms which could insure the steady and continuous flow of various resources and services among different social groups and among major social institutions. Stated more concretely, adequate technical and organizational facilities were needed, for communicating among different groups in the society, and for establishing and maintaining agencies and rules to insure some degree of continuous flow of services to these groups, regardless of the monetary balance of forces within the society.

The need also arose for rules or norms that were upheld by most groups, strata, and elites, and that could regulate and channelize their conflicts and competition; and agencies to enforce such rules were necessary.

Last, the need developed for the maintenance of some allegiance and orientation to the society's central symbols and values, on the parts of the various strata of the society, with their varied traditions and styles of life.

These requirements evolved within all the institutional spheres of the society, and, because of the development of the autonomy of the political sphere, also in the political sphere's interrelations with other institutional spheres in the society. The problems arising from the interrelation between the autonomous political sphere and differentiated institutional spheres created the potential for the development of more differentiated political activities and demands made by various social groups on the rulers and the political institutions.*

[3] *The Development of Autonomous Regulative Mechanisms*

The same social conditions which created the problems and needs we have enumerated also gave rise, in the historical bureaucratic societies, several new, distinctive types of regulative mechanisms. These attempted, with varying measures of success, to deal with several aspects of the problems.

These mechanisms may be broadly classified into two major types. The first type comprised "autonomous-social" mechanisms—i.e., regulative mechanisms developed by various groups and strata, and maintained mostly through their own activities and interrelations.

The second type comprised political mechanisms—i.e., mechanisms developed and upheld mainly by the political rulers. Some of the most important of these mechanisms were, as has been indicated, the bureaucratic administration and the organs of political struggle.

To understand how the various conditions we have described facilitated the institutionalization of these political mechanisms, we must analyze the ways in which the various autonomous mechanisms operated; the extent to which they were able to cope with the problems emerging from the differentiations of the social structure; with which problems they could deal and which of them conducted to the institutionalization of specific political mechanisms.

The most important of such autonomous "regulative" mechanisms were market exchange and monetary mechanisms, usually countrywide, that controlled the flow of the major unembedded economic resources among different groups and sectors; and internal autonomous mechanisms that regulated the internal activities of, and the relations among, the more differentiated groups. Among the most significant of these mechanisms were various types of representation, delegation of powers, or self-government; organs of municipal or associational government; formal or informal councils of different social orders, strata, or associations; and voluntary courts of arbitration, where both the internal affairs of various groups and the relations among them were settled by arbitration, bargaining, or competition among their respective representatives. (*See* [L] *Bratianu, 1938; Lopez, 1945; Boak, 1929; Mickwitz, 1936[a], 1936[b]; Abel, 1955; Bréhier, 1950, ch. iv, v;* [R] *Haring*

---

* The social problems which arose in these are described in the major historical works cited in this chapter, in Chapter 2 above, and in Chapters 7 and 8 below.

1947; Konetzke, 1953; [Y] *Sagnac, 1945; 1946; Coornaert, 1941, 1952;*
[S] *Labrousse, 1955.*)

The most important characteristic of these organs and mechanisms
was that they were not embedded in the structure of traditional-ascriptive groups and regulated according to traditional-ascriptive criteria.
Rather, they tended to crystallize in less rigid frameworks, whose membership was not predetermined by ascriptive rights, and which developed flexible, autonomous norms and regulations.

[4] Developments in Legal Organization

Next, there were several significant developments in the legal
sphere.

There were the great variety of details and differences in the legal
systems of the historical bureaucratic societies. However, most of them
shared several characteristics of primary importance for our discussion.
(*For some general problems of legal development relevant here, see*
[F] *Seidl, 1933;* [H] *Schiller, 1933;* [I] *Escarra, 1933;* [A] *Mühl, 1933;*
[F] *Wilson, 1954;* [I] *Bodde, 1954;* [J] *Ingalls, 1954.*) The most significant common characteristic was the continuous creation of legal precepts, contracts, bodies, and systems of rights, and of various tribunals
where these could be enforced or arbitrated ([Q] *Schultz, 1946;* [L]
*Bréhier, 1949[b]; Ostrogorsky, 1956[a], 1956[b]; Zacharia von Lingen-
thal, 1892;* [G] *Christensen, 1936, ch. vi, vii;* [R] *Haring, 1947* passim;
[Y] *Hanotaux, 1886; Lough, 1954, 1960; Sagnac, 1945, 1946*).

Concomitantly, formalization and unification tended to develop
in private civil law in general, and in the sphere of contracts in particular—China was, perhaps, the only exception. The best illustrations
of this development are found in the Roman Empire.

Most of these formalized and codified legal systems show some constituent orientations of specifity and of universalism. Many rules were
formulated which were held to apply to categories of persons or collectivities on the basis of generally defined characteristics, independent of
status in kinship, territorial, or ethnic groups. Some rights evolved for
entering contractual relations, whose consequences were defined as
independent of the kinship or local community relations of the respective contracting members. Thus, rights and obligations were created
that could be abstracted from the status and expectations of certain
particularistic solidary memberships (like kinship, tribal membership,
etc.), without destroying that membership.

The extent to which universalism and specifity developed in the
legal system was different in each of the societies examined. They

evolved least in Persia, and in China, where the scope of particularistic legal relations was, as we have seen, relatively wide. They were much more advanced in the Byzantine and Spanish-American empires—although there too they were often limited by the special treatment of rural population, and by the insistence that the members both of rural communities and of various urban associations had mutual responsibiliy. The ingredients of universalism and specificity developed far more in the French and English legal systems. But, even when these ingredients weɪe small, the legal system tended to create broad legal categories and systems of rights. Within these frameworks, there was inevitably much scope for struggle over rights, and for developing new, flexible contractual relations and obligations.

These were linked with the development of the legal profession that has been briefly discussed above, and with the profession's tendency to establish some autonomy of its own.

The various developments in the legal field were promoted both by the rulers and by many active social groups and strata, e.g., urban groups of religious and professional elites. In many cases, the rulers advanced trends which were already evolving among other strata of the population (especially among some legal and cultural elites) and in different urban centers. However, even when the rulers had played decisive roles in furthering such legal activities, organizations, and centers of learning, they very often became dependent on these organs and on the legal experts; and the rulers then faced the problem of how to control them.

[5] Developments in Patterns of Communication

Last, complex patterns of communication developed in these societies.

Communication usually tended to be organized on two major levels: the local level, especially that of the rural group; and the level of the urban and especially metropolitan centers. At the local, village level, the pattern of communication was relatively undifferentiated and traditional; it corresponded to that found in many primitive countries.

Among the upper and middle strata, a far more differentiated pattern evolved. There were many specific communicative situations not confined to ritual and social occasions. Various associations, informal meeting places, discussion groups, and salons are good examples of such communicative situations.

Moreover, special interlinking channels of communication between the localities and the political-urban centers were established; and, although the patterns of communication of the rural and lower urban groups were generally traditional and relatively undifferentiated, they were not entirely self-sufficient. Their "Little Traditions" became more and more dependent on the "Great Traditions" of these centers. They depended, to various degrees, on communications emanating from the urban centers and were to some extent oriented to certain central symbols and problems. In this way, these communications performed regulative and integrative functions. (*See* [L] *Sinogowitz, 1953[a], 1953[b]; Treitinger, 1958; Brightman, 1901; Barker, 1957; pp. 1–56; Ostrogorsky, 1956[a] passim; Diehl, 1927; [G] Christensen, 1936 passim. See also* [Y] *Sagnac, 1945, 1946; Göhring, 1947.*)

[6] The Inadequacy of the Autonomous Mechanisms from the Point of View of the Regulative Problems

The "autonomous" (non-political) regulative mechanisms operated mostly in and through the associations, professional groups, and elites that were analyzed above. Associations, groups, and elites performed many important functions in the organizing and regulating different market and exchange activities. They served as important channels for keeping various groups and strata in touch with the society's central spheres and with its ultimate values and symbols. They often provided meeting places, for the representatives and members of different groups, where some of their interrelations could be regulated. They were outlets of political and social activity for the more active elements within various groups and strata; and they channelized these activities, at least to some extent, within institutionalized frameworks. They also provided several points of contact between status hierarchies, and did so obliterating their distinctions.

However, these mechanisms alone could not solve all the major regulative and integrative problems that arose in these societies.

They could not, by themselves, regulate the relations among the political institutions and other institutions. They could not insure the flow of resources to the polity and thus assure the rulers of being able to implement their various goals. Neither could they secure the political rights and obligations of various groups vis-à-vis each other, or guarantee that their demands and rights would be accepted by the rulers. They could not adequately provide for over-all regulation of intergroup relations within wide territorial limits, and were inadequate to deal with matters demanding actual enforcement of legal decisions, obligations, and contracts.

Further, the very multiplicity of the elites and of the associationa̱ and professional activities—through which most of these mechanisms operated—and the inevitable competition among them, minimized the possibilities for these activities and organizations, in themselves, to regulate all their interrelations and conflicts. Many of these activities and associations aimed to insure the commitment of free resources to various groups in the society. However, their respective basic structures were based on flexible criteria of membership, patterns of activities, and orientation; this fact prevented them from entirely "freezing" the free resources available in any one major institutional field into a prescribed rigid organization.

In other words, the level of free-floating resources was, in the institutional structure of these societies, so all-pervasive that the internal regulative mechanisms and arrangements of any given sphere sector were incapable of fully integrating and channelizing them.

[7] *The Relation of the Development of Regulative Problems to the Institutionalization of Bureaucratic Administration*

We have now come to the explanation of the central part of our hypothesis, that is, the explanation of the relation between the major "external" conditions and the institutionalization of the major features of the political systems of the centralized bureaucratic empires.

As a result of growing differentiation and free-floating resources, many regulative problems developed, while the various autonomous (non-political) regulative mechanisms were inadequate to deal with all aspects of these problems. This created the conditions for the institutionalization of the main organizational features of the political systems.

These conditions made this institutionalization possible for three reasons:

1. The organizational patterns could help regulate the aspects of the problems with which the autonomous regulative mechanisms did not deal adequately.

2. They could provide the major groups and strata with varied services and with frameworks within which they could channelize their social and political aspirations and the potential generalized power they generated.

3. The performance of various regulative functions by these institutionalized organs could insure the continuous provision, in some measure, of those resources the rulers needed to implement their basic aims

and to uphold the autonomy of the political sphere and the framework of a unified polity.

What were, then, the concrete connections between the regulative problems which emerged as concomitants of the growing differentiation in the major institutional spheres of the society and the society's organs of administration and political struggle?

Continuous administrative organizations developed that were at least partially staffed by professional personnel whose activities were regulated, to greater or lesser degree, by mechanisms independent of other groups. These organizations insured that technical services and facilities were constantly available, on a societywide basis, to various groups of the society. They also facilitated the regulation of some aspects of the interrelations and potential conflicts among the main groups of the society; and they made these groups certain of having some continuous services, and of having their rights upheld, irrespective of momentary changes in their power relations.*

Similarly, the bureaucratic administrations also helped stabilize the relations among the political sphere, the ruler, and other groups in the society. They regulated the rulers' demands for different resources from the main social groups, insured some regularity and continuity in the mobilization of these resources, and provided the major social groups with certain continuous services they performed on behalf of the rulers.

[8] *The Relation of the Development of Regulative Problems to the Development of the Organs of Political Struggle*

However, the routine activities of the bureaucratic administration could not deal with *all* problems of regulation that arose, either between the rulers and the major social groups, or among various groups in the society. The administration were particularly unable to resolve the basic conflicts and political competition among different groups, and to cope with their attempts to influence the rulers' decisions and to participate in the political struggle.

Moreover, the very rules maintained by the bureaucracies to govern the provision of services to different strata in the society were not always "given." They themselves were objects of conflicts and struggles among groups—including the rulers—desiring to change them to suit their own respective interests.

---

* For description of the developments of the administration and of the chief organs of political struggle in general, and of representative institutions in particular, see the historical works cited in this chapter.

In these circumstances, the conditions for the institutionalization of the organs and channels of political struggle emerged. These organs had initially been created or promoted by the rulers for their own purposes; but their continuous functioning usually became dependent on their serving the needs of the major social groups as well. Gradually, within the organs, "rules of the political game" were evolved, that enabled those participating in the organs to engage in the different activities outlined in the preceding chapter. The rules also helped regulate the relations among the rulers and some of the major groups, among these different major groups.

The organs of bureaucratic administration were concerned mainly with insuring that resources would be provided to various groups, and that resources from them would be mobilized. The organs of political struggle dealt mostly with regulating political conflicts and struggle among groups, and their competition for relatively advanced political standing and influence over the rulers.

Despite this differentiation between routine bureaucratic activities and the channels of political struggle, a close relation necessarily existed between them. They both focused largely around the person of the ruler and around problems of implementing policy and political goals. Organizationally, they were usually very closely interlinked—often the various political councils served, as we have seen, as the apexes of the bureaucratic organizations. Similarly, the definition of many of the rules directing the administrations' actions was, in itself, as already indicated, frequently a subject of political struggle, in which the bureaucracy often participated.

Both the channels of political struggle and the bureaucratic organization developed close associations with juridical institutions. In all the societies studied, the administration and the organs of political struggle fulfilled certain juridical functions. In this way, they both, in conjunction with juridical institutions, provided a framework for upholding the various legal precepts and decisions frequently lacking in the autonomous regulative mechanisms outlined above. But these functions usually constituted only a part of the administration of justice; and conflicts for the right to fulfill them (e.g., defining the province of various juridical authorities, and limiting the juridical arbitration of both the king and the administration) were a constant feature of the political life of these societies. The bureaucracy and the participants in the organs of political struggle were interested in exercising juridical functions, because both realized that their activities could thus be fully recognized, and they could enjoy legitimation and actual power.

The organs of political struggle were usually very closely linked with the autonomous regulative mechanisms. These organs provided some social groups with opportunities for political activity and social advancement, and for making their own demands on the rulers and on each other. They supplied the members of many groups with chances for social mobility and advancement. In addition, they were fields in which these groups could pursue their own goals and resolve the problems created by their activities, interests, and interrelations.

In these societies, the organs of political struggle and the administrative agencies were both limited in operational scope by the same factors. One limitation was imposed by the traditional legitimation of the rulers. Another arose from the relatively wide scope of "traditional," undifferentiated political attitudes, and from the fact that a great proportion of the masses felt a basic, traditional identification with the rulers, and often exhibited apathy toward many aspects of the political struggle waged in the central organs.

However, these organs did perform basic functions in the political systems of these societies. They were the only means for resolving the problems arising from the concomitant developments of the political sphere's autonomy and of the limited differentiation in other spheres. The institutionalization of these political and administrative organs and their continuity provided the conditions necessary for maintaining the basic frameworks of the centralized polity and of these political systems.

In all these ways, the administrative agencies and the organs of political struggle were complementary to the different types of autonomous regulative mechanisms. They established the framework within which these mechanisms could operate, and legally sanctioned these operations. But the relative importance of the political and non-political regulative mechanisms, and of each of the political ones— i.e., of the channels of political struggle and the administrative agencies—varied greatly from society to society. These variations will constitute one of the major problems of our analysis.

[9] Summary of Explanation

Above, we have attempted to explain how the concomitant emergences of the autonomy of the political sphere and of the pervasive but limited differentiation of the social structure created the conditions for (1) the development and initial stabilization of the political systems of the historical bureaucratic empires; and (2) the institutionalization of the major organizational features of these political systems. We have shown that institutionalization was facilitated by the fact that the administrative and political organs helped resolve several regulative problems that arose from these concomitant developments and could not be handled by the autonomous regulative mechanisms alone. In addition, these conditions provided the administrative and political organs with the resources they needed to operate; and these organs, through supplying services to various strata of the population, may have facilitated the provision of these resources.

This does not mean that the evolution of such limited but pervasive differentiation of the general structure was necessarily followed by the development and institutionalization of the specific features of the political systems of the historical bureaucratic societies. As we have seen, in many cases the rulers' development of autonomous political goals and orientations was not "matched" by the development of the requisite level of social differentiation. In the same way, differentiation could develop in the social structure that was not matched by the rulers' development of the requisite political orientation; such a case is best illustrated by the example of the Greek city-states. We shall see that, in both cases, the major features of the political systems of the historical bureaucratic societies could not become fully institutionalized. In the next section we shall try to verify our hypothesis.

[10] *Verification of the Hypothesis*

A. THE CONDITIONS OF INSTITUTIONALIZATION AND OF LACK OF INSTITUTIONALIZATION OF THE POLITICAL SYSTEMS

As stated, our hypothesis postulates the dependence of the institutionalization of the major features of the political system of the centralized bureaucratic empire on the concomitant developments both of the tendency toward the autonomy of the political sphere (as manifested mainly in the rulers' aims and activities), and of the limited differentiation and free resources.

This hypothesis attempts to explain the relations between the independent variables and the dependent ones through a series of intervening variables. These are the development of certain problems in the social structure and of potential conflicts among groups, and the relative inadequacy of the autonomous (non-political) mechanisms which developed in these societies.

To verify this hypothesis, we must first show that the major features of the political systems of centralized bureaucratic societies are really institutionalized only when the two independent variables occur together, and not when either occurs by itself; and second, that the variations in the connections among the independent and dependent variables are related to some variations in the intervening variables. The data presented in Table 1* have been collected to test this hypothesis. The data contain first several cases in which the only independent variable that existed was the tendency to autonomy of political sphere, while the *pervasive* extent of differentiation did not develop in all institutional spheres of the society and free-floating resources.

The most important cases are the Mongol and Carolingian empires, and some of the Persian Ahmenid cases ([E] *Ehtécham, 1946; Delaporte and Huart, 1943; Christensen, 1936, ch. i*). In each of these, the ruler's efforts were not successful; and the institutionalization of the political systems of the historical centralized empires either did not develop or did not last for any length of time.

Second, for our analysis, the social conditions connected with the emergence of feudalism in Europe, particularly in Western Europe around the tenth and eleventh centuries are important. The degree of differentiation and of free-floating resources differed greatly in different institutional spheres. It was very small in the economic and stratification fields, and it was relatively great in the religious and cultural spheres and, to some extent, also in the political orientations of some groups—while the scope of the autonomy of the rulers was (after the decline of the Carolingian Empire) very small. These conditions, in spite of the high level of differentiation of the religion spheres, did not make the development of a centralized bureaucratic polity possible. ([D] *Bloch, 1939–40; Hintze, 1929; Coulborn, 1956.*)

Third, our data contain some cases where the development of certain high levels of differentiation did occur without being accompanied by the other independent variable, for example, in the Phoenician and the Greek city-states (and probably also by other city-states). Within most of the institutional spheres of city-state societies, a relatively high level of differentiation developed. At the same time, however, the ruling elite remained embedded in older kinship or "city-bound" limits and frameworks, and did not develop the tendency to autonomy of the political spheres. In the city-states at the height of development, there also evolved some embryonic forms of administrative agencies, of organs of concerted political action, and of more flexible and wider political orientations. However, these did not grow beyond the embry-

* See page 449 of the Appendix.

onic stage; and the traditional orientations of the elite impeded the development of a more unified polity. Only when (as occurred in Rome) there developed, from *within* the traditional (patrician) ruling elite, a more dynamic one with a strong tendency toward autonomous political goals—only then did these political organizations become institutionalized and a new, more differentiated political system develop. (*For Greece, see* [B] *Glotz, 1929; Toynbee, 1959, ch. iv–ix et passim; Ehrenberg, 1960, especially p. 1; Beyer, 1959; and Bibliography. For comparison with Rome, see especially* [Q] *Homo, 1950; Syme, 1939. On general problems of city-states, see* [A] *Oppenheimer, 1912;* [B] *Toynbee, 1959.*)

B. CONDITIONS INFLUENCING THE EXTENT OF DEVELOPMENT OF BUREAUCRATIC ADMINISTRATION AND CHANNELS OF POLITICAL STRUGGLE

Our analysis has demonstrated that the special features of the political systems of the historical bureaucratical centralized polity— channels of political struggle and administrative bodies—were institutionalized when there evolved concurrently the autonomy of political spheres and the pervasive but limited differentiation in the social structure. But the extents to which the autonomy of both the dependent and independent variables developed differed in different societies. If our hypothesis is valid, it should be possible to relate the differences in the development of the basic characteristics of the political system of a historical bureaucratical polity to the degree of differentiation of its social system and/or the autonomy of its political sphere. Let us now examine briefly to what extent our material supports our hypothesis.

In general, our data support the hypothesis. The detailed material presented and summarized in Tables 1 through 8* shows that, on the whole, the greater the autonomy of the ruler's political goals and the differentiation of the social structure, the greater also usually are: (1) the extent and evolution of centralized polity; (2) the emergence of autonomous bureaucratic organizations; (3) the development either of "non-traditional" (i.e., not embedded in traditional-ascriptive kingship, kinship, and territorial groups) channels of political struggle, or of channels which, though still formally embedded in traditional groups (and especially, in the king's court or bureaucracy), evolved more non-traditional (explicit or arbitrary) rules of membership; and (4) the non-traditional institutionalization of their powers.

---

* Pages 449-458 of the Appendix.

On more detailed examination, the data revealed in our case studies show that, in the "less" differentiated societies (like Sassanid Persia and Ancient Egypt), the channels of political struggle and the bureaucratic administration were not yet fully differentiated and organized as autonomous bodies. The channels of political struggle were largely identical with traditional court offices and circles and with higher administrative offices. In these, there was little explication of rules of struggle or of membership, although the rulers did attempt to break through such traditional institutions and circles and to infuse new blood into them. (*On Egypt, see* [F] *Drioton and Vandier, 1952; Kees, 1933[a]; Wilson, 1951; Otto, 1953; Meyer, 1928. On Persia, see* [G] *Christensen, 1936* passim; *Altheim and Stiehl, 1954* passim, *especially for the differentiations between the reigns of the "patrimonial" and the "centralistic" Kings; Altheim, 1955[a]; Faziolleh, 1938.*) The administration, although developed to some extent, was not yet very autonomous. However, it evinced, in distinguishing its roles and memberships from those of various status groups and in using wider criteria of recruitment, a relatively high degree of centralization, specialization, and organization.

In China, the extents of differentiation and of political goals of the rulers were already greater. There, autonomy of the administration, measured according to the criteria applied above, was much greater ([I] *Des Rotours, 1932, Introduction* et passim, *1947–48, Introduction* et passim; *Wang, 1949, Hucker, 1950; Kracke, 1953; Eberhard, 1948[a]* passim). The autonomous organs of political struggle had not emerged, at least officially, to such extents and as separate bodies; yet the rules of membership and operation were already more explicit—especially in practice, though not so much in ideology ([I] *Des Rotours, 1932, 1947–48; De Bary, 1957; Liu, 1959[a], 1959[c]*).

In the Byzantine Empire, differentiation in many social fields was far more extensive. In Byzantium, the organs of political struggle were very distinct (as evident in the Senate and circus parties), as were the rules of their operation. Also, the bureaucracy had advanced greatly in terms of distinctiveness of roles, autonomous criteria of recruitment, centralization, and specialization. ([L] *Ostrogorsky, 1929[a], 1956[a], 1956[b]* passim. *On the Senate and representative institutions, see* [L] *Bratianu, 1937, 1948[a]; Bréhier, 1949[b], pp. 89 ff.; Diehl, 1927. On the development of Byzantine bureaucracy, see* [L] *Ostrogorsky, 1956[a], 1956[b]* passim; *Bréhier, 1917, 1949[b] [livres II, III]; Diehl, 1927; Dendias, 1939; Stein, 1924, 1954; Ensslin, 1948; Moravcsik and Jenkins, 1949. For special departments, see* [L] *Dölger, 1927, 1956; Stein, 1919, pp. 141–160, 1923–25; Lemerle, 1949; Guilland, 1946[a],*

1946[b]; Andréadès, 1921[a]. On Roman administration, see [Q]
*Boak, 1955[a]; Mattingly, 1957; Last, 1936[a], 1936[b]; Miller, 1956;
Ensslin, 1956.*)

The European population of the Spanish-American Empire had
relatively highly developed channels of political struggle (shown, e.g.,
in municipal committees and in local councils), though the advance of
both such channels was limited by the strong centralistic tendencies
of the Spanish Crown. Participation in these channels was not usually
open to Indian population. The distinctive organization of the administration was relatively high; it was associated with the high level of
differentiation among the European elements, and with their imposition of low levels of differentiation on the Indian elements [R] *Gallo,
1944; Haring, 1947, ch. iv, v, vii–viii, ix; Zavala, 1943; Fisher, 1926,
1936; Simpson, 1934, 1938; Ots Capdequi, 1951; Borah, 1956*).

The highest level of distinctive organization of channels of political
struggle emerged in England (and, in lesser degree, in France). England's bureaucratic organization had also reached a relatively high
level of distinctiveness, though probably it was not much higher than
Byzantium's. Moreover, in England, although at least some of the administrative departments were relatively highly centralized, the administration's scope of activities and specialization was not very extensive.
(*On the development of French and Continental administration, see*
[S] *Lindsay, 1957[b]; Beloff, 1954;* [Y] *Zeller, 1948; Pagès 1928,
1932[a], 1932[b]; Doucet, 1948. For the somewhat earlier development
of the English administrative system, see* [Z] *Elton, 1953; Davies, 1937;
Clark, 1955. On the development of European representative systems,
see* [X] *Hintze, 1931[a], 1931[b];* [D] *McIlwain, 1932;* [Y] *Cobban,
1950; Sagnac, 1945, 1946; Ford, 1953; Göhring, 1947; Egret, 1952;
Zeller, 1948; Doucet, 1948. On England, see, e.g.,* [Z] *Pares, 1957;
Thomson, 1938; Namier, 1929, 1952.*)

Within each of the societies studied here, the bureaucracy's greater
development, specialization, and growing professionalization are usually connected with increasing differentiation in the social structure
and in the rulers' political needs. For instance, in China, the amplification of bureaucratic specialization was associated, during the Sung
Dynasties (A.D. 960–1279) and Ming Dynasty (A.D. 1368–1644) with increasing social and economic differentiation ([I] *Kracke, 1953; Hucker,
1950*). A similar development occurred, as we have seen, in Sassanid
Persia under Khosrou I. ([G] *Christensen, 1936, ch. vii; Altheim and
Stiehl, 1954; Altheim, 1955[a], 1955[b].*) There are abundant examples
of this tendency in English, French, and Prussian administrative history. (*See* [X] *Dorwart, 1953; Dorn, 1931; Fay, 1946; Hintze, 1901,
1903, 1915; Schmoller, 1898; Bruford, 1957.*)

[11] Some Additional Problems of Explanation

The material presented above has shown that, in each of the societies examined in which the two conditions emerged that our hypothesis postulates as basic, the major features of the society's political system were fully institutionalized. However, the extents to which these features were developed in general were different; and there were differences in the *relative* importances of their developments. Our data show that the extent to which *each* of these features, channels of political struggle, or administrative agencies and different aspects thereof, was developed and institutionalized varied, both somewhat independently in the same society, and in different societies. For example, there existed many differences between the extent of relative development of the bureaucratic administration and of the organs of political struggle; and there were differences in the degree of emphasis that a bureaucracy, whatever the extent of its general development, placed on either technical or regulative activities; and there existed also variations in the development of the different aspects of the organization of the channels of political struggle.

The existence of these differences inevitably poses certain questions. The first is whether they can be explained by our hypothesis. That is, to what extent can these differences be attributed to differences in either the extent or the type of development of the independent variable autonomy of political sphere, and differentiation of the social structures), or to differences in the operation of the intervening variables (intergroup conflicts and regulative problems, and operation of autonomous regulatory mechanisms)?

The second question is that of the extent to which such differences in the social and political structures can still be contained within the framework of the political systems of the historical bureaucratic societies. In other words, what influence do these differences have on the conditions of perpetuation of these systems? We shall discuss these problems in the remaining chapters of this volume.

[12] The Conditions for Development of Historical Bureaucratic Empires. The Conditions for Their Perpetuation

We have tested and verified our hypothesis about the conditions necessary to the institutionalization of the main features of the political systems of the historical bureaucratic societies. We have demonstrated that such institutionalization is contingent on the simultaneous developments of a limited autonomy of the political sphere (represented by the rulers' development of autonomous political goals), and of a limited but pervasive differentiation in all the society's major institutional spheres.

Our analysis has indicated the basic prerequisites or premises of the political systems of the historical bureaucratic empires. These can be defined as the maintenance of social conditions and institutional frameworks that make possible the continuous and simultaneous generation both of certain levels of free-floating resources and differentiated political activities and of traditional political attitudes, to be held by parts of the population, that would help maintain the rulers' traditional legitimation.

This necessarily raises the matter of the conditions for perpetuation of these political systems after they have been established and institutionalized. If our preceding analysis is correct, we may postulate that the perpetuation of these systems is largely dependent on the continuation of the same conditions as were necessary for their institutionalization—i.e., on the constant coexistence of certain levels of autonomous political goals and orientations, and of *limited but pervasive* differentiation of the social structure. However, we must consider whether the very institutionalization of the major features of the political systems of the historical bureaucratic societies assures the continued existence of these conditions. In other words, we must determine whether the establishment of a centralized polity; the institutionalization, operation, and functioning of the organs of political struggle and administration; and participation by the rulers and by various groups and strata in them—whether all these factors insure the continued existence of the basic conditions of these political systems.

The preceding analysis seems to indicate that the institutionalization of political systems does not in itself make the continuation of these conditions certain. The very structure of political processes in these societies often created various incompatibilities capable of underming such conditions. The incompatibilities were usually associated with the coexistence, among the rulers and the major strata, both of traditional and of more differentiated social and political interests and orientations.

The coexistence of these elements, combined with the possibility of constant shiftings in the relative strengths of different groups and strata, created circumstances in which several significant types of incompatibilities could develop within the social and political structures of these societies. For example, the differentiation in the social structure could be less than the degree demanded, as it were, by the rulers' political orientations. Or such differentiation could extend beyond the limits set by the traditional legitimation of the rulers; and various groups and strata could attempt to expand political participasion beyond the premises of these political systems—participation undermining the rulers' traditional legitimation.

In this context, we should remember that the regulative activities evolved by the organs of political struggle and by the bureaucratic administration constituted only one facet of several diverse regulative mechanisms developed, in these societies, in response to the problems created by growing differentiation. For example, their emergence coincided with the development—in varying degrees—of various autonomous regulative mechanisms; and the latter would compete, in a way, with the former, both for resources and for scope of activities.

Because the possibility of realizing these potential incompatibilities was inherent in the political structures of these societies—even in those in which the political systems were institutionalized— the systems could not always be certain that the resources necessary for their functioning would be available continuously. The resources' availability depended on the structure, interests, attitudes, and political activities of the rulers and of major groups and strata in the society, and on their relations to the basic prerequisites of the political system. Attitudes were, of course, greatly influenced by the differences in the structures and compositions of these groups, by the extent of their differentiation and specialization, and by the scale on which they used and depended on autonomous regulative mechanisms.

A specific composition of the political orientations and activities both of the rulers and of the major strata would be favorable to perpetuating the basic conditions necessary for the continuity of the political systems of the historical bureaucratic societies, while a different composition might have the opposite effect.

Hence, in order to understand the conditions necessary for the perpetuation or non-perpetuation of these political systems, we must analyze the political process—the variations in the political activities of the rulers and of the main groups—in them.

TWO

Conditions of Perpetuation

of the Political Systems of the

Historical Bureaucratic Empires

Plan of Part Two

The preceding discussion has indicated the main problems which will be our concern in the following chapters. Having substantiated the hypothesis which explains the prerequisites for the development of the political systems of the historical bureaucratic empires, we must now investigate the conditions necessary for the perpetuation of these systems. This investigation will first involve analyzing the main differences among the societies studied here; the principal features of the political systems of the centralized bureaucratic empires; and the nature of political powers—i.e., policies of the rulers and political activities of the major groups. We shall attempt to determine the relations between these differences and the variations of the basic characteristics in their societies' structure. That is, we shall analyze the extent to which the political sphere developed autonomy within them; the degree to which they differentiated their groups' social structures; the intensity of the regulative problems consequent on such differentiation; and the scopes of the autonomous mechanisms.

Second, we must investigate the conditions under which these variations tend to be conducive to the continuous functioning of the political systems, and the conditions under which they tend to undermine this continuity.

7

The Policies of the Rulers

[1] *The Problems of Perpetuating the Political Systems*

At the close of Chapter 6, we raised the subject of the conditions necessary for the perpetuation and continuity of the political systems of the historical bureaucratic societies. We saw that this continuity was not given or insured by the conditions necessary for the development of these political systems, nor by the initial institutionalization of their principal features instead, it was largely dependent on the social and political orientations of the rulers and of the major groups and their principal features. Instead, it was largely dependent on the social political orientations became manifested in the political struggle—in the political activities and organizations that arose in these societies. Therefore, we now should proceed to analyze this political struggle; to describe its chief participants and their political orientations, organizations, and activities; and to examine the ways that their participation affected both the structures of the various political institutions, and the continuity of the political systems, of the historical bureaucratic empires.

Let us begin by examining the framework of the political struggle in the historical bureaucratic polities, and by enumerating its main participants. These were the rulers arrayed against the major groups and strata—the bureaucracy, the aristocracy, the professional, religious, and cultural elites, the upper urban groups (especially the merchants and burghers), the middle and lower urban groups, the landed gentry, and the peasantry.

The actual framework for the political struggle was supplied, in most of the societies studied, by the policies of the rulers. Of course, these policies did not grow in a social vacuum; and in Chapter 6 we analyzed the principal social conditions influencing their development. Nevertheless, these policies usually constituted the most active and dynamic elements in the political process. They shaped the environment and setting to which other groups had to adjust and/or react—even though these groups were only rarely passive in the political struggle.

It is appropriate here to describe briefly the rulers and the political elites in these societies; the description will in some measure recapitulate points made in preceding chapters. In most of the countries examined, the political elites consisted of the ruler-king or emperor, his leading advisers and personal retainers, court officials, and (to some extent) heads of the different bureaucratic services.

The members of political elites—as distinct from all the upper strata of the country (the aristocracy, gentry, and bureaucracy)—were not selected according to rigid or formal criteria. They were recruited from many different social strata, like the aristocracy, some of the middle class, religious groups, and even the peasantry. In some cases (in Europe, Egypt, and Sassanid Persia, and, to a lesser degree, in Byzantium and China), the monarchs came from old, aristocratic royal families. In others (e.g., Rome, and—again, only to some extent—Byzantium and China), they also often came from different strata as usurpers or war lords.

Whatever its origin, the political elite was distinct from all social groups—including, in some measure, the bureaucracy to which some of its members belonged—by virtue of its specifically political outlook, aims, and behavior. It upheld and promoted the autonomy of the political sphere and of political goals already described and analyzed.

[2] *The Major Objectives of the Rulers*

What were the foremost objectives of the policies of the rulers and the political elites in the societies studied?

The respective concrete goals of rulers of the various historical bureaucratic societies varied greatly. They included territorial unification and expansion, conquest, enrichment of the polity, economic development, and maintaining or expanding a given cultural pattern.

Obviously, their objectives always incorporated what may be called
the universal or basic goals of any ruler—namely, maintaining his own
position of power against any opponents, and insuring the possibility
of mobilizing resources for his own needs. But whatever the rulers'
concrete aims, the rulers usually envisaged and implemented these
aims as autonomous political goals of a unified, centralized polity. This
very fact affected the nature of the rulers' general political orientations
and the nature of their concrete aims and policies. Any specific goal or
objective of the rulers of these societies may not have differed, in its
concrete details, from similar aims of patrimonial or feudal rulers.
But the rulers of the historical bureaucratic societies, to be able to
implement their goals, were forced—by virtue of their positions within
the structures of their societies and their general political orientations
—to evolve some new, additional *general* goals. These provided the
framework within which their more concrete policies and aims developed.

The first general goal was to establish and maintain a unified and
centralized polity and the ruler's sovereignty over it. At certain historical stages of these societies, establishing of such a polity might have
been a major goal in itself. In other stages, the continuous maintenance
of the polity constituted an important goal.

Then, the rulers of the historical bureaucratic societies developed
special orientations with regard to mobilizing resources. Their objective was to acquire the certainty that they could obtain *continuous* and
independent recruitment of resources from various strata in the society.
These rulers were, as we have seen, usually not interested only in implementing any one policy or concrete goal. In addition, they were
concerned with the possibility of executing their policies continuously
according to their changing needs and at their own discretion. Their
raison d'être—in their battles with traditional feudal or patrimonial
elements—was based largely on their abilities to implement continuously various policies, and to maintain a unified, centralized political
framework, and their flexibility in choosing policies and concrete goals.
Moreover, the rulers needed a constant supply of resources to maintain the administrative machinery, which constituted one basis of their
strength and the main medium for the continuous execution of their
policies.

As a result of their objectives and of their structural positions in
the societies, the rulers of historical bureaucratic empires always had a
basic interest in the continuous and independent mobilization of resources from other groups and strata. That is, they were interested in a
mobilization which would be largely independent both of the fixed
ascriptive rights and duties of these groups and strata, and of the wishes
of their members.

This interest was manifest in the rulers' desire either to concentrate most resources in their own hands (e.g., by storing goods and money and accumulating state property), or to further the development of various types of free-floating, mobile resources not tied to any ascriptive groups and thus able to be freely accumulated and exchanged. These resources could then be controlled and utilized at the ruler's discretion. In all the societies studied, the monarchs owned some "private" or feudal properties and resources; yet these were insufficient, and the rulers were continually confronted by the need to mobilize additional resources. Obviously, the more developed and differentiated the social structure, the more difficult it was for the rulers to monopolize all the needed resources. Thus, their ability to control continuously the free-floating resources became more crucial. They therefore endeavored to create situations in which such resources were continuously available, and wherein they could fully control and mobilize these resources whenever necessary for their own purposes.

The ruler of the centralized bureaucratic polity could realize his political objectives only in so far as there existed, in the society, power and resources that were neither entirely dependent on other groups, nor committed to their use, nor obtainable only through their good will. Although the rulers occasionally might have utilized such embedded and committed resources, continued reliance on them would necessarily have entailed the loss of the rulers' independence, and of their ability to formulate freely their aims and goals and to pursue their policies. Unlike rulers of many primitive patrimonial or feudal systems, the rulers of the bureaucratic polities were not willing to be merely the strongest and "first" among rulers or owners of similar clan or patrimonial units. Instead, these rulers strove to concentrate in their own hands, the main centers of power and control in the society.

The rulers and the bureaucracy united, when their respective interests did not conflict, to insure the continuous existence of free-floating resources of various kinds and their continuous control over them. They attempted to prevent any one group or stratum within the society from controlling the use of free-floating resources—whether wealth, prestige, communication, or political power and support itself —sufficiently to be able to challenge the rulers' control of them.

Because of this, the rulers and the bureaucracy in these polities always tended to regulate, make dependent on themselves, or reduce all other centers of power, thus minimizing their chances of becoming entirely autonomous or of monopolizing resources in the society. The rulers always tried to create strategic positions for themselves that would enable them to control most of the available resources. Max Weber has pointed out that every bureaucratic administration characteristically tries to "level out" various social differences. It is important, however, to note that this tendency is not limited to the bureaucratic administration; it occurs also, and perhaps mostly, in the political elites of bureaucratic polities ([I] *Weber, 1922, pp. 650 ff.*).

To summarize, the rulers of these polities exhibited a triple tendency:

1. They were interested in promoting free resources and in freeing resources from commitments to particularistic-ascriptive groups

2. They did not want these resources to develop beyond limits appropriate to their own traditional legitimation

3. They tried to control these resources—to commit them, as it were, to their own uses

Obviously, the respective degrees of success attained by the rulers' efforts varied greatly. However, most of these societies share some general tendencies in these directions. The exceptions are marginal patrimonial societies (like that existing, to some extent, in Sassanid Persia), and in cases during periods of disintegration of the bureaucratic polities.

All the aims and policies discussed illustrate the general tendency, common to the rulers of the historical bureaucratic polities, to develop a relatively high level of generalization of power. These rulers needed and desired to attain a state of affairs wherein political power—at least, the power potentially at their disposal—could be generalized, extended with relative freedom from traditionalistic restriction, and applied to various goals in accordance with the rulers' interests and considerations.

This tendency toward establishing a certain level of generalization of power is the single most universal characteristic of the rulers' policy orientations. It organized their activities in a pattern which distinguished them from the activities of rulers of less differentiated types of polity. However, this tendency was limited (as we shall discuss in greater detail) by the traditional elements inherent in the rulers' structural situations and orientations. This limitation makes the policies of these rulers distinct from those of more differentiated—especially, modern—societies.

[3] *The Social Setting of the Implementation of the Rulers' Aims*

To understand how the general tendencies and goals of the rulers were translated into concrete policies, we must recall the environment in which they were articulated and executed. The rulers' basic aims had to be realized in societies whose development of free-floating resources was limited. This limitation was imposed, first, by the great preponderance that different types of natural or semi-natural economy had in agriculture. This preponderance involved many consequences for the extent of economic development and expansion, the degree of social mobility, and the possible emergence of new strata and groups. It set obvious bounds to the creation of fluid resources and to the possibility of exchanging and accumulating means of exchange. These bounds constitute a principal difference between the historical bureaucratic systems and modern societies; in the latter, all economic activities and mechanisms tend to be focused around market exchange.

Second, despite all the inroads made by criteria of universalism and achievement, the social structures of these societies were still, as was indicated earlier, predominantly based on ascriptive criteria and hierarchically stratified. However, the basic traditional resources or polical support available to the various elites and other politically and socially active groups was greatly limited by the conditions mentioned.

The low level of differentiation in the social structure was not the only factor that limited the implementation of these policies of the rulers that were directed to furthering free resources. Limitations were also imposed by some of the rulers' own orientations—especially by their identification with many ascriptive and traditional aspects of their societies' social organizations and values, and by their strong emphasis on their traditional legitimation.

The actual policies of the ruling elites, and their viscissitudes, can be understood only in relation to all these conditions.

The degrees of social differentiation and free-floating resources varied from society to society. Thus, the policies of their ruling elites also differed in concrete details, even when some of their basic aims were similar. These differences will be considered when we analyze the manifestations of these policies in various social spheres.

Then we shall describe, in rather more detail, the principal policies undertaken by the rulers of the historical bureaucratic polities. Many elements of these policies can also be found in other types of political systems—in feudal, patrimonial, or even modern ones. At this stage of our analysis, we shall not consider the question of which of these policies are endemic to the historical bureaucratic polities; we shall proceed directly to the rulers' policies in the major institutional fields—economics, stratification, religion and education, law, and the political field itself. We shall determine how, and to what extent, the rulers' general political aims and tendencies were manifested in these policies, and which kinds of policies the rulers employed to implement their aims.

[4] *Policies of the Rulers in the Economic Field*

A. PRINCIPAL CHARACTERISTICS

The rulers had three basic and constant objectives in the economic sphere. The first was to monopolize, or at least insure the possibility of rapidly mobilizing sufficient economic and manpower resources to make it certain that any of their goals and policies would be constantly implemented and that their services would be maintained. The second main aim was the continuous control and regulation of economic resources. The rulers' third important objective was to maintain their *political* control over different groups in the society, as they frequently did, through utilizing various economic policies.

These goals could be implemented through a great variety of concrete policies and means. Basically, the rulers used the following means to realize them: (1) direct conscription of labor and promotion of state enterprises; (2) taxation; and (3) various financial monetary measures and policies.

We shall now consider the main economic policies and measures employed by the rulers of the historical bureaucratic societies, and the ways they served to achieve the rulers' economic goals.

First, let us deal with the ways the rulers solved the problem of making resources available to themselves. They had two possible alternatives: to accumulate them directly; or to encourage various groups and strata to develop resources, which the rulers would then regulate and control in such a way that they would have a sure, constant supply.

There are many cases illustrating the rulers' direct concentration of various resources in their own hands. One example is provided by the different types of monopoly that existed in many of the countries studied—both in the forms of state-owned mines, workshops, and merchant navy, and of exclusive control over the distribution of essential materials like salt and iron. ([G] *Christensen, 1936, ch. ii; Altheim and Stiehl, 1954, 1957, ch. i, ii, iii, [L] Andréadès, 1934; Bratianu, 1938; [R] Haring, 1927; Zavala, 1943; [I] Gale, 1930, 1931; Wilbur, 1943; Balázs, 1931–33, 1960.*)

The rulers' methods of insuring that maximum manpower would be available for their economic, administrative, and military activities consisted of mobilizing free or slave manpower for mines, galleys, and workshops (this was closely connected with the monopolies); and binding peasants to state-owned land and limiting their freedom of movement, thus assuring the state of having the necessary revenues and produce. These measures usually developed in those societies, or sectors thereof, where there was little economic differentiation and mobile manpower. Illustrations can be seen in Sassanid Persia ([G] *Ghirshman, 1954; Christensen, 1936; Altheim and Stiehl, 1954, 1957*) and among the Indian population in the Spanish-American Empire; and in relatively more developed societies, like Prussia and Russia, where the rulers, in co-operation with the aristocracy, attempted to limit the peasants' freedom and mobility and to bind them to the land ([X] *Carsten, 1954, 1955; Hintze, 1914, 1915; Beloff,* [W] *1953,* [S] *1954, ch. i, vi;* [W] *Young, 1957; Sacke, 1938[a], 1938[b]*). Measures binding various categories of people—peasants, artisans, etc.—to their vocations were enacted to insure both the basic productivity of the labor force and the revenues levied from it. Their purpose could have been to make certain that various population sectons performed public services. Prescriptive measures like this also occurred frequently in the late Roman and early Byzantine periods ([L] *Ostrogorsky, 1931; Charanis, 1944–45; Stein, 1928[a], 1928[b]*), during the Hellenistic monarchies, and (to a small extent) in the Spanish-American Empire ([R] *Simpson, 1934, 1938; Zavala, 1943; Ots Capdequi, 1934[a], 1934[b], 1939; Haring, 1927*).

The rulers had another means of assuring the supply of resources and manpower: establishing colonies and settlements of peasant soldiers, and thus making certain that the state would have sufficient military manpower. These colonies were not necessarily state owned; and they were closely associated with more complicated economic measures and policies, like various types of taxation. The policy of establishing such colonies evolved particularly in societies whose problems of frontier defense were of paramount importance. In Byzantium, one purpose of the famous system of *themes,* supposedly founded by Emperor Heraclius (reigned A.D. 610–641), was to provide adequate manpower for frontier garrisons. This was achieved by starting military colonies of free peasants, from which soldiers were compulsorily recruited (*Ostrogorsky, 1927, 1931; Stein, 1920, 1928[b]; Constantinescu, 1924; Lemerle, 1958; Gelzer, 1899; Setton, 1953; J. Darko, 1939; Stadtmüller, 1937; Baynes, 1952; Cassimatis, 1939*). A similar pattern was established in the Sassanid Empire by Khosrou I ([G] *Stein, 1920; Christensen, 1936, ch. viii; Altheim and Stiehl, 1954*), called "Khosrou of the Immortal Soul." The T'ang Dynasty (A.D. 618–905) also organized the militia along similar lines ([I] *Des Rotours, 1947–48, Introduction; Pulleyblank, 1955; Balázs, 1931–33*).

It is worth while to note that, in connection with these prescriptive measures and with taxation policies in general, the rulers and administrators developed (or inherited from preceding types of polities) various types of registrating and census-taking activities and organizations, that could even include property registration.

B. MAJOR TYPES OF TAXATION

Exclusive control of resources, through enterprises or direct prescription of available resources, was only one way in which the rulers implemented their economic objectives. In more differentiated societies and economic systems, this system involved many difficulties and was less capable of tapping and utilizing all available resources. Thus as concomitants of, and in addition to, such direct concentration of resources, the rulers also developed new, more complex policies. The latters' function was to make certain the mobilization of resources—not through the rulers' direct ownership of resources, but through developing, regulating, and controlling various economic forces. Some of the most important of the more complex policies were various fiscal and monetary ones, utilizing taxation as a major means to gain their ends.

As we have seen, the primary purpose of taxation frequently was to contribute to the rulers' accumulation of as many resources as possible. However, taxation was also instrumental to several long-range social and economic policies. The types used by the rulers of the historical bureaucratic societies were manifold. Two very important types were taxes on land and "personal" taxes—i.e., tax payable by every person (or members of different classes of persons): taxes on using different facilities, like roads, bridges, forests; taxes on different commodities; customs; and different kinds of tribute or extortion exacted from different classes of population. These taxes had usually originated in different historical circumstances and customs. The rulers adopted many of them from previous (feudal, patrimonial, or city-state) usages and were continued by them. But although many details persisted, on the whole the rulers transformed, although with varying degrees of consistency, the taxation systems used in each of the societies studied here. The transformation can be discerned in two different aspects of the organization of taxation and finance. First, the finances of the realm, usually distinct from court finances, were generally organized in a relatively unified framework and budget. Second, the purely tributary or "collecting" aspect of taxation became, in most cases, co-ordinated and incorporated with a wider, though not always fully coherent and consistent, framework of financial policies.

One of the principal objectives of taxation always continued to be purely fiscal and accumulative. But even the fiscal aspect became organized in this new framework. It did so in a way—distinct from the way of a patrimonial or conquest society—that took into account the economic interests of different groups, and was, at least somewhat, designed not only to advance mobilization of immediate resources, but also to attain the possibility of more continuous mobilization. As a consquence of this organization, taxation could become an important means of carrying out complex, flexible economic and social policies. Thus the rulers of these societies had much less tendency than the rulers of feudal or patrimonial societies to use financial and economic means (payments, negotiations, etc.) as instruments of internal political bargaining. Instead, they tended more to use financial policies as means of political control and social policy ([L] *Andréadès, 1921[b]; Stein, 1923; Dölger, 1927, 1956; [G] Faziolleh, 1938; Altheim and Stiehl, 1954, 1957; [Y] Zeller, 1923–25, 1948, 1952; [S] Beloff, 1954; [Z] Mousnier, 1951; [R] Haring, 1927, 1947; Ots Capdequi, 1934[a], 1934[b], 1939; Zavala, 1943, 1947[b]*).

C. THE PRINCIPAL USES OF TAXATION

What broader aims were served by taxation?

First, taxation was employed as a critical, although not invariably successful, tool for regulating the relations between land resources and population, and for providing an adequate supply of manpower. It was especially important as a regulator of manpower mobility. As such, it was used extensively in those countries where, and during periods when, because the population had decreased or become more mobile, vast areas were threatened with desertion.

For example, in times of depopulation—e.g., in the early Byzantine period, or in some periods in China—a revenue system developed that combined the land and poll taxes, thus binding the peasant to his land and the artisan to his shop. Adequately populated societies, on the other hand, characteristically separated these taxes and encouraged greater manpower mobility—especially movement toward the frontier regions. Populating the Empire's frontier regions and insuring their cultivation were the purposes of the famous tax reforms made by Heraclius in Byzantium ([L] *Ostrogorsky, 1927, 1930[a], 1931; but also Lemerle, 1958; Karayanopulus, 1956; Stein, 1928[a], 1928[b]*). Similar tendencies are revealed by the land tax regulation in T'ang China ([I] *Balázs, 1931–33, 1954[a]; Maspero, 1950[a]; Pulleyblank, 1955, ch. iv, v*). The reformed revenue systems effected by the distinction between poll and land taxes in Byzantium, and by the monetary unification of the land tax in T'ang China, were in both cases intended to expand the peasant class, assure them of secure tenure, encourage them to settle in the frontier regions, and make them supply more flexible, preferably monetary, resources to the state. Comparable wider economic-social aims, and not merely the immediate objective of acquiring more revenue, instigated some taxation reforms made by Khosrou I in Persia. These, however, were much less successful, because Persia's level of economic differentiation was initially low ([G] *Christensen. 1936, ch. viii; Stein, 1920; Altheim and Stiehl, 1954, 1957, ch. i, ii, iii*).

Second, a differential taxation policy was often, in effect, a "discriminatory" or "levelling" instrument capable of undermining the economic and political power of many strong groups (e.g., aristocracy, merchants). A taxation policy like this could thus regulate the distribution of power and economic facilities in the society. The major example of this levelling that recurred in some of the societies we are studying consisted of the efforts, made by the rulers and bureaucracies, to promote a free peasantry. The purposes of these efforts were to limit the power and expansion of landed aristocracy, and to provide the rulers, through the free peasants, with economic and political support and with military and administrative manpower.

The levelling tendency occurred in Sassanid Persia during the reigns of Kavadh I (A.D. 488–531) and Khosrou I (A.D. 531–579), although in Persia their efforts never met with any long-range success. The same tendency was also expressed in the renowned policies of the Byzantine emperors (from Heraclius through at least the reign of Constantine VII; that is, from A.D. 610 through 959) that severely limited the rights of the big landowners to buy land from the free owners of small holdings [L] *Ostrogorsky, 1929[a], 1930[a], 1956[a]* passim; *Guilland, 1953–55; Jenkins, 1953; Lemerle, 1958; Charanis, 1944–45, 1951; Diehl, 1943, ch. vii, viii, ix*). Similar tendencies were exhibited also in (1) China, where most of the dynasties continually tried to limit, by statute, the maximum amount of land that any one individual was permitted to possess ([I] *Balázs, 1953[b], 1954[b]; Maspero, 1950[a]; H. Franke, 1953[a]; K. Wang, 1956; Liang, 1956[a], Rieger, 1937*); (2) Rome, where attempts to protect the small Roman and Italian peasants from the encroachment by the latifundia were made ([Q] *Charlesworth, 1936; Momigliano, 1934*); and (3) the Spanish-American Empire, where many efforts were made to limit the power of the big *enconmienderos* and to insure some rights for the Indian communities. (*See for instance*, [R] *Zavala, 1943.*)

The levelling issue was less important in the European countries during the Age of Absolutism. The European aristocracy no longer monopolized economic and political powers, since the old type of self-sufficient aristocratic and manorial units had broken down.

Third, taxation often served the rulers and the bureaucracy by providing a means for regulating the different economic activities of various sectors and groups. This is best illustrated by the control of urban economy, whose aim was to make certain that the urban population would provide various resources for the rulers and for different groups in the society, and also that the rulers would control these latter groups. In many cases (especially in Europe), these policies of urban economy had originated in the towns and then had been adopted by the rulers of the centralized state.

In addition, taxation often served the rulers' more general (and not always fully articulated) aim of controlling, as far as possible, all the economically active groups, thus preventing them from constituting an independent economic power, and enabling the rulers to mobilize financial resources at will.

Fourth, taxation sometimes supplied various incentives for the development of economic resources and activities. In most of the societies we are studying, economic development was not very articulate as a fully conscious goal of policy. In Sassanid Persia, or even in Byzantium and China, economic development was mostly subordinated to political and cultural goals and considerations; in so far as economic activities were encouraged, this encouragement was given primarily for the political interests of the state ([G] *Altheim, 1955[a], 1955[b]; Christensen, 1936* passim; [L] *Ostrogorsky, 1931; Dölger, 1927, 1956; Danstrup, 1946[a], 1946[b]; Runciman, 1952; Boak, 1929;* [I] *Blue, 1948; Balázs, 1960*). Economic development was given prominence as a goal only in Europe and, to a lesser degree, in the Spanish-American Empire ([S] *Wilson, 1958; Heckscher, 1932; Viner, 1948; Beloff, 1954;* [R] *Ots Capdequi, 1932, 1939; Zavala, 1943*).

Taxing and directing trade often constituted an important factor in foreign policy and relations. Their regulation was considered essential to the maintenance of both political strength and free political maneuverability.

D. MONETARY AND FINANCIAL POLICIES

The rulers of the historical bureaucratic polities employed several economic means in addition to taxation for achieving their regulatory and fiscal objectives. The most important monetary and financial devices were the manipulation of currency and the system of compulsory or semi-compulsory loans. These devices were utilized, by the rulers of most of these societies, for mobilizing resources as well as for regulating and consolidating the sources of economic power; and they were sometimes used to further the development of economic resources. The monarch often manipulated currency so that, by coining his to compete with local currency, he could undermine the economic power of great land-owners and magnates. Frequently, too, currency was devalued, in order to provide the state with greater free-floating monetary resources at the expense of landed property-holding groups.

In these societies, the importance of monetary means and policies transcended that due the mere accumulation of financial assets by the rulers. The functioning of the royal administration was usually entirely contingent on its continuous possession of, or free access to, monetary means, and on the rulers' abilities to balance their budgets. Since the rulers thus depended greatly on flexible economic monetary means, and on being able to mobilize these continuously, they were extremely sensitive to any fluctuations in the supply and demand of money; regulating the supply of money became a major policy issue for most of them.

Hence, in all the societies we are examining, the rulers did not only "accumulate" money. They also, through a variety of means and expedients, attempted both to insure their steady supply of money and to control the conditions of its availability. Manipulating the value of money, and its devaluation and coinage, and controlling sources of credit became basic expedients of economic policy. In this way, the policies of the rulers themselves became vitally important for the functioning of the economy; but, at the same time, the rulers became greatly dependent on various fluctuations within the economy ([G] *Faziolleh, 1938; Altheim and Stiehl, 1954, 1957;* [L] *Andréadès, 1921[b]; Stein 1919, 1949, 1954; Lopez, 1945, 1951[a], 1951[b]; Segrè, 1940–41, 1942–43, 1945;* [I] *N. Li, 1956; Balázs, 1960; Blue, 1948;* [Z] *Lipson, 1929–30; Mousnier, 1951;* [Y] *Zeller, 1952*).

E. REGULATION OF PROVISIONS AND SUPPLY

The rulers' tendency to control many strategic regulatory points in the society, and to provide for the population in terms of certain basic expectations (and patterns of legitimation), was demonstrated also by their assumption of responsibility for maintaining the production and distribution of goods, especially of basic victuals. Assuming this responsibility is characteristic of rulers in many different types of societies. The rulers tended also to assume such responsibility in the majority of societies studied here—although sometimes, especially when the tendency impeded the economic development of some groups, it was opposed by such groups.

In the ancient Egyptian empires, the rulers' tendency to make themselves responsible was most evident in the system of granaries. This system provided the entire population with grain and food during droughts, and supplied foodstuffs to some parts of the urban population at "reasonable" prices. Similar, although less extensive, policies were undertaken in Sassanid Persia ([F] *Drioton and Vandier, 1952; Kees, 1933[a]; Edgerton, 1947[a]; [G] Altheim and Stiehl, 1954, 1957, ch. i, ii; Ghirshman, 1954*).

A system of granaries also existed in China. The products stored in the granaries were used to balance any excessive fluctuations in the prices of basic provisions ([I] *Blue, 1948; Balázs, 1931–33, 1953[a], 1960; Gale, 1930, 1931*).

In Byzantium, the government was responsible for providing necessities to the capital and other urban centers. In addition, it regulated prices, mostly for the benefit of the consumer. This device was used constantly by Roman and Byzantine emperors, from the fall of the Republic until the fall of Byzantium ([L] *Bratianu, 1934[a], 1938; Andréadès, 1934*).

Similarly, the government of the Spanish-American Empire always undertook to provide, or to direct the provision of, adequate and cheap foodstuffs to the urban centers ([R] *Guthrie, 1939*).

During the Age of Absolutism, European national governments adopted, adapted, and extended many traditional policies of regulating prices, providing victuals to urban centers, and accumulating resources adequate for the needs of their populations. The economic policies and ideologies of many statesmen of the period strongly emphasized the accumulation of wealth and the economic self-sufficiency of the state ([S] *Hauser, 1940; Wilson, 1958; Heckscher, 1932; Viner, 1948; [Z] Lipson, 1929–30; for an earlier example, see also Bisson, 1957*).

These supply policies manifested several of the goals of the rulers. Ideologically, they emphasized the ruler as the society's "provider." Also, they were directed toward effectively regulating social and economic life, maintaining a certain equilibrium between levels of supply and demand, and creating appropriate motivation for the maintenance of levels of consumption. Moreover, in many cases (e.g., in Byzantium), they could serve the ruler as instruments to keep politically disruptive or active elements of the urban population quiet.

F. MOBILIZATION OF ADMINISTRATIVE MANPOWER

We may now proceed to analyze the policies directed toward supplying manpower for the various state services, especially administration. Several of these policies were roughly parallel to economic policies. In addition to the conscriptive and prescriptive policies already described, the rulers employed two chief methods to achieve their goals. One was to recruit manpower through various kinds of direct remuneration—such as salaries, emoluments, and benefices. The other consisted of "farming out" taxes and selling offices ([L] *Kolias, 1939;* [S] *Swart, 1949*). These latter practices were prevalent, to varying degrees, in almost all the societies studied. They served the declared objective of recruiting personnel. In addition, they constituted modes of providing more revenue to the state, and of absorbing many active social elements into the state's political framework.

We must note that these recruiting policies were predicated on the existence of some mobile and flexible manpower; and the rulers employed them to make certain of having available an adequate part of this manpower in case of need.

G. SUMMARY OF ECONOMIC POLICIES

The above discussion has shown that the rulers of the bureaucratic societies employed a great variety of methods and policies in the economic field, to implement both economic and political purposes. A method or policy usually served several intermingled aims, not just one.

The foremost goals of the economic policies were common, though their relative importance varied, to the ruling elites of the societies we are investigating. We can summarize these goals as follows: (1) direct concentration of as many economic resources as possible under the control of the state; (2) regulating economic forces, and insuring the constant flow of free (i.e., mostly monetary) resources to the state; (3) encouraging economic development, and the state regulation of the growth of economic and investment potential, enabling the state to benefit from any wealth and increased productivity in the country; (4) discharging the state's responsibility for providing the population with major necessities, fulfilling the state's protective functions, and providing various services to the population and thus maintaining the rulers' general control over the society; and (5) using economic measures, as tools of political control, to weaken opposition to the rulers and to strengthen their potential supporters.

Some of these goals and policies existed also in other types of political systems. The objectives under (1) and (4), and, to a lesser degree, those under (5)—these occur in primitive, patrimonial, and feudal societies; and they also occur, to some extent, in city-states. True, the implementation of any such goal may, in details, vary greatly from one type of society to another; nevertheless, even here many similarities are discernible.

There are characteristics of economic policies that are distinctive and appear only in the policies of the rulers of historical bureaucratic policies. These distinguishing qualities emerge, first, in the rulers' policy of encouraging some, even though limited, free resources. They also appear in the rulers' attempts to control and regulate all the centers of free resources. On the whole, the mobilizing aspect—i.e., the aspect representing the rulers' efforts to mobilize maximum resources to implement their goals—seems to have been predominant in their economic policies. However, it was usually not possible for the rulers to mobilize all the resources they needed without first encouraging autonomous economic activities. Consequently, the rulers had to promote, on whatever scale, some autonomous economic activities; and these subsequently had to be regulated in their turn.

Most of the rulers' economic policies were implemented by the bureaucratic administration. The administrative implementation of many such policies resulted, within the administration itself, in growing specialization and departmental differentiation, and in some general rationalization of administrative techniques and usages. Thus, while these policies were in one sense manifestations of these societies tendency to generalized power, they in turn caused some development of the rationalization of administrative techniques and of the relations among administrative organs and other social spheres.

[5] The Rulers' Policies in the Military Field

We have noted that, among the aims of the ruling elites of the historical bureaucratic societies, the military and diplomatic objectives were usually very important. Territorial expansion and conquest, and "political-international" gains made through diplomatic maneuvers, were essential to the rulers of these societies and often constituted their primary political goals. During long periods in the history of these societies, policies oriented to achieving these objectives were predominant.

To realize such goals, the rulers had to develop several internal policies that centered on mobilizing and effectively controlling an army (and a diplomatic service). For both external and internal reasons, the rulers were interested in maintaining a standing army—or, at least, in being able to mobilize one rapidly—and desired this army to be their own and not the armed force of aristocratic or feudal retainers.

The rulers utilized several policies to attain these military goals. In most of these societies, the rulers' "private" (patrimonial or feudal) armies were not adequate for their needs. Therefore, the rulers were forced to have recourse either to one of two major methods of recruiting armies, or to some mixture of the two.

The first method was conscription to a "national" army, whose core consisted of professional or semi-professional soldiers and offices. The "national" army also included the peasant militias, which were particularly important in frontier districts. Such national armies existed in Sassanid Persia, especially after the reign of Khosrou I ([G] *Stein, 1920; Altheim and Stiehl, 1954*); in T'ang China, where the militia was also prevalent ([I] *Pulleyblank, 1955; Des Rotours, 1947–48; Michael, 1946*); and in the Byzantine Empire, which established it through the system of *themes* ([G] *Christensen, 1936, ch. viii; Stein, 1920;* [L] *Diehl, 1943, 1957, pp. 40–57; J. Darko, 1939; E. Darko, 1946–48*). National armies were less important in France and England ([S] *Roberts, 1956;* [A] *Speier, 1952*). Men were recruited for these armies by (1) forceful conscription, for example, by the press gang, (2) founding special military colonies, (3) establishing peasant colonies from which soldiers could be conscripted, and (4) general mobilization of manpower from various groups in the society.

Another major method of military recruitment used by these rulers was the employment of mercenary armies. Such mercenary armies could be of two types, which often overlapped. In Byzantium and China, and on a lesser scale in England and France, hired mercenaries were used ([L] *Bréhier, 1949[b]; Diehl, 1943*). The rulers obtained soldiers for the other type of mercenary armies by compromise—that is, by "farming out" recruitment to various landed magnates and aristocrats. This technique is best illustrated by the late Byzantine *pronoia,* and, though not so well, by the French and English post-feudal armies ([L] *Ostrogorsky, 1956[a], 1956[b]*).

In all these cases, the rulers had to control the military forces effectively and to minimize the possibilities of their becoming independent. These necessities raised a problem somewhat similar to that of controlling the bureaucracy. (The latter problem will be discussed later.) Obviously, however, the control of the military was much more complicated. This problem confronted the rulers with three possibilities: (1) the "feudalization" of the army, (2) usurpation by the military of the centers of government, and (3) rebellions and outbursts of the soldiery.

The rulers coped—in so far as they coped at all—with these potential difficulties by developing (1) a non-aristocratic army, directly organized by the rulers and dependent on them for provisions; (2) systems of controlling and supervising the army, and using it to control different strata of the population.

However, as we shall later observe in greater detail, these attempts by the rulers were not always completely successful.

[6] Policies of the Rulers in the Field of Social Organization and Stratification

The chief aims of the rulers of bureaucratic polities were translated into concrete policies next in the area of social organization and of distributing honor and prestige within the society—in other words, in the sphere of stratification. The rulers' most general goals in this sphere were, in broad outline, similar to their aims in other spheres. They wanted to weaken the strength and independence of the traditional (especially aristocratic) groups and strata, and to encourage development either of more flexible groups or at least of the strata opposing the aristocracy. On the other hand, they were anxious for the autonomous development of the encouraged strata to be confined within certain limits; and they wanted to control the movements of all these strata.

The rulers were especially interested in governing the avenues of mobility—and, in extreme cases, in eliminating mobility in order to preserve their own control over the population.

To implement the achievement of these general aims, the rulers of the historical bureaucratic polities evolved three general kinds of policies.

The first class of policies consisted of those designed to make the monarch the chief dispenser of social prestige, and thus to minimize various strata's self-sufficiency in this respect. The rulers constantly tried both to establish the degree of proximity and access to political power and position as the primary criterion of stratification, and, at the same time, to acquire or retain control over as many avenues to this access as possible. This was closely connected with the rulers' endeavors to formalize the status system and to monopolize such formalization. In other words, the rulers attempted to limit the power positions of the aristocratic groups in general and of the hereditary transmission of titles and positions in particular, and to make holding or transmitting the positions contingent on the rulers' will.

The second type of policies evolved because (for reasons we shall analyze later) it was not possible to realize the objectives of the first type in entirety. In so far as this was impossible, the rulers tended to try to insulate the holders of power in any one sphere, and to prevent them from exercising effective influence in other social spheres, and thus to limit the scope of their power. In cases like this, the rulers usually formulated policies designed to concentrate control over the top positions in any institutional sphere in their own hands, and to prevent the holders of the middle and lower positions from attaining these top positions.

The third kind of policies were the ones that repeatedly—although not always successfully or consistently—encouraged the middle and lower strata in their attempts to free themselves from excessive dependency on the aristocracy. Rulers enacted such policies to increase these strata's direct dependence on them, and to enhance their own positions as arbiters and mediators among conflicting strata. In some cases (e.g., in Prussia and in Russia), the rulers' attempts to control these groups led to growing prescription and regimentation of the lower strata. These were carried out by the rulers, with the help of some of the higher strata—e.g., the bureaucracy and aristocracy. These upper strata, however, also became dependent on the rulers ([X] *Carsten, 1954, 1955; Hintze, 1914, 1915; Beloff,* [W] *1953,* [S] *1954, ch. v;* [W] *Sacke, 1938[a], 1938[b]; Young, 1957*).

Our historical material supplies abundant examples of all three types of policies. The data demonstrate that the rulers' chief aims in this area were served, not only by special policies designed for this specific field, but also by policies stemming from other fields—like economy, politics, or religion.

A. ATTEMPTS TO MONOPOLIZE THE ALLOCATION OF POWER AND PRESTIGE

The first type of policy, that which attempted to establish the ruler as the chief dispenser of power and prestige, is best illustrated by the methods of distributing titles and honors in the Byzantine and Chinese empires, and also, though not to the same extent, by those used in Imperial Rome and Absolutist France. The Roman, Byzantine, and Chinese empires each had a double system of titles. One kind of title designated that its bearer had general attribute of belonging to a certain class—e.g., the senatorial and equestrian orders in Rome, titles like "clarissimi" in Byzantium, and the different ranks of mandarins in China. The other kind of title designated its bearer's particular function and office—the head position in a department or army unit, for example, or governorship of a province.

In the Chinese Empire, such a system had prevailed—probably dating from the Han Dynasty (206 B.C.–A.D. 22), and certainly from the late T'ang Dynasty. Noble and aristocratic titles became progressively more confined to the imperial family, and their bearers were deprived of real political power. Although China's system of grades was far more permanent and systematized than the system used in Byzantium, it, too, was characterized by a distinction between general grades and functional designations of offices, and by several limitations on the hereditary transmission of titles. (*On China, see* [I] *Des Rotours, 1932, 1947-48; Chang, 1955; Pulleyblank 1955; Kracke,*

1953. On Byzantine emperors, see [L] Diehl, 1927; Benesevic, 1926–28; Bréhier, 1949[b], pp. 81 ff.; Courtois, 1949; Ostrogorsky, 1956[a] passim.)

In Absolutist France (and other European countries, such as Spain), the policy of making the ruler distribute titles was clear. It was evinced by royalty's attempts to create new titles and offices, to distinguish between hereditary title and effective office, to recruit "new blood" by devices like the sale of offices, and to limit or forestall the possibility of hereditary transmission of the newly created positions. (*See [Y] Sagnac, 1945, 1946; Ford, 1953, p. 1; Pagès, 1928; [U] Desdevises du Dezert, 1925, 1927; [S] Beloff, 1954. On some English parallels, see [Z] Black, 1936; Williamson, 1953; Davies, 1937; Clark, 1955.*)

The rulers of many of these societies used another important means. This was to inflate the number of titles by constantly creating new titles and offices—thus minimizing the real or even symbolic value of many of them.

B. ATTEMPTS TO LIMIT THE POWER AND INFLUENCE OF THE UPPER (ARISTOCRATIC) GROUPS

The second type of policies limited the power and influence of any strong status group. This type existed, in different measure, in all the major historical bureaucratic societies. Its most important manifestations were that the landed nobility were gradually deprived of real political power and confined to activities in the economic field, while the middle classes were excluded from spheres of social (noble) prestige.

Thus, in the Sassanid Empire, to limit the feudal families' power, a special administrative class and a special class of "grandees and nobles" were created ([G] *Christensen, 1936, ch. i, ii, 1939; Altheim, 1955[a], 1955[b]; Benveniste, 1938*).

The Byzantine rulers also wanted to limit the political power of the aristocracy. They tried to do so by denying full political rights to the aristocracy and by differentiating between aristocratic titles and bureaucratic offices ([L] *Diehl, 1927, 1943; Ostrogorsky, 1956[a]* passim).

In China, the centralized Confucian state was usually opposed to the aristocratic families and tried to limit their influence. As a consequence of state policies, the aristocratic familiies became almost entirely extinct after the T'ang Dynasty (i.e., after A.D. 905), and reappeared, as part of the conquering group only after China had been subject to foreign conquests. Even in these cases, the foreign conquerors of China usually tried to keep their own kin and tribesmen from holding any prominent political positions in the Chinese system ([I] *Eberhard, 1948[a]* passim, *1952, ch. i, ii; Pulleyblank, 1955; Michael, 1942*).

During the first period of the Spanish-American Empire—i.e., the period immediately following the conquest—the Spanish Crown tried to minimize the possibility that an independent nobility could arise. The Crown bestowed noble and feudal titles rather freely, and tried to prevent their bearers from forming an independent aristocracy with political and economic powers. Similarly, the Spanish Crown sought to restrict the economic and political autonomy of the military entrepreneurs who had conquered Spanish America in its name. It hoped that the conquistadores would become town dwellers, who would not participate directly in production at the community level but would, rather, remain dependent on the Crown's carefully graded bounty. The conquistadores would thus have no local roots, but would be directly dependent on a group of officials operating from a central point. The chief device created to facilitate the attainment of these allied goals was the *encomienda*. The recipient of an *encomienda* was entitled to a specific amount of Indian tribute and services; but he was permitted neither to organize his own labor force nor to settle in Indian towns. Both the control of Indian labor and the allocation of tribute payments were to remain prerogatives exclusively of the royal bureaucrats ([R] *Zavala, 1943, 1944, 1951; Gallo, 1951[b], 1952; Konetzke, 1951[a], 1952, 1953; Simpson, 1934, 1938, 1950*). These policies of the rulers, like other of their policies, were not always successful, in later periods, the Crown's policies in this field were weakened. But, during the first stages of the Empire, these tendencies prevailed.

The most important examples of this kind of policies occurred in Absolutist Europe. It was especially well illustrated by France, whose rulers divested the ancient feudal nobility (i.e., the *noblesse d'épée*) of its political power and substituted the *noblesse de robe* as their principal administrative and political instrument. ([S] *See Beloff, 1954; [Y] Ford, 1953; Pagès, 1928. On some English parallels, see [Z] Black, 1936; Davies, 1937; Williamson, 1953; Clark, 1955.*)

C. PROMOTION OF THE MIDDLE AND LOWER STRATA

The third kind of policies comprised those designed for supporting or creating strata and status groups both lower than the aristocracy and opposed to it. These had various manifestations, of which many were related to policies in the economic and political fields. The best known instances are probably the great support late medieval and absolute kings extended to different bourgeois elements, these kings' attempts to abolish the feudal rights of land-owners, and their promotion of more freedom for the peasantry.

While all these policies were replete with contradictions (some of which will be analyzed later), their general aims are clear. We have observed, even in the Sassanid Empire with its small range of differentiation of the social structure, special new classes (e.g., the bureaucracy, and scribes) were encouraged—if not created—by the rulers.

In Byzantium, the great emperors of the seventh through eleventh centuries advanced the development of various middle groups—the landed gentry, members of legal profession, and some urban groups—from which they mobilized their bureaucracy and army ([L] *Guilland, 1946[a], 1953[a], 1953[b], 1954; Bréhier, 1924; Diehl, 1924, 1927, 1929, 1943; Diehl and Maredis, 1936* passim).

Since the Han Dynasty (206 B.C.–A.D. 221)—and especially since the Sung period (A.D. 960–1279)—the Chinese emperors encouraged the gentry and literati at the expense of aristocratic forces, and incessantly fought the aristocratic tendencies of the gentry. This is too well known to require detailed comment here.

In Imperial Rome, the equestrian order was constantly furthered by the rulers' allocations of political and administrative offices; at the same time, the senatorial order was increasingly divested of political power ([Q] *Alföldi, 1956, especially pp. 216–219, 223–229; Stein, 1927; Pflaum, 1950; Momigliano, 1934, ch. iii*).

Similar attempts, on the rulers' parts, to give impetus to the rise of various urban groups while simultaneously making them dependent on the central government, occurred in many other places. One was the Spanish-American Empire. The Spanish Crown increasingly endeavored to "urbanize" the settlers in Spanish America, to foster semi-municipal institutions like the *cabildo* (i.e., the municipal corporation), and to create a core for municipal autonomy ([R] *Chapman, 1942; Haring, 1947; Zavala, 1943; Ots Capdequi, 1932, 1934[a], 1941, 1945; Pierson, 1922; Konetzke, 1952*).

Perhaps the most interesting and important example of this third kind of policies is provided by the rulers' various attempts to create and maintain an independent free peasantry with small holdings, and to restrict land-owners' encroachments on these small holdings. We have analyzed the economic aspects of this kind of policies, particularly of their execution in Byzantium and China, in the appropriate section above. But the implications and objectives of such policies were not purely economic. One basic purpose of any policy classified in the third category was to create or strengthen the social stratum that was not merely dependent on, but also loyal to, the state, and that identified more strongly with the Emperor than with any lord. We must remember that the free peasants constituted the backbone of the national army or militia in each of these empires.

In this context, the several policies adopted by the Spanish authorities in the Spanish-American Empire are interesting. The most important was the policy of encouraging the organization of the Indian population into compact communities whose internal affairs were regulated by their members, and that were subject to the supervision and intervention of the royal officials. This policy led to the development of new Indian communities that were organized much more efficiently than the earlier (i.e., pre-Spanish conquest) ones had been. Another result was the emergence of a new class of Indian leaders, considered useful to the Crown, although, in later periods, they succumbed to the power of the great land-owners ([R] *Gallo, 1953; Zavala, 1943; Gongora, 1951; Miranda, 1951; Garcia, 1900; Gibson, 1955; Levene, 1953*).

The rulers also often developed such promotive policies with regard to the more urban groups, attempting to help them to advance in the economic and social spheres and to provide them with varying opportunities within the framework of the political institutions established by the rulers. In some cases, however, the rulers tended to place more emphasis on control and prescriptive orientations with regard to the lower strata, and to develop rigidly prescriptive policies whose object was to minimize these strata's flexibility and freedom of movement. The most significant examples of this tendency can be found in the later Roman Empire, and in Russia and Prussia during the seventeenth and eighteenth centuries.

[7] *The Legal Policies of the Rulers*

The basic goals held by the ruling elites of bureaucratic polities were also manifest in their legal policies. The respective policies concerning the legal field probably differed more from one society to another than policies involved with other fields; yet they shared some common features.

Most bureaucratic polities had many legal policies—although the relative prevalence and importance of each of them varied from case to case. Broadly speaking, the rulers' general objectives in the legal field were to minimize the legal autonomy of traditional groups and strata (e.g., the aristocracy, or the urban patriciate) and to advance the development of more complex and differentiated legal institutions and activities. At the same time, however, the rulers wished to maintain control over these institutions and to keep them, as far as possible, from autonomous growth (*Beloff* [W] *1953;* [S] *1954;* [W] *Sacke, 1938[a], 1938[b];* [X] *Carsten, 1954, 1955; Rosenberg, 1958; Hintze, 1914, 1915*).

The best-known policy employed to implement these goals was probably the codification and unification of law. Their purpose often was to regulate legal activities in various spheres, thus regulating the entire systems of social control these activities implied. (Although the policy of codifying and unifying laws was applied in non-bureaucratic polities—especially the ones where theocratic orientations were predominant—it was usually greatly advanced in the bureaucratic polities.) The following are some of the outstanding examples of this policy in the societies studid here: the Code of Justinian (compiled A.D. 529–535); the codifying activities of Basil I (*c.* A.D. 867–886) and of Leo VI (*c.* A.D. 886–912), also in Byzantium ([L] *Ostrogorsky, 1956[a]; Schulz, 1953, pp. 262–399; Zacharia von Lingenthal, 1892; Angelov, 1945–46; Lemerle, 1949*); the codes promulgated by most Chinese dynasties during the first years of their respective reigns ([I] *Balázs, 1954[a], 1959[a]; Bünger, no date, 1952*); the Spanish-American Empire's *Recopilacion de Leyes* ([R] *Levene, 1953; Zavala, 1943; Gongora, 1951; Miranda, 1951*); Absolutist Europe's great works of codification ([Y] *Doucet, 1948; Zeller, 1948*); and the attempts to formalize, rationalize, and codify laws in Sassanid Persia ([G] *Christensen, 1936, pp. 300 ff., 1939*). The ruling elite's codification of laws was oriented against diverse "popular" autonomous legal traditions, like those of the aristocracy and of different rural or urban patriciates. The legal codification by the ruling elite was also oriented toward preventing judges and members of the legal profession from autonomously and independently creating laws. It bore, therefore, an intimate relation to the ruling elite's attempts to bureaucratize the judicial and legal profession as much as possible.

The rulers' efforts to restrict the legal autonomy of various groups, and to concentrate most legal activities under their own control, were directed both against traditional-aristocratic and/or traditional groups, and against more differentiated legal groups. When the former kind was preponderant (as in Sassanid Persia), the rulers' efforts were mostly directed toward centralizing and monopolizing the majority of legal tradition and activity. As legal groups and institutions became more differentiated, the rulers tended more to establish special legal offices in the central administrations, and to maintain, through these offices, their control over the various legal groups.

The rulers implemented the attainment of these general goals by three major types of policy.

Policies of the first type were applied in the sphere of legal organization, both in the rulers' attempts to transfer powers of criminal prosecution from different groups to themselves and to the bureaucracy, and in their attempts to rationalize their central legal administration. This kind of policy was used in the following societies.

1. In Sassanid Persia, the kings tried to control, either personally or in conjunction with the clergy, most juridical and police functions.

2. In Rome, during the Principate (30 B.C.–A.D. 192), the *princeps* and the state officials appropriated progressively more legislative and juridical functions from the Senate and the elected officials ([L] *Pringsheim, 1950;* [Q] *Schiller, 1949[a], 1949[b], 1953; Jones, 1954*).

3. In Byzantium, criminal prosecution was largely the prerogative of the emperors and the bureaucracy ([L] *Bréhier, 1949[b], pp. 218-248; Schultz, 1953; pp. 262–299; Pringsheim, 1950; Collinet, 1947*).

4. In fourteenth-century England, the kings enlarged the compass under their jurisdiction by extending criminal law and procedure to feudal and civil law ([Y] *Chenon, 1929, II, pp. 452 ff.;* [Z] *Des Longrais, 1956*).

5. In Absolutist France, the monarch constantly abrogated the judiciary powers of "intermediary" groups like the provincial magistracies and parliaments, and then made these groups subject to royal legislation and judicial action. (*See* [Y] *Zeller, 1948; Pagès, 1928, 1932[b]; Sagnac, 1945; Rébillon, 1928; Ford, 1953, ch. i; and compare* [Z] *Black, 1936; Williamson, 1953; Zeeveld, 1948.*)

The second kind of policy the monarch used to restrict the legal autonomy of divers groups was the method of limiting the autonomy and scope of the legal profession's activities and/or subjecting these activities to strict royal supervision. This method was particularly prominent in Rome, Byzantium, and Absolutist Europe. Its policies were formulated as numerous regulations of every aspect of legal training and activity, and as limitations on the law-creating activities of the members of legal professions. For instance, in Absolutist Europe (especially France), the kings attempted to control and supervise the legal professions. In addition, the kings succeeded, by employing and extending Roman law, in using the legal professions to further their own policies and goals of centralization.

The third type of policy the ruling elites utilized to attain their objectives in the legal spheres was, perhaps, the most important. It comprised policies that limited, as much as possible, the sphere of civil procedure (to use modern terms), making the civil sphere subject to criminal jurisdiction and procedure—which could more easily be

monopolized by the rulers. For example, in Imperial Rome the juris-
dictional range of the officers of criminal prosecution appointed by
the *princeps* was constantly enlarged, at the expense of litigation by
private individuals or elective officers. This method was related to
the development of new concepts of state intervention in the legal
fields (*Jones, 1954*).

Civil-legal affairs were most completely subjugated by criminal
law in China during and after the Han Dynasty ([I] *Balázs, 1954[c];
Hulsewé, 1955; Bünger, no date, 1952; Twitchett, 1958; Bodde, 1954;
Escarra, 1936; Balázs, 1959[b]; Riasanovsky, 1937; Duyvendak, 1928,
1958; Cheng, 1956; Sprenkel, 1956*). Purely "private" or civil law and
legislation had minimal range in Chinese law; most legal enactments
were intended primarily to maintain the population's obedience to
the emperor and its compliance with the existing social order. Many
so-called civil suits were settled "out of court," through arbitration;
these suits served as instruments of direct political and social control,
rather than as tools for mediating and arbitrating among conflicting
interests. The rise of criminal law was facilitated by endemic characteristics of Chinese law. Legists' precepts combined with Confucianists' traditional "ethnical" orientation and their emphasis on
maintaining the existing social order. This mixture resulted in the
development of a very strong, paternalistic-moralistic criminal law,
while greatly impeding the evolution of civil law.

However, the rulers and bureaucracies of the historical bureaucratic polities could not always effect civil law's complete subjugation
to criminal law. Therefore, they usually developed policies for controlling the establishment of civil rights and civil jurisdiction. Such
a policy might be first, to limit the independent creation of legal
rights, claims, and obligations by private parties, and then to concentrate as many of these as possible under their own control. This
process was, of course, often intimately related to the policy of codification. Second, the rulers might often attempt to vest many legal
rights and claims directly in the state. This, too, was closely associated
with the rulers' general tendency to monopolize legal administration,
while rationalizing their monopoly by claiming it served the interests
of efficiency and political expediency.

[8] *The Rulers' Religious, Cultural, and Educational Policies*

Before analyzing the rulers' aims and policies in the cultural, religious, and educational fields, let us point out the basic attitude under-
lying their activities in these fields and also in the political field. This

attitude was formed by their desires to promote their own legitimation, to emphasize and enhance the prestige and sanctity of their position, to stress their adherence to their society's fundamental values
and symbols, and to establish their monopoly in the political, educational, and training areas.

In all societies studied here, the rulers attempted to portray themselves and the political systems they established as the bearers of special
cultural symbols and missions. They tried to depict themselves as transmitting distinct civilizations—either as reviving older, "national" cultures, or as conveying universal religious values. We have already noted
that such wider orientations and symbols were decisive factors in the
development and existence of the centralized bureaucratic polities. We
must emphasize the fact that the rulers of these societies invariably tried
to be perceived as the propagators and upholders of, and to present their
polities as the bearers of, these cultural orientations and traditions.
(*For examples concerning Persia, see* [G] *Christensen, 1936* passim;
Altheim, 1955[a], 1955[b]. On the Byzantine Empire, see [L] *Mitard,
1930; Bratianu, 1937; Sinogowitz, 1953[a]; Baynes, 1955, pp. 47–64;
Bréhier, 1937, 1949[b], pp. 1–52; Ensslin, 1939; Charanis, 1940–41[a];
Diehl, 1943, ch. iv; Grobar, 1937. On Moslem, see* [M] *Lewis, 1950;
Hodgson, 1960;* [N] *Schacht, 1955. On Europe, see* [Y] *Göhring, 1947;*
[S] *Beloff, 1954. On the Spanish-American Empire, see* [R] *Hanke,
1936[a], 1937; Parry, 1940.*) A concomitant of the rulers' wish to be
identified, as closely as possible, with their society's values and symbols,
was their desire to minimize any group's pretensions to having the right
to judge and evaluate the rulers or to sanction their legitimation.

However, many groups did try to exert influence on legitimizing
and controlling the rulers. Such a possibility was inherent in autonomy
of the religious field. The rulers' needs for political support also could
make them dependent on various forces in religion. Hence the rulers
had to create special activities and policies in order to realize their
aims. However, their endeavors were often limited, since their legitimation was basically traditional and religious, and also because the rulers
did not want the scope of political participation to be extended too
greatly.

The rulers' different orientations in the cultural and religious
spheres were expressed in two—sometimes contradictory—sets of policies. One set comprised policies of founding and promoting academies,
schools, and religious institutions. The other included many policies
of direct, strict control—and, sometimes, even of the suppression—of
independent cultural activities and institutions.

The rulers were interested in helping cultural, religious, and educational institutions to advance for the following reasons:

1. Such institutions could provide a great deal of support for the rulers' legitimation

2. They could be instrumental in creating a wider group consciousness and common identification—cutting across the local, kin, and ascriptive groups and symbols that connected the primordial images and traditions of various groups with the symbols of the rulers

3. They offered opportunities for manipulating symbols, identifications, and group loyalties that were important to the rulers as potential sources of political support for their goals and policies

4. They provided trained personnel to fill various bureaucratic positions and were a channel through which members of different groups attained political control

On the other hand, the rulers were concerned with controlling the cultural, religious and educational institutions. They wished to prevent these institutions from becoming independent centers of power, and to minimize their chances to realize their potential influence on various strata of population.

The ruling elite tried to control these cultural fields in many ways. They endeavored to maintain direct channels of communication with the more active—or, at least, potentially active—groups of the society; to limit their autonomous development; and to supervise the centers of learning and cultural creativity where cultural and religious symbols and values were formed that could be transmitted to the society's strata and groups. On the whole, the rulers were concerned primarily with directing and, if possible, monopolizing the various channels of communication, and of education of personnel, and of cultural creativity; they were less interested in allowing the *intensive* development of free-floating intellectual interests and cultural activities. The rulers wanted to preserve many traditional orientations and to restrict the emergence of an independent, critical public opinion. They often perceived free-floating intellectual activity as threatening the foundations of different groups' loyalty to them.

Since only a few autonomous cultural and religious institutions existed, and since these were largely embedded in the structures of traditional groups, the rulers frequently established themselves as the chief symbols and sole bearers of cultural and religious values and activities. In more differentiated societies which included many autonomous, distinct cultural groups and institutions, the rulers often tended to encourage and promote these—though, at the same time, they usually tried to limit their autonomy and to gain control of them.

Policies of governing and of suppressing autonomous cultural activities evolved as consequences of those factors. In Rome, the emperors' desires to subdue certain "philosophical" and literary groups, and the early Christian sects, resulted in the development of a suppression policy. In China, the rulers persecuted those religious groups, like the Taoists, the Buddhists, and the Confucian academies, that, at certain stages, seemed to be acquiring too much independent power ([I] *Hucker, 1958; Galt, 1951* passim; *Goodrich, 1953. On the political role of history-writing in China, see* [I] *Balázs, 1957; L. S. Yang, 1957[b]*). In Byzantium, the state of the great centers of learning was closely associated with the particular reigning emperor, and their vicissitudes were linked with his changing attitudes and policies ([L] *Hussey, 1937* passim; *Ostrogorsky, 1956[a]*).

In Europe, the same kings who founded and/or advanced academies and universities also attempted to monopolize them completely. The kings hoped that these institutions would become both centers of new semi-national consciousness and sources of the clerical personnel needed for the developing bureaucracy. At the same time, however, they tried to control, direct, and censure the institutions' activities.

Of special importance in this field are the rulers' policies concerned with the establishment of schools and training institutes that would serve as sources of recruits for their service. In almost all the societies studied here, the rulers tried to establish such institutions and to make them entirely dependent. In all these societies, the rulers were in great need of trained personnel—for their personal service and/or for the bureaucracy—and they were ready to utilize any and all available sources of trained personnel, including religious and professional schools, or even aristocratic houses. Moreover, the kings usually tended to create educational and training institutions that would provide them with the needed manpower. But the rulers always wanted also to limit the independence and autonomy of these institutions, to minimize their chances of becoming centers of independent power, and to exercise the maximum control over them. These desires resulted in the many cases when such schools were persecuted and in their manifold political vicissitudes. They also led rulers to make many efforts to create "closed" educational institutions under their direct supervision; the various palace schools especially the palace schools of the Ottoman Empire ([O] *Miller, 1941*) are the best examples of such institutions ([L] *Hussey, 1937; Fuchs, 1926;* [R] *Haring, 1947, ch. xi, xii*).

[9] *Policies of the Rulers in the Political Field*

All the major aims and tendencies of the rulers of bureaucratic polities were necessarily strongly reflected in the political field itself. We have considered some of these already here, we shall recapitulate them briefly from the point of view of our present analysis.

In the political field, the rulers were interested in (1) establishing and maintaining the centralized political frameworks; (2) encouraging political loyalty to themselves and advancing their own basic, traditional legitimation; (3) evolving some kind of new political consciousness, identified with their own rules and with their polities; (4) weakening traditional loyalties to aristocratic lords or to divers particularistic, patriomonial, or feudal units; (5) increasing the identification of different strata with their own regime and aims, and providing these strata with opportunities to advance within the framework of the political institutions of the centralized polities; (6) maintaining their political control over all politically important groups; and (7) creating instruments of powers and of implementing objectives—mainly in the form of various administrative units—and organizing them for maximum efficiency.

These aims of their rulers initiated the trends toward generalization of political power in these societies. We have seen the ways in which the Sassanid, Byzantine, and Chinese emperors and the Spanish, French, and English kings, trying to establish new political entities and symbols, created many channels of communication through which loyalty to these entities and symbols was fostered. (*See the literature cited on pp. 31–32.*) These rulers intended to diminish the political power of all groups which might compete with them and to regulate the political positions and powers of these potential competitors. Obviously, all their policies were designed to contribute to the realization of this objective. But, in addition, the rulers utilized specific policies of allocating political roles and power. These policies manifested several basic trends. One trend was toward the limitation of the power of the hereditary or semi-hereditary offices that existed in many feudal and patrimonial polities. The monarchs usually tried to divest these offices of any real political value and power, to create new offices and administrative bodies that would be entirely dependent on the rulers alone, and to control all avenues of advance in the political service. Such newly-created administrative bodies and organs that were dependent on the king and not on traditional (autocratic, religious) forces could be used against these forces. (*On France, see* [Y] *Zeller, 1948; Dupont-Ferrier, 1932; Doucet, 1948; Pagès, 1928. On England, see* [Z] *Richardson, 1952; Williams, 1935; Pickthorn, 1949; Beloff, 1938;* [L] *Bréhier, 1949[b];* [S] *Skalweit, 1957. On the Byzantine Empire, see* [L] *Ostrogorsky, 1956[a], ch. i, ii. On Persia, see* [G] *Christensen, 1936, ch. i, ii; Altheim and Stiehl, 1954, 1957; Altheim, 1955[a]. On the Spanish-American Empire, see* [R] *Haring, 1927, 1947; Ots Capdequi 1934[a]; Gallo, 1944; Zavala, 1943; Fisher, 1926, 1936.*)

But the establishment of new administrative organs was only the preliminary stage, and it usually entailed new problems of control for the rulers. Many of these organs often tended to identify themselves with some of the older, aristocratic or patrimonial groups. Moreover, the rulers attempted to attract the more active elements of different (especially non-aristocratic) groups and strata, to provide them with social, political, and economic opportunities within the polity in general and within the framework of the political and administrative institutions and organizations in particular. The rulers then had to develop new ways of controlling these organs and groups.

Several of these systems of control are of special interest. One was the wide use of eunuchs in many monarchies ([L] *Guilland, 1943, 1944-45;* [I] *Rideout, 1949*). Another was the attempt of the rulers to create and maintain a permanent core of officials of the "inner court," controlled directly by the rulers themselves. However, many of these officials gradually become relatively independent and lost contact with their rulers. This fact explains the frequent changes in the positions of different officials, and the continual creation of new positions and titles by the kings and ministers ([L] *Bréhier, 1949[b], ch. i, ii; Diehl, 1927; Boak and Dunlap, 1924; Guilland, 1946[b], 1954*).

The emergence of various controlling and inspecting officers—the commissaries, the intendants, the *visitores,* etc. ([X] *Hintz, 1903, 1907, 1914; Dorn, 1931; Dorwart, 1953;* [Y] *Pagès, 1932[b]; Zeller, 1939, 1944, 1947;* [R] *Fisher, 1926, 1929; Pierson, 1941; Parry, 1948; Haring, 1927; Ots Capdequi, 1945*)—is also significant. They evolved as "extraordinary" officers, charged with the execution of special missions. These were usually aimed at mobilizing special resources or at unifying and controlling administrative organization. In this context, the very widespread practice of not posting such officials in their own home districts is important.

The institution of the Chinese Censorate is particularly relevant at this point of our discussion. The Censorate developed as a body of internal control of the bureaucracy. The rulers, the bureaucrats, and the literati all attempted to use and manipulate it ([I] *Des Rotours, 1932, 1947–48; Hucker, 1950, 1959[a], 1959[b]; Li, 1936*).

Another significant method of control was represented by the development of the various systems of inner councils, restricted private councils, cabinets, etc., that characterized these societies' administrative histories. These different administrative organs changed rapidly—both because of growing needs and specialization, and because of the rulers' continual attempts to minimize their autonomy and to maintain control ([Y] *Pagès, 1928, 1932[b];* [S] *Beloff, 1954;* [Y] *Zeller, 1948;* [R] *Parry, 1948; Gallo, 1944; Fisher, 1926, 1929; Roscher, 1944; Haring, 1947, ch. iv, v, vi;* [I] *Ho, 1952*).

The rulers' difficulties in controlling the bureaucracies reflected more general problems of political control that developed in the historical bureaucratic societies. The rulers tried to control the political activities of the more vigorous groups, in order to reduce to minimum their chances of organizing into potent and independent political forces, and also to assure themselves of direct support from these groups. (*On the social policies, see* [L] *Barker, 1957; Guilland, 1954, 1953–55; Bréhier, 1924;* [R] *Konetzke, 1951[a], 1952;* [Q] *Alföldi, 1956;* [I] *Balázs, 1950, 1959[a]; Eberhard, 1952; Wittfogel, 1957.*)

When one of these rulers became aware of a potentially active group, he tried both to "buy it off" and to undermine its power through persecution, economic exploitation, and encouraging its competitors. In these situations, the rulers had to develop different techniques and organizations. They evolved several types of "party-political" activities —e.g., extensive propaganda, or manipulation of political cliques. They utilized several policies of mobilization and recruitment to attract talents from the more active elements to themselves and of providing these talents with possibilities for advancing, as described above. On the other hand, the rulers also often utilized repressive policies. The police were important instruments for executing these policies.

In many of the societies studied—especially in Byzantium and France, and to a lesser degree in Sassanid Persia and the Spanish-American Empire—the rulers organized police forces which performed a variety of functions. These included patrolling the streets, rounding up vagabonds and criminals, maintaining peace, and generally supervising markets and public order. In addition, the police were a very important instrument of political control. Police forces in particular, and the armed forces in general, could be used to suppress rebellions, to persecute "subversive" groups, etc.

In connection with the persecution of subversives, we should mention one type of police activity. This is the one executed by the so-called "police of morals," which occurred in embryonic form in Sassanid Persia and China (where its functions were closely related to the Censorate's), and in a more advanced form in Byzantium, Spanish America, and France. Functions of policing morals were fulfilled either by special police officers or by the police in conjunction with the clergy. The police of morals were a chief instrument of suppressing "subversive" religious organizations and groups, and popular and intellectual sects. They served a twofold purpose. First, they were designed to insure the population's behaving properly and in accordance with basic norms and precepts, and to discipline any deviations from proper behavior. On the other hand, they were also intended to suppress any "subversive" ideals that might lead to deviant behavior. The first aim was implemented by regular police activities; and the second, by persecuting many independent sects and centers of culture, and by the extensive censorship of printed matter. One may postulate that the development of the police of morals was closely related both to the diminishing self-control of many ascriptive groups, and to the growing importance of political activities oriented to the central political institutions.

[10] *Classification of the Major Types of Policies of the Rulers*

We have analyzed the fundamental objectives of the ruling elites and the policies used to implement them. Both the goals and the means of realizing them varied, from place to place and from period to period. The rulers often changed their policies—some of these shifts will be examined below in the chapters on comparative political process. Here, we are concerned chiefly with the more general types of policies.

Many of these policies were similar to policies used by rulers of patrimonial or feudal polities. However, the rulers of the centralized bureaucratic empires also evolved distinctive types of policies. These were endemic to this kind of society, and derived from the rulers' endeavors to maintain their specific orientations toward the autonomy of the political sphere, and to implement the objectives arising from these orientations.

The rulers' different instrumental policies can be distinguished according to several criteria.

The first criterion is founded in the distinction between technical services and creative and regulative services. Technical ones only provide or transfer services among different groups or sectors. The other kind of services aim also at regulating the major institutional spheres of society or at creating new structures within them. The chief technical policies are subdivided into the two following categories:

1. Technical-accumulative policies, which were designed for the primary function of directly exploiting (e.g., by collecting taxes and tributes) the several social spheres in order to accumulate resources and concentrate them for monopoly by the rulers.

2. Service activities, whose main functions were to supply technical services to different strata (e.g., regulating waterworks, or lines of communication), and to fulfil various police and judiciary functions

Before trying to classify the creative and regulative types of policies, we must distinguish between them.

Creative policies are those by which the rulers try to create, directly, special organizations and structures within different social spheres. The establishment of various types of state enterprises, of monopolies, and of semi-patrimonial or feudal domains illustrates this class of policies.

The regulative class of policies were not so concerned with creating new types of organization. Their chief functions were utilizing and serving the existing social organization or promoting new, autonomous developments within them. In addition, they were devices for regulating the society's various institutional spheres. They regulated manpower and the distribution of resources to different groups and institutions, established the criteria governing this distribution, and supervised the internal functioning of spheres and institutions.

Regulative policies may be classified according to the following criteria. The first criterion for classifying a regulative policy is its extent of *prescription,* as opposed to *promotion,* of various enterprises in different social spheres. By "prescriptive" policies, we mean those designed to regulate the social spheres for the purposes of supervising them strictly and of benefiting from them. "Promotive" policies are directed toward creating general conditions conducive to the development of different groups which are potential providers of the types of resources needed by the rulers.

The best examples of purely prescriptive policies are those that bind peasants to their lands, that maintain the requirement of hereditary membership in guilds, and other organizations, and that levy direct taxes on various urban groups. Promotive policies are best illustrated by Heraclius' taxation reforms in Byzantium by the tax land reforms in T'ang China that were directed toward creating conditions which would indirectly promote the flow of population to underpopulated and underdeveloped regions; and the various monetary and taxation policies inaugurated, under the aegis of mercantilism in France and England. Obviously, concrete policies often partake of both the prescriptive and the promotive qualities.

The second criterion involves the considerations governing the contents of regulative policies. The major possible considerations are: (1) general value orientations, e.g., toward maintaining certain moral standards or cultural patterns; (2) implementation of some collective or group goals; (3) power and maximization of the rulers' power positions; and (4) interests of different groups in the society.

The kinds of policies used to implement the rulers' political aims can also be distinguished according to the level of generalized political power that they engendered. The autonomy of the political sphere and the articulation of the rulers' autonomous political goals were not extensive in societies where the extremely simple creative and accumulative policies preponderated. Only the more complicated regulative policies represented a greater articulation of specific political goals and a higher level of power generalization, since such policies were contingent on the political sphere's distinctiveness in relation to other spheres in the society. The regulative policies were oriented toward governing strategic positions in several social spheres in order to insure the uninterrupted flow of resources and support to the rulers; they were not concerned with attaining direct "ownership" or direct control of these spheres.

These regulative policies were the most closely associated with the specific structures of the historical bureaucratic societies and with the specific aims and goals of their rulers. Both the promotive and the prescriptive policies of the rulers evolved in this context. The fact that both types evolved within the same context indicates some of the internal contradictions in the basic orientations of the rulers. We shall now investigate and analyze these contradictions.

[11] *Major Contradictions in the Policies of the Rulers*

As we have seen, the rulers of the centralized bureaucratic polities had several distinct objectives. First, they tried to promote a certain amount of "free-floating" resources; but they wanted to confine these within specified limits, so that they could not undermine the rulers' traditional legislation. Second, even when the rulers furthered the development of such resources, they were interested in maintaining their control over the resources and in minimizing the autonomy of those groups which produced them. Moreover, some of their goals—e.g., military expansion—could easily deplete the free-floating resources.

The rulers' aims and orientations might at times seem to have been mutually complementary. However, a double contradiction could easily develop between them. First, the ruler's traditional orientation and his more flexible orientation contradicted each other. Also, his more flexible orientation conflicted with his attempts to control the free strata and to use their resources for achieving his objectives—some of which, by their very natures, would deplete their resources.

The rulers were not always consciously aware of these contradictions. Nevertheless, these contradictions were always implicit in the rulers' structural positions in the problems and exigencies with which they had to deal, and in the concrete policies they employed to deal with them.

A. CONTRADICTIONS IN THE SYSTEMS OF STRATIFICATION

The contradictions were manifested first in the sphere of legitimation and stratification. As we have indicated, the rulers frequently tried to limit the aristocracy's power and to create new, more "flexible" status groups. But these attempts met several obstacles. Regardless of the extent of the rulers' independent activities in this field, of the number of new titles created, of the degree to which new strata were encouraged—the symbols of status used by the rulers were usually very similar to those of the landed, hereditary aristocracy or of the religious elites. Fundamentally, the legitimation of the rulers was a variation on traditional and/or charismatic themes, in which the rulers were accepted on traditional grounds and were expected to uphold the given cultural traditions. (An entirely new, secular, and "rational" type of legitimation, based on social groups or universalistic symbols and values, was never instituted in any of the historical bureaucratic empires. The concept was either too advanced for them and/or against their basic political interests, in that such a legitimation would necessarily involve extending the span of political participation.) Therefore, the monarchs were usually unable to transcend the symbols of stratification and legitimation both borne and represented by the very strata whose influence the rulers wanted to limit.

For instance, the French kings considered themselves the first gentlemen of the realm and identified *socially* with the aristocracy. The same was true of many Byzantine and Sassanid rulers; and strong "feudal" or "patrimonial" features persisted even in the style and symbols of the Chinese Empire.

The traditional nature of the rulers' legitimation entailed a number of significant consequences. First, it limited the mutual identification possible between the rulers and the lower strata of the population, and the possibility that the former could appeal to the later. The second consequence of the traditional nature of legitimation was even more important. Since the superiority and worth of aristocratic symbols and values were emphasized, many new strata or groups aspired to attain "aristocratization" through identifying themselves with these symbols and values. In this way, the opportunities of the middle and lower groups for mobility and advancement, and the power that the central political institutions had for attracting the more active elements of these groups, could become quite limited. One important facet of aristocratization was a feature of almost all the societies studied, and constituted an additional obstacle to implementing many of the rulers' aims. This was the overvaluation of landed property (and of the rentier-security connected with it—in Europe, especially of "noble" landed property) as a symbol of status— and related, similar feelings about other types of economic activity, which might otherwise have been more conducive to economic growth. The overvaluation of landed property also often resulted in a constricting of channels of mobility. This reaction usually followed an initial period of economic growth, expansion, and active dissociation from the regime and the ruling elite.

The contradictions in the rulers' policies and goals tended to have ramifications in another, different direction. However much the ruling elites were restricted by tradition, their policiees required them to create and propagate additional flexible free resources in different institutional fields. Such propagation either initiated or advanced many religious, intellectual, and legal groups, and "middle strata" whose value orientations differed from the traditional ones. Often, these elements were all very weak and succumbed easily to the influence of the more conservative groups and to the policies of the ruling elites. However, in many other cases they evolved into relatively independent centers of power, whose opposition to the ruling elites was only stimulated by their more conservative policies.

B. CONTRADICTIONS IN THE ECONOMIC FIELD

Similar contradictions may also be discerned in the rulers' relations to the economic structure. In this area, the ruling elites' long-term economic policies were often contradictory to their short-term economic policies.

Thus, for instance, two chief objectives of taxation—i.e., to mobilize resources necessary for a given goal, and to regulate or level the various centers of power in order to control the flow of free resources —were often conflicting. The big land-owners and merchants, who constituted important centers of economic power, frequently tried to intensify this contradition by providing the government with short-term allocations at the price of buttressing their own positions.

The ruling elites of many, if not all, bureaucratic polities were potentially dependent on the resources of the landed nobility or of the aristocraticized bureaucracy itself. Often, this dependence was caused not only by the general economic backwardness of these societies, but also largely by some of the rulers' own economic policies. In most cases, the ruling elites endeavored to control all the potential centers of investment (especially in trade and industry) and taxed them heavily. In this way, the rulers usually undermined the economic value of investment activities, depleted their strength, reduced the economic importance of centers of investment, and diverted a good portion of investment to land. Moreover, through excessive taxation and excessive expenditure on administration, court, and wars, the rulers often undermined the purchasing power of the masses, shrank the existing local markets, stimulated inflation, and directed the flow of capital away from the country.

Thus a basically paradoxical situation could exist wherein the rulers, by constant mobilization and regimentation, exhausted and depleted the very groups which constituted the mainstay of their economic strength and a source of flexible resources. The various urban groups, and sometimes the groups of small independent peasants with fairly easily marked property, were an obvious target for taxation and special levies. As the requirements of the state budget grew, the strength of these groups was gradually drained. This occurred in the late Roman Empire, during the later stages of the Byzantine Empire ([L] *Charanis, 1951[a], 1953[a]; Ostrogorsky, 1929[a], 1956[a]* passim; *Guilland, 1953–1955*), in many final stages of the dynastic "cycles" in China ([I] *Eberhard, 1945, 1952, ch. ii, iii; Sprenkel, 1952; Twitchett, 1956[a], 1956[b]*), and, to some extent, in the Spanish-American Empire ([R] *Haring, 1947; Ots Capdequi, 1941, 1951*).

A similar contradiction existed between the long-range and the short-range policies concerned with problems of administrative manpower. In many cases, not enough manpower was available for the execution of various administrative and political tasks. In other cases, inadequate communication and technical facilities made it very difficult to supervise administrative personnel effectively. In either situation, the rulers were forced to "farm out" different functions and positions—to local gentry and land-owners, or to officials who gradually became aristocratized.

C. THE SYSTEM OF SALES OF OFFICES: A CASE STUDY IN THE RESULTS OF THE CONTRADICTIONS IN THE RULERS' POLICIES

Contradictory components of the rulers' orientations and policies were sometimes manifested in the evolutionary courses taken by groups created or promoted by the rulers. The system of sales of offices provides the best example of the way a social group created or promoted by the ruling elite can become partially opposed to that elite's aims and basic political premises. The development of this system was closely connected with the entire process of recruitment into the bureaucracy.

This system emerged in most of the societies under consideration,

and was especially prominent in the Byzantine Empire ([L] *Kolias,
1939; Andréadès, 1921[a]; Leicht, 1937*), China, France and the other
European countries during the Age of Absolutism, and the Spanish-
American Empire ([R] *Parry, 1953*). It was usually introduced by the
rulers, as a method of solving their financial problems and admitting
new (non-aristocratic) elements into their service (thus diminishing
their dependence on aristocratic elements). However, in most of these
societies, the bureaucracy gradually began to regard bureaucratic offices as personal possessions, and either transmited them in their families or sold them in the market. As a result, the rulers, despite their
many efforts to the contrary, slowly lost control over bureaucratic
offices. Their diminishing control was caused by their increasing dependence on the political support of the groups from which officials
were recruited in this manner.

However, the rulers' great dependence on the more traditional
forces for manpower and economic resources was only one aspect of the
contradictions in their policies. When the rulers' aims were mutually
contradictory, these contradictions tended sometimes to work out in
different directions. The rulers also often tried to advance the economic
activities and strength of other urban groups or of the free, independent peasantry. Sometimes their efforts were entirely thwarted by the
economic and political strength of the traditional-aristocratic elements,
and by those among their own policies that enhanced the power of
these elements. In other cases—especially in European countries during the Age of Absolutism, and in the Spanish-American Empire—the
economically active groups ultimately proved stronger than the aristocratic groups and the aristocratized elite, and were able to overcome
the effects of the ruling elite's economically retarding policies. But—
with few partial exceptions, like traditional China—these strong economic groups could not be contained within the frameworks of the
rulers' policies. The economic groups, together with various intellectual elites, were crucial forces of influence for changes in the social
and political systems.

[12] Summary

We can now summarize the chief causes of the internal contradictions in the policies of the ruling elites of the historical bureaucratic
polities. These contradictions were due to certain attitudes inherent in
the rulers' political orientations and objectives, and to the relations
between these orientations and objectives and the resources that could
be acquired to implement their attainment.

The historical bureaucratic polities strongly emphasized the rulers' pursuit of definite, autonomous political goals. Hence their rulers were concerned with creating and mobilizing the resources necessary to realize these objectives, and tried to establish conditions for generalizing political power. But the available resources were often insufficient or incompatible with the rulers' basic social orientations. This contingency could arise in the cases both of material economic resources and of political support and identification. The less differentiated the economy and the more traditional the society's bases of legitimation, the less could "free" resources be made available to the polity and the more difficult was the realization of specific, differentiated poilitcal goals. On the other hand, in societies characterized by a greater degree of economic differentiation and development and a lesser degree of traditionalism, an incompatibility could exist between the orientations of the strata able to supply most of the economic resources and political support necessary for the realization of these goals, and the more traditional orientations and bases of legitimation of the ruling elites.

The contradictions in the rulers' internal policies were caused in some cases, by the prevalence of what may be termed "pre-bureaucratic" (traditional) elements, like, e.g., the aristocracy. Sometimes, also, they were caused by the conflicting orientations and goals of the rulers themselves. These necessarily gave rise to contradictory policies regarding the recruitment of resources, the development of various social strata, and the type of political support sought.

Internal contradictions of this nature were most clearly manifested in the rulers' attitudes toward the so-called "free" resources—a crucial area. The rulers were interested in establishing and maintaining a reservoir of free resources not committed to any traditional and particularistic group. However, the rulers did not want to further these resources' development to a point beyond their control. The rulers usually distrusted any strong autonomous tendencies exhibited by the social groups which constituted their sources of free resources. Their suspicion stemmed both from the traditional aspects of their values, and from their strong desires to retain the power to mobilize these resources at will.

Some potential internal contradictions with regard to free resources were inherent in the goals of the rulers. Among their objectives, goals like the promotion of economic interests or of middle and lower strata would conduce to the development of such resources. Other goals, like that of military expansion, would continually deplete them. It was in this area that the conflicts between main aims of the rulers, or mutual contradictions between their short-range and long-range policies, became important. Requiring immediate resources, and confronting the basic limitations of their economic systems, the rulers often felt forced to regiment the free resources in a way which could exhaust them.

In summary, while the rulers of these societies exhibited a strong tendency toward generalization of power they themselves also imposed many internal restrictions on this generalization. These limits were inherent in (1) the traditional orientations of the rulers, (2) the policies of control they employed to deal with political tasks and exigencies, and (3) the resources available to them for implementing their goals and policies.

In addition, the rulers' policies were also restricted as a result of the development of the political orientations and demands of various groups and strata.

This summary has taken us to the subject of the next chapter, namely, the political orientations and activities of the major groups in the historical bureaucratic policies.

8

The Political Orientations and Activities

of the Major Groups and Strata

[1] *The Major Groups Involved in the Political Struggle*

The policies of the ruling elites outlined in Chapter 7 constituted the basic framework of political struggle within the historical bureaucratic societies. When these polities were in the formative stage, these policies provided new institutional structures (the bureaucratic administration and channels of political struggle) and the chief points of reference for different groups and strata. Through the rulers' policies, the basic premises of the historical bureaucratic societies were articulated. However, the participation of all other groups in the political struggle was not necessarily confined to passively adjusting to the rulers' policies. In fact, most groups had their own basic interests and objectives, and some of these were closely related to the groups' structural positions in the societies; these entailed different attitudes toward the interests and policies of the ruling elites. The interaction between the policies of the ruling elites and the interests, attitudes, and objectives of the other major groups and strata provided the principal aspects of the political struggle.

We shall discuss two major kinds of groups here. The first type comprises "ecological" groups and strata, defined in terms of each one's locality, occupation, and way of life—namely, the landed groups (i.e., the aristocracy, gentry, and peasantry) and the main urban economic groups. The second type includes groups which are defined largely in terms of their functions—e.g., bureaucracy, army, religious and cultural elites, and professional groups.

Obviously, these two kinds of groups overlapped somewhere, in connection with different occupations, and we shall analyze the overlapping in each case. The two types of groups necessarily occupied different structural positions in society. These positions may have influenced the groups' attitudes toward the basic premises of the bureaucratic polity. In general, the "ecological" type was important chiefly in providing the resources needed by the polity, whereas, the "functional" type dealt chiefly with organizing, regulating, and channelizing these resources. The two frequently overlapped, especially in the area of provision of political support.

The political struggle was waged largely in the special channels that are characteristic of the bureaucratic polities, and also in other arenas, that existed in other types of societies. The arenas of political struggle were: (1) court circles and cliques; (2) the upper echelons of the bureaucracy, the higher and middle bureaucratic positions and organizations; (3) local provincial bureaucratic echelons and diverse institutions of local self-government; and (4) different representative or semi-representative institutions (e.g., the Roman Senate and popular assemblies, the Byzantine Senate and circus parties, and the European parliaments or councils of estates).

Each of these arenas was important and utilized by various groups to a different extent in each society.

Let us now examine the political attitudes and orientations of the major groups and strata participating in political struggle in these societies.

[2] *The Place of the Bureaucracy in Political Struggle*

A. ITS SOCIAL COMPOSITION

After the ruling elite, the first group participating in the political struggle in a bureaucratic society was the bureaucracy itself. True, the entire body of administrative officials never constituted a homogeneous and unified group whose members shared identical aims and outlooks. There were many social, economic, and regional differences among the various echelons of the bureaucracy. In addition, differing factions, groups, and outlooks often coexisted at its upper, more active levels.

The upper and middle echelons of the bureaucracy were usually recruited from upper or middle urban groups and gentry, upper peasant groups, and the army. The proportion of members from each stratum obviously differed in different echelons of the bureaucracy. The lower echelons were usually recruited from the lower urban groups, the peasantry, and the lower ranks of the army.

The extent of identification that members of the various echelons of the bureaucracy retained with the groups from which they had been recruited varied greatly from one society to another. However, in most of the societies studied, they had some social interests transcending the interest of performing their bureaucratic-organizational roles, and did not view these as purely occupational. There were very few cases in which purely bureaucratic "career-patterns" developed that were not embedded also in wider social and economic interests. The relative paucity of free resources, the great economic and social importance of landed interests, the relative preponderance of ascriptive status criteria, and the practice of defining mobility goals in terms of such ascriptive criteria—these all necessarily greatly influenced the outlooks of the officials in these societies, albeit in varying degrees in different cases. They frequently led the officials to use their positions as means of attaining economic and status objectives for themselves, their families, and, sometimes, the groups from which they had come.

As a result, bureaucratic officials' relations with other active economic and status groups were very close. The convergence or opposition of the bureaucracy, the rulers, and other social groups, and their mutual interests and conflicts, had great significance for the political activities of the bureaucratic groups. As indicated, the echelons of bureaucratic organs differed greatly in this respect, as we shall analyze when dealing with the patterns of recruitment into the bureaucracy used in the different societies.

However, in each of the societies studied, the bureaucracy—or at least its upper and middle echelons, because of their specific structural position and their proximity to the rulers and to different social strata —was often active in the political struggle. Its members were not merely technical or administrative executives. While the respective concrete issues in which they participated might vary in different cases, two basic foci may be discerned for the political struggle of bureaucratic echelons. One focus consisted of their relations to the rulers; the other, of their relations with the social groups and strata participating in the political struggle. (For a general, although not fully systematic, survey of this problem, see [A] Borch, 1954, especially pp. 21–159.)

B. THE MAJOR ORIENTATIONS
OF THE BUREAUCRACY

On the simplest level, the principal contentions between the active elements of bureaucracy and the ruling elite arose because the various echelons of the bureaucracy were concerned with insuring their pay, increasing their emoluments, being appointed to lucrative positions, and having security in their positions. In the history of each society studied here, the bureaucratic officials strove, either individually or collectively to attain these aims. They struggled to obtain for themselves, and when necessary to wrest from their opponents, the more lucrative and influential positions within the administration.

However, in addition, more fundamental issues emerged between the bureaucracy and the rulers. As a rule, these broader did not emerge during the first developmental stages of the bureaucratic polity; then the bureaucracy tended to identify with the king, and confine itself to the concrete aims listed above, without evincing many general interests of its own. Later, when the bureaucracy had evolved into a somewhat autonomous body with its own traditions, conflicts with the rulers tended to arise. These conflicts were focused, in general, on the bureaucracy's aspirations to attain autonomy and independence in the political, status, and economic fields.

The bureaucracy's aspirations toward some measure of autonomy as a status group and as a relatively independent political force were usually closely related to its claim to a legitimation distinct from the ruling elite's. In most of these societies, the upper and middle echelons of the bureaucracy had, especially after their initial stages of development, established their somewhat autonomous legitimation. This was mostly of a "legal-rational" or professional nature, as distinct from the more charismatic or traditional legitimation of the ruling elite. In some cases, the bureaucracy also claimed semi-aristocratic grounds for its legitimation.

In most of the countries studied, the bureaucracy developed, to some extent, an ideology emphasizing its own autonomy, and its direct ethical, professional (and, sometimes, even legal) responsibility for implementing the society's chief values and goals, in contrast to the vicissitudes of political experiences or of the arbitrary policies of the rulers ([A] *Borch, 1954* passim). This ideology did not fully emerge in some relatively underdeveloped societies—on the border between the feudal and the patrimonial and the centralized polities—like Sassanid Persia; and even in them some rudiments of specific professional—bureaucratic orientations existed ([G] *Christensen, 1933, 1936* passim;

Altheim, 1955[a]). It was clearly present in China, in the ideology of the responsibility of the officials ([I] *Des Rotours, 1932, 1947–48; Liu, 1957, 1959[a], 1959[b]; Bünger, no date; De Bary, 1957*). It was couched more in legal terms in Rome and Byzantium ([L] *Bréhier, 1949[b], 1950; Diehl, 1927; Barker, 1957 passim; Hussey, 1937*), where the Roman legal tradition left its imprint on the attitudes and behavior of the bureaucracy. In European countries, legal ideology and attitudes, and a strong *esprit du corps,* developed among the upper and middle bureaucrats; these emphasized their own specific positions and traditions. The bureaucracy's professional or semi-professional orientation evolved to an even greater extent in the European countries during the Age of Absolutism. *(See [S] Beloff, 1954; Lindsay, 1957[b]; [Y] Sagnac, 1945, 1946; Pagè, 1928; [A] Borch, 1954; [Y] Göhring, 1947; Lough, 1954, 1960.)*

C. THE AIMS OF THE BUREAUCRACY

THE POLITICAL FIELD. Several problems were created by the bureaucracy's claims to independence in the political field.

The first major issue involved the bureaucracy's political autonomy. It was manifested by the struggle over the degree of control that the rulers could exercise over the bureaucracy. Conversely, it could be indicated by the extent to which the bureaucracy—especially its upper echelons—could determine the basic policies governing their activities, and thus become, in a way, its own political master.

Within this general context, several concrete issues developed. The most important issues were: the measure to which the king's personal officers could effectively control the making of major political and administrative decisions in bureaucratic councils; the compass in which the king could act through independent agencies outside the usual bureaucracy; and the extent to which the bureaucracy itself determined the criteria governing the recruitment of its members.

The contention concerning these issues was evinced by various measures taken by the monarch. The ruler tried, for example, to maintain a body of personal officials and advisors who were independent of the bureaucratic machinery and cliques (of course, the bureaucracy made efforts to penetrate and influence these circles); to make wide use of eunuchs and other "independent" persons (e.g., priests), whose positions were highly ambivalent positions in the political struggle; and to create a core of officials of the "inner court," directly under his control, who would not be absorbed by the bureaucracy. Many of these officials eventually became relatively independent and lost touch with the king; this fact explains the frequent changes in the position of various officials, and the constant creation of similar positions and titles ([L] *Boak and Dunlap, 1924; Diehl, 1927; Guilland, 1946[a], 1949, 1950[a], 1953[a]; Des Rotours, 1926, 1932, Introduction, 1947–48, Introduction; Pulleyblank, 1955; Wang, 1949;* [G] *Christensen, 1939; Altheim and Stiehl, 1954).*

Another point of conflict that often developed between the king and the bureaucracy involved the existence and functions of a chief official and *general* council of officials, at the head of the bureaucracy, that acted as the major policy- and decision-making bodies in the polity. Frequently, the monarch tried to dispense with the official or council (as a corporate body), or to play one against the other; the bureaucracy, naturally, attempted to foster them. It is significant that conciliar centralization was greatest in Byzantium during periods of the aristocracy's relative dominance ([L] *Beck, 1955*); during these periods, the Senate was of relatively great importance ([L] *Bratianu, 1948[a]; Bury, 1910, pp. 106 ff.; Diehl, 1924; Ostrogorsky, 1956[a]* passim; *Vasiliev, 1952*); and in China, a council and, especially, a prime minister were most influential during periods when the bureaucracy dominated the ruler ([I] *Ho, 1952; Hucker, 1950* passim). In France, the Absolutist monarchs tried either to be their own prime ministers (e.g., Louis XIV), or else to force the various councils to accept ministers they chose as their leaders ([S] *Beloff, 1954;* [Y] *Pagès, 1932[a], 1932[b], 1937, 1938;* [X] *Hintze, 1903, 1914;* [Y] *Mousnier, 1938, 1948; Antoine, 1951).* The Prussian kings tended toward even more centralized supervision over their ministers, often forbidding them to work together. (*See* [X] *Dorn, 1931; Rosenberg, 1958; Hintze, 1915; Dorwart, 1953;* [A] *Finer, 1949, ch. xxviii;* [R] *Haring, 1947; Gallo, 1944; Ots Capdequi, 1951.*)

There were also many concrete problems related to maintaining discipline in, and control over, the bureaucracy. The ruler tended either to concentrate most of these matters in his hands or to delegate them to as many heads of departments as possible. This conflicted with the bureaucracy's tendency to establish its own regulations and organs—a tendency which also served as means of influencing the king's policy and attitude. The Chinese Censorate is, perhaps, the most important illustration of the bureaucratic tendency ([I] *Hucker, 1950, 1959[a], 1959[b]*). The French parliaments, in their regulating of sales of offices and dealing with other semi-disciplinary matters, and the Byzantine legalists involved in such activities, were also characterized by the same tendency ([L] *Bréhier, 1949[b], 1950, ch. ii, iii; Lemerle, 1948; Hussey, 1957;* [Y] *Pagès, 1928, 1938; Oliver-Martin, 1933; Rébillon, 1928; Lough, 1945, 1960; Zeller, 1944, 1948; Swart, 1949*). Among other things, these legalists often attempted to govern different aspects of the tenure and security of offices and to minimize the ruler's interference in these matters. It is relevant here to mention the many attempts the bureaucracy, or at least some of its upper echelons, made to gain control of the educational system—and particularly of those schools from which officials were recruited. The bureaucracy frequently attempted to maintain autonomous schools like these, and to get them a semi-monopoly in the field.

The rulers' attempts to control the bureaucracy were also evinced in their nominating various controlling officers from time to time. These would be sent out to supervise the local officials. The Byzantine inspectors, the Chinese officials of the Censorate, the French intendants, and the Spanish *visitores,* were all such officers. Most of them were *homines novi,* coming from outside the usual administrative hierarchy. The first nominees often were the special confidants of the king. However, as these offices gradually became institutionalized, the bureaucracy employed many devices to "install" them within its own folds. As a rule, the control of these officers constituted a constant issue of contention between the rulers and the bureaucracy.

Certain special posts within the bureaucracy—especially those bordering on the cultural sphere ([I] *Eberhard, 1957; and in general, Sprenkel, 1958*), like those of the astronomer in China or of the personal priests in ancient Egypt ([F] *Wilson, 1954)*—were also frequently used to influence the rulers and executive organs.

In the societies where representative institutions existed, the bureaucracy often essayed to gain control over some of them ([S] *Beloff, 1954; Zeller, 1939, 1947, 1948; Doucet, 1948;* [R] *Fisher, 1926, 1936; Haring, 1947; Gallo, 1944).* This is illustrated in France, for example, by the relations of the French parliaments (during the period when they were chiefly juridical institutions) to the *noblesse de robe.* Another example is provided by the bureaucrats' efforts, in the Spanish-American Empire, to acquire control of municipal offices and insure their compliance with the basic norms and values of the bureaucratic cliques. The bureaucracy, or some of its upper groups, had great success in influencing or even monopolizing several such institutions ([Y] *Ford, 1953; Sagnac, 1945, 1946; Egret, 1952;* [R] *Borah, 1956; Haring, 1947).*

This political struggle of the bureaucracy was waged mainly in the administrative organs and mechanisms designed to maintain the king's independence and his control over the bureaucracy; in these, the major policy decisions were usually made. The offices of the inner court, the higher councils of the bureaucracy, various "private" court cliques, and, in some countries, the main representative institutions, were the most important of these administrative features.

THE FIELD OF STATUS. The bureaucracy's aspirations in the field

of status constituted the second main general issue between the bureaucracy and the ruling elite. They centered around the problems of
the bureaucracy's independence and autonomy as a status group.

These ambitions necessarily entailed the bureaucracy's trying to
acquire high (chiefly aristocratic or semi-aristocratic) symbols of status
and to establish their hereditary transmission. However, except during
a period of utter decline in one of these polities, such attempts were
usually closely allied with various "legal" and semi-professional formu-
lations and ideologies, emphasizing the specific legal values and professional orientations of the upper echelons of the bureaucracy.

We have noted that the distribution of titles constituted a fundamental focus of the monarchs' policies in the field of stratification.
It also was a major source of conflict between ruler and the bureaucracy in the status area. The kings often endeavored to establish and
maintain the distinction between official designations of functions
within the bureaucracy and honorific titles denoting the official's general status in the hierarchy. While there was some correspondence
between the two, they were never identical. The distinction between
them served the rulers as a means of controlling both the bureaucracy
and the aristocracy of making them dependent on himself, and of
restraining them from monopolizing status and administrative positions. Sometimes the rulers used the honorific titles to compensate
others for loss of power, or to create new "nobles" more directly
dependent on them. *(See* [L] *Diehl, 1927; Diehl and Marçais, 1936;
Diehl et al., 1945; Guilland, 1946[a]*; [G] *Christensen, 1936; Ghirshman, 1954;* [R] *Konetzke, 1951[a], 1951[b], 1952.)*

To counteract these devices of the ruler, the bureaucracy often
strove to make titles more or less hereditary, to acquire proprietary
rights over its positions, and to develop a strong cohesion as a status-
group. For example, in Sassanid Persia, the rulers first attempted to
establish a royal officialdom distinct from the old feudal-aristocratic
families. Then the upper echelons of this new class developed quickly
into a rather closed *Aemteraristokratie*, strongly connected with parts
of the aristocracy ([G] *Christensen, 1936, especially ch. ix, x, 1939;
Altheim and Stiehl, 1954; Ghirshman, 1954;* [L] *Ostrogorsky, 1956[a]*
passim; *Jenkins, 1953; Beck, 1956).*

In Byzantium, the senatorial nobility, composed mostly of officials
and ex-officials, constantly tried to perpetuate itself. It attempted to
transmit its offices, positions, and wealth from generation to generation, and to evade, as far as possible, potential degradations by the
Emperor. It developed considerable class consciousness, which was
an important factor in the political evolution of the Byzantine Empire
([L] *Guilland, 1947–48, 1954; Diehl, 1927; Charanis, 1951[b]).*

In China, ostensibly, the official control of titles (through the examination system) was greatest. Nevertheless, the degree of monopolization of such positions by different gentry and other families was quite high, although it varied from one period to another. *(See* [I] *Chang, 1955; Eberhard, 1952; Sprenkel, 1952, 1958; Kracke, 1953, 1957, p. 110.)*

In its struggle for independent status, the bureaucracy often aligned itself with the religious and legal elites; at times, even with the aristocracy. But these alignments were not very stable, since their components' interests frequently diverged.

These general orientations of the bureaucracy necessarily had some repercussions on its stand regarding the making of policies. It is difficult to find any political orientation that prepondered in the bureaucracy. In general, however, the bureaucracy as a group showed a more traditional and legalistic attitude. It was far more bent on maintaining the given status quo than to taking initiative in the executive field— although, at times, it was from its ranks that the great reformers and innovators arose. The bureaucracy's more conservative and legal attitude was particularly evident in its relations to legal problems and reforms. It usually had great respect for legal tradition and inclined more toward systematization and codification, and was less predisposed to employ *ad hoc* measures, than were the kings or the great executive ministers. Hence the bureaucracy was often drawn into close contact with the legal profession, and sometimes even incorporated parts of it. However, often there were exceptions to this orientation—for instance, the great reformers.

THE FIELD OF FINANCE.   The bureaucracy and the rulers also clashed in the arena of economics and finance, since the officials wished financial independence in general and possession of their own offices in particular.

This struggle centered around two main issues. One concerned the extent of monarchal supervision and control of resources, and the amount of revenues the bureaucracy might derive from its offices beyond stipulated salaries and emoluments. This was usually connected with various aspects of farming out taxes. The other issue was the selling of offices by their incumbents.

The sale of offices was expedient for the rulers, because of the technical difficulties involved in centralized activity, and the necessity to mobilize as many flexible free-floating resources as possible. During the primary developmental stages of bureaucratic polities, selling offices was also an important means of breaking the aristocratic monopoly on positions, and instilling new (mostly bourgeois) blood and achievement criteria into the civil service. But after these stages, it created many new problems. It obstructed the monarchy's financial control of the bureaucracy, and often turned the offices into types of investment and private property ([L] *Kolias, 1939; Guilland, 1953[a]*; [S] *Lotz, 1935*; [Y] *Swart, 1949; Pagès, 1932[a]; 1938; Göhring, 1938*; [R] *Parry, 1953*). These problems naurally gave rise to a series of disputes and legal questions, to the emergence of an entire body of legal tradition and doctrine, and to political and social compromises. However, the issue itself continued to be a major focus of political struggle in most of the societies studied.

We must emphasize that these broader political and status orientations and aspirations were largely confined to the upper and middle echelons of the bureaucracies studied here, and evolved only in so far as autonomous traditions and cohesive groups developed within the bureaucracies. The lower-middle and lower echelons of the bureaucracy—the clerks, lower-grade technicians, and administrators did not usually participate in the more general struggles; nor did they always identify themselves with the broader aims. Their objectives were usually far more concrete—having security of office, payments, assurance of various emoluments, and, to some extent, possibilities of promotion.

Only when the lower and lower-middle echelons became somewhat professionalized—when their personnel had either legal or technical bureaucratic training, and they had evolved autonomous professional orientations—did they too begin to show some interest in the wider issues of struggle. This occurred on a small scale in Byzantium, where the middle echelons of the bureaucracy often participated in wider social or political movements. It occurred on a large scale in the Spanish-American Empire and France, where important professional legal echelons developed in the middle position of the bureaucracy ([Y] *Sagnac, 1945, 1946*; [R] *Haring, 1947; Ots Capdequi, 1951*).

D. THE RELATIONS OF THE BUREAUCRACY TO THE MAJOR POLITICAL AND SOCIAL GROUPS

The second front of the bureaucracy's political struggle was its relations with other social strata. Because of its special power position, the bureaucracy's relations with many strata could be of great political significance. What, then, were the relations and contacts that developed between the bureaucracy and the various social groups and strata? Was the bureaucracy characterized by policies or orientations of its own, or did it only represent the interests of the major strata? Were its various policies only reflections of these social groups, or were they manifestations of more autonomous tendencies? Was the bureaucracy merely the representative of the gentry and literati in China, of the landed and urban groups in Byzantium, of the rising bourgeoisie in Western Europe? In other words, was the bureaucracy an autonomous force in the political struggle vis-à-vis *both* the king and other groups in the society?

In order to answer this question, we must investigate several areas. First, we have to determine to what extent and under what conditions the upper bureaucracy was a unified body with homogeneous social and political orientations. Second, we must determine whether, if such homogeneity existed, it was connected with the predominance of any one social group in the bureaucracy.

Analysis of the available material indicates the difficulty of discovering whether, at any point of time, the entire bureaucracy of a given country had a homogeneous social-political orientation entirely distinct from the orientation of different groups or classes. Wang Yu Chuan has put this in a rather extreme way:

> In spite of the basic interests of its members, the bureaucracy did not constitute a homogeneous body. It was made up of a number of factions, all struggling for supremacy, which were formed on the basis of personal ambition for power and position or on the basis presented. The bureaucracy was maintained by the equilibrium of the forces between the various factions or by the domination of one of them ([I] *Wang, 1949*).

Thus, even in China, where the gentry's domination in the bureaucracy was most pronounced, there were always, within the gentry itself, different factions with different interests. They included various regional factions, factions of big and small land-owners, of different families, or of groups. Moreover, the pure gentry factions were not the only significant ones. Aristocratic or military groups were very important sometimes. Also, during several periods, especially during the Sung Dynasty's great period of economic expansion, various merchant groups came very close to being directly represented in the bureaucracy. In addition, several religious groups, like the Taoists and Buddhists, continuously struggled for influence within the bureaucracy. *(See [I] Des Routours, 1932, 1947–48, Introduction; Pulleyblank, 1955; Eberhard, 1945, 1948[a], 1951, 1952, ch. ii. iii; Balázs, 1952, 1959[a], 1960.)*

The composition of the upper echelons of the bureaucracy in most other societies studied were even more diversified. With the possible exception of its period of utter decline, when the bureaucracy became almost entirely aristocratized, the Byzantine Empire's bureaucracy was never entirely dominated by one major group or social stratum. Its members came variously from aristocratic, upper-bureaucratic, urban-professional, and gentry origins ([L] *Runciman, 1933;*

Bréhier, 1924, 1949[b] passim; *Andréadès, 1926; Diehl, 1906–08, 1929).*

In France and the Spanish-American Empire, the composition of the bureaucracy was also greatly varied. The aristocratic, *robe,* professional, and bourgeois elements all participated in the different echelons of the administrative structure—although in certain periods, the aristocratic or *robe* elements tended to monopolize several upper levels ([Y] *Ford, 1953; Sagnac, 1945, 1946; Egret, 1952;* [R] *Konetzke, 1951[a], 1951[b], 1952; Fisher, 1926, 1936; Haring, 1947; Zavala, 1943).* In Sassanid Persia many bureaucratic posts were in the hands of the landed aristocracy. However, many members of other groups found their way into the bureaucracy, which even tried to establish itself as an independent status group ([G] *Christensen, 1936, ch. vi– viii; Altheim and Stiehl, 1954, 1957; Massé, 1952, especially ch. iv).*

Thus, in terms of social composition and orientation, the upper bureaucracy was rarely a homogeneous group. However, it did frequently happen that various groups did attempt to dominate the bureaucracy, and succeeded in doing so for some time. But it was only in rare cases—usually, during periods of decline—that the bureaucracy became entirely dominated by any one social group.

This very lack of complete homogeneity in composition and social outlook emphasized the fact that the bureaucracy (or at least its upper and middle echelons) tended to develop and maintain, with regard to the major strata, some organizational and socio-political autonomy of its own. The extent to which this autonomy was maintained or developed varied greatly from case to case, but in general there were three chief manifestations—sometimes complementary and sometimes contradictory of this tendency to relative autonomy.

The first way this tendency was manifested was in the fact that, because of the bureaucracy's heterogeneous composition, the bureaucratic institutions and organizations provided a basic framework for regulating conflicts among its factions and other interests which they may have represented.

Most of these conflicts occurred within the framework of the bureaucratic organization, its rules and orientations. Different groups and factions might quarrel over the details of taxation or economic policy; however, they rarely denied the necessity of having some such policy or of upholding certain fundamental rules and frameworks of activity. These frameworks would not allow all the privileges that certain groups demanded, involving the denial of all legal rights to several lower strata of the population—although the bureaucracy itself might make heavy demands on these strata. Thus most such groups usually upheld some general common orientations and regulations, even when these were against the interests of the social strata closest to them—if only because the bureaucracy's own position vis-à-vis the rulers was largely dependent on its maintaining such orientations.

The second manifestation of the bureaucracy's tendency to autonomy consisted of its attempts to organize itself into a discrete status group—differing even from the strata from which it had been constituted with strong, sometimes semi-aristocratic, symbols of its own.

The major focus of the bureaucracy's efforts to attain status autonomy was its emphasis on the professional-occupational (and, sometimes, the power) aspects of bureaucratic activities as constituting a major distinctive source of social status, and on the development of a semi-professional ideology which attempted to stress professional autonomy and incorporate it in symbols of social status. This applies to almost all the countries studied here ([A] *Borch, 1954* passim; [L] *Bréhier, 1949[b]; Diehl, 1929*).

Even in China, where the gentry and the bureaucracy were as closely related as possible, they were not identical. The bureaucracy tended to differentiate itself somewhat from both the gentry and the literati, and to maintain a framework and policy of its own. The importance of holding a degree, the various legal and actual privileges connected with doing so, and the common outlook engendered by the examination life—all these led to some degree of differentiation between the literati in the bureaucracy and other groups, even those groups (like the gentry) with which they were very closely related and allied ([I] *Chang, 1955; Eberhard, 1948[a]* passim, *1952; Wittfogel, 1957; Pulleyblank, 1955*).

Thus in many cases the upper and middle echelons of the bureaucracy evolved into somewhat autonomous status groups. These limited the flexibility of the status system by impressing their own ascriptive criteria and values on it, and by monopolizing many high positions, sources of power and prestige, and the right to allocate them. The respective degrees of autonomy achieved by the bureaucratic groups varied from case to case. However, the bureaucracy in most of these societies aspired toward its realization in relation to other social strata and in relation to the rulers.

The last, and perhaps the most important, manifestation of the bureaucracy's tendency to autonomy occurred in its attempts to minimize the scope of the autonomous regulative mechanisms that developed in the society and to control them. However closely it was identified with the interests of any social group, the bureaucracy usually regarded unfavorably any attempts made by these groups to extend their own autonomy and the scope of their autonomous regulative mechanisms. The bureaucracy continuously attempted either to minimize their scope or to control them.

E. THE POSSIBILITIES OF DECLINE
OF AUTONOMY OF THE BUREAUCRACY.
REFORM MOVEMENTS WITHIN THE BUREAUCRACY

The above analysis has demonstrated the chief spheres in which the bureaucracy maintained some measure of autonomy vis-à-vis the rulers and other groups. Obviously, the particular society determined the extent to which such autonomy was maintained. In many instances, the bureaucracy became exclusively dominated by one group or coterie of groups; or it became entirely, or almost entirely, independent of the rulers. In many other cases, its autonomy and initiative were stifled and undermined by the rulers. We shall not consider all these variations, or the conditions under which they tended to develop, until a later chapter.

Here, we wish only to point out the ranges and spectrum of the different political attitudes of the bureaucracy, the crucial importance of its various claims to autonomy, and the possible implications of these claims for its basic political orientations.

It is significant that, in many of the cases in which the bureaucracy became both independent and corrupt, movements of reform and change were initiated within the bureaucracy itself—at times in conjunction with the monarch and at times in opposition to him. Reform movements were more or less oriented to the prevention of the bureaucracy's being completely subjugated by any strong group within the society, to the establishment of a more equitable pattern of service provision, and to more efficient patterns of mobilizing resources by the bureaucracy.

These attempts at reform are illustrated by well-known and well-documented cases—Wang An-shih of Sung China (A.D. 1069–1079) ([I] *Williamson, 1937; O. Franke, 1931, 1932; Lui, 1959[a], 1959[b]*, of San Mehmed Pasha of the later Ottoman Empire ([O] *Wright, 1935*), and of great European ministers during the Age of Absolutism *(for a general survey, see* [S] *Beloff, 1954;* [Y] *Pagès 1928)*. But these individuals often merely represented wider movements of reform, or at least orientations, in this direction. They all aimed at increasing the bureaucracy's efficiency and at securing its impartial execution of its duties and its devotion to the monarch's interests rather than to those of any other group. True, they did not always succeed in realizing these goals; the bureaucratic machine might remain "corrupt" and dominated by one group or clique. But this corruption could easily be the beginning of the end of the given political system—as illustrated by emergence of the famous "dynastic cycle" of Chinese history ([I] *Spren-*

kel, 1952; Eberhard, 1954; Balàzs, 1950; for a less cautious formulation, see Wang, 1936), the gradual shrinking and disintegration of the Byzantine and Ottoman empires ([L] *Ostrogorsky, 1956[a]; Vasiliev, 1952; Stein, 1954;* [O] *Gibb and Bowen, 1950, 1957;* [N] *Lewis, 1953),* or the political revolutions in Europe ([Y] *Pagès, 1928, 1932[b];* [S] *Beloff, 1954).* It is significant for our analysis that many of these downfalls were related to the bureaucracy's losing its power of independent action—that is, to its inability to maintain equilibrium between contending factions and social groups. These contentions finally led to the alienation of many social groups from the existing political framework.

When disintegration was followed by periods of reorganization, these usually were initiated by the reinstallation of a relatively autonomous, well controlled, and efficient bureaucratic organization. Such processes were well known and documented in China ([I] *Liu, 1959[a], 1959[b]; O. Franke, 1931, 1932; Hu, 1955; Sprenkel, 1952, 1958),* and developed also in France and the Spanish-American Empire ([Y] *Pagès, 1928;* [R] *Haring, 1947; Ots Capdequi, 1945;* on Persia, see [G] *Christensen, 1936, ch. viii; Altheim and Stiehl, 1954; Altheim, 1955[a], 1955[b], and although in somewhat different ways, during several periods of Byzantine history* [Y] *Pagès, 1928* passim; [L] *Ostrogorsky, 1956[a]* passim; *Bréhier, 1949[b], livres IV, VII,* passim).

Thus almost all these reform movements emphasized the importance of the bureaucracy's not becoming entirely subjugated by any one group. It should uphold more general rules and provide services to many groups and strata, to continue some of its functions in the polity.

The analysis is not meant to suggest that, in any of the societies studied, the principles of bureaucratic organization and activity did not favor some social strata over others. First, it is obvious that politically and socially passive groups—particularly the peasantry—did not exert any great influence on most of the bureaucracies, whose consideration of their interests was relatively minimal. There were some exceptions, especially in Byzantium from the seventh to the eleventh century, but these were extremely rare ([L] *Jenkins, 1953).*

Second, the bureaucracy itself, and the kings who directed it, usually did not go very far beyond the basic principles of status that existed within a given society. Rather, they tried to adjust their policies to the existing system of stratification—to modify it somewhat or to isolate some of its aspects, but not to abolish it entirely. Thus, in most of the cases studied, the ruling elite tended to uphold several basic aristocratic symbols of status and prestige and the general hierarchical structure of the status system. At the same time, however, the rulers' fundamental policies, and the bureaucracy's, in the field of stratification, were directed toward weakening the monopolistic position of various status groups. The very existence of these policies—though their successful implementation varied greatly from society to society—explains the fact that the bureaucracy usually, at times in co-operation with the rulers, at times in opposition to them, tried to fulfill some basic mediating and regulatory functions whose results were not entirely identical with the interests of any one group of stratum. Unless totally corrupt, the bureaucracy even tended to provide minimal protection for the interests of the lower groups and strata, and for their maintaining some stability and continuity in their expectations. Usually, it was only under special conditions, generally connected with the decline of the political system of the historical bureaucratic societies, that the bureaucracy was likely to become entirely subjugated to any social group of stratum. But the extent to which it did perform its functions and maintain some extent of autonomy varied greatly from case to case, as we shall analyze later.

The bureaucracy became the ruthless and "total" oppressor of the lower strata only during periods of decline—e.g., during the decline of the Chinese dynasties, during the last stages of Byzantine history, and in eighteenth-century France ([L] *Ostrogorsky, 1956[a], 1956[b]; Vasiliev, 1952; [Y] Cobban, 1957[b]; Barber, 1955; Pagès, 1928, 1932[b]*).

F. THE RELATIONS OF THE POLITICAL ACTIVITIES OF THE BUREAUCRACY TO THE BASIC PREMISES OF THE POLITICAL SYSTEM

We may now briefly summarize the basic attitudes of the bureaucracy about the premises of the bureaucratic historical polities. The political and social activities of the bureaucracy were situated between the rulers' basic aims and goals of the various active strata of the population. Its orientations, aims, and interests were related to the problems lying between these two poles. Its continuous functioning within the basic premises of the historical bureaucratic polities was greatly dependent on its keeping a "middle position" between these two poles and maintaining some degree of autonomy with regard to both. In so far as it did so, the bureaucracy performed its basic functions in the institutional framework of the historical bureaucratic societies and maintained a fundamentally positive attitude toward their key premises.

However, since it occupied an extremely strategic place in the political sphere, the bureaucracy could easily develop tendencies to acquire entirely independent and uncontrollable power and status positions, to monopolize these positions, and to minimize any effective control over itself and over the scope of activities of the various autonomous regulative mechanisms.

Since the bureaucracy had these inclinations, and tended to acquire ascriptive-hereditary status symbols, it could become an all-important opponent or stumbling block to the rulers' attempts to maintain their control over reservoir of free resources in the society.

The bureaucracy, by the very nature of its activities, could not—unless it had been totally aristocratized and had become itself the ruling elite—be in total opposition to the basic premises of the bureaucratic polity. However, it could effect great changes in the balance of power within this polity, and limit its possible development. In this way, the bureaucracy—which was, in a sense, the chief concrete instrument of generalizing political power—could easily develop inclinations which would fetter and restrict the society's generalization of power, and even undermine the conditions making for free resources available.

[3] The Place of the Army in the Political Struggle

A. ITS COMPOSITION

The army was also a frequent, active participant in the political struggles of the historical bureaucratic societies. From a purely formal point of view the army can, of course, be considered as a part of the bureaucracy. But when it engaged in the political struggle on its own, its attitudes and objectives could differ so widely from those held by the major bureaucratic groups that they deserve special treatment.

The army's importance as an independent force in the political struggle was different in each of the societies studied. In Rome, Byzantium, the Caliphate, and the Ottoman Empire, the army played a major role. In China, though in different periods, it enjoyed relatively great political significance, the army did not constitute a permanent, semi-legitimate (or at least accepted) factor in the political process ([I] *Michael, 1946; Des Rotours, 1926, 1947–48; Pulleyblank, 1955*). In France and the Spanish-American Empire, the army had little political importance. In Sassanid Persia, the army participated in the political struggle as a constituent of either the feudal or the bureaucratic groups ([G] *Christensen, 1936* passim; *Altheim, 1955[a], 1955[b]; Altheim and Stiehl, 1954, 1957*).

However, the fact that the army was possibly a latent independent political force was closely connected with several characteristics of the historical bureaucratic societies. First, almost all these polities—and especially the ones with collective expansionist goals that confronted major problems of external and internal security (e.g., the Sassanid, Byzantine, and Roman empires)—laid great emphasis on external relations, and, therefore, on maintaining adequate military forces.

Second, armies composed of professional soldiers, as well as mercenary and "citizen" armies (like these in Republican and early Imperial Rome, and in Byzantium) often became centers of mob activity and hotbeds of political propaganda.

Third, the rulers of many of these societies had to employ mercenary armies, because of the unavailability of free mobile manpower, the rulers' fear of "popular" armies, or the low level of technical and organizational knowledge. In some cases (as we shall discuss in a later chapter), these factors placed the mercenary armies in a powerful position, and enabled their leaders to have considerable political influence.

Finally, when the army (especially an army recruited by conscription, but sometimes a mercenary one) became a main avenue of mobility, it also acquired relatively great social and political importance in the society.

When discussing the army, one must distinguish the great masses of soldiers from the military elite and leaders. They often belonged to different social groups, both sharing political and social aspirations, and, possibly, tending to use military positions to attain their respective goals. When a "national" army developed—as one did in Byzantium during the seventh through tenth centuries ([L] *Bréhier, 1949[b]; Diehl, 1943; Diehl et al., 1945; Jenkins, 1953; Ostrogorsky, 1956[a]* passim; *Diehl and Marçais, 1936*), and in Persia under Khosrou I ([G] *Stein, 1920; Christensen, 1936, ch. viii*)—its members usually participated in political activities through the respective social groups to which they belonged (*e.g., for France, see* [Y] *Leonard, 1948*).

The most extreme example of this participation probably is the case of "religious" armies—like the Islamic armies and orders—that perceived themselves as the foremost bearers of the society's religious and political values. This kind of religious army sometimes blended with that type of army that evolved more autonomous political aspirations —the mercenary armies which often tried or hoped to usurp political power in the societies which they served ([N] *Cahen, 1957[a], 1957[b];* [M] *Hodgson, 1955, 1960; Grunebaum, 1954, 1955[a], 1955[b]*).

B. THE POLITICAL AIMS OF DIFFERENT ARMY ECHELONS

Even when the army constituted an autonomous political factor, there were usually great differences between the goals of its two chief components. The vast mass of soldiers—including non-commissioned and junior officers—were mostly interested in concrete economic and social matters. The most important of these were wage increases, security of pensions, procurement of lucrative offices in the bureaucracy, and, at times, security and special favors for their families. These soldiers could also be made to feel strongly about wider "patriotic" issues

—for instance, about foreign threats to a dynasty, or about religious controversy. But their wider interests were rarely spontaneous; as a rule, they were aroused by political or military leaders. Further, they were not permanent, or capable of being detached for long from more concrete issues. Thus many troop rebellions in Rome, Byzantium, etc., that proclaimed national, political and religious ideals, were usually much less stormy if the soldiers' demands for increases in pay, rights to land, etc., were met and/or their representatives succeeded in seizing positions of power. As a rule, only armies deriving from religious orders and sects, and maintaining a strong religious identification, evinced more sustained interest in wider political issues. These kinds of armies are best illustrated by the various "orders" that developed in the Abbaside (A.D. 749–1258) and Fatimite (*c.* A.D. 909–1171) caliphates.

The soldiers usually conducted their struggle within the framework of the army itself, by threatening to withdraw their services, by rebellions and mutinies, and by desertion. In some cases (e.g., Byzantium, China, and France), they also participated in more general rebellious movements.

The political aims of the military leaders were, of course, far more complicated, diversified, and related to central problems of the polity. Besides using their positions to enrich themselves and their families, the military leaders evinced political interest in obtaining the following:

1. Political influence, through appropriating advisory and bureaucratic positions

2. Concentration and, in so far as possible, monopolization of effective political power, through controlling the crucial offices

3. Control of the ruling elite, by controlling the monarch and the succession to the throne

4. In extreme cases, seizure of realm and rule

Obviously the political battles of the military leaders were waged in the most central arenas of court politics and in the upper echelons of the bureaucracy. They used various methods, but could all ultimately be reduced to the threat either to use their military forces against their opponents, or to withdraw their services. Since the army was often composed of members from many strata, such threats could have several wider social repercussions.

C. THE RELATIONS OF THE ARMY'S POLITICAL ACTIVITIES TO THE BASIC PREMISES OF THE POLITICAL SYSTEMS

In so far as the army played some independent role in the political struggle, to what extent did its different component elements identify themselves with the basic premises of the bureaucratic polity and the basic policies of the ruling elite? Superficially, most of these armies seemed to be fundamentally in accord with the *general* policies of the ruling elite—only within their framework was their own existence assured.

However, the army's strategic position within such framework could, under certain circumstances, lead to results which undermined the ruling elite's basic policies and political premises.

First, the great demands on resources consequent on maintaining armies could often bring about the diminution, and finally the disintegration, of the bureaucratic polities.

Also, the army frequently mistrusted both the autonomous regulative mechanisms developed by the major strata and the activities of the civil bureaucracy. Thus it often aspired to control them through directly usurping power.

Third, the army could play an important part in changing and subverting the polity's specific goals. Its strong power position enabled it to impose its own goals on the rulers. The army's significance was especially prominent when it usurped the ultimate power in the society. It was then able to change the basic goals of the polity and, accordingly, change the fundamental institutional framework of the polity. (*See* [N] *Cahen, 1957[a], 1957[b]; Hoeuerbach, 1950; [X] Craig, 1955. For some aspects of the social problem in the French army before the Revolution, see* [Y] *Girardet, 1953.*)

[4] The Place of the Aristocracy in the Political Struggle

A. ITS COMPOSITION

In addition to the ruling elite, the bureaucracy, and the army, the aristocracy was another major group that always participated in the political struggles of the societies analyzed. The aristocracy usually comprised great landed families interrelated by kinship ties, and, sometimes, ties of territorial proximity, common way of life, and common values. It held high, or the highest, positions, in the system of stratification, in honor, prestige, and, at times, power. The most important distinctions within the aristocracy were those of wealth and status; another crucial internal difference was the one between its "civil" and its military components. Such a distinction evolved, for instance, in Byzantium. Though the aristocracy was thus usually composed of several subgroups and, at its margin, tended to dovetail with the gentry, it still can on the whole be distinguished from other groups.

Within the structure of most bureaucratic societies, the aristocracy held a strategic position—even though its position was not always clearly

definable in terms of the polity's basic premises. The aristocracy's relatively great strength resulted from the fact that most bureaucratic polities had developed from political systems (in the majority of feudal or
patrimonial societies) dominated by aristocratic groups—like pre-Sassanid Persia, feudal (pre-Han; i.e., before 206 B.C.) China, and, obviously, feudal Europe.

Throughout the history of Sassanid Persia, strong aristocratic forces
existed in the forms of "old established" princely and feudal families.
During later periods of the Sassanid Empire, the aristocracy continued
in the growing *Aemteraristokratie,* whose economic and political
powers were not curbed, for any length of time, except during the reign
of Khosrou I ([G] *Christensen, 1933, 1936 passim, 1939; Ghirshman,
1954; Delaporte and Huart, 1943; Altheim, 1955[a], 1955[b]; Altheim
and Stiehl, 1954, 1957; Widengren, 1956).*

There was probably a greater turnover in the composition of the
aristocracy during the different periods of the Byzantine Empire's history. However, in Byzantium also, landed magnates, high officials, and
military leaders tried to establish themselves as an independent or
landed aristocracy, with strong holds over economic and political positions. Through the Empire's history, these aristocratic groups recruited
new elements from upper urban strata. *(See* [L] *Runciman, 1929, pp.
109 ff.; Charanis, 1951[b]; Jenkins, 1953; Guilland, 1947–48; 1954; Bréhier, 1949[b], 1950 passim; Ostrogorsky, 1956[a] passim; Vasiliev, 1952.)*

In China, aristocratic or feudal families existed in the Han period
(206 B.C.–A.D. 221). They survived, to some extent, during the T'ang
Dynasty (A.D. 618–905). However, by 905 they had become almost entirely extinct, although gentry families often attempted to extend their
landholdings and to attain aristocratic status—in the second, they were
not very successful. *(See* [I] *Pulleyblank, 1955; Stange, 1950. For a somewhat different view, see Eberhard, 1948[a], 1952; Balázs, 1948, 1950.)*
Later, it was mostly the conquest dynasties, like the Mongols and the
Manchus, that established various aristocratic families around the court
and the dynasty. These did not, however, become integrated into the
Chinese social structure *(see, e.g.,* [I] *Michael, 1942).*

In most European countries, the feudal aristocracies persisted in
some form. However, as we have already seen, they were greatly transformed and lost most of their political and economic (as distinct from
social) predominance ([S] *Lindsay, 1957[a]; Goodwin, 1953;* [Y] *Bloch,
1936; Carré, 1920; d'Avenel, 1901; Ford, 1953; Sagnac, 1945, 1946;* [U]
Desdevises du Dezert, 1925, 1927). In the Spanish-American Empire,
no "old" autochthonous aristocracy existed. Although a local creole aristocracy developed and became dominant in the social and economic
fields, its feudal tendencies were checked by the Crown and Crown

officials ([R] *Konetzke, 1951[a], 1951[b], 1952, 1953; Zavala, 1943; Levene, 1953*).

Because of the history of these societies the landed and aristocratic groups always participated actively in political struggle. For this reason, they constituted one of the most problematic elements in the political structure, especially in the initial stages of development of the polity. During these early stages, the goals of the aristocracy were often basically opposed to the fundamental premises of the bureaucratic polities, causing the ruling elite's policies to be directed against the aristocracy. This led to the aristocracy's having, in general, a negative or ambivalent attitude toward the ruling elite and toward the premises and goals of the bureaucratic polity.

In most of the societies we are examining, the aristocracy's ambivalence toward the premises of the centralized polities was evinced. However, its manifestations varied from one place to another, and from one period to another. There were two main types or stages of aristocratic opposition to the premises of bureaucratic polities and to the policies of their rulers. The first is characterized by open, or almost open, opposition. The second is characterized both by the aristocracy's relative adaptation to the frameworks of these polities and its attempts to obtain maximum benefits within these frameworks; and also by a continuation, in most cases, of some general negative orientation toward many facets of the fundamental premises of these political systems and of the rulers' policies. Although the distinction between the manifestations of these types or stages of opposition was not always clear-cut, they are analytically distinct.

B. ARISTOCRATIC OPPOSITION TO THE PREMISES OF THE POLITICAL SYSTEMS

FIRST TYPE. Initially, the aristocracy's opposition was manifested chiefly in its attempts to obstruct the ruling elite's realization of its autonomous goals. The aristocracy tried, for example, to establish independent political organizations, territorial unity, and expansion; and it attempted to diminish the availability of free resources to the ruler, and to narrow the range of the activities, both internal and external, of the rulers and the bureaucracy. The aristocracy therefore had a great interest in impeding the creation of new loyalties, symbols of solidarity, and identifications that would cut across strong particularistic (territorial, kinship, and status) groups to focus on the ruler as the center of the new community and state. The aristocracy wished to maintain a status system which would be largely independent of the ruler and based on the aristocracy's values, way of life, and position.

What were the concrete aims, orientations, and activities which manifested the aristocracy's political attitude?

One of the aristocracy's primary aims was to maintain its autonomy vis-à-vis the rising royal power and to limit the latter's resources and effectiveness. It employed several devices to achieve this objective. One was to weaken the economic chief support of the monarchy by appropriating many of its resources, channels of taxation, and mobilization of manpower, and to preserve several feudal or patrimonial traditions.

The aristocracy also strove to formalize and perpetuate its rights to offices in the royal council, and administration, and representative institutions. Of course, many of these institutions were employed by the monarchs to break the aristocracy's power and to enlarge the scope of participation in the political struggle. Many of them, however, had been carried over from the feudal or patrimonial antecedents of the historical bureaucratic polities. Through the perpetuation of its claims to these offices, the aristocracy often attempted to limit the monarchy's effectiveness and independence, and the distinctiveness of its political goals; and to retain its own influence on the making of major political decisions. For example, in Sassanid Persia even the new *Aemteraristokratie,* and the military aristocracy created after the reforms of various periods, developed into a semi-landed military group that succeeded in controlling the kings through its offices ([G] *Christensen, 1936, especially ch. viii, ix, x; Altheim and Stiehl, 1954; Ghirshman, 1954).* Similarly, the Byzantine and French aristocracies often attempted to monopolize strategic offices and to weaken the power of centralized monarchy ([L] *Ostrogorsky, 1956[a], 1956[b]; Charanis, 1951[a], 1951[b], 1953[a]; [Y] Pagès, 1928; Ford, 1953; Sagnac, 1946).*

These tendencies of the aristocracy generally developed mostly in the polities that were on the border between patrimonial and feudal societies, and bureaucratic polities. In ancient Persia, for example, aristocratic elements—whether landed or military aristocracy—frequently predominated in the state, used state machinery for their own purposes, and succeeded in limiting the rulers' power and the realization of their policies.

The aristocracy engaged in similar activities in China, during the transition from the Ch'in (225–206 B.C.) to the Han Dynasty, and, to a lesser extent, through to the T'ang period, until the bureaucratic Confucian system had been fully established ([I] *Pulleyblank, 1955; Stange, 1950).* The same occurred in Poland; and, to a lesser degree, in Hungary, where the nobility managed, for a very long time, to prevent any unified polity whatever from arising ([S] *Goodwin, 1953).*

However, these tendencies did not exist only in these borderline cases between bureaucratic and pre-bureaucratic polities, or during the primary stages of the establishment of centralized polities. They also emerged in many fully established bureaucratic societies. In these polities, the aristocracy could develop such tendencies at later stages of the polity's development. For example, the Byzantine aristocracy continually attempted to limit the monarchy's dependence of the monarchy and to impose its own goals on the monarchy, and to maintain its own positions and immunities. And, in most European Absolutist countries, the aristocracy was trying to limit the monarchy's effectiveness and its scope of independent activities as late as the eighteenth century ([S] *Goodwin, 1953; also* [Y] *Ford, 1953; Pagès, 1928*).

SECOND TYPE. The aristocracy's success in realizing its aims against the ruling elite and the bureaucracy was different in each society. But never (with the sole—and partial—exception of post-T'ang China) was the aristocracy entirely obliterated or prevented from exerting any social and political influence. Even in post-T'ang China, a number of royal and aristocratic families survived; and aristocratic tendencies, though not fully articulated, were evinced by various gentry families.

In Sassanid Persia the aristocracy suffered many vicissitudes, especially during the period of anti-aristocratic persecution under Khosrou I. Yet it reasserted itself toward the end of the Empire.

In Byzantium, the emperors during the seventh through tenth centuries tried to restrain the aristocracy from becoming too strong and from encroaching on the free peasants. However, from the eleventh century on, these efforts were less and less successful. The different aristocratic groups gained, both economically (through extending their landholdings) and politically, the upper hand. The last dynasties— the Commenibs (A.D. 1057–1059, 1081–1118) and Paleologi (A.D. 1261–1453) dynasties—were greatly dominated by different aristocratic groups ([L] *Guilland, 1953–55; Ostrogorsky, 1956[a]; Jenkins, 1953; Vasiliev, 1933, 1952*).

In most other countries, the aristocracy might have failed to achieve its primary objectives, and so had to adapt to the basic premises and frameworks of the bureaucratic polities. Even in such cases, however, it did not cease to exert important influence in diverse spheres and to participate in the political struggle. In their policies, the ruling elites themselves usually acknowledged, and even emphasized, the aristocracy's prominence in the social sphere. Its high social status enabled the aristocracy to participate in political struggles, even though it was obliged to pursue goals and employ means very different from those it had had during the initial stages of its opposition to the rulers. Thus there emerged the second stage, or type, of aristocratic opposition to the ruling elites of the bureaucratic polities.

In some European countries, like France, Spain, and Portugal, the aristocracy was greatly weakened politically and economically during the first period of the Age of Absolutism, but maintained its social predominance. It then became politically more active during the eighteenth century. In France, the alliance between the old (*d'épée*) and new (*de robe*) aristocracies led, after the death of Louis XIV (in 1715), to the "Aristocratic Reaction" that greatly weakened the stability of the regime ([Y] *Ford, 1953; Sagnac, 1945, 1946; Pagès, 1928; Barber, 1955*). In Prussia, after the first rift between the Hohenzollern and the old aristocracy had been closed in the eighteenth century, the aristocracy—after having been domesticated by the rulers for their service—became socially and politically predominant ([X] *Hintz, 1914, 1915; Carsten, 1954, 1955; Schmoller, 1898; Rosenberg, 1958*).

This stage usually developed, after the old landed aristocracy had been successfully subjugated, and partly transformed into an *Aemter-aristokratie,* by the rulers, or else after the rulers had created such an *Aemteraristokratie.* Then the various aristocratic groups became less concerned with the outright limitation of the polity's scope and objectives. They were chiefly interested in the optimum utilization of these frameworks for their own purposes—to increase their power, prestige, and wealth; and to maximize the aristocratic elements and symbols in the social and political structures. The aristocratic elements tried to achieve these objectives in many ways.

They still continued to attempt to monopolize various positions within the bureaucracy. The rulers were interested in limiting their control to the purely honorific positions—e.g., Chamberlain, or Constable of the Realm, in France. However, the aristocracy endeavored either to make these positions politically effective, or to penetrate and monopolize various other strategically important spheres of administrative political activity, like the army and the judiciary. In some cases, the aristocracy even tried to monopolize the king's council and decision-making power.

The aristocrats attempted—either intentionally or unintentionally, to guide many upper bureaucrats to aristocratic values and ways of life. Their methods ranged from combined social condescension and distance, intermarriage, and financial deals, to open political alliances and accepting some members of the upper bureaucracy into the aristocracy. This last method was employed in eighteenth-century France (the partial alliance of the *robe* and the *epée);* to a lesser degree in Prussia; and, perhaps to the greatest extent, in Byzantium from the eleventh century on. In Byzantium, the civil and military aristocracies tried to absorb most of the active elements from other strata and elites.

Various aristocratic families tried to utilize the economic facilities and opportunities provided by the rulers to expand their own economic interests. Sometimes they entered trade and manufacture; more often, they became agricultural entrepreneurs, changing many techniques of cultivation or orienting agricultural produce to the market. In some instances, as in Prussia and Austria, they combined these activities with the use of state power to enforce their rights against the peasants and to increase their authority over the serfs. In general, they tried to monopolize economic positions and opportunities at the expense of other groups ([X] *Hintze, 1914, 1915; Rosenberg, 1958;* [T] *Schenk, 1953; Blum, 1948; also,* [V] *Gohlin, 1953;* [S] *Redlich, 1953*).

Finally, the aristocracy often initiated or organized strong movements opposing those of the monarch's policies that might benefit other classes in the country. Two examples of this method are the opposition of the French aristocracy to the king's policies at the beginning of the eighteenth century; and the seizure of power by the Byzantine civil and military aristocracies in the eleventh century. *(See* [Y] *Ford, 1953; Pagès, 1928;* [L] *Ostrogorsky, 1956[a], 1956[b]; Vasiliev, 1952; Jenkins, 1953.)*

In so far as these attempts succeeded, they heightened the aristocracy's political power within the framework of the bureaucratic polities. They enabled the aristocracy to exercise greater influence in political councils, and to protect its specific economic and social interests.

C. THE RELATIONS OF THE POLITICAL ACTIVITIES OF THE ARISTOCRACY TO THE BASIC PREMISES OF THE POLITICAL SYSTEMS

The distinction between the two stages or types of aristocratic opposition to the basic premises of the bureaucratic polities and their rulers was not always clear-cut. Except in China and England ([Z] *Habakkuk, 1953; Namier, 1929, 1930, 1952; Pares, 1957;* [S] *Beloff, 1954, ch. ix*), the landed aristocracy, even when adapted to, and economically thriving in, the framework of the bureaucratic polity, was always somewhat opposed to some of its actual or potential orientations and social tendencies, to many of the rulers' policies, and to the rulers' promotion of free resources. Very often the aristocracy strongly resisted the materialization of potential participation by other groups in the political process, and opposed their autonomous political development —e.g., in eighteenth-century Prussia. In other words, the aristocracy was usually the social force most strongly combatting any extension of differentiation in the society and, in extreme cases, withstanding the concentration of power in the hands of the rulers and their free employment of power in pursuit of their objectives. In its less radical form, the aristocracy's opposition consisted of attempts to limit the potential development of latent free centers of power in other strata and these strata's use of power to realize their own goals and political aspirations. In such cases, the aristocracy often tried to foster and encourage the more traditional or prescriptive orientations of the rulers.

These political tendencies of the aristocracy were most evident in the relations it developed to other groups in the society, and in the significance these relations had for the political process in the society. The aristocracy was related to most groups in the society, including the peasants; the religious elites, with whom they came in contact both locally and at the center through participating in central political institutions; and urban groups, like merchants and manufacturers, with whom they had contacts for both economic and political reasons. The aristocrats probably constituted the "ecological" group which had the widest contacts with other strata and with functional elites. However, the aristocrats attempted to keep all these contacts on a traditional and particularistic basis of direct relations between themselves and the other groups and strata, and to remove them from the realm of central administrative and political activities. They also attempted to forestall the formation of direct relations between these groups and strata and the rulers. In this way, they influenced the stability and continuity of the historical bureaucratic polities.

The distinction between the two stages of aristocratic opposition to the premises of the political systems of the historical bureaucratic empires—the stage of complete open opposition of the alien-feudal or the patrimonial-aristocratic elements, and the stage of a relatively "domesticated" aristocracy working for its interests *within* the frameworks of these polities—was not always clearcut. However, some differences are discernible with regard to the respective types of political activities connected with each stage or type.

The first type, or stage, of aristocratic opposition to policies of centralization was usually offered on the local and provincial levels by lords, provincial governors, etc. These were trying to remain relatively independent of the central authorities at the royal court through "personal" family cliques and intrigues. The second type of aristocratic opposition was usually organized on a national level in either the bureaucracy or different representative institutions. At this stage, the aristocracy became far more cohesive and organized—largely as a result of the activities of the centralized monarchies, and within their institutional frameworks.

The first type of aristocratic, feudal opposition to the basic premises of the bureaucratic polities caused, in many cases (e.g., Sassanid Persia, the disorganization or fall of the centralized polities.

The second type of opposition was adapted to the frameworks of the bureaucratic polities and usually did not have such far-reaching or direct results. When it was potent—e.g., in Prussia, and to some extent in Byzantium—the aristocracy generally was content to use it to change the internal balance of power in its own favor. However, the aristocracy's opposition to the rulers could also give rise to social and economic processes which might in turn lead to the disintegration or transformation of the bureaucratic polity. This occurred particularly when the aristocracy had developed into a relatively closed status group and tended to keep the free resources available to the rulers at a minimum, and to alienate the ruling elite from the groups constituting the major sources of these resources.

In Byzantium, the polity's gradual disintegration was related to the aristocracy's rising power and to the shrinking supply of free resources in the society ([L] *Ostrogorsky, 1956[a], 1956[b]; Charanis, 1951[b], 1953[a]; Lemerle, 1958*).

In France, the overthrow of the *ancien régime* was closely connected with the growing aristocratization of the monarchy and the upper bureaucracy, and with the "Aristocratic Reaction" that followed Louis XIV's death ([Y] *Ford, 1953; Pagès, 1928; Cobban, 1957[a]; Carré, 1890, 1920; Bloch, 1936; Egret, 1952, 1955*). In England—and to a smaller degree in Prussia and in Russia—the aristocracy became adapted to and identified with the premises of the bureaucratic polity and did not precipitate its disintegration ([Z] *Ashley, 1952; Plumb, 1950; Mamier, 1929, 1930, 1952; Mathew, 1948;* [S] *Lindsay, 1957[a];* [Z] *Brock, 1957; Habakkuk, 1953*). However, in Prussia the realignment of the aristocratic forces with the monarchy during the late eighteenth century resulted in freezing the social and political structures and in weakening of the polity. These conditions precipitated the reform movements which developed there during the late eighteenth and early nineteenth centuries ([X] *Rosenberg, 1958; Hintze, 1914, 1915; Bruford, 1935, 1957*).

[5] *The Place of the Religious and Cultural Groups in the Political Struggle*

A. THEIR COMPOSITION

The various religious and cultural groups and elites' hierarchy also participated in the political struggle. These groups and elites were composed mostly of the heads and staff of religious institutions; of the members of different religious, especially monastic or semi-monastic, orders; of the leaders of sects and religious movements; and, in some cases, of more charismatic personalities as well—though obviously their interests differed greatly from the interests of the members of the established churches and religious institutions.

Another branch of the cultural elites comprised the heads of institutions of higher learning, like universities or academies, which could be either affiliated with or independent of religious institutons. In many of the societies studied here, the religio-cultural elites were relatively well organized—often according to bureaucratic patterns.

In our discussion of the social prerequisites of bureaucratic societies, we noted the great significance of wider cultural orientations in the structures of these societies. These orientations and values, and the groups and elites which held them, fulfilled very important functions in the creation of these necessary conditions. They were the great potential allies of the ruling elites in the latter's endeavors to remain identified with the political and cultural systems and their symbols. Further, they usually were the chief connecting links between the local traditions of vast strata of the population and the "Great Tradition" of the cultural and political centers.

Because they occupied this position in the social and political structure, the religious and cultural groups were usually drawn into the political struggle, and they could be neither neglected nor ignored by most of the contending parties. As a rule, these contending parties depended greatly on the religious and cultural elites to be instrumental in propagating the legitimacy of their interests and for the effective communication and transmission of their respective symbols. Moreover, the religious leaders and institutions also constituted centers of economic and political power in their own right.

For these reasons, the cultural and religious elites were active participants in the political struggle in these societies. Changes in the balance of power between the king and the bureaucracy, or between the king and some aristocratic forces, were often concomitants of vicissitudes in the fortunes of various religious institutions or sects. In ancient Persia, some branches of the Mazdaist church were intimately related to the landed aristocracy and/or the king; and an intimate relation also existed between the Mazdakite movement and the middle and lower classes, and, to a smaller extent, the reforming kings ([G] *Christensen, 1936, ch. iii, vi, vii, 1939; Mole, 1953; Massé, 1952; Klima, 1957*).

In Byzantium, during the iconoclastic controversy (eighth and ninth centuries), the Church joined forces with many anti-monarchal and popular movements ([L] *Bréhier, 1899, 1904; Ostrogorsky, 1929[a], 1930[b]; Dvornik, 1948; Runciman, 1955; Jugie, 1941*). In China, the

Taoists and Buddhists allied with various courts and central bureaucratic cliques, and with several gentry and provincial groups ([I] *Gernet, 1956; Wright, 1959; Pulleyblank, 1955*). In the Spanish-American Empire, the Church and missions often formed alliances with different bureaucratic cliques, and, even more important, with some Indian communities ([R] *Haring, 1947, ch. x; Mörner, 1953; Hanke, 1937, 1949, 1951, 1952; Desdevises du Dezert, 1914, 1917; Zavala, 1943*). During the Reformation and religious wars of sixteenth-century Europe, very close relations existed there also among various social and political groups and religious sects *(Clark,* [S] *1929–59; 1957* [Z], *1955;* [Y] *Königsberger, 1955;* [S] *Jedin, 1955; Leonard, 1955; Orcibal, 1955*).

B. MAJOR POLITICAL AIMS OF THE RELIGIOUS GROUPS

The principal political interests and orientations of the religious and cultural elites within the framework of bureaucratic polities can be easily discerned. The religious group's first concrete objective (obviously derived from their basic values) was to gain full official recognition and protection from the state—if possible, as the established religion; or else as a secondary, recognized, and protected one.

The religious elite's second objective was to maintain its independence in the performance of its major functions in the society. This independence usually implied (1) the possibility for the religious group and institution to be autonomous in their internal government, organization of activities, and recruitment of members; (2) the establishment of their relative autonomy with regard to propagating of their creed and to maintaining shrines, temples, and educational institutions; and (3) independent determination and transmission of the major religious values and dogma. The religious groups demanded autonomy mainly from the ruling elite and the bureaucracy. As discussed earlier, the latter usually aspired to control the religious elite's activities and to incorporate them into the general framework of their administrative activities.

The third major objective of the religious elites was closely related to the first. This was to preserve and extend their material bases (i.e., property), and to enhance their general positions in the society.

At least some members of the religious elite had still a fourth objective. This was to obtain positions of political and, at times, administrative importance and influence. Aside from personal ambition, those who had this objective were motivated by: (1) the desire to serve as the rulers' and administrators' spiritual guides, thus securing and maintaining their loyalty to the religious elite's values and symbols; and (2) the wish to increase the political and economic power of the religious institutions and groups.

The rulers of many bureaucratic polities (and the rulers of other types of polity) often employed clergymen in political offices, for an obvious reason. Since the clergy had (especially in Roman Catholic nations) few family ties and obligations, it was considered to have minimal direct involvement with any given group, including the bureaucracy itself. However, this second assumption was not always substantiated by the facts. The extent of the clergy's identification with any specific group engaged in the political struggle varied greatly from one society to another. It depended chiefly on the nature and measure of the religious organization's participation in political struggle, and on the clergymen's family and local connections.

Among some branches of the religious groups and leaders, another type of objective also tended to develop. That goal was to transform some of the fundamental premises of the polity, and to establish new policies based on religious values and on the predominance of religious leaders and communities.

C. MEANS OF POLITICAL STRUGGLE OF THE RELIGIOUS GROUPS

The religious and cultural groups and classes waged their battles in different ways and different places within the society, and used different weapons in their struggles. Since they had strategic positions and society-wide organizations and functions, they could act both on the local provincial level and on the more central levels. Because they had access to, and close relations with, all the strata of the population, they could easily influence them politically and mobilize their support.

The members of the religious elites also could, just as easily approach the more central arenas of political struggle—the court and the higher echelons of the bureaucracy. They often had direct access to the ruler or his chief adviser. They themselves could serve as advisers, and were frequently appointed to high posts in the bureaucracy. Thus they had ample opportunity to participate in court cliques and struggles, and to have a voice in many political decisions.

The religious elites could also organize their own centers of power and propaganda—these, as a rule, were very powerful. The various academies in China or Byzantium provide good examples ([L] *Hussey, 1937; Fuchs, 1926;* [I] *Galt, 1951* passim; *Hucker, 1951, 1959[a]; Wilhelm, 1951*). Moreover, the clergy frequently founded, or participated in, various political organizations. They also were active in representative institutions—particularly in assemblies of estates, where the religious elites acted either as a separate estate or in conjunction with other estates.

The religious elites tended to use almost all available means of political struggle. However, they resorted—more frequently than any other group except, perhaps, the ruling elite—to propaganda, to recruiting "public opinion," to obtain support for their stands and policies. Churches and centers of learning originated such propaganda, while the local religious activities (churches, preachers, missionaries, etc.) often served as its active channels *(see, e.g.,* [L] *Hussey, 1937, 1957; Barker, 1957; Baynes, 1955;* [I] *Reischauer, 1955).* This propaganda had major significance as a channelizer of free-floating social and generalized political power. It could direct this power in accordance with or in opposition to the rulers' goals, or deflect it entirely from political goals ([G] *Christensen, 1936, especially ch. vi–viii, 1939).* Therefore, the cultural and religious elites competed strongly with the ruling elite for its control—and the latter always attempted to control the former's activities in the field of communication.

D. BASIC ATTITUDES OF THE RELIGIOUS GROUPS TO THE CENTRALIZED POLITIES

The religious elites had a great variety of political interests and activities. This fact naturally raises the question of their basic attitudes about the premises of the political systems of the historical bureaucratic empires.

At first glance, it appears impossible to draw any general conclusions about these attitudes. The religious groups and elites allied themselves with many different groups, and would very often transfer allegiance from one group to another in the same society. Superficially, it seems possible that they did not necessarily evince any clear, continuous, and stable political orientation at all. For example, in some cases they apparently utilized their close relations with other groups to intensify their own political identification with the rulers, and to create new potential reservoirs of generalized power; in other cases, they apparently did precisely the opposite.

In a sense, this assertion is valid. The values and orientations of the religious and cultural elites usually transcended any one group or regime; and, although these elites did participate in the political struggle of the bureaucratic societies, they did not necessarily have a fixed allegiance to any of the other participants in this struggle.

However, this view does not comprehend all the pertinent aspects of the matter. We must remember that the religious and cultural elites fulfilled vital functions, in the social and political systems of these

societies and in the legitimation of the rulers. Therefore, their fundamental attitudes to the political system and its symbols were very significant for the regime, and were necessarily closely related to the
values, orientations, and ideologies of their creeds.

The more that traditional, particularistic, and non-transcendental
elements were included in the orientations and value structures of the
religious and cultural elites, and the more these were organized in
ways emphasizing the fusion of religious and political roles, the less
able they were to generate the wider cultural orientations so closely
connected with the basic premises of the historical bureaucratic polities.
One important example of such religious organization was the Mazdaist
church in Persia, which featured many particularistic elements and
traditions, and was often the powerful ally of the more patrimonial or
feudal elements. Such religious elites usually promoted those aspects of
the rulers' legitimation that were based on traditional values and
orientations. In cases like these, the religious and cultural elites did not
provide very strong support for the bureaucratic polity; they did usually provide the basic traditional legitimation of the rulers.

However, in the more differentiated societies under consideration,
a much closer relation existed between the basic orientations of the
religious elites and the basic premises of the historical bureaucratic
political systems. The wider orientations and the strong emphasis on
performance propagated by the religious elites created some of the basic
resources needed by these political systems.

Thus in all of the societies studied, the religious elites both upheld
the traditional legitimation of the rulers and supported in principle
some of the best of their more flexible political orientations and policies—despite their numerous conflicts with the rulers above concrete
problems. These functions were performed for instance, by the Byzantine church, throughout most of its history (with the partial exception
of the periods of the iconoclastic wars), for the emperors ([L] *Gelzer,
1907; Grégoire, 1948; Baynes, 1955);* by the Catholic Church, for the
French (non-Protestant) kings; and by the Confucian scholars, through
their teachings and religious activities, for the Chinese rulers ([I]
*Kracke, 1953; H. Franke, 1953;[b]; DeBary, 1957; Nivison and Wright,
1959).* This kind of legitimation was symbolized by rituals, coronation,
special prayers for the monarch, etc. In the Spanish-American Empire,
the conquest was ideologically justified by the Bull of Pope Alexander
III. Throughout the existence of the Empire, the religious and coloniz-
ing activities of the Church and missions were very important ([R]
*Hanke, 1937, 1951; Mörner, 1953; Desdevises du Dezert, 1914, 1917;
Haring, 1947, ch. x).*

However, the close association between the religious organizations and the political regime did not imply that the former were always the mainstay of the latter. The actual political participations of the religious groups indicated that they could easily develop political orientations and activities detrimental to the regime. These possibilities were rooted in some basic characteristics of the religious organizations in these societies.

E. THE BASIC PATTERNS OF THE PARTICIPATION
OF THE RELIGIOUS GROUPS
IN THE POLITICAL STRUGGLE

In their actual participation in political struggle, the religious elites tended to exhibit all the important orientations possible to have toward the basic premises of their respective political systems.

PARTICIPATION IN LEGITIMATE POLITICAL STRUGGLE. In most of the countries studied, the religious groups' political participation was, at least for certain periods of time, contained well within the basic premises and the framework of the given bureaucratic polity. Then the religious groups advanced the development of legitimate political struggle within the society, thus contributing to its continuity. There are many examples of the religious groups' active participation in the institutional frameworks of their societies—the Mazdaist church's political participation and its co-operation with the rulers and with different social groups, in Persia; the Church's political activity and co-operation with other groups in the Byzantine Empire; and, especially, the Confucians' and the Buddhists' engaging in the political struggle of the Chinese Empire.

However, in a historical bureaucratic society, the religious organization could serve both as a mainstay of the existing political regime and as a focus of social change and political passivity—in the latter way, undermining the basic premises of the society's political system. In many cases, religious orders and groups identified themselves with reform movements in the society. Sometimes the established religion supplied the impetus toward, or at least the justification of, these reforms. In Moslem countries ([M] *Lewis, 1950, 1953;* [N] *Cahen, 1955[a], 1957[a], 1958–59;* [M] *Hodgson, 1960; Grunebaum, 1946, 1954, 1955[a], 1955[b]; Brockelmann, 1943*), in Reformation Europe, and in some of the activities in the Spanish-American Empire, religious groups were the starting points of political change ([S] *Clark, 1929–59, 1957; Jedin, 1955; Leonard, 1955; Orcibal, 1955;* [Y] *Königsberger, 1955*). Furthermore, in all these societies the religious groups and organizations could stimulate attitudes of political passivity that could deflect political support from the rulers.

There are three basic reasons why the religious organizations and orientations in these societies could serve as foci or starting points of radical changes and of political passivity. All three derive from fundamental characteristics of the religious organizations of the historical bureaucratic societies—i.e., the differentiation of the religious sphere, its relative autonomy, and its continuous interaction with the political sphere.

In most of the societies studied, the value systems of the major religions were sufficiently differentiated to contain a strong ingredient of universalistic and/or transcendental orientations. They thus constituted potential sources of autonomous orientations, of change, and of dissent.

The complicated bureaucratic character of many religious organizations, and the great importance of written tradition and its exegesis, were fertile grounds for the growth of sectarian movements and orders. These sects and orders emerged in all these societies—sometimes at the very center of the established church, sometimes on the periphery.

PARTICIPATION IN REBELLIONS AND MOVEMENTS OF CHANGE. In many of the societies studied, several religious bodies and organizations competed with one another for prominence in the society. Often— e.g., the cases of the Christian, Moslem, and Buddhist churches—the contending groups were supranational, and had continent-wide interest and orientations cutting across given territorial and political units. In all such cases, many sectarian groups and religious movements could develop those religious orientations, accentuating both the ideological and the political elements within them.

These factors frequently predisposed some of the religious groups and elites to develop more extreme political orientations and to participate in radical political and social movements; they also made other groups (or the same groups, under different circumstances) inclined to develop basic political passivity.

The latent predilection for change that characterized some of the religious institutions, orders, and groups explained their frequent participation in "radical" social and political movements—e.g., in peasant uprisings, and in urban movements and conspiracies. Cooperation between "popular" movements and leaders of religious secret societies was common in rebellions in China ([I] *Balázs, 1952; Shih, 1956; Levy, 1955),* and also, to some extent, in Byzantium, and in peasant uprisings in France ([L] *Barker, 1957, pp. 184–194; Charanis, 1940–41[b];* [G] *Christensen, 1936, ch. vii; Klima, 1957).*

In other cases—e.g., in the Moslem world, and in Reformation Europe—religious groups helped to create new types of dynamic political organization. Some examples are the various religious political parties, secret societies, or orders ([N] *Lewis, 1950, 1953; Caben,*

1958–59; [M] *Hodgson, 1960; Brockelman, 1943; Grunebaum, 1954,*
1955[a]; [L] *Barker, 1957, pp. 26–51; Hussey, 1957; Bréhier, 1950;*
[G] *Christensen, 1936, ch. ix, x; Ghirshman, 1954; Widengren, 1956).*

PARTICIPATION IN PROMOTION OF POLITICAL PASSIVITY. Religious
organizations also could influence processes of change in the political
system. They did so by instigating or furthering the withdrawal of
active social and political identifications from the ruling elites, and
by developing political passivity and indifference. They were able
to do so because frequently the main referent of social identification
they inspired was the religious, and not the political, community. Of
course, the creation of universal religious symbols and values furthered
the evolution of wider political identification and loyalty. In addition,
there was a partial identification of Church and state in several of the
historical bureaucratic societies—e.g., in Sassanid Persia, Byzantium,
and China. But even then, in so far as these religions were characterized
by autonomous institutions and independent religious values, identification with the religious community and with transcendental values,
as distinct from loyalty to the political community, could develop. This
could cut across political boundaries and/or emphasize the importance
of the continuity of the church or sect, despite its political vicissitudes.

This applies particularly to certain orders and sects, and sometimes
also to churches, that arose within the religious compass. These were
able to promote, during political adversity and decline, or through
alliance with aristocratic forces, a distinctly apolitical attitude. These
orders and sects thus severed, in effect, the relation between the religious and the secular political images of man, and emphasized the
inherent wickedness of the political order. In this way, they could deflect much potential social fervor from participating actively in the
political process. While the apolitical attitude often minimized the
participation of religious groups in open and active rebellions, it also
often deprived the rulers of the active support and identification that
they might need.

It is significant that, in many of the societies studied, there were
religious organizations and churches that outlived the polities to which
they were allied and in which they functioned. For instance, the Mazdaist church in Persia survived, in different forms, the Arab conquest;
and the Eastern Christian Church outlasted the Byzantine Empire.

F. THE PLACE OF SECULAR CULTURAL ELITES IN THE POLITICAL STRUGGLE

Our discussion has thus far been devoted largely to religious
elites—to which we sometimes appended "cultural," to imply that religious or semi-religious elites (like the Confucianists) fulfilled the

major cultural functions. However, in many of the societies studied (e.g., in Byzantium, Western Europe, and, to some extent, China), the cultural functions were also performed by other groups—including the professional groups and elites, and the "lay intelligentsia" that emerged in several societies. In some cases, the professional elites and the intelligentsia were relatively weak and had only secondary importance in the social and cultural structures. They often depended greatly on the ruling elite to provide their sustenance, and to permit them to pursue their interests and to work at their crafts.

However, in other cases (e.g., in Byzantium and Europe), the professionals and intelligentsia were more prominent and played crucial parts in the legitimation of the political system ([L] *Bréhier, 1950; Hussey, 1937, 1957; Diehl, 1929*). The legal profession, in particular, attained this prominence and importance, as we shall later discuss in further detail. The Confucian literati in China constituted a unique secular-religious elite with immense influence on the society's whole institutional structure.

There were also societies where groups of lay intelligentsia (e.g., the lay "philosophers" in the Spanish-American Empire, and Absolutist Europe's intelligentsia) were even more active in the social and political changes that occurred. Their part in effecting the changes and transformation of the ancient régime is well known ([U] *Sarrailh, 1951*; [S] *Beloff, 1954*; [Y] *Cobban, 1957[a]*; [S] *Hartung and Mousnier, 1955*; [Y] *Sagnac, 1945, 1946*; [R] *Haring, 1947, ch. xi, xii; Leonard, 1942; Moses, 1926; Ots Capdequi, 1946[a]; Parra, 1933; Spell, 1935; Whitaker, 1942*).

These intelligentsia often encouraged and initiated reforms in the cultural and value orientations of different strata. In addition to their direct creative activities in the cultural field, they also occasionally served as rallying centers of forces constituting potential sources of political change. This occurred particularly in societies whose universalistic orientations were being secularized.

But the secular intelligentsia was not invariably politically active in the historical-bureaucratic societies. Under some conditions, it exhibited a passive, apathetic attitude about political affairs that was parallel, although not similar, to that of the religious elite. This attitude derived from universalistic transcendental concepts and ideals, and developed under adverse conditions. It is best illustrated by the political indifference of the Hellenic philosophers and mystics, and of the Roman Stoics *(see, e.g., [Q] Jones, 1955)*.

The Confucian literati are unique among the various religious and secular elites discussed here. They constituted a traditional-secular elite with strongly religious backgrounds and orientations. They were oriented toward upholding a differentiated cultural tradition which was not a "natural" growth of a folk-society. It had, rather, been evolved and elaborated by groups with a strong literary tradition and highly developed and organized institutions. The Confucian literati formed a cultural group that was differentiated and developed, and, at the same time, was bound by its own particularistic traditional orientations. Though they constituted a very active cultural and political elite, they could not develop any political orientations transcending the political community. On the contrary, they provided the basic legitimation of the regime and set up the fundamental framework of political orientations and ideologies. In relation to the rulers, they often constituted a more conservative and restraining political element. The constant interplay between them and the rulers was a principal focus of internal Chinese history ([I] *Balász, 1952, 1959[a], 1960; Kaltenmark, 1959[a]; Nivison and Wright, 1959; De Bary, 1957; Liu, 1959[a], 1959[b]*).

G. THE RELATION OF THE POLITICAL ACTIVITIES OF THE RELIGIOUS AND CULTURAL GROUPS TO THE PREMISES OF THE POLITICAL SYSTEMS

On the basis of the foregoing analysis, we can summarize the place of the religious and cultural elites in the political processes of bureaucratic polities.

Despite—or, perhaps, because of—their crucial position, the political orientations and concrete activities of the religious groups and elites were neither fixed nor homogeneous. Even when they were adherents of the same religion, they varied from place to place and from period to period. They ranged from being conservative, supporting existing rulers, and engaging in the concrete political game in process in a given polity, to withdrawing support, and exhibiting political apathy, and even encouraging participation in reform movements.

The problematic nature of cultural and religious groups and institutions was caused by the fact that, although they performed important regulative functions in polity and created some prerequisites for its development, their basic referent was not the polity as such. Their activities were primarily oriented toward their own specific values and toward the religious community, and both of these often transcended, or aimed to transform, the polity.

The religious groups did contribute, through developing various free-floating orientations, to the perpetuation of the bureaucratic polity's basic premises. At the same time, however, their activities could become detrimental to this continuity, either by deflecting potential support from the rulers or by becoming foci of processes of transformation and change in the systems.

[6] The Place of the Professional Elites
in the Political Struggle

A. THEIR COMPOSITION

Let us now discuss briefly the places different professional elites occupied in the political struggles of bureaucratic societies.

As we have observed, professional elites emerged in several of the societies studied. They were composed of a number of groups, whose respective importance varied in different societies, as did the importance of professional elites in general. Usually their most important members were those connected with the legal profession—judges, arbitrators, lawyers, and heads and staffs of legal academies.

The legal profession and its affiliates flourished in Byzantium ([L] *Bréhier, 1949[b], 1950; Zacharia von Lingenthal, 1892*), Absolutist Europe, and the Spanish-American Empire ([Y] *Sagnac, 1945, 1946; Ford, 1953; Barber, 1955;* [S] *Beloff, 1954;* [U] *Desdevises du Dezert, 1925, 1927;* [X] *Hintze, 1907;* [R] *Haring, 1947*). The autonomous organization of jurists was especially prominent in England ([Z] *Mathew, 1948; Trevelyan, 1944; Namier, 1929, 1930; Plumb, 1950; Ashley, 1952; Holdsworth, 1938; Clark, 1955; Davies, 1937*). In some societies—e.g., in China ([I] *Balázs, 1954[c]*), and, to some extent, in Byzantium—the majority of its members were in the government's employment. In these cases, their work in the legal departments, academies, and schools was their only means of evolving some measure of internal cohesion.

In China, and to a lesser degree in the Sassanid Empire as well ([G] *Christensen, 1936, pp. 300 ff.*), some legal specialists also served as informal arbitrators and mediators in urban and rural districts. They did not develop any marked professional ideology and were not organized in specific professional groups.

In other societies, however, members of the legal profession were organized more autonomously—in their own colleges and associations, which exerted a great deal of influence on, and acted within, the framework of governmental institutions. Thus members of the legal profession were prominent in the committees of notables in France, the Spanish-American Empire, and England. Their predominance was smaller, though still marked, in Byzantium.

The second major professional elite was the medical one. As a rule, doctors also were organized in colleges and associations supervised, in different measures, by the state. Medical colleges and associations existed in rudimentary form in the Sassanid Empire ([G] *Christensen, 1936, especially ch. ii; Ghirshman, 1954*) and evolved somewhat more in China ([I] *Balázs, 1954[a]*). They were far more organized in Byzantium ([L] *Bréhier, 1950; Grumel, 1949; Hussey, 1937*), Western Europe, and the Spanish-American Empire, where they were also affiliated with the universities and academies ([Y] *Barber, 1955; Sagnac, 1945, 1946;* [U] *Sarrailh, 1951;* [S] *Lindsay, 1957[a];* [R] *Haring, 1947*).

At times, architects, astronomers, and other types of practitioners and experts were considered as professional elites. However, their importance and consequence in the society were minor, and their organizations were usually much weaker.

In general, in many of the societies studied here (e.g., Persia and China), the professional groups were relatively weak and their development was arrested in the embryonic stage. Their degree of autonomy and their potential power were limited, and they were subservient to the bureaucracy, to the religious elites, or to both.

However, in Western Europe, the Spanish-American Empire, and (somewhat) in Byzantium, the professional groups were more fully developed. They were more differentiated from other groups, had more autonomy, and exerted greater political influence ([Y] *Sagnac, 1945, 1946; Lough, 1954, 1960;* [S] *Lindsay, 1957[a];* [Y] *Barber, 1955; Ford, 1953;* [Z] *Mathew, 1948; Davies, 1937; Clark, 1955;* [R] *Haring, 1947*).

B. THE POLITICAL GOALS OF THE PROFESSIONAL ELITES AND THEIR RELATIONS TO THE BASIC PREMISES OF THE POLITICAL SYSTEMS

What were the professional group's major political aims and orientations? Initially, we must point out that they had some resemblance to, but were often more limited than, the goals and orientations of the religious elites.

The concrete objectives of professional groups focused on attaining relative autonomy, extending the scope of their activities, and insuring their status positions and remunerations, and economic security. In societies where they were stronger and more autonomous, they tried also to establish and maintain their own self-government, their own independent supervision of internal affairs, and their determination of the criteria of admission to the profession.

To implement their objectives, the professions often allied themselves with parts of the cultural elites—particularly with the centers of learning and the universities. They frequently demanded autonomy in the name of wider values and symbols. Thus, in Byzantium, the legal profession joined forces with wider cultural groups in the various cultural-political trends emerging around the University ([L] *Hussey, 1937; Fuchs, 1926; Barker, 1957, Introduction*). In France, members of the legal profession were closely allied with the *parlements;* and, during the eighteenth century, they participated somewhat in the salons and intellectual movements.

This brings us to the problem of the basic attitude that the professional groups had toward the premises of centralized bureaucratic polities. The professions' functions were always somewhat technical and derived from the fundamental premises of the institutional and power structures in which they themselves were not the most powerful element. This is best illustrated by the case of the legal profession. Unlike many religious and cultural elites, the legal profession was highly dependent on the institutional framework provided by the state for carrying on the majority of its activities; and it did not always have immanent orientations transcending the community and polity. However, when the legal profession was more autonomous, it was able to evolve an orientation and loyalty to general, sometimes universalistic, principles inherent in the legal system. In such situations, its proximity to the central ruling elite, and its orientations toward the universalistic aspects of law, enabled some branches of the legal profession to perform a somewhat independent role in, and to exert some independent influence on, the institutional structure of the society. This was the case of the jurists in England, and, to a smaller extent, in France, the Spanish-American Empire, and the Byzantine Empire ([Y] *Sagnac, 1945, 1946*).

The relative power position of any one of these professional elites, and its amount of active participation in the political process, depended on many factors. In general, these were: the extents of its own autonomy and wider social orientations; the strength, composition, and value orientations of the various cultural elites and "lay intelligentsia"; and the more active social strata. In so far as the value orientations of the predominent cultural elites were strongly bound by tradition, in so far as the structure of the religious elite was relatively monolithic, and in so far as these elites' relations with the ruling elite were peaceful and co-operative—the power and influence of the professional elites were limited, even though they might have some autonomy in their own fields.

On the other hand, when active social groups existed who were characterized by a more independent political attitude, some parts of the legal professions might join them, and might even form the vanguard of their struggle. Thus the magistrates and *parlements* in France became involved in the political struggle between the Jesuits and the adherents of Gallicanism, and in the "Aristocratic" Reaction in the eighteenth century. The role of the judges in the political struggles in England between the parliament and the king is too well known to require amplification.

The possibility that the professional, and especially the legal, elites could become more widely politically active was latent in some of the inherent orientations of the more flexible legal systems, and in the professional groups' place in the social and political systems of their societies.

The professional groups' identification with the basic premises of these systems was thus often great. However, it did not necessarily entail their identifying with the actual scope of political and administrative regulation, or with the aspirations of the political rulers and administrations to extend such scope. On the contrary, the legal elites frequently championed the more autonomous social-regulative mechanisms—especially those of autonomous legal arrangements and of market activities—and attempted to formalize legal rights that could insure the functioning of these mechanisms. Because of this, they often participated in political activities and movements whose objectives were to secure basic political rights and to widen political participation. Under some conditions, they even became foci or symbols (as in England) of such activities and struggles ([Z] *Davies, 1937; Clark, 1955; Ashley, 1952*).

The professional groups' principal political orientations and attitudes, and their structural positions in the society, also determined the arenas and channels in and through which they engaged in political struggle. By virtue of their structural proximity to the centers of political power, they concentrated their political activities chiefly in the more central arenas of political struggle—e.g., the court, the bureaucratic juridical institutions, and, in some cases, the semi-representative juridical institutions like the French *parlements*. When they participated in local affairs, they conducted their struggle (which, at this level, was focused on problems of the autonomy of professional associations) primarily in the municipal institutions.

When it happened that members of professional groups overstepped their professional confines, they participated in more dynamic types of political organization—e.g., social and political movements, and semi-party organizations—as well.

[7] The Place of the Urban Economic and Social Group in the Political Struggle

A. THEIR COMPOSITION

We shall now consider the political orientations and objectives of the urban groups which were, in varying measures, active in the political struggle of bureaucratic societies.

The three major specific urban groups were: (1) the middle-class elements, like merchants, bankers, financiers, manufacturers, and artisans; (2) many upper rural groups (e.g., the gentry in China, members of the equestrian order in Rome, or the rich peasants in Byzantium) who dabbled in finance and trade, were both interested in and connected with urban centers, and lived in the cities at least part of the year; (3) the lower and unsettled groups of the urban population—the different parts of the urban proletariat ([S] *Labrousse, 1955;* [Y] *Coornaert, 1941; Mousnier, 1955;* [R] *Haring, 1947, ch. ix; Bagu, 1949*).

The numerical strength of the urban population was different in each of these societies; but it was predominant in none of them. These societies were all predominantly agricultural. Nevertheless, the cities were a major factor in their economic, social, and political structures.

The various types of social organizations—like guilds, merchant associations, and cultural associations—developed chiefly in the cities. Since urban groups were located at the center of social, cultural, and political activities and were closely associated with various elites and professions, they could exert influence out of proportion to their numerical strength within the population. The purely economic urban groups—artisans, merchants, and manufacturers—could sometimes be influential in fields which apparently did not directly concern them. Also, they could become organized into wider social strata with articulated political consciousness, and, at times, even engage in intensive and organized political activity of their own.

Except in Western Europe, the urban groups (unlike the political elite or the aristocracy) were rarely independent forces during the formative stages of these societies. However, during and after the societies' formation, they frequently contributed to the evolution of the institutional framework of the bureaucratic society. Their structural positions often placed the urban groups among the most influential and important groups in the society.

The development of the bureaucratic polity and administration created conditions conducive to the expansion of certain pursuits of different urban groups. Often, the rulers, by opening new horizons of economic expansion and growth of international trade, by establishing bureaucratic organization, and by pursuing political goals, enabled and encouraged urban groups to expand their activities. In some cases (e.g., in Western and Central Europe), the rulers of bureaucratic polities even tried to compel the cities to become a part of these wider political frameworks, and adjusted—and, consequently, changed—their economic activities and social and political orientations accordingly.

B. MAJOR POLITICAL GOALS OF THE URBAN GROUPS

The most important political orientations, concrete issues, and demands of the urban strata were the following:

1. They demanded that the rulers minimize and regulate the taxes levied from them, and themselves tried to obtain economic allocations from the government, in the forms of contracts, subsidies, materials, and manpower.

2. The urban groups often tried to influence the general trend of the rulers' economic policies in favor of a given group or aspect of economic activity. The most recurrent examples of this issue were the controversies concerning protected *vs.* free foreign trade, and concerning price regulation and control *vs.* free internal trade.

3. The urban groups wanted efforts made to promote their wider interests in economic development and expansion, and in maintaining their own ways of life.

4. Various urban groups—including guilds, merchant associations, and sometimes entire municipalities—endeavored to retain their autonomy and self-rule, defending these against the encroachments of the political elites. They also attempted to prevent the ruling elite from regulating the recruitment and supervision of their members and from controlling their economic activities and internal affairs. The urban groups wished to secure the possibility of establishing wider urban self-government and political autonomy, and the maintenance and enhancement of their status. In this context, the many endeavors made by the urban groups to establish and continue their own educational institutions, or to influence those major educational institutions established by the rulers, are significant.

Obviously, the different urban groups did not necessarily share the same interests and orientations. There were repeated divergences, and even conflicts—between small and big merchants, between manufacturers and labourers and handworkers, etc. The urban proletariat often rebelled against the patricians and the guilds, while different associations and guilds frequently competed with one another. In so far as the urban groups' claims to autonomy were oriented also toward exerting influence in the municipal government, any emergence of conflicting claims would facilitate the rulers' extension of their power and scope of regulation.

An additional fundamental social and political objective of the urban groups was that of insuring that they would have widespread possibilities of social, economic, and political mobility, and access to elite positions.

These issues were set within the basic framework of the rulers' policies. In addition, the urban groups sometimes evolved political orientations, and supported political positions, that transcended this framework. The most important among these were:

1. The urban groups' attempts to attain an authorized position, in the political institutions, in the processes of decision- and policy-making

2. Their efforts to influence the general formulation and execution of policies

3. Their attempts, on both local and central levels, to strengthen their status position by obtaining official recognition of hereditary, semi-hereditary, or oligarchic status criteria, and thus to attain a recognized, sanctioned place in the political structure

4. Their trying to effect changes in the structures of the political institutions, and to influence the determination of the basic criteria of social stratification and political participation

5. Their furthering the scopes of various autonomous mechanisms at the expense of explicit political and bureaucratic regulations

The various urban groups' evolution of these orientations was related to their active and intensive participation in political affairs and their generation of specific, highly differentiated forms of political organization. The urban groups' political activities could develop in two diametrically opposed directions.

First, the development could go in a conservative, traditional direction, occasioning the limitation of the scope of universalistic criteria and reinforcing the ascriptive foundations of the society. This kind of tendency was evinced, as a rule, by urban groups—and especially upper urban patriciates—chiefly interested in enchancing and maintaining their own positions, privileges, and independence. Such reactionary urban patriciates existed in seventeenth- and eighteenth-century France ([Y] *Sagnac, 1945, 1946; Ford, 1953; Barber, 1955)*, in the Spanish-American Empire ([R] *Haring, 1947, ch. xii; Borah, 1956)*, and, to a certain extent, in Byzantium. In all these societies, several upper urban bourgeois groups tried to acquire high, and in some measure hereditary, status by exerting organized political pressure on the central authorities. In order to do so, the bourgeois groups frequently became allied with aristocratic elements. This type of alliance existed, for instance, in the case of the upper urban classes in Byzantium ([L] *Ostorgorsky, 1956[a]; Diehl, 1929*); it is also manifested by the relation between upper urban groups and the various aristocratic groups in seventeenth- and eighteenth-century France ([Y] *Ford, 1953; Pagès, 1928; Barber, 1955; Coornaert, 1941*).

In addition, many lower urban groups often participated in uprisings, rebellions, and demonstrations. In this way, they formed starting points or incubators of many processes of change.

The second direction that could be taken by the participation of urban groups in the central political struggle was oriented toward furthering the development of social differentiation, of free-floating economic and political power, of the range of autonomous regulative mechanisms and of broader scope of political participation.

As a rule, these wider orientations and activities evolved when the purely economic urban groups united with various other active groups —like the religious, cultural, intellectual, and professional elites—and formed a wider, more flexible stratum. When this occurred—as it did to some extent in the Abbaside Empire ([N] *Cahen, 1953; 1955[a], 1958–59*) and in Byzantium ([L] *Bratianu, 1938; Ostrogorsky, 1956[a]; Diehl, 1924; Hussey, 1957; Manojlovic, 1936;* [R] *Haring, 1947*), and especially in France and England—the urban groups had, in effect, come out of their local environments, greatly increased their country-wide contacts, and become oriented to, and continuously active in, country-wide political institutions ([Y] *Barber, 1955;* [S] *Labrousse, 1955; Beloff, 1954;* [Y] *Pagès, 1928; Ford, 1953;* [U] *Desdevises du Dezert, 1925, 1927; Sarrailh, 1951; Ortiz, 1955;* ([Z] *Clark, 1955; Mathew, 1948*). These developments naturally engendered clashes among various urban strata. The internal cohesions of individual cities and of their local institutions were replaced by wider associations and organizations that cut across particular municipalities and urban groups.

C. THE MAIN ARENAS OF THE POLITICAL STRUGGLE OF THE URBAN GROUPS

We may now consider the main arenas in which the urban groups conducted their political struggle and activities, and these groups' main types of political organization.

The first such arena comprised local settings and offices of the bureaucracy, where the urban groups could influence the execution of policies and gain various favors.

The second arena consisted of divers institutions of municipal self-government, that the urban groups endeavored to maintain and utilize as weapons in their struggles with the rulers.

The third arena comprised the circles close to the ruler, the upper political elite, and the groups of actual decision- and policy-makers, that the urban groups tried to infiltrate or influence. Within this arena, various individuals and families endeavored to attain and occupy important political positions, either ministerial or advisory.

The fourth arena was the bureaucracy. The urban groups attempted to be admitted to it and wished, if possible, to monopolize its important offices. They would then be in a position to influence the formulation and execution of policies.

The fifth arena was composed of social movements and organized political pressure groups. These constituted a wider and more heterogeneous type of political organization, one not confined only to local issues.

The sixth arena (existing mainly in the close relation to the fifth) comprised various representative or semi-representative institutions.

These last two arenas lead us to the problem of the types of political organization developed by the urban groups.

Some of the organizational types were at times specific to the urban population. The most interesting of these are probably the Byzantine circus parties, and the parallel organizations which existed in many other cities (e.g., in some Hellenistic cities). However, the expressly political types of organization (i.e., political clubs and rudimentary political parties) that evolved in the urban centers of Europe and the Spanish-American Empire were even more significant.

The extent to which these different arenas were employed varied greatly from one society to another. It was largely determined (as we shall see in greater detail in Chapter 9) by the strength, internal cohesion, organization, and economic resources of the urban groups, and by their interrelations with other elites. In Persia and China, and in smaller measure in the Byzantine and Spanish-American empires, the urban groups' political struggles and organizations were generally only local. The urban groups in Byzantium (through participating in the circus parties), and even more so in Europe, managed, by extending their contacts with the cultural elites and the intelligentsia, to generate more articulated and dynamic forms of political orientation and activity.

D. THE RELATION OF THE POLITICAL ACTIVITIES OF THE URBAN GROUPS TO THE BASIC PREMISES OF THE POLITICAL SYSTEMS

In summary, the urban groups' main relations and orientations toward the basic premises of the bureaucratic polities and toward their rulers' policies were as follows. The full development of the urban groups was, to some extent, contingent on the institutional frameworks established by the rulers and by their policies. On the other hand, the urban groups were a major mainstay of bureaucratic polities.

The urban groups' activities were crucial in the generation of the conditions favorable to the expansion and institutionalization of the chief characteristics of the historical bureaucratic polities. They provided many of the resources—finances, manpower, and political support—on which these bureaucratic polities depended. In addition, the institutional frameworks of these polities were usually conducive to the development of the activities of many urban groups. Also, the bureaucratic administration offered them opportunities to advance, thus fostering their mobility aspirations.

Moreover, the political attitudes of these groups were often permeated with wider orientations and universalistic values. They often found the institutional framework of the bureaucratic polity congenial, with its emphasis on developing free resources.

Obviously, the urban groups actually developed these various attitudes toward the basic premises of the bureaucratic polity to a different extent in each society. Also, such attitudes were usually characteristic of the more active urban groups. These groups had wider interests and orientations, came in closer contact with different elites and professions, and participated in expressly political movements. As a rule, the lower groups—e.g., the small artisans, seasonal laborers, and urban proletariat—evinced far more passive orientations. They did not achieve any notable degree of political articulation—except in secret societies and uprisings, insurrections and rebellions.

But this *potential* great convergence between the political orientations of the more active urban groups and the basic premises of the bureaucratic polity did not mean that the former invariably complied with the concrete details of the rulers' policies—or even with the principles of political participation—in any given state. The latent possibility that the urban elements might oppose the basic premises of the political system of the historical bureaucratic societies was rooted in several factors. The urban elements tended to foster the scope of their own autonomous regulative mechanisms—especially that of self-government. The urban groups also wished to maintain various economic mechanims and autonomous activities, and often in opposition to the wish of the rulers and the bureaucracy to extend the range of the political regulative mechanisms. This possibility of the opposition was noted also by the fact that the universalistic orientation of the urban groups could transcend the institutional frameworks of the historical bureaucratic polity.

The interests and orientations of the urban groups and the policies and objectives of the rulers were irreconcilably opposed in two instances. The first irreconcilable incompatibility emerged whenever the urban groups limited their concerns to local problems and did not participate in or take interest in the wider frameworks that the rulers wished to further. Such apathy, on the part of groups which were among the major potential providers of resources for the political institutions, could have significant repercussions on the stability and development of these polities.

The second incompatibility emerged when some urban groups—especially, in conjunction with some elites—became important centers of an intensive political struggle for enlarging the scope of political participation and/or the range of autonomous regulative mechanisms. In such a situation, the various urban groups, when they had managed to overcome—at least temporarily—some of their internal differences, and to unite and co-operate with other active groups, could easily have evolved into bearers of social change and political reform.

[8] The Place of the Gentry in the Political Struggle

The last entries on our list of possible participants in the political struggle in bureaucratic societies are the non-aristocratic rural groups, namely, the gentry and the peasantry.

A. COMPOSITION OF THE GENTRY

The category of landed strata included—placed between the aristocracy and the peasantry, or in the peasantry—the various gentry groups. Members of the gentry may be defined as the more prosperous peasants, or as the smaller landlords, who were somewhat related to aristocratic groups but comparatively independent of them. They generally consisted of middle-range proprietors, *rentiers,* and landlords. Their interests in the land were at least partly commercial, and they were inclined to be strongly market oriented. As a rule, these groups were not restricted by the legal limitations imposed on other parts of the peasantry.

Apparently the gentry in Sassanid Persia—that is, the Dekhans—had some, albeit limited, importance. In Byzantium, many groups of upper peasants arose, though they were not always fully differentiated from other, lower peasant groups ([G] *Christensen, 1936, ch. ii; Altheim and Stiehl, 1954; Stein, 1928*). They emerged especially after the reforms of Heraclius in the seventh century, and survived throughout Byzantine history—though they began to decline in the eleventh century, and slowly but surely continued to decline ([L] *Guilland, 1953–55; Ostrogorsky, 1956[a]; 1956[b]; Vasiliev, 1952; Charanis, 1951[a], 1953[a], 1953[b]; Bréhier, 1927–29*).

In the Spanish-American Empire, the gentry comprised low- and middle-range *encomienderos* and the heads of Indian villages ([R] *Gibson, 1955; Zavala, 1936[a], 1943, 1949; Haring, 1947; Miranda, 1941–42; Konetzke, 1951[a], 1952, 1953*).

In France, from the fourteenth century on, many groups of wealthy peasants emerged and became an important feature of the rural situation. However, they did not always prosper—as evinced by their plight during the eighteenth century—nor did they necessarily constitute a discrete stratum ([Y] *Sagnac, 1945, 1946; Goubaert, 1956*).

Only the Chinese and the English gentry succeeded in attaining significant political prominence. In China, approximately from the Han Dynasty (206 B.C.–A.D. 221) onward, a class of gentry developed that dominated the rural setting and executed most tasks of local government. Also, most of the officials were drawn from this class. In England, the gentry (e.g., the "local" non-aristocratic landholders) emerged as an important stratum largely in the later Tudor period; and since then, they have played an important part in the nation's political life ([Z] *Tawney, 1954, Trevor-Roper, 1953; Campbell, 1945; Clark, 1955; Davies, 1937; Ashley, 1952; Hughes, 1952*). Although they were initially closely related to the aristocracy, during the sixteenth century they began to emerge as the backbone of rural life and of agricultural economic entrepreneurship.

B. THE POLITICAL ACTIVITIES OF THE GENTRY AND THEIR RELATION TO THE BASIC PREMISES OF THE POLITICAL SYSTEMS

The gentry's interests and political orientations were complex. They evinced several aristocratic tendencies and aspirations, and might ally themselves with various aristocratic groups or become aristocratized. However, the aristocracy were inclined to encroach on the gentry's landholdings and social and political positions and, as a rule, endeavored to maintain the aristocracy as occupying a higher stratum, from which they preferred to exclude the gentry. Only in exceptional cases —such as post-eighteenth-century Prussia—did there emerge some basic identity of the gentry's and the aristocracy's interests. However, this was occasioned and facilitated by the "taming" of the aristocracy effected by the rulers.

The gentry characteristically had a comparatively strong market orientation, interests in money rents and in various commercial pursuits, and latent rivalry with the aristocracy. These qualities generally predisposed the gentry in favor of the basic premises of bureaucratic polities and of those policies of the rulers that tended to support trade relations and to strengthen the positions of middle-status groups. Moreover, the gentry often derived direct benefit from the development of the bureaucracy, because its members occupied various positions within it.

Thus the gentry usually had good cause to support the rulers and their centralizing policies, and in many cases it was among their chief mainstays. We have noted how the rulers in Byzantium, China, the Spanish-American Empire, France, and England endeavored to establish and further gentry groups. So long as these endeavors were successful, the rulers usually enjoyed the gentry's loyalty, and benefited from its economic and manpower resources and from its important contributions in the field of rural local government. The gentry, combined with the wealthier independent smaller peasants, determined the supply of various free resources by the agricultural economic sector. If these two groups were allowed to maintain their independent positions and economic activities and were able to set the social and cultural tone of the countryside, the rulers could be more or less certain of receiving adequate economic and manpower resources, cultural identification, and political support. Hence, a decline of the gentry and upper peasant group often reflected either the shrinkage of resources or the complete transformation of the political system.

Basically, the gentry's principal political activities and orientations were similar to those of the urban groups. They were concentrated on attaining social and economic benefits, influencing the government's economic policies to attain positions within political institutions in their favor, and maintaining some measure of autonomy in local self-government. As a rule, the gentry waged its campaigns either on the local level (in institutions of local government, through contact with local officials, etc.), or at the center (through bureaucratic court cliques and in the main bureaus). However, the gentry's participation in social and political movements was, on the whole, less intensive and continuous than that of several urban groups. Members of the gentry engaged in wider social and political movements only under relatively exceptional circumstances. Even in China and England, where the gentry managed to establish wider and more central contacts, only some very select members succeeded in penetrating into the central bureaucratic, political, and cultural groups; the majority remained within the boundaries of their localities. Within these boundaries, they organized, conducted, and maintained various types of social, cultural, and religious activities and organizations. In these ways, they could also advance some of the wider cultural and political orientations within their respective local settings.

However, because of their structural position and their vested interests in landed property, the gentry's basic political attitude within the framework of bureaucratic polities was usually relatively conservative. When this conservative attitude led them to join forces with the aristocracy or to allow it to subjugate them by their becoming its retainers (as in later Byzantium), the gentry sometimes became the targets of peasant uprisings—in which some members of the gentry sometimes participated as leaders. On the other hand, under certain circumstances, the gentry evinced more radical tendencies, allied themselves with the more extremist elements of the urban groups and the religious elite, and participated actively in political movements. Such cases, although very rare, were manifestations of the more dynamic potential of gentry groups.

[9] *The Place of the Peasantry in the Political Struggle*

A. COMPOSITION OF THE PEASANTRY

Numerically, the middle and lower peasant groups were the largest part of the rural population.

In none of the societies studied here did the strictly rural non-gentry constitute a homogeneous stratum. If we ignore the merely local variations and differences, we can distinguish three major peasant groups: (1) the relatively free peasants, proprietors of some landholdings; (2) the types of dependent peasants, e.g., serfs and (3) the expropriated and unattached agricultural laborers. In the historical bureaucratic polity, the peasantry probably carried the greatest burdens of taxation and of military mobilization. At the same time, it was, as a rule, politically the most passive and inarticulate, and the least organized, stratum. Although intensive internal political activities might be conducted in each village or groups of villages, these activities were largely isolated and insulated from the central political processes of the society. Through many generations, these villages were the strongholds and the perpetuators of the various "Little Traditions." In some cases, the peasantry provided personnel for lower local services—particularly for the lower echelons of the bureaucracy and the army, and for the secondary officers of the local government.

The peasantry became politically active only rarely. Even when it did, it did not usually become active independently, but mostly in conjunction with other groups and strata, like the army or religious movements.

As discussed earlier, in the bureaucratic societies the ruling elites' policies showed great preoccupation with the social and economic status and activities of the peasantry. However, the rulers' efforts to promote the peasantry's welfare were not always successful; and the rulers often yielded to the demands of the landed aristocracy.

Within the frameworks of the rulers' policies and their vacillations, the political orientations and attitudes of the peasantry developed. Their principal objectives were usually the following:

1. To ease the burden of taxation, whether imposed by feudal lords or by the state

2. To buttress their relative economic independence by protecting their property against encroachments by large land-owners

3. To attain personal freedom and abolish their servile status

4. To maintain somewhat independent cultural traditions and some amount of rural and group autonomy of self-government, against the infringements both of the bureaucracy and of centralized and unifying religious organization

5. To be represented in the government organs, in the army, and especially in local government (This aim was rather vague and comparatively inarticulated among most peasant groups.)

In some exceptional cases—e.g., in France on the eve of the Revolution, and in England—certain peasant groups engaged in articulated and politically organized social movements and organizations, directed toward the realization of political objectives and toward reforming the allocations of political rights and representation. (*On France, see* [Y] *Sagnac, 1946; Egret, 1955; On England, see* [Z] *Tawney, 1912, 1954; Trevor-Roper, 1953; Davies, 1937; Clark, 1955.*) The peasants frequently participated in religious and semi-religious movements, secret societies, and cults with some indirect political bearing—e.g., in China and in Sassanid Persia.

They often took part in rebellions, and sometimes even inaugurated them, under the leadership either of their own people or of alienated bureaucrats, gentry, or religious leaders. The numerous peasant uprisings in China provide probably the best-known example, but similar, although perhaps less organized and articulated, rebellions broke out in all the societies studied. (*For China, see, e.g.,* [I] *Balázs, 1948, 1950; Shih, 1956; Levy, 1956; Eichhorn, 1954.*)

The main foci and arenas of the peasants' political activities were:

1. Local government offices, wherein the peasantry attempted to influence the execution of various policies (especially those concerning

taxation and manpower mobilization) by exerting pressure on local officials

2. Less frequently, central government organs, where the peasant groups aired their grievances and endeavored to influence policy-making in general, and that concerning problems of maintaining the free independent peasantry in particular

3. Circus parties and other political organizations, in which the peasants and rural elements participated but were not of primary importance

4. The army, which in some cases—like Rome and Byzantium—provided the peasants with the opportunity to assert themselves

The peasants had several weapons at their disposal. These included:

1. Turning to large land-owners for protection, and thus both depriving the state of their manpower and taxes, and withdrawing their military and agricultural services. Although this was primarily a passive resistance, it was the peasantry's chief weapon and, in the long run, its use had major repercussions on the structure of the society

2. Participating in uprisings and rebellions, which were very frequent in most of the societies studied. These uprisings constituted the most specific form of articulation of any potential dynamic political attitude of the peasantry

3. Engaging in wider, well-organized social and political movements, organizations, and parties—as the peasantry did, e.g., in France and England. This weapon, however, was rarely employed by the peasant groups

B. THE RELATION OF THE POLITICAL ACTIVITIES OF THE PEASANTRY TO THE BASIC PREMISES OF THE POLITICAL SYSTEMS

The peasantry's basic attitudes and relations to the premises of the historical bureaucratic polities were extremely unstable, and were far more contingent on vacillations of the rulers' policies than were those of any other group within the society. On the whole, the peasantry identified themselves with the rulers and their policies, so long as the rulers endeavored to promote the peasantry's economic, and their relatively limited and inarticulate political, interests.

To the degree that the rulers' efforts failed and the peasantry's interests were neglected, the peasants increased their passivity and indifference toward wider political issues and toward the symbols and policies of the rulers of centralized bureaucratic polities. The peasants would instigate or participate in uprisings and rebellions, or else transfer their allegiance to landed aristocrats, feudal and semi-feudal elements, and provincial and local symbols. In some exceptional cases, they also participated in radical, reform-oriented movements.

However, the peasantry rarely constituted an active and independent factor in the processes of internal change and transformation of these societies. They were a neutral element, which rarely had recourse to organized political activity, and had such recourse largely, when it was dictated by active elements.

The largest and economically fundamental stratum within the bureaucratic societies was thus both politically inarticulate and basically neutral or indifferent to the key premises of these polities. Obviously, the fact is of great consequence for the understanding of the conditions of stability and change in such societies. The peasantry's apathy greatly limited the processes of social and economic differentiation, restricted the availability of free resources, and circumscribed the extent of power generalization possible in these societies.

[10] The Major Types of Political Orientations of the Principal Groups and Strata and Their Relations to the Basic Premises of the Political Systems

What were the principal attitudes of the various strata toward the basic premises of the bureaucratic polities and toward the rulers' policies? We may distinguish, on the basis of the material presented above, four such principal attitudes.

The first attitude was evinced chiefly by the aristocracy. It was one of opposition to the polity's basic premises, and was manifested mainly in attempts to diminish the free-floating resources and to lower the level of generalized power in the polity.

The second attitude was passivity toward these premises—an attitude of "empirical" adaptation to the demands of the administration and central authorities. This attitude was most evinced by the peasants, and frequently by other groups interested only in maintaining their own limited local autonomy and their immediate economic interests.

The third attitude was most prevalent in the bureaucracy, and in parts of the urban groups and the professional and cultural elites (with the partial exception of elements of the last). It consisted of their basic identification with the premises of the given bureaucratic system, and their willingness to fight for their interests within its framework and to channelize their own power potential *within* the framework of existing political institutions and of policies set up by the rulers.

The fourth attitude was most developed among the more differentiated urban groups and elites. It favored changes in extending the range of political participation beyond the premises of the more differentiated groups. This attitude was manifested by attempts to alter the basic premises and values of the system, to widen the patterns of political participation within it, and/or to find referents of political orientation that transcended the given political system.

These four attitudes did, of course, often overlap in actuality. As we have frequently demonstrated, the concrete attitudes of each group and stratum varied in different societies and periods. Moreover, the attitudes of any one group were never homogeneous and stable. Nevertheless, those four types constitute the possible basic attitudes existing, in different degrees, among the different groups and strata.

Any one group's primary attitude was largely determined by the group's composition and structural position, and by the potential or real benefits and outlets it could obtain within the framework of the bureaucratic polities and the rulers' policies.

Different social groups and strata in the centralized bureaucratic societies featured these various attitudes toward the basic premises of these polities. This fact is a manifestation of their initial institutions' inadequacy to guarantee the perpetuation and continuity of these regimes. Although, under certain conditions, the political activities of different groups contributed greatly to the continuity of such a regime, in other circumstances they might have been detrimental to it. In the next chapters, we shall attempt to determine and analyze the conditions under which the different types of political activities could develop, and second, the conditions under which these activities contributed to, or undermined, the continuity of these regimes. Before this, however, we have to attempt a systematic classification of these different political issues, activities, and organizations.

[11] *Classification of Major Types of Political Issues*

Above, we have described and analyzed the political orientations and activities of the principal groups in the historical bureaucratic societies. In discussing each group or stratum, we analyzed its place in the social structure, the potential range of its political orientations and activities, and the compatibility or incompatibility of these orientations and activities with the political systems of the historical bureaucratic societies. This analysis inevitably raises the question of the extent to which the political activities and organizations analyzed above were specific to the political system of these societies.

On superficial examination, several characteristics appear common both to the political struggle in the historical bureaucratic societies studied here and to the political struggle in any other type of society. Many of the groups we have examined—e.g., the aristocracies, burghers, gentry, and peasantry—also existed in feudal societies, and their political activities in the bureaucratic polities sometimes seem to be identical with their activities in patrimonial, feudal, or city-state polities. To analyze both the similarities and the differences between the political processes of the same group respectively in these and other types of societies, it is worth-while first to present a systematic classification and analysis of the principal types of issues of political struggle and of political organization and activity that developed in the historical bureaucratic societies.

We shall begin by analyzing the main issues of political struggles that developed in bureaucratic societies.

These issues, the chief objectives of the political struggle, are differentiated, specifically political issues, according to the following criteria, which attempt to indicate the extent of their development as such:

1. The compass of the issue, in terms of the groups to which it is related and the extent to which it cuts across different groups

2. The degree to which the issue is specifically articulated as a *political* issue

3. The generality of the principle or the criterion involved in the issue

4. The political institution and arena toward which the issue is oriented and related

The most important issues of political activity and struggle in the societies studied here were of the following types:

1. Issues concerned with influencing policy formulation or execution in so far as it affected the concrete and immediate interests of various individuals and groups. Some good examples of this type of issue include urging direct distribution and allocation of rewards and facilities—e.g.,subsidies, posts, etc.—by the rulers and the bureaucracy; and the attempts to reduce the rulers' concrete demands—e.g., taxes or demands for manpower.

2. Issues concerned with influencing policy-making in terms of various groups' more general and continuous orientations and interests. These issues involve a more complicated and less concrete level of articulation of political demands: the claims are expressed in terms

of wider, more continuous interests and values; and different groups try to influence the rulers' long-term policies in favor of their own objectives and interests. For instance, the aristocracy's basic political orientations focused on limiting the scope of the rulers' autonomous political goals. Merchants or big land-owners often tried to sway the polity's concrete goals toward territorial expansion, promotion of investment, and international trade and concessions. Religious groups fought for full recognition and institutionalization of their status.

3. Cutting across these two issues were the attempts, made by individual groups and cliques, to seize power through usurping it or through designating the successor to the throne. In some cases, these attempts were manifestations only of personal or clique aspirations; in others, they represented wider issues, aspirations, and interests.

4. The fourth kind of major issue comprised various groups' concerns or aims to maintain and develop their own autonomy in different spheres vis-à-vis other groups—particularly vis-à-vis the ruling elite and the bureaucracy.

The autonomy they sought was one of two main types. One may be called "passive autonomy"—i.e., striving to "be left alone," to have minimal contacts with the political elite and bureaucracy, and evincing no aspiration to participate in the political process or decisions. This kind of autonomy is very much akin to what Wittfogel ([I] *1957, p. 108 ff.*) has described as the "beggar democracy" of the rural and urban groups.

The second type of autonomy was, from the political point of view, more articulated and dynamic. The aspirations it signified were not limited to desiring non-interference from the ruling elites and the bureaucracy. These were also aspirations to achieve some measure of active participation in the peripheral, if not some of the central, spheres of political life, and to be allowed to develop or maintain many autonomous regulative mechanisms without undue interference from the rulers or the bureaucracy.

5. The fifth political issue found in centralized bureaucratic societies involved attempts by different groups to acquire or establish some fundamental legal rights which would make them, in some respects, legally independent of the rulers. These attempts were focused on the legalization of (a) autonomy, as discussed above; (b) more general legal rights, e.g., due process of law, non-violation of property, etc.; (c) autonomy of independent legal bodies and courts of law; and (d) general, "universal" human or political rights. These last claims were, however, a later development, and were usually connected with the evolution of the more "radical" political orientations to be discussed under point 7 below.

6. The sixth issue in the political struggle concerned the objectives of different groups—to attain some recognition and official standing with regard to political decision-making, to be represented in the higher echelons of the political institutions, and to be considered in the determination of political goals. This kind of goal differed in essence from the ones already discussed. It signified more than aspirations toward attaining privileges, rights, and facilities from a ruling elite which monopolized political decision-making, or aspirations toward mere usurpation of power by any one group or by the substitution of one group of rulers for another. Rather it represented the desire to influence, or even to determine—through achieving official strategic positions in the political institutions—the distribution of power, or, at least, the principles governing the allocation of power and the choice of the polity's goals and policies.

This aim evolved mainly on the margins of the political systems of the societies studied here. One of its chief manifestations consisted of attempts to control the executive by dictating the allocation of financial resources to the rulers. Such attempts ranged from sporadic efforts to maintain temporary control over expenditure to efforts to have continuous control over the budget. Another manifestation of this aim consisted of attempts to supervise the appointment of ministers of the Crown.

7. Closely related to the aim just discussed was the one directed at extending the scope of political participation and at changing, at least to some extent, the basic political framework, values, and patterns of political participation.

[12] Classification of Major Types of Political Organizations

The chief types of political organization in the historical bureaucratic societies may be classified according to the following criteria:

1. The extent to which the organization was specific to political activities and differed from other social activities and groupings

2. The permanence and durability of the political organization

3. The number, type, and homogeneity or heterogeneity of the social groups participating in the organization; and the organization's consequent ability to channelize the free-floating political power existing in the society and to aggregate, within its framework, different political interests

4. The degrees of legitimation of the organization, and of its activities in the social and political systems

These criteria indicate the main (most frequent) types of political organization.

The first type consisted of individual or group representation, and petitioning, in regard to concrete, specific problems.

In this kind of political organization, the "represented" individuals and groups did not participate fully in the political sruggle as an independent (even though weak) force. They were, rather, a passive petitioning force or group, with no permanent and independent place in the political activities, reacting to these activities only in so far as they touched upon their personal interests.

This type of organization was usually associated with a distinctive type of leadership, involving an *ad hoc* group representation before the rulers, and the leaders' appearance as supplicants and petitioners. As a rule, the leaders were delegated by the group because they occupied more or less fixed positions within it. They did not organize the political potential their group had in relation to the rulers into any distinct or specific unit. Their leadership and representational activities were entirely embedded in the structures of the existing social groups, and usually did not constitute a discrete political activity.

A second type of political organization and activity was very common in these societies. This was the court or bureaucratic clique, usually composed of members of the ruling family, eunuchs, aristocrats, or upper bureaucrats. Such organizations resembled, in some respects, the preceding type—despite their obvious differences in regard to proximity to the center of power and to participation in the executive and administrative processes. Their similarity derived from the facts that, in many of these societies, these cliques and persons were not recognized as legitimate contenders for power, and that, in many cases, these cliques represented "fixed" kinship and territorial groups. Even more often, however, such a clique was indeed a sort of representative of different and varied social groups and strata. They were, therefore, among the most important, permanent, and active elements in the political struggle of the majority of these societies—especially when there were few legitimate channels and organizations for this struggle. In such cases, these cliques performed the crucial functions of aggregating, within their framework, somewhat different types of political interests, and of articulating them in the central channels of political struggle.

The political institutions of these societies contained positions that were, in a way, conducive to the development of such cliques. These were (1) the offices of the "inner court" and the royal household (e.g., the harem); (2) controlling offices; and (3) semi-independent offices, e.g., the court astronomer's, religious offices, or positions linked with external, independent organizations.

These cliques engendered a somewhat new type of political and group leadership. This comprised both semi-specialists and experts in political intrigue and influence, and people who either considered themselves representatives of certain groups (families, localities, etc.) or had been asked to perform certain mediating or semi-representative functions. However, their representative and mediating functions were neither fully recognized and accredited nor occasioned by any fixed positions in these groups. They were derived chiefly from their official positions as advisers, attendants of the monarch, or holders of bureaucratic or military positions. Most of them became politically ambitious (either for themselves or for their allies and friends), which, as a rule, was responsible for their engaging in clique intrigues. At least some of them turned for support to the "inner court" circle, the bureaucracy, and to powerful families or urban and rural groups. Consequently, they were in turn "approachable" by all these groups. Thus, the clique of organization often represented an embryonic stage of autonomous party-political activity.

The concrete objectives of these cliques were very frequently of a different order from the issues occasioning the petition made by representatives of particular groups. Their chief objectives were as follows:

1. To influence policy-making and decisions concerning concrete issues affecting the immediate interests and, in some cases, also the wider and more permanent concerns, of themselves or of other groups and strata

2. To install members of different groups in court offices and in the bureaucracy, so they could attain power and influence and thus benefit the group

3. To influence the determination and implementation of various policies, especially in so far as they had any bearing on the interests or values of different groups

The major focus of such clique activities was often the struggle around the problem of succession to the throne or, sometimes, of nominating the main ministers. The cliques, either in conjunction with more rebellious movements or on their own initiative, sometimes even planned the overthrow of a ruler or a dynasty.

A third type of political activity and organization was the continuous and semi-permanent representation of various groups in a special political framework. This type is best illustrated by the popular assemblies—e.g., the Roman and Byzantine Senates, and the European Assemblies of Estates. Many religious institutions were represented, though in a less articulated form, at the royal court, by virtue of the special positions of their members.

This was a more organized and permanent type of political activity and organization, and a much more diversified form of articulating different political interests and aggregating them in a common framework. However, organizations of this type were still rigidly linked to specific groups; so they had little possibility of unhampered manipulation of free-floating political forces and attitudes. Nevertheless, this form of representation allowed some manipulation of free-floating power. First, the representative offices were often already semi-independent politically, and in themselves constituted a focus of political struggle. Second, the representatives might be able, or required, to act as intermediaries between the king and different groups, and to mobilize resources and political support from these groups. Moreover, these representatives funcioned within the framework of special, distinct political institutions which had been legitimized in the society and which conferred some distinct political status upon them.

The same representatives also sometimes became relatively independent political leaders, and organized political cabals and cliques that served them as means of mobilizing support for different groups and strata.

The next type of social and political organization—which, in a way, cut across former stages, and also constituted a new development—consisted of social-political movements and rebellions of various kinds. The most universal characteristic of these movements was their ability to organize, in a comparatively common framework, rather varying and diverging groups. These movements were led by popular leaders, ephemeral-charismatic personalities, Robin Hoods, religious mystics, military bandits, and sometimes dissatisfied and disaffected aristocrats and bureaucratic war lords ([G] *Christensen, 1936, ch. vii; Klima, 1957*).

These social-political movements differed greatly in stability, continuity, continuous leadership, and the extent of internal articulation of special political issues.

Within this general category, two special subtypes should be mentioned. One was the "secret society"—a society, usually with some sort of religious orientation, that engaged in clandestine activities, and sometimes joined a rebellion or a popular outburst. The best examples of secret societies are provided by China ([I] *Groot, 1903; Levy, 1956; Eichhorn, 1954*), although similar examples can be found in other societies.

The second subtype was the militant religious sect or order (best illustrated by the Moslem "Order of Assassins") ([M] *Hodgson, 1955*). Such a group, in addition to its avowed religious aims, sometimes sought to overthrow a political system, to assassinate a ruler, or to establish a new religious polity.

To some extent, these groups and movements bordered on being either eruptive and passing movements and rebellions or more fully articulated and independent political organizations. Most of them were only partially, if at all, legitimate, and often evolved into open rebellions. Their emergence was frequently occasioned by the lack of any legitimate outlets and channels for political struggle. Some of these movements, however, did undergo metamorphosis into more durable types of political organization.

The last stage of political organization in the historical bureaucratic societies was the rise of special and permanent groups, which were organized for political purposes and featured some expressly political programs. (Obviously, in many instances, political organizations of this type were closely linked to the representation stage—especially to its more "advanced" or complicated developments.) The organizations in this category differed from one another in permanence, in the generality or specificity of their goals, and in the amount of heterogeneity of the social strata participating in them.

These groups were characterized by a relatively high degree of aggregation of different types of political interests and of their articulation, in terms of political issues, in the central channels of political struggle.

The outstanding characteristics of the new kind of leadership engendered and entailed by this form of political organization were: (1) differentiation of different levels of leadership (especially local and countrywide); (2) development of "free" leadership not attached in a fixed way to any ascriptive group; (3) establishment of nationwide or society-wide contacts among members of similar and different strata and among different leaders; and (4) semi-institutional competition between different groups of leaders. These developments prevailed most in the European countries studied and, to some extent, in the Spanish-American Empire. Although far less advanced, they also emerged in Byzantium and in late Republican and early Imperial Rome. (*See* [Y] *Königsberger, 1955; Sagnac, 1946;* [Z] *Namier, 1929, 1930, 1952;* [L] *Marica, 1949; Manojlovic, 1936;* [R] *Whitaker, 1942; Parry, 1957.*)

It is mostly this type of organization that featured regular and methodized attempts to mobilize continuously the potential political support of different associations, and of non-ascriptive groups and strata. Though existing in rudimentary form in the less differentiated types of political organizations, this approach became fully articulated only in the comparatively permanent and expressly political one.

The different types of political organization have been presented here in order of complexity (with the partial exception of the various social-political movements, whose exact positions could not be designated because they bordered on both preceding and subsequent stages). For the sake of clarity, in the analysis each type was considered as strongly differentiated from the others—although, in reality, political organizations frequently had the characteristics of more than one type.

[13] *Classification of Major Types of the Means of Political Struggle*

The chief means employed in the political struggle in the historical bureaucratic societies were similar to the ones used in any kind of society. The rulers' methods included distributing facilities and rewards, considering the interests of various groups when making decisions and implementing policies, and the differential use of coercion. The means employed by the subjects consisted largely of supplying different resources and support to the rulers.

But the particular ways in which these means were organized necessarily differed from one type of society or political system to another; and some were endemic to the bureaucratic societies studied. The basic characteristics of a given society determine the specific kinds of means of political struggle that are most prominent in it. From this point of view, the major significant factors in the political structure of the historical bureaucratic societies were in the crucial importance of the free-floating resources and support, and in the rulers' attempts to control these resources while at the same time maintaining some basic, unconditional support and legitimation.

Accordingly, in these societies, the subject strata and groups employed the following major means in their political struggle:

1. Withdrawing basic, unconditional support, and developing apathy toward the rulers

2. Denying the rulers direct resources, whether of manpower and finance—through desertion, non-payment of taxes, or non-performance of tasks and offices—or of political support

3. Undermining the continuous development of all free-floating resources by migrating or submitting to feudal lords

4. Organizing free resources (especially, contingent political support) in such a way as to injure—or at least not benefit—the ruling elite

5. Blocking the channels of communication, influence, and supply between various social strata and the rulers

6. Developing apathy, and *indirect* withdrawal of resources. (This was sometimes very close to 1 and 5)

[14] *The Types of Political Issues and Organizations Related to the Basic Premises of the Political Systems*

We have described and analyzed the major types of political issues, organizations, and leadership that emerged in the historical bureaucratic societies. Several of these existed both in these societies and in less differentiated ones—primitive, patrimonial, or feudal societies. However, some were found especially in the historical bureaucratic societies. Among such characteristic *issues* of political struggles, the most important were:

1. Attempts to influence the scope and direction of the polity's goals

2. The development of specifically articulated political goals and broader issues and interests that cut across the concrete interests of any fixed group

3. The attempts some groups made not only to change the concrete benefits allocated to them and their relative position within a fixed status hierarchy, but also to alter, to some extent, certain of the principles of stratification, and to impose some of their own specific values on the status hierarchy

4. The efforts to reform the existing social and political structure, political goals, and system of values, and to broaden the scope of political participation

One major way of organizing political activities was evolved in the historical bureaucratic societies, but did not arise in less differentiated types of political systems. This was the type of organization which either represented a relatively fluid group or was composed of members of different groups and directed by the appropriate kind of leadership.

The means of political struggle most specific to the political systems of the historical bureaucratic societies were those which blocked the transmission of free resources and of political support to the rulers, and could give rise to semi-organized apathy toward the rulers' policies and toward the basic premises of these polities.

These more differentiated and specifically political types of issues of political struggle and of political organization and leadership were very closely related. That is, they usually (as we shall see in detail later)

tended to develop together, although in some cases—especially during rebellions and sectarian movements—they also occurred separately.

But the most important characteristic of these societies' kind of political system is not the mere development of these more differentiated types of political activities, organizations, and issues. It is their coexistence, within *the same* frameworks and organizations, with much less differentiated political attitudes. In all the societies studied here, these "developed," "articulated," "differentiated" types of political activity and organization existed along with the less differentiated types. But they did not merely coexist, each type isolated in its own insulated compartment. Of course, on the local levels the less differentiated and articulated types of political activities usually preponderated. But these were linked to the central political organs through the more differentiated and articulated types of political activity. The more differentiated and articulated political activities, in a sense, encompassed the less differentiated ones in their framework and provided them with connections to the central political activities. This linkage probably constituted the single most important characteristic of the political systems of the historical bureaucratic societies. It also explains all the major groups which have, in these societies, engaged, at different periods, in all types of political activities—and it was through all these activities that they articulated their basic attitudes to the fundamental premises of the political systems. In the next chapter we shall analyze the variations in these activities in the societies studied here.

9

The Social Determinants

of the Political Processes

, A Comparative Analysis

[1] Introduction. The Major Variables
Influencing the Political Process

In the preceding chapters we have analyzed the extent of development of the major features of the political systems of the historical bureaucratic societies, the different types of policies of the rulers, the basic political orientations of the major social groups, and the potential range of their actual political activities.

In this chapter, we shall attempt to analyze, in a systematic way, the conditions that influence the development of the types of political organizations, orientations, and activities described in the preceding chapters. By "conditions," we mean the different values or constellations of the fundamental independent variables presented in our hypothesis—namely, the autonomy of the political sphere, as manifested in the types of goals of the rulers; and the extent of differentiation of the social structure, as manifested in the social organizations of the major social groups in evolving various autonomous regulative mechanisms.

These variables influenced all the principal aspects of the political struggle—i.e., the policies of the rulers, and the political participation of groups and strata in the society. Obviously, each of these variables is more closely related to one aspect of the political process than to the other. Thus, the rulers' policies were more influenced by their own goals than by the political participation of the groups. And the social structures and orientations of these groups had more influence on their participation of the political process than on the rulers' policies. It can be assumed that the types and amounts of resources needed by the rulers, their reactions to external and internal exigencies, and their demands on the various strata in the society, are all mostly influenced by their goals, which thus, in effect, created the basic framework of political process in these societies. On the other hand, the extent and type of differentiation of the social structure and of groups within it influenced the range of these groups' political orientations and activities, and of their demands on the rulers, and thus exercised influence on the rulers' policies.

However, we must beware of oversimplifications. We shall see in greater detail how the rulers' different orientations and goals also influenced the political participation of different groups and strata, and how the compositions of the latter in turn influenced the rulers' polities. We shall also consider the ways that both the rulers' policies and the major groups' political activities and orientations affected the extent to which the organs of political struggle and of the bureaucracy, and the scope of their activities, evolved. Our systematic analysis of the effects of these variables on the development of different political activities in the historical bureaucratic societies will facilitate our further analysis of the conditions of perpetuation or change of these political systems.

[2] *The Major Types of Rulers' Goals*

To begin, let us examine the rulers' goals and orientations and the main tasks and exigencies related to them.

Broadly speaking, one may distinguish *two main kinds*—often very closely connected—of rulers' goals. One type comprises the collective goals which the rulers purported to implement. These goals included maintaining and propagating a given cultural tradition, territorial expansion, and economic enhancement of the polity. All these collective objectives existed in every historical bureaucracy, but the relative importance of each one varied from one society to another. The other major type comprises the "natural" aims of any ruling elite to maintain its position of power and authority.

The concrete relation between the two types of goals was varied and manifold. In general, however, the rulers' accomplishments in implementing collective goals, and their ability to deal with the internal and external exigencies of society, constituted an important condition of the maintenance of their legitimation in the societies studied here. The criteria of this legitimation—i.e., the principal values and standards according to which they upheld their power, and to which they and their actions were appraised in the society—greatly influenced, among other factors, the nature and extent of the resources the rulers needed to implement their goals, and the amount and type of support they could expect from their subjects.

Accordingly, the different rulers' goals must be considered in close connection with the value orientations prevalent among the main groups of a society and propagated by the rulers themselves.

What is the relation between the value orientations prevailing in the society and the rulers' goals, and how does it influence the political process in the society? What aspects of the value orientations are most important from this point of view?

For our discussion, the most profitable approach to classifying value orientations is to distinguish the basic referent of each major political goal, i.e., for what purpose, or for whose good, it was implemented. This approach initially may seem naïve—superficially, these political goals appear obviously to have been implemented to maintain the rulers' positions and the functioning of the political system. However, the very postulate of the existence of and the necessity for legitimation of the rulers implies the existence of the problem of determining other referents in all the societies studied here (and, probably, in all political systems). In the societies of our concern, the problem is especially acute because of the differentiation between the political and cultural spheres, the relative autonomy of each, their continual interaction, and the rulers' constant search for support.

Accordingly, the main referents of political order may be:

1. A cultural order or tradition encompassing the rulers, the polity, and the different strata of society

2. The rulers and/or the polity as a distinct unity

3. Different groups in the society

4. Systems of values that must be propagated by the polity and society

In our subsequent analysis, we shall refer to a polity in which any one of these value referents of political activity is predominant as a polity with "cultural," "political," "political-collective," "economic-social," etc., goals. Similarly, in describing different types of policies, political activities, organizations, and orientations, we shall often use adjectives like "simple," "complicated," "wider," etc., without further elaborating the description of these policies and political activities. This shorthand will be employed whenever these adjectives, which refer to the classification of policies and political activities developed in former chapters, can be fully understood in the given context.

Tables 1–20 indicate the relations between the main types of rulers' goals and different levels of differentiation of the social structure, and the chief types of rulers' policies and of political participation and orientations of the major groups in the society. The material of these tables will be discussed and analyzed in detail in the following paragraphs, where we shall refer—mostly for illustrative purposes—to those six to eight societies that have been discussed in the preceding chapters. However, the analysis will be based on all the societies analyzed in the tables.

[3] "Cultural" Orientation and Goals of the Rulers

Let us begin by examining the historical bureaucratic systems dominated by the cultural or "pattern maintenance" orientation. In other words, societies strongly emphasizing the maintenance of the given tradition, order, and patterns of culture, as constituting the basic framework within which the chief functions of the polity are fulfilled and to which political goals must—in theory, at least—be subordinated.

This type of cultural orientation—hereafter called the "cultural-particularistic"—must be distinguished from another. The second type comprises those cultural orientations directed at missionary-religious (or secular) activity—spreading the "true faith," with the help of the given collectivity and its political activities. The primary analytical difference between these two types of cultural orientations lies in their basic references and criteria of political activity.

The cultural-particularistic orientation emphasizes the maintenance of a given cultural tradition and order within the boundaries of a specific collectivity to which this tradition is related, and the absorption of all alien elements into this tradition and collectivity.

The second type of orientation was most clearly ilustrated by the Islamic states. It was directed toward spreading a certain universal faith or creed beyond the limits of any given collectivity, imposing this faith on other collectivities, and/or founding new collectivities based on adherence to the faith.

Often, the concrete manifestations of these two types of cultural orientations tended to overlap, particularly in the later stages of institutionalization of new "universal" creeds. This was demonstrated by the development of Islam during the later stages of the Abbaside (and Fatimite) Caliphate and of the Ottoman Empire. The cultural-universalistic aims or goals became at least partially transformed into cultural-particularistic orientations, placing more emphasis on maintaining the existing cultural traditions.

In many primitive societies, the cultural-particularistic orientations preponderated. However, in the historical bureaucratic societies we are examining, these orientations developed on the bases of the differentiation between the political and the cultural spheres and the relative autonomy of each. Hence the cultural order which they upheld was not a "given traditional" one, but a much more differentiated and flexible one. Sometimes the influence of these orientations was clearly evident even when they were not among the highest in the hierarchy of political goals. This occurred in several Church and Crown activities in the Spanish Indies, and, to a smaller extent, in the cultural activities and attempts to establish a homogeneous cultural framework in Byzantium. However, the influence of the cultural orientations was obviously far more pronounced in those relatively few cases wherein they were the most important objectives—especially in the Chinese and in the Ancient Egyptian empires ([F] *Frankfort, 1948, 1951; Drioton and Vandier, 1952; Edgerton, 1947[a], 1956; Otto, 1953; Kees, 1933[a], 1952; Meyer, 1928; Spiegel, 1950; Stock, 1949; Wilson, 1951*). In the latter, these goals were relatively undifferentiated, traditional, and based on a great degree of fusion between the political and the religious orientations.

Therefore, for the sake of clarity, we shall confine our analysis of the influence of these orientations on the political process in more differentiated political systems to the Chinese case. However, many of its aspects are similar to those of other polities where these goals were of some importance.

[4] The Influence of Cultural Orientations and Goals in the Chinese Empire

How, then, did these relatively non-traditional and differentiated cultural-particularistic value orientations influence the political process, especially in the Chinese Empire?

A. INFLUENCE OF CULTURAL ORIENTATIONS AND GOALS ON THE PATTERNS OF LEGITIMATION OF RULERS

The best starting point for analyzing the political process in a culturally oriented system is the examination of the nature of the legitimation of its rulers. (*See* [I] *Kracke, 1953; H. Franke, 1953[b]; Lee, 1954; De Bary, 1957; Liu, 1957, here adapted from Lee, 1954; O. Franke, 1925, 1930–52; Bodde, 1953, 1956; Weber, 1922; Dubs, 1938[b].*) The emphasis on cultural values and goals usually involved designating either a hereditary or a new group as the age-old upholders of the specific cultural tradition. Even when new dynasties arose, they still tended to stress their relation to the ancient forebears or monarchs. who symbolized, as it were, the "Golden Age." But the ruler's legitimation was based neither on pure "traditionalism" nor only on hereditary transmission; it was founded mainly on his acceptance of the "Mandate of Heaven," and his behavior according to that Mandate and its precepts.

The charismatic character of the Chinese dynastic ruler has often been emphasized. The emperor, commonly called the "Son of Heaven," received his empire from Heaven and ruled in accordance with Heaven's will. He was answerable neither to his subjects nor to any laws that they might enact. Ideally, he was responsible for a benevolent and natural order which would enable the people to live in peace and prosperity. Any strange or disastrous occurrence in nature—such as a solar eclipse, a comet's appearance, an avalanche, and, of course, a famine—was traditionally regarded as a heavenly omen admonishing the ruler. On such an occasion, the reigning emperor's usual procedure was to issue a decree expressing his deepest regret for his possible neglect of duty, and to seek advice, especially from his censors. The Confucian scholars serving in the court were only too glad to take this opportunity to reassert the Confucian principle of government and to reinforce their own positions in the administration.

Since it was based on the principle of justice, the authority of the sovereign was evidently subject to debate, question, and challenge. If the ruler did not select a qualified and worthy administration, and consequently failed to bring about the well-being of the people, the people's resultant loss of faith in him may have deprived him of all his prerogatives. He then ceased to be a sovereign, and became "a mere fellow"—to use Mencius' terminology. Confucian ethics contained numerous arguments justifying revolt against such a ruler.

This type of legitimation influenced the political process in Chinese society. Such cultural orientation, and the basic legitimation it entailed, greatly influenced the formulation both of the rulers' concrete goals and of the types of resources these demanded.

In any historical bureaucratic state, the rulers were in need of many kinds of material resources (especially manpower and economic resources) to realize their power and to pursue various political goals. But, because of the strong cultural orientations, the amount of resources the rulers needed was sometimes relatively small. Rulers in such polities generally were expected to place less emphasis on political-collective goals, like territorial expansion, military aggrandizement, and economic enhancement. These objectives were very expensive; when they had been relegated to secondary importance, the rulers required fewer costly resources.

We do not mean that collective aggrandizement, expansion, etc., were not considered as important goals by the rulers of China (or of Ancient Egypt). However, it is significant that they were usually expressed in cultural terms and formulated as subordinate to cultural values and orientations. Even if an emperor was interested in purely military, expansionist goals, his capacity to implement them was largely dependent on culturally oriented groups. The emperor was thus obliged to take into account his own basic legitimation, which emphasized such cultural orientations ([I] *Balázs, 1950, 1959[a]; Eberhard, 1948[a], 1952; Pulleyblank, 1954*).

Throughout Chinese history, multifarious tensions arose between the rulers and the Confucian literati and bureaucrats, on this very point. The emperors were inclined to emphasize a larger variety of collective, expansionist goals. The Confucian literati and bureaucrats tended to limit these objectives and to emphasize cultural goals and ideologies. This controversy was a major focus of the political struggle in China.

However, the existence and continuity of such controversies attest to the great importance the cultural orientation had in determining political processes in China. Even in those periods of Chinese history (especially in the later, "modern" period that began during the Sung Dynasty) when the rulers' autocratic power increased at the expense of the Confucian literati, the emperors never entirely abandoned the Confucian ideology; nor were they able to rule entirely without the help and assistance of the Confucian bureaucrats ([I] *Hulsewé, 1955; Hucker, 1950, 1959[a], 1959[b]; De Bary, 1957; Twitchett, 1957[c]; Balázs, 1952, 1959[a]; Pulleyblank, 1954*). The Confucian ideology established the basic ideal of a unified empire, and provided the institutional and cultural framework for maintaining unity.

In a similar way, the cultural orientations that prevailed in Chinese society influenced the emperors' basic political orientation, goals, and needs in the internal sphere.

Of course, the Chinese emperors needed monetary and manpower resources for more reasons than to attain their "collective" goals. These resources were necessary for conducting basic administrative activities as well. However, these activities had only a relatively narrow scope, because the general orientation toward cultural goals tended to emphasize both the autonomy of local and family groups and their political passivity. The legitimation of the Chinese emperor required that he take care of his subjects and keep them under surveillance; but the ideological orientations of the polity roused little active continuing political participation among the population. Usually, the extent of direct, active political support that the rulers claimed and acquired was comparatively small. The dominant ideology stressed the traditional and moral nature of legitimation, whose provisions did not require the rulers actively to solicit support. Passivity and acceptance were generally attributed to the potentially more active strata, like the bureaucracy, town dwellers, or gentry. As a rule, the rulers assumed that the different strata were loyal to the polity and its goals, and usually did not deem it necessary to involve these strata in active party politics, or in the determination of actual policies.

The rulers were primarily interested in preserving, through various ritual and educational activities, the allegiance of these strata ([I] *De Bary, 1957; Eberhard, 1948[a], 1952, 1957; Balázs, 1952, 1959[a]; Reischaeur, 1955*). The chief emphasis was on maintaining cultural conduct and organization proper according to basic cultural and ethical precepts.

However, administrative, executive, and policy problems were not ignored. Rather, the solution of these problems was considered implicit in appropriate cultural and moral behavior. Chinese ideology often assumed that proper administrative conduct and orientations would almost automatically solve all practical problems. In addition, however, it was taken for granted that the solutions of these problems would contribute to the perpetuation of the proper cultural order. In other words, Chinese ideology had a peculiar attitude both toward concrete problems of administration and order, and toward the rulers' methods of resolving them. Precisely because instrumental and administrative problems and objectives were conceived as being in themselves, of relatively small account the emperor's inability to deal with them was perceived as a certain indication that he could no longer cope with *any* problems whatever; and that, therefore, his claim to legitimation was no longer justified ([I] *Bingham, 1941; Biel-enstein, 1953[a], 1953[b]; Gale, 1929, 1930, 1931; Des Rotours, 1932, 1947–48; Sprenkel, 1958; Liu, 1959[a]*).

B. INFLUENCE OF CULTURAL ORIENTATIONS AND GOALS ON THE CONCRETE POLICIES OF THE RULERS

These basic political attitudes and orientations were manifested in the concrete policies the rulers developed. In the field of internal affairs, regulative policies preponderated that were aimed at main-taining the ruling elite's control over the distribution of economic resources, the strong "paternalistic" criteria of land allocation, the control of economic supply and demand, the monopoly of some essen-tial commodities, and the supervision and insulation of the more active economic groups. In general, the policies strongly stressed the relative self-sufficiency of various territorial and professional groups, minimized "free interrelations between them, and regulated their interrelations through insulating and controlling different groups. Even when the rulers encouraged trade activities, they attempted, with varying de-grees of success, to control them and to isolate the merchants socially and politically ([I] *Balázs, 1953[a], 1953[b]; 1954[a], 1960; Blue, 1948; Gale, 1929, 1930; Liu, 1959[a]* passim; *O. Franke, 1931, 1932, 1933[a], 1933[b]; Duyvendak, 1928, 1958* passim; *Stange, 1950*).

Thus, the policies of China's ruling elite may be characterized as generally creative-accumulative and regulative; very few were promo-tive policies. The regulative policies were very much directed toward maintaining the social and political status quo.

It is very significant that the Confucian scholars were strongly opposed to the state's direct promotion of economic enterprises, whether by monopolistic control or outright ownership. They feared it would result in the merchants' concentrating and monopolizing power, to the detriment of agriculture. Instead, the Confucians usually advocated small private trade, under only very general regulations. In other words, they favored the regulatory-prescriptive over the pro-motive policies. Although many emperors occasionally framed policies directed at the direct promotion of economic activities by the state, the Confucians' attitude usually limited their potency ([I] *Gale, 1929, 1930, 1931; Blue, 1948; Balázs, 1953[a], 1960; Liu, 1959[b]*). Pro-motive policies were, as a rule, successfully implemented only in the field of agricultural taxation and colonization. They were, in that area, because their goal was the indirect regulation of the supply of agricultural manpower and taxation ([I] *Rieger, 1937; Balázs, 1953[b], 1954[a]; H. Franke, 1953[a]*).

In the cultural field, the rulers were obviously very interested in monopolizing or controlling cultural-religious activities, and in the "cultural" and "moral" supervision of the population. Similarly, the rulers tried to control the status system emphasizing cultural achievement—in China, through the system of examinations—as the major criterion of status, and by supervising the examination system and the cultural organizations ([I] *Des Rotours, 1932, 1947–48; Chang, 1955; Hucker, 1950, 1959, 1959[a], 1959[b]; Liu, 1959[a], 1959[b]; Busch, 1955*).

In the field of external politics, the Chinese emperors often sought territorial expansion and engaged in many wars. However, they frequently—if not always—declared their purpose as the consolidation of the Empire, or the maintenance of its cultural unity. Even if these cultural motives were expressed only for propaganda purposes, they clearly influenced the actual framing and implementation of policies. Moreover, since the ideal of a unified empire could be realized only in the Confucian framework, the rulers had to employ cultural groups and strata in the unification of territories, etc.; they thus strengthened still more the positions of these strata.

The official criteria which guided the formulation of regulative policies were related primarily to issues of maintaining the cultural order, and—at least overtly, to a much smaller extent—to considerations of exigencies and internal power politics ([I] *De Bary, 1957; Holzman, 1957*). Officially, ostensibly few policies were actively concerned with the interests and goals of various strata, whose well-being was considered to be implicit in the perpetuation of the general cultural order ([I] *Blue, 1948; Balázs, 1959[a], 1960*). But, as we shall see, the real situation often differed greatly from this "ideal."

The great emphasis on regulative policies, on cultural considerations in framing these policies, and on the political passivity of the population—necessarily entailed a very limited development of organs of political struggle. The "official" political struggle that emerged was concentrated mostly in royal council and secretariat, and was waged mostly by court and bureaucratic cliques. Formally, these organs served only as advisory bodies to the kings; they had no autonomy of their own, and only limited political struggle was waged openly in them ([I] *Des Rotours, 1932, 1947–48; Rideout, 1949; Pulleyblank, 1954, 1955; Hucker, 1950, 1958, 1959[a], 1959[b]; Liu, 1957; 1959[a]*). In fact, however, the reality was more complicated and these organs usually became foci of continuous political struggle.

The picture presented above is simplified, in that, throughout the course of Chinese history, the importance and influence of the Confucian groups and ideals fluctuated greatly. Their fluctuations can be traced mainly through the different dynasties. During the earlier dynasties—e.g., the Han (206 B.C.–A.D. 221) and T'ang (A.D. 618–905)—the framework of the Confucian state had not yet been fully established; and the rulers very often supported other religious groups (e.g., the Buddhists) or tried to oust the Confucian scholars from any influential positions in the court. It was only under the Sung (A.D. 960–1279) that the Neo-Confucian ideology became predominant, leaving its imprint on the entire institutional structure of the state. But this predominance was gained through enhancing of royal autocracy and through diminishing the independence of the Confucian officials—who became, at least as individuals, subjected considerably to royal absolutism ([I] *Kracke, 1953, 1955;* Aspects de la Chine, *1959* passim; *De Bary, 1957; Hucker, 1958, 1959[a], 1959[b]; Twitchett, 1957[a]; Miyakawa, 1955; Bünger, 1936*).

Moreover, both during China's periods of division, and especially during its periods under the rule of foreign dynasties, the Yüan (A.D. 1260–1368) and the Ch'ing (A.D. 1644–1912), the basic political orientations of the foreign rulers were not greatly influenced by the Confucian ideology. And yet, despite all these changes and differences, the basic framework of the Confucian state that had gradually emerged has never been abolished in China, although it has undergone many variations and differences of emphasis. Even the foreign dynasties had, at least in their internal policies, to accommodate themselves to this framework in great measure.

C. INFLUENCE OF CULTURAL ORIENTATIONS AND GOALS ON THE POLITICAL ACTIVITIES AND ORIENTATIONS OF THE MAJOR GROUPS

In our analysis of the other aspect of the political process in culturally oriented societies—namely, the political attitudes and activities of the main social strata—our discussion, once again, will refer chiefly to China.

The emphasis on cultural orientations greatly influenced the nature of the political issues in which the major groups and strata were involved. It also set definite limits to the articulation of the issues, rules, and organization of the political struggle.

Chinese political ideology assumed that cultural and ethical norms included all precepts of appropriate political behavior and policies. Therefore, opposition to, or controversy over, policies was justified only when they were incompatible with these precepts. While this was obviously an "ideal" and purely ideological assumption, it was prevalent and strong enough to prevent the development of any explicit, open conflict over policies, and thus precluded the need for formulating rules for such conflict. In principle, all such controversies had to be regarded as interpretations and applications of the basic cultural precepts ([I] *De Bary, 1957; Liu, 1957, 1959[b]; Nivison, 1959; Nivison and Wright, 1959* passim; *Gale, 1929; Blue, 1948; Balázs, 1953[a], 1954[c]*).

However, precisely this ideology, and the concomitant political passivity, about articulating political issues and demands, necessarily occasioned major differences in the degrees of political participation of various groups and strata. Thus, as already mentioned, it enhanced the position of the groups which were most concerned with cultural values and with direct exercise of power respectively—namely, the literati and different branches of the bureaucracy.

Since cultural objectives were strongly stressed, cultural groups and institutions were crucially important. They could then become regarded—by themselves and by other groups—as the principal organs to whom the rulers were answerable. Moreover, determining the proper cultural tradition and the proper precepts for coping with various problems could be a major political issue. Consequently, the cultural and bureaucratic groups were among the most active participants in the political struggle; and the bureaucracy—particularly, some of its central and/or semi-ritual offices—became the most important arena of political struggle. In this connection, the bureaucratic posts engaging in cultural, administrative, and moral supervision—such as the Censorate and the ritual offices in China—were especially significant. Officially, these groups could not participate in any active political struggle, since the official ideology denied the very existence of such a struggle. Nevertheless, they were often considered, both by others and by themselves, to be repositories of the legitimation of the regime and of its rulers. In general, groups serving as channels of control necessarily became the foci of the political struggle of various cliques ([I] *De Bary, 1957; Liu, 1957, 1959[b]; Eberhard, 1957*).

Thus, although culturally oriented polities ostensibly were characterized by having only the relatively simple types of issue or organization of political activities—e.g., direct petitioning or clique activities, whose aim was to insure the allocaton of benefits and the maintenance of local autonomy—the reality was more complicated. Although the clique type of political organization was the most prominent in China, it screened, as it were, more intensive and articulated kinds of political orientations. This fact is closely associated with the high level of flexibility and non-traditionalism in Chinese cultural orientations and goals. The cliques were often concerned with wider problems and issues (e.g., framing basic economic and internal policies), even though their aims were usually formulated in terms of limited objectives and/or interpretations of cultural precepts.

Throughout Chinese history, therefore, several major wider questions were the foci of dispute, discussion, and political controversy. The most important among them were: (1) the legitimate behavior of the prince, or the difference between prince and despot; (2) law *vs.* custom and morality in public and private behavior; (3) the qualities, responsibilities, and autonomy of ministers, especially those of the prime minister; (4) the political roles of eunuchs; (5) the criteria of recruitment to and promotion in the civil service and local government; (6) the conduct proper to officials; (7) land reform, taxation, and encouraging other types of economic activities; and (8) the establishment of schools and academies. (*On this, see* [I] *De Bary, 1957; also Hucker, 1958; Liu, 1959[a]; Haenisch, 1944; H. Franke, 1940; Wilhelm, 1935–36, 1951.*)

In China, a wide "canonical" and interpretative literature existed concerning cultural precepts on the foregoing questions, as well as many statutes defining proper "political" and bureaucratic behavior. The existence of this literature was a manifestation of the rise of many forces with wider orientations, and the consequent need to formalize laws and regulations in order to accommodate these forces within the framework of the elites' basic cultural goals.

The articulation of wider political issues in spite of the ideological denial of political struggle was also manifested by several political means employed in these societies. Several active groups—especially branches of the bureaucracy and the literati—frequently tried to organize extensive propagandist enterprises. The most important were conducted by academies and schools during their struggles with cliques, eunuchs, and "tyrannical" emperors. Propagandist activities were both widespread and effective, particularly among the literati, the gentry, and even some upper peasant groups ([I] *Galt, 1951* passim; *Hucker, 1958, 1959[a]; Nivison, 1959.*)

D. TECHNOLOGICAL AND GEOGRAPHICAL FACTORS

The maintenance of such a relatively low level of political activity and participation was greatly facilitated by certain geographical and technological conditions. Technology in general, and military technology in particular, was not highly developed. This factor combined with the fact that several parts of the geographically huge empire were very interdependent, mainly through the system of irrigation. The combination of these elements facilitated the rulers' continuous maintenance of some measure of central control. It also aided the several regions and social units to attain and keep relatively great autonomy without enabling them to evolve into entirely independent and autonomous centers of power ([I] *Lattimore, 1951; Balázs, 1959[a], 1960*).

Of course, the extent to which the type of political process described may be attributed to technological factors, and how much political and cultural institutions limited technological development, are moot points. However, there is no doubt that the two interacted very closely. Nor is there any doubt that the predominance of the cultural orientation and of the consequent types of political activities was greatly facilitated by a level of general and military technology that enabled the ruler to maintain efficient but limited control, while also impeding active groups in the society from acquiring powerful technological or communicative means.

In this area too many variations occurred during different periods in Chinese history. The place and importance of the Confucian literati in relation to other religious groups and military leaders changed continually. Within the polity, there were constant shifts in the relative importances of different regional groups and families. For example, the urban groups rose to relative prominence under the Sung, and then declined again later. During periods of war or dissolution, the military leaders gained importance rapidly. However, all these fluctuations were made within the relatively flexible political framework, whose main features survived these changes ([I] *Kracke, 1955;* Aspects de la Chine, *1959* passim; *Hucker, 1958, 1959[a], 1959[b]; Liu, 1959[b]; O. Franke, 1945; Eberhard, 1948[a]; Stange, 1950*).

[5] *Summary of the Influence of Cultural Orientations and Goals on the Political Process*

The characteristics of the political struggle in societies (or sectors thereof) with predominantly cultural goals can be summarized through an analysis of the process of power generalization within them. Several features of these societies—the existence of a relatively high degree of social differentiation and of some autonomy of the political orientations—were conducive to a great generalization of power. However, these conditions were counteracted, to some extent, by the cultural referents of political activity. The preponderance of cultural orientations imposed restrictions both on various groups and on the rulers. Since this framework contained many institutions—such as the Chinese examination system and bureaucracy—binding both the rulers and the most active groups to the confines of common cultural orientations and activities, it helped greatly to regulate tensions between them.

The intensity of tensions between different groups' (and rulers') latent power and the basic cultural orientations was in proportion to the degree of differentiation of the social structure. The great difference, relevant to our discussion, between the Chinese and the Ancient Egyptian empires emerges from this relation. In Ancient Egypt, the general level of differentiation (especially between the political and the religious spheres) was relatively minor. Hence the political passivity of most social groups was not only an ideological assumption; in Egypt, the assumption corresponded to reality much more than it did in China. As a result, the Egyptian rulers' creative and prescriptive policies could be executed without meeting so many difficulties as in China.

However, when more flexible differentiated strata began to develop in these societies, they could not be accommodated easily within the framework of the more rigid goals and political institutions. We shall return to this problem in the chapter on change ([F] *Drioton and Vandier, 1952; Edgerton, 1947[a], 1956; Stock, 1949; Becherat, 1951; Wilson, 1951; Meyer, 1928; Otto, 1953; Kees, 1933[a], 1933[b], 1934, 1935; Spiegel, 1950*).

[6] The Major Types of Exigencies Developing in Culturally Oriented Polities

To elucidate the nature of these tensions and the limits within which they could be accommodated by these political systems, it will be worth-while to analyze some of the major exigencies which confronted the political systems.

Obviously, culturally oriented societies and their rulers often confronted difficulties and problems originating in external factors largely beyond their control, like wars and invasions. But, in these societies as in others, their emphasis on certain goals and values could engender sensitivity to special types of exigencies and could create special difficulties in dealing with them.

We have noted that the predominance of cultural goals in a society entailed specific kinds of administrative and security problems, of internal and external exigencies and tensions. Some causes of internal difficulties in these polities are the following:

1. General pressure on resources caused by the extravagances of the emperors and the bureaucracies

2. The rulers' and bureaucracies' faulty administration and inefficiency in dealing with concrete administrative problems. This is closely connected with 1 above

3. Crises focusing around the distribution of power among different groups and regions

4. Crises in the relations between the rulers and the cultural elites, or strong competition among these elites ([I] *Sprenkel, 1952; Balázs, 1948, 1950, 1952, 1959[a], 1960; Eberhard, 1948[a]; Stange, 1950*)

The foreign exigencies created by external pressure gave rise to problems of security and of maintaining the empire's unity and the ruling dynasty's stability.

The politically active groups' attitude to these problems and exigencies was, in some measure, determined by their predominantly cultural orientations. In general, it was founded in the assumption that, if the rulers' conduct and the realm's organization were governed by cultural-ethical precepts, the security of the polity would be more or less assured. Consequently, these groups' attitude toward military activities and organizations was one of suspicion and misgiving. At the same time, the regimes were often unable to control military forces or to maintain an efficient military establishment. Military administration was, to some extent, beyond the scope of the general administration. During periods of crisis, the military could become quite independent, and able easily to overthrow the incumbent regime and found a new one. Throughout Chinese history, for example, several military leaders played a very important role during periods of dynastic change and of external war—although they only recently developed any autonomous political orientation ([I] *Michael, 1946; Des Rotours, 1926, 1947–48, Introduction; Pulleyblank, 1955*).

The rulers dealt with internal and external difficulties in various ways. As a rule, they utilized a combination of repressive and "moral" persuasive measures, and attempted to revise policy and to reform bureaucracy ([I] *Liu, 1959[b]; Sprenkel, 1952, 1958; Pulleyblank, 1954, 1955; Eberhard, 1948[a]; Stange, 1950*). The rulers were obliged to resolve problems constantly, for any particular difficulty they failed to overcome could easily cause extensive change in the society and even their own fall. Thus, internal exigencies might lead to rebellion and attempts to usurp power; and foreign exigencies might increase the power of military governors, leaders, and war lords, and/or conquest by foreign powers. The consequences of unsolved difficulties were, of course, connected with the processes of change taking place in these societies; they will be systematically discussed in the relevant chapter.

[7] The Major Types of Collective-Executive Goals

Let us now analyze the influences that other types of value orientations and of referents of political activity and political goals had on political process in bureaucratic societies. One of the most prevalent general orientations—especially of the rulers—of these societies was toward the enhancement of the political community as an end in itself. This orientation was common to the majority of bureaucratic societies; it was the predominant orientation of many of the rulers, and a basic subsidiary goal for most of them. This type of orientation emphasized the autonomy and pre-eminence of the political sphere, while simultaneously stressing the polity's claims to be in direct relation to the realm of cultural values.

The respective manifestations of this orientation differed greatly in these societies, and were expressed by emphasis on correspondingly different goals. The differences between them are of some analytical importance. The chief concrete manifestations apparently were the following:

1. An emphasis on purely political-collective goals, like conquest, territorial expansion, and maintaining a strategic position in international diplomacy. This emphasis occurred in Sassanid Persia ([G] *Christensen, 1936; Altheim and Stiehl, 1954; Altheim, 1955[a], 1955[b]; Ghirshman, 1954*) and in Byzantium (*see e.g.* [L] *Ostrogorsky, 1956[a]* passim; *Vasiliev, 1952; Bréhier, 1947, 1949[b], 1950*) through most of their histories. It was, of course, very prominent in conquered empires, such as the Ottoman, where it was, however, linked to religious goals; or in the Spanish-American Empire, where it was somewhat connected with cultural and economic goals (as it was in many Absolutist regimes in Europe) ([R] *Haring, 1927, 1947; Hanke, 1949; Parry, 1940; Ots Capdequi, 1941; Zavala, 1943*).

2. An emphasis on the economic strength and expansion of the polity per se. This type of economic goal must be analytically distinguished from the emphasis on economic development and advancement of social groups or of the entire population (or "society"). The latter pertained to the economic advancement of the individual, of groups of individuals, or of the society—but not of the polity as such. The former type was concerned with economic advancement and development as a means of improving the polity or as a subsidiary

goal of the polity as such. True, the emphasis on economic development of the polity usually denoted an approach differing from
purely political-collective goals. Such an orientation to the economic
well-being of the polity was usually related to the somewhat wider
conception of the polity as a discrete entity, one not entirely identical
with the rulers although represented by them.

The distinction between these two types of economic goal is
analytical. It could not always be discerned in concrete cases where,
at times, they coincided. The best examples of the overlapping of
these orientations are provided by many Absolutist European states.
As a rule, the so-called mercantilist policies of seventeenth- and eighteenth-century France and Prussia were governed chiefly by the first
type of economic goal. However, the second type gradually infiltrated
some elements in France ([S] *Hartung and Mousnier, 1955; Morazé,
1948; Wilson, 1958; Heckscher, 1932; Heaton, 1937; Viner, 1948;
Treue, 1957* [X] *Schmoller, 1910;* [Y] *Cole, 1939, 1943*). In England,
during the same period and prior to the Great Rebellion, both types
of economic goals were prevalent, and there was a trend toward the
predominance of the second. (*See* [S] *Beloff, 1954; Viner, 1948;* [Z]
*Ashley, 1952; Plumb, 1950; Nef, 1940; Lipson, 1929–30; Davies, 1937;
Clark, 1955.*)

3. The expansion of the collectivity as representing universalistic
values, and the perpetuation of the collectivity's cultural or religious
values. The outstanding instance of this type of cultural orientation
is provided by the Islamic states, and especially the Abbaside and
Fatimite Caliphates, and to some extent the Ottoman Empire ([O]
Gibb and Bowen, 1950, 1957; Wittek, 1938; [N] *Lewis, 1953*). France
and England were also somewhat oriented toward this type of cultural
goal, as expressed in France in the Enlightenment and in the doctrine
of "Enlightened Absolutism" and in England by some of the internal
activities and orientations of Protestant groups ([S] *Hartung and
Mousnier, 1955; Beloff, 1954*).

Such cultural orientations, but less intensive and with less of a
missionary goal, existed in Sassanid Persia, especially during the reigns
of the first kings and of Khosrou I; in Byzantium, until the beginning
of its decline ([L] *Diehl, 1943; Barker, 1957*); and, to a greater extent,
in the activities of the rulers and Church in the Spanish-American
Empire ([R] *Hanke 1949; Parry, 1940; Ots Capdequi, 1941; Zavala,
1943; Haring, 1947*).

Obviously, in concrete cases these different "cultural" orientations
could overlap widely—with each other, and with the purely cultural-
particularistic orientations discussed above. Analytically, however, each
is distinct.

4. An emphasis on the mere perpetuation of the polity and the rulers, on the maintenance of the status quo of the political system.

In general, the different types of political-collective goals frequently overlapped, and their relative importance could vary in any given society. For instance, in Byzantium, the political-collective goals were usually predominant; however, the relative importance of military, economic, and cultural goals varied during different periods. (*See, e.g.,* [L] *Hussey, 1957 Ostrogorsky, 1956[a]; Diehl, 1943.*) In the Spanish-American Empire, cultural goals declined in importance after the second century of its development ([R] *Haring, 1947; Ots Capdequi, 1945, 1946[a]; Parry, 1940, 1957*). In France, emphasis continually vacillated between stress on pure collective expansion, and a broader conception of the polity's greatness, that included actual and potential economic strength as well as cultural attainments ([Y] *Sagnac, 1945, 1946; Lough, 1954, 1960; Pagès, 1928*).

[8] *The Influence of Collective-Executive Goals on the Patterns of Legitimation of the Rulers*

To understand fully the repercussions that these orientations and goals had on political process, we should first examine the systems of legitimation that tended to develop in connection with them. These systems varied greatly in details from one society to another.

In most of the polities studied, legitimate rule was allocated, as it were, to hereditary rulers. The most outstanding exceptions are Rome and Byzantium, where the crown was, at least in some periods, officially elective, and the Senate, the people, and the army participated in different and diverse ways in the election. Even in polities like the Spanish Empire and the French monarchy, where legitimate rule was hereditary, the values which had to be realized by the rulers and the patterns of behavior to which they had to conform were greatly varied and complex. The rulers were required to be able to implement collective goals and activities, to maintain administrative services, order, and justice, and to perpetuate certain traditions and religious values and institutions. They were also required to fulfil the equivocal function of implementing the nation's political goals and enhancing its glory—whose definition was very often vague and open to diverse interpretations. Like other countries, those that emphasized collective goals were characterized by an intimate relation between the monarch's duties and conduct and the ideals and symbols prescribed by religion. The former were defined in terms of the latter. Justice, order, the welfare of the people and the state—these were often translated into religious and cultural rituals, like coronations and festivals, that emphasized the relations between kingship and religion.

However, legitimation of rulers of collective-executive oriented polities differed from that of rulers of culturally (pattern-maintenance) oriented societies, in the nature of the demands that it required them to fulfil. They were supposed to maintain a given order of nature or to perpetuate a given cultural pattern. In addition, they were obliged to promote certain affairs and certain aspects of social and political life, to be active in a variety of fields, and, often, to further the polity "as such." The rulers themselves even emphasized this obligation. Moreover, they continuously stressed, and were expected to implement, several types of goals. The emphases on general enhancement of the collectivity, on the polity of the embodiment of values—as an autonomous referent of values and orientations—implied the rulers' responsibility for advancing a multiplicity of goals, and the lack of clear and unequivocal criteria for evaluating and judging rulers. (*See, e.g.,* [L] *Bréhier, 1949[b], p. 1; Sinogowitz, 1953[b]; Baynes, 1955, ch. iii; Ensslin, 1939; Charanis, 1940–41[a]; [G] Christensen, 1936; and especially Altheim and Stiehl, 1954; Altheim, 1955[a], 1955[b]; [R] Hanke, 1945; Parry, 1940; [S] Beloff, 1954 passim.*)

In most of these societies, therefore, the pattern of legitimation of the rulers, and the values according to which they expected to be appraised (and were very often judged), were neither uniform nor simple. This fact presented various groups with the opportunity to make many demands on the rulers; in some cases, it made possible some secondary shifts to these groups as the main referents of political goals and activity. This pattern of legitimation existed even in many conquest societies; e.g., in societies whose centralized bureaucratic political systems had been established by conquest. Once such a polity had been established, if its rulers wanted to perpetuate the viability of their systems, they evolved a similar pattern of legitimation—even though the extent to which the conquered groups could hold the rulers answerable was, of course, limited.

[9] *The Influence of Collective-Executive Goals on the Policies of the Rulers and on the Political Orientations of the Major Strata*

Let us now consider some of the general effects that the various types of collective orientation, and the patterns of legitimation connected with them, had on political process in bureaucratic societies. Their influence was apparent in the major policies framed by the ruling elites. These policies closely reflected the kinds and amounts of resources needed by the ruling elites. In a collectively oriented socity, the rulers' need for "material" (economic and manpower) resources was far greater than this need in culturally oriented polities at similar levels of economic development and societal differentiation. The collective and political goals and concrete tasks pursued by the rulers (such as military and bureaucratic activities) usually entailed great expenditure of such resources. The need to mobilize them necessarily expanded the range of administrative activities and organs, and increased the need of additional manpower and resources for them.

Moreover, the rulers of collectively oriented countries required far more articulated political support. This was so for several reasons, which were connected with the nature of their legitimation and with the fact that the demands made on them by different groups could be relatively great.

The need for great and varied support was also engendered by the multiplicity, complexity, and mutability of goals. These very frequently caused changing policies, and increased the rulers' need to get support from those in their entourage and from wider strata for such changes, and their need to explain these changes through various channels of propaganda. Another factor contributing to the rulers' great need for support was the very strong emphasis on the autonomy of the political sphere and of the ruling elite, as against the still active traditional and aristocratic goals.

Thus political process in the collectively oriented countries was usually far more variegated and complex than it was in those emphasizing cultural orientations. Its complexity was reflected in the great articulation of political goals, in the development of more highly articulated and varied policies, in the number of strata participating in political activity and leadership, and in the nature of the issues and channels of political struggle. Thus the various collectivist orientations, and the collective-executive goals they engendered caused, as a rule, comparatively higher levels of generalization of power, with regard both to the rulers' choice and definition of goals, and to the resources they needed.

This picture was somewhat different in the cases of conquest societies. Their rulers also required many resources, but, by virtue of the initial conquest situation, they could minimize the amount of *political* support they needed from the conquered—so long as they received such support from within their own (conquering) groups. *(See, for instance,* [Q] *Boak, 1955[a]* passim; [R] *Zavala, 9143; Haring, 1947;* [O] *Stavrianos, 1957[a], pp. 1–2, 1957[b].)*

The development of emphases on various types of political-collective goals was usually facilitated, although not necessarily caused, by certain technological and geopolitical conditions—by much exposure to other states or to migratory movements, by being situated at an international intersection, by a limited territory, and by certain levels of technology enabling the rulers to establish their control over such territory. But the relations between these geographical and technological factors and the rulers' goals and policies was never simple or unilateral. Each influenced the other in constituting the "external" frameworks and seeking of these political systems.

[10] *The Influence of the Different Types of Collective-Executive Goals on the Policies of the Rulers*

However, regardless of their over-all similarity when compared with political processes in cultural-particularistic oriented societies, the political processes in countries oriented to collective goals were obviously not identical; and at least some of the differences between them can be attributed to their different goal emphases. These emphases or orientations can be distinguished according to the amount of different levels of generalized power they generated. That is, they can be distinguished according to the extent to which they contained universalistic and activistic orientations, which consequently made possible a greater complexity of goals, and shifted, in some measure, the referent of political activities to some groups in the society, or to "objective," transcendental, universalistic values.

According to this hypothesis, political struggle would have a small scope in those societies whose rulers' collective goals were greatly restrained by traditional fetters. On the other hand, the scope of political struggle would be greater in societies in which traditional fetters were small; and also in polities whose general emphasis was either on economic values and some enhancement of the several groups within the society, or on the propagation of universalistic values and orientations, as distinct from emphasis on purely political-collective ports.

Let us now examine the support our data give to these general suppositions about the relations between different types of collective goals and orientations and the various aspects of political process in these societies.

First, we shall briefly compare the types of policies framed by the rulers of countries oriented to political-collective goals, like military expansion. In such cases, the rulers formulated chiefly accumulative-prescriptive and regulative policies, largely oriented toward their direct control of different centers of power. This occurred in Sassanid Persia during the first periods of its history ([G] *Christensen, 1936; Altheim and Stiehl, 1954*); in early Byzantium ([L] *Ostrogorsky, 1931; Stein, 1919; Lemerle, 1958*) during the first stages of development of the Spanish-American Empire (when the continent was exploited for the direct benefit of the Spanish Crown) ([R] *Zavala, 1943; Ots Capdequi, 1939; Haring, 1927, 1947; Gallo, 1944*); and in Prussia during the expansionist and diplomatic phase of Absolutism ([X] *Hintze, 1915; Carsten, 1954, 1955; [S] Beloff, 1954*). In these cases, the rulers' policies were designed, almost entirely, to aid them in directly accumulating the power and resources that were their immediate political and economic needs; these policies were made with very little regard for the interests of other groups. The rulers often tried to bind the peasants to the land or to prevent their mobility, in order to insure manpower resources or to create state-controlled industrial enterprises. The more traditional the orientations of the ruler, the more pronounced were these attempts. True, the greater the differentiation in this countries, the smaller was the ability of the rulers to use only accumulative and prescriptive measures, and also to have recourse to various regulative policies. But, in so far as their own interests and orientations were concerned, the rulers resorted to "creative," accumulative measures as much as possible.

Wherever or whenever economic enhancement of the country, creation of economic potential, or maintenance and diffusion of a given culture were emphasized, the rulers framed more regulative and promotive policies. These policies were manifestations that some consideration was being given to the interests and demands of other groups. For example, in Byzantium, although economic considerations were always subordinate to political ones, during the Macedonian (A.D. 867–1057) and Isaurian (A.D. 717–802) dynasties several policies developed that were directed toward enhancing the free peasantry; there were even some—if weak—promotive policies concerned with industry and culture ([L] *Ostrogorsky, 1956[a]* passim; *Guilland, 1953–55; Bratianu, 1938; Runciman, 1952; Hussey, 1937*). In Sassanid Persia, Khosrou I's more complex cultural-political goals were connected with more regulative-prescriptive, and not only creative and accumulative, policies concerning the peasantry ([G] *Christensen, 1936; especially, Altheim and Stiehl, 1954, ch. ii, 1957, ch. i, ii, iii; Stein, 1920; Altheim, 1955[a], pp. 73–125, 1955[b], pp. 94–115*). In the Spanish-American Empire, whenever the continent's internal problems and continuous development were considered in addition to its direct exploitation by the Crown or the conquerors, regulative policies evolved with regard to alloting land and mobilizing labor (the *encomienda* and *repartimiento*), and trade and industry were encouraged through concessions and exemption from taxes ([R] *Ots Capdequi, 1939, 1941; Zavala, 1943; Haring, 1947; Simpson, 1934, 1938, 1950; Gongora, 1951; Konetzke, 1952, 1953*). In mercantilist England and France, promotive policies developed that concerned subsidies, an elastic tariff system, and finances. The mercantilist policies were, somewhat, bearing in mind the potential interests of different groups and strata; and, in mercantilist thought, there evolved a degree of differentiation between the welfare of the community and that of the rulers. In England, after the Glorious Revolution, policies had an even more promotive nature—e.g., direct taxation, and the encouragement of a free banking system. There were policies expressly concerned with the interests of the main groups represented in Parliament—i.e., the landed aristocracy, the gentry, and the merchants.

The predominance of orientations and goals emphasizing the welfare and interests of diverse social groups implied a shift, in the main referent of political activities, from the rulers and the polity to various groups within the society. However, such goals attained even partial preponderance, in the historical-bureaucratic polities studied, only in extremely rare and special cases. The two major examples of such cases were the maritime powers in seventeenth- and eighteenth-century England and Holland. There, the more active social and political groups succeeded, within limits, in making the state serve their own purposes and goals—like promoting trade or providing security ([S] *Beloff, 1954; Wilson, 1958; Heckscher, 1932;* [Y] *Cole, 1939, 1943;* [S] *Heaton, 1937; Viner, 1948;* [Z] *Ashley, 1952; Plumb, 1950; Mousnier, 1951; Clark, 1955; Nef, 1940 Namier, 1929, 1930, 1952*).

Though these kinds of orientations and goals were rarely predominant, even a relative emphasis on them influenced several aspects of the rulers' policies. First—as illustrated above, by England and Holland—in such cases a tendency developed to emphasize the state's provision of many services to more active and stronger groups in the society ([S] *Beloff, 1954, ch. vii*).

Secondly, implementing such goals necessitated using promotive policies. We have already discussed the importance of these policies in England. In Byzantium and China, promotive policies pertaining to the rural population were, in some measure, occasioned by the ruling elites' concern for the well-being of the peasants, and by the necessity to maintain certain basic conditions for the material well-being of the society ([L] *Guilland, 1953–55; Ostrogorsky, 1929[a], 1931;* [I] *Pulleyblank, 1955; Balázs, 1953[b], 1954[a]*).

Third, when framing and implementing these policies, a ruling elite necessarily had to take the interests of many groups and strata into account. This necessity was often a result of pressure exerted by the representatives of these groups and strata ([S] *Wilson, 1958; Beloff, 1954; Hartung and Mousnier, 1955; Heckscher, 1932; Clark, 1957;* [Z] *Ashley, 1952; Plumb, 1950; Nef, 1940; Namier, 1929, 1952; Pares, 1957; Mousnier, 1951*).

As we have already explained, the broad correlation between types and differentiations of goals and types of policies was largely caused by the resources needed by the rulers, the forces the rulers created or encouraged, and the nature of the legitimation they claimed and on which their rule was based. All these factors created potential frameworks for different groups to develop a wider scope of political participation. The degree to which this potential framework was realized depended on the sets of factors which we shall now investigate.

[11] *The Influence of the Different Types of Collective-Executive Goals on the Political Activities of the Major Groups*

Let us now attempt a more detailed analysis of the political activities and attitudes of groups and strata in the historical bureaucratic polities oriented to various collective goals.

When the rulers' needs and policies were more complicated, they provided a potentially wider range of political struggle. Their more differentiated and flexible needs necessarily made the rulers depend more on the strata and groups that were largely responsible for the "production" of the required resources—the economically and politically active groups, and the professional and cultural elites. Consequently, these groups could, and often did, participate vigorously in the political struggle. They voiced more demands, oriented themselves to wider political issues, and found more articulate forms of political organization.

Tables 1–10 show that the compass of the political struggle, measured by the complexity and articulation of political issues and activities and by the development of political-legal rights, was smallest, other conditions being equal, in those societies where the goals of the rulers were restricted by traditional fetters and/or where the complexity of the goals of the rulers and the universalistic elements in those goals were smallest—i.e., when the collective-cultural and collective economic goals were relatively important. This is manifested both by the extent to which the autonomous organs of political struggle developed in the various societies, and by the scope and articulation of the political activities of various groups.

This hypothesis is substantiated by a brief comparison of these processes in Persia, Byzantium, the Spanish-American Empire, France, and England. In all of these, there was a trend toward evolving autonomous organs and a political struggle enlarging the scope of the political struggle. These were least developed in Sassanid Persia ([G] *Christensen, 1939; Altheim and Stiehl, 1954*). Even there, however, the aristocracy, the upper bureaucracy, and the religious elites engaged in some relatively active and articulated political activities. The political struggle in Byzantium was more extensive; it was characterized by active participation of the bureaucracy, the upper urban groups, the religious elites, and, in some circumstances, the peasantry. There were also several specific organs of political struggle that were, in some measure, supported by the rulers ([L] *Ostrogorsky, 1956[a]; Vasiliev, 1952; Bréhier, 1917, 1948[a], 1948[b]; Bratianu, 1938; Manojlovic, 1936*).

In the Spanish-America Empire, the political struggle was confined to local matters. This limitation was due to its "conquest" nature and to the predominantly exploitive attitude and adaptive-integrative policies of the Spanish Crown. It was also due to the ethnic heterogeneity of the subjects ([R] *Haring, 1947; Parry, 1957; Borah, 1956*). Matters of principle were largely decided in the metropolis. Locally, the most prominent and politically articulated groups were the Church, the local aristocracy, and the upper urban classes. Because of the peculiarities of the colonial conquest situation, the Indians' level of political activity was far lower than the internal differentiation of their countries warranted ([R] *Gibson, 1955*).

In England and France the institutionalization of the specific organs of political struggle was greater. The scope of political struggle (as we shall discuss in greater detail when dealing with the effect of social differentiation on the political struggle) was much broader and more articulated, and oriented to broader and more complex issues. The cultural elites, the intelligentsia, and the urban groups were particularly active in it. (*See, e.g.,* [Y] *Sagnac, 1945, 1946;* [Z] *Ashley, 1952; Plumb, 1950; Namier, 1929, 1930, 1952; Pares, 1953, 1957; Browning, 1948; Brock, 1957;* [S] *Lindsay, 1957[a]; Beloff, 1954.*)

The relation existing between goals stressing the well-being of various social groups and the compass of the political struggle is almost self-evident. Where these goals had some significance, the more articulated types of political struggle existed. This is only natural, since the different groups and strata had to articulate their demands if these were to be considered.

[12] The Patterns of Political Participation in Societies Oriented to Universalistic Religious or Cultural Goals

Within the general framework of the processes and problems engendered by different types of collective goals, the political dynamics connected with the preponderance in society of orientations to the dissemination of universalistic values and religions are especially significant. The most important illustrations of the orientation to collective goals are provided by the Abbaside (A.D. 749–1258) and, to some extent, Fatimite (c. A.D. 909–1171) caliphates; by the primary stages of the Ottoman Empire [O] *Wittek, 1938; Stavrianos, 1957[a], p. i, 1957[b]; Gibb and Bowen, 1950; Fisher, 1941; Inalcik, 1954; Kissling, 1953, 1954; Köprülü, 1935*); and, though to a much smaller degree, by the Spanish-American Empire (especially by the activities of its missionaries) ([R] *Haring, 1947, ch. ix; Mörner, 1953; Desdevises du Dezert, 1917*); and by France and England during the sixteenth through eighteenth centuries ([S] *Hartung, 1937, 1957; Hartung and Mousnier, 1955; Lhéritier, 1923; Lefebvre, 1949; Wittram, 1948*). In France, as we have seen, it was evident, in various claims to intellectual predominance made during the age of "Enlightened Absolutism." In England, it was manifested in several aspects of Protestant and Puritan activities directed toward imposing certain cultural values on the political system—and, later, in the gradual establishment of religious tolerance as an end in itself.

Orientation toward disseminating universal values and religions partly determined the nature of the legitimation of the rulers, and that of the support they needed and solicited. It also gave rise to groups which considered themselves to be perpetuators of these values, and, consequently, judges of the rulers. Obviously, this kind of orientation greatly enhanced the position and status of the cultural and religious elites, and occasioned their active political participation.

However, the most important feature of regimes dominated by this orientation was the opportunity—even though it was not a fully institutionalized one—offered, to numerous groups, to proclaim themselves representatives of the relevant universal and religious values. When the dissemination of universalistic values was emphasized as the main (or a main) goal of the ruling elite and collectivity, this emphasis implied that participation in achieving this objective would be widespread. In turn, such widespread participation implied that those engaging in it would make political demands on the rulers. Moreover, their struggles with "traditional" elements not fully identified with these values and goals—e.g., tribal and aristocratic elements—made the rulers relatively dependent on broader strata and groups, particularly on sects and groups of religious or lay intellectuals.

These groups very often impeded the rulers' attempts to institutionalize, stabilize, and routinize their rule; and they often demanded that the rulers continue to devote themselves to disseminating the religion, whatever the political cost. Thus, a society's religious ideology could inspire and encourage different social forces and group to demand changes and reforms. Such conditions produced several political processes and movements whose natures were usually contingent on the extent of differentiation of the society in which they occurred. (These will be analyzed in more detail in Chapter 12.)

Sometimes, the religious ideology led to militant sectarian-religious political activities. However, in other circumstances—e.g., in the later Islamic period (during the so-called "Islamic Middle Ages")—it gave rise to growing political passivity. (*See* [M] *Hodgson, 1960; Lewis,* [M] *1950,* [N] *1953,* [M] *1954,* [O] *1958,* [N] *Cahen, 1955[a], 1957[a], 1957[b],* [M] *Grunebaum, 1954, 1955[a], 1955[b]; Levy, 1957;* [N] *Arnold, 1924;* [M] *Schacht, 1950; Gabrielli, 1950; Rosenthal, 1958;* [N] *Samadi, 1955[b];* [O] *Stavrianos, 1957[a], pp. 1–2, 1957[b].*)

Thus, there was a broad correlation between complexity of the rulers' goals, and the amount of universalistic elements in them, and the scope range of different strata's political participation. However, this broad correlation does not take many variations into account. The rulers' goals created a potential framework for the development, by different groups, of a wider political participation. But these groups' political orientations and aspirations could be more intensive and wider than the framework created by the rulers—as was the case in the Spanish-American Empire, France, and England; and on a smaller scale, and in a more fragmentary way, in Byzantium during the seventh through eleventh centuries and in China. On the other hand, these groups' orientations were sometimes inadequate—more traditional than the political framework set up by the rulers—this was somewhat true in Persia, or in Byzantium during the early sixth and seventh, and the late fourteenth centuries. The political orientations and activities of the various groups in a society were not determined solely by its rulers' goals. Additional conditions could influence them.

Before we can analyze these other conditions, we must consider some additional problems related to the types of goals of the rulers.

[13] The Nature of the Exigencies Developing in Polities with Collective-Executive Goals

The first problem we must investigate is the nature of the political exigencies that developed within the historical bureaucratic polities where various types of political-collective goals preponderated.

In these, as in all other societies, many exigencies could arise easily that derived entirely from external circumstances beyond the society's control. Nevertheless, the rulers' goal emphasis tended to develop a special sensitivity to two types of exigency. One was external-political, resulting from the impact of foreign political forces on the political situation of the polity; the other was internal.

Political systems with strong political-collective goals were very sensitive to external exigencies—much more so than polities whose goals were cultural. In many societies dominated by these political-collective orientations, the very nature of these goals conduced to the *Primat der Aussenpolitik;* the impact of external forces frequently became, in them, the starting point of internal changes.

Internal exigencies may be divided into two classes. The first class comprised internal administrative problems, created mostly by the need to mobilize extensive resources in order to achieve the rulers' various goals and policies. Problems in this class frequently arose in connection with external exigencies—for example, in connection with the inability or unwillingness of certain strata to meet the rulers' demands for resources they required for their projects of military expansion or defense. The significance of these internal exigencies explains the important role of the military. This military importance is illustrated by the positions of the local army commanders in Sassanid Persia ([G] *Altheim and Stiehl, 1954, p. 2; Christensen, 1936);* by the commanders of the army or the military dynasties (e.g., the Comnenus Dynasty [A.D. 1057–59; A.D. 1081–1185]) in Byzantium ([L] *Ostrogorsky, 1956[a]; Guilland, 1953–55);* and by the various caliphates that ultimately succumbed entirely to military rule ([N] *Cahen, 1957[a], 1957[b]).*

The second type of internal exigencies emerged when various strong internal forces, initially promoted by the rulers, had reached the point where the existing political institutions could no longer accommodate them.

Any discussion of the exigencies related to the society's predominant goal orientation must inevitably involve the related problems of social and political change. Our detailed analysis of the latter will be presented in the chapter devoted to change.

[14] *The Conditions for Developing Goals of Self-Maintenance and Their Influence on the Political Process*

We have, till now, been concerned with the influence that the rulers' goals exerted on the policies of the rulers and on the political activities of different strata. Specifically, we have tried to analyze the influences of goals which contained some explicit cultural contents or orientations. However, the rulers of all the polities studied also had, as concomitants of these goals, the goals of self-maintenance, of perpetuating their own status and power.

But only in exceptional cases were the activities and ideologies of the ruling elites of the historical bureaucratic societies oriented chiefly (or exclusively) toward self-maintenance. Although goals of self-maintenance were ubiquitous, they became predominant only under certain conditions. Ideologically and politically, they were usually considered secondary—i.e., not as constituting ends in themselves, but, rather, as means of implementing the polity's main goals and of maintaining the rulers' power positions.

Self-maintenance preponderated—temporarily—as chief goal in these polities when they were threatened by external danger or internal disintegration. For example, if a ruler's position were strongly opposed by many groups, he would consequently be primarily concerned with making it secure; and he would then stress the goals of self-maintenance. Still, even under such conditions, the self-maintenance goals were seldom fully legitimized or acknowledged. However, the rulers placed much emphasis on preserving the status quo (even when this was coupled with attempted reforms) during the final periods of the Byzantine and Spanish-American empires, and during social and political upheavals in China ([L] *Ostrogorsky, 1956[a]; Stein, 1954;* [R] *Ots Capdequi, 1945; Parry, 1957; Haring, 1947, ch. xvii;* [I] *Duyvendak, 1928; Balázs, 1948, 1950; Hucker, 1958; Liu, 1949[a]*).

Second, the rulers may have been oriented primarily to the maintenance of the status quo sometimes, after having successfully expanded their polities and created new forms of political activity, but this was neither an open nor an official goal. Their chief interest was to stabilize the regime. This is most evident in conquest societies and empires whose rulers, after their initial successes, desisted from making further campaigns and endeavored to insure the status quo and the durability of the given society. In all these cases, such orientations were usually legitimated by the rulers' alleged implementation of various collective and cultural goals. A relatively strong emphasis on self-maintenance emerged in the political orientations of the Spanish-American Empire [R] *Haring, 1927, 1947; Ots Capdequi, 1939, 1941; Zavala, 1943)* and the Ottoman Empire ([O] *Köprülü, 1935; Wittek, 1938; Lybyer, 1913; Fisher, 1941)* following the first waves of conquest; and in China, after the establishment of new dynasties. The rulers of the seventeenth- and eighteenth-century Prussia and Russia also stressed self-maintenance. They did so after having initiated modernization programs whose effects were to incite the opposition of the aristocracy and to arouse the political aspirations of the lower classes, especially the peasantry ([X] *Rosenberg, 1958; Bruford, 1935, 1957; Carsten, 1954, 1955, 1959)*.

A ruler's orientation toward self-maintenance obviously influenced the types of policies that he chose to put into effect. It was responsible for his tendency to acquire total control over different spheres, according to his own power considerations, and to develop strong prescriptive policies toward those strata which he perceived either as opposed to him or as possessing the potential to become independent of him.

Also, their emphasis on goals of self-maintenance led the rulers to frame and implement party-political policies. These were chiefly concerned with propaganda; they were directed toward inculcating basic loyalty to, and winning support for, the rulers. The rulers often attempted to appropriate the symbols and values of the society's political-cultural traditions. These activities attained special prominence during periods when the rulers' choices of policies were severely opposed and controversial, and the rulers were consequently in dire need of support. Thus, party-political and propagandist policies were very pronounced during the iconoclast schism in Byzantium ([L]*Bréhier, 1904, 1938; Ostrogorsky, 1929[b], 1930[b]; Hussey, 1937; Barker, 1957)*, during the wars of religion in France and England ([Y] *Königsberger, 1955;* [Z] *Ashley, 1952; Namier, 1929, 1930, 1952; Pares, 1953, 1957; Walcott, 1956)*, and during strife between the emperors and the Confucian scholars and ministers in China (e.g., [I] *Hucker, 1958, 1959[a]; Liu, 1959[a]*). They also became somewhat prominent in Prussia and Russia during the seventeenth and eighteenth centuries ([X] *Carsten, 1954, 1955; Hintze, 1915; Rosenberg, 1958;* [S] *Beloff, 1954;* [W] *Young, 1957; Nolde, 1952–53)*. In all these cases (especially in the last), such policies were associated with powerful prescriptive policies directed both against the older aristocratic groups and against groups (like the peasantry or urban groups) whose political aspirations could have been stimulated by the processes of modernization introduced by the rulers. These prescriptive policies had the most manifestations in the legal and political fields—e.g., the rulers' attempts to make the status system inflexible; in their attempts to disrupt the autonomous channels of communication of different groups and strata, and to minimize the possibilities of contacts among them.

The most restrictive policies usually evolved when the rulers' self-maintenance orientations were closely associated with purely political-collective goals (as was the case in many conquest states). The combination of these two orientations usually resulted in the rulers' development of prescriptive and control policies to the maximum, and in their establishing patterns of political control very similar to the traditional conception of "Oriental despotism" ([I] *Wittfogel, 1957; Eberhard, 1958; Eisenstadt, 1958; Pulleyblank, 1958*).

An examination of the ways that the relative predominance of the self-maintenance orientation of the polity influenced the political activities of the polity's groups and strata reveals that, in so far as these groups and strata identified themselves with the rulers, or were successfully coerced to comply with the rulers' demands—their interest in wider issues and activities were reduced or minimized. The most active political groups and strata then adjusted their activities and demands to the framework established by the rulers' policies and aims. However, frequently the chief groups did not identify themselves with the rulers' goals, and opposed their attainment. In such cases, grave external exigencies sometimes developed that led to various processes of change. These processes will be analyzed in a later chapter.

[15] *The General Influence of Different Levels of Social Differentiation on the Political Process*

Hitherto we have examined the influence that different types of orientations and goals of the rulers had on the political process in historical bureaucratic societies, with the object of demonstrating the ways that these orientations and goals determined the rulers' policies, the political framework that the rulers established, and the resources they needed. We have also shown the ways that these different types of orientations and goals affected the degree both of political participation of divers groups and of the extent to which the autonomous organs of political struggle evolved. We have seen that the rulers' goals provided, at most, general frameworks or directions for the political participation of different groups. The manifestations of their participation were dependent mostly on their social composition and orientation.

A. GENERAL INFLUENCE OF DIFFERENT
LEVELS OF DIFFERENTIATIONS

Our analysis indicates that the main aspects of the compositions and orientations of the chief groups that influenced the nature of their political participation were those most closely related to the amount of social differentiation in the polity. We have demonstrated that most regulative and integrative problems engendered by differentiation of the social structure were closely related to the free-floating—economic, manpower, social, and political—activities and resources in the polity. Hence, we may assume that the same conditions that were most directly connected with the development of free-floating resources and activities also constituted a major determinant of the chief groups' political orientations. The extent of such societal differentiation in one of the historical bureaucratic empires may be measured by determining the degree to which, in the particular empire, the following had developed:

1. The market and exchange economy
2. The universalistic and achievement criteria, and the mobility
3. The flexibility of the status system
4. The universalistic value orientations, and the autonomous cultural organizations oriented to activistic participation in the society
5. The cultural and professional elites evincing universalistic orientations and activistic participation

The amount of societal differentiation could affect the political orientations of any given group in two ways. Through influencing the group's internal structure and its structural position in the society, it could set the ranges of the group's basic political attitudes. Second, it also affected the broader institutional framework within which the group operated and the concrete problems it faced; it could thus influence the articulation of the group's concrete political activities. In particular, the general extent of differentiation could influence the connections developing among different groups, and the possibilities of establishing wider frameworks of political activities, and of linking the more traditional with the more differentiated types of political orientation and activities. In these ways, the amount of differentiation of the social structure affected the levels of generalized power that were generated by the various strata. The higher this level, the more differentiated and articulated were the political orientations and activities of the several social groups and strata.

We have, accordingly, formulated our basic hypothesis in these terms. The more prevalent and extensive the societal differentiation, then—other conditions being equal—the greater (1) the flexibility of the rulers' policies and the basic frameworks of political activity they provided; (2) the various groups' and strata's interests in wider general issues and in more complex political participation; (3) the level of organization of the political struggle, in relatively distinct political organizations and by distinct political leadership; (4) the number of strata and groups participating in the central political struggle; and (5) the amount of political-legal rights they acquired.

[16] *The Influence of Different Levels of Differentiation on the Political Activities of Various Groups*

We shall first compare the effects social differentiation had on the political participation of the chief social groups and strata in different societies or within the same society. We shall try to demonstrate that scope of political participation of each type of group or stratum was dependent both on the extent to which the internal structure of such a group or stratum was differentiated according to the main criteria mentioned, and on the amount of differentiation in the general institutional framework within which such a group operated.

In other words, we shall undertake a detailed analysis of the relation among the degrees of differentiation, achievement, orientation, and status flexibility within different strata and groups, and of the amount and nature of these strata's participation in the political struggle.

A. THE ARISTOCRACY

Since the aristocracy was among the most ascriptive strata, its interests as a rule did not accord with growing differentiation in the society. At the same time, the aristocracy was usually among the politically more active strata. However, its political activity was usually oriented to limiting other strata's autonomous and free political participation, and to maintaining the simpler types of political issues and organization at the local and the central levels. At the local level, the aristocracy conducted its political activities largely through direct (personal or group) relations with other groups. At the central level, it participated in the political struggle chiefly through different types of cliques.

The more traditional and undifferentiated the structure of an aristocratic group, the narrower its range of specifically political orientations and the more these were patterned according to "traditional" un-differentiated ways—even when the aristocracy was (as it often was) the society's most active group politically. Thus, the most traditional types of aristocratic political activites occurred in Sassanid Persia, for example ([G] *Christensen, 1936; Ghrishman, 1954; Altheim and Stiehl, 1954, pp. 2–3)*; and during the first stages of absolute monarchies in Europe (fifteenth and sixteenth centuries, when the aristocracy had a marked patrimonial feudal character. The aristocracies engaged in more differentiated and articulated political activities in Byzantium, Spanish America and in Europe—especially in England and Prussia, and somewhere in France—during the eighteenth century ([L] *Ostrogorsky, 1956[a]; Stein, 1919, 1928[b], 1954;* [R] *Konetzke, 1951[a], 1952; Haring, 1947; Parry, 1957;* [S] *Goodwin, 1953)*. There, the social basis and structure became more differentiated, and bore more relation to market economy and to more differentiated social structure.

However, the degree of differentiation of the general social structure in a polity also influenced the aristocracy's political activities, which became more differentiated and articulated as the differentiation of the general social structure grew. Thus, in Persia, with the beginning of the Sassanid Dynasty—and especially during the reigns of Kavadh I (A.D. 488–531) and Khosrou I (A.D. 531–579)—the aristocratic groups had to engage in wider party politics, participate in more general political activities, and abandon their purely feudal attitudes ([G] *Altheim and Stiehl, 1954; Christensen, 1936* passim; *Widengren, 1956)*.

In Byzantium, during the sixth through eleventh centuries, the aristocratic groups participated in the party politics at court. The Senate and the bureaucracy evolved certain articulated political organization and activities, in the form of cliques, and participated in their own internal groups and parties. However, during periods of aristocratic preponderance and the Empire's decline, the aristocracy tended to concern itself more with the direct usurpation of power. It emphasized the ascriptive-territorial rights against the demands of the central government ([L] *Ostrogorsky, 1956[a]* passim, *1956[b]; Guilland, 1947–48, 1954)*.

Similarly, comparison of the Prussian with the French and the English aristocracies reveals that the latter—and especially the English —acted within the framework of relatively differentiated social structure. They developed much more articulated types of political activities, even though these activities were primarily conservatively oriented ([X]*Hintze, 1915; Rosenberg, 1958;* [S] *Goodwin, 1953* passim; *Lindsay, 1957[a])*.

A chapter will be devoted to the political attitudes of the bureaucracy. Therefore, let us analyze the political activities of the cultural, professional, and religious elites.

B. CULTURAL, RELIGIOUS,
AND PROFESSIONAL ELITES

As we have discussed, the cultural, religious, and professional (when these last were at all important) elites conducted numerous types of political activities. These ranged, from simple petitioning and limited struggles for concrete benefits and for the maintenance of their own restricted autonomy, to the most articulated kinds of political participation.

The extent to which religious groups and institutions engaged in political activity was largely determined by several interdependent variables. First, the basic political orientations of such a group and the range of its political activities, were greatly influenced by several aspects of its internal structure. the most important of these were the degrees to which: (1) universalistic orientations and activistic principles were predominant in the religion; (2) the state constituted an important referent of religious activity; and (3) the religious group's internal differentiation, organization, and cohesion, and its autonomy and distinctiveness from other social and political spheres, had developed.

The Mazdaist church was the most conservative religious group in our sample— the least differentiated from the political structure, and identifying with the state. It largely confined itself to the simple, not very highly articulated type of political activity within the court and provinces, concerned primarily with maintaining its given place in the social and political structure. The social-religious movement that developed as a reaction to the Church—i.e., the Mazdaite movement— was politically the least articulated of the many movements discussed here ([G] *Nyberg, 1938; Christensen, 1925, 1936, pp. 110 ff.; Coulborn, 1958–59; Klima, 1957*).

The Chinese Confucian elite was far more cohesive, and very actively oriented to the state and to political activity. At the same time, it exhibited powerful particularistic orientations, and had no central organization of its own. It participated mainly in those political activities which were oriented to the simpler issues and types of political activity; or it exerted influence on policies, according to their predominant particularistic values and criteria, within the given political framework. Members of the Confucian elite were more active in organized groups, cliques, and institutions (e.g., the Censorate, offices of the Secretariat, etc.) that were important foci of the political struggle— even though the scope and articulation of their activities were rather restricted ([I] *Liu, 1957, 1959[b]; Hucker, 1958, 1959[a]; De Bary, 1957; Bąlázs, 1952, 1959[a]; Nicolas-Vandier, 1959[a], 1959[b]; Kal-*

tenmark, 1959[a]; Pulleyblank, 1954). The Taoist and Buddhist groups, with their greater passivity and other-worldliness, participated, as a rule, in the simpler and less articulated kinds of political activity. The various movements which originated within them were also politically relatively unarticulated, and were either transient and temporary, or parts of wider rebellions directed at seizing the throne and re-establishing the former bureaucratic pattern. Most of these rebellions did not engender any extensive political passivity and deflection of political support from the polity. Rather, they emphasized and maintained the level of passivity that was expected of the lower groups in Chinese society ([I] *Wright, 1959; Maspero, 1950[b], 1950[c]; Gernet, 1956; Pulleyblank, 1955; Kaltenmark, 1959[b]; Demiéville, 1959[a], 1959[b]*).

The Byzantine church had far more autonomous and unversalistic orientations, and had a strong organization of its own. However, its autonomy was greatly restricted by its strong ties with the state and by its acceptance of the state's (and the emperor's) puissant position in the religious sphere. The Church participated greatly in the central political institutions in the Senate, the court, and the bureaucracy. In addition, it inaugurated basic political issues (e.g., during the iconoclastic wars), fulfilled many vital political and administrative functions, and was often concerned with wider issues of policy. However, because it contained strong other-worldly elements, and because of the rise of politically passive monasticism, and the Church's acceptance of the state's cultural position, its political activity was largely confined within frameworks and organizations established by the existing political institutions. In extreme cases, the Church engaged in the promotion of widespread political passivity. Although the various social-religious movements which developed within the Church (e.g., the monastic orders) were often active within the political framework established by the rulers, they did not create any new or wider types of political activity and orientations; and they often bred political passivity. Similarly, the rebellious movements arising during the fall of the Byzantine Empire were also relatively inarticulated, politically, and were greatly inspired by utopian ideologies and symbols ([L] *Hussey, 1937, 1957; Barker, 1957; Bréhier, 1948[a], 1948[b], 1950*).

The Catholic Church in the Spanish-American Empire and in France was characterized by its great degree of universalistic orientation, by its claims to judge the polity according to the transcendental criteria of which the Church was the bearer, and by its high extent of autonomous organization. Consequently, the Church exhibited a great deal of political militancy, and participated actively in the representative institutions and the higher government councils. In the Spanish-American Empire, the Church did not, on the whole, create new types of political activity. However, it played a major part in framing policies pertaining to the Indians, and was largely responsible for their humane treatment. Thus, the Church participated actively in the political struggle—propagating wider values and principles, on the one hand; and fighting for its place in the government and for monopoly in the cultural field, on the other ([R] *Haring, 1947, ch. ix; Mörner, 1953; Hanke, 1949, 1951, 1952; Desdevises du Dezert, 1915*).

Except for the Islamic states, the Protestant groups exhibited the most political militancy, organization, and articulation of political issues, during the Wars of Religion and the English Civil War (1642–49). The Protestant groups were characterized by strong universalistic and political activistic orientations, sectarian organization, and activist worldly tendencies. The last were manifested in the groups' active participation in the political struggle, their formation of relatively articulated political groups and organizations, and their repeated attempts to reform the basic pattern of participation in, and organization of, the political system ([Y] *Königsberger, 1955*; [S] *Beloff, 1954*; [Z] *Ashley, 1952; Plumb, 1950*; [S] *Clark, 1929–59*, [Z] *1955; Davies, 1955; Ogg, 1934, 1955; Trevelyan, 1930–34; Hill, 1955; Jordan, 1932; Sykes, 1934; Tawney, 1926*).

The Islamic groups, which were analyzed earlier, exhibited the most militant universalistic orientations of all. Within them, the universalistic-missionary orientation was very powerful, as was their emphasis on the state as the framework of the religious community, though in a way subordinate to it. On the other hand, there was no over-all organization or cohesion of the religious groups and functionaries. As a result, political participation was relatively limited, confined mostly to court cliques and participation in the bureaucracy; or else sectarian activities evolved that were extreme, and directed either at destroying the existing regime and establishing a new and religiously "pure" and true one, or at becoming bearers of political passivity ([N] *Lewis, 1950, 1953; Cahen, 1957[a], 1957[b]*).

However, the exact political activities of the religious and cultural groups were also determined by the extent of general differentiation of the social structure within which they acted and by the types of goals of the rulers. Thus, the more this structure was differentiated the wider were the articulation and the political activities of the religious (and cultural) elites.*

* Full bibliographical data for this section have been indicated in the preceding section.

Thus the Mazdaist church developed more active and articulated types of political and propagandist activities during the reigns of Kavadh I and Khosrou I, when social differentiation was growing.

In Byzantium, Church activities reached their heights in the seventh through tenth centuries, when the whole social structure of the Empire became highly differentiated, especially during the iconoclast wars in the eighth and ninth centuries. At the same time, the scope of the Church's political activities was more restricted to clique activities and personal relations to the rulers and its emphases on other-worldly orientations and political activity were greater during the Empire's periods of decline, when the general level of differentiation was lowered.

Similarly, the Confucian elite's operations were more articulated and active, during periods of growing differentiation in the social structure under the T'ang (A.D. 618–905) and Sung (A.D. 960–1279), earlier periods. In European countries, the activities of the Catholic Church in France and Spain, and of the Protestant churches and groups in England, France, and Holland, provide analogous illustrations.

Political passivity, emphasis on other-worldliness, and deflection of political support from the polity were all latent in many of the religions studied here. These, too, became most articulated in periods of political decline and social disorganization.

The political activities of the intelligentsia and the cultural and professional elites were contingent upon the same factors that determined the religious groups' political participation. For the intelligentsia and elites, the decisive factors were the degree of their own autonomy, and the number of flexible, universalistically oriented strata and groups. Consequently, in the less differentiated societies these groups. exhibited political passivity. Only in the more differentiated societies did they participate actively in the political struggle. Thus, these groups' political activity, participation in wider movements, articulated organization, and interest in wider political issues were great in England and France, smaller in the Spanish-American Empire, and smaller still in China and Byzantium.

C. URBAN GROUPS

The same fundamental conditions also influenced the types of political activities engaged in by the major urban groups. Their less developed and articulated political activities were directed at attaining local autonomy and various direct economic benefits. These activities were predominant wherever these urban groups were comparatively undifferentiated; confined largely to their local settings; not related to wider, differentiated settings; and accepted most of the polity's basic claims to constitute the chief embodiment of wider values and referent of political activities.

In Sassanid Persia ([I] *Balázs, 1954[a], 1960; Kracke, 1953, 1955; Liu, 1959[b]*) and in China, the urban groups' potentially wider orientations were kept from realization by the policies of the rulers and the bureaucracy, and by the basic cultural orientations of the polity. The same conditions obtained, though to a much lesser extent, in the Spanish-American Empire and in the urban centers of Byzantium and France. In all these countries, there were many urban centers whose differentiation was limited in extent. They accordingly displayed a high level of conservatism and a low level of articulated political participation.

In Byzantium ([L] *Ostrogorsky, 1956[a]; Vasiliev, 1952; Bratianu, 1938; Diehl, 1905, 1924, 1929; Bréhier, 1917*) and more particularly, in England and France, more extensive and articulated political participation by the urban groups also developed. It manifestations were the urban groups' orientations to wider issues and to acquiring legal political rights. It was directly related to the greater differentiation of economic and social activities—of the whole social setting, and of their own structure—to their growing acceptance of wider universalistic values, and to their development of a self-concept of themselves as the bearers of these values. The urban groups tended to evolve more active and articulated types of political activities whenever the relative extent of general differentiation of the social structure in which they acted was great. This was illustrated in Byzantium during the sixth through tenth centuries, in China under the Sung ([I] *Balázs, 1960; Kracke, 1953, 1955*), and, most of all, in the European countries (especially Western European ones) in the seventeenth and eighteenth centuries ([S] *Labrousse, 1955;* [Z] *Clark, 1955,* [S] *1957; Lindsay, 1957[a]; Briggs, 1956;* [Z] *Beloff, 1938*). Under such conditions, the specific political orientations of the urban groups became connected with the wider orientations of various cultural and professional elites, and, through them, were channelized into more differentiated and articulated kinds of political activities.

It is interesting to note that, where the urban groups were relatively undifferentiated and strongly ascriptive, they often participated in sporadic, politically unarticulated rebellions and uprisings. This occurred in Byzantium and in China, and, to much smaller extent, in Europe ([L] *Charanis, 1940–41[b], 1953[a]; Barker, 1957; Ostrogorsky, 1956[a]; Vasiliev, 1952; Diehl* et al., *1945;* [S] *Labrousse, 1955; Beloff, 1954*).

D. THE GENTRY AND THE PEASANTRY

Our general hypothesis about the influence of social differentiation on the extent of political participation is also substantiated by the analysis of the political activities of the gentry and peasantry. As we have seen, the political activities of these groups were generally confined to the local levels, and were neither very articulated nor extensive. (In many cases, there was little difference between the gentry and some peasant groups.) A higher degree of articulation was attained only under special conditions. The necessary conditions obtained when these groups became internally more differentiated and evolved wider orientations; or when the general level of differentiation of the social structure in which they participated was great, and their representatives were incorporated and partially integrated in wider institutional frameworks. Thus, those groups of Chinese gentry who became somewhat integrated in the literati-bureaucratic framework engaged in more articulated political activities. The same was true of the English gentry, which gradually became integrated with the central political institutions—i.e., with the House of Commons or the various institutions of local government. On a smaller scale, these developments occurred in the Spanish-American Empire, where the less influential colonists and the heads of Indian communities were represented in local political activities and in the bureaucracy.

The peasantry achieved a high degree of articulation in Byzantium, during the reigns of those emperors who tried to establish an independent peasantry. They attained a somewhat lower degree in China and in Europe in general, especially in England. As a rule, these groups did not become internally differentiated or integrated into wider frameworks, but remained within the confines of their narrow localities. Then they often participated in various unorganized or semi-organized rebellions and in outlawry.

The foregoing illustrations and analyses establish the acceptability of our hypothesis concerning the relations among the extent of differentiation of the social structure, the levels of generalized power generated by the main strata, and the degree to which these strata's political orientations and activities were articulated. We have tried to show that this relation operated both through the internal differentiation of such types of groups and through the general differentiation of the social structure.

However, the internal differentiation of each group appears to have been more important in determining the group's basic political attitudes. The influence exerted by the extent of "general" differentiation was, for the most part, limited to determining which of the potential political orientations of any given group would become most articulated; it did not create any new orientations.

It also follows from this analysis that the degree of differentiation need not have been equal in all sectors of the same society; and, therefore, that differences may have existed between the respective extents of political participation of the same type of stratum in different societies. For instance, the peasantry was more passive in England and France than in Byzantium, while the urban classes were more active in the former than in the latter.

[17] *The Effects of Different Levels of Differentiation on the Policies of the Rulers*

The preceding analysis has indicated the ways that the political participation of different strata was largely determined by the extent of the society's internal differentiation. However, this factor's influence was not confined to the political participation of different strata; it also affected, in some measure, the policies of the rulers. In order to examine this, we may again profitably compare societies, whose respective dominant orientations and political goals were similar, that differed in the respective levels of differentiation of their social structures.

Policy-making was partly determined by the extent of differentiation for two major reasons. First, social differentiation, and the consequent political attitudes of various groups, sometimes had a great deal of influence on certain aspects of the rulers' legitimation. The influence could be exerted especially on the designation of the ruling elite, the degree to which its legitimation was traditional charismatic or elective and non-traditional, the extent to which it was answerable to different social groups, and the part these groups had in its designation.

Second, the greater the social differentiation, the more developed and powerful the strata were upon which the rulers depended for resources. Thus, the greater was the rulers' potential obligation to consider the interests of these strata when formulating policies.

Therefore, when the extent of differentiation within a society increased—and other conditions, especially the extent of compatibility between the rulers' orientations and those of the main strata, being equal—the interests of various groups were taken more into account, semi-officially or officially, in the processes of policy- and decision-making, and the scope of the official or semi-official channels through which these interests could be represented and expanded.

In Sassanid Persia, the articulated accommodation of the interests of various groups was very small. Their only official means of representation were directly petitioning the king, or rebelling against him. *(See [G] Christensen, 1936; Delaporte and Huart, 1943 passim; Altheim and Stiehl, 1954; Altheim, 1955[a], 1955[b]; Ghirshman, 1954.)* In China, the official consideration of different groups' interests was also comparatively rare. However, in China, unofficial representation "interests" were much more commonly taken into account.

In Byzantium, different groups achieved a far greater measure of representation in the political process, and their articulated goals and interests had more influence on the policies of the rulers, than in Sassanid Persia or China. The consideration given to the interests of the urban and upper rural European population of the Spanish-American Empire was relatively great. However, the interests of the less articulated native population were much less—if at all—taken into account. The official accommodation of different groups—with the partial exception of that of the colonial aristocracy—diminished during the seventeenth century, as a result of the growing petrification of the social-political structures of both the metropolis and the colonies ([R] *Haring, 1947; Ots Capdequi, 1939, 1941, 1945 1946[a]; Zavala, 1943; Parry, 1957*). In France and—more particularly—in England, groups and their interests were considered far more, and had many more representation channels at their disposal. In France, several urban groups and the *noblesse de robe* attained some measure of semi-official and institutionalized accommodation in the *parlements,* the assemblies of estates, and the bureaucracy ([Y] *Sagnac, 1945, 1946; Pagès, 1928; Barber, 1955*). In England, many urban groups, as well as the gentry acquired significant and influential representation in Parliament ([Z] *Plumb, 1950; Ashley, 1952; Namier, 1929, 1930, 1952; Pares, 1957; Brock, 1957; [S] Beloff, 1954*).

Moreover, the greater the differentiation of their own and of the general social structure, the greater also were the scope of different groups' participation in the organs of political struggle and their demands to have some of their political rights recognized. As we have seen, such political participation was minimal in Sassanid Persia, and much higher in Byzantium; and, in Europe—especially in England and France (and, to some extent, in the Spanish-American Empire)—it reached its developmental zenith.

The extent of social differentiation usually also affected those policies dealing with the provision of certain resources—manpower and economic resources, and political support—to the rulers. Other conditions being equal, then the greater this differentiation, the less important were the creative or purely regulative policies, and the more were policies politically more articulated—whether promotive or prescriptive.

This general hypothesis can be tested by analyzing first, the effects of social differentiation on the political process in culturally oriented societies. China will serve as our point of departure. There was greater differentiation of the social structure during the Sung (960–1279) and Ming (1368–1644) dynasties than during the T'ang Dynasty (618–905). This led to the adoption of numerous comparatively promotive policies in the economic (trade) field; and, simultaneously, to the establishment of more extensive control over the more active groups and over the strata of the population ([I] *Liu, 1959[b]; Kracke, 1953, 1955; Twitchett, 1957[b], 1957[c]; Miyakawa, 1955; Rieger, 1937, H. Franke, 1953[a]*). Similarly, the more promotive-regulative agricultural policies were initiated during those periods (as during the T'ang) when the scope of differentiation and mobility in the rural sectors grew ([I] *Balázs, 1953[b], 1954[a]; Pulleyblank, 1955*).

In comparison with the Chinese Empire, the Ancient Egyptian Empire had a less differentiated polity, and it was oriented predominantly to very traditional, non-differentiated goals. The Egyptian rulers were accordingly strongly inclined to resort to accumulative and creative-prescriptive policies; they framed few, if any, regulative and promotive ones ([F] *Kees, 1933[a]; Drioton and Vandier, 1952; Otto, 1953*).

Social differentiation had similar effects on those policies of the rulers that dealt with provision of resources in societies with different types of political-collective orientations and goals. In many of these societies, the development of social differentiation gave rise to more flexible policies—even when the goals themselves did not change much.

In all these societies—with the partial exceptions of France and England—there were various types of creative, accumulative, and traditional prescriptive policies. Their purpose was to found state workshops and monopolies, to impose certain direct taxes, and to recruit manpower for the army and for public works. These policies were most important in the undifferentiated societies. They were prevalent, for example, in Sassanid Persia, where they were manifested in the founding of cities, royal workshops, and industries; in a rather rigid system of peasants' bondage to the soil; and in the several ways of obtaining taxes from the peasants by diverse registration systems. Policies of this sort were utilized during the transition from the late Roman Empire to the early Byzantine Empire ([Q] *Boak, 1955[a]; Jones, 1955; Kraemer, 1953; Westerman, 1955*), and, to some extent, during the latter's decline ([L] *Ostrogorsky, 1929[a]*), *1931, 1956[a], 1956[b]; Lemerle, 1958; Stein, 1919, 1954*).

They also preponderated during the primary stages of the Spanish-American Empire, before the *encomiendas* and the flexible systems of mobilizing Indian labor had been fully established. The *repartimiento,* the monopolies, the imposition of taxes and revenues on trade and mining—were manifestations of the persistence of the prescriptive and creative policies throughout the history of this Empire. These policies were made necessary, in part, by the exploitive purposes of the Spanish Crown and by the great gap between the European and native populations ([R] *Ots Capdequi, 1934[a], 1939, 1941; Zavala, 1943, 1945; Haring, 1922, 1927, 1947; Simpson, 1934, 1938, 1950; Konetzke, 1946, 1949[a], 1951[a], 1951[b], 1952, 1953; Gongora, 1951; Miranda, 1941–45, 1951; Chaunu, 1956; Hanke, 1936[b]; Barber, 1932).*

However, in the less differentiated countries, these creative and accumulative-prescriptive policies were not the only ones—and their importance waned as the differentiation of the social structure grew. Even in Sassanid Persia, as the differentiation in the economic and social structures increased toward the reigns of Kavadh and Khosrou I, and the activity of the kings concomitantly increased, more regulative-prescriptive policies developed with regard to the peasantry, aristocracy, and urban circles ([G] *Stein, 1920; Altheim and Stiehl, 1954[a]; Christensen, 1936).*

In seventeenth- and eighteenth-century France and (especially) England—the most differentiated societies in our sample—promotive policies, in addition to regulative, grew in importance. A comparison of the financial policies of these two nations during this period also bears out our hypothesis. In France, purely regulative policies were far more prominent; in England, promotive policies were much more predominant ([Z] *Nef, 1940; Mousnier, 1951;* [S] *Beloff, 1954; Wilson, 1958).*

In France, most monetary policies emphasized direct taxation and subsidies. In England, there were more promotive types of financial policy, proposing indirect taxation, banking operations, and a tariff system conducive to the development of trade.

For our hypothesis, the development of taxation policies in general, and of those concerned with agrarian problems in particular, is of special interest. The transition from purely regulative and accumulative policies, combining poll and land taxes to more "liberal" regulative-promotive policies, separating these taxes, was usually connected with growing differentiation in the social structure, diminution of the scope of purely ascriptive, self-sufficient, agrarian units, and increasing interaction among different groups. This connection existed in Byzantium and T'ang China, and in Sassanid Persia during Khosrou I's great administrative and taxation reforms ([L] *Ostrogorsky, 1931; Stein, 1920).*

[18] *The Differentiation in the Social Structure and the Development of Different Types of Rulers' Goals*

It might be claimed that the effect of social differentiation on policy-making was the development of a complexity of goals, which we examined earlier. It might be claimed that we have not succeeded in holding the orientations and goals of the rulers constant while analyzing the effects of social differentiation, because these two variables—the complexity of goals, and the differentiation of social structure—are identical, at least so far as their effects on the policies of the rulers are concerned.

Of course, the complexity of the rulers' goals may be considered one manifestation of general differentiation of the social structure. And its development may be attributed, to some extent, to the pressures of the more differentiated and complex social groups and to the rulers' attempts to accommodate them. Nevertheless, the complexity of the rulers' goals is not identical with the measure of social differentiation; nor do they necessarily develop to the same degree. They may vary, in degree, independently of one another. Growing differentiation of the social structure may create various pressures on the rulers to take the interests of different groups into account—but it need not give rise to a change in the complexity of the rulers' major cultural orientation and goals.

For example, the social structure in Byzantium was comparatively highly differentiated during the Empire's periods of greatest prosperity. Nevertheless, the rulers were still oriented primarily to political-collective goals, and displayed relatively little regard for economic enhancement. Another instance is provided by the Spanish-American Empire, where the complexity of the rulers' goals was not proportionate to the extent of social differentiation. This unbalance was due to the different (metropolitan and local, Spanish and Indian) levels of the political struggle, and to the differences of the approaches and interests of the Crown and the colonies respectively. Similar examples are provided mainly by France and England, and by China—where, as already indicated, the emphasis on cultural goals engendered attempts to prevent any political consequences of social differentiation.

In other words, the political aspirations and value orientations of various "differentiated" (so far as they have bearing on political activity) groups were not always harmonious with the rulers' general value and political orientations. Nor were they always fully translated into the goals and policies of the rulers. True, as we have demonstrated above, these aspirations and the problems they generated had to be taken into account by the rulers when formulating concrete policies. But they could be considered only as a sort of external conditions, and not as fully legitimate participants in the political process.

Analogously, the rulers sometimes demonstrated a great complexity of goals, without the existence of a corresponding level of differentiation of the social structure of the society. This is illustrated by various societies in the process of transition from patrimonial to bureaucratic systems, whose rulers wished to attain complex goals in spite of aristocratic and traditional opposition. This was often the case during Sassanid history.

There was often a very close relation between the extent of complexity of goals and the extent of social differentiation. However, as demonstrated above, these two variables could fluctuate somewhat, independently of one another, and could influence the scope of political struggle in different directions.

This brings us to the last problem we shall investigate in this chapter—namely, the compatibility or harmony between the rulers' goals and the interests of the main groups and strata in the society, and the influence of this compatibility on the political process.

[19] *The Influence of Incompatibility between the Political Goals of the Rulers and Those of the Major Strata on the Political Process*

Hitherto, we have implicitly assumed that the general political orientation of the rulers was basically compatible with that of the most active social groups and strata, and that the concrete political activities of the various strata were in harmony with the frameworks of political struggle provided by the political institutions. With the obvious exception of outright rebellions and outbursts (which have not yet been systematically analyzed), we have assumed that most of the active groups could find, within the framework of existing institutions, adequate channels for voicing and implementing their political goals and aims— even if this did not necessarily indicate that this situation was either permanent or complete.

Only when analyzing the major types of exigencies that arose in various societies did we mention more explicitly, although not in detail, the possibility of discord between the rulers and groups in the society. Here, we touch on some of the problems of changes within the historical bureaucratic societies—when no basic harmony between rulers and subject groups exists, different processes of change evolve within these societies. We shall analyze these processes in the penultimate chapter of this volume; but it will be worth while to devote some pages here to a short, preliminary analysis of the general effects that such lack of harmony had on some aspects of the political process in the historical bureaucratic societies.

The most important single effect of such incompatibility was the growing emphasis the rulers put on what we have called "self-maintenance" goals, with a very strong "punishment orientation" toward different strata. The rulers retaliated against these groups with severe disciplinary policies, and attempted to annihilate or at least to neutralize all potential centers of power and political activity, or else to subjugate them entirely. In some cases, the political struggle became extremely intense. Then both the rulers and the bureaucracy made every effort to suppress it, through implementing restrictive policies and through attempting to acquire total control of all the main spheres of social life. Situations of this extreme incompatibility occurred in China, during the last phase of the T'ang Dynasty, and, in general, during periods of rebellion and during the last stages of other dynasties, when oppressive policies were attempted. Similar prescriptive-disciplinary measures were used by the rulers of the Byzantine Empire against the aristocracy, and by the French and English monarchs during the wars of religion and in the primary stages of absolutism.

Repressive-prescriptive policies had the greatest compass when the rulers' original goals political-collective—oriented toward military conquest and expansion, or toward strengthening the polity by various processes of "modernization"—and social groups opposed them. The political-collective types of goals and policies developed in cases of conquest, as in the Ottoman Empire ([O] *Gibb and Bowen, 1950, 1957; Stavrianos, 1957[a], p. 1, 1957[b]; Köprülü, 1935; Wittek, 1938*), or in cases like Prussia and Russia. There, the rulers' establishment of a semi-modern political and economic framework was opposed by the traditional (aristocratic) groups. It also, at the same time, could enhance the political power of various lower groups, who could then attempt to shake off the strong control of the rulers. Thus, in Prussia and Russia, the monarchs strongly opposed municipal governments and representative institutions, instituted powerful regimentation in the economic field, and established firm police supervision over many groups of the population ([X] *Carsten, 1954, 1955, 1959; Hintze, 1915;* [S] *Beloff, 1954;* [X] *Rosenberg, 1958;* [W] *Nolde, 1952–1953; Sacke, 1938*).

In all these cases institutional incompatibility developed among the level of generalized power (manifested in the political institutions), the policies of the rulers, and the political aspirations of different groups in the society. In other words, forms of political activity existed that did not accord with the types of political organization permitted or requested by the rulers. From such incompatibility, different processes of change sometimes arose.

[20] Summary

The main argument of this chapter may be recapitulated as follows. Our inquiry was concerned with several variables which seemed to influence the extent and scope of the political process in the historical bureaucratic societies. These variables were: (a) the major cultural orientations prevailing in a society and influencing the goals, tasks, and legitimation of the rulers and the exigencies facing them; and (b) the extent of differentiation of the social structure and political orientation of the chief social groups.

Tables 1–20 summarize briefly the materials presented in greater detail; some show the differential effects that different combinations of the rulers' goals and the levels of differentiation of the social structure had on the rulers' policies and on the political orientation and participation of the major groups.

The preceding analysis has demonstrated the points listed below.

1. The scope of political struggle, and the evolution of autonomous organs of political struggle, were relatively limited in societies or periods in which cultural pattern-maintenance orientations preponderated and a given cultural tradition and order were perceived as the main referents of political activities.

2. The range of political struggle was greater in societies or periods oriented predominantly to the polity as the main referent of political activities—i.e., when types of collective goals were emphasized. Within the general framework of these orientations and goals, the scope of political struggle and the development of the organs of this struggle were most narrow where or when purely political-collective goals prevailed. They were wider where or when the economic enhancement of the country was emphasized, or the polity's propagation of a faith or universalistic system of values was stressed.

3. The scope of the political struggle and the development of the organs of the struggle were widest in societies which emphasized the enhancement and material enrichment of the community, its sectors, and its individual members, and considered the polity as an instrument of these groups; and/or societies in which these groups became the principal bearers of universalistic values and thus also the chief referents of political activity. However, such orientations developed,

within the framework of the historical bureaucratic society, only in an embryonic form.

4. The scope of political struggle, and especially the extent to which different groups participated in it, were functions of the extent of differentiation of the social structure, measured by the development of free market economy, flexible criteria, and universal value orientations.

5. The scope of political struggle was asymmetrical in those societies in which the rulers' goals were incompatible with their political orientations.

In these societies, the rulers' policies were relatively highly articulated, while, at the same time, the rulers tried to frame them to minimize articulation of the political activities of the major groups and strata. The rulers' success in these endeavors depended on the relative strengths of the rulers and of the principal strata; however, such contradictory orientations and activities usually evolved in connection with the development of processes of change in the political system.

The first three variables influenced, in a fairly direct way, the policies of the rulers, and created certain frameworks for working out the political participation of different groups. The last variable directly influenced the scope of such potential participation, while creating certain demands on the formulation of policies.

These variables were interconnected by one fundamental intervening variable—namely, the extent of power generalization. We proposed above that the greater the extent of generalized power, the wider the scope of the political struggle in the society. We have observed that generalization of power denotes a tendency to wield power according to what we may term inherent "rational" considerations, without traditional and ascriptive restrictions. Therefore, we may state that the more prevalent this tendency, the more complicated, articulated, and autonomous will be the different types of political activity and organization.

This assumption is fully supported by the hypotheses summarized and analyzed above. These hypotheses referred to several variables, each capable of affecting the extent to which this tendency toward unfettered use of power developed. The natures of the legitimation, orientation, goals, and tasks of the rulers determined the amount and type of power they needed and the ways in which they wielded it. Thus, the priority of the respective goals, and their definitions could decide the extent and use of the power needed by the rulers. We have seen how the different types of orientations and goal emphases were related to different levels of generalized power. We have noted that, when the particularistic and ascriptive elements preponderated in the definitions of goals, the level of generalized power was lower; correspondingly, it was lowest when cultural (pattern-maintenance) orientations prevailed. The level was higher when "pure" collective goals were stressed, and highest when goals were characterized by the priority of universalistic and achievement elements in their definitions.

Similarly, as the differentiation of the social structures increased, the higher was the level of potential generalized power that was realized among different strata, and the more complicated and articulated were their political activities.

The tendency toward generalization of power can thus be considered as the common denominator of all the major variables discussed. However, this does not mean that the levels of generalization of power engendered by the goals of the rulers and by the extent of differentiation in the social structure are necessarily identical in every society. In so far as they were not identical, various processes of change were generated. This tendency to generate various processes of change will be subsequently analyzed.

10

The Place of the Bureaucracy

in the Political Process

[1] *The Basic Characteristics of the Bureaucracy.*
Their Influence on Its Political Orientations

In the preceding chapters, we have analyzed the conditions which influenced the development of different constellations of the political process in the historical bureaucratic societies in two main aspects—the policies of the rulers, and the political activities of the major groups in the society. Since the bureaucracy—particularly its upper and middle echelons—played a crucial role in the social and political structures of these societies, its political orientations, goals, and activities, and the conditions that determined them, demand special attention.

This chapter will be devoted to the political orientations of the bureaucracy. However, we shall not be able to deal with all the numerous aspects of the organization of bureaucracy—e.g., the extent of specialization of activities and departments, or the development of specialized training—or to investigate the various social conditions which affected them. At this stage of our discussion, we shall consider these aspects only in so far as they are directly related to the place of the bureaucracy in the political process.

In Chapter 8 (Section 2), we discussed the major political orientations and interests of the upper and middle echelons of the bureaucracy. We demonstrated that the principal political orientations of the bureaucracy, in so far as they transcended its members' desires for personal benefits and influence, were focused mainly on the attainment of some autonomy vis-à-vis the rulers or the foremost social strata.

These political aspirations were only rarely fully and consciously oriented toward undermining the historical bureaucratic system. However, under certain conditions, the bureaucracy could, through its attempts to maximize its own autonomy and power, undermine the foundations of the bureaucratic policies and generate processes of change within them.

In order to analyze the major types of political orientations of the bureaucracy, and the conditions conducive to their development, we must briefly recapitulate some of the principal characteristics of the bureaucracy's development and organization. We have seen that the bureaucratic administrations in the historical bureaucratic societies were posed between the rulers, who wanted to use them for their own needs and purposes, and some of the major groups and strata from which the rulers (and the administrations themselves) wanted to mobilize resources. These groups and strata usually also tended to develop some expectations of services from the bureaucracy.

Thus, the bureaucratic administrations, in order to fulfil their functions for the rulers, had to take care of some needs of the leading and most active social strata. The bureaucracy had to provide them continuously with various services, and to regulate somewhat their relations with the rulers. In conjunction with these different demands and pressures, the bureaucratic administrations (especially their higher echelons) evolved many of their specific organizational characteristics, particularly their organizational and professional autonomy.

This tendency to some autonomy was manifested in two major aspects of the bureaucracy's activities and organization. First, the bureaucracy usually established and maintained certain general usages or rules and standards of service—to take into consideration some general interests of the population, and to withstand the pressure of those interested in changing it, continuously or intermittently, for their own benefit. Second, most of these bureaucracies tended to develop a conception of themselves as servants of the state or of the community (even if the "State" was symbolized mainly by a dynasty) and not only as *personal* servants of the rulers ([A] *Borch, 1954; Weber, 1921; Finer, 1949, pp.*

724–740, 794–810; [X] *Schmoller, 1898; Rosenberg, 1958; Hartung, 1941;* [I] *Des Rotours, 1932, 1947–48;* [Y] *Zeller, 1948; Pagès, 1928).*

The bureaucracy's autonomy was, however, often distrusted by the rulers. They usually tried to restrict it, to retain some measure of political control over it, and to minimize the possibility of its developing relatively independent political goals and activities.

Thus, while carrying out their different tasks the bureaucratic administrations were confronted with the need to strike some balance between these different pressures and tendencies. The conflict was especially acute between their own tendencies to establish some extent of organizational and social autonomy, and the tendencies of the rulers and some of the major strata to control and exert pressure on them. The attainment of balance between these tendencies and pressures was not always easy. If one of the tendencies became preponderant—as often occurred—it could undermine or weaken the others. It would accordingly influence the scope and direction of the bureaucracy's activities. Such possibilities could occur for several reasons—all of them connected with the basic conditions of development of the bureaucratic administrations in these polities, and with the fact that, from its very beginning, the bureaucracy was caught in the political struggle in the polity.

First, the power that bureaucracies acquired in societies where, as a rule, there existed few "constitutional" limits on power, and where access to power was relatively limited, placed the members of the bureaucracy in especially privileged positions. Second, in these societies, great emphasis was placed on certain ascriptive symbols of status. This emphasis necessarily tempted the members of the bureaucracy either to use their positions to acquire such symbols, or else to make their positions into bases of these symbols. Third, the comparatively low level of economic development and social differentiation made possible only the slight development of specialized professional roles that were adequately remunerative.

As a result, the different echelons of these bureaucracies often tended to distort many of their customary or explicit rules, and to divert many of their services for their own benefit and/or for the benefit of some social groups with whom they became identified. They thus became both alienated from other strata and groups in the society and oppressive toward them. In other words, they displaced their goals of serving the rulers and/or several of the social strata, and emphasized instead goals of self-interest and aggrandizement.

On the other hand, the relative political weakness of many political groups, and the bureaucracy's great dependence on the kings, often impaired and undermined the autonomy of the bureaucracy. The rulers could totally subjugate the bureaucracy through diverting all its activities to their own exclusive use, without allowing it to perform any continuous services to different strata in the society or to uphold any general rules of providing services.

[2] *The Major Types of Political Orientations of the Bureaucracy. The Patterns of Their Activities*

The preceding discussion indicates that the major types of political orientations that could be developed by a bureaucracy in the historical bureaucratic societies were as follows:

1. Maintaining service orientations to both the rulers and the major strata (In the societies studied here, usually, greater emphasis was placed on serving the rulers)

2. Evolving into a merely passive tool of the rulers, with little internal autonomy or performance of services to the different strata of the population

3. Displacing its goals of serving the various strata and the polity, in favor of goals of self-aggrandizement or usurpation of power exclusively for its own benefit and/or the benefit of a group with which it became closely identified

4. Replacing its goals of serving the major strata with goals of self-aggrandizement and attainment of political power, while maintaining goals of serving the polity and the rulers

Of course, the bureaucracy in each of the historical bureaucratic polities usually exhibited a mixture or overlapping of all these tendencies or orientations. However, as a rule, a particular tendency preponderated for at least part, if not the whole, of each polity's history. Our chief concern here is with such relative predominance and its influence on the continuity of the society's political systems.

To discuss the political orientations of the bureaucracy, we must also consider the ways these were related to the scope of its activities. When we discussed the social conditions of the historical bureaucratic polities, we observed that, in general, this scope, measured according to the institutional spheres in which it was active and according to the extent of specialization of departments, was closely related to the degree to which the basic conditions of these societies had developed. In other words, it was related to the extent of differentiation of the institutional structures of these societies, and to the compass of the autonomy of political sphere within them.

However, in our previous discussions, we did not distinguish among the several types of activities in which the bureaucracy could engage—

especially between technical or regulative activities. Although the bureaucratic administration in any of the historical bureaucratic societies obviously participated in both types, the relative predominance of each kind could vary greatly from one case to another. Moreover, the criteria according to which regulative goals were considered effective, and those judging which groups which had benefited from them, necessarily varied considerably. These variables were—as we shall see in more detail later—the ones influenced by the bureaucracy's political orientations and activities.

[3] Service-Oriented Bureaucracies

We shall begin by describing the major types of political orientations and activities of the bureaucracies that emerged in the historical-bureaucratic societies ([L] *Bréhier, 1949[b]; Ostrogorsky, 1956[a]; Hussey , 1957; Diehl and Marçais, 1936; Diehl et al., 1945; Runciman, 1929; Stein, 1954; Charanis, 1951[a]*).

First, we shall analyze those cases in which the bureaucracy maintained its service orientation both to the rulers and to certain of the major strata—although, in the societies with which we are concerned, there always was a greater emphasis on serving the rulers. The bureaucracy evolved and maintained such political orientations and tendencies in Sassanid Persia, especially during its first historical phases and during the reign of Kavadh I (A.D. 488–531) ([G] *Christensen, 1936, pp. 201–235, 1939, pp. 114–1118; Altheim and Stiehl, 1957, pp. 55–75*); in the Byzantine Empire, through most of the seventh through tenth centuries ([L] *Bréhier, 1949[b]; Diehl, 1927; Stein, 1954, pp. 113–138; Ostrogorsky, 1956[a]*); in the Spanish-American Empire, during the first 150 years of its existence ([R] *Haring, 1927, 1947, ch. vii, viii, xi; Gongora, 1951; Zavala, 1943; Konetzke, 1951[a], 1951[b], 1952, 1953; Gallo, 1944; Hanke, 1936[a]; Ots Capdequi, 1934[a], 1934[b], 1945, 1951; Vida Viceus, 1957*); In France, especially in the period from the *Fronde* (1648–1653) until approximately the end of the seventeenth century ([Y] *Sagnac, 1945, 1946; Pagès, 1928, 1932[b]; Barber, 1955; Zeller, 1948; Doucet, 1948*); in England, after the Glorious Revolution (1688–1689) ([Z] *Brock, 1957; Plumb, 1950; Ashley, 1952; Trevelyan, 1944*); in the Chinese Empire, throughout the first and middle periods of most of its dynasties ([I] *Des Rotours, 1932, 1947–48; Sprenkel, 1958; Kracke, 1953; Balázs, 1952, 1959[a]; Chang, 1955; Liu, 1957, 1959[a], 1959[b]*); and in the Abbaside Caliphate, until the eleventh century ([M] *Levy, 1957;* [N] *Cahen, 1955[a], 1955[b], 1957[a], 1957[b];* [M] *Brockelmann, 1943; Lewis, 1950*).

In most of these cases, the bureaucracy maintained some degree of internal organizational autonomy. At the same time, the rulers' ultimate control over it was not weakened—although many tensions and quarrels always developed both within the bureaucracy and between it and the rulers. Within the bureaucracy, continuous and general usages or even explicit rules of service, appointment, and promotion were maintained. Also, within it, some relatively strong professional and even departmental *esprit du corps*, and some extent of internal colleagueship and reponsibility, evolved. In addition, various internal supervisory and disciplinary bodies emerged that attempted to maintain the standards of discipline and service.

At the same time, the rulers were usually successful in retaining their control over the service-oriented bureaucracies. The rulers did so through special officials (private officials of the inner courts, special *intendants*, or *visitores*); through exercising relatively strong control over allocation of budget and over private traffic in offices; and through participating directly in the process of decision-making within the upper echelons of the bureaucracy.

[4] *Subjugation of the Bureaucracy by the Rulers*

The second chief type of political orientation that the bureaucracy in a historical bureaucratic society could have was characterized by the bureaucracy's total subservience to the king. This orientation precluded the bureaucracy's providing almost any—except some minor technical—services to the major strata of the population. This orientation is best illustrated by the bureaucracy of Prussia during the seventeenth and eighteenth centuries ([X] *Dorn, 1931; Hintze, 1900, 1901, 1915; Rosenberg, 1958; Dorwart, 1953; Schmoller, 1870, 1898; Carsten, 1954, 1955, 1959; Bruford, 1935, 1957*), and that of the Ottoman Empire, especially during its first 150 years ([O] *Lybyer, 1913; Stripling, 1942; Gibb and Bowen, 1950, 1957; Stavrianos, 1957[a], 1957[b]; Wittek, 1938*). The bureaucracy had this orientation, although in embryonic form, in conquest empires, like the Spanish-American Empire during early stages ([R] *Gallo, 1944; Haring, 1927, 1947; Zavala, 1943; Ots Capdequi, 1941, 1951; Vida Viceus, 1957*); during periods of rapid change and reorganization of royal power, in Sassanid Persia under Khosrou I ([G] *Christensen, 1936, pp. 358–436; Altheim, 1955[a], 1955[b]; Altheim and Stiehl, 1954; Fry, 1956*); and in Byzantium, during times of great external dangers—especially during A.D. 610–641, in the reign of Heraclius ([L] *Ostrogorsky, 1956[a], pp. 83–110*).

In these cases, the rulers' puissance over the bureaucracy was manifested, first, in the organization of the bureaucracy, which characteristically had a very small degree of internal autonomy. This crucial characteristic had many manifestations. One such was the continual shifting, without any fixed general rules, of officials from place to place and office to office. Another was the rulers' destruction of any distinct career patterns, and their maintenance of strong discipline that was often arbitrary, and not based on any general criteria. Still another manifestation was the rulers' breaking up of any departmental or professional *esprit du corps* and co-operation, and their insisting on the bureaucrats' being the "personal" servants of the ruler and of the "State" as personified by the ruler ([X] *Dorn, 1931; Rosenberg, 1958; Hintze, 1901, 1915; Schmoller, 1898;* [O] *Lybyer, 1913; Gibb and Bowen, 1950, 1957*). The rulers' powerful, and often ruthless, direction of the bureaucracy made it remain for some time—especially during the first stages of the establishment of new polities—a relatively efficient instrument for implementing the attainment of the rulers' chief goals, like mobilizing resources, unifying the country, and suppressing opposition. In the long run, however, this "strong hand" of the rulers often diminished the efficiency of the bureaucracy, quashed the initiative of officials, and gave rise to over-formalistic attitudes and activities. It also led the officials to engage in many subterfuges and tricks in trying to avoid the rulers' control. Further, it often resulted (as we shall see later) in the growing rapacity and self-assertion of the bureaucracy.

[5] *Displacement of Service Goals by the Bureaucracy. Tendency to Autonomy and Self-Orientation of the Bureaucracy*

The third principal type of political orientation in a bureaucracy stressed the bureaucracy's own autonomy and self-interests—sometimes to an extent that involved its evasion of all political supervision from above and/or its displacing its goals of service to different strata. When this kind of orientation obtained, the upper echelons of the bureaucracy attempted to act almost exclusively in their own self-interest, or in the interest of groups or strata with which they had become allied or identified. They tried, in so far as possible, to minimize their service orientation and their professional and political responsibilities.

This tendency toward the bureaucracy's political and social autonomy occurred in a number of our case studies. Its most extreme manifestations took place during the periods of aristocratic predominance in Sassanid Persia ([G] *Christensen, 1936* passim, *especially ch. x; Altheim and Stiehl, 1954, 1957; Widengren, 1956*); in the decadent stages of the Chinese dynasties, when the bureaucracy became rapacious and almost fully identified with specific gentry groups ([I] *Chang, 1955; Michael, 1955; Sprenkel, 1952, 1958; Balázs, 1950, 1959[a]; J. T. C. Liu, 1959[a], 1959[b]; 1959[c]; Hu, 1955; Eberhard, 1945, 1948[a]*); during the final period of the Byzantine Empire ([L] *Charanis, 1951[a]; Ostrogorsky, 1929[a], 1956[a], 1956[b]*); and during the aristocratic reaction in eighteenth-century France ([Y] *Lough, 1954, 1960; Ford, 1953; Barber, 1955; Sagnac, 1945, 1946; Pagès, 1928, 1932[b]*). Somewhat less extreme manifestations occurred at the close of the Hapsburg era; during the decline of the Spanish-American Empire ([R] *Ots Capdequi, 1941, 1945; Haring, 1947, ch. vii; Parry, 1957*); and in the later stages of the Abbaside Caliphate ([N] *Cahen, 1955[b], 1957[a] 1957[b]; Lewis, 1950*).

The bureaucracy's having this type of socio-political orientations was usually connected with several developments in its internal structure. These developments were all rooted in the partial or total transformation of the administration into a relatively inefficient, self-seeking group, concerned mostly with working to achieve maximum benefits for itself, and paying only minimum attention to public duties or efficiency. The most important manifestations of these developments were the following:

1. Recruiting bureaucratic personnel largely through nepotistic channels within the bureaucracy itself

2. The bureaucratic officials' conception of their posts as mainly (or merely) sinecures, and as their private, even hereditary, property; and the development of an intensive, unrestricted, and unregulated traffic in offices

3. A consequent expansion of bureaucratic personnel beyond the numbers needed to perform its tasks, and a tendency toward what, in modern usage, may be called the implementation of "Parkinson's law"

4. The rapid proliferation of departments, and growing difficulties in co-ordination among them

5. Weakening of the effectiveness of the bureaucracy's activities

6. Increasing formalization and ritualism in bureaucratic practice, both in the bureaucracy's internal relations and in its relations with its clients

[6] *Self-Orientation of the Bureaucracy Combined with Service Orientation to the Polity*

A fourth type of political orientation tended to develop in the bureaucracies of the historical bureaucratic societies. This type was characterized by the bureaucracy's strong self-orientation (i.e., orientation toward self-aggrandizement in the social, economic, and political spheres), in combination with service orientation to the polity and the rules—and an almost complete lack of any service orientation to other strata or social groups.

There were two chief classes, in the societies we are examining, of such semi-usurpatory bureaucracies which still retained some political responsibility and services performance.

One of these classes existed in the less developed, more traditional societies. These include ancient Egypt ([F] *Drioton and Vandier, 1952; Edgerton, 1947[a]; Hayes, 1953; Kees, 1933[a], 1933[b], 1935; Maspero, 1890; Moulet, 1946; Otto, 1953; Bagnani, 1934*), and Sassanid Persia ([G] *Christensen, 1936, ch. i, iv; Altheim, 1955[a]; Altheim and Stiehl, 1954*) in its patrimonial stages—i.e., in the first two periods of its history, when a relatively autonomous bureaucracy was often closely allied with a traditional, semi-patrimonial ruler. The second class is best exemplified by Prussia and Austria in the late eighteenth and early nineteenth centuries, when the bureaucracy, together with some of the aristocratic groups, developed a *modus vivendi* with the kings within the framework of a fairly differentiated bureaucratic polity ([X] *Rosenberg, 1958; Hintze, 1914;* [S] *Beloff, 1954*).

In both these cases, the bureaucracy's organizational pattern and its patterns of activities differed, in some important respects, from either totally subservient or totally aristocratized ones. In most of our examples, the bureaucracy exhibited many characteristics of a relatively closed group whose membership was restricted largely to those from upper social groups. Nevertheless, at the same time, it maintained a relatively efficient administrative structure. It had some type of departmental division of labor and some internal system of supervision enabling it to further, with relative efficiency, various policies and political goals. Moreover, in most of the bureaucracies cited, the several echelons tended to preserve a certain professional or service ideology and status image, in which service to the polity was, at least to some extent, emphasized ([X] *Schmoller, 1870, 1898; Dorwart, 1953; Rosenberg, 1958;* [F] *Drioton and Vandier, 1952;* [G] *Christensen, 1936, ch. i* et passim; *Altheim and Stiehl, 1954; Altheim, 1955[a], 1955[b]*).

[7] The Criteria of Social Composition and Position of the Bureaucracy in the Status System

The preceding analysis indicates that the type of political orientation that a specific bureaucratic administration tended to develop was very closely related to the bureaucracy's standing within the society—

especially, its relations to the rulers and to various strata in the society. Therefore, in order to understand the conditions of development of the bureaucracy's political orientation, we must first examine its position in the social structure.

This position may be examined in terms of the following criteria:

1. The place the main echelons of the bureaucracy had in the society's hierarchy of status and power

2. The extent to which the bureaucracy, or its upper and middle echelons, constituted an independent status group—or, conversely, the extent to which its different echelons were considered parts of other social strata

3. When the bureaucracy (or its different echelons) constituted an independent status group, the criteria for distinguishing it from other strata—in particular, the extent to which the bureaucracy's proximity to the ruler and its exercise of power served as such criteria, and the degree to which, in such cases, the bureaucracy was alienated from other social groups

4. Conversely, when the bureaucracy (or its upper echelons) were considered as parts of other ecological or status strata, the qualities that distinguished it (or them) from other subgroups in the same strata

[8] *The Social Conditions and Composition*
of the Bureaucracies

A. DIFFERENT TYPES OF SERVICE-ORIENTED BUREAUCRACIES

The available material, shown in Table 17,* indicates the existence of a very close relation between the social position of the bureaucracy (and especially of its upper echelons) and its major political orientations. The available historical data also indicate that one of the principal mechanisms connecting them comprised the patterns and avenues of recruitment into the bureaucracy.

The data reveal that the bureaucracy's maintenance of service orientation to both the rulers and the major strata was contingent on its dependence on the rulers, and on its being partially incorporated into, or at least not alienated from, various flexible and "free" strata.

The greatest incorporation of the bureaucracy within flexible, non-traditional upper and middle urban and peasant (or gentry) groups occurred in England and China. The bureaucracy in each country was

* See Appendix.

largely viewed as a part of these strata. It used the same major symbols of status and participated in simliar styles of life—although the bureaucracy developed and emphasized its distinctive occupational roles and career patterns. In England and China, the specific bureaucratic careers usually ranked as possibilities within the range of occupational and status roles open to members of the upper and middle strata.

In England, engaging in an administrative career was an acceptable way of life for members of the upper rural classes. To a smaller measure, it was also acceptable for some members of the upper urban classes ([Z] *Trevelyan, 1944; Mathew, 1948; Brock, 1957; Namier, 1929, 1930, 1952; Ashley, 1952*).

In China, the bureaucracy was greatly subordinated, in every instance, to the ruler, and obtained part of its prestige from him. However, it emphasized, through the system of examination, the criteria of classical (Confucian) education as the main determinants of status. The Chinese bureaucracy was generally considered to be a part of the wider literati group and was largely, though not entirely, rooted in the gentry. Its official prestige was derived from the examination degrees, and from the devotion to the Confucian ideals that it shared with the literati. The extent to which the Chinese bureaucracy constituted an entirely autonomous group, differentiated from the gentry, is still an object of debate. But there can be little doubt that very strong interrelations existed between these two facets of a common cultural tradition. (*See* [I] *Chang, 1955; Eberhard, 1945, 1948[a], 1948[b], 1952; Sprenkel, 1952, 1958; Balázs, 1950, 1959[a], 1960; see also Michael, 1955; Wittfogel, 1957.*)

Though its incorporation was less fully developed, the bureaucracy was incorporated in various middle and social strata in France during the reign of Henri IV (1589–1610) and immediately afterward. This commingling occurred especially with respect to the middle echelons of the bureaucracy, in the relation between the evolving *noblesse de robe* and the rising urban groups ([Y] *Sagnac, 1945, 1946; Ford, 1953; Barber, 1955; Pagès, 1928, 1932[a]*).

In such cases, the members of the higher and middle echelons of the bureaucracy were recruited from among the higher and middle flexible strata—i.e., mostly from upper and middle urban groups, from professional circles, and from the gentry and upper peasant groups. They continued, as a rule, to maintain close solid relations with their groups of origin. They frequently formed an important channel for linking the more traditional groups, and the provinces, with the more differentiated types of political activity that had developed at the centers of the polities.

A somewhat different social pattern emerged in the service oriented (with special emphasis on services to the rulers) bureaucracies of Sassanid Persia under the reigns of Kavadh I (488–531) and Khosrou I (531–575); during the early and middle stages of the Byzantine Empire; in the Spanish-American Empire; and in the Abbaside Caliphate ([G] *Christensen, 1936; Altheim and Stiehl, 1954, 1957; Altheim, 1955[a], 1955[b]; Bréhier, 1949 [b], 1950; Ostrogorsky, 1956[a]; [R] Haring, 1947; [N] Cahen, 1955[b], 1957[a]; [M] Levy, 1957*). The upper echelons of the bureaucracies tended to develop into fairly autonomous status groups which emphasized either their service and political positions, and/or their power, as the chief criteria of their distinctiveness. In these cases, the bureaucracy constituted a nearly discrete group stressing its own criteria of status. Nevertheless, it continued to maintain some relations with the different upper and middle urban, professional, gentry, and upper peasant groups, from whom many of its members were recruited. In most of these societies, the members of the bureaucracy were not alienated from these strata. In fact, they constituted an important link between these groups and the central political institutions—even when the bureaucracy and these strata were not entirely identical, and/or there were great differences of style of life, and of social and political participation between them.

For example, in early and middle Byzantium, the bureaucracy constituted a comparatively independent status group, oriented principally toward implementing the achievement of the emperor's goals and policies. It was subject to his strict supervision, and tended to emphasize service both to him and to the polity. In conjunction with these characteristics, its members usually stressed the occupation of a bureaucratic office as a basic status criterion. In the social sphere, the bureaucracy was relatively autonomous and distinct from other groups; but it was closely associated with some major social strata— especially with the upper peasant groups, and with merchant and urban professional and cultural groups. This description applies to the bureaucracy during seventh- through tenth-century Byzantium (with, perhaps, the partial exception of the reign of Heraclius [610– 641]), which was then at its prime. Only during the Empire's decline, when the state was weakened and the aristocracy grew powerful, did the bureaucracy become intimately associated with the aristocracy. It then became, to some extent, incorporated into the aristocracy, thus becoming alienated from the more differentiated middle groups, and oppressive toward them and toward lower groups ([L] *Bréhier, 1924, 1948[b], 1949[b], ch. iii, iv; Ostrogorsky, 1929[a], 1956[b], pp. 271– 491, 1956[b]; Lemerle, 1958; Charanis, 1951[a]*).

A similar situation developed in the Spanish-American Empire. The bureaucracy initially constituted a separate group, differentiated from both the Spanish settlers and the natives, and emphasizing the fact that the Crown had granted it autonomous status. But it was also closely affiliated with the upper-class local settlers and with the groups of local aristocracy. As in Byzantium, the bureaucracy of the Spanish-American Empire inclined toward aristocratization and assimilation into the upper strata when the power of the rulers—and, consequently, their ability to implement their goals—became weaker ([R] *Ots Capdequi, 1941, 1945; Konetzke, 1951[a], 1951[b], 1952, 1953; Haring, 1947, ch. xvii; Parry, 1957*).

Until the middle of the tenth century, the bureaucracy of the Abbaside Caliphate manifested a similar trend toward some measure of social autonomy. This was based on its services to the rulers and on its power positions; but it was linked with a relatively close and positive relation to various (especially middle urban and rural) groups.

In these societies too, the upper and middle echelons of the bureaucracy were usually recruited from middle urban and rural groups. However, the process of recruitment was selective in a special way. It predisposed to emphasize the distinctiveness of the bureaucratic career pattern, to remove the recruits from their groups of origin, and to weaken their relations with these groups—even if no special attitudes of alienation were developed or stressed.

B. BUREAUCRACIES SUBSERVIENT TO THE RULERS

The bureaucracy's subservience to the rulers was usually a concomitant of its constituting a discrete status group whose principal distinctive social characteristic was its strong emphasis on power and service to the rulers. Although they were socially autonomous, and had status based on their special positions, politically such bureaucracies were subject to the rulers' supervision. During the first stages of the Ottoman Empire, both the political subservience and the social autonomy of the bureaucracy were insured by the system of having it composed mostly of members who were the sultan's personal slaves, and had been recruited from alien elements ([O] *Gibb and Bowen, 1950, 1957; Stavrianos, 1957[a], parts i, ii, 1957[b]; Wittek, 1938; Miller, 1941*). In seventeenth-century Prussia, the Hohenzollerns established a widespread bureaucratic organization entirely subordinate to the ruler. This bureaucracy derived its status and power from its relation to the ruler, and was markedly hostile—in the first stages of its development—to the aristocracy, to the older town autonomies, and to the various *staende* organizations ([X] *Carsten, 1954, 1955, 1959; Hintze, 1915; Rosenberg, 1958; Bruford, 1957*).

In situations like these, the upper and middle echelons of the bureaucracy were usually recruited from the lower or from the very weak middle strata, and sometimes from alien groups. They were removed from their groups of origin; and the process of recruitment stressed their alienation and their complete distinctiveness from any traditional social status. Then—at least for the period during which the rulers were able to control it—the bureaucracy, alienated from the strata from which many of its members were recruited, developed definite punishment orientation toward them. It usually evolved monolithic status aspirations, and strove—frequently with the rulers' encouragement—to establish a status hierarchy, based largely on criteria of power, whose sole apex it would become.

However, such a bureaucracy's dependence on the king hindered it in trying to achieve the full realization of its aspirations to autonomous power and status. As long as the rulers maintained their firm control over it, the bureaucracy could not usually develop into a separate and cohesive status group. Its members and their families were frequently subject to the vicissitudes and arbitrariness of the monarch's will. Therefore, as the bureaucracy developed and became more stabilized and diversified, it often tried to find ways to assert its own status. It also sought allies among some groups—especially the aristocratic—which could provide it with symbols of status and social standing against the rulers ([O] *Lewis, 1958; Gibb and Boden, 1950, 1957;* [X] *Rosenberg, 1958; Hintze, 1914*).

C. SELF-ORIENTED BUREAUCRACIES

When the upper echelons of a bureaucracy developed tendencies toward displacement of their goals of service to various strata and/or to the rulers, they did so usually in connection with the bureaucracy's evolving into a strongly ascriptive stratum. This stratum became either an independent semi-aristocratic or "gentry" stratum (emphasizing power as a status criterion), or a part of an existing aristocratic stratum. It became alienated, at least, to some extent, from the rulers. This kind of development occurred in the periods of decline in Byzantium ([L] *Stein, 1954; Ostrogorsky, 1956[a]; Vasiliev, 1952; Guilland, 1954; Charanis, 1951[b]; Bréhier, 1949[b]*), from the thirteenth century until its fall in 1453, and in the Abbaside Caliphate ([N] *Cahen, 1957[a], 1957[b]*); during the aristocratic reaction in eighteenth-century France ([Y] *Ford, 1953; Pagès, 1928; Barber, 1955*); and, to a smaller degree, during the declines of several Chinese dynasties (*in addition to the literature cited above, see* [I] *Stange, 1950*).

In cases like these, the bureaucracy usually inclined to weaken and de-emphasize the distinctiveness of its occupational and career patterns, and its professional ideology and self-concept as the nation's servant. It tried to lend its positions the basic attributes of aristocratic status and to make its offices private hereditary possessions or fiefs. It also attempted to confine eligibility for serving in the bureaucracy to members of bureaucratic families, and to minimize the degree to which it was answerable to various strata, and, in extreme cases, to the rulers.

An aristocratized bureaucracy maintained some orientation toward public service only in so far as it was neither alienated from the rulers nor strongly opposed to some of the other strata. These conditions obtained in ancient Egypt and, in less measure, in Prussia and Russia during the seventeenth and eighteenth centuries.

[9] *The Influence of the Rulers' Goals and of the Relation between the Rulers and the Major Strata on the Development of Different Types of Political Orientations of the Bureaucracy*

We have seen that each of the principal political orientations of the bureaucracy was connected with the specific positions its members occupied in the social structure. We shall now try to determine the specific conditions which influenced the nature of the social standing of the bureaucracy and, through this, affected its political orientations and patterns of activities.

The picture here is, necessarily, very complex. The same major variables which we demonstrated, in Chapter 9, influenced the political orientations and activities of the main groups—i.e., the extent of differentiation and the goals of the rulers—of course affected the bureaucracy's political orientation. However, the bureaucracy had a special position in the political and social structures of these societies. Because of this fact, it was the constellation of the political forces and process in the society—especially, the extent of compatibility between the rulers' goals and the leading groups' political orientations—that was crucially important in determining the development of the bureaucracy's social status and political orientations.

The great complexity of the relevant data is shown in Table III* and in Tables 16–20* and does not make easy correlations possible. However, we may offer general tentative suggestions based on the materials in this table and, especially, on the material of our case studies.

* See Appendix.

We shall begin with a brief analysis of the effect that the rulers' major goals had on the social standing and political orientation of the bureaucracy.

When the chief goals of the polity were mainly political-collective, the bureaucracy tended to emphasize its own autonomous status position. Political-collective goals stressed the autonomy and the special position of the rulers—who were, in a sense, the principal bearers of these goals—and, therefore, also of the bureaucracy which served the rulers. When most of the polity's goals were cultural or economic (e.g., in China, in the Abbaside Empire, or in England), the bureaucracy tended to become incorporated into wider, relatively flexible groups and strata.

However, in any polity, the predominant goals of the rulers provided only the framework within which the social and political orientations of the bureaucracy (and its patterns of activities) could evolve. The concrete development of its orientations depended largely on the conditions specified above—namely, the compatibility between the goals of the rulers and those of the major groups, and the amount of differentiation of the social structure.

When the goals and interests of the major strata were basically incompatible with those of the rulers, the bureaucracy, aided by the rulers, tended to develop power as its most important autonomous criterion of status. The bureaucracy either became entirely autonomous, alienated from other strata, and greatly dependent on, and subservient to, the rulers; or it tried to find a *modus vivendi* with some of these strata. The alternative was decided by the relative strengths of the rulers and of these "opposing strata." When the opposing strata were not very powerful or politically active—or when the rulers had sufficient power to repress them and make them politically passive—the bureaucracy (especially its higher echelons) tended to establish power as the chief criterion of status, and to attain autonomous status on the basis of this criterion. The two best examples of such development included in our data are provided by Prussia and the Ottoman Empire. In each, the bureaucracy had originally been an independent group or stratum, differentiated from all other strata and oriented against the aristocracy, the town, and estates. It had initially been considered as the monarch's means of implementing his goals, and had derived its status entirely from him and from its service to him. However, both the social autonomy and political subservience of the bureaucracy diminished, in time, as a result of the financial and social stability its members attained, and in close connection with a realignment of the relations between the rulers and some of the aristocratic groups and forces ([X] *Carsten, 1950, 1955, 1959; Hintze, 1915; Bruford, 1935, 1957; Rosenberg, 1958*).

When the opposing strata were stronger, and the rulers weak and unable to control them—as was the case in many periods of decline of the historical polities—the bureaucracy tended to ally itself with these (mostly aristocratic) groups, at the expense of both the rulers and other strata, and developed a tendency to displace their service goals. (These cases will be discussed in greater detail below.)

On the other hand, the greater the compatibility between the rulers' foremost goals and the major strata's political orientations, the greater it seems, was the tendency of the bureaucracy to become incorporated into a free stratum, or at least not to be alienated from one. This compatibility also predisposed the bureaucracy to maintain its service orientation to the rulers and the free strata. The bureaucracy's latent aspirations to social and political autonomy were kept from emerging by the strength of the rulers and of the flexible strata. At the same time, however, the interaction between different strata and the rulers, and the very multiplicity of these strata—when the latter were relatively powerful—exerted pressures on the bureaucracy, and enabled it to evolve some organizational and occupational autonomy and an autonomous professional image. And, simultaneously, the bureaucratic occupational patterns were easily incorporated into the general style of life of these strata. The bureaucracy's maintenance of service orientation was fullest when the flexible middle strata were strong and comparatively dominant in the social structure—i.e., when the differentiation of the social structure was relatively great. Good examples of this situation are provided by Byzantium during the seventh through twelfth centuries; by China during most of its history; and by Western Europe in the seventeenth century.

The bureaucracy could also evolve a similar orientation when the scope of differentiation of the social structure was small and the aristocracy, or an aristocratized bureaucracy, constituted the predominant social strata. However, this orientation then could develop only when a basic compatibility existed between the political goals of the rulers and those of the politically active aristocracy and the most passive orientation of the weak middle strata. In such cases, the aristocracy, although relatively predominant in the social and economic hierarchy, was somewhat "domesticated" within the framework of the bureaucratic polity. Its own power and economic positions were largely dependent on the existence of these frameworks; it thus usually attained some *modus vivendi* with the rulers.

As we have already discussed, there were two main types of aristocratized service bureaucracy. One developed in the traditional, comparatively· non-differentiated societies, like ancient Egypt and Sassanid Persia. In these societies, the bureaucracy usually developed in one of two major directions. When the autonomous, aristocratic patrimonial hierarchy was relatively strong (as it was, e.g., throughout most of Sassanid Persia's history), it usually assimilated and absorbed the upper echelons of the bureaucracy. However, if the aristocracy was weak (as in Egypt) or oppressed by the rulers (as happened during the first periods of Sassanid Persia, and especially during the reigns of Kavadh I and Khosrou I), the upper echelons of the bureaucracy tended to develop into a more autonomous stratum, somewhat emphasizing power as an autonomous criterion of status. Even in such cases, however, the predisposition to adopt an aristocratic style of life generally prevailed— although the new aristocracy was largely an aristocracy of service or *Aemteraristokratie* ([F] *Drioton and Vandier, 1952; Kees, 1933[a]; Otto, 1953;* [G] *Christensen, 1936* passim; *Altheim and Stiehl, 1954, 1957; Ghirshman, 1954*).

In cases like these, the lower and middle echelons of the bureaucracy usually were recruited from the society's marginal groups or from outside. Whatever their personal prestige and power, they rarely evolved into an independent stratum. These bureaucratic echelons were—to the extent that they tried to achieve economic position and security—in the same category as the lower strata (e.g., the peasantry or, in a way, outside the main status hierarchy of the society).

The second type of aristocratized service bureaucracy is best illustrated by Prussia, from the time of Frederick the Great (1740–1786) on. It also emerged, to a smaller extent, in Austria and Russia during the eighteenth and nineteenth centuries ([X] *Rosenberg, 1958; Hintze, 1914;* [W] *Young, 1957; Beloff, 1953,* [S] *1954;* [T] *Schenck, 1953; Macartney, 1957*). In Prussia, the bureaucracy was initially oriented toward the ruler and power, and against the aristocracy; it was an avenue of social advancement for the middle classes. However, under Frederick the Great, there was an aristocratic reaction on the part of the rulers, and the bureaucracy was increasingly infused with aristocratic elements. Similar developments took place in Austria and Russia.

In these cases, the rulers' control over the bureaucracy, and the bureaucracy's service orientation, were not entirely weakened as a result of the latter's partial aristocratization. They were, in fact, greatly increased by the rulers' dependence on the bureaucracy and by the political power of both the bureaucracy and the aristocratic group. These increases followed a period during which both the aristocratic groups and, to a lower degree, the (traditional) towns became adjusted to the demands of the rulers, benefitting economically from the political framework. During the same period, the rulers themselves, after flirting with various middle groups, stressed their conservative orientations and their distrust of some of the more flexible groups. At the same time, these groups continued to be important in the social structure ([X] *Rosenberg, 1958; Carsten, 1954, 1955, 1959*).

A total displacement of service goals by an aristocratized bureaucracy usually developed largely in those cases when the policies of the rulers depleted or alienated the various sources of free-floating resources and political support; and where, as a result, the rulers became progressively less able to uphold their distinct political orientations and goals, and progressively more dependent on different conservative aristocratic forces. These forces attempted to monopolize the most important economic and political positions in the society. By doing so, they furthered the dwindling of the flexible strata or their alienation from the framework and symbols of existing political institutions. In such cases, the bureaucracy usually tried either to incorporate some of these strata with its own status hierarchy based on the criterion of power or to develop as an independent aristocratic stratum and acquire many of the symbols of aristocratic status.

Such conditions could emerge in societies, like the Ottoman Empire and (to a smaller extent) the Spanish-American Empire, whose bureaucracy was initially subservient to the rulers. They also could evolve in those societies, like Byzantium, the Abbaside Empire, and France, where, for relatively long periods of time, a service-oriented bureaucracy had existed.

[10] *Changes in the Political Orientations of the Bureaucracy. Attempts to Reform the Bureaucracy*

The conditions connected with the development of the different types of political orientations of the bureaucracy were not fixed. In any society, they could change throughout its history and their changes necessarily brought about changes in the social standing and political orientation of the bureaucracy.

In many of the societies studied here—perhaps, in most of them—the developing bureaucracy's initially strong subservience to the rulers was frequently replaced by the bureaucracy's more differentiated service orientation to both the rulers and the major strata. This occurred, for instance, in Byzantium after the eighth century, and in the Spanish-American Empire during the first two centuries of its development. Sometimes—especially when the polity was threatened by external dangers—however, the bureaucracy's service orientation became weakened, and its subordination to the rulers developed or was re-established.

In many other cases, the rulers attempted to check the tendencies of the aristocracy to self-aggrandizement. The periodic attempts made, by the rulers or by some of their active ministers, to effect reforms of the bureaucracy, are very instructive in this connection. Many reforms—e.g., those of Frederick William I (1688–1740) in Prussia ([X] *Dorwat, 1953; Rosenberg, 1958*); of Wang An-shih (A.D. 1021–1086) in China [I] *Liu, 1957, 1959[a], 1959[b], 1959[c]; on other Chinese reforms, see* [I] *Stange, 1934, 1939; O. Franke, 1931, 1932; Dubs, 1939; Williamson, 1937*); of Heraclius (A.D. 610–641) and of Leo III (717–740) and Leo IV (886–912) in Byzantium ([L] *Ostrogorsky, 1956[a], ch. ii, iii; Bréhier, 1949[b], livres II, III; Stein, 1954*)—were directed at re-establishing the rulers' control over the bureaucracy, and against the bureaucracy's upper echelons' growing usurpation of power and displacement of service goals. Frequently, the reforms were aimed against those structural characteristics of the bureaucracy which were perceived as the most important manifestations of its total independence—especially against the following:

1. The narrowing of the bases of recruitment to the bureaucracy
2. The conception of the bureaucratic position as a sort of sinecure
3. Over-formalization and ritualization
4. Proliferation of unco-ordinated activities and departments, and lack of control

It is significant that, in each polity where bureaucratic reform was attempted—especially, in each where the reforms were successful—the rulers were aided, in trying to make the reform, by different social groups. This aid was forthcoming particularly from the rising middle classes—or, in some cases, like Byzantium, from the rural middle classes.

One change in the bureaucracy's political orientations occurred most often, and was most prevalent, in the societies studied here. That was the metamorphosis, during the periods of decline of the political systems, of either a ruler-centered or a service oriented bureaucracy, into a self-centered aristocratic or semi-aristocratic body.

[11] The Influence of the Bureaucracy's Service Orientation on Its Patterns of Activities

The preceding analysis has demonstrated and substantiated the thesis that the bureaucracy's political orientations, in a centralized bureaucratic political system can be fully understood only in connection with the bureaucracy's status and function in the social structure, and its relation to the constellation of political forces within that structure.

The nature of the bureaucracy's political orientation and patterns of activities was greatly affected by its social position within the society. In turn, this position was influenced: (1) by the extent of differentiation of the social structure; (2) by the major goals of the rulers; and (3) most important of all, by the relative strength of the major social strata vis-à-vis both the rulers and one another, and by the amount of compatibility between the rulers' goals and these strata's political orientations. Also, we have observed that the social and political conditions affecting, in any society, the development of the political orientations of the bureaucracy were not fixed; rather, they tended to change according to the relative strengths of the social forces and the outcome of the political struggle among them.

The bureaucracy's different political orientations and activities could also, because of the bureaucracy's crucial position in the political struggle in the historical bureaucratical polities, have had many repercussions on these very conditions, and on the changes in the constellation of political forces, in the society. In order to understand these possible repercussions fully, we should analyze the patterns of activities developed by the different types of bureaucracies in these societies.

As we have seen, the general scope of the activities of the bureaucracy was largely determined by the general amount of differentiation in the social structure of the respective societies, and by the major goals. However, as we have also seen, the bureaucracy's political orientations greatly influenced several facets of its activities—particularly the relative importance of technical or of regulative activities.

Thus, those bureaucracies that maintained orientations of service toward rulers and chief strata emphasized both technical and regulative activities. The degree to which one of these bureaucracies stressed one kind over the other, and the criteria according to which such regulation was implemented, depended on two factors. The first was the relative predominance of the rulers or the major strata in the political field; the second was the scope of the autonomous regulative mechanisms developed by the different strata.

In Tables 17–20, we have summarized the available data on this point. Using these as our bases, we may proceed with our analysis.

For instance, in cases—like Byzantium or the Spanish-American Empire—where the rulers were predominant, the bureaucracy provided many technical services to the population. At the same time, it also implemented many regulative policies in the major institutional spheres—i.e., in the economic, political, and cultural areas—that were chiefly guided by the interests of the rulers. On the other hand—e.g., in England, particularly after the Glorious Revolution (1688–1689); and, to a more limited degree, in China—in a polity where several of the social groups and strata were very powerful, the bureaucracy placed more emphasis on providing technical services, stressing only the in- direct control of major social strata and of the major institutional spheres The bureaucracy's regulative activities were also greatly affected by the interests of the politically strong strata.

Thus, as a rule, when the bureaucracy's regulative activities were stressed, the extent to which the major groups enjoyed political partici- pation in the organs of political struggle was small. Where both regula- tive and technical activities were emphasized, the extension of the scope of the bureaucracy's activities was usually also evident in the in- creasing participation by the chief strata in the organs of political struggle.

The second factor which determined the relative importance of the bureaucracy's regulative or technical activities was the range of the autonomous regulative mechanisms developed by the principal social strata in the major institutional fields. The greater the scope of the activities of these autonomous mechanisms, the smaller was the scope of the bureaucracy's *regulative* activities. In so far as the compass of the self-regulation of these groups was relatively small, or they were contented with the rulers, the scope of the regulative activities of the bureaucracy was greater.

Other conditions being equal, then, the economic self-regulation of different groups (as manifested by the development of economic associations, organizations, and guilds, and in autonomous market arrangements and mobilization of financial resources) usually involved limitation of bureaucratic activities in the economic field to: (1) tech- nical activities, like defense, legal services, and maintenance of com- muncations; and (2) providing foreign resources, and supervising the flow of various economic resources to other institutional spheres.

The economic self-regulation of different groups definitely influ- enced the scope of the regulative activities of the bureaucracy. This statement is substantiated by an examination of the ranges and types of bureaucratic activity that developed in: (1) the local self-regulation of the Chinese gentry; (2) the semi-autonomous urban centers (e.g., Byzantine trading posts, Hellenistic cities, and cities of early Absolutist Europe; (3) the urban economies of the eighteenth-century maritime societies (e.g., Holland [(S) *Beloff, 1954, ch. ix*]) and (4) the market oriented economic activities of aristocracies adjusted to and accom- modated by the bureaucratic polity, as in Prussia ([X] *Carsten, 1950, 1955; Hintze, 1914*).

Sometimes the stratification system of the major groups and strata was largely self-regulating, in terms of maintaining independent cul- tural patterns and status hierarchies vis-à-vis those of the rulers. Then the activities of the bureaucracy in the sphere of stratification were confined, as a rule, to the legal enforcement of existing rights, and the prevention and/or punishment of deviant behavior (as defined by the precepts of the various groups).

In England, for example, the aristocracy, the gentry, and the urban groups gradually developed their own status systems and values. There, the bureaucracy and the ruling elite did not usually regulate the existing hierarchy—they largely maintained and enforced it. On the other hand, in France, most of the foremost groups (except the *noblesse d'épée*) developed only weak autonomous status criteria. The French central authorities (i.e., the court and the bureaucracy) not only enforced existing status distinctions, but also created many new status symbols and groups. These bestowed rank and nobility for the several middle groups, until the bureaucracy began to usurp their positions and to develop into an autonomous and semi-aristocratic status group. (*On England, see* [Z] *Trevelyan, 1944; Mathew, 1948; Ashley, 1952;* [S] *Goodwin, 1953. On France, see* [Y] *Zeller, 1948; Sagnac, 1945, 1946; Pagès, 1928; Barber, 1955.*) China provides another interesting case in point. There, the local status systems were relatively autonomous, and free from external regulation. However, the central status system, governed by ethical (Confucian) and political values and based on criteria of merit (degrees and examinations, and bureaucratic positions), was for the most part regulated and enforced by the bureaucracy (*Balázs, 1950, 1959[a]; Chang, 1955*).

When the extent of autonomous intergroup and intragroup legal regulation was great—as manifested in numerous "autonomous" devices of arbitration, and in the relative independence of the juridical institution and/or legal profession—the juridical and legal activities of the bureaucracy dealt chiefly with administering justice and with codifying, institutionalizing, and enforcing laws. Thus, in England, various autonomous legal institutions and traditions developed that largely prevailed against the encroachment of different types of administrative jurisdiction ([Z] *Holdsworth, 1938; Davies, 1937; Clark, 1955*). In China, legal autonomy was great at the local levels and minimal at the central ones. There, the bureaucracy's local legal activities were chiefly technical, whereas its activities at the center were comprehensive and regulative ([I] *Des Rotours, 1932; Sprenkel, 1952, 1958; Escarra, 1933, 1936; Balázs, 1954[c]*).

In France, the autonomous legal bodies—i.e., the *parlements* and the courts of law—tried in every way to prevent the judicial administration of the central authorities from being extended. In this, they were only partially successful in the sixteenth century. Hence, in France, the scope of the central authorities' administrative-judicial activity increased constantly, though the *parlements* were able to obstruct it from time to time. The French *parlements* revived, though only partially during the later eighteenth century, when they formed a focus of the aristocratic reaction—but even then, they could not greatly hinder the juridical power of the administration ([Y] *Cobban, 1950; Zeller, 1948; Pagès, 1928; Sagnac, 1945, 1946*). In Byzantium, where legal institutions had little autonomy, and in Sassanid Persia, where they had almost none, there were very comprehensive systems of judicial administration ([L] *Bréhier, 1949[b]; Ostrogorsky, 1956[a]*).

[12] *The Influence of the Bureaucracy's Orientation to the Rulers and to Its Self-Aggrandizement on Its Patterns of Activities*

In the types of bureaucracies which minimized the service orientations to groups and strata, and, strongly emphasized either service to the rulers and/or self-aggrandizement, as a rule, regulative activities preponderated, and only minimal stress was laid on technical services.

Thus, when the bureaucracy was entirely subservient to the ruler— as it was, e.g., in Prussia or in the Ottoman Empire—it tended to evolve certain regulative activities under his direction. These activities aimed to insure the power positions of the ruler and of the bureaucracy—and the resources they needed—against most of the (potentially active) social strata ([O] *Lybyer, 1913; Stavrianos, 1957[a]*, parts i, ii; *Gibb and Bowen, 1950;* [X] *Rosenberg, 1958; Dorn, 1931; Hintze, 1915*). The most important of these regulative activities were as follows:

1. Attempts to regulate, *in toto*, most of the social spheres. These were directed at providing different groups and strata with technical services, and also at establishing the general principles governing the regulation of social, economic, political, and cultural activities, and/or at creating many new types of such organization and activities.

2. Attempts to penetrate into many social spheres and groups, even if they did not seem to require these specific services of the bureaucracy.

3. Attempts to develop different legal activities directed at regimenting and prescribing of many aspects of social life.

4. Attempts to develop various party-political and propagandist activities. The chief purpose of these was to control, and even monopolize, the free-floating political potential in the society, and to minimize the possibility that independent centers of power would evolve.

A very similar pattern of activities emerged in those bureaucracies which tended to displace goals of service in favor of goals of self-interest and aggrandizement. In such cases, the bureaucracy usually developed usurpatory, regulative-prescriptive activities. These served, mostly, the interests both of the upper echelons of the bureaucracy itself, and of the groups with which it allied itself against the rulers and other groups and strata. Then, the bureaucracy's regulative-prescriptive activities did not, as a rule, touch on the privileges and special interest of the strata—particularly, of the aristocratic groups, and some upper echelons of traditional elites—with which it was allied. However, the bureaucracy's activities frequently were very oppressive toward other strata.

Moreover, in these cases, the bureaucracy's activities were not geared toward implementing any prevalent political goals or any consistent set of policies. They tended to serve the diverse, often discrepant, interests of different bureaucratic and aristocratic groups. Hence, such a bureaucracy usually exhibited much smaller degrees of efficiency and unified policy than did oppressive bureaucracies during their initial stages of being totally subservient to the rulers.

As a rule, those bureaucracies which combined a tendency to *partial* usurpation of power and strong autonomy, with orientations toward performance of public services, also emphasized strong regulation of most aspects of the social life in the society. However, usually it was not so oppressive and self-oriented as the regulation by the totally aristocratized bureaucracies. Generally, in such a situation, the different echelons of the bureaucracy maintained some professional ideology and image. In these, service to the polity was strongly emphasized; hence, the bureaucracy's regulative activities were often guided by consistent policies and goals.

[13] *The Influence of the Activities of the Bureaucracy on the Basic Social Conditions of the Political Systems*

In the preceding analysis, we have shown, in greater detail, the ways the activities of the bureaucracy were able to influence the basic social conditions of the political systems of the historical bureaucratic societies, and the constellations of political power and the political process within them.

In so far as the bureaucracy kept its basic service orientations both to the rulers and to the major strata, it usually contributed to the continuity and stability of the regime—especially to maintaining the fundamental conditions of the centralized bureaucratic regimes. In the societies or periods in which the bureaucracy preserved such service orientations, the rulers could, with the bureaucracy's help, maintain their own positions and the positions of those strata that supported them. The rulers were also thus able to restrain those strata which were opposed to the basic prerequisites of the centralized political systems. In so far as the bureaucracy could monopolize the highest social, political, and economic positions, and to minimize its own political responsibility and accountability to the rulers and/or the major flexible strata, it usually tended to contribute to the weakening of these frameworks in many ways. (These ways will be analyzed in detail in the following chapters.)

The above analysis has also indicated the bureaucracy's rather paradoxical relation to the basic prerequisites necessary for the functioning of the political systems of the historical bureaucratic societies.

The bureaucracy, because of its central regulative functions in the historical bureaucratic society, performed very important tasks in the internal control of free-floating power and in insuring a continuous and ordered flow of free-floating power and resources. However, to the degree that the bureaucracy became a semi-independent stratum or was not effectively controlled in the political field, it could itself become an omnivorous consumer of these free resources. It could then have greatly impeded the functioning of the diverse autonomous regulative mechanisms and become an obstacle to the continuous flow of regulated and controlled generalized power.

This ambivalent or paradoxical relation of the bureaucracy to the functional prerequisites of the political systems of the historical bureaucratic societies was manifested in the conditions conducive to the growth of the scope of the bureaucracy's activities, when compared with the conditions which increased the possibilities for the bureaucracy to usurp political power and social position.

The general scope of the bureaucracy's activities, and its technical activities in particular, was closely related to increased differentiation, growing development of free resources, and the rise of different mobile strata in the society. However, the scope of its *regulative* activities was in inverse proportion to the social and political strength of these strata. The range of the bureaucracy's technical activities usually expanded with the growth of social differentiation. Nevertheless, the extent of the bureaucracy's ability to become a socially and politically independent group was severely limited by the fact that this social differentiation was connected with the growing social, economic, and political self-regulation of the principal social groups, and with the existence of politically powerful rulers and groups. The clearest manifestation of this feature was the inverse proportion usually existing between the regulative activities of the bureaucracy and the scope of the activities of the organs of political struggle and of the political activities of the groups within them.

Thus, the conditions that gave rise to the extension of the bureaucracy's technical and service activities were not necessarily compatible with those which made its usurpation of political control and its displacement of service-goals possible. The lack of such necessary compatibility was inherent in the structural position of the bureaucracy and in the bases for its growth. It was intrinsic in the fact that the bureaucracy was both a functional group performing relatively specific functions, and a group closely related to the bases of power, and thus able to monopolize power positions and evolve into an independent social stratum that could impede the continuity of these political systems.

The exact ways in which these orientations and activities of the bureaucracy were connected with processes of change in the political systems of the historical bureaucratic societies will be considered in the next chapters.

11

The Place of the Political Process

in the Social Structures

of the Centralized Empires

[1] *The Interlinking of Traditional and Differentiated*
Political Activities in the Political Process

In the preceding chapters, we analyzed the conditions under which
the different types of political orientations of the rulers and of the
major groups developed.

For fuller comprehension of the ways that the principal groups'
different political activities and orientations could contribute to the
functioning of the political systems of the historical societies, or could
undermine the basic premises of these systems, we must analyze, in
greater detail and more systematically, the place the political process
occupied in the social structures of these societies.

As we have seen, the relative autonomy of the political sphere, the tendency toward generalization of power, and the articulation of distinct political goals, all increased the political sphere's dependence on resources from other spheres. At the same time, these factors made the supply of such resources more problematical, and contingent on various conditions and changes in the political relations among different groups in the society.

The historical bureaucratic polities were characterized by the coexistence of "free-floating" and traditional resources, and of political forces and orientations. This *coexistence* was a fundamental prerequisite for the functioning of these systems. This, in addition to the fact that the rulers were interested in maintaining both their traditional legitimation and their monopoly of political decision-making, and in implementing, within this framework, more differentiated and politically autonomous goals and policies, made the rulers especially sensitive to the problems related to the development of the free-floating resources and to their relations to the more traditional aspects of the social structure.

The chief sources of free-floating resources and the primary bases of potential generalized power were concentrated largely in those sectors of the society that were not regulated by ascriptive and particularistic criteria. These sectors were also more articulated politically, and thus could attempt to further their independent political goals and to undermine the traditional legitimation of the rulers. On the other hand, the relative paucity of these free-floating resources, combined with the existence of many "traditional" forces, could easily cause the free-floating resources to dwindle, and widespread political apathy to develop on the part of the most active strata. This could cause the predominance of the traditional—largely aristocratic—elements, whose intensive political activity could easily be directed against those prerequisites that made it possible for the bureaucratic polities to continue to function.

Hence it became crucial to the rulers to regulate and channel the more active groups and free-floating forces, and to link them constantly to the more traditional forces in common political frameworks and organizations. The rulers' effective exercise of political power was largely dependent on their ability to maintain such regulation. However, this maintenance was possible only in so far as rulers took the needs and orientations of these active groups into account. Their specific needs and orientations were expressed through their linking the less differentiated political activities and orientations to the more differentiated and articulated ones, just as the rulers were in need both of traditional legitimation and of more differentiated generalized power and support.

As indicated above, the policies of the rulers and political activities and organizations of the major groups were both manifestations of the two aspects of generalization of power that tended to evolve in the historical bureaucratic societies. These two aspects of generalization of power were always closely interrelated. However, they were not necessarily always fully compatible. As a result, the rulers were continually confronted with the problem of finding ways and institutionalized channels through which the generalized power potential created by the various strata could be transferred into the political framework and accommodated by their policies.

[2] The Channelization of the Political Activities of the Major Groups and Strata

In order to understand the rulers' great concern with channelization, crystallization, and maintenance of the required level of generalized power, we must consider the potentially crucial importance that many interrelations, struggles, and tensions among different groups and strata had for the political process in the historical bureaucratic societies.

In this respect, the historical bureaucratic polities differed from primitive, feudal, and patrimonial ones. In many primitive societies, the internal and mutual interrelationships among different groups constituted the foremost expression of the political process. This was particularly applicable when political positions and activities were not greatly differentiated from other offices and functions. However, as the political activities and roles became more differentiated and more developed in primitive, feudal, or patrimonial societies—and the more special ruling groups emerged in these societies—the greater became the areas of social relations and organizations that were somewhat insulated from the central political process and, in a way, indifferent or passive toward it. To a great extent, this also occurred in large areas of social life in the historical bureaucratic societies, particularly in those in which the politically unarticulated strata—the peasants, some of the urban groups—were concentrated. These areas were characterized by the least developed and articulated political issues and organizations.

However, in the historical bureaucratic societies, there evolved—albeit to different degrees in different societies—fields of social life whose regulation became directly important to the political process. These areas were characterized by a high degree of differentiation, extensive interdependence and contacts among various groups, and by those groups' tendency to develop wider social and political orientations. Moreover, the close interrelations among these different areas made linking them in common political frameworks crucially important for the political process.

As we have discussed, many regulative and integrative problems, and many foci of conflict among various groups, arose in the more differentiated areas of social life. Since many of these groups constituted primary sources of free-floating resources and centers of potential generalized power, their interrelations, the ways in which they were linked with the less differentiated groups, the types of consensus attained by them or the foci of conflict among them, all became vitally important to the political process. All these intergroup processes were significant for both the extent to which these groups depended on the polity and the demands they made on the polity. In addition, these same intergroup processes could determine the types of resources that the groups made available to the polity, and the problems which would become crystallized into political issues.

The degree to which these problems, issues, and social conflicts became directly relevant to the political process varied widely, as we have seen, from one historical bureaucratic society to another. Whatever the respective variations, however, in each of these societies, there always remained—to a far greater extent than in modern societies— many strata which, by virtue of their structural positions, were politically unarticulated, and areas of life whose problems were regulated without regard to the political process of the total society. However, in the historical bureaucratic societies, in comparison with less differentiated societies, the extent to which group relations were crystallized into political issues was relatively great.

[3] *The Institutionalization of Norms of Political Struggle and of Political Consensus*

In the historical bureaucratic societies, the social conditions enumerated above created both the potential and the limitations for the development of generalized power whose channelization constituted a major problem for the political institutions of these societies. What were, then, the concrete ways through which, after this potential political power had been realized, its channelization was effected?

The foremost way was through formulating and institutionalizing various norms of political behavior and process. In the preceding analyses, we emphasized the contentious—the "struggle"—aspect of the political process. However, we must remember that, in this same process, some common norms, some degrees of consensus and agreement among various groups, were also worked out. Both autonomous (i.e., non-political), and political and bureaucratic, mechanisms developed which dealt with regulating these problems and conflicts, and with evolving and institutionalizing the appropriate norms. Although these different types of mechanisms differed from, and often competed with, one another, they were closely interrelated and interconnected. In many cases, the articulation and formulation of such norms, and the institutionalization of such channels, became directly related to, and a significant aspect of, the political struggle and process, and the policies of the rulers.

Thus, in these societies, the constant functioning of the political institutions in which the rulers had the monopoly of decision-making depended on the degree to which their framework permitted various social groups to develop at least some autonomous-regulative activities. At the same time, the autonomous regulation of the interrelations among the major groups in the society could not be fully worked out without reference to the framework established by the political institutions. Thus the legal codes and norms evolved by different groups, or their attempts to establish their respective rights in various social spheres, were often achieved within the frameworks of the bureaucracy and the organs of political struggle; and they constituted, as already discussed, important facets of the issues of political struggle. And the complex, specifically political issues of this struggle, and types of political organization, provided the major links among the social and political orientations and activities of the major groups, and among the central political institutions. These general issues—the more flexible policies and the more articulated types of political organization—enabled the various social groups and strata to organize themselves, to articulate and regulate some of their own political goals, and to control their relations and conflicts with other groups in the society. By their very nature, the norms evolved in this process were not too rigid; they thus made the continual reorganization and rearticulation of intergroup problems and conflicts possible.

Within this context, the bureaucratic administration always performed vital functions. It provided continuous services to the major strata, and insured certain specific rights would continue whatever the balance of political forces at any given moment. The bureaucracy thus upheld some general norms of political and legal behavior and activities. Similarly, the organs of political struggle performed a vital function in the development and institutionalization of these more flexible norms.

However, it was necessary to link these more differentiated political activities with the less differentiated ones. As a result, two kinds of basic norms of political struggle emerged in these societies. These denote the two levels of political consensus that existed in these societies.

The political consensus that was evolved in these societies did not focus on the principal common symbols alone. The trend was toward differentiating the basic legitimation of the rulers (kings, etc.) from their concrete policies and the policies of the various government organs. This trend's manifestations were the distinctions made between the norms regulating basic loyalty to the ruler and the norms pertaining to attitudes about different concrete policies, and the shifting interrelations among various social groups and between them and the rulers.

Although the first type of norms and values was usually very traditional and ascriptive, the other was far more flexible and given to change. Much of the political struggle was focused on the concrete definitions and derivations of the latter types.

Moreover, the fact that the traditional element or orientation persisted in the legitimation of the rulers did not necessarily imply that the rulers were precluded from engaging in the political struggle concerning the definition of the second type of norms. On the contrary—the rulers were always, continually involved in political controversy. They received a much smaller amount of unconditional support than was available to the rulers and systems of less differentiated societies. In the historical bureaucratic empires, therefore, the rulers became involved in party politics and competed with other political leaders; they thus found it necessary to take into account the political orientations and activities of the more active groups and strata. In this way, the potential generalized political power that existed among many strata, when realized and translated into political goals and issues, constrained the rulers' endeavors to generalize power and to utilize it more or less indiscriminately. These limitations on the rulers' absolutist tendencies were intrinsic in the very process of institutionalizing generalized power. They differed from the limitations that were due to the prevalence of traditional forces and that restricted the development of generalized power. However, both kinds of limitation, and a third (discussed below), always coexisted in the historical bureaucratic societies. They effected, through the political activities and orientations of the major social groups, the functioning and continuity of these societies' political systems. The endemic coexistence of these different types of limitation on generalized power is characteristic of the political systems of the historical bureaucratic polities, and is also a fundamental prerequisite of their continuity.

[4] The Relations of Various Groups and Strata to the Basic Prerequisites of the Political Systems and to the Conditions of Their Perpetuation

To summarize our discussion of the political process, both in the social structure of the historical bureaucratic polities and in the maintaining of the conditions conducive to the perpetuation of their political systems, we should relate this discussion to the analysis of the attitudes that the various groups and strata had toward basic prerequisites of these political systems. We may investigate the extent to which the different strata furthered the development and maintenance of levels of generalized power and of the political institutions appropriate for these bureaucratic polities, and the extent to which these strata impeded such development.

Following our preceding analysis, we may distinguish between different types of limitations on and oppositions to the rulers' tendency toward generalization of power.

The first type comprised the following: (1) possible scarcity of free-floating resources and bases for such generalized power; (2) active opposition by different groups; and (3) various strata's political passivity and lack of active support. This type of limitation could easily impede the rulers' endeavors to attain the desired level of generalization of power.

The second type of limitation was imposed on the rulers' exercise of generalized power by the integrative and regulative problems of certain groups and strata who identified with the basic premises of a given system, acted within its framework, and developed within its articulated political orientation. The political participations, aspirations, and goals of these groups, their mutual conflicts, the operation of the diverse autonomous regulative mechanisms—these inevitably imposed important boundaries to the rulers' tendency to generalization of power.

In addition, the existence of certain levels of generalization of power might have been impeded by the traditional orientations and attempts of the rulers themselves to achieve a more extended control over the power potential and political goals of the more active social strata.

The continuous coexistence of these three types of limitations on the rulers' tendency to generalization of power was imperative for the continuity of the political systems of the historical bureaucratic empires.

The first and third kinds could, by themselves, undermine the conditions and premises of centralized bureaucratic societies. The second, when combined with the others could be a critical factor conducing to the continuity of these societies.

Our preceding discussion has demonstrated the ways that the more differentiated and flexible aspects of the political process could generate the conditions necessary for maintaining the type of limitations, imposed by the groups and strata who identified with the specific system, on generalization of power. Through these, they operated to insure the continuous interchange of relations between the polity and other parts of the society; in turn, this interchange made the functioning of these political systems certain. The more flexible political institutions could, in some measure, cope with shifts in the allocation and concentration of resources. The more articulated and flexible kinds of political organization and leadership, when effectively linked to the less differentiated kinds, contributed to the uninterrupted functioning of these political institutions. They constituted the chief method of reconciling the political goals of different groups to the level of generalized power generated by the rulers' political aims and goals. In so far as conditions were propitious to their development, they could be important agents of the system's malleability and of helping to insure its continuity.

Developments within the bureaucracy were necessarily crucial in this connection. The bureaucracy's maintenance of its services and service orientations could insure the constant accommodation of different groups in the existing political framework. Also, the services the bureaucracy rendered could provide one of the most important mechanisms for channeling the social and political aspirations of many groups. As a result, however, the possibility grew that the bureaucracy's goals of service would be displaced by goals of self-aggrandizement, and so did the possibility that it would usurp power. These possibilities, if realized, would lead to the bureaucracy's evolving into some "closed" social semi-aristocratic stratum. This would have a most detrimental effect both on the chances of accommodating different groups within the framework of the existing political institutions, and on the possibility of institutionalizing the requisite level of generalized power.

Thus the bureaucracy was a focal point in the political process in the historical bureaucratic societies. The repercussions of the continuous interactions between the activities and orientations of the rulers and the main strata and those of the bureaucracy were critically important to the maintenance or undermining of the continuity of the political systems of these societies.

These various types of attitudes toward the fundamental prerequisites of the political systems of the historical bureaucratic polities sometimes explained the different kinds of activities in which the rulers engaged against their opponents, and the fact that these reaction activities of the rulers usually contained, as we have noted, two different elements.

The first element in the rulers' reaction activities comprised their attempts to control the generalized power engendered by the more flexible and differentiated strata, to monopolize all the regulative activities related to such levels of societal differentiation, and to maintain their own level of generalized power—at the expense, as it were, of these more active strata, and through negating their relative autonomy. In other words, the rulers always tried to monopolize all the main functions of articulation and aggregation of the more differentiated political interests.

The second element in the activities of the rulers consisted of their attempts to revert to more traditional levels of legitimation and generalization of power, and to impose *traditional* limitations on the generalization of the power of the more flexible strata.

It is symptomatic of the basic conditions of the historical bureaucratic societies, and of the dual orientations of their rulers, that these two elements always coexisted in the rulers' activities directed at preserving their own monopoly of control and power.

12

Processes of Change

in the Political Systems

[1] *Processes of Change in Group Structure*
and in Political Organization

In the preceding chapters, we have analyzed the principal political activities and orientations of the major groups in the historical
bureaucratic societies. We have discussed their range of variations. We
have considered the place of the political process in the social structure of these polities, and the ways in which differential participation
in this process could, in principle, either contribute to or endanger
the functioning and continuity of these political systems.

We have been concerned with the major differences in the political
attitudes and activities of the chief participants in political process in
the historical bureaucratic societies, and with the conditions under
which these differences tended to develop. The analysis of these differences necessarily poses the question of the extent to which they
could be contained within the framework of the political institutions
of the historical bureaucratic societies, or to which they were com-

patible with the continuity of the basic premises of any such political system.

To analyze these problems, we must remember that these different political orientations and activities developed, as has already been indicated, under specific social conditions. These conditions were not, however, within the confines of any given society, static or unchangeable. Within each of the historical bureaucratic societies, these conditions themselves changed continuously—as did the political attitudes and activities of the major participants in the political process. To understand the processes of continuity or change of these political systems, we must first describe and analyze the main types of change which occurred in historical bureaucratic societies. Then we must determine the ways in which they were organized and structured as social processes and conditions under which these types of change developed. Last, but not least, we must investigate the relation of the political process to these processes of change—i.e., the ways in which these changes were manifested in the political process, and the extent to which they could be regulated and accommodated by the society's political institutions.

Most of the important changes that developed within these societies were connected with, or rooted in, changes in the group structure, especially in the following:

1. Changes in intergroup structure in the society, manifested in either the emergence of new groups, or in changes in the relative strength and predominance of different groups. The best illustrations of such changes in the historical bureaucratic societies are: the rise, and growing or diminishing strength, of professional, cultural, and religious elites and institutions; and shifts in the relative strengths of the monarch *vs.* the aristocracy and of the aristocracy *vs.* the urban groups and the free peasantry, or shifts in the relative strength and independence of the bureaucracy.

2. Intragroup changes—i.e., shifts in the internal structure, composition, strength, and alignments of the major groups and strata. For example, such shifts occurred in the relative predominance of civil or military elements within the bureaucracy, or in the emergence of semi-autonomous military groups.

Whatever the exact genesis of any of these processes of change, they were always connected with some degree of dislocation of some groups from the existing institutional framework of the society. Such dislocation was usually evident in the attempts made by a group to change its relative place in the institutional structure, and in the growing conflicts between different groups; in the rupture of the major lines of communication between such groups and the prevalent institutional structure; and in these groups' endeavors to establish new channels which would be more in accordance with their aspirations.

This kind of dislocation usually developed concurrently within both ecological strata and functional groups and elites. When they evolved in ecological groups and strata, these dislocations were usually manifested in the rupture of the lines of communication from the political institutions and from many functional groups and elites. They were sometimes also discernible in the development of symbols of group identity that were disconnected from the basic symbols both of the polity and of other groups. When occurring in the functional groups and elites, this kind of dislocation was also usually manifested in the articulation of new symbols and norms, and in the breaking off of communication, between the functional groups and elites, and the rulers and those strata loyal to the rulers, with their symbols, and orientations; and in the search for new strata, or "clientele," among which new symbols and norms could be disseminated. In such cases, a shift in the group's conception of the basic references of political activity was often generated.

All these changes necessarily created conflicts—whether potential or actual—between at least some of the society's major groups and strata. They necessitated the continuous development and reformulation of institutional activities and arrangements dealing with the regulation or resolution of these conflicts. Hence they were closely related to the political process in these societies and were manifested in various changes within the political institutions. The most important of these were the following:

1. Changes in administrative, political, and ministerial personnel.

2. Changes in the relative predominance of any group in the political arena, in terms of the group's influence on policy decisions, its acquisition of various benefits from the political authorities, or its possible influence on the definition of at least some of the rulers' long-term goals.

3. Direct assumption and usurpation of political power and decision-making by different groups—e.g., military groups, eunuchs, or some upper bureaucratic groups. This type of change was either personal (as when a ruler was deposed by a member of his own family or court) or dynastic—or it involved the elevation of a new dynasty, representing one of these groups, to the throne.

4. Rebellions, sectarian activities, outbursts, and revolutions of different kinds.

[2] The Articulation of Processes of Change through Political Activities and Leadership

The changes in group structure were linked to changes in the political institutions through the different types of political activities that tended to emerge in these societies. The most important of these political activities were the following:

1. The rise of divers kinds of leaders who advocated new policies and a certain redistribution of benefits and power within the society and its political institutions. The orientations and activities of these leaders were limited to one stratum or were directed toward encompassing several strata. But, to some extent, all these types of leaders tended to emphasize, generate, or develop some general symbols—even if they stressed the values or interests of one group or stratum more than those of another. Frequently, the rulers themselves, their representatives, or members of the ruling elite played such leadership roles.

2. Attempts made by these leaders to find support among different groups and strata, to co-operate with different elites and functional groups, to "tap" various free-floating resources, and to organize and channelize them to augment their own power. These attempts were manifested in (a) the leaders' endeavors to develop various types of social and political organizations of different degrees of articulation; (b) to attain political influence and power in the political institutions; and (c) to obtain support from many of the cultural, professional, and religious groups and elites; to forge new symbols of social and political identication; to develop varied types of associations and organizations; to become themselves representatives of certain values; and to redefine the relations between the society's "Great" and "Little" traditions.

3. These leaders' attempts to establish, through co-operation with or coercion of different groups and elites, regulatory and integrative organizations and institutions to which different groups and strata had to have recourse in order to regulate their conflicts. In some cases, the leaders (especially the rulers themselves, in so far as they engaged in party politics of this type) may have stirred up conflicts between groups, in order to force these groups to apply to themselves for arbitration and mediation.

Through all these activities, the various kinds of leaders were trying to channelize and control the main types of resources required by the polity, and to effect some changes—whether basic or not—in the relations between the political and the other social spheres.

[3] *Major Types of Change*

These activities constituted the channels through which different groups were linked with, or dislocated from, the political-institutional structure. Thus, the orientations and activities of these social and political leaders were crucially important in directing the processes of change. From this point of view, we can distinguish between several major types of such processes.

A. ACCOMMODABLE CHANGE

The first type consisted of changes which could, to a large extent, be accommodated within the basic premises and institutions of the political system of any given historical bureaucratic society. This type constituted, mostly, changes in the definition of diverse concrete roles in the political institutions, in the structure of various groups participating in them, and, to some extent, of some concrete norms and arrangements of the political institutions. This type did *not* extend to the *basic* norms, symbols, and levels of activity of the central political institutions.

B. TOTAL CHANGES

In contrast with this type of change, some of the major dynastic changes (especially those connected with the usurpation of ultimate power by new groups)—and, in particular, the changes which gave rise to transformation of the polity—could not be accommodated by the existing frameworks of political institutions, legitimation, and symbols. Such processes of "total" or of "unaccommodable" change of the political institutions were characterized, not only by changes of different roles and groups, but also by changes in the basic norms, symbols, and value orientations of the political system.

In this second type of change, the dislocated groups were not reaccommodated within the framework of the basic norms of the existing political system. Instead, new political norms, frameworks, and symbols developed; and the continuity of the political symbols and ideology was broken. This breach was usually manifested in an awareness of the instability and the inadequacy of the political order.

C. MARGINAL CHANGES

Between these two types of change just discussed, there often developed a marginal type, exemplified chiefly by different kinds of rebellions and sectarian activities. These were characterized by two qualities. One was that their orientations and symbols usually negated the existing political order and its basic premises. The other was their inability to create a new kind of effective political symbols, organizations and activities largely because of their inadequate political articulation and leadership.

In actual cases, these different types of change often overlapped. For example, there was the overlapping between personal and dynastic changes and between dynastic change and transformations of the polity. Sometimes, the accumulation of the accommodable or marginal types of change could bring about the total transformation of the political system. The extent to which this happened and the conditions under which different types of change occurred will be the subject of our subsequent analysis.

[4] The Basic Prerequisites of the Political Systems of Centralized Empires

What, then, were the conditions under which these different types of change tended to develop in the historical bureaucratic societies?

In order to be able to analyze these conditions, we must first recapitulate briefly the analysis of the basic prerequisites of the political systems of the historical bureaucratic empires that we have already expounded.

The basic prerequisites for the functioning of these political systems were that the rulers were provided concomitantly with both traditional, unconditional support, and various types of free-floating resources and support. The constant development and provision of such free-floating resources—*within the limits* of the basic traditional legitimation—were, as we have seen in our preceding discussion, a basic condition of the continuous functioning of these political systems, of the maintenance of adequate levels of generalized power, and of having some measure of flexible consensus within them.

However, in order to maintain the conditions requisite for the continuing growth of both free resources and traditional legitimation in the different institutional spheres, the political sphere had to create or facilitate the conditions necessary for the constant development of such limited free-floating resources.

We have seen that the maintenance of these requisite conditions was linked to the development, in addition to certain accumulative and creative policies, of the regulatory and promotive policies which we have already discussed. The most important of these policies were those which—while directed toward regulating the major social strata and maintaining certain levels of traditional support for the rulers—at the same time enabled these strata and functional groups to work out their own norms and regulations, to establish their own interrelations with other subgroups, and to retain some scope of autonomous activity and creativity. In this way, the different groups and strata were able to develop continuously both some of the more flexible political activities and the "traditional" acceptance of the basic premises of the institutions of the political systems.

Among these policies, the most important in the economic sphere were those which, through taxation policies and monetary manipulation, encouraged the development of the level of productivity necessary to the continuous development of free resources. Thus, certain levels of technological knowledge, saving, capital, and skilled and mobile labor had to be assured for effective production; and certain needs and demands had to be generated among different strata and groups in order to create potential markets for the fruits of the productive units.

Among the "social" policies, the most important in this respect were those which assured (1) the provision of a general framework within which different status hierarchies could evolve and coexist; (2) the creation of means for maintaining and regulating relations among different groups; and (3) the creation of facilities for the permissive use, by these groups, of different types of influence, power, and symbols of prestige which would make possible, and implement, the legitimate articulation of the goals and aspirations of various groups in political terms.

In the cultural sphere, the most important policies were those which assured (1) the provision of general institutional frameworks that made possible the development of religious and cultural institutions, the dissemination of religio-cultural values in the society, and the maintenance of adequate communication channels between the centers of cultural life and the various groups of the population; (2) permissiveness to develop separate, distinct loyalties around the different cultural symbols and institutions; and (3) support for religious and cultural elites in terms of sanction for, and promotion of, their basic norms and values.

These services and flexible frameworks to other social spheres and groups must be constantly provided by the political institutions, as must *limited* free-floating economic and manpower resources, as well as political support and over-all traditional legitimation to the polity, by these groups and strata, if the functioning of this type of political systems at the requisite level of generalized power was to be assured. In other words, the ability of the political system of any historical bureaucratic society to accommodate changes and shifts in the relative position and composition of different groups, and in their political orientations and activities, depended largely on the system's continuous reception of adequate but limited free resources, and on its making political decisions which provided the framework for the development, within major social groups, of such resources. In so far as this interchange between the policies of the rulers and the political activities of the major groups were interrupted at any one of these poles, the given political system could break down.

In the fulfilment of all these functions, the major organs of political struggle and the bureaucracy performed crucial operations. In so far as the organs of political struggle provided the frameworks for legitimate articulation of differentiated political orientations, and in so far as the bureaucracy continuously provided some of its basic services and maintained some extent of service orientation, they fulfilled two important functions: they insured the supply of the requisite resources to most social groups; and they regulated their relations with each other and with the polity. Thus, the organs of political struggle and the bureaucracy tended to insure the constant implementation of divers regulative promotive policies, the continuous development of various free resources within different social strata, and the uninterrupted flow of these resources to the polity.

[5] *The Basic Conditions of the Perpetuation*
of the Political Systems. The Places of the Policies
of the Rulers and of the Political Activities of the Major
Groups in the Perpetuation of These Conditions

Having thus recapitulated our analysis of the major premises of the historical bureaucratic societies, we may now analyze the general conditions under which the different processes of change developed in these societies and the more specific conditions connected with each major type of change.

We have already seen that the various processes of change that emerged within the historical bureaucratic societies were rooted in the very conditions of their development—in the *limited autonomy* of the political sphere and of the different social spheres and groups, on the one hand; and in the interaction between these different spheres, on the other. In these societies, these processes of change were inherent in the endemic tendencies toward generalization of power—in the rulers' tendencies to develop generalized power, in order to use it for the implementation of different political goals; and in the tendencies of various groups and strata to evolve their own autonomous social orientations and political goals, and to channelize this generalized power for implementing their goals and orientations.

Next, the processes of change that developed in these societies were rooted in the constant tension and contradiction between the free-floating resources and flexible orientations, on the one hand, and the more traditional orientations and interests, on the other. We have seen that these tensions and contradictions were features both of the political attitudes and policies of the rulers, and of the political activities and orientations of the principal social strata.

More concretely, we may describe the chief factors that generated processes of change in historical bureaucratic societies as follows:

1. The rulers' needs for different types of resources, and especially their growing dependence on various flexible resources

2. The rulers' attempts to maintain their own positions of control, in terms both of traditional legitimation and of effective political control over the more flexible forces in the society

3. The possibility of the emergence, in most of these societies, of what has been called *Primat der Aussenpolitik* (*see, e.g.,* [G] *Altheim, 1955[b], pp. 124 ff.*), and the consequent relatively great and constant sensitivity of the internal structures of these societies to external pressures, to political and economic developments in the international field

4. The rulers' resulting needs to mobilize resources in order to deal with problems arising from changes in military, diplomatic, and economic international situations

5. The evolution, among the major strata, of various autonomous orientations and goals, and their respective demands on the rulers

Among these different needs and demands, various tensions and contradictions could develop that would lead to different kinds of political activities and changes.

[6] *The Major Foci of Contradiction in the Political Process*

A. THE POLICIES OF THE RULERS

The focal point of these possible contradictions was comprised of the developments of both autonomous political goals and autonomous groups with active political orientations. The development and implementation of such autonomous goals sometimes led to divers contradictory policies. These policies could possibly deplete those groups which were the main providers of free resources in these societies, or alienated them from the basic premises of their political systems—in this way minimizing the viability of the systems.

This possibility was innate in several aspects of these goals. Strong political-collective goals, by their very nature, required implementation by extensive economic and manpower resources. If the society's economy was relatively underdeveloped, the economic resources of many of its comparatively mobile sectors could easily be strained in implementing these goals. In a society whose economy was more developed, these goals could increase the rulers' dependence on economically active strata which might have been difficult to control.

The rulers' excessive demands and their growing expenditure, the consequent taxation and inflation, the rulers' attempts at over-centralization and overplanning, sometimes, if not checked, struck hardest at those groups whose economic positions were based on more flexible resources—thereby draining these resources. These groups became depleted by such taxation and by the inflation resulting from growing governmental expenditure. This was especially true in an economy of limited resources that could nevertheless depend greatly on fluctuations in international monetary developments—without being able to cope fully with their effects.

This depletion assumed different, varying forms: outright demographic apathy and consequent shrinking of manpower (see, for instance, [Q] Boak, 1955[b]); weakening of the more independent economic elements and their subordination to more conservative, aristocratic-patrimonial (or feudal) elements; and the diminishing or flight of mobile capital.

Second, the very emphasis on such autonomous goals and on the traditional orientation of the rulers—with which they were always connected—minimized the importance of purely economic activities and long-range economic considerations, and subordinated them to the need for immediate resources. Rulers who upheld political-collective goals framed policies that frequently tended to discriminate against long-term economic investment and development in favor of immediate fiscal and manpower needs. These conditions in turn made the political and economic systems even less able to deal with problems arising out of international economic fluctuations—changes in the availability of money and metals, in trade routes, etc.

Third, the emphasis on political-collective goals usually enhanced the prestige and power of those elements and strata customarily engaged in such activities (mainly, the military and the aristocracy). It further weakened the free strata—both the peasants, who became more dependent on the aristocracy, and the urban groups and elites, whose free-resources became depleted.

As results of developments like this, there was often a shrinkage of the available supply of free or flexible resources; a lowering of the general level of productivity; and/or the alienation, of the economically and socially more active strata, from the rulers and their policies and from the political institutions of the society. Such alienation was frequently intensified by the fact that many parts of these polities had often been incorporated through conquest. Thus, whatever passive loyalty may have been engendered at certain stages of their development, it was frequently undermined because of the various prescriptive policies of the rulers.

Similar developments occurred in the fields of status, religion, and culture. The rulers' emphasis on traditional legitimation and/or prescriptive control of various groups (especially obvious in conquered provinces) could diminish the flexibility of the status systems, obstruct processes of mobility within the society, and either weakened some of the more active urban, cultural, religious, and professional groups, and/or alienated them from the existing political framework, its values and symbols. In more traditional societies, the rulers' emphasis on traditional legitimation and prescriptive control could alienate strongly the religious and professional elites from the symbols of the polity; it could cause them to deflect their interest from political issues and orientations; and ultimately it could result in the evolution of less flexible and more traditionalistic political orientations and leaders. In the more differentiated societies, the alienation of the active groups from the symbols of the polity could lead to the emergence of new foci of intellectual and social activities, directed toward establishing new principles of political organization and participation, and new major referents of political activity. In either case, it could result in growing dissociation between different strata—especially between the more traditional and the more "active" differentiated ones. It also often gave impetus to the development of various sectarian, apolitical, and religiously militant groups.

Fourth, the emphasis on political-collective and military-expansion goals sometimes resulted, in combination with the dwindling supply of free resources, in the rulers' inability to deal with various exigencies (e.g., external pressure and need for numerous resources), and in growing dependency on foreign powers and elements. For instance, in the absence of internal strata which could be mobilized for military service, the rulers often resorted to alien mercenaries. Or the absence or depletion of economically active groups often attracted foreign merchants.

These mercenaries and/or merchants were easily able to acquire strategic importance in economic and military matters.

B. THE POLITICAL ORIENTATIONS
OF THE MAJOR GROUPS

The processes of change we have described above were not results solely of the rulers' policies in the historical bureaucratic societies. They also developed as consequences of changes in the compositions and relative strengths of diverse groups. In this context, the extent to which many flexible groups evolved that had wider, universalistic orientations and a relatively high potential for political articulation and activity, was especially important. A paradoxical reciprocal relation usually developed between these and the policies of the rulers. At the initial stages of the growth of the bureaucratic polities, their rulers were usually interested in the limited promotion of such free strata. However, additional growth of these strata, plus both increasing external exigencies and the problems of controlling these strata, frequently combined to make the rulers' policies more prescriptive in later stages of development.

In situations related to growing internal needs and external exigencies, the rulers were often caught on the horns of the basic dilemma inherent in their own political orientations, goals, and policies. This dilemma was posed by the rulers' contradictory interests: one was in the development of some level of "free" resources; the other was their desire to maintain traditional legitimation and to establish complete control over the different strata. To the extent that the rise of "free" groups concurred with the intensification of the rulers' external and internal needs and exigencies, the rulers' tendency toward control could easily predominate. This increased the power of the traditional forces, sharpened the conflicts between them and the free strata, and either destroyed the more "free" groups and strata or alienated them from the rulers.

When this occurred, the rulers usually exhibited a growing tendency toward emphasizing "self-maintenance" goals, developing various prescriptive policies, and over-planning at the center—and these things, as we have noted in Chapter 7, were always related to the predominance of these goals. Although most of these prescriptive policies were couched in ideological terms and purported to aim at maintaining the "traditional" loyalty to the rulers, they necessarily went beyond pure "traditionalism." Thus, while often the professed goal of the rulers was to restore traditionalism, they were obliged to resort to numerous prescriptive measures and policies that could not take a lower, traditional level of political activity for granted and were directed toward the political suppression of the more active strata. The rulers necessarily employed a higher level of generalized power than would have been warranted by purely traditional considerations; and yet, they continually used traditionalistic symbols. Policies like these reflected the contradiction within the rulers' aims and goals—the contradiction which could ultimately undermine the continuous functioning of the main organs of the political systems of the historical bureaucratic societies. This contradiction weakened the organs of political struggle and of bureaucratic administration and impaired their capacity to perform their basic tasks —i.e, to mobilize adequate resources for the polity, and to regulate the relations among different groups in the society and between them and the polity. In this way, it ultimately undermined also the very prerequisites necessary for the functioning of these political systems.

Thus, in all the societies studied, the exigencies created by the goals and policies of the rulers and by their potential conflicts with the autonomous political orientations developed by various groups strata built up a pressure which usually led to processes of change. These processes included, potentially, accommodable change, the partial or total undermining of the basic premises of the political systems of the historical bureaucratic polities, and their transformation. However, the extent to which these potentials were realized varied from society to society and from time to time.

₀[7] *The Basic Conditions and ₍Characteristics of Processes of Accommodable Change*

We can now consider and analyze the specific conditions which give rise to the respective types of change—the accommodable, the total and the various marginal types—in the historical bureaucratic societies.

On the basis of our preceding analysis, we may assume that these specific conditions are shaped by different constellations of the major aspects of the political process, as already outlined. These aspects are as follows: (1) the major policies of the rulers and their repercussions on the relative strengths of different strata; (2) changes in the relative strengths of different strata, resulting from internal economic, religious, or political developments; (3) the occurrence of internal and external exigencies; (4) the effects that the policies framed by the rulers in response to such exigencies had on the relative strengths of different groups in the society; (5) the composition and social orientations of the major elites and of political leadership; and (6) the extents of interchange and mobility among different groups and strata in the society.

Accordingly, we may postulate that various types of accommodable change tended to develop in so far as concurrently: (1) the policies of the rulers, the exigencies which they faced, and the costs of dealing with them did not strain the existing resources beyond certain limits—i.e., either that the cost of implementing policy was not too high, or that the "free" strata were sufficiently numerous and strong to bear the burden without losing the bases of their existence; (2) the rulers were always able to give some amount of encouragement to the society's more active groups and strata, and did not either overemphasize their own traditional legitimation or exercise excessive control and restriction over flexible groups; and (3) the aspirations and orientations of these flexible groups were more or less limited and did not evolve beyond certain points compatible with an attitude which viewed the polity or the rulers as the basic referent of their political activities and orientations.

Thus, processes of accommodable change were connected with social conditions which made possible the *continuous* maintenance of some fundamental harmony between the orientations of the various political leaders and the basic premises of the polity within whose framework they acted—a marked continuity in the chief symbols, legitimation, and basic politico-cultural ideology of the polity. The political process that developed in such cases was characterized by the fact that the political leaders and the groups they organized were receptive to the rulers' demands for support. They felt that they could find adequate satisfaction for their aspiration in the rulers' offers to carry out changes of personnel, organization, and policy.

Moreover, there usually developed processes of sponsored mobility, which could be regulated and absorbed within the existing social and political structure and which assured the flow of the more active social elements from the major strata into this structure.

The conflicts which developed, in these cases, between different groups and their interests could be regulated, by the rulers and by the different elites, through the norms and activities of the major political and regulative institutions of the society. These conflicts did not undermine the flexible orientations and frameworks common to different groups—especially to the more traditional and the more differentiated ones—in the society. Throughout these activities, the different types of political organization and leadership—which linked the more traditional with the more differentiated groups and strata—remained intact, even when their specific natures and organizations underwent many changes. When these changes occurred, the main channels of mobility, extending from various more active groups and from the provinces to the central elites, were maintained unimpaired.

Similarly, the bureaucracy and the organs of political struggle were enabled to continue functioning properly by the social and political activities of the major groups in the society, and by the constant recruitment of political and administrative personnel from the more active strata.

In all these cases, the specific interrelations between the polity and other social spheres in the historical bureaucratic societies were not radically transformed. For instance, whatever the relative predominance of the respective groups in the polity (aristocracy, urban groups, religious elites, etc.), the social structure remained sufficiently differentiated and flexible to make the continuous provision of a certain supply of free-floating resources and of social mobility possible. At the same time, the requisite traditional orientation and forces were also maintained within the society. Moreover, any changes which developed in the rulers' policies remained similarly flexible and "promotive" enough for free resources to be maintained at the requisite levels. This made it certain that flexible frameworks and leadership would be sufficient. It also combined or bound together the more conservative and the more flexible groups and elements, and assured the recruitment of elites, thus making possible the continuous fostering of the more flexible orientations within most of the groups.

In this connection, it is especially important that, in each case of accommodable change, the changes in the bureaucracy's political orientation did not go beyond certain limits. The changes never negated entirely some service orientation, especially to the rulers (and, to a lesser extent, to the groups). This fact enabled the bureaucracy to continue to perform some of its basic functions in the political system.

[8] *Accommodable Change in China*

A. ANALYSIS OF MAJOR TYPES

China presents a good example of a society in which processes of accommodable change occurred and of the concrete conditions under which they tend to develop. In China, throughout many centuries (until the end of the nineteenth century and the meeting with the West), accommodable and marginal (rebellious and dynastic) changes constituted the principal types of change. On the other hand, all the marginal types of change either evaporated or merged in the processes of accommodable change, becoming reintegrated into the basic framework of the political institutions.

In China, as in all centralized bureaucratic polities, the primary factors that gave rise to many societal and political changes were the rulers' policies, the changes in them, the various exigencies confronting the polity, and the ways in which the rulers dealt with them. In Chapters 7 and 8, we pointed out that the rulers of China—like those of many other types of bureaucratic polity—tended to emphasize collective goals, such as military security and expansion, some economic enhancement, etc. The costs of pursuing and implementing these varied collective goals, and, in general, of maintaining the administrative system under agrarian economic conditions, periodically strained the society's economic resources. The consequences of this periodic strain were often to bring about the destruction of the small peasantry, to increase the power of the landlords and warlords, and to result in the exploitation of the merchants. However, in China, the pressure on resources and their consequent diminution were not so widespread and acute as in Iran, Byzantium, and other ancient empires. Several factors limited the Chinese rulers' potential needs for many types of resources.

First, the relatively low level of technological development greatly limited, as we have seen, both the necessity for material resources and for political support and the scope of political and administrative activities of the rulers. Then, too, local self-government and the masses' political passivity were strongly emphasized; and the reliance on the literati and gentry for the fulfilment of various governmental and semi-governmental tasks was crucial. True, these factors were not, in themselves, always strong enough to restrain the rulers and prevent them from framing extravagant policies—although in many cases they were effective in doing so. However, they did guarantee the possibility of reorganizing the state, following rebellious reactions to extravagant policies, on the basis of the existing social groups and institutional frameworks. They thus prevented the radical transformation, or even the destruction, of the framework of the empire. Moreover—in close connection with the technological, geographical, and political conditions enumerated above—the *Primat der Aussenpolitik* was weaker in China than in any of the societies studied here; and the external and military exigencies, although continually arising, did not assume the same basic importance for the political structure as they did in other countries.

The second major factor responsible for processes of change consisted, in China as in other societies studied here, of shifts in the relative strength of different groups or families, bureaucratic cliques, or regional groups, and of alterations in their internal structures. These variations were frequently allied with shifts in the international situation and relations, or with international economic developments. In connecton with this fact, it is most important that most of these groups did not develop autonomous goals and organizations that could not be fully accommodated by the relatively flexible institutional frameworks of the bureaucracy and literati groups.

In relation to this, it is especially important that the three vital tendencies capable of undermining the existing institutional framework never developed beyond the embryonic stage in China. The first of these was the potential trend toward feudalization or patrimonial decentralization. Such a tendency was sometimes exhibited by the gentry and the older aristocracy. It appeared very often in the later periods of many Chinese dynasties, when continued prosperity, coupled with growing needs of the government, enabled many gentry groups to extend their landholdings at the expense of the peasants and to escape, to some extent, the supervision of the central government. However, this tendency did not become predominant in any period after the T'ang (i.e., after A.D. 905), because the gentry groups were so dependent on the central administrative organs—for maintaining some of the hydraulic works, for insuring the possibility of interrelationships between different parts of the Empire, and for political positions and privileges for themselves and for members of their families ([I] *Eberhard, 1945, 1948[a], 1951; Stange, 1950; Chang, 1955; Michael, 1942; Balázs, 1952; Lattimore, 1951*).

It is true that marked changes occurred in the land-owning system in China. Under the Ming (A.D. 1368–1644), especially, a strong trend toward the building up of large estates and the diminution of the free peasantry developed. However, even these changes—which were, to some degree, counteracted by the policies of the rulers—did not result in the emergence of an aristocrat stratum ([I] *Twitchett, 1957[a], 1957[c]*).

Another potential which never fully materialized in China was the tendency toward complete independence of the urban-merchant and professional groups. In different periods of Chinese history, there were changes in the relative positions of these groups in the social structure; and during some periods, their power and influence caused the rulers to take their interests into account in formulating policies. Nevertheless, they never became a fully autonomous and politically independent social force. Even when they were relatively powerful—e.g., during the Sung period (A.D. 960–1279)—the urban groups were accommodated chiefly by widening the channels of mobility, thus permitting their entry into the gentry and literati strata and into the bureaucracy ([I] *Balázs, 1954[a], 1960; Eberhard, 1948[a]*; [A] *Weber, 1920–21*).

The third potential tendency was the trend toward the development of activistic, universalistic religious and cultural orientations. This tendency had its roots in some features of the Confucian academies and among the Buddhist sects during the T'ang period. However, it too was never realized except in its incipient stages ([A] *Weber, 1920–21;* [I] *Wright, 1959; DeBary, 1953; Levenson, 1953, 1958*).

If the "feudal" tendencies had evolved beyond embryonic stages, they could have led to the development of a more ascriptive and less differentiated social structure. If the potential trend of the urban and intellectual groups had been more fully matured, it could have resulted in wide universalistic orientation. However, they were usually accommodated by the existing institutional and cultural framework—even if this framework had to find rather special places for them. Their accommodation was manifested (as we shall discuss subsequently) in changes in political and bureaucratic personnel, in allocation of benefits to them, and in the general drafting of policies which took into account, to some extent, the changing interests and strengths of different groups.

The same can be said of the principal marginal types of change that occurred in China—namely, rebellions, and the development of provincial governors into semi-autonomous war lords. Each was connected with the major kinds of internal and external exigencies to which the Chinese Empire was exposed. The internal usually arose from the growth of cliques, the corruption of the bureaucracy, and/or heavy taxation. The external were due to the growing pressure of outside forces—e.g., population pressure on the frontiers of the Empire. These two types of exigencies very often appeared together, one reinforcing the other. They could frequently lead to dynastic changes and to the temporary—even if long-lasting—dismemberment of the Empire. The various marginal types of change were repeatedly closely related to the accommodable changes analyzed above—e.g., clique intrigues at court, or family feuds and struggles between aristocratic and gentry groups.

From the point of view of political organization, these rebellions and military outbursts did not usually feature a markedly different or new level of political articulation. (*See* [I] *Shih, 1956; Eberhard, 1945; Levy, 1959; Eichhorn, 1954; Chiang, 1954; Frisch, 1927; Haloun, 1949–52; Bielenstein, 1953[a], 1953[b]; Bingham, 1941; Hsia, 1956; Parsons, 1957; Muramutsu, 1960.*) The rebellions were often sporadic or undertaken by various cults and secret societies which, while developing many symbols of social protest, incorporated relatively little active articulation of political issues and activities. Their specific symbols included strong apolitical, anhistorical, and semi-mythical or utopian elements. These were, as a rule, bound to the existing value structure and orientations. Thus these rebellions usually provided only secondary interpretations of the existing value structure and did not innovate any radically new orientations. In so far as they had any sort of active political orientations and aims, these were, on the whole, set within the existing political framework. Usually, they aimed at seizing the government and the bureaucracy, and at establishing new governments on the same pattern.

The political orientations of the military governors and war lords were usually also set within the existing value and political frameworks ([I] *Des Rotours, 1926, 1947–48, Introduction; Pulleyblank, 1955; Levy, 1956; Bingham, 1941; Parsons, 1957*). Although they strove for a greater extent of independence from, or the seizure of, the central government, they never envisaged the establishment of a new type of political system. As a rule, they did not even incline toward the complete militarization of the structure of the government; they were, rather, interested in gaining the control of the existing political institutions for themselves, their families, and their cliques.

In certain periods, such developments and the activities of the military government occasioned the extreme results of the dismemberment of the Empire—the establishment of several different states, in which the force of the Confucian tradition and institutions was often weakened. However, even within these states many tendencies evolved toward the unification of the Empire, which remained, in a way, the ultimate political ideal. These inclinations were greatly encouraged by the Confucian literati; they "naturally" implied the reinforcement of the traditional institutional structure.

It is, perhaps, of even greater interest that even the more marked changes in the institutional history of China—i.e., the principal dynastic changes—did not result in significant transformations of the basic symbols and institutions of the political order. As we have seen, generally these changes were also occasioned by an intensification and combination of internal and external exigencies. Often they were related to more pervasive changes in the social and economic structure ([I] *Frisch, 1927; Bingham, 1941; Dubs, 1938[a]; Eberhard, 1945, 1948[a]; Bielenstein, 1953[a], 1953[b]; Stange, 1950*). However, in China—as contrasted with other societies studied here—these changes never, through an accumulation of circumstances and exigencies, burst the existing institutional framework. It is true that these dynastic changes were frequently associated with marked changes in emphasis on the different concrete goals of the rulers, with the relative importance of different groups, and with some changes in the administrative structure. We have noted that, after the Sung (and especially under the Ming and Yüan [A.D. 1260–1368] dynasties), the Chinese government took on a more despotic character. It minimized the political power of individual literati and of bureaucratic groups, and enhanced the absolutism of the rulers—who also effected several changes in the administrative structure, in order to insure their own control over it ([I] *Miyakawa,*

1955; Liu, 1959[b]; Hucker, 1950, 1951, 1959[a]; Aspects ˙de le Chine, 1959, part i et passim).

However, even the rulers of these later dynasties could not do without the body of the literati and the bureaucracy, even though they denigrated the individual bureaucrat. Thus they accepted, at least in principle, both the basic cultural orientations and legitimation of the *Confucian order* and the limitations it imposed on the scope of their own direct political measures concerning the masses of the population and the political activity of these masses.

Even the conquering foreign dynasties which ruled over China—especially the Yüan and the Ch'ing (A.D. 1644–1919)—had to accomodate themselves to the framework of this tradition. Their basic political orientations were not shaped by it; these were governed—especially in external affairs—by different considerations. In internal affairs, however, they had to rely on the already existing institutional framework ([I] *Eberhard, 1948[a]; Wittfogel, 1951*).

Both the rebellions and the dynastic cycles effected alterations in numerous details of the institutional and territorial structures of the Chinese Empire, and were related to many important shifts in the relative power positions of different groups or regions. However, they did not change the fundamental structure of the political order—the nature of the basic interrelations between the political institutions and the other major institutional spheres in the society.

B. THE MAJOR SOCIAL CONDITIONS FAVORING ACCOMMODABLE CHANGE IN CHINA

What is the explanation of the fact that in China—until the Empire's breakdown, in the twentieth century, under the impact of the West—all the significant kinds of change were accommodated within the framework of the existing political symbols and institutions? Can we specify the constellation of the major components of the social structure and political process of the historical bureaucratic societies that was operative in China that minimized the intensity of the processes of change there?

We believe that this fact was primarily due, within the limits imposed by the geographic and technological conditions enumerated above, to certain endemic factors in the Chinese social structure. These were the predominantly cultural orientations of the differentiated Chinese polity and society; the prevalence of the ideals of the Confucian social order; and the relation between these orientations and the rulers' policies, and those between the political orientations of the major strata.

China's predominantly cultural goal orientations helped preserve the stability of its social-political structure in two crucial ways. Their acceptance by the greater part of the population constituted a firm and seemingly unique basis for maintaining the unity of the Empire (at least as an ideal). Also significant was the specific social position of the literati who represented these values and upheld them.

The literati were a peculiar combination of a functional group and elite and a semi-ecological stratum—they were closely, although not exclusively, connected with the gentry. The functional aspect of the composition and activities of the literati has been well stressed by Balázs, who has aptly described them in the following words:

> La position de lettre dans la société ne dépend pas en dernière analyse ni de sa formation, ni de ses privilèges héréditaires, ni de sa propriété ou de sa fortune, familiale ou individuelle, mais fait ses éléments constitutifs de sa situation découlant de la fonction qu'elle exerce effectivement sur tous les plains de la société ([I] *Balázs, 1952*).

At the same time, through its relation to the gentry, the literati—and ultimately the bureaucracy—inclined to identify with some of the ecological strata, especially with the so-called gentry ([I] *Eberhard, 1948[a], 1952; Chang, 1955*). The literati's double social status, or orientation, together with their position vis-à-vis the rulers, enabled them to fulfil several critical regulative and integrative functions in the society, particularly in relation to the political institutions. The literati's very existence as an elite group was contingent upon the persistence of the ideal of a unified empire; and their activities were closely associated with the bureaucratic and administrative apparatus. On the other hand, however, their special position enabled the literati to influence the political orientations and activities both of the rulers and of the leading strata of the population. They exerted this influence, in ideological terms, through upholding the ideal of a common hierarchical social-cultural order binding both on the ruler and on these strata.

The literati served also as a channel of sponsored mobility within the system. They absorbed many active elements from the gentry, urban, military, and even peasant groups into the existing social and political structure. Thus they insured that such mobility would be functional from the point of view of the existing structure and also controlled by it.

Through this influence, and through the development of various mechanisms which will be analyzed shortly, the literati were able to minimize the full development of the internal contradictions inherent in the goals and orientations of the rulers and of the principal strata. First, they often attempted to prevent the rulers from framing extravagant policies, and especially to restrain them from trying to establish

a charismatic traditional legitimation, with strong military orientations, without regard to Confucian values. They endeavored to restrict
the purely executive and military goals pursued by the rulers, so that
the amount of manpower resources required for implementing such
goals was small in proportion to the total population. The literati constantly checked those types of political participation and direct identification with the monarch that were not mediated by the bureaucracy
and themselves. At the same time, through their activities, the literati
limited the extent of free resources and support needed by the rulers.
Their degree of success in these efforts varied greatly; and in many
actual cases, their influence on *concrete* details and execution of policy
was limited. However, even then, the rulers were not able to effect
any significant changes in the basic scope and framework of the existing
political and cultural orientations. The pressures and strains inherent
in the pursuit of various political-executive goals tended to diminish
the available supply of resources, in China as in other bureaucratic societies. However, this depletion was less severe in China than in other
historical bureaucratic polities; and in China, reorganization was possible within the framework of the existing political institutions.

Second, the literati combines their support of the ideal of a
common hierarchical social order with the performance of regulative-
functional activities. Close relations of the literati with ecological
groups helped in the evolution and maintenance of the various mechanisms through which the literati often could check the growth of these
contradictory elements within the social structure that could lead to
the emergence either of pre-bureaucratic tendencies (e.g., tendencies
to feudalization) or of wider free-floating universalistic forces. The
very existence of the literati and their close connection with the
imperial bureaucracy provided an important channel of mobility for
different groups in the society. The literati and the bureaucracy provided a point where the more active elements in both rural and urban
groups could meet, and minimized the possibility that ungovernable
conflicts and/or too strong negative orientations toward the basic
premises of the polity among different strata would develop.

Moreover, the persistence and development of Confucian ideology
among the literati frequently restrained various corruptive and semi-
feudal inclinations within the bureaucracy itself. These also served as
starting points for many tries to reform the bureaucracy, tries made
after periods of corruption and relative disintegration ([I] *Williamson,
1937; Liu, 1959[a], 1959[b]; Stange, 1934, 1939; O. Franke, 1931, 1932;
Dubs, 1938[a], especially pp. 171 ff., 216 ff., 1939*).

In summary of our discussion so far, we can assert that the crucial position and activities of the literati were responsible for two principal features of the conditions of change in Chinese society. First, they explain the fact that the rulers and the bureaucracy never exerted pressure, on the country's supply of resources, strong enough to demolish the bases of the limited free-floating resources necessary for maintaining the centralized bureaucratic polity. Second, they indicate how the society's political and regulative institutions contained sufficient mechanisms and forces enabling them to regulate and accommodate both the emergence of new groups and changes in the structure and orientations of existing political institutions.

Such accommodation was effected through several mechanisms. These were all related to the specific value orientation of the society and to the structure and activities of the literati and the bureaucracy ([I] *Chang, 1955; Eberhard, 1945, 1948[a]; Stange, 1950; Balázs, 1952, 1959[b], 1960; Pulleyblank, 1960*). The most important of these mechanisms were the following:

1. Absorbing some members of different groups into the strata of the literati and into the bureaucracy
2. Considering their interest in policy-making, e.g., granting special permissiveness in the economic and status fields
3. Promoting their interests, e.g., the dissemination of cultural values or the development of trade relations
4. Providing adequate facilities and services, thus making certain of their continued identification of themselves with the maintenance of the state framework

C. COMPARISON OF CHANGE IN CHINA WITH THAT IN THE ANCIENT EGYPTIAN EMPIRE

In the case of China, we have attributed the existence of the accommodable type of change to the predominance of a differentiated (nontraditional) cultural orientation, to the persistence of the ideology of a common hierarchical order, and to the specific characteristics of the stratum representing these values and orientations. To test the validity of our explanation, it will be profitable to analyze briefly the types of change which occurred in the Ancient Egyptian Empire and the conditions responsible for them.

The Ancient Egyptian Empire (especially the Old Empire) also showed strong cultural orientations and goals ([F] *Drioton and Vandier, 1952; Otto, 1953; Wilson, 1951; Edgerton, 1947[a]*). But these orientations and goals were neither so differentiated nor so distinctly articulated as the autonomous political goals in China. The conception of a cultural-political order that they represented was of a far more traditional, non-differentiated nature. The social characteristics of the groups which were the bearers of these values were closely connected with this. The various priestly groups, and particularly the temple priests, constituted semi-independent territorial groups with strong inclinations toward becoming an aristocratized bureaucracy. Because of the great traditionalist and ecological orientations and bases of organization of these groups, they were not strongly bound to the basic premises of a bureaucratic territorial organization, and could become dissociated from the framework of the centralized polity. They were unable to deal, adequately and continuously, with the internal and external exigencies which, exerting pressure on the Ancient Egyptian Empire, led to its dismemberment into smaller patrimonial states. The pressure of the rulers' policies and needs on the existing strata and their resources was very often so great that it sapped their strength and left them unable to provide the free-floating resources requisite for the uninterrupted functioning of the bureaucratic polity. Hence the history of the Ancient Egyptian Empire contains many instances of processes of dismemberment into smaller patrimonial units. However, at the same time the force of the Pharaonic tradition and the basic Egyptian concept of cultural-political order was so strong that, for centuries, they constituted a focus of revival and continuity whenever internal political unifying forces emerged.

In both Egypt and China, there was a long continuity of the main cultural symbols of the polity and of the conception of cultural-political order. However, in Egypt (unlike China), this continuity was accompanied by marked institutional discontinuity in the structure of the political institutions, participation of different groups in the political process, and even in some aspects of the rulers' legitimation ([F] *Drioton and Vandier, 1952; Otto, 1953; Kees, 1933[a], 1934[b], 1935, 1952; Becherat, 1951; Spiegel, 1950; Stock, 1949; Meyer, 1928; Erman, 1923*).

Thus cultural orientations, because of their influence on the legitimation goals of the rulers and the political orientations of the main strata, in themselves constituted an important element of continuity and facilitated accommodable change. Yet it is the extent of the society's internal flexibility and differentiation, and of the flexibility and social characteristics of the stratum bearing these values, that is of crucial importance in terms of accommodation of change. For only such flexibility can insure the possibilities of continuously accommodating diverse types of political change and of minimizing the internal contradictions in the orientations both of the ruler's and of the different strata.

[9] *Major Conditions Related to Development of Processes of Marginal and Total Change*

We have enumerated the conditions that explain, in the case of China, both the prevalence of accommodable change and the ultimate reintegration of the marginal types of change (rebellious and dynastic changes) into the major types of accommodable change and into the existing political framework.

The conditions conducive to and responsible for the development of the accommodable types of change could emerge and persist on different levels of societal differentiation—e.g., in societies with low levels of articulation of generalized power and political activity, as well as in societies with higher levels of differentiation, power generalization and political activity, political participation, and growth of other flexible, active groups.

In all the societies we are examining, during relatively long periods the shifts in the power and positions of different groups did not undermine the framework of the centralized polity. However, these conditions did not obtain for long. In each of these societies, whatever the level of differentiation of its respective social structure, tensions and ruptures developed. These gave rise not only to various types of accommodable change, but also to other kinds of change—such as rebellions and outbursts, as well as, ultimately, changes which brought about the transformation of the political system of the particular historical bureaucratic society.

Moreover, in many of these societies, the different types of marginal change—rebellions, usurpations, and dynastic changes—did not become reintegrated into the existing political order. Instead, they either gave rise to its dissipation or became integrated into movements which led to transformations of the polity.

In Persia, the relatively centralized empires of the Ahmenids and the Sassanids (A.D. 226–641) disintegrated into several independent patrimonial provinces and/or were dismembered under the onslaught of foreign forces ([G] *Christensen, 1936, ch. ix, x; Ghirshman, 1954; Altheim, 1955[b]*). The same sort of thing occurred in the Ancient Egyptian Empire. In Byzantium, as we have seen, the process of gradual disintegration of the Empire began in the eleventh and twelfth centuries, and continued ([L] *Ostrogorsky, 1956[a], 1956[b]; Vasiliev, 1952; Diehl et al., 1945; Charanis, 1940–41[b], 1953[a]; Stein, 1924*). In the Spanish-American Empire, France, and England, the political systems of the historical bureaucratic societies became transformed through internal revolutions ([R] *Haring, 1947;* [S] *Beloff, 1954;* [Y]

Cobban, 1957[b]; [Z] Brock, 1957; [Y] Sagnac, 1945, 1946; Pagès, 1928).

We must determine the exact conditions which gave rise to these rebellions, and, more important, to transformations of the political systems of these empires. Some indications can be negatively derived from our above analysis of processes of accommodable change. It can be postulated that the processes of rebellion and of "total" change—of transformation of the political system—could evolve in proportion to the failure of the various "limiting" or mediating mechanisms and conditions (e.g., orientations to the same social order that are common to the rulers and the main strata, or the functioning of some elite group as continuous mediators between the rulers and the major strata), operative in the cases of accommodated change, to operate. Under what conditions did such mechanisms fail to become fully and continuously institutionalized within the structure of these societies?

The first principal condition for their failure was the prevalence, among both the rulers and the leading strata, of political and social orientations which focused on the polity and/or on some of the social groups as the main referents of non-traditional, differentiated political activity. Such activity emphasized the aggrandizement and development both of the polity and of these groups as the main foci of political activity and/or saw, in the polity or some of the social groups, the primary bearers of any values which directed political activity. Under these circumstances, very strong differences and antagonisms could easily emerge between the major referents of the political orientations of the rulers and those of the leading strata. The rulers emphasized their own complete autonomy and independence in this respect. However, the various groups perceived themselves as the chief direct bearers of active political values and activities. Or some of the foremost strata or groups evolved orientations that were largely apolitical, and considered certain non-political groups, such as churches or religious organizations, to be the major foci or referents of social and even political activity.

When such cases, occurred, any common political orientation which the rulers and the different groups shared, and the different political and social mechanisms which upheld such common orientations, often became undermined, with the result that the potential contradictions in their respective orientations could be sharpened and emphasized. This possibility was much greater when the rulers and the principal strata and elites were not ethnically or culturally-religiously homogeneous.

The second major condition conducive to the lack of continuous institutionalization of "mediating" mechanisms consisted of certain characteristics and social orientations of the leading elite groups in a society—especially of the extent to which the economic bases and social and cultural orientations of these elites were derived from social settings which were independent of the development of the institutional frameworks of the historical bureaucratic polities or which transcended the major symbols and institutions of these polities.

The most important concrete manifestations of such possibilities were as follows:

1. The prevalence of cultural, religious, bureaucratic elites with strong aristocratic and ecological bases and orientations, which sometimes became disconnected from the institutional framework of the political systems of the historical bureaucratic societies and deflected political support and regulative activities from these institutions.

2. The evolution and prevalence of elites and professional groups which, through processes of differentiation, technological and economic development, and strong emphasis on universalistic values, became dislocated from traditional ecological strata. They were then, unable to regulate the conflicts arising among such groups or to channelize their activities into existing political institutions.

3. The possibility of the emergence of continuous and intensive conflicts among different elite groups.

4. The growing importance of ethnically "foreign" elements in the constitution of different elites.

If these two crucial conditions obtained in a historical bureaucratic society they could result first in tensions between the relative levels of development of the various strata and groups and of the political framework set up by the rulers.

Second, they could result in its rulers becoming more sensitive to various external and internal exigencies and less able to cope with them. When this sensitivity to external exigencies occurred, it was largely rooted in the great emphasis on executive-political goals, and the rulers' consequent increasing pressure on the resources necessary for the implementation of these goals.

Obviously, the pressure of external exigencies was often determined by purely external factors and forces; and in some cases, the very pressure of these external forces was decisive in the fate of the polity. Nonetheless, in many of the cases studied here, both the sensitivity to these pressures and the ability to deal with them were greatly influenced by the internal social and political forces and the given polity.

[10] *Political Processes Attendant on the Development of Processes of Marginal and Total Change*

The conditions we have enumerated were often prominent in the structure of the historical bureaucratic societies. Their prevalence could facilitate the development, within a society, of political processes which could lead to rebellions and to total change. The most important characteristics of these processes were as follows:

1. The activities of various types of political leaders, the level of generalized power, and the types of activities and organizations fostered by them, were continuously incompatible with the basic framework of the existing political institutions—that is, the basic referents of the political activity of these institutions were incompatible with those of the various leaders.

2. Different strata, groups, and leaders did not respond to the demands for resources and support made by the rulers and the political institutions.

3. The main elites and functional groups, or some of their parts, became alienated from the existing political institutions. This alienation was manifest (a) in their attempts to transform the major societal-cultural symbols, and the relation between these symbols and those of the polity; and (b) in their organization of new types of social, economic, and political activities and organizations that could not be contained by the existing political frameworks.

4. Dissociation grew between the more traditional, undifferentiated and the more flexible groups. The common frameworks, activities, and organizations of political leadership that had interlinked the more traditional and the more differentiated groups and strata were undermined. Conflicts between different groups in the society were intensified.

5. It was difficult to regulate these conflicts within the framework of the existing norms and regulative institutions. This difficulty was demonstrated by the attempts, on the part of the rulers or of various leaders, to suppress or prohibit any such conflicts, and/or by the generally ineffective control of such conflicts. This inability to regulate these conflicts was often due to the different levels of development and differentiation of the more active social groups, on the one hand, and of the political institutions set up by the rulers, on the other hand.

6. The channels of mobility in the society were blocked or frozen —especially those channels which had facilitated recruitment, into the central elites, from different groups and from the provinces.

In all these cases, a hiatus evolved between the "demand" and "supply" of political activities. In other words, the political institutions (the rulers and the chief political organs) were unable—often despite various prescriptive measures—to recruit adequate and loyal personnel for political and administrative positions and to maintain adequate channels of communication with the more active groups of the society. In addition, the bureaucracy evolved strong tendencies to displacement of goals of service and to aristocratization. These inclinations undermined its effectiveness and its function as a link between the different strata and the central political institutions.

The organs of the political systems of the historical bureaucratic societies were impeded in their functionings, and their activities became undermined. These organs—whether organs of political struggle or of the bureaucratic administration—were not able to mobilize effectively the resources necessary for the functioning of the polity. However, on the other hand, they also could not effectively control the interrelations among different social groups and between them and the polity. All these processes were conducive to the emergence of changing interrelations between the polity and the major social spheres.

In some cases, the social strata and groups no longer provided the rulers either with the basic traditional support and legitimation or with the free-floating resources they needed. At the same time, the policies of the rulers were no longer directed toward promoting free-floating resources; or else the existing political institutions no longer supplied the frameworks and conditions requisite for the development of free resources in the chief institutional spheres. Independent creativity on the part of divers groups was not facilitated—in fact, it was constricted by various types of prescriptive policy.

In other cases, groups and strata in the society evolved many free-floating resources and orientations that could not be accommodated by the existing permissive framework of the political institutions. These tended to weaken the bases of the rulers' traditional legitimation. All these were connected with the lack of ability of the central institutions either to sponsor and/or to regulate social mobility within the society. Sometimes, the attempts of the central institutions to sponsor a certain amount of mobility from within the various strata were unsuccessful because of the paucity of active elements within these strata. In other cases, there was an overflow of such active elements that could not be regulated within the existing institutions.

[11] *The Relation of External and Internal Conditions in the Processes of Marginal and Total Change*

The conditions facilitating the development of extensive marginal and total changes existed, in varying degrees, in all the societies studied here except China (and with the partial exceptions of the Ancient Egyptian Empire and England). As we have seen, in all these societies there were longer periods during which these conditions were not predominant or fully operative and during which, therefore, processes of accommodable change evolved. But the prerequisite conditions for the other types of change were prevalent in the social structure of these societies. Because of their prevalence, in each of these polities some processes evolved ultimately which led to its transformation.

The extent and tempo in which these general conditions occasioned processes of total change of the political institutions of a given historical bureaucratic society depended on inherent structural reasons, on accidental reasons, and on a combination of the two. One of the more inherent or internal structural reasons was the extent of compatibility between the relative levels of development and differentiation of the political institution and of the various strata and between the orientations of the rulers and those of the leading strata. (This has been analyzed, especially in its relation to the political process in these societies, in Chapters 7, 8, and 9.)

An important, mostly accidental or external reason, comprised the different amounts of external pressures (major movements and conquests of nomads or international economic fluctuations). Another was the degree to which ethnic heterogeneity had existed, from the beginning, in a given society. By definition, most of the accidental reasons developed outside the frontiers of the particular polity. But even these accidental reasons exerted their influence principally through internal factors, and precipitated the different processes of change through the accentuation of the internal contradictions analyzed above. While the tempo and intensity of these accidental pressures usually depended on outside forces, the internal conditions of any specific bureaucratic society could influence the "attraction" of such forces to its frontiers.

Of course, some "external" conditions, like the basic geographical or geopolitical factors, frequently constituted a fundamental part of the immediate environment of these societies and of their political self-consciousness. These provided important facets of the medium through which the external and internal exigencies were interrelated.

In general, some combination of external and internal pressures and exigencies precipitated the change of the political system of the historical bureaucratic society. Hence, the greater the intensity of the internal contradictions and of the pressure of external exigencies with which the internal forces of the society could not deal, the quicker and more intensive were the intensity and accumulation of processes of change in the society and the tempo of transformation of its political systems.

Because of the relatively small number of cases and the lack of clear indices (except, perhaps, of the temporal duration of a given system) of the speed of such change, it is difficult to examine fully this general hypothesis. However, a cursory examination of the facts presented in Chapter 9, which considered the comparative political processes, apparently lends tentative support to this hypothesis. For instance, in the Ancient Egytian Empire, where the intensity of external exigencies and internal contradictions was relatively small, the tempo of change was slow; it tended to become accentuated whenever either the external exigencies or the internal contradictions became intensified. In Byzantium, the processes of change became more intensive when the pressure of external exigencies emphasized the internal contradictions, while the latter in their turn weakened the possibility of dealing with the former ([L] *Ostrogorsky, 1956[a], 1956[b]; Vasiliev, 1952; Diehl* et al., *1945; Jenkins, 1953; Stein, 1924;* [Q] *Boak, 1955[a]* passim; *Jones, 1955*). Similarly, in the Spanish-American Empire, the combination of the international constellation and of internal pressures precipitated the war of independence ([R] *Haring, 1947, ch. xviii; Parry, 1957*). It was in periods of internal strife, as in the later periods of Sassanid Persia and of the Roman Empire, that the sensitivity to external exigencies tended to grow ([G] *Christensen, 1936, ch. x; Altheim and Stiehl, 1954*).

It is not easy to prove the quantitative aspects of our hypothesis. Nonetheless, the data clearly show that, in all the societies in which these conditions existed, such processes of change evolved; and that these processes of change were systematically connected with the development of the aforementioned condiitons.

As already indicated, there were—beyond the characteristics and conditions common to all the processes of change connected with the development of rebellions and with the transformation of the political systems of the bureaucratic societies—many variations in the conditions under which such *different* processes tended to evolve and mature. The exact ways in which the contradictions in the rulers' orientation and policies and the tensions between them and the major strata worked out varied, from case to case, according to the relative strength of the principal factors entering into the making of these contradictions. These factors were the following:

1. The strength of the pressures of the rulers, the intensities of the external exigencies with which the rulers had to deal and of their demands for resources, and their development of prescriptive control policies

2. The exact groups or institutional spheres that were depleted because of factor 1 and the level of their differentiation and development; and, conversely, the spheres or groups that were still able to maintain some amount of flexible orientation, organization, and social differentiation

3. The extent to which some kind of organized political leadership emerged within the different groups, strata, and institutional spheres,

and the nature of the social and political orientations of this leadership

4. The availability of different types of elites and leaders, and their fundamental political orientations

Differences in the constellations of these factors were among the most important determinants influencing the outcome of the process of change—i.e., determinants of which, of the different types of marginal and non-accommodable changes, would develop in a given situation.

[12] Analysis of Marginal Types of Change

First, let us consider some of the more marginal types of change—such as the different rebellions and usurpations of ultimate political power by military groups—and see what constellations give rise to them.

A.   MILITARY   USURPATION

The first type that we shall analyze is the usurpation of ultimate political power by a military group—as occurred in the Abbaside Caliphate and in the Roman Empire ([N] *Cahen, 1957[a], 1957[b]*; [M] *Brockelman, 1943; Lewis, 1937; Hodgson, 1955, 1960*; [Q] *Boak, 1955[a]* passim; *Jones, 1955; Charlesworth, 1936; Kraemer, 1953; Westerman, 1955; Alföldi, 1956*). Usurpation of this kind tended to develop when the combined pressures of the policies of the rulers, of the bureaucracy, and of the more conservative and aristocratic groups on the free strata became connected with growing external exigencies, with ethnical and/or religious estrangement between the rulers and the active strata of the population, and with great ethnical heterogeneity of the latter. Under such conditions, the more active strata became depleted of any effective political leadership. Dissociation between urban and rural centers generally increased. Political apathy, and sometimes many other-worldly orientations, emerged in many of the religious groups which developed among these strata. In connection with this depletion and apathy, there was a continuous flux of foreign elements into the centers of the realms. The foreign military groups had initially had the status of mere mercenaries, hirelings, and personal helpers of the rulers. But gradually, as the native strata were depleted and the external and internal exigencies grew, they succeeded in infiltrating some of the most important political posts (e.g., as eunuchs, military commandants, and viziers) and, finally, in totally usurping the ultimate political power.

As has been indicated, such usurpation can be considered as a border case between accommodable change and the transformation of the political system. At least superficially, most of these usurpers upheld some of the principal symbols of legitimation of the former political system. More often than not, they maintained and utilized the existing institutions and organizations. However, at the same time they usually effected far-reaching alterations in these institutions and organizations. The most important of these were: (1) the ousting of numerous groups from the political arena; (2) a general lowering of the level of political participation; and (3) the prevention, by means of many prescriptive and oppressive policies, of further societal differentiation and of the rise of new free strata (*see, for instance,* [N] *Cahen, 1957[a], 1957[b]*).

It is significant that there is no known case when a more flexible polity was re-established following such usurpation. Also, the system established by this kind of usurpation most closely resembles the ideal type of Oriental despotic regime.

B. REBELLIONS

Cases of military usurpation were very often connected both with the transformation of the historical bureaucratic polities and with rebellions and outbursts of different kinds that preceded them and paved their way. Let us, therefore, now analyze some of the conditions associated with the development of such rebellions.

Rebellions of various kinds erupted in all the societies studied here. Sometimes they were simple uprisings of discontented peasants or urban proletariats. Sometimes they were characterized by strong religious orientations and organizations—whether in the guise of sectarian groups or secret (cult) societies. In some cases—in Persia, for example ([G] *Ghirshman, 1954; Christensen, 1925, 1936; Klima, 1957, especially ch. viii*), and, especially, among the Byzantine "Zealots" of the fourteenth century—diverse religious-social utopian elements and orientations were included ([L] *Charanis, 1940–41[b], 1953[a]; Barker, 1957; Ostrogorsky, 1956[a]; Vasiliev, 1952*). Most of them usually developed under specific constellations of the more general conditions of change analyzed above.

The most important conditions responsible for their development were the following:

1. Strong pressures on different strata of the population (especially on the lower groups, which are socially less differentiated and politically less articulate), and the depletion of their economic basis and organized, traditional leadership

2. Dissociation of these strata from those elites and functional groups which hitherto connected them with the central political institutions

3. Growing dissociation of the "lower" strata from the more active (usually urban) "middle" strata, and petrification of channels of mobility connecting the two

4. The rise, because of these dissociations, of autochthonous, "primitive," "nativistic" leaders—who stressed religious-social, semi-utopian symbols, and organized secretarian units, but at the same time were able neither to create permanent and articulated political organizations and programs nor to initiate regulative and integrative activities based on any wider political, economic, or cultural orientations

These rebellions may thus be described as manifestations of the dislocation and alienation of various relatively low-status and undifferentiated groups which, because of the low level of generalized power at their disposal, were unable to create new and permanent types of political organization. Simultaneously, they became disconnected from any central sphere, whose representatives were incapable of channelizing their power potential.

The extent to which rebellions affected the existing system was contingent upon the duration of their causes. Thus, when the contributing factors were transient—even if repeated in long-term periods— the outbursts could die out without leaving any noticeable mark on the institutional structure of the society. When, however, a rebellions' causes were endemic and long-lasting—and particularly when the depletion of the less differentiated strata of any active social or political leadership was continuous—it could gradually prepare the way for the total undermining of the basic premies of the historical bureaucratic polity, for its dismemberment or transformation.

Such rebellions or outbursts could lead to the gradual dissipation of the forces of a regime and to its dismemberment, or they could become re-integrated into wider and more articulated political processes— whether those connected with "accommodable" or total change. Which of these paths a rebellion actually took depended greatly on the availability of different types of leaders and elites and of the regulative frameworks they maintained.

[13] *General Conditions of the Transformation of the Political System of the Historical Bureaucratic Societies into Pre-bureaucratic Polities*

This brings us to the analysis of the principal types of transformation of the political systems of the historical bureaucratic societies. As we have indicated, changes of the political system could develop in two directions. One led to systems based on a much lower, limited level of generalized power and to regression to pre-bureaucratic types of political systems. The other led to the development of more differentiated bureaucratic (i.e., what is usually called "modern") political systems.

Let us begin by analyzing the specific characteristics of the political process that was related to the transformation of historical bureaucratic polities that resulted in the development of some type of pre-bureaucratic polity. This kind of transformation evolved under the following conditions:

1. Relatively limited social differentiation (especially in relation to the needs of the rulers) in at least some of the major institutional spheres, and a consequent continuous depletion of the few available free resources

2. The prevalence of relatively strong traditional and *power-oriented* elements in the system of legitimation of the rulers, and their resulting inability to tolerate a high level of flexible groups and political orientations in the society

3. The existence of several elite groups (especially religious and administrative-political elites) and of older aristocratic elements, with some levels of organizational capability and with *potentially* traditional and/or apolitical orientations

In different societies, of course, there were great variations in the respective extents to which each of these characteristics or conditions developed. These differences necessarily influenced the nature of the pre-bureaucratic political system that emerged. Before discussing that, however, we shall consider the common features of the changes that led toward the development of *all* types of pre-bureaucratic political polity.

A. THE CASE OF THE BYZANTINE EMPIRE

Before we proceed to do so, however, it will be worthwhile to illustrate these processes by describing some cases. The processes which caused the downfall of the Byzantine Empire may serve this purpose (*following* [L] *Ostrogorsky, 1956[a[, and Charanis, 1940–41[b], 1953[a]*).

In the course of the ninth and tenth centuries, the free village community was seriously endangered by the tremendous expansion of the large estates—lay, ecclesiastical, and monastic. This development was clearly perceived as a threat to the interests of the state by the enlightened emperors of the tenth century. Romanus Lecapenus (d. A.D. 948) declared in one of his *Novels*:

> It is not through hatred and envy of the rich that we take these measures, but for the protection of the small and the safety of the small and the safety of the

Empire as a whole. . . . The extension of the power of the strong . . . will bring about the irreparable loss of the public good, if the present law does not bring a check to it. For it is the many, settled on the land, who provide for the general needs, who pay the taxes and furnish the *army with its recruits*. Everything falls when the many are wanting.

But the series of strong measures which Romanus I and his immediate successors took in order to check this development finally ended in failure. After the death of Basil II in 1025, there was no longer any question of protecting the small independent peasant against the encroachments of the powerful. Free villages still existed in the thirteenth century, but they probably were not very numerous.

The tremendous expansion of the large estates during the ninth and tenth centuries, which led gradually to the absorption of most of the holdings of the small peasant proprietors, had similar effects on the military estates. The emperors of the tenth century who tried to save the small peasant proprietors sought also to protect the soldiers, but their measures proved as ineffective in the latter case as they did in the former. The decline of the free soldiers was finally consummated in the eleventh century, as a result of the struggle between the military aristocracy and the civil bureaucracy. It was in connection with this that the semi-feudal system of *pronoia* developed.

In the thirteenth century, the vast majority of the rural population of the Empire were dependent peasants known as *paroikoi*. It is significant for our analysis that, in these later centuries, the number of land-bound *paroikoi* also greatly increased on the state lands—a manifestation of the state's lessening interest in the free peasant.

Thus, the society of small farmers and of artisans, organized and regulated for the interest of all, was undermined by the social struggle of the tenth century and by the political and military disasters of the military aristocracy in the eleventh. Indeed, this social struggle was a principal reason for the Empire's fall from its pre-eminent position. Concomitant with these rural developments, several trends in urban life and economy also combined to undermine the stability of the social structure of the Empire.

At the end of the eleventh century, Byzantine trade began to undergo drastic changes from which it never recovered. The Seljuk conquest of Asia Minor (A.D. 1071) altered the whole of Byzantine economy by robbing Constantinople both of the source of its corn supply and of numbers of the solid peasant population—one of the chief foundations of its strength. Moreover, the constant war in Asia Minor upset its land and even its coastal trade. At the same time, the presence of the Normans in southern Italy meant piratical raids on the prosperous Greek peninsula and was a very real danger to all the European provinces of the Empire. Meanwhile, the Italian merchant cities were steadily increasing their fleets and encroaching more and more on eastern markets.

Finally, the effect of the Crusades on the trade of Byzantium was immense—even if not immediate. At first, Constantinople was on the Crusaders' main route, and their coming and going, though trying for the Byzantine police, brought new buyers to the city's markets. But the ultimate result of the movement was to reopen the ports of Syria, that had been closed to European traders for five centuries. This provided a new route so that Oriental goods could reach Western Europe without passing through Imperial territory.

These developments in the trade relations of the Byzantine Empire were connected and intensified by the various measures of economic—especially monetary—policy undertaken by the Byzantine rulers. In its general outline, the history of Byzantine currency in the period after the Seljuk victory at Manzikert (1071) closely resembles the history of Spanish currency after the introduction of bullion: a strong inflationary trend, periodically interrupted by ultimately futile attempts at deflation through a "reform of the coinage." The results were ample room for the free play of Gresham's Law, confusion in monetary standards, and a disastrous impact on the general economy (*adapted from* [A] *Hoselitz, 1956*).

This over-all unfavorable effect of price instability acted on agriculture, industry, and commerce. It gave rise to numerous and sharp fluctuations in prices, upset calculations, stifled initiative, impeded the vigorous conduct of business enterprise, and wrought havoc on the economic life of the country—particularly on agriculture, whose terms of trade in relation to industry deteriorated.

These destructive results of the monetary trends in the later Byzantine Empire were rooted in the basic economic policies and orientations of its rulers—and especially in that policy by which they attempted, for political reasons, to keep the *bezant* stable throughout the Empire's history. Thus it seems that the seeds of Byzantium's economic decline were being cultivated, in the consideration which governed economic policy, in the period of the Empire's greatest glory (*following* [L] *Lopez, 1951[a], 1951[b], and* [A] *Hoselitz, 1956*).

The stability of the *bezant* may have been a symptom, if not a cause, of Byzantine economic stagnation. Although there were no serious obstacles in the Byzantine Empire to the growth of commerce and industry, there were no notable increases in production and consumption. Only the silk industry showed any tendency to develop along capitalistic lines—and silk was definitely a luxury.

The high prices that prevailed in the Byzantine Empire affected foreign trade unfavorably. Byzantine mints could replenish their stock only through foreign gold obtained by trade. The government attempted to prevent the export of gold and to retain as much foreign gold as possible.

The gold income barely offset the drains of tributes and bribes that the Byzantine diplomacy used profusely, and of the payments deriving from the Empire's excess of imports over exports. This fact helps to explain the Byzantine merchants' reluctance to risk making large investments and to meet foreign traders in foreign markets. Their defensive attitude impeded the expansion of the foreign trade—the one thing which, alone, could have attracted larger currents of gold. This vicious circle could have been broken by monetary inflation or by an expansion of credit, either of which could have stimulated the home production of cheap exportable goods; "but the bezant remained stable and credit did not grow" ([L] *Lopez, 1951[a]*).

Thus, as Europe recovered and expanded, the Byzantine Empire was forced to depreciate its coinage. The inferior *bezants* did not stimulate a decadent economy. "Credit had not developed in times of relative prosperity and it could hardly expand in an age of general distress" ([L] *Lopez, 1951[a]*).

The strong political control of economic activities caused Byzantium to export capital in the forms of "gifts" to foreign princes and payments to foreign soldiers; another form was the flight of private capital. Controls of this kind, so far as they were effective, tended to create stability rather than either progress or decadence.

In this context, taxation and the loss of capital are interrelated. Industry was stagnating or declining, and trade was almost exclusively in the hands of foreigners. So, funds, collected through taxation and exported—as tribute, and as bribes or as payments for foreign mercenaries or for armies in foreign countries—constituted that much loss of actual or potential capital to the agrarian Empire.

The decline of domestic over foreign trade was also associated with a general progressive atrophy of internal commercial relations. The old markets and fairs lost their importance and, in many instances, were completely abolished. The growing landed estates became more self-sufficient and curtailed both their purchases from the cities and their deliveries to them. There was a large-scale return to "natural economy"—i.e., a system in which the ordinary market mechanism operated only with great difficulty and frequent breakdowns. In this system, the total amount of transactions which continued to take place, as well as unilateral payments of taxes or services, were made in kind rather than in money. Of course, this does not imply that money ceased to function as a general means of exchange—we have seen how important price developments were as factors in the economic stagnation of agrarian states. One important reaction against monetary instability, stagnating production, and the atrophy of commercial channels was a relative increase in barter and natural economy (as opposed to money economy).

All these developments were coupled with growing external pressures. The combination led, from the thirteenth century onward, to a gradual shrinking of the Byzantine Empire, to the growing predominance of the aristocracy, and to the depletion of the peasantry and the lower urban groups. The many uprisings and rebellions—particularly those of the Zealots—that occurred in various urban and rural centers in the fourteenth century testified to the growing disaffection of the masses and to their alienation from the political system of the Empire.

B. THE DECLINE OF THE OTTOMAN EMPIRE

Similar trends—though different in details and constellation—also emerged in other empires: in the Roman Empire, in the Sassanid Empire, and in many of the Caliphate states, during their periods of decline ([Q] *Jones, 1955; Boak, 1955[b]; [G] Christensen, 1936; Altheim, 1955; [N] Cahen, 1957[a], 1957[b]*). B. Lewis, in his analysis of the decline of the Ottoman Empire, stresses some similar broad trends ([O] *Lewis, 1958* passim). It is worth while to present his analysis of the Ottoman Empire here. This analysis shows the trend that conduced to the decline of an empire that, while it disintegrated through secessions and rebellions, later became transformed—at its core—into a more differentiated, modern system.

Precisely in the late sixteenth century monetary and financial crisis developed, the government was compelled to embark on a great expansion in its salaried personnel and a great increase in expenditure in coin. When Mehemmed the Conqueror had faced a monetary crisis, he had reduced the numbers of paid soldiers and increased the numbers of cavalry *sipahis,* whose services were rewarded with fiefs and not coin. But in the changed conditions of warfare of the sixteenth and seventeenth centuries, this had ceased to be possible. The greatly increased use of firearms and artillery necessitated the maintenance of larger and larger paid professional armies, and reduced the relative importance of the "feudal" cavalryman.

The price was appalling. Faced with a growing expenditure and a depreciating currency, the demands of the treasury became more and more insatiable. The underpaid and oversized salaried personnel of the State—civil, military, and religious—had greater and greater difficulties in making ends meet, with the inevitable effects on their honesty, their prestige, and their further recruitment. Though the feudal cavalryman was no longer needed by the army, his disappearance was sorely felt in the countryside, as the old Ottoman agrarian system, of which he had once been the keystone, tottered and collapsed. In place of the *sipahi,* who resided in or near the fief in which he had a hereditary interest, palace favourites, parasites, and speculators became the recipients of fiefs, sometimes accumulating great numbers of them, and thus becoming, in effect, absentee owners of great latifundia. Other fiefs reverted to the Imperial domain. But the growing inefficiency and venality of the bureaucracy prevented the formation of any effective state system for the assessment and collection of taxes. Instead these tasks were given to tax-farmers, whose interposition and interception of revenues became in time a prescriptive and hereditary right, and added to the number of vast and neglected latifundia.

The shrinking economy of the Empire thus had to support an increasingly costly and cumbersome superstructure. The palace, the bureaucracy and the religious hierarchy, an army that in expenditure at least was modern, and a parasitic class of tax-farmers and absentee landlords—all this was far more than the mediaeval states or even the Roman Empire had tried to support; yet it rested on an economy that was no more advanced than theirs. The technological level of agriculture remained primitive, and the social conditions of the Turkish countryside after the sixteenth century precluded the appearance of anything like the English gentleman-farmers of the seventeenth century whose experiments revolutionized English agriculture.

These developments are not peculiar to Turkey. The fall in money and rise of prices, the growing cost of government and warfare, the sale of offices and farming of taxes—all these are known in other Mediterranean and adjoining states, where they contributed to the rise of a new class of capitalists and financiers, with a growing and constructive influence on governments.

In Turkey too there were rich merchants and bankers, such as the Greek Michael Cantacuzenos and the Portuguese Jew Joseph Nasi—the Fugger of the Orient, as Braudel called him. But they were never able to play anything like the financial, economic, and political role of their European counterparts. Part of the cause of this must undoubtedly be found in the progressive stagnation of Ottoman trade, to which allusion has already been made. But that is not all. Most if not all of these merchants were Christians or Jews—tolerated but second-class subjects of the Muslim State. However great their economic power, they were politically penalized and socially segregated; they could obtain political power only by stealth, and exercise it only by intrigues with demoralizing effect on all concerned. Despite the scale and extent of their financial operations, they were unable to create political conditions more favourable to commerce, or to build up any solid structure of banking and credit, and thus help the Ottoman government in its perennial financial straits.

With the steady decline in bureaucratic efficiency during the seventeenth and eighteenth centuries, the former system of regular land surveys and population censuses was abandoned. The central government ceased to exercise any check or control over agriculture and village affairs, which were left to the unchecked rapacity of the tax-farmers, the lease-holders, and the bailiffs of court nominees. During the seventeenth century some of the more permanently established lease-holders began to coalesce with the landowners into a new landed aristocracy— the *a'yan-i memleket,* or country notables, whose appearance and usurpation of some of the functions and authority of government were already noted in the seventeenth century. While agriculture declined, industry fared little better.

In the military Empire, at once feudal and bureaucratic, which they had created, the Muslims knew only four professions—government, war, religion, and agriculture. Industry and trade were left to the non-Muslim conquered subjects, who continued to practice their inherited crafts. Thus the stigma of the infidel became attached to the professions which the infidels followed, and remained so attached even after many of the craftsmen had become Muslim. Westerners and native Christians, bankers, merchants, and craftsmen, were all involved in the general contempt which made the Ottoman Muslim impervious to ideas or inventions of Christian origin and unwilling to bend his own thoughts to the problems of artisans and vile mechanics. Primitive techniques of production, primitive means of transportation, chronic insecurity, and social penalization, combined to preclude any long-term or large-scale undertakings, and to keep the Ottoman economy at the lowest level of competence, initiative, and morality ([O] *Lewis, 1950*, passim).

[14] *Political Processes Connected with the Transformation of the Political Systems of Historical Bureaucratic Societies into Pre-bureaucratic Polities*

On the basis of the preceding analysis we may now approach the general analysis of the processes connected with the transformation of the political system of the historical bureaucratic empires into some type of pre-bureaucratic system.

By definition, this transformation was characterized by a shrinking supply of the free economic and manpower resources available. This was manifested by the depletion of mobile manpower; by the decreasing importance of exchange and of monetary means; by the growing political apathy of many groups; and by the lack of adequate personnel to perform the major bureaucratic and administrative tasks. This diminution of free resources was usually initiated by the excessive demands of the rulers and by the conflicts between the more flexible and the aristocratic groups, and created a vicious circle in the political and social processes of these societies. As a result of this initial depletion or alienation of free resources, the rulers employed various expedients. These included oppressive taxation, farming out of taxes, and making "bargains" with local governors. The recourse to these ultimately minimized the rulers' control over administrative personnel and obstructed their direct approach to strategic sources of free resources. In addition, it increased the burden of these *rentier* groups on the economy. Consequently, divers new, less differentiated (more patrimonial or feudal) types of economic organization developed, and these succeeded in attracting or subordinating many of the strata and groups ([L] *Ostrogorsky, 1929[a], 1956[a]* passim; *Jenkins, 1953; Charanis, 1953[a]; Zakythinos, 1947–48;* [G] *Christensen, 1936, ch. viii, ix; Ghirshman, 1954; Altheim and Stiehl, 1954, 1957; Altheim, 1955[a], 1955[b];* [F] *Drioton and Vandier, 1952; Kees, 1933[a], 1933[b]*).

Developments like these were usually accompanied by general dislocation of different strata from the central political institutions and from professional and functional groups and religious organizations. This dislocation was evinced by the diminishing scope of their activities and by the weakening both of universalistic and/or "activistic" political orientations or of more differentiated economic activities. A similar dislocation arose between some of the more differentiated functional groups and elites. The major ecological groups and strata became dissociated from one another, and the aristocratic elements became prominent. The latter continued to disrupt the frameworks of the central political institutions and those integrative and regulative institutions which upheld relatively flexible norms. In addition, in most societies undergoing this type of change, the cultural-religious organizations tended to develop a strong apolitical bent in their activities, symbols, and value orientations.

As a rule, these developments incurred certain results. These were a general regression in the levels of political organization and in the articulation of political aims and issues of different strata; a growing passivity on the part of many of these strata; an increasing oppression of the lower groups; and the gradual emergence of new, traditional, or "restrictive" types of leadership. Such leadership was usually strongly affiliated with the new types of aristocratic-economic leaders, who were able to draw and attract the relatively passive groups and strata and organize them within new ecological and political frameworks ([L] *Ostrogorsky, 1952, 1954, 1956[a], 1956[b]; Charanis, 1940–41[b], 1953[a]; Barker, 1957; Hussey, 1957; Vasiliev, 1952, especially p. 563 ff.; Stein, 1924; Kantorowicz, 1956; [G] Ghirshman, 1954; Christensen, 1936*). This was always connected with certain patterns of mobility— usually with the draining off of the active elements within most strata.

The political apathy was closely connected with the disruption of the communication between the bearers of the "Great" and "Little" traditions—with growing dissociation between the symbols of political authority and the primordial human and collective symbols borne by the "Little Traditions." Consequently, either new traditions and symbols evolved, or the older traditions became transformed through re-emphasis of their traditional-particularistic or other-worldly apolitical elements.

One of the most important manifestations of this widespread dislocation consisted of the persistence and perservation of many groups and organizations, despite and throughout the changes of the polity. This manifestation was best illustrated by the persistence of different religious organizations and institutions after the disintegration of the centralized monarchies; by the continuous evolution of new sects, with strong other-worldly orientations, and of religious organizations, from within these major organizations; and by the perseverance and continuity of many urban centers and associations. These groups and organizations often were the cultural and political centers for the newly emerged non-flexible economic groups and organizations.

Developments within the bureaucracy always played an important part in these processes. In most of these situations, the bureaucracy tended to evolve into a semi-aristocratic, traditionally oriented group. It monopolized many potential centers of free, flexible resources; developed several prescriptive policies, directed primarily toward increasing its own benefits; became a progressively heavier burden on the economy; and threw off, to a large degree, any central political control. In these ways, the bureaucracy usually contributed to the further dwindling of the free resources in these societies ([L] *Ostrogorsky, 1954, 1956[a], 1956[b]; Vasiliev, 1952; Diehl,* et al., *1945; Bréhier, 1945, 1947; Lemerle, 1958; Kantorowicz, 1956;* [N] *Lewis, 1953;* [G] *Christensen, 1936,* especially ch. *vii, x; Altheim, 1955[a], 1955[b]; Ghirshman, 1954;* [F] *Drioton and Vandier, 1952*).

[15] *Major Types of Pre-bureaucratic Polities into Which Historical Bureaucratic Societies Were Transformed*

The processes described above, in some cases—e.g., in some of the Central Asian states—led to the simple disintegration of the polity and its subjection to foreign invasion, or to its power's being usurped by a foreign military group. In other cases, these processes contributed or resulted in the evolution of a more crystallized kind of pre-bureaucratic political system. As we indicated above, the exact type of pre-bureaucratic polity which evolved differed greatly from case to case. The major forms of political systems which evolved in our cases were: (1) smaller, patrimonial units, as in "middle periods" in Egypt ([F] *Drioton and Vandier, 1952; Stock, 1949; Spiegel, 1950; Remondon, 1955; Kees, 1934; Farina, 1921; Edgerton, 1951*) or Persia; (2) semi-feudal aristocratic states, as in Byzantium ([L] *Ostrogorsky, 1956[a]; Vasiliev, 1952; Diehl* et al., *1945,* and, to a smaller extent, Sassanid Persia ([G] *Altheim and Stiehl, 1954* passim; *Christensen, 1936; Ghrishman, 1954*); or (3) a kind of feudal system, as, particularly, in Europe ([D] *Bloch, 1939–40; Hintze, 1929*).

All such changes were related to the depletion of the free, flexible resources requisite for the continuous functioning of the bureaucratic polity. However, in different cases there were many variations with respect to the extent to which the resources were depleted, the institutional sphere in which this depletion was most marked, and which elites and functional groups remained oriented to universalistic values. These differences had immense influence on the nature of the type of pre-bureaucratic polity which developed from those processes of change in each case. Although a full analysis of the relation between the former and the latter is beyond the scope of our work, some tentative and preliminary hypotheses can be offered here.

Regression to decentralization and patrimonial types of systems, as in Persia or the Ancient Egyptian Empire, occurred when the pressure of expansionist political goals and exigencies was so great that it almost completely exhausted the supply of free-floating economic resources. The pressure also deflected any active political support from the centralized polity, while leaving almost intact some of the more traditionally oriented elites and groups. This happened most frequently in societies both with an initially low level of economic development and with strong traditionalistic and ascriptive elements in the rulers' system of legitimation and in the initial composition of the major elites. In these societies, the draining of free resources usually occasioned marked changes in the political system but not in the cultural sphere. In the latter, some continuity persisted—largely because of the initial traditional orientation that prevailed ([G] *Christensen, 1936; Altheim, 1955; Altheim and Stiehl, 1954; Ghrishman, 1954;* [F] *Drioton and Vandier, 1952; Stock, 1949; Kees, 1933[b]*).

The gradual aristocratization and disintegration of the bureaucratic polity that occurred, e.g., in Byzantium, were also related to the excessive costs of implementing expansionist policies. However, they took place in a more differentiated internal system and a highly sensitive and insecure international situation. The relatively higher level of economic, social and cultural differentiation, as well as the continouously precarious international situation, resulted in costly and extravagant policies which tended to exhaust existing resources. However, since the society was much more differentiated, independent patrimonial units could not be established by means of simple territorial divisions. Thus the centralized framework was preserved—but at the cost of aristocratization from within and conquest from without. The internal aristocratization resulted in concentrating economic productivity in semi-feudal units, shrinking internal trade activities, and incessantly withdrawing free resources from the central political institutions. These weakened the state until it was no longer able to withstand foreign invasion, and facilitated alliances between powers, war lords, and the invaders ([L] *Ostrogorsky, 1952, 1954, 1956[a], 1956[b]; Vasiliev, 1952; Diehl* et al., *1945; Zakythinos, 1947–48, 1948*).

Feudalization—i.e., the process which terminated in the development of some type of feudal structures—was related to a depletion of economic resources. This took place in a setting of constant political exigencies, coupled with the perseverance of wider, often universalistic religious orientations and political ideals (e.g., ideals of universal empires). These, in turn, were conducive to the persistence of evolution of several binding forces (e.g., the rise of a common nobility and chivalry stratum, codes of chivalry) and of universal churches. They persisted in these systems beyond the confines of narrow local units and created a more complex—even if, in a way, unbalanced—social political structure than in other types of pre-bureaucratic politics ([D] *Bloch, 1939–40; Hintze, 1929; Coulborn, 1956; Ganshof, 1947; Boutruche, 1959*).

[16] *The Transformation of the Political Systems of Historical Bureaucratic Systems into More Differentiated Political Systems*

The second principal kind of structural change in the historical bureaucratic empires was the type which gave rise to more differentiated kinds of bureaucratic polity. It may be discerned chiefly in European countries—especially in France, England, and the Spanish-American Empire; and, to a smaller extent, in Islam during the transition from the Omayyad (to A.D. 1031) to the Abbaside Caliphate.

The occurrence of this kind of change was correlated with certain factors very similar to those discussed above. These were the internal contradictions in the orientations and policies of the rulers; the rulers' growing need for resources; the reactions different social groups had to the consequent pressures exerted on them; and the rulers' attempts to counteract and control any advanced emergence of "free" groups by different kinds of prescriptive policies and emphasis on self-maintenance goals. Thus, in many respects the developments which led to the transformation of these polities were similar to those which occasioned the development of some types of pre-bureaucratic political systems.

For example, in eighteenth-century France, the monarchy became discernibly weaker. At the same time, the aristocracy (both the *noblesse d'épée* and *noblesse de robe*) became more powerful; the economic difficulties of the peasants increased; and the avenues of mobility from the growing middle to the upper groups were frozen. ([Y] *See Sagnac, 1945, 1946; Pagès, 1928; Barber, 1955; Ford, 1953;* [S] *Beloff, 1954. For Spain, see also* [U] *Hamilton, 1954; Sarailh, 1951; Trevor-Davis, 1957; Suárez, 1950.*) In the Spanish-American Empire during the late eighteenth century, there was also a similar weakening of the machinery of government; a general economic decline, leading to depopulation (especially among the Indians); strengthening of the landed aristocracy; and growing alienation between the Creole upper groups and the Spanish officials, and between at least some of the rising middle classes and the aristocracy ([R] *Haring, 1947, ch. vii; Parry, 1957; Thomas, 1956; Whitaker, 1942, 1955; Moses, 1919, 1926; Vida Viceus, 1957; Christelow, 1942, 1947*).

However, in these societies, these factors were accompanied by others not found in the societies whose transformation went in the pre-bureaucratic direction. The factors which, when coupled with these treated above, were responsible for changes culminating in the establishment of a more differentiated bureaucratic polity were the following:

1. A considerable extent of economic and social differentiation, and a high level of technological development and economic productivity —such as prevailed particularly in the Absolutist European societies, to a lesser degree in the early nineteenth-century Spanish-American Empire, and even less in the first period of the Abbaside Dynasty.

2. Strong emphasis on the economic strength and development of the state as constituting a distinct goal of the polity and the society, as manifest chiefly in the various mercantilist theories and policies. True, the economic development of the society generally was viewed primarily as a means to the ultimate political aggrandizement and strengthening of the state. However, the latter goal was not conceived in terms of mere accumulation of state resources, but in terms of a general increase in the over-all productivity and enrichment of the state ([S] *Viner, 1948; Wilson, 1958; Heckscher, 1932; Heaton, 1937; Morazé, 1948*).

3. The prevalence, among the most active groups of the society, of a distinct type of value orientation. This was characterized by strong universalistic elements and an active political-social ideology—e.g., the new universalistic religion of Islam in the Arab Caliphates, or the ideologies of the Age of Absolutism in Europe (especially those related to the epoch of so-called "enlightened" absolutism ([S] *Hartung, 1937, 1957; Hartung and Mousnier, 1955; Beloff, 1954; Lefebvre, 1949; Wittram, 1948;* [T] *Müller, 1937; Peterka, 1937;* [Y] *Oliver-Martin, 1933;* [U] *Alcázar, 1933*).

4. The development of various highly differentiated groups, with universalistic orientations, which gradually began to consider themselves as the major bearers of these values and as the main group referents of political activity. Many of these groups displayed a relatively high degree of articulation of political goals and organization. This was evinced in their more articulated types of political issues, organizations, and struggles; and in their distinction between religious and ideological systems and their emphasis on dynamic secular ideologies

that would make clear and politically articulate demands on the political sphere ([Y] *Cobban, 1957[a], 1957[b]*; [S] *Beloff, 1954*; [Z] *Brock, 1957*).

The evolution of groups like the last constituted a principal difference between the processes of change which led to pre-bureaucratic types of polity and those which culminated in the establishment of more differentiated bureaucratic systems. In the former case, the main functional elites and groups lost many of their flexible orientations and frameworks. Consequently, they not only failed to restrict the dislocation of different ecological groups and strata from the more flexible political institutions of the bureaucratic polities—they actually furthered both this dislocation and the growing dissociation between different more traditional and more differentiated strata. In the second case, many active, functional, and elite groups emerged that were potentially able to provide new, more flexible, and universalistic regulative principles. They supplied new frameworks, into which the various dislocated groups and strata could be re-absorbed and regulated according to wider, universalistic principles. Moreover, the development of economically active groups of merchants, financiers, etc.—which were also politically active, and which were, through connection with different elites, also relatively integrated in the central political life of the community—could assume crucial importance from the point of view of dealing with some of the effects of the economic fluctuations connected with the policies of the rulers. They could minimize the flow of capital abroad, deflect many of the social and economic groups from becoming politically passive, and absorb many of their more active elements.

As a result of the developments we have been discussing, the existing political frameworks and policies of the rulers no longer sufficed to regulate the interrelations between the new groups and elites or to accommodate their political orientations and goals. At the same time, the political orientations of the more active groups were both inadequate and too intensive for the existing institutional framework, which they therefore tended to undermine.

The social and political trends in the bureaucracy always played an important part in the emergence of these conditions. In most of these societies, the bureaucracy evolved into some kind of aristocratized or semi-aristocratized group. It was then able to monopolize the highest social, political, and economic positions, and to minimize its political responsibility and responsiveness to the rulers and/or to the principal flexible strata.

Sometimes, as in the case of the French, *noblesse de robe*, it became almost fully aristocratized and strongly opposed to the more absolutist tendencies of the king ([Y] *Ford, 1953; Pagès, 1928, 1932[b]; Barber, 1955;* [R] *Haring, 1947, ch. vii; Vida Viceus, 1957; Griffin, 1949*). In other cases—e.g., in Prussia, Austria, and (to a lesser degree) Russia—the bureaucracy maintained more basic identification with the rulers and was, in a way, accommodated to the basic framework of the polity. However, it strove to freeze and restrict the extent of social differentiation. The bureaucracy thus contributed to the blocking of channels of mobility of the middle and lower strata and to the minimizing of their participation. In each of the polities where the bureaucracy followed this pattern, it contributed either to the dwindling of free resources and strata, or to the growing alienation of free strata from the existing political institutions.

It is significant that, among the societies studied here, only in England—and, to a lesser degree, in Holland and the Scandinavian countries—did the bureaucracy not evolve along these lines This resulted chiefly from the small scope of the bureaucracy's activities. In turn, this smaller scope was due both to the high extent of self-regulation and political articulation of the principal strata in these countries, and to their great influence on the goals of the polity. The fact that their bureaucracies did not undergo processes of aristocratization and alienation explained many aspects of the type of "gradual" political change to which these countries were subject ([S] *Beloff, 1954, ch. ix;* [Z] *Brock, 1957*).

[17] *Major Types of Transformations of the Political Systems of Historical Bureaucratic Empires into More Differentiated Political Systems*

The impetus to changes that occasioned more differentiated bureaucratic systems could develop from divers groups and institutional spheres in the society and it did develop in societies where different levels of general differentiation existed. It is beyond the scope of this chapter to analyze all the possible variations; we shall present only a very brief and preliminary consideration of some of them.

Let us begin by examining the changes wrought, in a society with relatively low levels of political organization and social and economic differentiations, by the emergence of universalistic creeds and sects. This occurred, e.g., during the transition from the Omayyad to the Abbaside Caliphate and under the Abbasides ([N] *Dennett, 1939, 1950; Lewis, 1950; Cahen, 1954, 1957[a], 1957[b];* [M] *Brockelmann, 1943;* [N] *Samadi, 1955[a]*).

Such conditions usually generated processes leading to the establishment of flexible, religiously oriented polities. These tended, during relatively short periods, to maintain a high level of social and political activity. The short duration of this high level of political activity was caused by: (1) the ultimately low level of economic development and social differentiation; (2) the different levels of flexibility and free resources in the cultural and the economic spheres; (3) the continuous implementation of the rulers' excessive political and military policies; and (4) the growing political and ethnical heterogeneity of the most active groups. This last factor was due to the spread of universal religions and to the rulers' dependence on these new groups rather than on the more traditional groups in their own society. These developments gave rise to a large extent of dissociation of religious activities from political and economic organizations. The concomitant increasing pressures of the rulers' policies then gave rise to growing alienation between the rulers and the various socially and religiously active strata ([N] *Cahen, 1957[a], 1957[b], 1958–59;* [M] *Hodgson, 1960;* [N] *Lewis, 1950, 1953*). In such cases, after flexible frameworks had emerged and expanded, the periods of such development were usually followed by growing miiltary rule and usurpation, the polity's decline and dismemberment, or the establishment of transient sectarian orders and states.

The dismemberment of the Spanish-American Empire provides a good example of the effects of limited economic development, a relatively strong intellectual universalistic orientation, and the activity of a few active strata, in a society characterized by a higher level of differentiation. There, the intellectual-political ferment of relatively small elite groups, closely associated with certain economically active groups operating within a generally underdeveloped economy, led both to the severance of ties with the metropolis and to the establishment of new political regimes. However, each of these new regimes exhibited, with respect to the level of institutionalized, generalized power, a marked continuity with the antecedent regime. They were characterized by: (1) the development of formal constitutions; (2) the relative concentration of effective power in the hands of small groups; (3) the political passivity of the masses; and (4) continual instability caused by conflicts among the ruling groups and by the exclusion of wider groups from political participation, and by the widespread political apathy ([R] *Haring, 1947, ch. vii; Moses, 1908, 1919, 1926; Parry, 1957; Thomas, 1956; Vida Viceus, 1957;* [U] *Suárez, 1950*).

Among the societies studied here, a relatively stable, non-traditional type of differentiated bureaucratic polity developed only in Europe —particularly in France and England. This was due to the fact that, in Europe, the impetus toward more differentiated orientations emerged simultaneously from different institutional spheres. This was manifested as follows:

1. Intense economic development, productivity, and rationalization among the peasant as well as the urban strata ([A] *Brunner, 1956, especially ch. iii, iv, v; Nef, 1958, especially ch. ii;* [S] *Wilson, 1958; Beloff, 1954; Hartung, 1957; Lindsay, 1957[a];* [T] *Müller, 1937; Peterka, 1937;* [Y] *Olivier-Martin, 1933; Cobban, 1957[a], 1957[b];* [U] *Alcázar, 1933;* [Z] *Brock, 1957*)

2. Evolution of both the rural and the urban centers of differentiated economic power into centers of relatively autonomous political power

3. The emergence of high levels of political organization and activity represented by secular, differentiated leadership and elites that conducted cultural and economic activities and were politically oriented ([S] *Labrousse, 1955;* [Y] *Cobban, 1957[b]; Sagnac, 1946;* [Z] *Plumb, 1950; Mathew, 1948*)

4. Close interrelation between the functional elites and the leading strata, and their association in common cultural and political activities

5. Strong universalistic elements in the legitimation, goals, and policies of the rulers, combined with relative flexibility of the political systems

The great extent of societal and economic differentiation, coupled with the universalistic orientations and ideologies, conflicted strongly with the policies of the rulers. The latter did not want to encourage the evolution of free strata and elites beyond certain limits. The resultant conflict undermined the basic premises of the historical bureaucratic societies and led to far-reaching changes. These factors laid the foundations for the emergence of more differentiated, "modern" political systems. The ultimate transformation or breakdown of the old system was usually effected by a marginal type of change— a rebellion or outburst, like the Civil War in England, or the French Revolution. The basic political and institutional frameworks, and the chief symbols of the polity, were preserved through such a change only in England. There, the flexibility of the political institutions; the strong alliance between the rulers and the growing, very active middle groups; the flexible structure of the aristocracy; the relative weakness of the bureaucracy and the narrow scope of its activities; the geographic isolation, which lessened the pressure of foreign policies— all these combined to obliterate the marks of the Civil War. The fundamental character of the polity was continuously maintained, even through the Glorious Revolution (*see* [Z] *Clark, 1955; Trevelyan, 1944; Ashley, 1952; Plumb, 1950; Pares, 1957; Namier, 1952*).

Thus, development of the bureaucracy in Europe was due not to the work of forces entirely different from those existing in other countries. It was, rather, the result of the simultaneous evolution of several conditions which elsewhere usually developed separately—and, probably, to a qualitatively more extensive development of some of these conditions. In other words, in Europe there occurred extensive, parallel, and similar developments of a high order in the economic, political, and value-cultural spheres, facilitated and encouraged by a flexible political framework.

[18] *Summary*

We have presented our hypotheses concerning the relations of the types of change undergone by historical bureaucratic societies to various social-economic conditions and to the internal contradictions in the orientations of both the rulers and the major strata. If they are correct, they substantiate the thesis that each level and type of social differentiation and each constellation of the principal components of the political process of the historical bureaucratic societies were connected, not only with a different level or type of political activity, but also with different types of potential or actual change.

We have substantiated the thesis that the various types of societal and political change that emerged within the historical bureaucratic societies could be systematically related to the basic social-economic conditions of these societies and to the basic types of political process that developed within them. We have seen that the processes of change in these societies were rooted in the following conditions:

1. The *relative, limited* development of free-floating resources and the autonomy of the political sphere

2. The internal contradictions in the orientations and policies of the rulers and in the political orientations and goals of the leading socal strata

3. The exigencies to which these systems were exposed and sensitive, caused by the nature of the rulers' goals, the emphasis on the autonomy of the political sphere, and the social composition and orientations of the main strata

Of course, there were many variations with regard to the detailed nature and immediate causes of these exigencies. Many of them were largely contingent upon fortuitous historical and external circumstances (e.g., population movements) outside the given polity. Nevertheless, we have shown that the general nature of the exigencies to which a specific system became exposed and was especially sensitive was, at least to some extent, rooted in its basic social conditions and political characteristics. Moreover, we have demonstrated that the particular forms taken by the processes of change were largely determined by the political activities, issues, and organizations within the society. Thus, these changes did not consist in sudden, inexplicable eruptions and outbursts. Rather, they were inherent in, and part and parcel of, the structural characteristics and political process of the society in which they occurred.

The internal contradictions which developed within the less differentiated historical bureaucratic political systems were related to the evolving of more creative-prescriptive types of policy, and to the consequent depletion of free economic resources and the withdrawal of active political support from the differentiated polity. In the more differentiated polities, on the other hand, the internal tensions were usually connected with shifts, in the conception of the chief referents of political activity, from the polity to universalistic value systems and/or to various social groups—and, consequently, with aspiration toward more differentiated political systems with a different basic pattern of political decision-making.

Accordingly, we have shown that just as the conditions responsible for processes of change varied from one historical bureaucratic society to another so also the direction and outcome of these processes varied, in terms of the type of political system (whether a pre-bureaucratic or a more differentiated bureaucratic polity) in which they culminated.

13

Conclusions

[1] *Summary of the Argument*

In this chapter, we shall attempt to summarize briefly the main thread of our analysis. We shall also try to indicate some more general conclusions, about the interrelations between the political system and social structure, that can be derived from this analysis.

As we stated at the beginning of this book, our main concern was to provide a sociological analysis of the historical bureaucratic empires, to describe their basic characteristics, and to analyze the social conditions under which they developed and functioned, and the social and political processes which made their continuity possible or which brought about their changes.

The starting point of our analysis was the discussion of the conditions under which the political systems of historical bureaucratic empires became institutionalized. The most important of these conditions were found to be: (1) the tendency of the rulers toward implementing autonomous political goals; and (2) the development of certain (even if relatively limited) levels of differentiation and free-floating resources in *all* the major institutional spheres of the society.

Only when these two conditions obtained concurrently—even if developed to different degrees—was it possible for the basic premises of the political systems of the historical bureaucratic societies to evolve constantly and to be institutionalized, in the forms of a centralized polity, organs ·of political struggle, and bureaucratic administration.

The fundamental organizational features of these systems—i.e., the organs of political struggle and of bureaucratic administration—can be considered as ways or mechanisms which insure the continuous interplay between the political and other chief institutional spheres in these societies. However, the effective functioning of these organs, and the perpetuation of these political systems, were contingent on the continued prevalence of the basic conditions described above. In any of the historical bureaucratic societies, their continued prominence was dependent on the nature of the political process that developed in the society: first, on the policies of the rulers; second, on the orientations, goals, and political activities of the principal strata; and third, on the interrelations between these two. Through the uninterrupted interaction of the policies of the rulers with the political activities of the major strata, the fundamental prerequisites necessary for the functioning of the historical bureaucratic polities and the effective operating of their principal organs could be maintained.

We have seen, however, that within the orientations, goals, and activities of the rulers, and within the major social and political orientations of the chief strata, there were contradictory elements concerning their attitudes toward the basic premises of the political systems of the historical bureaucratic societies. Thus, the rulers sometimes displayed many traditional and control orientations and utilized various prescriptive policies to an extent that undermined both the continuous development of free-floating resources in the leading social groups and their linking to the more traditional groups and strata. In some cases, within each of the major strata there also existed both traditional and more autonomous—whether passive or active—orientations and goals that transcended the institutional premises of these polities. These contradictory components of the orientations of both the rulers and the principal strata were reinforced to the extent that their respective orientations and goals were incompatible, and also by various external factors and exigencies. The constant interactions of these different forces created the primary problems and strains in the political structure of the empires. They generated various processes of change capable of undermining the balance between traditional and more differentiated types of social structures, and the close interlinking between them and the functioning of the organs of political struggle and of bureaucratic administration.

These processes of change were of different kinds. These types were distinguished primarily on the basis of the extent to which they could be accommodated within the fundamental framework of the political institutions of the historical bureaucratic empires.

Processes of accommodable change occurred when the contradictions between the orientations and policies of the rulers and the goals and activities of the major strata were not greatly strained. Then the basic conditions and prerequisites of these political systems were continuously maintained—even when many changes took place in the actual composition and strength of different groups and in the policies of the rulers. In such cases, the various political and administrative organs continued to function, interrelating the political sphere with other social spheres—although there were, necessarily, alterations in many of the details of their functioning.

In some of the historical bureaucratic empires, the contradictions in the respective orientations and activities of the rulers and the major strata, and in their interrelations, became so strong that they undermined the basic conditions and premises of the historical bureaucratic polities. This resulted in processes of transformation of the political systems—i.e., processes of total change—in the direction of less differentiated and flexible political systems. The different specific political and administrative organs of these polities were not able to perform their functions of interrelating the political sphere with other social spheres and of insuring the mutual flow of resources among them. One crucial aspect of such a breakdown of this interchange was the tendency of the bureaucracy itself to displace its service goals to the rulers and to major strata—emphasizing goals of self-aggrandizement, and thus seriously imparing its own efficiency.

[2] *The Relations between the Political System and the Other Parts of the Society. The Tendency to Political Autonomy and Generalization of Power*

The analysis presented in this book may also throw some light on more general problems—the interrelations between the political institutions and the society at large, the place of the political institutions in the social structure, and the contingencies connected with the potential development of the autonomy of the political sphere.

Our analysis began with the assumption that the political system constitutes a special subsystem or domain of the society. This domain is necessarily dependent on other subsystems of the society. In order to be able to function at all, the political system needs various things

—e.g., economic and manpower resources, legitimation and support for its activities, identification with its goals—that can be supplied only by other parts or institutions of the society.

The relations between the political system and other subsystems of the society are focused in the organization of the political process, i.e., in the demands made by the holders of political power on the major strata and in the interchange of activities and services between them.

However, the political subsystem has some degree of autonomy. It evinces tendencies and orientations of its own in relation to other subsystems or institutions of the society—and these, in their turn, are dependent on the outputs from the political subsystem. This relative autonomy of the political subsystem is most clearly discernible in the tendency or orientation to the exercise of power. Power is, as it were, the major autonomous component of this domain. There are two basic manifestations of such exercise of power: the holders of power are able (1) to use various resources for the implementation of different goals and (2) to mobilize human resources at will—those who exercise power (the "rulers") can impose their will on others.

Thus, to analyze the ways in which the political system may tend to stress or evolve its own autonomy, we must examine the ways in which political power can develop without being encumbered. The tendency toward the unhindered, uninhibited use of power has two chief manifestations, which, although often interrelated, are analytically distinct.

The first manifestation is in what may be called the pure arbitrariness of political power—as evinced in the ruler's personal rule and discretion over other people's lives, in the possibility of the ruler's becoming "despotic." Examples of this kind of despotic, arbitrary, personal power can, of course, be found in many different types of societies and political systems, ranging from the most primitive to the most developed. In many political systems, we find incidences of rulers' attempting to exercise power arbitrarily—albeit in different degrees and with varying amounts of success. Whether or not their attempts were checked or limited depended on circumstances.

However, these attempts do not, in themselves, indicate very much about the second and more central aspect of autonomous development of political power. This aspect consists in the uses, besides that of direct arbitrary rule over other people, to which power is applied—in other words, the types of goals that are implemented by the utilization of power and mobilization of resources. In many of the simpler societies, even if the rulers behave despotically, they are nevertheless greatly restricted—in their formulation of goals, and in implementing them—by the traditional values and by the amount of social differentiation in the society. These factors are able to limit the political activities of the rulers in two ways. The first way is through the resources which are made available to the ruler. The second way is through the very values and cultural orientations predominant in the society—these can prevent the rulers from formulating any autonomous goals that are not related to these values and are not largely embedded in the structure of the major social groups. The level of *generalized* power is, in these simpler societies, relatively low. Thus the two aspects of autonomy of power—the arbitrary use of power in personal ruler-ruled relations, and the application of political power for specifically political goals—are not necessarily identical or concomitant.

From the sociological point of view, obviously, the latter aspect of generalization of power is of greater interest. Therefore, the study of the conditions under which it may develop is central to the sociological analysis of political systems. Thus, the analysis of the political systems of the historical bureaucratic empires is of special significance and relevance.

[3] *The Limitations on the Tendencies of Generalization of Power in the Political Systems of the Historical Bureaucratic Empires*

The special analytical interest of the historical bureaucratic societies derives partly from the fact that there emerged within them a growing differentiation of the social structure, and the differentiated social groups had increasingly more recourse to the political system. The divers social goals and aspirations of these groups became closely related to the political process and were, in some degree, translated into political goals. On the other hand, the traditional aspects of the legitimation of the rulers were still predominant, and some traditional orientations existed among almost all the strata. This fact greatly restricted the extent of interpenetration of the (relatively differentiated) political and social spheres, and enabled each of them to maintain a great deal of distinctiveness and separateness. Despite their growing interdependence, they remained not only autonomous but discrete, and did not totally interpenetrate one another.

This was evinced in the organization of the political process in these societies and in the relation between the political process and the social structure—in the fact that many of the groups and strata were somewhat isolated from the central political process, but that at the same time this isolation was only partial.

Hence, the study of these political systems can help us to analyze the conditions under which the tendency of political sphere to autonomy, to generalization of power, develops, and the different types of restraints on this tendency which can evolve in different social settings.

As we have seen, the development of the tendency toward generalization of power is greatly facilitated by the emergence of social differentiation and by the growth of free-floating resources. It is greatly checked by the extent to which social differentiation and free-floating resources are underdeveloped, by the prevalence of many traditional forces and orientations, and by general political passivity. Thus, whatever degree of personal despotism and arbitrariness might be evinced by the ruler of one of these societies, its application to societal goals is necessarily confined by these conditions. However, it is even more relevant for our analysis that, within these political systems, other types of limitations on the tendency to generalized power also emerged. These limitations evolve in close association with the very conditions which facilitate the growth of the tendency—i.e., under conditions of increasing differentiation of the social structure and the development of free-floating resources.

The rulers of the historical bureaucratic societies became, in terms of the maintenance of their legitimation, in a way more dependent on societal forces than were the rulers of more traditional societies. This dependence is due to the facts that the basic differentiation between the social, cultural, and political spheres—while these spheres still remained distinct—as well as the very tendency of the ruler to the formulation of autonomous political goals, made the problem of the relation of the political goals of the rulers to the value orientation prevalent among the different social groups more acute. As a consequence, the legitimation of the rulers was largely contingent on the expectations and demands of the various groups and strata—expectations and demands that were often couched in the terms of these value orientations.

The claims and expectations of the groups and strata were, at least somewhat, "translated" into their political goals; they were channelized through the groups' participation in the political process. Thus, from the very beginning, the rulers' tendency toward generalization of power was confronted with the problems accruing from the development of a similar or parallel tendency among the ruled.

The rulers of these political systems always had to take into consideration the fact that the different social groups tended also to evolve quite specific political aspirations. While, in less differentiated societies, the great amount of embeddedness of political roles in other groups prevents making a sharp distinction between rulers and ruled in purely political terms, the relative growth of an autonomous political sphere hastened the development of both the rulers' own tendencies to generalization of power and parallel tendencies among the ruled.

This is closely connected to an additional point, namely, to the relation between the development of the tendency toward generalization of power, and the various regulative and integrative problems arising as results of the evolution of social differentiations. As we have observed, the same conditions which led to social differentiation and to the development of free resources also created divers regulative problems concerning conflicts and relations among the chief groups and strata of the society. Many facets of the political institutions—especially the development of the bureaucracy and of the channels of political struggle—can be considered in terms of providing services to various groups and of regulating their relationships.

Thus, the tendency to generalization of power of the rulers in the historical bureaucratic empires was limited not only by the paucity of free resources and by the existence of many traditional forces. It was also restricted by the internal regulative problems which emerged as a result of the growing differentiation of the social structure. As a rule, the trend in these cases was toward some convergence between the tendency of the rulers to maximize generalization of power and the growing tendency of various groups to translate their social aspirations into political goals.

However, in the historical bureaucratic societies, such convergence was never complete. The differentiated political and social spheres remained distinct, each keeping, so to speak, its separate identity. Among both the traditional and the more differentiated groups, referents of political activity developed that somewhat transcended the existing polity. Even when these referents were oriented to it, they remained, to some degree, autonomous and independent.

The political goals of the various groups became more articulated as social differentiation increased. However, no matter how articulated they were, they never became fully incorporated in the political sphere —i.e., they never set the goals of the polity, chose the rulers, or took over political decision-making. Hence, the central political process was, to some extent, isolated from the internal social and "political" processes of many groups and did not touch on all the possible aspects of social life of these groups.

The social and political spheres remained distinct, and the extent to which different groups had recourse to the polity remained circumscribed. This limitation was greatly facilitated by the close interlinking of the traditional and more differentiated groups and strata.

These limitations of the autonomy of the political sphere are most clearly discernible in the ambivalent attitudes of the rulers themselves to generalization of power. We have noted that, even when the rulers of the historical bureaucratic societies formulated maximal totalitarian prescriptive policies, they still tended to cloak these policies in some traditional guises—in this way restraining their despotic and totalitarian tendencies.

It follows that the limitations on the generalization of power of the rulers, on the total autonomy of the political sphere, are fundamentally dependent on the autonomy and distinctiveness—whether traditional or more differentiated—of social groups.

The less differentiated the society is, and the more the traditional orientations are predominant within it, the smaller the direct contact tends to be among the more differentiated political roles and organizations and the different social spheres. The autonomy of the political spheres is then restricted by the traditional elements; but *within* the relatively differentiated political sphere, the holders of political power need not be greatly dependent on various social groups. The greater the differentiation of the social structure, the greater becomes the potential contact between it and the social spheres. Also, in the latter case, various more complex limitations tend to develop on the rulers' tendency to generalization of power, and, at the same time, on the potential recourse of the social groups to the polity.

Within the historical bureaucratic empires, both types of limitations coexisted. By their very relationship, they reinforced one another—although this same relationship could also undermine the continuity of these systems. However this relationship did not persist in the more developed, differentiated political systems.

The existence of such relationships created the special conditions of continuity of these systems and their special "systemic" vulnerabilities. As in all political systems, this continuity was dependent on the provision of the necessary resources and support to the polity from other spheres of the society and on the creation, by political decisions, of conditions conducing to such provision. But the specific ways in which the political systems of the historical bureaucratic empires depended on both differentiated and traditional resources and support created the endemic types of sensitivity of these systems, as analyzed in the preceding chapter.

[4] *The Tendencies to Generalization of Power in More Differentiated (Modern) Political Systems*

The same forces that created the more dynamic types of limitations on generalization of power and on autonomy of the political sphere were also most closely related to the processes of change in these societies. The further evolution of these forces could have caused changes of these political systems and led to the development of new types of political systems—systems in which many of the limitations on generalization of power and on the autonomy of the political sphere that we have observed in the historical bureaucratic empires could be, in a way, overcome. This possibility is inherent in the emergence of more differentiated, modern political systems. These systems are characterized by the weakening of the distinction between the goals of the rulers and the political aspirations of the ruled, and by the development of types of political institutions and processes directed toward incorporating the social and political aspirations of different groups into the goals of the polity.

In the historical bureaucratic systems, the rulers held the monopoly of authoritative political decision-making. The political aspirations of the ruled were manifest only in potential, but not fully institutionalized, demands on the rulers—demands which only the rulers could translate into political goals. In the modern systems, the *formal* political difference between rulers and ruled becomes continually obliterated; both develop as relatively direct holders or representatives of political power, orientation, and demands. The process of political decision-making becomes largely vested in a somewhat new type of ruling elite—an elite whose foremost claim to legitimation is that its members represent different groups of the society, their values and orientations. This new kind of elite attempts to incorporate these values and aspirations in the political process and to translate them into the ultimate goals of the polity. The two principal aspects of the process of generalization of power—the goals of the polity (rulers) and the political aspirations of the several groups in the society—become, in modern societies, much more closely interrelated and interconnected, even though they can never be totally submerged in one another. In this way, the interrelations between the political and other subsystems or institutions of the society become much more close; and the various mechanisms which regulate and channelize these interrelations—such as constitutions, mechanisms of voting, organized political parties—become much more articulated. At the same time, these very mechanisms emphasize the growing interdependence and potential identity between the highly differentiated political and the other institutional ("social") spheres.

All these conditions facilitate and maximize the different tendencies to generalization of power. They thus create a constant state of tension between the highly differentiated, autonomous, "social" sphere—which develops its own strong political orientations—and the similarly differentiated and autonomous political sphere. These tensions are resolved in different ways in different types of modern political regimes. However, all of them—democratic, totalitarian, or any mixed types—are necessarily fraught with the continuous possibilities of change, since, in all of them, these tensions continue and no solution of them can be accepted as final and unchangeable.

In modern societies, all the fundamental tensions between traditional, differentiated, and transcendental orientations of political activity, and between the recourse to the polity as the chief basis of values, become more identified, and much more fully articulated and delicately balanced. However, this can also increase the claims of the polity to be the sole representative of such values.

Under these general conditions, some of the possibilities of total generalization of power become apparent—although even here their "totality" may be more apparent than real. The interdependence and interpenetration of the *differentiated* political and other subsystems of the society create the possibility that the societal institutions will be "totally" subjugated by the political, and, so to speak, absorbed by the political institution.

In the area of legitimation, this interdependence has the potential to cause, easily, a shift in the main referents of political activities—from different autonomous groups, traditions, and transcendental values, to certain political groups and institutions that then may become the chief direct expressions of values and orientations of political activities. In this way, the polity itself may become the ultimate and direct expression of such values and orientations; it may absorb all autonomous groups and value orientations into itself, and largely abolish their autonomy with regard to the political institution.

The several regulative problems, which emerge in connection with the growing social differentiation and the increasing interdependence between the differentiated political and other social institutions, are intensified. Their intensification can give the polity the impetus to try to monopolze all such regulative mechanisms, to identify them with purely political mechanisms, and to suppress any of their autonomy or the potential aspirations of divers social groups to autonomous political influence. Such suppression is usually not made in terms of denial of the political orientations of the ruled; it is made in terms of channelizations of these orientations in the monopolistic political institutions of the elite. Thus, the tensions between traditional, differentiated, and transcendental orientations of political activity may become, in these types of modern societies, transposed—incorporated into a monolithic state structure which is built on the close interpenetration of the differentiated political and other institutional spheres. The different aspects of the tendencies to generalization of power become, at least somewhat, incorporated into this monolithic political structure. It attempts to monopolize, regulate, and dictate the flow of inputs and outputs between the political and other social institutions.

These totalitarian developments are not inevitable results of the evolution of modern political systems. However, their emergence is potential; the possibility is innate in the growing social differentiation; in the weakening of the differences between the *political* activities and rights of the rulers and the ruled; and in the increasing interdependence between differentiated, non-embedded institutional spheres.

Only under these conditions can the latent despotic and totalitarian power—the first, albeit partial and ambivalent, manifestation of which occurred in the political systems of the historical bureaucratic empires—become completely realized and fully developed; but also only under these conditions can the potentialities for the fuller free participation of different social groups in the political process—the partial manifestation of which also occurred in the political systems of the historical bureaucratic empires—be fully developed.

Appendix

General Remarks

on Analytical Tables

1. In Tables I, II, and III, the main relevant variables pertaining to thirty-two societies are categorized. Five of these societies are pre-bureaucratic; twenty-seven exhibit the characteristics of the political system of the historical bureaucratic societies. As the variables of the pre-bureaucratic societies are of interest only for validating the hypothesis about the condition of development and institutionalization of these systems (Part I of this volume), they have been analyzed in detail only in Table I and not in Tables II and III.

2. The scales of categories used in our numerical analyses are appropriate only to historical bureaucratic societies. Therefore, the least developed of those societies (the Inca) has been assigned the lowest marks, and the most developed (England), the highest. In some societies, mostly pre-bureaucratic, some variables have such low values that they have been marked zero in order to differentiate between them and other bureaucratic societies whose variables have higher values. Conversely, if we were to analyze a modern society in our tables, we would have to give it higher marks than our scales provide for in many cases.

3. In most cases, we have tried to delineate the developments occurring in different periods in the history of the societies we have studied here. The reader will find the historical limits of each period in Note a for each society. When there is no adequate information on developments, or the developments have no significance for our purposes, only one general value has been given.

4. When attaching numerical values to our variables, we took two considerations into account: (a) the extent to which the material at our disposal would allow for a certain degree of elaboration; and (b) the importance of fine distinctions for our pur-

poses. In cases where the available material is considerable and the variables important, an analysis in nine numerical categories has been attempted. In other cases, only five or even three numerical categories have been used. Whenever the number of categories usually satisfactory for our purposes did not permit an important distinction to be made, we have had to construe "mediate values" falling in between two full numerical categories; these consist of a dominant value and a secondary one (the latter has been enclosed in parentheses).

5. The analytical tables refer to the parts of this volume in the following order: Table I refers to Part I; Table I-A refers also to Chapter 11 in Part II; Table II refers to Chapters 7 to 9 in Part II; Table III refers to Chapter 10.

6. In the definitions and descriptions of the scheme in the general outlay of our variables and categories, only those variables and categories have been considered whose meaning has not been made clear in the text; for the rest, the reader is referred to the appropriate chapters of the text.

7. A dash (—) has been used to designate the absence of a variable in a society.

8. Lack of information has been indicated by a question mark.

9. If a secondary tendency was very low in importance, it has been put in parentheses; for example, in Variable IX-B.1 in Table I-D, the category "Technical" has been used with regard to the existence of some conscious political orientation in this direction, whereas the same symbol in parentheses designates the existence of only minimal technical services.

10. Although most of the societies studied contained an upper peasant group similar to the gentry, the gentry has been analyzed as a special group only in those societies where it constituted an articulated social group.

11. In Table I, Variable III, the differentiation of four institutional groups has been analyzed. The last, comprising the cultural-secular groups, has been analyzed only in those societies where it had some political importance; its analysis has been omitted in Variable IV of the same table, dealing with the crystallization of institutional groups, because it was not expected that such a process would occur in the societies dealt with here.

12. In Table I-D, we distinguish, with respect to Variable IX-A, between a central and a local level of bureaucratic activity. In cases where the difference is unimportant or unknown, only one row of values is given, signifying general bureaucratic activity in various institutional spheres of the society.

13. The notes following Tables I, II, and III pertain to the individual columns in the tables and are grouped by specific societies.

Definitions of Variables Used in Analytical Tables

TABLE I

I. Autonomy of political goals of ruler; i.e., extent of ruler's independence from ascriptive and traditional prescription in the setting up of political goals

II. Traditional legitimation of ruler; i.e., extent of ruler's legitimation by ascriptive traditional values and culture

III. Differentiation of social structure; i.e., existence of specific institutions and groups
A. Spheres

In defining the various spheres, the following indices were taken into consideration:

1. ECONOMIC
    a. Activities: agriculture, industry, trade, finance
    b. Roles: craftsmen, traders, bankers
    c. Organizations: manufacturing concerns, guilds, trading companies
    d. Mechanisms: self-regulating markets

e. Values and norms
  (1) personal enrichment, economic growth and development
  (2) Norms of property transaction

f. Elites: big traders, bankers, industrialists

2. POLITICAL

a. Activities: administration, party-political activity
b. Roles: administrators, propagandists, political advisers
c. Organizations: parties
d. Mechanisms: autonomous self-government, arbitration between and within groups, regional political institutions
e. Values and norms
  (1) Political power
  (2) Norms of political behavior
f. Elites: political and administrative elites

3. LEGAL

a. Activities: judicial processes, legal activities
b. Roles: judges, advocates
c. Organizations: legal machinery
d. Mechanisms: autonomous legal systems
e. Values and norms
  (1) Sanctity of robe
  (2) Judicial rights, generalized and abstract legal norms
f. Elites: judges, legal specialists

4. RELIGIOUS

a. Activities: religious rites and ceremonies, ecclesiastical and theological activities
b. Roles: priests, theologians, monks, heads of temples, members of sects, bishops
c. Organizations: sects, organizations, churches
d. Mechanisms: ecclesiastic synods
e. Values and norms
  (1) Salvation, pious life
  (2) Ideals and religious norms
f. Elites: heads of religious organizations and orders; bishops

5. EDUCATION AND CULTURE

a. Activities: education, academic, artistic, philosophical
b. Roles: teachers, philosophers
c. Organizations: school systems
d. Values and norms
  (1) Cultured personality
  (2) Educational and cultural ideas and norms
e. Elites: professors, cultural elites

6. STRATIFICATION

a. Development of groups and associations in society
  (1) Specific functional groups (e.g., artisan and merchant guilds, merchant associations, religious and cultural associations)
  (2) "Social" and cultural–social groups (social clubs, recreational associations)
  (3) Solidary integrative groups (cult groups, mutual aid associations)
  (4) General ascriptive solidarities
b. Status; i.e., extent of development of specific occupations, political and legal rights, religious affiliation, and education as criteria of status
c. Specific elite in major institutional spheres; i.e., development of communicative and leadership positions, such as politicians, preachers, economic magnates, professors
d. Specific status symbols for groups and associations; i.e., differentiations of symbols of rank and precedence, codes of conduct and etiquette, and specific styles of life for various classes and professional groups

B. *Groups*

  a. ECOLOGICAL GROUPS:
  1. Peasantry
  2. Gentry
  3. Aristocracy
  4. Urban groups

In analyzing the differentiation of each ecological group, the following indices were used:

1. Diversification of the group's resources
2. Differentiation of economic activities
   a. From other groups
   b. Within the group
3. Differentiation of economic organization
   a. From other groups
   b. Within the group
4. Participation in market economy
5. Differentiation of political organization and leadership; i.e., extent of groups' participation in parties/assemblies, differentiation of group representation
6. Diversification of political affiliation of members; i.e., extent of members' differential affiliation with various parties and cliques
7. Differentiation of religious organization and leadership; i.e., extent of differentiation in the same social group of various types of religious sects, orders, and hierarchies, distinct from those in other groups and from one another
   a. From other groups
   b. Within the group
8. Diversification of religious affiliation of members; i.e., extent of members' differential affiliation with various religious sects and orders
9. Differentiation of status criteria; i.e., extent of development of specific criteria of status differentiating the group from other groups and sub-groups within the group from one another
   a. From other groups
   b. From one another
10. Differentiation of social sub-groups
    a. Within the group
    b. Between the group and other groups
11. Differentiation of individual status; i.e., extent of non-ascriptive individual status differentiation as against ascriptive status of whole group or sub-group

   b. INSTITUTIONAL GROUPS:
      5. Legal profession
      6. Military profession
      7. Religious profession
      8. Cultural-secular profession

In analyzing the differentiation of each institutional group, the following indices were used:

1. Differentiation of professional roles
   a. From other, non-professional roles
   b. From one another
2. Differentiation of professional organization and leadership
3. Differentiation of sub-groups within professional group; i.e., various military services (e.g., infantry, cavalry, war elephants, fleet), legal schools and traditions, academies of religion and science
4. Development of professional standards; i.e., differentiation of specific codes of conduct and professional etiquette
5. Differentiation of specific status of professional group in society

IV. Crystallization of institutional groups; i.e., extent of autonomy of institutional groups from ecological groups (e.g., differentiation of military groups from aristocracy and local groups, differentiation of legal from religious groups)
   1. LEGAL PROFESSION
   2. MILITARY PROFESSION
   3. RELIGIOUS PROFESSION
   4. CULTURAL-SECULAR GROUP

V. Development of free-floating power in society; spheres:
   1. ECONOMIC
   2. POLITICAL
   3. LEGAL
   4. RELIGIOUS
   5. EDUCATION AND CULTURE
   6. STRATIFICATION

The following indices were used for each sphere:

1. Extent of development of free-floating resources (money and various types of exchangeable commodities)
2. Extent of development of free-floating population (free rural population; religiously, politically, and legally non-committed populations)
3. Extent of universality of norms and values
4. Extent of flexibility of institutional organizations

5. Extent of mobility in institutional spheres
6. Extent of development of non-ascriptive and universal status criteria

VI. Centralized polity

In defining this variable the following indices were used:

    A. *Extent of differentiation of ruling group from ascriptive and ecological groups*

    B. *Extent of direct citizenship in broader society*

    C. *Fixed delineation of society's boundaries*

    D. *Control of central over local political units*

    E. *Extent of legal sovereignty of ruler*

VII. Differentiation of political roles

    A. *Producers; i.e., legislative, administrative, party-political roles: extent of development of specific roles of ruler in political sphere*

    B. *Consumers; i.e., citizens, voters: extent of development of passive but specific political roles of subjects*

VIII. Development of channels of political struggle

    A. *Types of channels of political struggle; i.e., the main mechanisms carrying the political process in society*

The following categories were used in this analysis:

    1. PARLIAMENT
    2. RULER'S COUNCIL
    3. SENATE
    4. BUREAUCRACY
    5. COUNCIL OF VASSALS
    6. CITY COUNCIL
    7. TERRITORIAL GROUPS
    8. ARMY
    9. RULING FAMILIES

    B. *Degree of embeddedness of channels; i.e., extent to which channels of political struggle lack differentiation from other social groups such as king, family, kinship, and territorial groups*

        1. TRADITIONAL CHANNELS: TRIBES, TERRITORIAL GROUPS

        2. TRADITIONAL CHANNELS AND SPECIAL POLITICAL ORGANS: TRIBES, TERRITORIAL GROUPS AND KING, COURT, COUNCIL

        3. SPECIAL POLITICAL ORGANS: KING, COURT, COUNCIL

        4. SPECIAL POLITICAL ORGANS—SEPARATE: KING, COURT, COUNCIL AND NON-EMBEDDED

        5. SEPARATE: NON-EMBEDDED

    C. *Membership in channels of struggle*

        1. GROUPS

            (1) Peasantry
            (2) Gentry
            (3) Aristocracy
            (4) Urban groups
            (5) Legal profession
            (6) Military profession
            (7) Religious profession
            (8) Cultural-secular group
            (9) Bureaucracy

The following categories were used in this analysis:

    a. No participation
    b. Continuous participation
    c. Sporadic participation
    d. Rare participation

        2. EXPLICATION OF RULES OF MEMBERSHIP IN CHANNELS OF STRUGGLE; I.E., EXTENT OF CLEAR DEFINITION OF RULES BY WHICH GROUPS OBTAIN MEMBERSHIP WITHIN CHANNELS OF POLITICAL STRUGGLE

The following categories were used in this analysis:

    a. Explicit traditional
    b. Explicit legal
    c. Non-explicit traditional
    d. Non-explicit arbitrary

    D. *Powers of channels of political struggle*

        1. EXTENT OF POWERS; I.E., EXTENT OF INFLUENCE OF CHANNELS ON RULERS' POLICIES

The following categories were used in this analysis:

    a. Approval of rulers' decisions

b. Advisory

c. Decision

d. Control post factum

e. Execution

2. SCOPE OF POWERS; I.E., SCOPE OF MATTERS DEALT WITH AND BY CHANNELS

The following categories were used in this analysis:

a. Policy

b. Budget

c. Appointments

d. Legislation

e. Self-regulation

f. Control of administration

g. Election

3. INSTITUTIONALIZATION OF POWERS; I.E., EXTENT OF CLEAR-CUT DEFINITION OF POWERS

E. *Explication of rules of political struggle between ruler and groups*

In defining the categories, the following indices were used:

1. EXISTENCE OF RULES OF ARBITRATION

2. EXISTENCE OF RULES OF PETITIONING

3. EXTENT OF FORMALIZATION OF POLITICAL BEHAVIOR FOR EACH INDEX

a. Between ruler and groups

b. Between various groups

The following categories were used in this analysis:

1. NON-EXPLICIT—TRADITIONAL

2. EXPLICIT—TRADITIONAL

3. NON-EXPLICIT—NON-TRADITIONAL

4. EXPLICIT—NON-TRADITIONAL

IX. Scope of bureaucratic activity

A. *Spheres*

1. CENTRAL LEVEL

(1) Economic

(2) Political (including diplomatic)

(3) Legal

(4) Religious

(5) Educational and cultural

(6) Stratification

2. LOCAL LEVEL

(1) Economic

(2) Political

(3) Legal

(4) Religious

(5) Educational and cultural

(6) Stratification

B. *Type of bureaucratic activity in sphere*

The following categories were used for each sphere:

1. TECHNICAL: ACTIVITY REFERRING TO THE PERFORMANCE OF SERVICES AND MAINTENANCE OF CONDITIONS FOR FUNCTIONING OF DIFFERENT GROUPS

2. REGULATIVE: ACTIVITY FOCUSING IN REGULATION OF MAJOR INSTITUTIONAL SPHERES AND CENTERS OF POWER IN SOCIETY

3. BALANCED: EQUILIBRIUM BETWEEN REGULATIVE AND TECHNICAL POLICY

C. *Autonomy of bureaucratic organization; i.e., extent of independence and distinctiveness of bureaucracy from other social groups and spheres*

In defining this variable, the following indices were used for each sphere:

1. ROLES

2. GOALS

3. RULES

D. *Extent of professionalization of bureaucratic roles*

In defining the categories, the following indices were used:

1. EXTENT OF DEFINITION OF ROLES

2. EXTENT OF PERMANENCE OF OFFICE TENURE

3. DEVELOPMENT OF PROFESSIONAL IDEOLOGY

4. EXTENT OF HIERARCHIZATION OF BUREAUCRATIC APPARATUS

5. EXTENT OF INTERNALITY AS AGAINST EXTRANEOUSNESS OF CRITERIA OF RECRUITMENT (E.G., PROFESSIONAL QUALIFICATIONS AGAINST SALE OF OFFICES)

E. *Types of remuneration of bureaucracy*

The following categories were used in this analysis:

1. PATRIMONIAL REMUNERATION BY RULER
   a. Grant
   b. Ad hoc
   c. Continuous
   d. Tax-farming

2. REMUNERATION BY CLIENT
   a. Bribes
   b. For services
3. HONORARY

F. *Extent of functional departmentalization; i.e., extent of differentiation and specialization of governmental departments*

TABLE II

I. Major orientations and references of ruler's goals; i.e., major frames of reference of ruler's goals, defining content, complexity, and heterogeneity of these goals as follows:

A. *Content*
B. *Complexity*
C. *Heterogenity*

The following categories were used in this analysis:

A. *Cultural ascriptive (particularistic)*
B. *Collective reference*
   1. POLITICAL-COLLECTIVE
   2. ECONOMIC-COLLECTIVE
   3. CULTURAL-COLLECTIVE
   4. SELF-MAINTENANCE POLICY
   5. SOCIAL-GROUPS REFERENCE

II. Autonomy of political goals of ruler (See Table I, Variable I.)

III. Extent of differentiation (See Table I, Variable III.C.)

IV. Self-regulation of groups
   A. *Traditional*
   B. *Non-traditional*

In defining the categories, the following indices were used:

a. *Intra-group regulations*
   1. TRADITIONAL SELF-GOVERNING AGENCIES
   2. ECONOMIC AUTARCHY
   3. AUTONOMOUS LEGAL INSTITUTION
   4. STRATIFICATIONAL AUTONOMY
b. *Intergroup regulations*
   1. REGULATION BY OTHER SOCIAL GROUPS

2. REGULATION BY AUTONOMOUS LOCAL RULERS
3. REGULATION BY RELIGIOUS INSTITUTIONS

In almost every index the self-regulation may be either traditional or non-traditional:

1. Traditional: maintained within ascriptive frameworks and norms, such as kinship and territorial groups, guilds, etc.
2. Non-traditional: maintained by non-ascriptive mechanisms, such as markets, special political organizations, self-government and arbitration procedures of different groups

V. Extent of political participation of groups

A. *Intensity of political participation of groups; i.e., scope of group's activity in political struggle*
   1. PEASANTRY
   2. GENTRY
   3. ARISTOCRACY
   4. URBAN GROUP
   5. LEGAL PROFESSION
   6. MILITARY PROFESSION
   7. RELIGIOUS PROFESSION
   8. CULTURAL-SECULAR GROUP
   9. BUREAUCRACY

B. *Articulation of political goals of groups; i.e., generalization of political orientation of group as against demands for immediate concrete rewards (same groups as above)*

C. *Extent of crystallization of political organizations in society*

D. *Extent of participation of groups in political organizations (same groups as above)*

E. *General extent of participation of groups: Summary of variables V.A.–V.C.*

VI. Rebellions*

VII. Types of policies used by ruler for the implementation of his goals

The following categories and indices were used in this analysis:

A. *Creative policies*

  1. CREATION OF NEW SOCIAL GROUPS
  2. CREATION OF NEW ORGANIZATIONS AND MECHANISMS
  3. REPLICATION OF EXISTING SOCIAL ORGANIZATIONS AND MECHANISMS
  4. CREATION OF NEW SYMBOLS AND VALUES

B. *Accumulative policies*
   (only in economic sphere)

  1. ACCUMULATION OF RESOURCES

  a. Money
  b. Manpower
  c. Commodities

---

* This is not an analytical variable but it was inserted in order to point out differences between societies in which the political struggle was institutionally channelized and societies in which it was manifested in violent outburst of rebellions.

C. *Regulative policies*

  1. REGULATION OF SUPPLY OF

  a. commodities
  b. money
  c. land

  2. REGULATION OF CONDITIONS OF SUPPLY OF MANPOWER
  3. REGULATION OF CONTRACTS
  4. REGULATION OF DETAILS OF BEHAVIOR AND UNHOLDING OF NORMS
  5. REGULATION OF RELATIONS BETWEEN GROUPS

D. *Prescriptive policies*

  1. PRESCRIPTION OF BEHAVIOR TO GROUPS
  2. RESTRICTION OF GROUPS
  3. LEVELING
  4. DESTRUCTION OF GROUPS

E. *Services supplied by ruler*

  1. BASIC COMMODITIES
  2. PUBLIC UTILITIES
  3. INTERNAL ORDER AND EXTERNAL SECURITY
  4. AMENITIES FOR RELIGIOUS ACTIVITY
  5. LEGAL SERVICES

F. *Promotive policies: encouragement of activities and development of social groups by*

  1. DIRECT HELP
  2. FAVORABLE LEGISLATION
  3. ENACTMENT OF SPECIAL PRIVILEGES

TABLE III

I. Differentiation of groups—general
   (See Table I; Variable III-B.)

II. Extent of political participation of groups
   (See Table II; Variable V-A.)

III. Relative strength of groups and ruler

The following categories were used in this analysis:

  a. Ruler stronger
  b. Groups stronger

IV. Relative strength of aristocracy vs. middle and low groups

The following categories were used in this analysis:

  a. Aristocracy stronger
  b. Balanced strength
  c. Groups stronger

V. Compatibility of goals of groups and ruler

The following categories were used in this analysis:

  a. Compatible active
  b. Compatible passive
  c. Incompatible active
  d. Incompatible passive

VI. Self-regulation of groups and state
(See Table II; Variable IV.)

A. *Traditional*
(See Table II; Variable IV-A.)

B. *Non-traditional*
(See Table II; Variable IV-B.)

VII. Type of activity of bureaucracy

The following categories were used in this analysis:

    a. Technical
    b. Regulative

VIII. Autonomy of bureaucratic organization
(See Table I-D; Variable IX-C1.)

IX. Social status of bureaucracy

A. *Extent of embeddedness of bureaucracy; i.e., differentiation of bureaucracy from other groups and strata*

The following categories were used in this analysis:

    a. Embedded in central polity
    b. Embedded in aristocracy
    c. Embedded in middle groups
    d. Embedded in gentry
    e. Non-embedded

B. *Criteria of status of bureaucracy; i.e., criteria of bureaucracy's status*

The following categories were used in this analysis:

    a. Power criteria
    b. Educational-cultural criteria
    c. Professional criteria
    d. Symbols of mobility

X. Political orientation of bureaucracy; i.e., major groups or institutions serving as reference of political activity and orientation of bureaucracy

The following categories were used in this analysis:

    a. Ruler-oriented
    b. Group-oriented
    c. Self-oriented
    d. Self- and polity-oriented

XI. Relative strength of bureaucracy and ruler

The following categories were used in this analysis:

    a. Ruler stronger
    b. Balanced strength
    c. Bureaucracy stronger

Definitions of Scales Used in the Tables

TABLE I

Variable	Scale	Definition
I	1-2	Almost total dependence
	3-4	Independence in framework of ascriptive and traditional limitations
	5	Great independence
II	1	No traditional legitimation
	2	Some traditional legitimation
	3	Full traditional legitimation
III	1-3	Little or no differentiation
	4-6	Moderate differentiation
	7-9	High differentiation
IV	1	Institutional group wholly embedded in ecological groups
	2	Institutional group somewhat differentiated from ecological groups
	3	Institutional group wholly differentiated from ecological groups

TABLE I *(Cont'd.)*

Variable	Scale	Definition
V	1-3	Low development of free-floating power in institutional spheres
	4-6	Medium amounts of non-differentiated free floating power in institutional spheres
	7-9	High amounts of differentiated free-floating powers in institutional spheres
VI	1-2	Low centralization; semi-feudal organization of polity
	3-4	Medium centralization, especially in central parts of kingdom
	5	High centralization
VII	1	Lack of differentiation of political producers
	2	Differentiation of a few roles of political producers
	3	High differentiation of political producers
VIII	1	Total lack of institutionalization
	2	Some but not full institutionalization
	3	Full institutionalization
IX	1	Low
	2	Medium
	3	High

TABLE II

Variable	Scale	Definition
II	1-5	From non-autonomous to autonomous
III	1-9	From low to high differentiation
IV	1	No self-regulation
	2-3	Medium degree of self-regulation in some or most institutional spheres
	4-5	High degree of self-regulation in almost all institutional spheres
V.A	1	Low intensity
	2	Medium intensity
	3	High intensity
B	1	Low degree of articulation: mostly demands for direct rewards and autonomy in management of their own affairs; attempts to seize power in society
	2	Medium degree of articulation: mostly demands for influence in policy making and autonomy in determination of values and status criteria; attempts to seize power in society
	3	High degree of articulation: mostly demands for general, especially legal, rights and for influence in political decision-making

TABLE II *(Cont'd.)*

Variable	Scale	Definition
C	1	Lack of crystallization: development of cliques
	2	Medium crystallization: development of assemblies, group representation, secret societies, religious social movements
	3	High crystallization: development of special organization (parties)
D	1	Low participation of group in political organizations
	2	Medium participation of group in political organizations
	3	High participation of group in political organizations
E	1	Low participation of groups in political struggle
	2	Medium participation of groups in political struggle
	3	High participation of groups in political struggle
VI	1	No rebellions
	2	Few rebellions
	3	Many rebellions

TABLE III

Variable	Scale	Definition
I	1-9	Low to high differentiation
II	1-3	Low to high degree of participation
VI	1-5	Low to high self-regulation
VIII	1-3	Low to high autonomy

List of Abbreviations Used in Tables

Ac.	Active		Bu.	Budget
Acc.	Accumulative		Bur.	Bureaucracy
Ad.	Advisory			
Ap.	Approval of ruler's decisions		C.ad.	Control of administration
App.	Appointments		Cent.	Central political authority
Ar.	Arbitrary		City	City council
Aris.	Aristocracy		Coll.	Collective
Arm.	Army		Com.	Compatible
As.	Ascriptive		Con.	Continuous
Ass.	Assembly		Cont.	Control post factum
			Coun.	Ruler's council
Bal.	Balanced		Court	Court circle
Bri.	Bribes		Crea.	Creative

Cul.	Cultural		Parl.	Parliament
			Pass.	Passive
Dec.	Decision		Pat.	Patrimonial remuneration by ruler
			Pet.	Petitionary
Ec.	Economic		Pol.	Policy, Political
Ed.	Educational-cultural		Pow.	Power
El.	Election		Pres.	Prescriptive
Emb.	Embedded		Prof.	Professional
Ex.	Explicit		Prom.	Promotive
Exec.	Execution			
			Ra.	Rare
Fa.	Tax-farming		R.fa.	Ruling family
			Reg.	Regulative
Gent.	Gentry		Rul.	Ruler
Gr.	Grant			
Group	Groups		Self	Self-regulative, Self-oriented
			Sen.	Senate
Hoc	Ad hoc		Sep.	Separate
Hon.	Honorary		Serv.	Services
			Soc.	Social groups
Inc.	Incompatible		Sp.	Special
			Spor.	Sporadic
Le.	Legal			
Leg.	Legislation		Tax.	Taxation
			Tech.	Technical
Mid.	Middle		Ter.	Territorial groups
			Tr.	Traditional, Traditional channels
N.	Non-, No		Trans.	Transitional from traditional to nontraditional
Nob.	Nobility			
			Vass.	Council of vassals
Or.	Oriented			
Par.	Participation			

Tables

TABLE I.

Social Conditions of the Institutionalization of the Political Systems

A. PRE-BUREAUCRATIC SOCIETIES

Variable	Greece[a]	Mongols[a]	Feudal Europe[a]	Ahmenids[a]	Carolingian Empire[a]
I. Autonomy of political goals of ruler	0(1)	4	1	1(2)	4
II. Traditional legitimation of ruler	1	3	1	3	1
III. Differentiation of social structure					
A. Spheres—General	4	1	2	2	2
1. Economic	4	1	2	2(3)	2
2. Political	2	1	2	2	2
3. Legal	3	0	2	2	2
4. Religious	4	1	6	2	6
5. Education and culture	4	1	2	1	2
6. Stratification	5	1(2)	2	2	2
B. Groups—General	4(5)	1(2)	3	2	4
1. Peasantry	4	2	1	1	1
2. Gentry	—	—	—	—	—
3. Aristocracy	?	2	3	3	2
4. Urban groups	5	1	1	2	1
5. Legal profession	2	—	2	1	2
6. Military profession	—	—	—[b]	—	—[b]
7. Religious profession	3	1	5	2	4
8. Cultural-secular group	5	—	—	—	—
IV. Crystallization of institutional groups					
1. Legal	1	—	1	1	1
2. Military	—	—	—	—	—
3. Religious	1	0	1	2	1
4. Cultural-secular	1	—	—	—	—
V. Development of free-floating power:					
Spheres—General	4	0	3	2	3
1. Economic	4	1	1	2	1
2. Political	4	0(1)	1	2	1
3. Legal	3	0	2	1	2
4. Religious	4	0	5	2	5
5. Education and culture	5	0	3	2	3
6. Stratification	4	0(1)	2	2	2
VI. Centralized polity	1	1(2)	1	2	2
VII. Differentiation of political roles:					
A. "Producers"	2	1	1	1	1
B. "Consumers"	3	1	1	1	1

TABLE I. *(continued)*
Social Conditions of the Institutionalization of the Political Systems

B. HISTORICAL BUREAUCRATIC SOCIETIES

Inca Empire[a]	Ancient Egypt[a]			Sassanid Persia[a]				Ptolemies	Seleucids[a]	T'ang Dynasty[a]		
	I	II	III	I	II	III	IV			I	II	III
1	2	2	1	2	1	3	1	3	3	4	4	2
3	3	3	3	3	3	3	3	2/3b	2/3b	3	3	3
2	2	3	2	3	2	3(4)	2	3	4	4	4	4
1	2	3	2	3	2	4	2	4	4	4	4	4
1	2	3	2	3	2	4	2	3	4	4	5	5
2	1	1	1	2	2	2	2	2	3	3	3	3
4	2	3	4	3	3	3	3	7	6	4	3	3
2	1	2	2	2	2	3	2	3	4	5	5	5
2	2	3	2	3	3	4	3	3	5	4	4	4
1(2)	2	3	2	2	2	3	2	3	4	4	4	4
1	1	2	1	2	2	3	2	*1*	2	3	2	2
–	–	–	–	2	2	4	2b	–	–	4	5	5b
3	2	2	3	2	2	3	2	?	4	4	3	3
1(2)	1	3	2	3	2	4	2	3	6	3	4	5
–	1	2	2	2	2	2	2	–	–	–	–	–
–b	1	2	3	2	2	2	2	5	5	3	4	5
3	2	3	3	3	3	4	3	6	5	4	3	3
–	–	–	–	–	–	–	–	–	–	–	–	–
–		1			1			–	–	–	–	–
–		2			1			3	3	1	2	3
2		3			1			2	3	2	1	1
–		–			–			–	–	–	–	–
1	2	3	1	2	2	3	2	2	4	3	4	5
1	2	3	2	3	2	3	2	2	3	3	4	2
2	2	3	2	2	2	4	2	2	3	3	4	6
1	1	2	1	2	2(1)	2	2(1)	1	3	3	3	4
2	1	1	2	2	2	3	2	3	5	3	2	4
1	1	1	1	2	2	4	2	2	4	4	3	5
1	1	3	2	2	2	3	2	3	5	3	4	5
3	1	2	1	3	1	2(3)	1	4	2	4	3	1
2	1	2	1		1(2)			2	2	3	3	3
1	1	1	1		1			1	2/1c	1	1	2

TABLE I. (*continued*)

Social Conditions of the Institutionalization of the Political Systems

B. HISTORICAL BUREAUCRATIC SOCIETIES								
Variable	Sung Dynasty[a]			Yuan Dynasty[a]	Ming Dynasty[a]	Ch'ing Dynasty[a]	Maurya[a]	
	I	II	III				I	II
I. Autonomy of political goals of ruler	4	4	2	4	4	4	3	4
II. Traditional legitimation of ruler	3	3	3	3	3	3	3	2
III. Differentiation of social structure								
A. Spheres—General	5	5	5	5	5	5	5	
1. Economic	5	5	5	5(6)	5(6)	5(6)	5	
2. Political	5	5	5	5	5	5	3	
3. Legal	3	3	3	3	3	3	4	
4. Religious	3	3	3	4	3	3	8	
5. Education and culture	6	6	6	4	4	4	6	
6. Stratification	5	5	5	5	5(6)	5(6)	8	
B. Groups—General	5	5	5	5	5	5	4	
1. Peasantry	3	3	3	2	3	3	3	
2. Gentry	5(6)	5(6)	5(6)	6[b]	6[b]	6[b]	—	
3. Aristocracy	3	3	3	4[c]	2	3	4	
4. Urban groups	5	5	5	5(6)	6	6	5	
5. Legal profession	—	—	—	—	—	—	—	
6. Military profession	3	3	5	4	4	4	7	
7. Religious profession	3	3	3	4	2	2	7	
8. Cultural-secular group	—	—	—	—	—	—	—	
IV. Crystallization of institutional groups								
1. Legal	—	—	—	—	—	—	—	
2. Military	2	2	3	1	2	2	3	
3. Religious	2	1	1	2	1	1	3	
4. Cultural-secular	—	—	—	—	—	—	—	
V. Development of free-floating power Spheres—General	5	5	6	5	5	5	4	
1. Economic	4	4	2	5	4	4	4	
2. Political	4	4	6	2	3	3	1	
3. Legal	3	3	4	3	3	3	3	
4. Religious	2	2	3	4	2	2	9	
5. Education and culture	4	4	5	3	3	3	6	
6. Stratification	5	5	6	5	5	5	3	
VI. Centralized polity	4	3	1	4	4	4	2	3
VII. Differentiation of political roles								
A. "Producers"	3	3	3	3	3	3	2	
B. "Consumers"	1	1	2	1	1	1	1	

TABLE I. *(continued)*

Social Conditions of the Institutionalization of the Political Systems

B. HISTORICAL BUREAUCRATIC SOCIETIES

Gupta[a]	Mogul Empire[a]			Byzantine Empire[a]			Abbassids[a]		Saffawids[a]		Ottomans[a]		
	I	II	III	I	II	III	I	II	I	II	I	II	III
2	3	4	4	4	5	3(4)	3	1	1	3	2	4	3
3		3/1^b		3	2	3	2	3	1	3	3	2	3
5	3	4	3	5	6	4	5	4	4	5	4	5	5
5	3	5	3	5	6	4	6	3	2	6	5	6	6
3		3		4	6	3	3	3	2	3	3	4	5
4		2		6	7	5	6	7	5	5	6	6	5
8		3/8^c		7/3	6/4	8/2^b	2/6	3/6^b	3/5	5/5^b	3/6	6/6	6/6^b
8		3		4	6	7	4	4	4	4	5	7	6
8		3/8^c		4	7	5	5	4	3	4	5	5	6
4	3	4	3	4	7	6	5	6	4	5	4	6	6
3		3		3	6	2	2	2	2	2	3	2	2
—	—	—	—	—	—	—	—	—	—	—	—	—	—
4		4		4	7	6	?		4	2	5	3	3
5	3	5	3	6	7	5	7	5	2	6	5	6	6
—	2			5	7	7	5	5^e	4	5^e	4	7	7^e
5	3	5	5^d	3	4	5	3	6	2	4	3	7	6
7		7^e		7	7	8	—	—	—	—	—	—	—
—	—	—	—	2	5	4	—	—	—	—	—	—	—
—		2^f		2			1		1			2	
2		1^d		2			1			2	1	1	3
3		3^e		2			—		—		—	—	—
—		—		1			—		—		—	—	—
4	3	4	2	3	6	3(4)	5	4	3	5	5	4	3
4	4	6	2	2	5	1(2)	2	3	2	5	5	4	3
1		2		5	3	4	5	3	2	5	4	4	3
3		2		5	7	4	8	8	4	6	7	7	7
8		4		3	5	3	6	6	5	3	6	5	4
6	3	3	1	3	7	5	5	5	3	3	3	3	3
2	4	5	2	2	5	3	4	3	3	4	4	3	2
3	2	4	3	2	4	1(2)	3	1	2	4	3	4	2
2		2		2			2	2	2	2	2	2	2
1		1		2			1	1	1	1	2	1	2

TABLE I. (*continued*)

Social Conditions of the Institutionalization of the Political Systems

B. HISTORICAL BUREAUCRATIC SOCIETIES

Variable	Moslem Spain[a] I	II	Rome[a] I	II	III	Spanish-American Empire[a] I	II	III	Austria[a]
I. Autonomy of political goals of ruler	2	3	3	4	4	5	4	5	5
II. Traditional legitimation of ruler	2	1	2	2	1	1	1	1	2
III. Differentiation of social structure									
A. Spheres—General	4	5	5	4	3	3/3	6/4	7/4b	6
1. Economic	5	6	5	5	3	4/3	6/4	6b/3	5
2. Political	3	3	5/5	4/6	3/6b	3/3	6/4	7/4b	3
3. Legal	4	5	4	5	6	3/3	6/4	7/4b	8
4. Religious	3/5	4/5b	5	5	6	6	7	7	6
5. Education and culture	4	5	4	5	3	2/2	6/5	7/6b	8
6. Stratification	5	4	5	4	3	3/3	6/4	7/4b	5
B. Groups—General	6	6	5	4	4	4/3	6/4	7/3b	6
1. Peasantry	3	3	2	2	3	2	3	2	5
2. Gentry	—	—	—	—	—		4	4c	—
3. Aristocracy	7	5	4	1	1	7	6	6	7
4. Urban groups	6	6	6	5	3	5/4	6/4	7/4b	6
5. Legal profession	4	4c	2	3	4	3	6	7	8
6. Military profession	5	6	5	5	5	1	1	1	6
7. Religious profession	—	—	3	3	4	5	6	7	6
8. Cultural-secular group	—	—	4	3	1	—	—	—	7
IV. Crystallization of institutional groups									
1. Legal	1	1	1	1	1	1	1	1	1
2. Military	2	2	1	2	3	1	1	1	1
3. Religious	—	—	2	1	1	1	1	1	1
4. Cultural-secular	—	—	1	1	1	—	—	—	1
V. Development of free-floating power: Spheres—General	4	4	5	4	4	3	5	6	7
1. Economic	4	4	6	5	3	2	5	6	5
2. Political	6	6	5	2	7	4	5	7	6
3. Legal	3	3	5	5	3	4	5	6	7
4. Religious	3	3	6	6	7	5	5	5	9
5. Education and culture	4	4	4	5	3	2	5	7	8
6. Stratification	3	4	4	4	7	2	6	6	5
VI. Centralized polity	2	4	3	4	2	2	4	4	4
VII. Differentiation of political roles: A. "Producers"	2	2		3		2/1	3/2	3/1b	3
B. "Consumers"	1	1		2		2/1	2/2	3/1b	2

TABLE I. (*continued*)

Social Conditions of the Institutionalization of the Political Systems

B. HISTORICAL BUREAUCRATIC SOCIETIES

I	Spain[a] II	I	Sweden[a] II	III	I	Russia[a] II	III	I	Prussia[a] II	I	France[a] II	III	I	England[a] II	III
3	4	5	5	4^b	5	3	4	5	4	4	5	3	5	4	5
3	2	2	1	1	1	2	1^b	2	1	2	2	1	2	2	1
6	5	6	8	8	5	4	6	5	7	6	(7)	8	6	7	9
6	4	6	7	8	5	4	6	6	8	6	7	8	6	8	9
6	3	7	9	8	3	3	4	2	4^b	6	5	7	6	7	9
4	4	4	6	8	3	3	5	4	6	6	7	8	8	8	9^b
		{3	5	4}				{4	3^c}						
6	7	{6	8	7^c}	6	6	6	{6	8}	6	5	5	5	7	8
6	3	6	8	8	4	3	5	5	7	5	6	8	5	6	8
8	7	6	6	8	5	7	8	5	8	5	6	8	6	7	9
5	4	5	6	7	5	4	5	5	6	6	6	7	6	7(8)	8(9)
4	4	7	4	8	4	3	3	3	5^d	5	5	6	6	7	8
−	−	−	−	−	−	−	−^c	−	−^e	−	−	−	5	8	9
4	6^b	4	8	6	5	6	7	6	7	7	6	7	6	7	7
6	3	3	5	6	5	3	4	8	6	5	6	8	6	8	9
4	4	3	5	6^d	2	2	3	3	5	7	7	8	5	7	9
7	3	7	6	6^d	6	3	5	8	8	5	5	5	3	5	6
8	8	4	5	5	5	5	5	4	4	6	6	6	6	7	6
6	4	5	8	8	3	3	5	4	6	4	6	8	5	7	8
1	1	1	1	1	1	1	1	1	1	1	2	2	1	1	1
2	1	2	1	1	1	1	1	1	1	1	1	1	1	1	1
3	2	1	1	1	2	2	2	1	1	2	2	2	1	1	1
1	1	1	1	1	1	1	1	1	1	1	1	1	1	1	1
6	3	5	7	7	3	2	4	4	5	6	5(6)	8	6	8	9
7	6	3	5	8	3	3	4	3	4	5	6	7	6	8	9
5	2	4	8	6	2	3	4	2	3	7	5	8	6	7	9
3	3	6	7	8	3	2	3	4	4	5	6	7	7	8	9
2	2	6	8	7	2	2	4	8	8	6	4	5	6	8	8
7	3	5	6	8	4	2	3	4	6	4	6	8	5	7	9
		{5	7	8}						{6	7	8}			
7	5	{5	7	5^e}	4	2	2	6	4	{6	7	6^b}	6	8	9
3	4(5)	4	3	5	4	3	3	5	4	4	5	5	5	5	5
	2	2	3	3	2	2	3	3	3	2	3	3	2	3	3
	2	2	2	3	2	1	1	2	3	1	2	2	2	2	3

TABLE I. (*continued*)

Social Conditions of the Institutionalization of the Political Systems

C. DEVELOPMENT OF CHANNELS OF POLITICAL STRUGGLE (VARIABLE VIII)				
Variable	Greece	Mongols	Feudal Europe	Ahmenids
VIII. A. Type of channels*				
1	city	coun.	coun.,vass.,court	vass.
2	—	vass.	—	court,coun.
3				
B. Degree of embeddedness of channels	tr.	tr.	tr.	tr.
C. Membership				
1. Groups				
(1) Peasantry	cont.	n.par.	cont.,spor.	n.par.
(2) Gentry	—	—	—	—
(3) Aristocracy	cont.	cont.,spor.	cont.	cont.
(4) Urban groups	cont.	n.par.	spor.	n.par.
(5) Legal	n.par.	—	n.par.	n.par.
(6) Military	—	—	—	—
(7) Religious	n.par.	n.par.	cont.	—
(8) Cultural-secular	n.par.	—	—	—
(9) Bureaucracy	—	—	—	—
2. Explication of rules of membership	ex.tr.	ex.tr.	ex.tr.	ex.tr.
	ex.le.	n.ex.ar.		n.ex.ar.
D. Powers of channels				
1. Extent of powers*				
(1)	ap.ad.cont.	ad.	ad.dec.	ad.dec.
(2)	—	cont.	—	—
(3)	—	—	—	—
2. Scope of powers*				
(1)	All items[b]	pol.ap.	pol.	pol.bur.leg.
(2)	—	—	bu.ap.le.	—
(3)	—	—	—	—
(4)				—
(5)	—	—	—	—
3. Institutionalization of powers	3	0(1)	2	2
E. Explication of rules of political struggle between ruler and groups	n.ex.tr.	n.ex.n.tr.	n.ex.tr.	n.ex.tr.

* According to degree of importance.

TABLE I. (continued)

Social Conditions of the Institutionalization of the Political Systems

C. DEVELOPMENT OF CHANNELS OF POLITICAL STRUGGLE (VARIABLE VIII)

Carolingian Empire	Inca Empire	Ancient Egypt			Sassanid Persia			
		I	II	III	I	II	III	IV
coun.,vass.	r.fa.	court			coun.		court	
court	—	bur. coun.			bur.	—	vass.	
sp./sep.	tr.	sp.pol.			tr.sp.	tr.sp.	sp.pol.	tr.
n.par.	n.par.	n.par.			n.par.			
—	—	—			n.par.			
cont.	ra.	spor.			cont.	—	spor.	
ra.	n.par.	n.par.			n.par.			
spor.	—	n.par.			n.par.			
spor.	—	spor.			n.par.			
—	n.par.	cont.			spor.			
—	—	—			—			
—	n.par.	cont.			cont.			
ex.tr.	ex.tr.	n.ex.tr.			ex.tr.			
n.ex.ar.		n.ex.ar.			n.ex.ar.			
ad.	dec.	ad.			ad.			
—	—	—			dec.			
—	—	—			—			
pol.	el.	le.			le.c.ad.			
leg.	c.ad.	app.			—			
c.ad.	—	—			—			
—	—	—			—			
1	1	1			1			
ex. tr.	n.ex.tr.	n.ex.tr.			n.ex.tr.			

TABLE I. (*continued*)

Social Conditions of the Institutionalization of the Political Systems

Variable	Ptolemies	Seleucids	I	T'ang II	III
VIII. A. Type of channels*					
1	—	ter.		court	
2	—	—	bur.	bur.	arm.
3	—		r.fa.	—	ter.
B. Degree of embeddedness		sp.pol.	tr/sp.	tr/sp.	sp.sep.
of channels					
C. Membership					
1. Groups					
(1) Peasantry	n.par.	n.par.	n.par.	n.par.	n.par.
(2) Gentry	—	—	cont.	cont.	cont.
(3) Aristocracy	?	spor.	cont.	cont.	cont.
(4) Urban groups	n.par.	cont.	ra.	ra.	spor.
(5) Legal	—	—	—	—	—
(6) Military	n.par.	n.par.	ra.	ra.	spor.
(7) Religious	n.par.	n.par.	spor.	ra.	ra.
(8) Cultural-secular	—	—	—	—	—
(9) Bureaucracy	n.par.	n.par.	cont.	cont.	cont.
2. Explication of rules of membership	—	ex.le.	ex.tr.	ex.tr.	n.ex.ar.
D. Powers of channels					
1. Extent of powers*					
(1)	—	dec.	ap.	ap.	dec.
(2)	—	—	ad.	ad.	ad.
(3)	—	—	cont.	cont.	cont.
2. Scope of powers*					
(1)	—	self	c.ad.	c.ad.	c.ad.
(2)	—	—	pol.	pol.	pol.
(3)	—	—	app.	app.	app.
(4)	—	—	—		
(5)	—	—	—		
3. Institutionalization of powers	No powers	1	2	2	1
E. Explication of rules of political					
struggle between ruler and groups	n.ex./n.tr.	n.ex./n.tr.	ex.tr./n.tr.	ex.tr./n.tr.	n.ex.tr./n.tr.

* According to degree of importance.

TABLE I. *(continued)*

Social Conditions of the Institutionalization of the Political Systems

C. DEVELOPMENT OF CHANNELS OF POLITICAL STRUGGLE (VARIABLE VIII)

I	Sung II	III	Yuan	Ming	Ch'ing	Maurya I	II
	court		court.,r.fa.	court.,r.fa.	court.,r.fa.	court.,r.fa.,ter.	
bur.	bur.	arm.	bur.	bur.	bur.	—	
r.fa,	—	ter.	r.fa.	—	—	—	
tr/sp.	tr/sp.	sp/sep.	tr/sp.	tr/sp.	tr/sp.	tr/sp.	
n.par.	n.par.	n.par.	n.par.	n.par.	n.par.	n.par.	
cont.	cont.	cont.	cont.	cont.	cont.	—	
spor,	spor.	spor.	cont.	n.par.	rare	cont.	
spor.	spor.	cont.	spor.	spor.	spor.	n.par.	
—	—	—	—	—	—	—	
spor.	spor.	cont.	spor.	spor.	spor.	?	
n.par.	n.par.	n.par.	spor.	n.par.	n.par.	cont.	
—	—	—	—	—	—	—	
cont.	cont.	cont.	cont.	cont.	cont.	n.par.	
ex.tr.	ex.tr.	n.ex.ar.	ex.tr.	ex.tr.	ex.tr.	n.ex.tr.	
ap.	ap.	dec.	ap.	ap.	ap.	?c	
ad.	ad.	ad.	ad.	ad.	ad.		
cont.	cont.	cont.	cont.	cont.	cont.	—	
pol.	pol.	c.ad.	c.ad.	c.ad.	c.ad.	?c	
c.ad.	c.ad.	pol.	pol.	pol.	pol.	—	
app.	app.	app.	app.	app.	app.	—	
—			—	—	—	—	
2	2	1	2	2	2	1	
ex.tr./n.tr.	ex.tr./n.tr.	n.ex.tr./ex.tr.	n.tr./ex.tr.	n.tr./ex.tr.	n.tr./n.ex.tr.	n.tr./n.ex.tr.	

TABLE I. (*continued*)

Social Conditions of the Institutionalization of the Political Systems

C. DEVELOPMENT OF CHANNELS OF POLITICAL STRUGGLE (VARIABLE VIII)				
Variable	*Gupta*	I	*Mogul Empire* II	III
VIII. A. Type of channels*				
1	court.,r.fa.,ter.	r.fa.	vass^g.,	court,ter.
2	—	—		
3	—	—		
B. Degree of embeddedness of channels	tr./sp.	tr./sp.		
C. Membership				
1. Groups				
(1) Peasantry	n.par.	n.par.		
(2) Gentry	—	—		
(3) Aristocracy	cont.	cont.		
(4) Urban groups	n.par.	n.par.		
(5) Legal	—	n.par.		
(6) Military	?	spor.		
(7) Religious	cont.	n.par.		
(8) Cultural-secular	—	—		
(9) Bureaucracy	n.par.	—^{h}		
2. Explication of rules of membership	n.ex.tr.	n.ex.ar.		
D. Powers of channels				
1. Extent of powers*				
(1)	?^{b}	?		
(2)				
(3)	—	—		
2. Scope of powers*				
(1)	el.^{c}	?		
(2)	—	—		
(3)	—	—		
(4)	—	—		
(5)	—	—		
3. Institutionalization of powers	1	1		
E. Explication of rules of political struggle between ruler and groups	n.ex./n.tr.	n.ex./tr.		

* According to degree of importance.

TABLE I. *(continued)*

Social Conditions of the Institutionalization of the Political Systems

C. DEVELOPMENT OF CHANNELS OF POLITICAL STRUGGLE (VARIABLE VIII)						
Byzantine Empire			Abbassids		Saffawids	
I	II	III	I	II	I	II
sen.	bur.	court	court	ter.	ter.	court
—			—		—	
—			—		—	
sp./sep.	sp.pol.	sp.pol.	sep.	sp.pol.	tr.	sep.
n.par.			n.par.		n.par.	
—			—		—	
cont.			?		spor.	
spor.			cont.		ra.	
spor.			spor.		ra.	
spor.			cont.		spor.	
spor.			—		—	
n.par.			—		—	
cont.			cont.	spor.	ra.	cont.
ex.tr.	n.ex.ar.	n.ex.tr.	ex.tr.		n.ex.tr.	n.ex.ar.
cont.	ap.	ap.	dec.		dec.	
dec.	ad.	dec.	ex.ec.		ex.ec.	
—	ex.ec.	ex.ec.	—		—	
pol.	el.	pol.	app.		app.	
—	—	—	c.ad.		c.ad.	
—	—	—	self		self	
—	—	—	le.		le.	
—	—	—	—		—	
3	2	1	1		1	
ex.n.tr.	ex.tr./n.tr.	ex.n.tr.	ex.n.tr.		n.ex.tr.	n.ex./n.tr.

TABLE I. *(continued)*

Social Conditions of the Institutionalization of the Political Systems

C. DEVELOPMENT OF CHANNELS OF POLITICAL STRUGGLE (VARIABLE VIII)					
Variable		Ottomans		Moslem Spain	
	I	II	III	I	II
VIII. A. Type of channels*					
1	ter.	coun.	ter.	ter.arm.	
2	r.fa.			—	
3	arm.			—	
B. Degree of embeddedness of channels	sp.pol.	sep.	sp.pol.	sp.pol.	sp.pol.
C. Membership					
1. Groups					
(1) Peasantry	n.par.			n.par.	
(2) Gentry	—			—	
(3) Aristocracy	spor.			cont.	
(4) Urban groups	spor.			spor.	
(5) Legal	ra.			ra.	
(6) Military	cont.			cont.	
(7) Religious	—			—	
(8) Cultural-secular	—			—	
(9) Bureaucracy	spor.	cont.	cont.	spor.	
2. Explication of rules of membership	n.ex.tr.	n.ex.ar.	n.ex.ar.	ex.tr.	
D. Powers of channels					
1. Extent of powers*					
(1)	exec.dec.			dec.	
(2)	ap.			exec.	
(3)	dec.			—	
2. Scope of powers					
(1)	ad.			app.	
(2)	app.			c.ad.	
(3)	c.ad.			self	le.
(4)	pol.			—	
(5)	self			—	
3. Institutionalization of powers	2			1	
E. Explication of rules of political struggle between ruler and groups	ex.tr./n.tr.	ex.tr./n.tr.	ex.n.tr.	n.ex.tr.	

* According to degree of importance.

TABLE I.   (continued)

Social Conditions of the Institutionalization of the Political Systems

C. DEVELOPMENT OF CHANNELS OF POLITICAL STRUGGLE (VARIABLE VIII)

	Rome			Spanish-American Empire			Austria	Spain	
	I	II	III	I	II	III		I	II
coun.arm.				coun.city			ter.bur.	coun.ter.par.bur.	court.
—				bur.			—	—	
—				—			—	—	
sp.pol.	sp.pol.	sp.pol.	sp.pol.	sp./sep.	sp./sep.	sp./sep.	sp.pol.	sp.pol.	sp.pol.
ra.				n.par.			ra.	n.par.	
—				—			—	—	
spor.				cont.			spor.	spor.	cont.
cont.				spor.			spor.	cont.	spor.
n.par.				ra.			cont.	n.par.	
cont.				n.par.			cont.	n.par.	
ra.				n.par.			cont.	spor.	ra.
n.par.				—			n.par.	n.par.	
spor.				cont.			cont.	cont.	ra.
ex.le.				ex.le.			ex.le.	ex.tr.	n.ex.ar.
exec.	ap.	dec.		ad.			exec.	ap.	ad.
dec.	exec.	exec.		exec.			ad.	pet.	exec.
—	—	—		—			—	exec.	
app.	self	el.		pol.			pol.	tax.	pol.
el.	app.	pol.		le.			le.	le.	
—	—	—		—			—	el.	
—				—			—	—	
—				—			—	—	
3				2	3	3	2–4	2	1
n.ex.n.tr.				n.ex.n.tr.			n.ex.n.tr.	ex.n.tr.	n.ex.n.tr.

TABLE I. (*continued*)

Social Conditions of the Institutionalization of the Political Systems

		Sweden				Russia	
C. DEVELOPMENT OF CHANNELS OF POLITICAL STRUGGLE (VARIABLE VIII)							
Variable		I	II	III	I	II	III
VIII. A. Type of channels*							
1		par.coun.			sen.	coun.,court	par.,court,arm.
2		bur.			—		
3		—			—		
B. Degree of embeddedness of channels		sep.	sep.	sep.	sp.pol.	sp.pol.	sp.pol.
C. Membership							
1. Groups							
(1) Peasantry		ra.cont.ᶠ			ra.	n.par.	n.par.
(2) Gentry		—			—		
(3) Aristocracy		cont.ᶠ			cont.		
(4) Urban groups		ra.			spor.		
(5) Legal		n.par.			n.par.		
(6) Military		n.par.			n.par.		
(7) Religious		cont.			ra.		
(8) Cultural-secular		n.par.			n.par.		
(9) Bureaucracy		cont.	ra.	n.par.	cont.		
2. Explication of rules of membership		ex.le.			n.ex.tr.	n.ex.ar.	n.ex.ar.
D. Powers of channels							
1. Extent of powers*							
(1)		ap.	cont.	ap.	ex.	ad.	ad.
(2)		ad.	dec.	ad.	—	ap.	ex.
(3)		exec.			—	—	—
2. Scope of powers*							
(1)		tax.	bu.	tax.	pol.	el.	el.
(2)		leg.	leg.	pol.	c.ad.	pol.	pol.
(3)		pol.			—	c.ad.	c.ad.
(4)		c.ad.			—		
(5)		self			—		
3. Institutionalization of powers		2	3	3	2	1	2
E. Explication of rules of political struggle between ruler and groups		ex.tr. n.tr.			n.ex.tr./ n.tr.	n.ex.n.tr.	n.ex.n.tr.

* According to degree of importance.

TABLE I. *(continued)*

Social Conditions of the Institutionalization of the Political Systems

C. DEVELOPMENT OF CHANNELS OF POLITICAL STRUGGLE (VARIABLE VIII)

Prussia		France			England		
I	II	I	II	III	I	II	III
bur.		court,ass.,par.,coun.,bur.			coun.	coun.,par.	—
—		—	—	—	—	—	—
—		—	—	—	—	—	—
sp.pol.	sp.pol.	sp./sep.	sp./sep.	sp./sep.	sp./sep.	sp./sep.	sep.
n.par.		cont.	ra.	ra.	cont.		
—		—	—	—	cont.		
cont.		cont.	spor.	cont.	cont.		
cont.	spor.	cont.	ra.	spor.	cont.		
n.par.		n.par.	spor.	cont.	spor.		
n.par.		n.par.			n.par.		
n.par.		ra.	spor.	ra.	cont.	spor.	n.par.
n.par.		n.par.			n.par.		
n.par.	spor.	ra.	spor.	spor.	cont.	spor.	ra.
n.ex.ar.	ex.le.	n.ex.ar., ex.le.			n.ex.ar., ex.le.		
exec.		ap.	ad.	dec.	ap.	dec.	dec.
ad.	dec.	exec.			ad.	cont.	exec.
—	—	—	—	—	—	—	—
pol.	app.	pol.			bu.	bu.	pol.
—	—	—	—	—	leg.	pol.	leg.
—	—	—	—	—	–	self	app.
—	—	—	—	—	—	—	c.ad.
—	—	—	—	—	—	—	self
3		2	3	2	2	3	3
n.ex.n.tr.		n.ex.n.tr.	n.ex.n.tr.	ex.n.tr.	n.ex.n.tr.	ex.tr./n.tr.	ex.tr./n.tr.

TABLE I (*continued*)

Social Conditions of the Institutionalization of the Political Systems

D. EXTENT OF DEVELOPMENT OF BUREAUCRATIC ACTIVITY (VARIABLE IX)

Variable	Greece	Mongols	Feudal Europe	Ahmenids	Carolingian Empire
IX. Scope of bureaucratic activity					
A. Spheres—General	0	0	1	1	2
1. Central level					
(1) Economic	0(1)	1	1	2	2
(2) Political	0(1)	1	1	2	2
(3) Legal	0	0	1	2	2
(4) Religious	0	0	1	1	2
(5) Educational and cultural	0	0	1	1	1
(6) Stratification	0	0	1	1	1
2. Local level					
(1) Economic	0	1	2ᶜ	0	2
(2) Political	0	1	2	0	2
(3) Legal	0	0	0	0	1
(4) Religious	0	0	0	0	1
(5) Educational and cultural	0	0	0	0	1
(6) Stratification	0	0	0	0	1
B. Type of bureaucratic activity in sphere*					
1. Economic					
(1)	...	...	...	...	...
(2)	...	...	...	...	...
2. Political					
(1)	...	...	...	...	...
(2)	...	...	...	...	...
3. Legal					
(1)	...	...	...	...	...
(2)	...	...	...	...	...
4. Religious					
(1)	...	...	...	...	...
(2)	...	...	...	...	...
5. Educational and cultural					
(1)	...	...	...	...	...
(2)	...	...	...	...	...
6. Stratification					
(1)	...	...	...	...	...
(2)	...	...	...	...	...
7. General					
(1)	...	...	...	...	...
(2)	...	...			

* According to degree of importance.

TABLE I. (continued)

Social Conditions of the Institutionalization of the Political Systems

D. EXTENT OF DEVELOPMENT OF BUREAUCRATIC ACTIVITY (VARIABLE IX)

Inca Empire	Ancient Egypt			Sassanid Persia				Ptolemies	Seleucids
	I	II	III	I	II	III	IV		
3		1				1		3	2
1	1	2	1			2		3	2
3	1	2	1			2		3	2
3	1	1	1			2		3	3
3	1	2	1			1(2)		2	3
3		1				1		1	1
1		1				2		1	1
3		1				2		0	0
3		0				1		0	0
3		0				1		0	0
2		0				1		0	0
2		0				1		0	0
1		0				1(2)		0	0
tech.		bal.				reg.		tech.	tech.
—		—				tech.		reg.	reg.
tech.		reg.				reg.		tech.	tech.
reg.		—				—		—	—
tech.		—				reg.		tech.	tech.
—		—				tech.		—	—
tech.		reg.				bal.		reg.	reg.
reg.		tech.				—		—	—
reg.		—				bal.		—	—
tech.		—				—		—	—
—		reg.				reg.		—	—
—		-				tech.		—	—
bal.	bal.	reg.	reg.(tech.)	reg.	reg.	reg.	reg.	tech.	tech.
—		—		tech.		tech.		—	—

TABLE I. *(continued)*

Social Conditions of the Institutionalization of the Political Systems

D. EXTENT OF DEVELOPMENT OF BUREAUCRATIC ACTIVITY (VARIABLE IX)						
Variable		T'ang			Sung	
	I	II	III	I	II	III
IX. Scope of bureaucratic activity						
A. Spheres—General	3	3	2	3	3	2
1. Central level						
(1) Economic	3	3	1	3	3	3
(2) Political	3	3	2	3	3	2
(3) Legal	3	3	2	3	3	2
(4) Religious	2	3	2	3	3	2
(5) Educational and cultural	3	3	2	3	3	2
(6) Stratification	2	2	2	2	2	2
2. Local level						
(1) Economic	2	2	1	2	2	1
(2) Political	2	2	3	2	2	3
(3) Legal	3	3	3	3	3	3
(4) Religious	2	2	2	2	2	2
(5) Educational and cultural	2	2	2	2	2	2
(6) Stratification	2	2	1	2	2	1
B. Type of bureaucratic activity in sphere*						
1. Economic						
(1)	reg.	reg.	reg.	reg.	reg.	reg.
(2)	tech.	tech.	tech.	tech.	tech.	tech.
2. Political						
(1)	tech.	tech.	tech.	tech.	tech.	tech.
(2)	reg.	reg.	reg.	reg.	reg.	reg.
3. Legal						
(1)	tech.	tech.	tech.	tech.	tech.	tech.
(2)	reg.	reg.	reg.	reg.	reg.	reg.
4. Religious						
(1)	reg.	reg.	reg.	reg.	reg.	reg.
(2)	tech.	tech.	tech.	tech.	tech.	tech.
5. Educational and cultural						
(1)	tech.	tech.	tech.	tech.	tech.	tech.
(2)	reg.	reg.	reg.	reg.	reg.	reg.
6. Stratification						
(1)	reg.	reg.	reg.	reg.	reg.	reg.
(2)	tech.	tech.	tech.	tech.	tech.	tech.
7. General						
(1)	reg.	reg.	reg.	reg.	reg.	reg.
(2)	tech.	tech.	tech.	tech.	tech.	tech.

* According to degree of importance.

TABLE I. (continued)

Social Conditions of the Institutionalization of the Political Systems

	Yuan	Ming	Ch'ing	Maurya I	Maurya II	Gupta	Mogul Empire I	Mogul Empire II	III
D. EXTENT OF DEVELOPMENT OF BUREAUCRATIC ACTIVITY (VARIABLE IX)									
	3	3	3	3		2		2	
	3	3	3	3		2	2	2	3
	3	3	3	3		2		3	
	3	3	3	3		3		2	
	2	3	3	1	3	1	1	1	3
	3	3	3	1		1		1	
	2	2	2	1		1	1	1	2
	2	2	2	0		0		0	
	2	2	2	0		0		0	
	3	3	3	0		0		0	
	2	2	2	0		0		0	
	2	2	2	0		0		0	
	2	2	2	0		0		0	
	reg.	reg.	reg.	reg.		tech.		tech.	
	tech.	tech.	tech.	tech.		—		reg.	
	tech.	tech.	tech.	reg.		tech.		tech.	
	reg.	reg.	reg.	tech.		reg.		reg.	
	tech.	tech.	tech.	tech.		tech.		tech.	
	reg.	reg.	reg.	reg.		reg.		—	
	reg.	reg.	reg.	—	reg.[d]	—	—	—	reg.[i]
	tech.	tech.	tech.	—	tech.[d]	—	—		
	tech.	tech.	tech.	—	—	—	—		
	reg.	reg.	reg.	—	—	—	—		
	reg.	reg.	reg.	—	—	—	—	—	reg.
	tech.	tech.	tech.	—	—	—	—		—
	reg.	reg.	reg.	reg.		tech.	tech.	tech.	reg.
	tech.	tech.	tech.	tech.		reg.	reg.	reg.	tech.

TABLE I. (*continued*)

Social Conditions of the Institutionalization of the Political Systems

D. EXTENT OF DEVELOPMENT OF BUREAUCRATIC ACTIVITY (VARIABLE IX)							
Variable	Byzantine Empire			Abbassids		Saffawids	
	I	II	III	I	II	I	II
IX. Scope of bureaucratic activity							
A. Spheres—General		3		2		2	
1. Central level							
(1) Economic	3	3	2	3		3	
(2) Political	2	2	3	3		3	
(3) Legal	3	3	3	2		3	
(4) Religious	2	2	2	1		3	
(5) Educational and cultural	2	3	2	2		2	
(6) Stratification	2	3	2	3		3	
2. Local level							
(1) Economic		1		2		2	
(2) Political		1		2		3	
(3) Legal		2		1		2	
(4) Religious	2	1		2			
(5) Educational and cultural		2		1		2	
(6) Stratification		1		1		2	
B. Type of bureaucratic activity in sphere[*]							
1. Economic							
(1)		reg.		tech.		tech.	
(2)		tech.		reg.		reg.	
2. Political							
(1)		reg.		tech.		reg.	
(2)		tech.		reg.		tech.	
3. Legal							
(1)		reg.		tech.		reg.	
(2)		—		reg.		tech.	
4. Religious							
(1)	reg.			—		reg.	
(2)	—			→		tech.	
5. Educational and cultural							
(1)	tech.			tech.		tech.	
(2)	reg.			—		—	
6. Stratification							
(1)	—			reg.		reg.	
(2)	—			—		—	
7. General							
(1)	reg.	reg.	reg.	bal.	reg.	reg.	bal.
(2)	—	tech.	—	—	—	—	—

[*] According to degree of importance.

TABLE I. (continued)
Social Conditions of the Institutionalization of the Political Systems

D. EXTENT OF DEVELOPMENT OF BUREAUCRATIC ACTIVITY (VARIABLE IX)

Ottomans			Moslem Spain		Rome			Spanish-American Empire		
I	II	III	I	II	I	II	III	I	II	III
3			2		1	1	2	1	3	2
3			3		1	1	3	1	3	2
3			3		1	2	3	1	3	2
3			2		2	2	2	1	3	2
3			1		1	1	3	1	2	2
2			2		1	2	1	1	2	2
1			1		2	2	3	1	3	2
2			2		1	2	3	1	3	2
2			2		1	2	3	1	1	1
2			1		1	1	2	1	1	1
2			1		2	2	3	1	1	1
1			1		1	2	1	1	2	1
2			1		1	2	3	1	2	1
tech.			tech.		tech.			reg.		
reg.			reg.		reg.			tech.		
tech,			tech.		tech.			reg.		
reg.			reg.		—			tech.		
tech.			tech.		tech.			reg.		
reg.			—		—			tech.		
reg.			tech.		reg.			reg.		
tech.			—		—			tech.		
tech.			tech.		tech.			reg.		
—			—		—			tech.		
reg.			—		reg.			bal.		
—			—		—			—		
reg.	bal.	reg.	?	tech.	tech.	bal.	reg.	reg.	reg.	reg.
(tech.)		(tech.)		reg.	reg.		tech.	tech.	tech.	(tech.)

TABLE I. *(continued)*

Social Conditions of the Institutionalization of the Political Systems

D. EXTENT OF DEVELOPMENT OF BUREAUCRATIC ACTIVITY (VARIABLE IX)						
Variable	Austria	Spain			Sweden	
		I	II	I	II	III
IX. Scope of bureaucratic activity						
A. Spheres—General	3	2	1(2)	2	2	2
1. Central level						
(1) Economic	2	1	2	2	3	1
(2) Political	2	3	2	1	2	1
(3) Legal	3	3	2	2	2	3
(4) Religious	2	2	2(3)	2	1	2
(5) Educational and cultural	2	1	2	3	2	2
(6) Stratification	?	2	1	1	2	1
2. Local level						
(1) Economic	3	1	1	2	2	1
(2) Political	3	2	2	1	2	1
(3) Legal	3	2	2	2	2	2
(4) Religious	3	1(2)	1(2)ᶜ	2	1	2
(5) Educational and cultural	3	1	1	2	2	2
(6) Stratification	1	1	1	1	1	1
B. Type of bureaucratic activity in sphere*						
1. Economic						
(1)	reg.	reg.		reg.	reg.	reg.
(2)	—	—		—	tech.	—
2. Political						
(1)	tech.	reg.		—	tech.	—
(2)	reg.	—		—	reg.	—
3. Legal						
(1)	tech.	tech.		reg.	tech.	tech.
(2)	reg.	—		tech.	reg.	—
4. Religious						
(1)	reg.	tech.		reg.	—	reg.
(2)	—	reg.		—	—	—
5. Educational and cultural						
(1)	reg.	reg.		reg.	tech.	tech.
(2)	tech.	reg.		tech.	reg.	—
6. Stratification						
(1)	—	tech.		—	reg.	—
(2)	—	—		—	—	—
7. General						
(1)	reg.	reg.	reg.	reg.	bal.	reg.
(2)	tech.	tech.	—	tech.	—	tech.

* According to degree of importance.

TABLE I. *(continued)*

Social Conditions of the Institutionalization of the Political Systems

D. EXTENT OF DEVELOPMENT OF BUREAUCRATIC ACTIVITY (VARIABLE IX)

Russia I	Russia II	Russia III	Prussia I	Prussia II	France I	France II	France III	England I	England II	England III
3	2	3	2	3	2	3	2	2	2	1
2	1	2	2	3	1	3	2	2	1	1
3	2	2	2	3	1	3	2	2	2	1
3	2	3	3	2	2	3	2	2	1	1
2	2	3		1	1	2	1	3	3	2
2	2	3		1	1	3	2	2	1	1
3	3	3	1	2	1	2	1	2	1	1
2	1	2	2	1	2	2	2	1	1	1[d]
2	3	2	2	3	2	2	2	1	1	1
2	1	2	2	2	2	2	2	1	1	1
2	2	2	1		1	1	1	1	1	1
1	1	1	2	2	1	1	2	1	1	1
2	2	2	1		1	2	2	1	1	1

Russia I	Russia II	Russia III	Prussia I	Prussia II	France I	France II	France III	England I	England II	England III
reg.		reg.	reg.	reg.				bal.	tech.	tech.
—				tech.	tech.			reg.		
reg.			reg.		reg.			reg.		
tech.					tech.			—		
tech.			reg.	tech.	tech.			reg.	tech.	tech.
—				—	reg.			—	—	
reg.				—	reg.			reg.	tech.	tech.
—				—	tech.			tech.		
reg.			tech.		reg.			reg.	tech.	tech.
—				—	tech.			tech.		
tech.				reg.	reg.			tech.		
reg.				—	tech.			—		
reg.	reg.	reg.	reg.	reg.	reg.	reg.	reg.	reg.	reg.	tech.
(tech.)	—	(tech.)	(tech.)	tech.	tech.	—	tech.	tech.	tech.	

TABLE I. (continued)

Social Conditions of the Institutionalization of the Political Systems

D. EXTENT OF DEVELOPMENT OF BUREAUCRATIC ACTIVITY (VARIABLE IX)

Variable	Greece	Mongols	Feudal Europe	Ahmenids	Carolingian Empire
C. Autonomy of bureaucratic organization—general	0(1)	0(1)	1(2)	1	0
1. Roles	0(1)	1	1(2)	1	0
2. Goals	0(1)	1	1	1(2)	1
3. Rules	0(1)	0(1)	1	1	0
D. Extent of professionalization of bureaucratic roles	0(1)	0(1)	1	1	1(0)
E. Type of remuneration of bureaucracy*					
1.	hoc.	pat.	gr.	pat.gr.	gr.hoc., con.
2.	con	hoc.	pat.hoc.	—	—
3.	hon.	—	—	—	—
4.	—	—	—	—	—
5.	—	—	—	—	—
F. Extent of functional departmentalization	1	0(1)	0	1(2)	1

* * gr.hoc. fa.

Variable	I	T'ang II	III	I	Sung II	III
C. Autonomy of bureaucratic organization—general	3	3	3	3	3	3
1. Roles	2	3	3	3	3	3
2. Goals	2	2	2	2	2	2
3. Rules	3	3	3	3	3	3
D. Extent of professionalization of bureaucratic roles	3(2)	3(2)	3(2)	3(2)	3(2)	3(2)
E. Type of remuneration of bureaucracy*						
1.	con.			con.gr.		
2.	bri.			bri.		
3.	—	—	—	—	—	—
4.	—	—	—	—	—	—
5.	—	—	—	—	—	—
F. Extent of functional departmentalization	3	3	3	3	3	3

* According to degree of importance.

TABLE I. *(continued)*

Social Conditions of the Institutionalization of the Political Systems

D. EXTENT OF DEVELOPMENT OF BUREAUCRATIC ACTIVITY (VARIABLE IX)

Inca Empire	Ancient Egypt			Sassanid Persia				Ptolemies	Seleucids
	I	II	III	I	II	III	IV		
1	1	2	1		1			1	1
1	1	2	1	1	1	2	1	1	1
1	0	1	2			1		1	1
1		0				1		1	1
1		1			1			2	1
pat.		gr.		pat.	pat.	**	pat.	gr.	gr.
gr.		fa.		**	**	pat.	*+	bri.	—
—		con.				—		—	—
—		pat.				—		—	—
—		hoc.				—		—	—
2	1	2	1			1(2)		3	1

Yuan	Ming	Ch'ing	Maurya		Gupta	Mogul Empire		
			I	II		I	II	III
3	3	3	1		1	1		
2	3	3	2		2	1		
2	2	2	1		1	1		
3	3	3	1		1	1		
3(2)	3(2)	3(2)	1		1	1		
con.gr.	con.gr.	con.gr.	con.		con.	gr.		
bri.	bri.	bri.	—		—	con.		
—	—	—	—		—	—		
—	—	—	—		—	—		
—	—	—	—		—	—		
3	3	3	2	3	1	1	2	1

TABLE I. *(continued)*

Social Conditions of the Institutionalization of the Political Systems

D. EXTENT OF DEVELOPMENT OF BUREAUCRATIC ACTIVITY (VARIABLE IX)

Variable	Byzantine Empire			Abbassids		Saffawids	
	I	II	III	I	II	I	II
C. Autonomy of bureaucratic organization—general	2	2(3)	2	2		2	
1. Roles	2	3	2	3	2	1	2
2. Goals	2	2	3	2		2	
3. Rules	2	3	2	1		1	
D. Extent of professionalization of bureaucratic roles	2	3	2	2	2(1)	1	2
E. Type of remuneration of bureaucracy*							
1.	gr.			fa.		fa.	
2.	con.			con.		gr.	
3.	—			bri.		bri.	
4.	—			—		—	
5.	—			—		—	
F. Extent of functional departmentalization			1	3	2	1	3

Variable	Austria	Spain		Sweden		
		I	II	I	II	III
C. Autonomy of bureaucratic organization—general	1(3)	2	2	2	2	2
1. Roles	3	2(3)	2	3	2	3
2. Goals	2	1	1	1	2	1
3. Rules	3	2	2	2	2	3
D. Extent of professionalization of bureaucratic roles	2	2	1		2	
E. Type of remuneration of bureaucracy*						
1.	con.	gr.		con.	con.	
2.	—	con.		fa.	—	—
3.	—	hoc.		serv.		
4.	—	hon.		—		
5.	—	—		—		
F. Extent of functional departmentalization	3	2	2	2	3	2

* According to degree of importance.

TABLE I. *(continued)*

Social Conditions of the Institutionalization of the Political Systems

D. EXTENT OF DEVELOPMENT OF BUREAUCRATIC ACTIVITY (VARIABLE IX)

I	Ottomans II	III	Moslem Spain I	II	Rome I	II	III	Spanish-American Empire I	II	III
2(1)	2(3)	2(1)	1		1(2)	1(2)	2(3)	1	3	3
2	3	2	1		1	1	3	1	3	3
	2		1		1	1	2	1	3	3
	1		1		2	2	2	1	3	3
	2		1	2	1	2	3	1	3	3
fa.			fa.		con.			fa.		
con.			con.		bri.			con.		
bri.			bri.		gr.			bri.		
—			—		fq.			—		
—			—					—		
2	3	1	2	3	3			1	3	3

I	Russia II	III	Prussia I	II	France I	II	III	England I	II	III
1(2)	1	1(2)	2	3	1	2	3	2	2	2(3)
2	1(2)	2	3	3	1	2	3	2	2	3
1	1	1	2	3	1	2	3	2	2	1
2	1	2	2	3	1	2	2	2	2	2
	2(1)		2	2	1	3	2	1	2	2
con.			con.	con.	con.			con.		
hon.			hoc.	fa.	bri.			hon.		
bri.			hon.	—	—			—		
—			—	—	—			—		
—			—	—	—			—		
1(2)	1(2)	2	2	3	1	3	3	3c		

TABLE II.

Scope of Political Struggle in the Historical Bureaucratic Societies

Variable	Inca Empire	Ancient Egypt		
		I	II	III
I. Major orientations and references of ruler's goals				
A. Content	cul.as.	cul.as.	cul.as.	cul.as.
B. Complexity	—	pol.coll.	pol.coll.	pol.coll.
C. Heterogeneity	—	—		
II. Autonomy of political goals of ruler	1	2	2	1
III. Extent of differentiation—general	1(2)	2	3	2
1. Peasantry	1	1	2	1
2. Gentry	—	—		
3. Aristocracy	3	2	2	3
4. Urban group	1(2)	1	3	2
5. Legal	—	1	2	2
6. Military	—[b]	1	2	3
7. Religious	3	2	3	3
8. Cultural-secular	—	—	—	—
IV. Self-regulation of groups				
A. Traditional	3	4	3	4
B. Nontraditional	1	1	2	1
V. Extent of political participation of groups				
A. Intensivity—general	1	1	1	2
1. Peasantry	1		1	
2. Gentry	—	—	—	—
3. Aristocracy	1(2)	1	2	1
4. Urban group	1		1	
5. Legal	—	1	1	2
6. Military	—	1	1	2
7. Religious	1	1	2	1
8. Cultural-secular	—	—	—	—
9. Bureaucracy	1	1	2	2
B. Articulation of political goals of groups—general	1	1	2(1)	1(2)
1. Peasantry	1	1	1	1
2. Gentry	—		—	
3. Aristocracy	1	1	2	1
4. Urban group	1	1	1	1
5. Legal	—	1	1	2
6. Military	—	1	1	2
7. Religious	1	1	2	1
8. Cultural-secular	—		—	
9. Bureaucracy	—	1	2	1
C. Extent of crystallization of political organization in society	0		1	

TABLE II. *(continued)*
Scope of Political Struggle in the Historical Bureaucratic Societies

Sassanid Persia				Ptolemies	Seleucids	T'ang		
I	II	III	IV			I	II	III
		pol.coll. cul.coll.[c] self		self ec.coll. —	self pol.coll. —	cul.as. pol.coll. self	cul.as. pol.coll. —	cul.as. pol.coll. self
2	1	3	1	3	3	4	4	2
2	2	3	2	3	4	4	4	4
2	2	3	2	1	2	3	2	2
2	2	4	2[b]	—	—	4	5	5
2	2	3	2	?	4	4	3	3
3	2	4	2	3	6	3	4	5
2	2	2	2	—	—	—	—	—
2	2	2	2	5	5	3	4	5
3	3	4	3	6	5	4	3	3
—	—	—	—	—	—	—	—	—
		4		2	4	3	3	4
		1		2	4	2	2	3
1	2	2(1)	2	1	2	1	1	1(2)[c]
1	2(1)	1	1	2	1	2	2	2(3)
1	2(3)	2	1	—	—	1	1	1(2)[c]
2(1)	2	2	2	1	2	2	2	2(3)
						2(3)	2	2
1	1	2	1	1	2	0(1)	1	1[c]
						1(2)	2(1)	2(1)
1	1	1	1	—	—	—	—	—
1	2	1	2	1	1	1	1	2
1	2	2	2	2	1	2	1	2
—	—	—	—	—	—	—	—	—
1	1	2	1	1	1	1	1(2)	1(2)[c]
						2	2(3)	2(3)
1(2)	1	2(1)	1	1	1	2(1)	2(1)	2
1	1	1	1	1	1	1	1	1[d]
1	1	1(2)	1	—	—	1(2)	1(2)	1(2)
2(1)	2	2	2(3)	1	2	1	1	1
1	1	1(2)	1	1	2	1(2)	1(2)	1(2)
1	1	1	1	—	—	—	—	—
1	2	1	2	1	1	1	1	1
1(2)	2(1)	2	1	2	1	1	1	1
		—		—	—	—	—	—
2(1)	1	2(1)	1	1	1	2(1)	2(1)	2
		1		0	0(1)	1(2)	1(2)	2

TABLE II. (*continued*)

Scope of Political Struggle in the Historical Bureaucratic Societies

Variable	I	Sung II	III	Yuan	Ming
I. Major orientations and references of ruler's goals					
A. Content	cul.as.	cul.as.	cul.as.	cul.as.	cul.as.
B. Complexity	pol.coll.	pol.coll.	pol.coll.	pol.coll., self	pol.coll., self
C. Heterogeneity	self	—	self	—	—
II. Autonomy of political goals of ruler	4	4	2	4	4
III. Extent of differentiation—general	5	5	5	5	5
1. Peasantry	3	3	2	2	3
2. Gentry	5(6)	5(6)	5(6)	6	6
3. Aristocracy	3	3	3	4[d]	2
4. Urban group	5	5	5	5(6)	6
5. Legal	—			—	—
6. Military	3	3	5	4	4
7. Religious	3	3	3	4	2
8. Cultural-secular	—	—	—	—	—
IV. Self-regulation of groups					
A. Traditional	3	3	4	3	3
B. Nontraditional	2	2	3	2	2
V. Extent of political participation of groups					
A. Intensitivity—general	{ 1 / 2	1 / 2	1(2)[c] / 2(3)	{ 1[e] / 2 }	{ 1[e] / 2 }
1. Peasantry	1(2)	1(2)	2(3)	1(2)	1(2)
2. Gentry	{ 1(2) / 2(3)	1(2) / 2(3)	1(2)[c] / 2(3)	2(3)	2(3)
3. Aristocracy	1	1	2	2[d]	1
4. Urban group	{ 1 / 2	1 / 2	1[c] / 2	{ 1[e] / 2 }	{ 1[e] / 2(1) }
5. Legal	—	—	—	—	—
6. Military	{ 1 / 1	1 / 2	1[c] / 2	1(2)	1(2)[c]
7. Religious	1	1	1	2	1
8. Cultural-secular	—	—	—	—	—
9. Bureaucracy	{ 1(2) / 2(3)	1(2) / 2(3)	1(2)[c] / 2(3)	{ 1[e] / 2 }	{ 1[e] / 2 }
B. Articulation of political goals of groups—general	2	2	2	2	2
1. Peasantry	1	1	1[d]	1[g]	1[d]
2. Gentry	2(1)	2(1)	2(1)	2(1)	2(1)
3. Aristocracy	1	1	1	1	1
4. Urban group	2	2	2	2(1)	2(1)
5. Legal	—	—	—	—	—
6. Military	1	1	1	1	1
7. Religious	1	1	1	1	1
8. Cultural-secular	—	—	—	—	—
9. Bureaucracy	2	2	2(3)	2	2
C. Extent of crystallization of political organization in society	2(1)	2(1)	2	1(2)	1(2)

TABLE II. (*continued*)
Scope of Political Struggle in the Historical Bureaucratic Societies

Ch'ing	Maurya I	Maurya II	Gupta	I	Mogul Empire II	III
cul.as.		pol.coll. cul.coll.	pol.coll.		pol.coll.	
pol.coll., self	self	—	self		self	
—	—	—	—	—	—	—
4	3	4	2	3	4	4
5	4		4	3	4	3
3	3		3		3	
6	—		—	—	—	—
3	4		4		4	
6	5		5	3	5	3
—	—		—		2	
4	7		5	3	5	5d
2	7		7		7e	
—			—	—	—	—
3	5		5		5	
2	1		1		1	
{ 1d / 2 }	1		1		1	
1(2)	1		1		1	
2(3)	—		—		—	
2c	3		3		3	
{ 1d / 2 }	1		1		1	
—	—		—		—	
1(2)e	?		?		—	
1	1		3d		1	
—	—		—		—	
{ 1d / 2 }	1		1		1	
2	1		1		1	
1g	1		1		1	
2(1)	—		—		—	
1	2		2		1	
2(1)	1		1		1	
—	—		—		—	
1	?		?		—	
1	2(3)		2(3)		?	
—	—		—		—	
2	1		1		1	
1(2)	1		1		2	

TABLE II. (*continued*)

Scope of Political Struggle in the Historical Bureaucratic Societies

Variable	I	Byzantine Empire II	III	Abbassids I	II
I. Major orientations and references of ruler's goals					
A. Content	pol.coll.	pol.coll.	self	cul.coll.	
B. Complexity	self	cul.coll.,ec.coll.	pol.coll.	self	
C. Heterogeneity	—	—	—	pol.coll.	
II. Autonomy of political goals of ruler	4	5	3	3	1
III. Extent of differentiation—general	4	7	6	5	6
1. Peasantry	3	6	2	2	2
2. Gentry	—	—	—	—	—
3. Aristocracy	4	7	6	?	
4. Urban group	6	7	5	7	5
5. Legal	5	7	7	5	5ᶜ
6. Military	3	4	5	3	6
7. Religious	7	7	8	—	—
8. Cultural-secular	2	5	4	—	—
IV. Self-regulation of groups		⎰ 4 ⎱			
A. Traditional		⎱ 2ᶜ ⎰			4
B. Nontraditional		3ᵈ			3
V. Extent of political participation of groups					
A. Intensity—general	1	2(3)	2	2(3)	2(3)
1. Peasantry	1	2	1	1	1(2)
2. Gentry	—	—	—	—	—
3. Aristocracy	3	3	3	2	1
4. Urban group	1(2)	2	2(1)	3	2
5. Legal	2	2	2	2	2(3)
6. Military	1	2	2	2	3
7. Religious	2	2(3)	2	—	—
8. Cultural-secular	1	1	1	—	—
9. Bureaucracy	2	3	2	3	3
B. Articulation of political goals of groups—general	1(2)	2	2(1)	1(2)	1
1. Peasantry	1	2	1	1	1
2. Gentry		—			—
3. Aristocracy	2	2	2	2	2
4. Urban group	1	2	1	2	2
5. Legal	2	2	2	1	1
6. Military	1	1(2)	1	1	1
7. Religious	2	3	3	—	—
8. Cultural-secular	2	3	2	—	—
9. Bureaucracy	1	2	2	1	1
C. Extent of crystallization of political organization in society	1(2)	2	2(1)	2	1

TABLE II. (continued)
Scope of Political Struggle in the Historical Bureaucratic Societies

	Saffawids		Ottomans			Moslem Spain	
I		II	I		III	I	II
	self cul.coll.	pol.coll., self cul.coll.	pol.coll., self cul.coll.	pol.coll., self —			cul.coll. self
—	—	—	—	—		—	—
1	3	2	4	3		2	3
4	5	4	6	6			6
2	2	3	2	2			3
—	—	—	—	—			—
4	2	5	3	3		7	5
2	6	5	6	6			6
4	5c	4	7	7c			4c
2	4	3	7	6		5	6
—	—	—	—	—		—	—
—	—	—	—	—			—
	3		4				4
	2		2				3
	2	1(2)	2	3			2(3)
	1	1	1	1			1
	—	—	—	—			—
	2	3	1	1			3
	2	1	2	3			2
	2	2	2	3			2
	3	1	2	3			3
	—	—	—	—			—
	—						
	2	1	3	3			1
	1	1	1	1(2)			1(2)
	1	1	1	1			1
	—	—	—	—			—
	2	1	1	1			2
	1	1	1	2			1(2)
	1	1	1	2			1
	1	1	1	1			1
	—	—	—	—			—
	—	—	—	—			—
	1	1	1	1			1
	2(1)	2(1)	1	2			2(1)

TABLE II. *(continued)*

Scope of Political Struggle in the Historical Bureaucratic Societies

Variable		Rome			Spanish-American Empire	
	I	II	III	I	II	III
I. Major orientations and references of ruler's goals						
A. Content	pol.coll.	pol.coll.	pol.coll.	self,pol.coll.	pol.coll.	pol.coll.
B. Complexity	cul.poll.	cul.coll.	self	cul.coll.	cul.coll.	ec.coll.
C. Heterogeneity	self	self	–	–	ec.coll.	cul.coll.
D.	–	–	–	–	–	soc.gr.[c]
II. Autonomy of political goals of ruler	3	4	4	5	4	5
III. Extent of differentiation—general	5	4	4	{ 4 3	6 4	7 3[b] }
1. Peasantry	2	2	3	2	3	2
2. Gentry		–		–	4	4[c]
3. Aristocracy	4	4	1	7	6	6
4. Urban group	6	5	3	{ 5 4	6 4	7 4[b] }
5. Legal	2	3	4	3	6	7
6. Military	5	5	5	1	1	1
7. Religious	3	3	4	5	6	7
8. Cultural-secular	4	3	1		–	
IV. Self-regulation of groups						
A. Traditional	4	3	2	{ 1 5	1 3	1 3[b] }
B. Nontraditional	2	1	3	{ 1 1	2 1	3 1[b] }
V. Extent of political participation of groups						
A. Intensitivity—general	2	1	2	2	2	3
1. Peasantry	1	1	ı	1	2	1
2. Gentry		–		1	1	1(2)
3. Aristocracy	3	1	1	3	2	2
4. Urban group	1	2	2	1	2	3
5. Legal	No participation			1	2	3
6. Military	2	1	3	No participation		
7. Religious	1	1	2	2	3	2
8. Cultural-secular	2	1	1	–	–	–
9. Bureaucracy	1	1(2)	2	1	2	2
B. Articulation of political goals of groups—general	2	1	2	2	2	3
1. Peasantry	1	1	1	1	2	1
2. Gentry	–	–	–	1	1(2)	1
3. Aristocracy	3	1	1	3	2	2
4. Urban group	2(1)	2	1	1	2	3
5. Legal	1	1	1	1	2	3
6. Military	2	1	3	1	1	1
7. Religious	1	1	2	2	3	2
8. Cultural-secular	2	1	1	–	–	–
9. Bureaucracy	1	1(2)	2	1	2	2
C. Extent of crystallization of political organization in society	2(3)	1	1(2)	1(2)	2	2(3)

TABLE II. (continued)
Scope of Political Struggle in the Historical Bureaucratic Societies

Austria	I	Spain / II	I	Sweden / II	III
pol.coll.	pol.coll.	pol.coll.		pol.coll.	
ec.coll., cul.coll.	cul.coll.	self		—	
—	ec.coll.	cul.coll.		—	
—	—	—		—	
5	3	4	5	5	4[b]
6	5	4	5	6	7
5	4	4	7	4	8
—		—		—	
7	4	6[b]	4	8	6
6	6	3	3	5	6
8	4	4	3	5	6[d]
6	7	3	7	6	6[d]
6	8	8	8	5	5
7	6	4	5	8	8
3	4	2		3	
2	2	2		4	
2	3	2	3	3	3
2	3	1	3	2	3
—		—		—	
2	3	3	2	3	3
2	3	2	2	2	2
3	1	1	1	1	1
3	1	1	1	1	1
2	3	2	3	2	2
2	1	1	1	3	2
3	3	2	2	1	1
1(2)	2	2	2	3	2
1	1	1	1	2	2[g]
—		—		—	
1	3	2	3	3	3
1	1	1	1	2	1
2	1	1	1	1	1
1	1	1	1	1	1
3	2	2	3	2	2
3	3	1	1	3	3
3	1	1	1	1	1
1(2)	2	2(3)	2	2(3)	2(3)

TABLE II. (*continued*)

Scope of Political Struggle in the Historical Bureaucratic Societies

Variable	I	Russia II	III	Prussia I	II
I. Major orientations and references of ruler's goals					
A. Content	pol.coll.	self	pol.coll.	pol.coll.	pol.coll.
B. Complexity	ec.coll.	—	ec.coll.		self
C. Heterogeneity		—			—
D.		—			—
II. Autonomy of political goals of ruler	5	3	4	5	4
III. Extent of differentiation—general	5	4	5	5	6
1. Peasantry	4	3	3	3	5[d]
2. Gentry		—	—[e]		—[e]
3. Aristocracy	5	6	7	6	7
4. Urban group	5	3	4	8	6
5. Legal	2	2	3	3	5
6. Military	6	3	5	8	8
7. Religious	5	5	5	4	4
8. Cultural-secular	3	3	5	4	6
IV. Self-regulation of groups					
A. Traditional		2		3	2[f]
B. Nontraditional		3		2	2
V. Extent of political participation of groups					
A. Intensitivity—general	2	2	3	2	2
1. Peasantry	1	2	3	1	1
2. Gentry	—			—	
3. Aristocracy	2	3	3[d]	2	3
4. Urban group	2	1	2	2	2(1)
5. Legal	1	1	1	2	1
6. Military	1	3	2	1	1
7. Religious	2	2	2	1	1
8. Cultural-secular	1	1	3	1	2
9. Bureaucracy	2	2	3	1	2
B. Articulation of political goals of groups—general	1	1	2	2	2
1. Peasantry	1	1	1	1	1
2. Gentry	—	—	—		—
3. Aristocracy	1	2	3	2	3
4. Urban group	1	1	2	2	2
5. Legal	1	1	1	2	1
6. Military	1	1	1	1	1
7. Religious	2	1	2	1	1
8. Cultural-secular	2	2	3	1	3
9. Bureaucracy	1	1	2	1	2
C. Extent of crystallization of political organization in society	1(2)	1(2)	1(2)	2(1)	2

TABLE II. (continued)
Scope of Political Struggle in the Historical Bureaucratic Societies

I	France II	III	I	England II	III
pol.coll.	pol.coll. ec.coll. cul.coll.	pol.coll. ec.coll. cul.coll. soc. gr.	pol.coll. cul.coll.	pol.coll. ec.coll. – –	pol.coll. soc. gr.
4	5	3	5	4	5
6	6	7	6	7(8)	8(9)
5	5	6	6	7	8
–	–	–	5	8	9
7	6	7	6	7	7
5	6	8	6	8	9
7	7	8	5	7	9
5	5	5	3	5	6
6	6	6	6	7	6
4	6	8	5	7	8
4	2	2	2	1	1
2	3	3	3	4	5
2	2	3	2	3	3
1	2	2	2	2	2
		–	2	3	3
3	2	3	3	3	3
2	1	3	2	2	3
2	2	3	3	2	2
2	No participation		2	No participation	
2	2	2	2	3	2
1	2	3	1	1	2
1	2	3	1	1	1
2	2	3	2(3)	2(3)	3
1	1	1	2	1	1
–	–	–	2	3	3
2	3	3	3	2	2
2	2	3	2	2	3
1	2	3	3	2	1
1	No articulation		3	No articulation	
3	2	2	3	3	2
1	2	3	1	1	2
1	2	3	1	1	1
2	2(1)	2(3)	2	2(3)	2(3)

TABLE II. *(continued)*

Scope of Political Struggle in the Historical Bureaucratic Societies

Variable	*Inca Empire*	I	*Ancient Egypt* II	III
D. Extent of participation of groups in political organization—general	1	1	2	2(1)
1. Peasantry	1	1	1	1
2. Gentry	—		—	1
3. Aristocracy	1	2	2	2
4. Urban group	1	1	1	1
5. Legal	—	1	1	1
6. Military	—	1	2	2
7. Religious	1	1	2	2
8. Cultural-secular	—		—	
9. Bureaucracy	1	1	2	2
E. General extent of participation of groups	1	1	2(1)	1(2)
VI. Rebellions	1	1	2	2
VII. Types of policies *				
1.	acc.	acc.crea.	acc.crea.	acc.crea.
2.	pres.	reg.serv.	reg.pres.	reg.
3.	serv.	pres.	serv.	pres.serv.
4.	serv./reg.	—		
5.	—	—		
6.	—	—		

Variable	I	*Sung* II	III	*Yuan*	*Ming*
D. Extent of participation of groups in political organization—general	2	2	3	2	2
1. Peasantry	1	1	2	1	1
2. Gentry	2	2	3	2	2
3. Aristocracy	1	1	2	2	1
4. Urban group	2	2	2	2	2
5. Legal		—		—	—
6. Military	2	2	3	2	2
7. Religious	1	1	2	2	1
8. Cultural-secular	—	—	—	—	—
9. Bureaucracy	3	3	3	3	3
E. General extent of participation of groups	1(2) / 2(1)	2(1) / 2(1)	1(2) / 2	1(2) / 2	1(2) / 2
VI. Rebellions	1	2	3	1	1
VII. Types of policies*					
1.	reg.	reg.	reg.	reg.	reg.
2.	serv.	serv.	pres.	acc.	serv.
3.	prom.	acc.	serv. ᵉ	serv.	prom.
4.	acc.	pres.	prom.	pres.	pres.
5.	pres.	prom.	crea.	prom.	acc.
6.	crea.	crea.		crea.	crea.

* According to degree of importance.

TABLE II. (continued)
Scope of Political Struggle in the Historical Bureaucratic Societies

I	Sassanid Persia II	III	IV	Ptolemies	Seleucids	I	T'ang II	III
2(1)	2(1)	2	2(1)	1	1	2	2	3
1	1	1	1	1	1	1	1	2
(1)	1	2(1)	1	—	—	2	2	3
1	2(3)	2	2(3)	1	1	3	2	2
1	1	1(2)	1	1	2	1	1	2
1	1	1	1	—	—	—	—	—
1(2)	2	1(2)	2	1	1	2	3	3
2(1)	2(1)	2	1(2)	1	1	2	1	2
		—		—	—	—	—	—
2	2	2(3)	1	1	1	3	3	3
						{ 1	1(2)	1 }
1(2)	1(2)	2	1	1	1	{ 2(1)	2(1)	2 }
1	2(3)	2(1)	2(3)	2(3)	1(2)	1	1	3
crea.	crea.	crea.	crea.	acc.	reg.	reg.	reg.	reg.
acc.	acc.	reg.	pres.	pres.	pres.	serv.	serv.	pres.
pres.	pres.	pres.	reg.	reg.	prom.	prom.	pres.	serv.
reg.	reg.	prom.	—	serv.	—	crea.	acc.	acc.
—		—		—	—	acc.	prom.	prom.
—			—		—	pres.	crea.	crea.

Ch'ing	Maurya I	II	Gupta	Mogul Empire I	II	III
2	1		1		2	
1	1		1		1	
2	—		—		—	
2	3		e		3	
2	1		1		1	
—	—		—		—	
2	e		1		—	
1	3		3		e	
—	—		—		—	
3	1		1		1	
{ 1(2)						
2 }	1		1		1	
1	1		1		3	
reg.	reg.	serv.	acc.	acc.	acc.	reg. pres.
serv.	acc.	crea.	serv.	reg.	reg.	acc.
acc.	serv.	acc.	reg.	—	—	—
pres.	—	reg.	—	—	—	—
prom.	—	—	—	—	—	—
crea.	—	—	—	—	—	—

TABLE II. (*continued*)

Scope of Political Struggle in the Historical Bureaucratic Societies

Variable	Byzantine Empire I	II	III	Abbassids I	II
D. Extent of participation of groups in political organization—general	2(1)	2	2(1)	2	2
1. Peasantry	1	2(1)	1	1	1
2. Gentry	—	—		—	—
3. Aristocracy	3	2	2	1	1
4. Urban group	3	2	2	2(3)	2(3)
5. Legal	2	2	2	1	1
6. Military	1	2	1	1	1
7. Religious	2	2	2	—	
8. Cultural-secular	1	2	1	—	
9. Bureaucracy	2	2	2	1(2)	1(2)
E. General extent of participation of groups	2(1)	2	2(1)	2	1(2)
VI. Rebellions	1	2	3	2	3
VII. Types of policies*					
1.	reg.	reg.	reg.	pres.	crea.
2.	pres.	prom.	pres.	crea.	acc.
3.	serv.	serv.	serv.	prom.	reg.
4.		pres.	—	reg.	—
5.	—	—	—	—	—
6.	—	—	—	—	—

Variable	Rome I	II	III	Spanish-American Empire I	II	III
D. Extent of participation of groups in political organization—general	2(3)	1(2)	2	2	2	3
1. Peasantry	1	1	1	1	2	1
2. Gentry	—	—	—	1	1(2)	1(2)
3. Aristocracy	3	1	1	3	2	2
4. Urban group	3	2	1	1	2	3
5. Legal	1	1	1	1	2	3
6. Military	3	2(1)	3	1	1	1
7. Religious	1	1	1	2	3	2
8. Cultural-secular	2	1	1	1	3	3
9. Bureaucracy	1	1(2)	2	1	2	2
E. General extent of participation of groups	2	1	3	1(2)	2	2(3)
VI. Rebellions	2	1	3	1		
VII. Types of policies*						
1.	reg.	prom.	prom.	acc.	reg.	reg.
2.	prom.	serv.	pres.	pres.	acc.	acc.
3.	serv.	pres.	crea.	—	pres.	prom.
4.	crea.	crea.	serv.	—	—	serv.
5.	—	—	—	—	—	—
6.	—	—	—	—	—	—

* According to degree of importance.

TABLE II. (continued)
Scope of Political Struggle in the Historical Bureaucratic Societies

	Saffawide		Ottomans			Moslem Spain	
	I	II	I	II	III	I	II
		1	2(1)	1	2		1
	1	1	1	1	1		1
	−	−	−	−	−		−
	1(2)	1	1	1	1		1
		2	2	1	2(3)		2
		1	1	1	1		1
		1	2	2	2		1
		−	−	−	−		−
		−	−	−	−		−
		1	1	1(2)	2		1
	2	1	3(2)	2	2		2(1)
		2		2			2(3)
	reg.	pres.	reg.	crea.	prom.		crea.
	−	prom.	pres.	prom.	pres.		reg.
	−	crea.	crea.	reg.	reg.		prom.
	−	{ acc., serv., reg. }	−	serv.	−		acc.
	−	−	−	−	−		−
	−	−	−	−	−		−

Austria		Spain		Sweden		
		I	II	I	II	III
1			1(2)	2	3	2
1			1	1	2	2[h]
−			−		−	
1			2	2	3	2
1			1	2	3	3
1			1	1	1	1
1			1	1	1	1
2			2	2	1	1
1		2	1	1	3	3
2(3)		1	2	1(2)	1(2)	2
2		2	2	2	3	2
1		1	2	1	1	1(2)
reg.		acc.	acc.	reg.	reg.	reg.
serv.		reg.	pres.	prom.	crea.	prom.
prom.		pres.	reg.	crea.	pres.	serv.
acc.			−	acc.	serv.	pres.
−			−	−	−	−
−			−	−	−	−

TABLE II. *(continued)*

Scope of Political Struggle in the Historical Bureaucratic Societies

Variable	I	Russia II	III	Prussia I	II
D. Extent of participation of groups in political organization—general	1	1(2)	2	1	1(2)
1. Peasantry	1(2)	1(2)	2	1	1
2. Gentry		—			—
3. Aristocracy	1	2	3	2	3ᵍ
4. Urban group	1	1	1	1	1
5. Legal	1	1	1	1	1
6. Military	1	1	1	1	1
7. Religious	2	1	1	1	1
8. Cultural-secular	1	1	2	1	1
9. Bureaucracy	1	1(2)	2	1	2
E. General extent of participation of groups	1(2)	1	2	2	2
VI. Rebellions	3	2	3		1
VII. Types of policies*					
1.	acc.	acc.	reg.	pres.	pres.,reg.
2.	crea.	pres.	reg.acc.	crea.	reg.
3.	prom. reg.	pres.	pres.	reg.	prom.
4.	serv.	crea.	prom.	acc.	serv.
5.		—		serv.	acc.
6.		—		—	—

* According to degree of importance.

TABLE II. *(continued)*

Scope of Political Struggle in the Historical Bureaucratic Societies

	France				*England*	
I	II	I		I	II	III
1	1	2		2(3)	2(3)	3
1	1	1		2	1	2
	—			2	2	3
3	2	3		3	3	3
1	1	1		2	2	3
1	2	3		3	2	1
	No crystallization				No crystallization	
1	1	1		3	3	2
1	1	3		1	1	2
2	2(1)	2(3)		2(1)	2	1
2	1(2)	2(3)		3	2	3
1	2	2		1	3^g	1
reg.	prom.	reg.		reg.	reg.	prom.
—	pres.	pres.		acc.	prom.	serv.
—	acc.	serv.		prom.	serv.	
—	crea.	—			—	
—	—	—			—	

TABLE III.

Social Position of the Bureaucracy, Scope of Its Activities, and Its Place in the Political Struggle

Variable	Inca Empire	I	Ancient Egypt II	III
I. Differentiation (general) of groups	1(2)	2	3	2
II. Extent of political participation of groups	1	1	2(1)	1(2)
III. Relative strength of groups and ruler	rul.	rul.	rul.	rul.
IV. Relative strength of aristocracy vs. middle and low groups	aris.	aris.	bal.	aris.
V. Compatibility of goals of groups and ruler	com.ac.	com.pass.	com.ac.	com.pass.
VI. Self-regulation of groups and state				
A. Traditional	3	4	3	4
B. Nontraditional	1	1	2	1
VII. Type of activity of bureaucracy*				
1.	bal.	bal.	reg.	reg.(tech.)
2.	—	—	—	—
VIII. Autonomy of bureaucratic organization	1	1	2	1
IX. Social status of bureaucracy				
A. Extent of embeddedness of bureaucracy*				
1.	cent.	cent.	cent.	aris.
2.	—	aris.	—	—
B. Criteria of status of bureaucracy	nob.	nob.,prof.	nob.	nob.prof.
X. Political orientation of bureaucracy	rul.	self pol.	self pol.	rul.
XI. Relative strength of bureaucracy and ruler	rul.	rul.	rul.	bur.

* According to degree of importance.

TABLE III. (continued)
Social Position of the Bureaucracy, Scope of Its Activities, and Its Place in the Political Struggle

I	Sassanid Persia		IV	Ptolemies	Seleucids	I	T'ang	III
	II	III					II	
2	2	3	2	3	4	4	4	4
1(2)	1(2)	2	1	1	1	1 2(1)	1(2) 2(1)	1 2
bal.	groups	rul.	groups	rul.	rul.	rul.	rul.	groups
aris.	aris.	groups	aris.	?	?	bal.	groups	groups[d]
com.pass.	inc.ac.	com.pass.	inc.ac.	inc.pass.	com.pass.	com.ac.	com.ac.	inc.ac.
		4		2	4	3	3	4
		1		2	4	2	2	3
reg. tech.	reg.	reg. (tech.)	reg.	tech. reg.	tech. reg.	reg. tech.	reg. tech.	reg. tech.
		1		1	1	3	3	3
cent. aris.	cent. aris.	cent.	cent. aris.	mid. cent.	mid. aris.		gent. —	
nob.	nob.(prof	prof.nob.	prof.nob.	?	?	ed.	ed.	ed.
self,pol.	self	rul.	self	?	?	rul.group	rul.groups	self
bal.	bal.	rul.	bur.	bal.	rul.	rul.	rul.	bur.

TABLE III. (*continued*)

Social Position of the Bureaucracy, Scope of Its Activities, and Its Place in the Political Struggle

Variable	I	Sung II	III	Yuan	Ming
I. Differentiation (general) of groups	5	5	5	5	5
II. Extent of political participation of groups	1(2) / 2(1)	2(1) / 2(1)	1(2) / 2	1(2) / 2	1(2) / 2
III. Relative strength of groups and ruler	rul.	rul.	groups	rul.	rul.
IV. Relative strength of aristocracy vs. middle and low groups	groups	groups	groups	aris.	groups
V. Compatibility of goals of groups and ruler	com.ac.	com.ac.	inc.ac.	com.ac.	com.ac.
VI. Self-regulation of groups and state					
A. Traditional	3	3	4	3	3
B. Nontraditional	2	2	3	2	2
VII. Type of activity of bureaucracy*					
1.	reg.	reg.	reg.	reg.	reg.
2.	tech.	tech.	tech.	tech.	tech.
VIII. Autonomy of bureaucratic organization	3	3	3	3	3
IX. Social status of bureaucracy					
A. Extent of embeddedness of bureaucracy*					
1.		gent.		gent.aris.	gent.
2.		—		—	—
B. Criteria of status of bureaucracy	ed.	ed.	ed.	ed.,nob.	ed.
X. Political orientation of bureaucracy	rul.groups	rul.groups	self	rul.groups	rul.groups
XI. Relative strength of bureaucracy and ruler	rul.	rul.	bur.	rul.	rul.

* According to degree of importance.

TABLE III. (*continued*)

Social Position of the Bureaucracy, Scope of Its Activities, and Its Place in the Political Struggle

Ch'ing	Maurya		Gupta		Mogul Empire	
	I	II		I	II	III
5	4		4	3	4	3
1(2) 2 }	1		1		1	
rul.	rul.		rul.		rul.	
groups	aris.		aris.		aris.	
com.ac.	com.pass.		com.pass.	com.pass.	com.pass.	inc.ac.
3	5		5		5	
2	1		1		1	
reg. tech.	reg. tech.		tech. reg.	tech. reg.	tech. reg.	reg. tech.
3	1		1	1		
gent.	cent.		cent.	—	cent.	
—	—		—	—	—	
ed.	?		?	pow.	nob.	
rul.groups	rul.		rul.	rul.		
rul.	rul.		rul.	rul.		

Table III. *(continued)*

Social Position of the Bureaucracy, Scope of Its Activities,
and Its Place in the Political Struggle

Variable	Byzantine Empire			Abbassids	
	I	II	III	I	II
I. Differentiation (general) of groups	4	7	6	5	6
II. Extent of political participation of groups	2(1)	2	2(1)	2	1(2)
III. Relative strength of groups and ruler	groups	rul.	bal.	rul.	groups
IV. Relative strength of aristocracy vs. middle and low groups	aris.	bal.	aris.		groups
V. Compatibility of goals of groups and ruler	com.pass., inc.pass.	com.ac.	com.pass., com.ac.	com.ac.	inc.pass.
VI. Self-regulation of groups and state					
A. Traditional		{ 4 2^{c} }			4
B. Nontraditional		3^{d}			3
VII. Type of activity of bureaucracy					
1.	reg.	reg.	reg.	bal.	reg.
2.		tech.			—
VIII. Autonomy of bureaucratic organization	2	2(3)	2		2
IX. Social status of bureaucracy					
A. Extent of embeddedness of bureaucracy*					
1.	cent.	cent.	cent.	cent.	mid.
2.	mid.	mid.	aris.	—	
B. Criteria of status of bureaucracy	pow.	ed.	nob.	ed.	pow.
X. Political orientation of bureaucracy	rul.groups	rul.group	self		rul.groups
XI. Relative strength of bureaucracy and ruler	rul.	rul.	bur.		rul.

* According to degree of importance.

Table III. (*continued*)

Social Position of the Bureaucracy, Scope of Its Activities, and Its Place in the Political Struggle

Saffawids		Ottomans			Moslem Spain	
I	II	I	II	III	I	II
4	5	4	6	6	6	6
2	1	3(2)	2	2		2(1)
groups	rul.	bal.	rul.	groups	groups	rul.
aris.	groups	aris.	groups	groups	aris.	groups
inc.ac.	com.pass.	com.ac.	com.ac.	inc.ac.	inc.pass.	com.pass.
	3		4		4	
	3		2		3	
reg.	bal.	reg.	bal.	reg.		tech.
	—	(tech.)		(tech.)		reg.
	2	2(1)	2(3)	2(1)	1	
	mid.	cent.	cent.	n.emb.		aris.
—			—			—
ed.	pow.		pow.ed.			pow.ed.
self	self,pol.	rul.	self,pol.	self		self,pol.
bur.	rul.	rul.	rul.	bur.	rul.	

TABLE III. *(continued)*

Social Position of the Bureaucracy, Scope of Its Activities, and Its Place in the Political Struggle

Variable	Rome I	Rome II	Rome III	Spanish-American Empire I	Spanish-American Empire II	Spanish-American Empire III
I. Differentiation (general) of groups	5	4	4	{4 3	6 4	7 3[b]}
II. Extent of political participation of groups	2	1	3	1(2)	2	2(3)
III. Relative strength of groups and ruler	groups	rul.	groups	bal.	rul.	groups
IV. Relative strength of aristocracy vs. middle and low groups	bal.	groups	groups	aris.	bal.	bal.
V. Compatibility of goals of groups and ruler	inc.pass.	com.ac.	inc.pass.	com.ac.	com.pass.	com.pass., inc.ac.
VI. Self-regulation of groups and state						
A. Traditional	4	3	2	{1 5	1 3	1 3[b]}
B. Nontraditional	2	1	3	{1 1	2 1	3 1[b]}
VII. Type of activity of bureaucracy*						
1.	tech.	bal.	reg.	reg.	reg.	reg.
2.	reg.		tech.	tech.	tech.	(tech.)
VIII. Autonomy of bureaucratic organization	1(2)	1(2)	2(3)	1	3	3
IX. Social status of bureaucracy						
A. Extent of embeddedness of bureaucracy*						
1.	cent.	n.emb.	n.emb.	cent.	n.emb., aris.,mid.	n.emb.,aris.
2.	—	cent.		—		
B. Criteria of status of bureaucracy		pow.		ed.prof.	{prof.nob. pow.}	prof.nob.[b]
X. Political orientation of bureaucracy	rul.	rul.	self,pol.	rul.	rul.groups	self
XI. Relative strength of bureaucracy and ruler	rul.	rul.	rul.	rul.	bal.	bur.

* According to degree of importance.

TABLE III. *(continued)*

Social Position of the Bureaucracy, Scope of Its Activities,
and Its Place in the Political Struggle

| Austria | Spain | | Sweden | | |
	I	II	I	II	III
6	5	4	5	6	7
2	2	2	2	3	2
rul.	rul.	bal.	rul.	groups	rul.
bal.	low aris.	high aris.	groups	aris.	groups
com.pass.	inc.pass.	com.ac.	inc.ac.	com.ac.	com.pass.
3	4	2		3	
2	2	2		4	
reg.	reg.	reg.	reg.	bal.	reg.
tech.	tech.	—	tech.	—	tech.
1(3)	2	2	2	2	2
cent.	cent.	aris.	cent.	aris.	n.emb.
—	—		—		
prof.	prof.pow.	nob.	pow.	nob.	prof.
rul.	rul.	groups/self	rul.	groups	self,pol.
rul.	rul.	bal.	rul.	bal.	rul.

TABLE III. (*continued*)
Social Position of the Bureaucracy, Scope of Its Activities, and Its Place in the Political Struggle

Variable	Russia I	Russia II	Russia III	Prussia I	Prussia II
I. Differentiation (general) of groups	5	4	5	5	6
II. Extent of political participation of groups	1(2)	1	2	2	2
III. Relative strength of groups and ruler	rul.	groups	bal.	rul.	rul.
IV. Relative strength of aristocracy vs. middle and low groups	bal.	aris.	aris.	aris.	aris.
V. Compatibility of goals of groups and ruler	inc.pass.	com.ac.	com.ac.	inc.pass.	com.ac.
VI. Self-regulation of groups and state					
A. Traditional		2		3	2^f
B. Nontraditional		3		2	2
VII. Type of activity of bureaucracy*					
1.	reg.	reg.	reg.	reg.	reg.
2.	(tech.)	—	(tech.)	(tech.)	tech.
VIII. Autonomy of bureaucratic organization	1(2)	1	1(2)	2	3
IX. Social status of bureaucracy					
A. Extent of embeddedness of bureaucracy*					
1.	cent.	cent.	aris.	cent.	aris.n.emb.
2.	pow.	pow.	nob.^{e}	pow.(prof.)	pow.prof.(nob.)
B. Criteria of status of bureaucracy					
X. Political orientation of bureaucracy	rul.	groups,rul.	groups rul.	rul.	self,pol.
XI. Relative strength of bureaucracy and ruler	rul.	bal.	bal.	rul.	bal.

* According to degree of importance.

TABLE III. (*continued*)
Social Position of the Bureaucracy, Scope of Its Activities, and Its Place in the Political Struggle

| | France | | | England | |
I	II	III	I	II	III
6	6	7	6	7(8)	8(9)
2	1(2)	2(3)	3	2	3
bal.	rul.	groups	rul.	rul.	groups
aris.	bal.	groups	bal.	aris.	bal.
inc.ac.	com.pass.	inc.ac.[d]	com.pass.	{ com.pass. / inc.ac. }	com.ac.
4	2	2	2	1	1
2	3	3	3	4	5
reg.	reg.	reg.	reg.	reg.	tech.
—	tech.	tech.	tech.	tech.	—
1	2	3	2	2	2(3)
cent.mid.	mid.cent.	aris.mid.	cent.	aris.mid.	aris.mid.
pow.prof.	nob.prof.	nob.	pow.nob.	pow.nob.prof.	pow.nob.prof.
rul. groups	rul.	self	rul.	groups	groups
rul.	bal.	bur.	rul.	rul.	rul.

Notes to the Analytical Tables

GREECE

a. Fifth century B.C. (Periclean and post-Periclean Athens).
b. Official assembly had great powers.

MONGOLS

a. Beginning of thirteenth century (period of Genghis Khan).

FEUDAL EUROPE

a. Tenth to thirteenth centuries, specifically with reference to France.
b. Army composed of various groups whose higher ranks were aristocratic.
c. Activity at local courts.

AHMENIDS

a. Sixth to fourth centuries B.C.

CAROLINGIAN EMPIRE

a. Era of Charlemagne (770–814).
b. Army composed of various groups, the highest ranks being aristocratic.

INCA EMPIRE

a. Eve of the Spanish Conquest (first quarter of sixteenth century).
b. The group is not analyzed separately, since it is not differentiated from the aristocracy.

ANCIENT EGYPT

a. (Ancient and Middle Empires till the end of the "second intermediary period.")
   I. 2778–2065 B.C. (Ancient Empire until first intermediary period).
  II. 2065–1785 B.C. (Middle Empire).
 III. 1785–1580 B.C. (second intermediary period).

SASSANID PERSIA

a.   I. A.D. 226–310
   II. A.D. 310–488 (from Shapur II until reign of Kovadh; period of decline of centralized power).
 III. A.D. 488–579 (reign of Kovadh and Chosroes).
 IV. A.D. 579–650 (period of decline).
b. By "gentry," we mean the *dekhans*.
c. The cultural-collective orientation of rul-

er's goals comes close to a cultural particularistic orientation.

PTOLEMIES

a. 300–30 B.C. (approximately from the end of the Diodachian Wars to the Roman Conquest).

b. Legitimation in respect to Greek population (upper symbols) is distinguished from legitimation in respect to native population (lower symbols).

SELEUCIDS

a. 300–100 B.C. (approximately from the end of the Diadochian Wars to the Roman Conquest).

b. See note b to Ptolemies.

c. Political roles in the Hellenistic cities (upper symbols) are here distinguished from those in the autochthonic population (lower symbols), which was relatively more passive.

T'ANG DYNASTY

a. The T'ang Dynasty extended from A.D. 618 to A.D. 907. To indicate the cyclical changes which arose within the dynasty, the T'ang period has been divided into the following three sub-periods:

I. 618–755. This phase represents the peak of centralized power, the decline of which sets in with the rebellion of An-Lu-shan (755).

II. 756–874. Huang Ch'ao's rebellion, which began in 874, marks the beginning of the disintegration of the T'ang regime.

III. 875–907. This final phase saw the rise of more or less independent military satrapies.

b. The term "gentry" covers the gentry in the narrower sense of the term as well as the literati and all other social elements which entered the bureaucracy and/or the group of literati; in some of the following variables, the gentry is called the "middle group."

c. Upper symbols signify ideological definition of political activities and struggle; lower symbols—their actual intensity.

d. Ideological definition of articulation of goals of political struggle is low for all periods of Chinese history and for all groups; the description refers to actual situation.

e. Especially with reference to considerable promotion of peasantry.

SUNG DYNASTY

a. The Sung period comprised two dynasties, the Northern Sung (960–1127) and the Southern Sung (1127–1279). We have indicated the dynastic decline which began in the latter part of the Southern Sung. Comparable phases of decline heralded the disintegration of subsequent dynasties as well; but, since these phases represent cyclical rather than secular phenomena, we have not indicated their appearance in these dynasties.

The Sung Dynasties have been divided into the following three sub-periods:

I. 960–1127.

II. 1127–1250 (*ca.*)

III. 1250–1279.

b. See note b under T'ang Dynasty.

c. See note c under T'ang Dynasty.

d. See note d under T'ang Dynasty.

e. "Promotion" here refers to ruler's activities toward cities.

YÜAN DYNASTY

a. The Yüan, or Mongol, Dynasty ruled China from 1279 to 1368. This period represents the fusion of Mongolian "nomadic feudalism" with the traditional Chinese bureaucratic system; the latter system was generally predominant (*see Schurman, 1957, p. 2*).

b. See note b under T'ang Dynasty.

c. Refers to the Mongol aristocracy.

d. Refers to the conquering Mongol aristocracy.

e. See note c under T'ang Dynasty.

f. Refers to conquering Mongol army.

g. See note d under T'ang Dynasty.

MING DYNASTY

a. The Ming Dynasty reigned from 1368 to 1644.

b. See note b under T'ang Dynasty.

c. See note c under T'ang Dynasty.

d. See note d under T'ang Dynasty.

CH'ING DYNASTY

a. The Ch'ing Manchu Dynasty reigned from 1644 to 1912.

b. See note b under T'ang Dynasty.

c. Refers to the conquering Manchu aristocracy.

d. See note c under T'ang Dynasty.

e. Refers to conquering Manchu army.

f. See note d under T'ang Dynasty.

MAURYA

a. I. 327–274 (264) B.C. Chandra-Gupta to ascendancy of Aśoka; period of organization of bureaucracy.

II. 273(263)–236 B.C. Aśoka's reign; high point of bureaucratic development. A third period, from 235 to 174 B.C. (from Aśoka's death to the disintegration of the Maurya Empire) is not considered because of the lack of suitable information.

b. Traditional legitimation diminishes because of Brahman antagonism to introduction of Buddhism by Aśoka.

c. There is no clear evidence about the extent and scope of power of channels of political struggle.

d. It seems that in the early part of dynasty's rule there was no activity in the religious sphere.

e. Activity of religious profession intensified, because of Brahman opposition to Aśoka's religious policy.

GUPTA

a. A.D. 320–495, from ascendancy of Chandra-Gupta to the death of Budha-Gupta. Principal reference: period between Samudra-Gupta and Chandra-Gupta, which is the period of the highest development.

b. No clear evidence exists on the extent of powers of channels of struggle.

c. At least one case is known when the ruler was elected by council of royal family members and dignitaries; there is no knowledge of other powers of channels of struggle.

d. High intensity because of continuation of Brahman reaction which began in rule of Aśoka. (See under Maurya, notes b and e.)

MOGUL EMPIRE

a. I. 1526–1554. Baber and Humayun; founding of Empire; beginning of bureaucratic organization.

II. 1556–1657. Akbar, Jahangia, and Shah Jehan; highest development of Empire.

III. 1657–1705. Aurangib—decline of Empire.

b. First symbols for Mongols, second for Indians.

c. First symbols for Moslems, second for Hindus.

d. Embedded in aristocracy.

e. Only Hindus; for Moslems, see legal profession.

f. Referring to legal-religious profession *ulemâ*.

g. Only in period I.

h. No differentiation of bureaucracy as a group from aristocracy and military profession.

i. Bureaucratic activity only in Aurangib reign.

BYZANTINE EMPIRE

a. I. 330–610 (from foundation of Constantinople to Heraclius I).

II. 610–1025 (period of maximum development).

III. 1025–1453 (period of increasing aristocratization till decline and fall).

b. Upper symbol for differentiation of organization, lower symbol for differentiation of ideology.

c. Upper symbol for cities, lower for villages.

d. Mainly cities.

ABBASSIDS

a.   I. 750–847 (from rise of dynasty till after al-Wathik, height of centralized bureaucracy).

   II. 847–940 (from al-Mutawakkil till the rise of the Buyuwids and disintegration of the Empire).

b. Upper symbols for differentiation of organization, lower symbol for differentiation of ideology.

c. The *ulemâ* are treated under the heading of "legal profession." It is understood this group functions in Islamic society also as a religious elite.

SAFFAWIDS

a.   I. 1502–1587 (from Ismail till rise of 'Abbas I; rule based on allegiance of tribal elements).

   II. 1587–1736 (from 'Abbas I to the Afghan occupation, height of centralized bureaucracy).

b. Upper symbol for differentiation of organization; lower symbol for differentiation of ideology.

c. The *ulemâ* are treated under the heading of "legal profession"—see note c under Abbassids.

OTTOMANS

a.   I. 1451–1520 (Mehmed II to Selim I, pre-bureaucratic regime, period of military expansion).

   II. 1520–1566 (Suleiman I, period of maximal centralization of bureaucracy).

   III. 1566–1789 (Selim II to Selim III, period of progressive stagnation).

b. Upper symbol for differentiation of organization, lower symbol for differentiation of ideology.

c. See note c under Abbassids.

MOSLEM SPAIN

a.   I. 750–912 (from the rise of the Marwanid Ummayads till Abd-ar-Rahman III, the polity based mainly on aristocratic-tribal elements).

   II. 912–1000 (from Abd-ar-Rahman III, when Caliphate of Cordoba was at its height, to period of progressive disintegration).

b. Upper symbol for differentiation of organization, lower symbol for differentiation of ideology.

c. See note c under Abbassids.

ROME

a.   I. 27 B.C.–A.D. 96 (Julio Claudius and Flavius).

   II. A.D. 96–193 (enlightened emperors).

   III. 193–350 (the military autocracy till the approximate end of the importance of the Western Empire).

b. Upper symbols refer to organization, lower symbols to ideology.

SPANISH-AMERICAN EMPIRE

a.   I. 1520–1580 (from the Conquests to the middle of Phillip II's reign).

   II. 1580–1759 (Philip II to Ferdinand VI).

   III. 1759–1820 (Charles III to Independence).

b. Upper symbols refer to Spaniards, lower symbols to native population.

c. By "gentry," we allude to the smaller *encommendieros* and the heads of the Indian communities who were promoted by the Spaniards.

d. Ruler's reference to social groups was not part of his ideology, but he was led to it by pressure exerted by these groups.

AUSTRIA

1740–1790 (Maria Theresa and Joseph II).

SPAIN

a.   I. 1520–1621 (height of absolutism).

   II. 1621–1701 (decline of absolutism till the War of the Succession).

b. The analysis here refers to the upper aristocracy. The development of the *hidalgo*, the lower aristocracy, was in the opposite direction—they are promoted by the kings in the sixteenth century and participated in various departments of government. In the seventeenth century, the rising upper aristocracy took the *hidalgo's* place.

c. The clergy participated in the administration.

d. In first period, lower aristocracy stronger; in second period, higher aristocracy stronger.

SWEDEN

a. I. 1523–1720 (height of absolutism).
    II. 1720–1770 ("Age of Freedom").
    III. 1770–1809 (enlightened absolutism).

b. Includes goals of classes represented in Parliament and Council, especially in second period.

c. Upper symbol for differentiation of organization, lower symbol for differentiation of ideology.

d. The military and legal professions were, to a large extent, the creation of the absolutist monarchy, especially of Gustav Adolph.

e. Second line symbolizes specific development in aristocracy. This class becomes more rigid in the third period and does not absorb any more new elements. Diversification of activity lessens as against developments in other groups.

f. Peasants are continuously represented in Parliament, but only rarely in council and committees. Burghers are represented in parliament and committees, but only rarely in council. The aristocracy is continuously represented in all institutions.

g. The clergy often act as the mouthpiece of the peasantry.

h. Peasant organization exists, but leadership is frequently drawn from other strata.

RUSSIA

a. I. 1682–1725 (Peter the Great).
    II. 1725–1761 (decline of absolutism and unstability).
    III. 1761–1796 (Catherine the Great, enlightened absolutism).

b. Traditional legitimation important during all periods as regards peasantry.

c. The kulaks are analyzed in the framework of peasants.

d. Political activity of aristocracy is channelized by the army and bureaucracy.

e. Bureaucratic rank determines social rank.

PRUSSIA

a. I. 1640–1740 (from Great Elector to Frederick Wilhelm I).
    II. 1740–1792 (Frederick II, enlightened absolutism).

b. Rise on provincial level.

c. Differentiation of organization is distinguished from differentiation of ideology.

d. Rise refers to peasants on royal domains.

e. The *Junkers* are analyzed in the framework of the aristocracy.

f. Refers only to decline of guilds.

g. Refers to self-organization of aristocracy only on provincial level.

FRANCE

a. I. 1589–1660 (Henry IV to the personal rule of Louis XIV).
    II. 1660–1715 (Louis XIV).
    III. 1715–1789 (Louis XV to the Revolution).

b. Aristocracy (second symbol) is here distinguished from other groups. Rigidity in aristocracy increases in third period, whereas social nobility develops in other groups.

c. Ruler's reference to social groups was not so much an explicit and voluntary part of his ideology as it was a *de facto* result of the pressures of these groups on the ruler.

d. In first period, incompatibility stems from the aristocracy; in the third period, from the middle groups.

ENGLAND

a. I. 1509–1640 (absolutist rule of Tudors and early Stuarts).
    II. 1660–1688 (Restoration of the Stuarts).
    III. 1689–1783 (the "Glorious Revolution," the Hanoverians, to the reforms resulting from the loss of the American colonies).

b. Considerable difference in sphere between activity in center, which is carried out by professionals, and activity at local level, which is carried out by "justices of the peace" whose duties include also various non-legal activities.

c. Rules of membership in struggle in councils during first two periods are arbitrary.

In the third period, they are explicit and legalistically formulated.

d. On local level, there exist elected or locally appointed functionaries, whose offices must be confirmed by central authority.

e. Departmentalization at the center.

f. Refers to the Civil War of 1642.

TABLE 1
Relations among Autonomy of Ruler's Goals, Differentiation of Institutional Spheres, and Extent of Development of Centralized Polity

Centralized Polity	DIFFERENTIATION OF SPHERES					
	1-3	4-6	7-9	1-3	4-6	7-9
	Autonomy of Ruler's Goals: 0			Autonomy of Ruler's Goals: 1		
1		Greece		Feudal Europe Egypt III Sassanid II, IV	Abbasid II	
2				Ahmenid	Saffawid I	
3				Inca		
	Autonomy of Ruler's Goals: 2			Autonomy of Ruler's Goals: 3		
1	Egypt I	T'ang III Sung III			Byzantium III	
2	Egypt II	Moslem Spain I		Sassanid III Mogul I	Seleucid Maurya I Ottoman III	
3	Sassanid I	Gupta Ottoman I			Abbassid I Rome I Spain I Russia II	
4				Ptolemies	Saffawid II Moslem Spain II	
5						France III
	Autonomy of Ruler's Goals: 4			Autonomy of Ruler's Goals: 5		
1	Mogul II					
2	Carolingian Rome III	Byzantium I		Spanish-American I		
3	Mogul III	T'ang II Sung II Maurya II Russia III				Sweden II
4		Spain II T'ang I Sung I Yüan Ming Ch'ing France I Mogul II Ottoman II Rome II Spanish-American II	Prussia II		Austria Sweden I Russia I Byzantium II	Spanish-American III
5			Sweden III England II		Prussia I France II England I	England III

TABLE 2
Relations among Autonomy of Ruler's Goals, Differentiation of Institutional Spheres, and Activities of Bureaucracy

	DIFFERENTIATION OF SPHERES					
Activities of	*1-3*	*4-6*	*7-9*	*1-3*	*4-6*	*7-9*
bureaucracy	*Autonomy of Ruler's Goals: 0*			*Autonomy of Ruler's Goals: 1*		
0		Greece				
1				Feudal Europe Ahmenid Egypt III Sassanid II, IV		
2				Inca	Abbassid II Saffawid I	
	Autonomy of Ruler's Goals: 2			*Autonomy of Ruler's Goals: 3*		
1	Egypt I, II Sassanid I			Sassanid III	Rome I	

2		Sung III
		Gupta
		Moslem
		  Spain I
		T'ang III
				Ptolemies
				Mogul I
					Seleucid
					Abbassid I
					Saffawid II
					Moslem-
					  Spain II
					Spain I
					Russia II
						France III

3		Ottoman I			Maurya I Byzantium III Ottoman III	
	Autonomy of Ruler's Goals: 4			*Autonomy of Ruler's Goals: 5*		
1	Mongols Carolingian	Rome II Spain II		Spanish- American I		England III
2	Mogul III Rome III	Mogul II France I	Sweden III England II		Sweden I Prussia I England I	Spanish- American III Sweden II
3		T'ang I, II Sung I, II Yüan Ming Ch'ing Maurya II Ottoman II Spanish- American II Russia III Byzantium I	Prussia II		Austria Russia I France II Byzantium II	

TABLE 3
Relations among Autonomy of Ruler's Goals, Differentiation of Institutional Spheres, and Extent of Autonomy of Bureaucracy

Autonomy of bureaucracy	*DIFFERENTIATION OF SPHERES*					
	1-3	*4-6*	*7-9*	*1-3*	*4-6*	*7-9*
	Autonomy of Ruler's Goals: 0			*Autonomy of Ruler's Goals: 1*		
0		Greece				
1				Feudal Europe Ahmenid Inca Egypt III Sassanid II, IV		
2				Abbas. II Saff. I		
	Autonomy of Ruler's Goals: 2			*Autonomy of Ruler's Goals: 3*		
1	Egypt I Sassanid I	Gupta Moslem Spain I		Sassanid III Ptolemies Mogul I	Seleucid Maurya I Moslem Spain II Rome I Russia II	
2	Egypt II	Ottoman I			Byzantium III Abbassid I Saffawid II Ottoman III Spain I	
3		T'ang III Sung III				France III
	Autonomy of Ruler's Goals: 4			*Autonomy of Ruler's Goals: 5*		
0	Mongols Carolingian					
1	Mogul III	Maurya II Mogul II Rome II Russia III France I		Spanish-American I	Austria Russia I	
2	Rome III	Ottoman II Spain II Byzantium I	Sweden III England II		Sweden I Prussia I France II England I Byzantium II	Sweden II England III
3		T'ang I, II Sung I, II Yüan Ming Ch'ing Spanish-American II	Prussia II			Spanish-American III

TABLE 4

Relations among Autonomy of Ruler's Goals, Differentiation of Institutional Spheres, and Type of Bureaucratic Activity

DIFFERENTIATION OF SPHERES

Type of bureaucratic activity	Autonomy of Ruler's Goals: 1		Autonomy of Ruler's Goals: 2		Autonomy of Ruler's Goals: 3		
	1-3	4-6	1-3	4-6	1-3	4-6	7-9
Technical-regulative				Gupta	Ptolemies Mogul I	Seleucid Moslem Spain II Rome I	
Balanced	Inca		Egypt I			Abbasid I Saffanid II	
Regulative-technical	Egypt III		Sassanid I	T'ang III Sung III Ottoman I	Sassanid III	Maurya I Ottoman III Spain I	France III
Regulative	Sassanid II, IV	Abassid II Saffawid I	Egypt II			Byzantium III Russia II	
No data				Moslem Spain I			

Type of bureaucratic activity	Autonomy of Ruler's Goals: 4			Autonomy of Ruler's Goals: 5		
	1-3	4-6	7-9	1-3	4-6	7-9
Technical						England III
Technical-regulative		Mogul II Ottoman II Rome II				
Balanced					Sweden II	
Regulative-technical	Mogul III Rome III	T'ang I, II Sung I, II Yüan Ming Ch'ing Maurya II Spanish-American II Russia III	Sweden III Prussia II England II	Spanish-American I	Austria Sweden I Russia I Prussia I France II England I Byzantium II	Spanish-American III
Regulative		Spain II France I Byzantium I				

TABLE 5
Relations among Autonomy of Ruler's Goals, Differentiation of Institutional Spheres, and Extent of Embeddedness of Channels of Political Struggle

The numeric sub-columns (1-3, 4-6, 7-9) fall under the spanning header **DIFFERENTIATION OF SPHERES**.

Autonomy of Ruler's Goals: 0, 1, 2

Embeddedness of channels of political struggle in	Autonomy of Ruler's Goals: 0			Autonomy of Ruler's Goals: 1			Autonomy of Ruler's Goals: 2		
	1-3	4-6	7-9	1-3	4-6	7-9	1-3	4-6	7-9
Traditional channels	Ahmenid, Inca, Feudal Europe	Greece			Saffawid I				
Traditional channels and special political organs				Sassanid I			Gupta		
Special political organs				Sassanid II, IV; Egypt III	Abbasid II		Egypt I, II	Austria, Russia I, Prussia I, Byzantium II; Moslem Spain I, Ottoman I; T'ang III, Sung III	
Special political organs—separate							Spanish-American I	France II, England I	Spanish-American III
Separate (not embedded)								Sweden I	Sweden II, England III

Autonomy of Ruler's Goals: 3, 4, 5

Embeddedness of channels of political struggle in	Autonomy of Ruler's Goals: 3			Autonomy of Ruler's Goals: 4			Autonomy of Ruler's Goals: 5		
	1-3	4-6	7-9	1-3	4-6	7-9	1-3	4-6	7-9
No channels	Ptolemies			Mangols					
Traditional channels		Maurya I							
Traditional channels and special political organs	Rome III			Mogul III	T'ang I, II, Sung I, II; Yüan, Ming, Ch'ing, Maurya II, Mogul II				
Special political organs	Mogul I, Sassanid III	Seleucid, Byzantium III, Ottoman III, Moslem Spain II, Rome I, Spain I, Russia II			Rome II, Spain II, Russia III				Prussia II
Special political organs—separate			France III	Carolingian	Byzantium I, Spanish-American II, France I				England II
Separate (not embedded)		Abbassid I, Saffawid II			Ottoman II				Sweden III

TABLE 6

Relation among Autonomy of Ruler's Goals, Differentiation of Institutional Spheres, and Explication of Rules of Membership in Channels of Political Struggle

Rules of membership	*DIFFERENTIATION OF SPHERES*					
	1-3	4-6	7-9	1-3	4-6	7-9
	Autonomy of Ruler's Goals: 0			*Autonomy of Ruler's Goals: 1*		
Explicit-traditional		Greece		Feudal Europe Ahmenid Inca Sassanid II, IV	Abassid II	
Explicit legal		Greece				
Non-explicit traditional				Ahmenid Egypt III	Saffawid I	
Non-explicit arbitrary				Egypt III Sassanid II, IV		
	Autonomy of Ruler's Goals: 2			*Autonomy of Ruler's Goals: 3*		
No channels				Ptolemies		
Explicit traditional	Sassanid I	Moslem Spain I		Sassanid III	Abassid I Moslem Spain II Spain I	
Explicit legal					Seleucid Rome I	France III
Non-explicit traditional	Egypt I, II	Gupta Ottoman I			Maurya I Byzantium III	
Non-explicit arbitrary	Sassanid I Egypt I, II	T'ang III Sung III		Mogul I Sassanid III	Saffawid II Ottoman III Russia II	France III
	Autonomy of Ruler's Goals: 4			*Autonomy of Ruler's Goals: 5*		
Explicit traditional	Mongol Carolingian	T'ang I, II Sung I, II Yüan Ming Ch'ing Byzantium I				
Explicit legal	Rome III	Rome II France I Spanish-American II	Sweden III England II Prussia II	Spanish-American I	Austria Sweden I France II England I	Sweden II England III Spanish-American III
Non-explicit traditional		Maurya II			Russia I	
Non-explicit arbitrary	Mongols Carolingian Mogul III	Mogul II Ottoman II Spain II Russia III France I	England II		Prussia I France I England I Byzantium II	England III

TABLE 7

Relations among Autonomy of Ruler's Goals, Differentiation of Institutional Spheres, and Explication of Rules of Political Struggle between Ruler and Group

DIFFERENTIATION OF SPHERES

	Autonomy of Ruler's Goals: 0			*Autonomy of Ruler's Goals: 1*			*Autonomy of Ruler's Goals: 2*		
	1-3	4-6	7-9	1-3	4-6	7-9	1-3	4-6	7-9
Non-explicit traditional		Greece		Feudal Europe Ahmenid Inca Egypt III Sassanid II, IV	Saffawid I		Egypt I, II Sassanid I	Moslem Spain I Gupta	
Explicit traditional									
Non-explicit, transition from traditional to non-traditional								T'ang III Sung III	
Explicit, transition from traditional to non-traditional								Ottoman I	
Explicit non-traditional					Abbasid II				

TABLE 7 (Cont'd.)

	Autonomy of Ruler's Goals: 3			Autonomy of Ruler's Goals: 4			Autonomy of Ruler's Goals: 5		
	1-3	4-6	7-9	1-3	4-6	7-9	1-3	4-6	7-9
Non-explicit traditional	Sassanid III	Moslem Spain II Maurya I			Maurya II				
Explicit traditional				Carolingian					
Non-explicit, transition from traditional to non-traditional								Russia I	
Non-explicit non-traditional	Ptolemies Mogul I	Seleucid Saffawid II Rome I Russia II		Rome III Mogul III	Rome II Spanish-American II Spain II Russia III France I Mogul II Mongol	Prussia II	Spanish-American I	Austria Prussia I France II England I	Spanish-American III
Explicit, transition from traditional to non-traditional					T'ang I, II Sung I, II Yüan Ming Ch'ing Ottoman II	Sweden III England II		Sweden I Byzantium II	Sweden II England III
Explicit non-traditional		Byzantium III Abbassid I Ottoman III Spain I	France III		Byzantium I				

TABLE 8

Relations among Autonomy of Ruler's Goals, Differentiation of Institutional Spheres, and Institutionalization of Powers of Channels of Political Struggle

Institutionalization of powers	*DIFFERENTIATION OF SPHERES*								
	Autonomy of Ruler's Goals: 0			*Autonomy of Ruler's Goals: 1*			*Autonomy of Ruler's Goals: 2*		
	1-3	*4-6*	*7-9*	*1-3*	*4-6*	*7-9*	*1-3*	*4-6*	*7-9*
1				Inca Egypt III Sassanid II, IV	Abbasid II Saffawid I		Egypt I, II Sassanid I	T'ang III Sung III Gupta Moslem Spain I	
2				Feudal Europe Ahmenid				Ottoman I	
3		Greece							

TABLE 8 (Cont'd.)

	Autonomy of Ruler's Goals: 3			Autonomy of Ruler's Goals: 4			Autonomy of Ruler's Goals: 5		
	1-3	4-6	7-9	1-3	4-6	7-9	1-3	4-6	7-9
0					Mongol				
1	Sassanid III Mogul I	Seleucid Maurya I Byzantium III Abbassid I Saffawid II Moslem Spain II Russia II		Carolingian Mogul III	Maurya II Mogul II Spain II				
2		Ottoman III Spain I	France III		T'ang I, II Sung I, II Yüan Ming Ch'ing Ottoman II Russia III France I		Spanish-American I	Austria Sweden I Russia I England I Byzantium III	
3		Rome I		Rome III	Rome II Spanish-American II Byzantium I	Sweden III Prussia II England III		Prussia I France II	Spanish-American III Sweden II England III
No channels	Ptolemies								

TABLE 9
Relations among Main Types of Policies of Ruler and Type of Reference of Ruler's Goals

Type of reference of ruler's goals	Policies primarily accumulative or creative			
	Regulative	Prescriptive	Promotive	Services
Cultural-ascriptive	Egypt I, II, III	Inca		
Political-collective				
Political-collective and economic-collective			Russia I	
Political-collective and cultural-collective	Sassanid III Spain I	Sassanid I, II Sassanid IV		
Cultural-collective	Abbassid II Moslem Spain I, II			
Political-collective and self-maintenance	Mogul I, II	Spanish-American I Spain II	Ottoman II	Gupta
Self-maintenance	Russia II	Ptolemies		

Type of reference of ruler's goals	Policies primarily regulative				
	No secondary policies	Accumulative creative	Prescriptive	Promotive	Services
Cultural-ascriptive		Yüan	T'ang III Sung III		T'ang I, II Sung I, II Ming Ch'ing
Political-collective	France I	Sweden II		Sweden I, III	
Political-collective and economic-collective		Spanish-American Russia III	France III	England II	Austria
Political-collective and cultural-collective		Spanish-American England I		Byzantium II Rome I	
Cultural-collective					
Political-collective and self-maintenance		Maurya I	Mogul III Byzantium I Ottoman I		
Self-maintenance	Saffawid II		Seleucid Byzantium III		

Reference of goals	Policies primarily prescriptive			Policies primarily promotive	
	Accumulative or creative	Regulative	Promotive	Prescriptive	Service
Political-collective	Prussia I				
Political-collective and economic-collective				France II	
Political-collective and cultural-collective				Rome II	
Political-collective and social groups				England III	
Cultural collective	Abbassid I				
Political-collective and self-maintenance		Prussia II		Ottoman III Rome III	
Self-maintenance			Saffawid II		

Note: In each case the primary policies are given in the first line, the secondary policies in the second line. In Maurya II, policies of ruler are primarily service, secondarily accumulated or creative, while goods are cultural-collective.

TABLE 10
Relations between Type of Reference of Ruler's Goals and Autonomy of Ruler's Goals

Type of reference	Autonomy of Ruler's Goals				
	1	2	3	4	5
Cultural-ascriptive	Inca Egypt III	Egypt I, II T'ang III Sung III		T'ang I, II Sung I, II Yüan Ming Ch'ing	
Political-collective				Sweden III France I	Sweden I, II Prussia I
Political-collective economic-collective			France III	Russia III England II	Spanish- American III Austria Russia I France II
Political-collective and cultural-collective	Sassanid II, IV	Sassanid I	Sassanid III Rome I Spain I	Rome II Spanish- American II	England I Byzantium I
Political-collective and social groups					England III
Cultural-collective	Abbassid II	Moslem Spain I	Abassid I Moslem Spain II	Maurya II	
Political-collective and self-maintenance	Ottoman I	Gupta	Mogul I Ottoman III Maurya I	Mogul II, III Ottoman II Rome III Spain II Prussia II Byzantium I	Spanish- American I
Self-maintenance	Saffawid I		Ptolemies Seleucid Byzantium III Saffawid II Russia II		

TABLE 11

Relations among Differentiation of Groups, Autonomy of Ruler's Goals, and Main Types of Policies of Ruler

Main types of policies	Autonomy of Ruler's Goals				
	1	2	3	4	5
	Low Differentiation (1-3)				
Accumulative or Creative	Inca England III Sassanid II, IV	Egypt I, II Sassanid I	Ptolemies Mogul I Sassanid III		
	Medium Differentiation (4-6)				
Accumulative or Creative	Abbassid II	Gupta Moslem Spain I	Spain I Russia II Moslem Spain II	Mogul II Spain II Ottoman II	Spanish- American I Russia I
Regulative	Saffawid I	T'ang III Sung III Ottoman I	Seleucid Maurya I Byzantium III Rome I	T'ang I, II Sung I, II Yüan Ming Ch'ing Spanish- American II Russia III Prussia II France I Byzantium I	Austria Sweden I, II England I
Prescriptive			Abbassid I Saffawid II	Prussia II	Prussia I
Promotive Services			Ottoman III	Rome II, III Maurya II	France II
	High Differentiation (7-9)				
Regulative		France III	Sweden III England II	Spanish- American III Byzantium II	
Promotive				England III	

TABLE 12

Relations among Differentiation of Groups, Type of Reference of Ruler's Goals, and Intensity of Political Participation of Groups

Reference of ruler's goals	INTENSITY OF POLITICAL PARTICIPATION OF GROUPS								
	Low Differentiation (1-3)			Medium Differentiation (4-6)			High Differentiation (7-9)		
	1	2	3	1	2	3	1	2	3
Cultural-ascriptive	Inca	Egypt III			T'ang I, II, III Sung I, II, III Yüan Ming Ch'ing				
Political-collective					Prussia I France I England I	Sweden I, II		Sweden III	
Political-collective and economic-collective					Austria Russia I France II	Russia III		Spanish-American III France III England II	
Political-collective and cultural-collective	Sassanid I			Rome II	Rome I Spanish-American II	Spain I		Byzantium II	
Cultural-collective					Maurya II Abbassid I, II Moslem Spain I, II				
Political-collective and social groups									England III
Political-collective and self-maintenance	Mogul I, II	Sassanid II, III, IV		Maurya I Gupta Mogul II Byzantium II Ottoman I	Ottoman II Rome III Spanish-American I Spain II Prussia II	Ottoman III			
Self-maintenance	Ptolemies				Seleucid Byzantium III Saffawid I, II Russia II				

TABLE 13

Relations among Differentiation of Groups, Type of Reference of Ruler's Goals, and Participation of Groups in Political Organization

Reference of ruler's goals	PARTICIPATION OF GROUPS IN POLITICAL ORGANIZATION								
	Low Differentiation (1-3)			*Medium Differentiation (4-6)*			*High Differentiation (7-9)*		
	1	2	3	1	2	3	1	2	3
Cultural-ascriptive	Inca Egypt I	Egypt II, III			T'ang I, II Sung I, II Yüan Ming Ch'ing	T'ang III Sung III			
Political-collective				Prussia I France I	Sweden I	Sweden II		Sweden III	
Political-collective and economic-collective				Austria Russia I	Russia III			France III England II	Spanish-American III American III
Political-collective and cultural-collective		Sassanid I, II, III, IV		Rome II Spain I	Rome I Spanish-American II England I			Byzantium II	
Political-collective and social groups									England III
Cultural-collective				Maurya II Moslem Spain I, II	Abbasid I, II				
Political-collective and self-maintenance		Mogul I, III		Maurya I Gupta Ottoman II Spain II Prussia II	Mogul I Byzantium I, III Ottoman I, III Rome III Spanish-American I				
Self-maintenance	Ptolemies			Seleucid Saffawid I, II	Byzantium III Russia II				

TABLE 14

Relations among Differentiation of Groups, Type of Reference of Ruler's Goals, and Articulation of Political Goals of Groups

Reference of ruler's goals	Low Differentiation (1-3) 1	2	3	Medium Differentiation (4-6) 1	2	3	High Differentiation (7-9) 1	2	3
Cultural-ascriptive	Inca Egypt I, III	Egypt II			T'ang I, II, III Yüan Ming Ch'ing Sung I, II, III				
Political-collective					Sweden I Prussia I France I			Sweden III	
Political-collective and economic-collective				Austria	France II Russia III			England II	France III Spanish-American III
Political-collective and cultural-collective	Sassanid I, II, IV	Sassanid III		Rome II	Rome I Spanish-American II Spain I England I			Byzantium II	
Political-collective and social groups									England III
Cultural-collective				Maurya II Abassid II Moslem Spain I, II	Abassid I				
Political-collective and self-maintenance	Mogul I, III			Maurya I Gupta Mogul II Byzantium I Ottoman I, II, III	Rome III Spain II Prussia II Spanish-American I				
Self-maintenance	Ptolemies			Seleucid Russia II	Byzantium III Saffawid I, II				

TABLE 15

Relations among Differentiation of Groups, Autonomy of Ruler's Goals, and Intensity of Political Participation of Groups

Autonomy of ruler's goals	INTENSITY OF POLITICAL PARTICIPATION OF GROUPS								
	Low Differentiation (1-3)			Medium Differentiation (4-6)			High Differentiation (7-9)		
	1	2	3	1	2	3	1	2	3
1	Inca Egypt III	Sassanid II, IV			Abbassid II Saffawid I				
2	Egypt I, II Sassanid I			Gupta Ottoman I	T'ang III Sung III Moslem Spain I				
3	Ptolemies Mogul II	Sassanid III		Maurya I	Seleucid Byzantium III Abbassid I Saffawid II Moslem Spain II Rome I Russia II	Ottoman III Spain I		France III	
4	Mogul III			Mogul II Byzantium I	T'ang I, II Sung I, II Yüan Ch'ing Rome II, III Spanish-American II Spain II Russia II France I Ottoman II Maurya II	Russia III			Sweden III England II
5					Austria Prussia I Russia I France II England I Spanish-American I	Sweden I		Byzantium II	Spanish-American III England III Sweden II

TABLE 16

Relations among Differentiation of Groups, Autonomy of Ruler's Goals, and Articulation of Political Goals of Groups

Autonomy of ruler's goals	ARTICULATION OF POLITICAL GOALS OF GROUPS								
	Low Differentiation (1-3)			Medium Differentiation (4-6)			High Differentiation (7-9)		
	1	2	3	1	2	3	1	2	3
1	Inca Egypt III Sassanid II, IV			Abbassid II Saffawid I					
2	Egypt I Sassanid I	Egypt II		Gupta Ottoman I Moslem Spain I	T'ang III Sung III				
3	Ptolemies Mogul I	Sassanid III		Seleucid Maurya I Abassid I Moslem Spain II Ottoman III Russia II Saffawid II	Byzantium III Rome I Spain I				France III
4	Mogul III			Maurya II Mogul II Ottoman II Rome II Byzantium I	T'ang I, II Sung I, II Yüan Ming Ch'ing Rome III Spanish-American II Spain II Russia III Prussia II France I			Sweden III England II	
5				Austria Russia I Spanish-American I Sweden I Prussia I France II England I				Byzantium II	Spanish-American III Sweden II England III

TABLE 17

Relations between Political Orientation of Bureaucracy
and Extent of Embeddedness of Bureaucracy

Embeddedness of Bureaucracy in	POLITICAL ORIENTATION OF BUREAUCRACY TO					
	Ruler	Group	Ruler and Group	Self	Self and Polity	No data
Central political authority	Inca Sassanid III Maurya I, II Gupta Mogul I, II, III Ottoman I Rome I Spanish- American I Austria Spain I Sweden I Russia I Prussia I England I		Russia II		Egypt II Ottoman II	
Central political authority and aristocracy				Sassanid II Sassanid IV Byzantium III	Egypt I Sassanid I	
Central political authority and middle group	France II		Byzantium I, II Abassid I France I	Abassid II		Ptolemies

Aristocracy	Egypt III	Spain II
		Sweden II
			Russia III	Spanish-
				    American III
					Moslem
					    Spain I, II
					Prussia II	

Aristocracy and middle group		England II, III	Spanish- American II	France III		Seleucid
Middle group					Saffawid I, II	
Gentry			T'ang I, II Sung I, II Yüan Ming Ch'ing	T'ang III Sung III		
Not embedded	Rome II			Ottoman III	Rome III Sweden III	

TABLE 18
Relations between Political Orientation of Bureaucracy and Types of Bureaucratic Activity

Types of Bureaucratic Activity	Ruler	POLITICAL ORIENTATION OF BUREAUCRACY TO				
		Group	Ruler and Group	Self	Self and Polity	No data
Technical		England III				
Technical-regulative	Gupta Rome I Mogul I, II				Moslem Spain II	Ptolemies Seleucid
Balanced	Inca Rome II	Sweden II	Abassid I		Egypt I Saffawid II Ottoman II	

Regulative-technical	Egypt III
	Sassanid III
	Maurya I, II
	Mogul III
	Ottoman I
	Austria
	Spanish-
	  American I
	Spain I
	Sweden I
	Russia I
	Prussia I
	France II
		England II	T'ang I, II
			Sung I, II
			Yüan
			Ming
			Ch'ing
			Byzantium II
			Spanish-
			  American II
			Russia III
				T'ang III
				Sung III
				Ottoman III
				Spanish-
				  American III
				France III
					Sassanid I
					Rome III
					Sweden III
					Prussia II	

Regulative		Spain II	Byzantium I Russia II France I	Sassanid II, IV Byzantium III Abassid II Spain II	Egypt II Saffawid I	
No data					Moslem Spain I	

TABLE 19
Relations among Type of Reference of Ruler's Goals, Differentiation of Groups, and Extent of Embeddedness of Bureaucracy

Embeddedness of Bureaucracy in	*Cultural-ascriptive Reference*			*Political-collective Reference*		
	1-3	4-6	7-9	1-3	4-6	7-9
Central political authority	Inca Egypt II			Sassanid III	England I Sweden I Russia I	
Central authority and aristocracy	Egypt I			Sassanid I, II, IV		
Central authority and middle group					France I	
Aristocracy	Egypt III				Sweden II	
Gentry		T'ang I, II, III Sung I, II, III Yüan Ming Ch'ing				
Not embedded						Sweden III

Embeddedness of Bureaucracy in	*Political-collective and Economic-collective Reference*			*Political-collective and Cultural-collective reference*		
	1-3	4-6	7-9	1-3	4-6	7-9
Central political authority		Austria Russia I			Maurya I Rome I Spain I	
Central authority and middle group		France II				Byzantium II
Aristocracy		Russia III	Spanish American III			
Aristocracy and middle group			England I France III		Spanish-American II	
Not embedded					Rome II	

Embeddedness of Bureaucracy in	*Political-collective and Social-group Reference*			*Political-collective and Self-maintenance Reference*		
	1-3	4-6	7-9	1-3	4-6	7-9
Central political authority				Mogul I, III	Ottoman I, II Spanish-American I Gupta Mogul II	
Central authority and middle group					Byzantium I	
Aristocracy					Spain II Russia II	
Aristocracy and middle group			England II			
Not embedded					Ottoman III Rome III	

Embeddedness of Bureaucracy in	*Cultural-collective Reference*			*Self-maintenance Reference*		
	1-3	4-6	7-9	1-3	4-6	7-9
Central political authority		Maurya II			Russia II	
Central authority and aristocracy					Byzantium III	
Central authority and middle group		Abassid I, II		Ptolemies		
Aristocracy		Moslem Spain I, II				
Aristocracy and middle group					Seleucid	
Middle group					Saffawid I, II	

TABLE 20

Relations among Types of Reference of Ruler's Goals, Compatibility of Goals of Ruler and Groups, and Extent of Embeddedness of Bureaucracy

Embeddedness of Bureaucracy in	Cultural-ascriptive Reference				Political collective Reference			
	Compatible Goals		Incompatible Goals		Compatible Goals		Incompatible Goals	
	Active	Passive	Active	Passive	Active	Passive	Active	Passive
Central Political Authority	Inca, Egypt II					Sassanid III, England I	Sweden I	Prussia I
Central Authority and Aristocracy		Egypt I				Sassanid I	Sassanid II, IV	
Central Authority and Middle Group						France II		
Aristocracy		Egypt III			Sweden II			
Gentry	T'ang I, II; Sung I, II; Yüan; Ming; Ch'ing		T'ang III; Sung II					
Not embedded						Sweden II		

Embeddedness of Bureaucracy in	Political-collective and Economic-collective Reference				Political-collective and Cultural-collective Reference			
	Compatible Goals		Incompatible Goals		Compatible Goals		Incompatible Goals	
	Active	Passive	Active	Passive	Active	Passive	Active	Passive
Central Political Authority	Russia III	Austria				Maurya I		
Central Authority and Middle Group		France II		Russia I				
Aristocracy		Spanish-American III			Byzantium II			
Aristocracy and middle group		England II	France III			Spanish-American II		
Not embedded					Rome II			Rome I, Spain I

	Political-collective and Social-group Reference	Political-collective and Self-maintenance Reference
Central Political Authority	Abassid I; Ottoman I, II	Gupta; Mogul I, II; Mogul III
Central Authority and Middle Group	Abassid II	Byzantium I; Ptolemies
Aristocracy	Spain II; Prussia II	
Aristocracy and middle group	England III	
Not embedded		Ottoman III; Rome III

	Cultural-collective Reference	Self-maintenance Reference
Central Political Authority	Maurya II	Russia II
Central authority and aristocracy		Byzantium III
Aristocracy	Moslem Spain II	Moslem Spain I
Aristocracy and middle group		Seleucid
In middle group		Saffawid I; Saffawid II

Bibliography

The following bibliography is classified according to the societies analyzed in the text. General works related to the subject of the book are also included. The most detailed—although certainly not exhaustive—sections are about the non-European societies presented in the case studies, such as the Chinese Empire, the Byzantine Empire, the Spanish-American Empire, the Sassanid Empire and, to a smaller extent, the Abbassid Empire.

The lists of works about Europe in general, and about France, England, and Russia in particular, are much less detailed. They are mostly limited to basic works on these societies and to more specialized works that are related to the specific problems dealt with in the text. Even fewer works concerned with societies analyzed only in the tables are listed.

Abbreviations of Journals

AJS	American Journal of Sociology	JAOS	Journal of the American Oriental Society
ASR	American Sociological Review		
BSOAS	Bulletin of the School of Oriental and African Studies	JAS	Journal of Asiatic Studies
		JRAS	Journal of the Royal Asiatic Society
BZ	Byzantinische Zeitschrift		
FEQ	Far Eastern Quarterly	REB	Revue des études byzantines
HAHR	Hispanic American Historical Review	RH	Revue historique
		TP	T'oung Pao
		VSWG	Vierteljahrschrift für Sozial und Wirtschaftsgeschichte
HJAS	Harvard Journal of Asiatic Studies		
HZ	Historische Zeitschrift	ZDMG	Zeitschrift der Deutschen Morgenländischen Gesellschaft
JA	Journal Asiatique		

Outline

A. General

1. POLITICAL SOCIOLOGY

ALMOND, G. A. (1960), "A Functional Approach to Comparative Politics," in Almond, G. A., and Coleman, J. S. (eds.), *The Politics of the Developing Areas*, Princeton, pp. 5-64.

APTER, D. F. (1958), "A Comparative Method for the Study of Politics," *AJS*, LXIV, 221-238.

BEER, S. H. (1958), "The Analysis of Political Systems," in Beer, S. H., and Ulam, A. B. (eds.), *Patterns of Government*, New York, pp. 3-51.

BORCH, H. (1954), *Obrigkeit und Widerstand: Zur politischen Soziologie des Beamtentums*, Tübingen.

EASTON, D. (1957), "An Approach to the Analysis of Political Systems," *World Politics*, X, 383-400.

—— (1959), "Political Anthropology," in Siegal, B. (ed.), *Biennial Review of Anthropology*, Stanford, Calif., pp. 210-262.

EISENSTADT, S. N. (ed.) (1954), *Political Sociology* (in Hebrew), Tel Aviv.

—— (1958), "The Study of Oriental Despotism as Systems of Total Power" (review of Wittfogel, K. A., 1957), *JAS*, XVII, 435-447.

—— (1959), "Primitive Political Systems," *American Anthropologist*, LXI, 200-220.

FINER, H. (1949), *The Theory and Practice of Modern Government*, New York.

FRIEDRICH, C. J. (1950), *Constitutional Government and Democracy*, Boston.

LEVY, M. J. (1952), *The Structure of Society*, Princeton, N.J., especially ch. X.

MC IVER, M. (1926), *The Modern State*, Oxford.

MOSCA, G. (1947), *Elementi di scienza politica*, Bari.

—— (1958), *Ciò che la storia potrebbe insegnare: Scritti di scienza politica*, Milan.

OPPENHEIMER, F. (1912), *Der Staat*, Munich.

PARSONS, T. (1960), "Authority, Legitimation, and Political Action," in *Structure and Process in Modern Societies*, New York, pp. 170-199.

—— and SMELSER, N. J. (1956), *Economy and Society*, London.

PULLEYBLANK, E. G. (1958), Review of K. A. Wittfogel, *Oriental Despotism*, *BSOAS*, XXI, 657-660.

REDFIELD, R., and SINGER, M. (1954), "The

Cultural Role of Cities," *Economic Development and Cultural Change*, III, 53-74.

RIGGS, F. W. (1957), "Agraria and Industria: Towards a Typology of Comparative Administration," in Siffin, W. J. (ed.), *Towards the Comparative Study of Public Administration*, Bloomington, Ind., pp. 23-116.

ROBERTS, J. M., and ALMOND, G. A. (1957), "The Political Process in Primitive Societies" (mimeo), Stanford, Calif.

SMELSER, N. J. (1959), "A Comparative View of Exchange Systems," *Economic Development and Cultural Change*, VII, 173-182.

SOCIÉTÉ JEAN BODIN (1954-55), *Recueils*, V, VI, VII, La Ville, Bruxelles.

SPEIER, H. (1952), *Social Order and the Risks of War*, New York.

SUTTON, F. X. (1955), "Social Theory and Comparative Politics" (mimeo), Social Science Research Council, New York.

WEBER, M. (1920-21), *Gesammlte Aufsätze zur Religionssoziologie*, Tübingen.

⸺ (1922), *Wirtschaft und Gesellschaft*, Tübingen.

⸺ (1924[a]), *Gesammlte Aufsätze zur Sozial- und Wirtschaftsgeschichte*, Tübingen, especially ch. 1-3.

⸺ (1924[b]), *Wirtschaftsgeschichte*, Munich.

WILSON, C. H. (1957), *Profit and Power*, London.

WITTFOGEL, K. A. (1957), *Oriental Despotism*, New Haven.

2. HISTORICAL WORKS

BRUNNER, O. (1956), *Neue Wege der Sozialgeschichte*, Göttingen.

COULBORN, R. (1958), "The State and Religion: Iran, India, and China," *Comparative Studies in Society and History*, I, 44-57.

HOSELITZ, B. (1956), "Economic Stagnation in Agrarian Empires" (mimeo), Harvard University Center of Far Eastern Studies, Cambridge, Mass.

MÜHL, M. (1933), *Untersuchungen zur altorientalischen und althellenischen Gesetzgebung*, Leipzig.

NEF, J. U. (1958), *Cultural Foundations of Industrial Civilization*, Cambridge.

NICHOS, J. H., et al. (1959), "Debate—The State and Religion," *Comparative Studies in Society and History*, I, 383-387.

SCHILLING, W. (1957), *Religion und Recht*, Zurich and Vienna, especially ch. II, 2.

SOCIAL SCIENCE MONOGRAPHS (1958), *Irrigation Civilizations: A Comparative Study*, Pan-American Union, Washington, D.C.

STRAYER, R. J. (1958), "The State and Religion: Greece and Rome, the West, Islam," *Comparative Studies in Society and History*, I, 38-43.

TURNER, R. (1941), *The Great Cultural Traditions: Vol. I, The Ancient Cities*, New York.

WITTFOGEL, K. A. (1932), "Die natürlichen Ursachen der Wirtschaftsgeschichte," *Archiv für Sozialwissenschaft und Sozialpolitik*, LXVII, 466-492, 599-609, 711-731.

⸺ (1938), "Die Theorie der Orientalischen Gesellschaft," *Zeitschrift für Sozialforschung*, VII, 90-122.

B. The Greek City-States

ADCOCK, F. E. (1939), "The Reform of the Athenian State," in *The Cambridge Ancient History*, vol. IV, pp. 26-58.

BEYER, W. C. (1959), "The Civil Service of the Ancient World," *Public Administration Review*, XIX, 243-249.

BOWRA, C. M. (1957), *The Greek Experience*, London.

CALHOUN, G. M. (1913), *Athenian Clubs in Politics and Litigation*, Austin, Tex.

CLOCHE, P. (1951), *La démocratie athénienne*, Paris.

EHRENBERG, V. (1960), *The Greek State*, New York.

FERGUSON, W. S. (1940[a]), "The Oligarchical Movement in Athens," in *The Cambridge Ancient History*, vol. V, pp. 312-347.

——— (1940[b]), "The Fall of the Athenian Empire," *ibid.*, pp. 348-375.

GLOTZ, G. (1926), *Ancient Greece at Work*, London.

——— (1929), *The Greek City*, London.

GOMME, A. W. (1939), *Essays in Greek History and Literature*, Oxford.

HEICHELHEIM, F. M. (1938), *Wirtschaftsgeschichte des Altertums*, Leiden.

JONES, A. H. M. (1940), *The Greek City from Alexander to Justinian*, Oxford.

THOMSON, G. (1946), *Studies in Ancient Greek Society*, London.

TOD, M. N. (1940), "The Economic Background of the Fifth Century," in *The Cambridge Ancient History*, vol. V, pp. 1-32.

TOYNBEE, A. J. (1959), *Hellenism: The History of a Civilization*, London.

C. The Mongol Empire

BACON, E. E. (1954), "Types of Pastoral Nomadism in Central and Southwest Asia," *Southwestern Journal of Anthropology*, X, 44-68.

HAENISCH, E. (1933), "Die letzten Feldzüge Cinggis Han's und sein Tod; nach der ostasiatischen Uberlieferung," *Asia Major*, IX, 503-533.

——— (1941), "Kulturbilder aus Chinas Mongolenzeit," *HZ*, CLXIV, 21-49.

——— (1943), *Die Kulturpolitik des Mongolischen Weltreichs*, Berlin.

KRADER, L. (1955), "Principles and Structures in the Organization of the Asiatic Steppe-Pastoralists, *Southwestern Journal of Anthropology*, XI, 67-92.

——— (1958), "Feudalism and the Tatar Polity of the Middle Ages," *Comparative Studies in Society and History*, I, 76-99.

LATTIMORE, O. (1947), "Inner Asian Frontiers: Chinese and Russian Margins of Expansion," *Journal of Economic History*, VII, 24-52.

——— (1951), *The Inner Asian Frontiers of China*, New York.

PELLIOT, P. (1951), *Histoire des Campagnes de Gengis Khan Cheng-Wou Ts'in-Tscheng Lou*, Leiden.

SCHRAM, M. J. (1954), *The Mongols of the Kansa Tibetan Frontier*, Philadelphia.

SPULER, B. (1948), *Die Mongolenzeit*, Berlin.

——— (1950), "Geschichte Mittelasiens," in Waldschmidt, E., *et al.*, *Geschichte Asiens*, Munich, pp. 309-360.

VERNADSKII, G. (1938), "The Scope and Contents of Chinghis Khan's Yasa," *HJAS*, III, 337-360.

——— (1939), "Tuwaini's Version of Chingis Khan's Yasa," *Annales de l'Institut Koudakov*, XI, 35-45.

——— (1953), *The Mongols and Russia*, New Haven.

VLADIMITSOV, B. Y. (1948), *Le régime social des mongols*, Paris.

——— (1950), *Life of Chinghis Khan*, London.

VREELAND, H. H. (1954), *Mongol Community and Kinship Structure*, New Haven.

D. European Feudalism

BISSON, T. N. (1957), "Coinages and Royal Monetary Policy in Languedoc during the Reign of St. Louis," *Speculum*, XXXIII, 443-470.

BLOCH, M. (1931), "Féodalité, vassalité, seigneurie: À propos de quelques travaux récents," *Annales*, III, 246-260.

——— (1937), "La genèse de la seigneurie: Idée d'une recherche comparée," *Annales*, IX, 225-227.

——— (1939-40), *La société féodale*, Paris, 2 vols.

BOSCH, K. (1960), Über soziale Mobilität in der mittelalterlichen Gesellschaft," *VSWG*, XLVII, 306-332.

BOUTRUCHE, R. (1939), "Aux origines d'une crise nobiliaire: Donations pieuses et pratiques successorales en Bordelais du XIIIième au XVIième siècle," *Annales*, XI, 161-177, 257-277.

——— (1959), *Seigneurie et féodalité; le premier âge des liens d'homme à homme*, Paris.

CAHEN, C. (1960), "Reflexions sur l'usage du mot de 'féodalité,'" *Journal of the Economic and Social History of the Orient*, III, 2-20.

CAM, H. M. (1940), "The Decline and Fall of British Feudalism," *History*, XXV, 216-233.

——— (1954), "Mediaeval Representation in Theory and Practice," *Speculum*, XXIX, 347-355.

COULBORN, R. (ed.) (1956), *Feudalism in History*, Princeton, N.J., pp. 188-214, 236-324.

CRONNE, H. A. (1940), "The Origins of Feudalism," *History*, XXIV, 251-259.

GANSHOF, F. L. (1937), "Note sur les origines de l'union du bénéfice avec la vassalité," in *Etudes d'histoire dédiées à la mémoire de Henry Pirenne*, Brussels, pp. 173-189.

——— (1947). *Quest-ce que la féodalité?*, Brussels.

HINTZE, O. (1929), "Wesen und Verbreitung des Feudalismus," *Sitz. der Preussischen Akademie der Wissenschaften, Phil.-hist. Klasse*, pp. 321-347.

LOT, F. (1933), "Origine et nature du bénéfice," *Annuario de historia del derecho español*, X, 175-185.

MC ILWAIN, C. H. (1932), "Medieval Estates," in *The Cambridge Medieval History*, vol. VII, pp. 665-713.

MITTEIS, H. (1953), *Der Staat des Hohen Mittelalters: Grundlinien einer vergleichende Verfassungsgeschichte des Lehnzeitaltes*, Weimar.

MOR, C. G. (1952), *L'età feudale*, Milan.

SANCHEZ-ALBORNOZ, C. (1942), *En torno a los origenes del feudalismo*, Mendoza.

SESTAN, E. (1946), "L'Italia nell'età feudale," in Rota, E. (ed.), *Questioni di storia medioevale*, Milan, pp. 77-127.

STENTON, F. M. (1935), "The Changing Feudalism of the Middle Ages," *History*, XIX, 289-301.

STEPHENSON, C. (1954), *Mediaeval Institutions: Selected Essays*, Ithaca, N.Y.

STRAYER, J. R. (1956), "Feudalism in Western Europe," in Coulborn, R. (ed.), *Feudalism in History*, Princeton, N.J., pp. 15-25.

———, and COULBORN, R. (1956), "The Idea of Feudalism," *ibid.*, pp. 3-11.

———, and TAYLOR, C. H. (1939), *Studies in Early French Taxation*, Cambridge.

THALAMAS, A. (1945), *Les origines de la société française*, Paris.

——— (1951), *La société seigneuriale française (1050-1270)*, Paris.

TOYNBEE, A. P., KROEBER, A. L., *et al.* (1950), *Conference on Feudalism*, Institute for Advanced Study, Princeton, N.J.

E. Ahmenid, Carolingian, and Inca Empires

1. AHMENIDS

CHRISTENSEN, A. E. (1936), *L'Iran sous les sassanides,* Copenhagen, ch. I.

DELAPORTE, L., and HUART, C. (1943), *L'Iran antique,* Paris.

EHTÉCHAM, M. (1946), *L'Iran sous les Achéménides,* Fribourg.

GALLING, K. (1937), *Syrien in der Politik der Achaemeniden,* Leipzig.

JUNGE, P. J. (1941-42), "Satrapie und Natio: Reichsverwaltung und Reichspolitik im Staate Dareios' I," *Klio,* XVI, 1-55.

MELONI, P. (1951), "La grande rivolta dei satrapi contro Artaserse II (370–359 A.C.). *Rivista storica italiana,* LXIII, 5-27.

2. CAROLINGIAN

BLOCH, M. (1952), "Les réformes monétaires carolingiennes," *Annales,* XXIV, 13-19.

GANSHOF, F. L. (1939), "Bénéfice and Vassalage in the Age of Charlemagne," *Cambridge Historical Journal,* VI, 147-175.

HALPHEN, L. (1947), *Charlemagne et l'empire carolingien,* Paris.

JUSSELIEN, M. (1922), "La chancellerie de Charles le Chauve," *Le moyen âge,* XXXIII, 1-91.

TESSIER, G. (1938), "Variétés," *Le moyen âge,* II, 14-81.

3. INCA

BAUDIN, L. (1928), *L'empire socialiste des Inka,* Paris.

——— (1955), *La vie quotidienne au temps des derniers Incas,* Paris.

BRAM, J. (1941), *An Analysis of Inca Militarism,* New York.

CUNOW, H. (1896), *Die Soziale Verfassung des Inkareichs,* Stuttgart.

KIRCHHOFF, P. (1949), "The Social and Political Organization of the Andean Peoples," in Stewart, J. H. (ed.), *Handbook of South American Indians,* vol. V, pp. 294-311.

MARKHAM, C. (1910), *The Incas of Peru,* London.

MASON, A. (1957), *Ancient Civilizations of Peru,* London.

MOORE, S. F. (1958), *Power and Property in Inca Peru,* New York.

F. The Ancient Egyptian Empire

ALLIOT, M. (1950), "Réflexions sur le pouvoir royal en Egypte depuis Téti jusqu'à Ahmosis," *Journal of Near Eastern Studies,* IX, 204-214.

BADAWY, A. (1952), "Le travail dans l'Egypte pharaonique," *Cahiers d'histoire égyptienne,* IV, 167-193.

BAGNANI, G. (1934), "Il primo intendente del pallazzo, Imenhotpe, detto Huy," *Aegyptus,* XIV, 33-49.

BECHERAT, J. VON (1951), *Tanis und Theben: Historische Grundlagen der Ramsessidenzeit in Ägypten,* Glückstadt.

BEYER, W. C. (1959), "The Civil Service of the Ancient World," *Public Administration Review,* XIX, 243-249.

CHEHATA, C. (1954), "Le testament dans l'Egypte pharaonique," *Revue historique de droit français et étranger,* XXXII, 1-23.

DRIOTON, E., and VANDIER, J. (1952), *L'Egypte (Les peuples de l'Orient mediterranéen,* vol. II), Paris.

EDGARD, D. O. (1960), "Die Beziehungen Babyloniens und Ägyptens in der mittel-babylonischen Zeit und das Gold," *Journal of the Economic and Social History of the Orient,* III, 38-55.

EDGERTON, W. F. (1947[a]), "The Government and the Governed in the Egyptian Empire," *Journal of Near Eastern Studies,* VI, 152-160.

——— (1947[b]), "The Nauri Decree of Seti I: A Translation and Analysis of the Legal Portion," *ibid.,* VI, 219-230.

——— (1951), "The Strikes in Ramses III's Twenty-ninth Year," *ibid.,* X, 137-145.

——— (1956), "The Question of Feudal Institutions in Ancient Egypt," in Coulborn, R. (ed.), *Feudalism in History,* Princeton, N.J., pp. 120-132.

ERMAN, A. (1923), *Ägypten und Ägyptisches Leben im Altertum,* Tübingen.

FARINA, G. (1921), "Rivolgimenti politici nell'antico Egitto," *Aegyptus* II, 3-17.

FRANKFORT, H. (1948), *Kingship and the Gods,* Chicago.

——— (1951), *The Birth of Civilization in the Near East,* London.

HAYES, W. C. (1953), "Notes on the Government of Egypt in the Late Middle Kingdom," *Journal of Near Eastern Studies,* XII, 31-39.

HELLEK, W. (1954), *Untersuchungen zu den Beamtentiteln des Ägyptischen alten Reiches,* Glückstadt.

KEES, H. (1933[a]), "Ägypten," in *Handbuch der Altertumskunde, Kulturgeschichte des Alten Orients,* Munich, vol. III, ch. 1.

——— (1933[b]), "Beiträge zur altägyptischen Provinzialverwaltung und der Geschichte des Feudalismus," *Nachrichten von der Gesellschaft der Wissenschaften zu Göttingen, Phil.-hist. Klasse,* III, 579-598.

——— (1934), "Herihor und die Aufrichtung des thebanischen Gottesstaates," *ibid.,* I, 1-20.

——— (1935), "Zur Innenpolitik der Saitendynastie," *ibid.,* n.s., I, 95-106.

——— (1940), "Beitrage zur Geschichte des Vezirats im Alten Reich," *ibid.,* n.s., IV, 40-54.

——— (1952), "Wandlungen des Ägyptischen Geschichtsbildes," *Journal of Near Eastern Studies,* XI, 157-163.

——— (1953), *Das Priestertum im Ägyptischen Staat vom Neuen Reich bis zur Spätzeit,* Leiden and Cologne.

LEEMANS, W. F. (1960), "The Trade Relations of Babylonia and the Question of Relations with Egypt in the Old Babylonian Period," *Journal of the Economic and Social History of the Orient,* III, 21-37.

MASPERO, M. G. (1890), "La carrière administrative de deux hauts fonctionnaires égyptiens vers la fin de la IIIième dynastie," *JA,* XV, 269-428.

MEYER, E. (1928), "Gottesstaat, Militärherrschaft und Ständewesen in Ägypten," *Sitz. der Preussischen Akademie der Wissenschaften, Phil.-hist. Klasse,* XXVIII, 495-532.

MOULET, P. (1946), *La vie quotidienne au temps des Ramsès (XIIIième–XIIième siècles),* Paris.

OTTO, E. (1953), *Ägypten: Der Weg des Pharaonenreiches,* Stuttgart.

PIRENNE, J. (1948), "L'écrit pour argent et l'écrit de cession dans l'ancien droit égyptien," *Revue internationale des droits de l'antiquité,* I, 173-188.

REMONDON, R. (1955), "Problèmes militaires en Egypte et dans l'Empire à la fin du IVième siècle," *RH,* LXXIX, 21-38.

SCHARFF, A. (1936), "Der Historische Abschnitt der Lehre für König Merikarê," *Sitz. der Bayerischen Akademie der Wissenschaften, Phil.-hist. Abteilung,* n. s.

SEIDL, E. (1933), "Law, Egyptian," in *Encyclopedia of the Social Sciences,* vol. IX, pp. 209-211.

——— (1939), *Einführung in die ägyptische Rechtsgeschichte bis zum Ende des Neuen Reiches, I: Juristischer Teil,* Glückstadt, Hamburg, and New York.

SPIEGEL, J. (1950), *Soziale und weltanschauliche Reformbewegungen im alten Ägypten,* Heidelberg.

STOCK, H. (1949), *Die erste Zwischenzeit Ägyptens,* Rome.

——— (1955), *Studien zur Geschichte der Archäologie der 13 bis 17 Dynastie Ägyptens,* Glückstadt.

VOYOTTE, J. (1954), "Trois généraux de la XIXième dynastie (à propos de l'égyptien "Suta," KUB, III, 57)," *Orientalia,* XXIII, 223-231.

WEILL, R. (1932), "Compléments pour la fin du moyen empire égyptien," *Bulletin de l'institut français d'archéologie orientale,* XXXII, 7-52.

WILSON, J. A. (1951), *The Burden of Egypt,* Chicago.

——— (1954), "Authority and Law in Ancient Egypt," supplement, *JAOS,* LXXIV, 1-8.

WINLOCK, H. E. (1943), "The Eleventh Egyptian Dynasty," *Journal of Near Eastern Studies,* II, 249-283.

G. Sassanids

ADONIZ, N. (1937), "L'aspect iranien du servage," *Recueils de la Societé Jean Bodin,* II, 135-153.

ALTHEIM, F. (1955[a]), *Reich gegen Mitternacht,* Hamburg.

——— (1955[b]), *Gesicht von Abend und Morgen,* Frankfurt.

——— (1956), "Arsakiden und Sassaniden," in Valjavec, F. (ed.), *Historia Mundi,* Berne, vol. IV, pp. 516-541.

ALTHEIM, F., and STIEHL, R. (1954), *Ein asiatischer Staat: Feudalismus unter den Sassaniden und ihren Nachbarn,* Wiesbaden.

———, and STIEHL, R. (1957), *Finanzgeschichte der Spätantike,* Frankfurt.

BAILEY, H. W. (1943), *Zoroastrian Problems in the Nineteenth Century Books,* Oxford.

BENVENISTE, E. (1932), "Les classes sociales dans la tradition avestique," *JA,* CCXXI, 117-134.

——— (1938), *Les images dans l'ancien Iran,* Paris.

BIANCHI, V. (1958), *Zaman i Ohrmazd-Lo Zoroastrismo nelle sui origini e nella sua essenza,* Turin.

BROWNE, E. G. (1951-53), *A Literary History of Persia,* Cambridge.

CHRISTENSEN, A. (1925), *Le règne du roi Khawadh et le communisme mazdakite,* Copenhagen.

——— (1933), "Die Iranier," in Alt, A., et al., *Kulturgeschichte des alten Orients,* Munich, vol. III.

——— (1936), *L'Iran sous les Sassanides,* Copenhagen.

——— (1939), "Sassanid Persia," in *The Cambridge Ancient History,* vol. XII, pp. 109-137.

COULBORN, R. (1958-59), "The State and Religion: Iran, India, and China," *Comparative Studies in Society and History,* I, 44-57.

DELAPORTE, L., and HUART, C. (1943), *L'Iran antique,* Paris.

DHALLA, M. N. (1938), *History of Zoroastrianism,* New York.

FAZIOLLEH, M. (1938), *L'évolution des finances iraniennes,* Paris.

FRY, R. N. (1956), Review of Altheim, F., and Stiehl, R. (1954), *Central Asiatic Journal,* II, 298-302.

GHIRSHMAN, R. (1954), *Iran,* London.

HENNIG, W. B. (1951), *Zoroaster,* Oxford.

KLIMA, O. (1957), *Mazdak: Geschichte einer sozialen Bewegung im sassanidischen Persien,* Prague.

MASSÉ, H. (1939), Review of Christensen, A. (1936), *Journal des savants,* pp. 165-168.

——— (ed.) (1952), *La civilisation iranienne,* Paris.

MENASCE, R. P. DE (1955), "L'église mazdéenne dans l'empire sassanide," *Journal of World History,* II, 554-565.

MOLE, M. (1953), Deux aspects de l'orthodoxie zoroastienne," *Annuaire de l'institut de philologie et d'histoire orientales et slaves*, XII, 289-324.

NYBERG, H. S. (1938), *Die Religionen des Alten Iran*, Leipzig.

STEIN, E. (1920), "Ein Kapitel vom Persischen und vom Byzantinischen Staat," *Byzantinisch-neugriechische Jahrbücher*, I, 50-89.

WIDENGREN, G. (1956), "Recherches sur le féodalisme iranien," *Orientalia Suecana*, V, 79-182.

H. Hellenistic Dynasties: Ptolemies and Seleucids

ATKINSON, K. C. (1952), "Some Observations on Ptolemaic Ranks and Titles," *Aegyptus*, XXXII, 204-215.

BEVAN, E. R. (1902), *History of the House of Seleucus*, London.

—— (1927), *History of Egypt under the Ptolemies*, London.

BIKERMANN, E. (1938), *Les institutions des Séleucides*, Paris.

BOUCHÉ-LECLERCQ, A. (1913-14), *Historie des Séleucides (323–64 avant J. C.)*, Paris.

CARY, M. (1951), *History of the Greek World*, London.

COOK, S. A., et al. (eds.) (1928), "The Hellenistic Monarchies and the Rise of Rome," in *The Cambridge Ancient History*, vol. VII.

—— (1930), "Rome and the Mediterranean," *ibid.*, vol. VIII.

HARPER, G. M., JR. (1934[a]), "Tax Contractors and Their Relation to Tax Collection in Ptolemaic Egypt," *Aegyptus*, XIV, 49-61.

—— (1934[b]), "The Relation of Αρχίογης, Μέτοχοι and Εγγοσι to Each Other, to the Government and to the Tax Contract in Ptolemaic Egypt," *ibid.*, XIV, 269-285.

HEICHELHEIM, F. M. (1938), "New Light on the Influence of Hellenistic Financial Administration in the Near East and India," *Economic History*, IV, 1-12.

MENTEVECCHI, O. (1937), "Contributi per una storia sociale ed economica della famiglia nell'Egitto greco-romano," *Aegyptus*, XVII, 338-349.

—— (1935-49), "Ricerche di sociologia nei documenti dell'Egitto greco-romano," *ibid.*, XV, 67-122; XVI, 3-84; XIX, 11-54; XXIV, 131-159; XXVII, 3-25; XXVIII, 129-168.

ROSTOVTZEFF, M. (1941), *The Social and Economic History of the Hellenistic World*, Oxford.

SCHILLER, A. A. (1933), "Law, Hellenistic and Graeco-Egyptian," in *Encyclopedia of the Social Sciences*, vol. IX, pp. 229-235.

SEIDL, E. (1952), "Neue Studien zum Eid im Ptolemäischen Recht," *Aegyptus*, XXXII, 311-323.

TARN, W. W., and GRIFFITH, G. T. (1953), *Hellenistic Civilization*, London.

J. China

Aspects de la Chine (1959), Paris.

BAGHI, P. C. (1950), *India and China: A Thousand Years of Cultural Relations*, Bombay.

BALÁZS, E. (1931-33), "Beiträge zur Wirtschaftsgeschichte der T'ang-Zeit (618-906)," *Mitteilungen des Seminars für Orientalische Sprachen zu Berlin*, XXXIV, 2-92; XXXV, 2-73.

—— (1948), "Entre révolte nihiliste et

évasion mystique; les courants intellectuels en Chine au IIIième siècle de notre ère," *Études Asiatiques*, II, 27-55.

—— (1950), "La crise sociale et la philosophie politique à la fin des Han," *JP*, XXXIX, 83-131.

—— (1952), "Les aspects significatifs de la société chinoise," *Études Asiatiques*, VI, 77-87.

—— (1953[a]), *Le traité économique du "Souei-Chou": Études sur la société et l'économie de la Chine médiévale*, Leiden.

—— (1953[b]), "Transformations du régime de la propriété dans la Chine tartare et dans la Chine chinoise aux IVième–VIème siècles, A.D.," *Journal of World History*, I, 417-427.

—— (1953[c]), "Les foires en Chine," *Recueils de la société Jean Bodin*, V, 77-89.

—— (1954[a]), "Le régime de la propriété en Chine du IVième au XIVième siècles; état de la question," *Journal of World History*, I, 669-679.

—— (1954[b]), "Les villes chinoises," *Recueils de la société Jean Bodin*, VI, 225-240.

—— (1954[c]), *Le traité juridique du "Souei-Chou": études sur la société et l'économie de la Chine médiévale*, Leiden.

—— (1957), "Chinesische Geschichtswerke als Wegweiser zur Praxis der Bürokratie," *Saeculum*, VIII, 210-223.

—— (1959)[a]), "La pérennité de la société bureaucratique en Chine," in *International Symposium on History of Eastern and Western Cultural Contacts* (mimeo), Tokyo, pp. 31-39.

—— (1959[b]), "Le droit chinois (I et II)," in *Aspects de la Chine*, Paris, pp. 195-203.

—— (1959[c]), "Confucius," *ibid.*, pp. 142-146.

—— (1960), "The Birth of Capitalism in China," *Journal of the Economic and Social History of the Orient*, III, 196-217.

BECKMANN, K. (1939), *Li Kang: Ein Staatsmann im Kampf zwischen konfuzianischer Beamtenpflicht und politischer Aufgabe*, Berlin.

BIELENSTEIN, H. (1953[a]), *The Restoration of the Han Dynasty*, Stockholm.

—— (1953[b]), *The Fall of a Chinese Dynasty*, Canberra.

BINGHAM, W. (1941), *The Founding of the T'ang Dynasty*, Baltimore.

BLOFIELD, J. (1948), *The Jewel in the Lotus: An Outline of Present Day Buddhism in China*, London.

BLUE, R. C. (1948), "The Argumentation of the Shih-Huo Chih," *HJAS*, XI, 90-100.

BODDE, D. (1953), "Harmony and Conflict in Chinese Philosophy," in Wright, A. F. (ed.), *Studies in Chinese Thought*, Chicago, pp. 19-80.

—— (1954), "Authority and Law in Ancient China," supplement, *JAOS*, LXXIV, 46-55.

—— (1956), "Feudalism in China," in Coulborn, R. (ed.), *Feudalism in History*, Princeton, N.J., pp. 49-92.

BOODBERG, P. (1939), "Marginalia to the Histories of the Northern Dynasties," *HJAS*, IV, 235-270.

BÜNGER, K. (1936), "Das Verhältniss zwischen Partie und Staat in China," *Zeitschrift für ausländisches öffentliches Recht und Völkerrecht*, VI, 286-303.

—— (1946?), *Quellen zur Rechtsgeschichte der T'ang-Zeit*, Peking.

—— (1947), "Über die Verantwortlichkeit der Beamten nach klassischem chinesischem Recht," *Studia Serica*, VI, 159-191.

—— (1952), "Die Rechtsidee in der Chinesischen Geschichte," *Saeculum*, III, 192-217.

BUSCH, H. (1955), "The Tung-lin Academy and Its Political and Philosophical Significance," *Monumenta Serica*, XIV, 1-163.

CAMMANN, S. (1953), "Presentation of Dragon Robes by the Ming and Ch'ing Courts for Diplomatic Purposes," *Sinologica*, III, 193-202.

CHAN, D. B. (1959), "The Role of the Monk Tao-yen in the Usurpation of the Prince of Yen (1398–1402)," *Sinologica*, VI, 83-98.

CHAN, W. T. (1951), "Neo-Confucianism," in MacNair, H. F. (ed.), *China*, Berkeley, Calif., pp. 254-266.

—— (1953), *Religious Trends in Modern China*, New York.

CHANG, C. L. (1955), *The Chinese Gentry*, Seattle.

CH'EN, K. (1952), "Anti-Buddhist Propaganda during the Nan-Ch'ao," *HJAS*, XV, 166-192.

—— (1954), "On Some Factors Responsible for the Anti-Buddhist Persecution under the Pei-ch'ao," *HJAS*, XVII, 261-273.

—— (1956), "The Economic Background of the Hui-ch'ang Suppression of Buddhism," *HJAS*, XIX, 67-105.

CH'EN, M. C. (1951), "The Greatness of Chou (*ca.* 1027–221 B.C.)," in MacNair, H. F. (ed.), *China*, Berkeley, Calif., pp. 54-72.

CHENG, F. T. (1956), "Sketch of the History, Philosophy, and Reform in Chinese Law," *Studies in the Law of the Far East and Southeast Asia*, Washington, D.C.

CHI, C. T. (1936), *Key Economic Areas in Chinese History, as Revealed in the Development of Public Works for Water Control*, London.

CHIA, C. Y. (1956), "The Church-State Conflict in the T'ang Dynasty," in Zen, E. T., and De Francis, J. (eds.), *Chinese Social History*, Washington, D.C., pp. 197-207.

CHIANG, S. T. (1954), *The Nien Rebellion*, Seattle.

CHOU, Y. L. (1945), "Tantrism in China," *HJAS*, VIII.

CHU, T. T. (1957), "Chinese Class Structure and Its Ideology," in Fairbank, J. K. (ed.), *Chinese Thought and Institutions*, Chicago, pp. 235-251.

COPLAND, D. B. (1948), *The Chinese Social Structure*, Sydney.

CREEL, H. G. (1931), "Confucius and Hsün-Tzu," *JAOS*, LI, 23-32.

DE BARY, W. (1953), "A Reappraisal of Neo-Confucianism," in Wright, A. F. (ed.), *Studies in Chinese Thought*, Chicago, pp. 81-111.

—— (1957), "Chinese Despotism and the Confucian Ideal: A Seventeenth Century View," in Fairbank, J. K. (ed.), *Chinese Thought and Institutions*, Chicago, pp. 163-204.

—— (1959), "Some Common Tendencies in Neo-Confucianism," in Nivison, D. S., and Wright, A. F. (eds.), *Confucianism in Action*, Stanford, Calif., pp. 25-49.

DEMIÉVILLE, P. (1959[a]), "Le Bouddhisme chinois," in *Aspects de la Chine*, pp. 62-166.

—— (1959[b]), "Le Bouddhisme sous les T'ang," *ibid.*, pp. 171-175.

DES ROUTOURS, R. (1926), "Les grands fonctionnaires des provinces en Chine sous la dynastie des T'ang," *TP*, XXIV, 219-315.

—— (1932), "Le traité des examens," traduit de la *Nouvelle histoire des T'ang*, vol. II, ch. XLIV-XLV, Paris.

—— (1947-48), "Traité des fonctionnaires et traité de l'armée," *ibid.*, vol. VI, tome I-II, ch. XLVI-I, Leiden.

—— (1955), "La religion dans la Chine antique," in Brilliant, M., and Angrain, R. (eds.), *Histoire des religions*, vol. II, Paris.

DUBS, H. H. (1938[a]), *Pan Ku: The History of the Former Han Dynasty*, vol. I, Baltimore.

—— (1938[b]), "The Victory of Han Confucianism," *JAOS*, LVIII, 435-449.

—— (1939), Wang Mang and His Economic Reforms, *TP*, XXXV, 263-265.

—— (1940), "A Military Contact between Chinese and Romans in 36 B.C.," *TP*, XXXVI, 64-81.

—— (1944), *Pan Ku: The History of the Former Han Dynasty*, vol. II, Baltimore.

—— (1951), "Taoism," in MacNair, H. F. (ed.), *China*, Berkeley, Calif., pp. 266-290.

DUYVENDAK, J. J. L. (1928), *The Book of the Lord Shang: A Classic of the Chinese School of Law*, London.

—— (1958), *Wegen en vormen van de Chinese geschiedenis*, Amsterdam.

EBERHARD, W. (1932), "Zur Landwirtschaft der Han-Zeit," *Mitteilungen des Seminars für orientalische Sprachen*, XXXV, 74-105.

—— (1940), "Bemerkungen zu statistischen Angaben der Han Zeit," *TP*, XXXVI, 1-26.

—— (1945), "Wie wurden Dynastien gegründet? Ein Problem der chinesischen Geschichte," *Dil ve Tarih-Cografya Fakültesi Derigesi* (Ankara) III, 361-376.

—— (1948[a]), *A History of China*, London.

—— (1948[b]), "Some Sociological Remarks on the Systems of Provincial Administration during the Period of the Five Dynasties," *Studia Serica*, Supplementary Volume, 1-18.

—— (1948[c]), "Die Beziehungen der Staaten der T'o-pa und der Sha-t'o zum Ausland," *Annales de l'Université d'Ankara*, II, 141-216.

—— (1948[d]), *Chinas Geschichte*, Berne.

—— (1951), "Remarks on the Bureaucracy in North China during the Tenth Century," *Oriens*, IV, 280-299.

—— (1952), *Conquerors and Rulers: Social Forces in Medieval China*, Leiden.

—— (1956), "Data on the Structure of the Chinese City in the Pre-Industrial Period," *Economic Development and Cultural Change*, IV, 253-269.

—— (1957), "The Political Function of Astronomy and Astronomers in Han China," in Fairbank, J. K. (ed.), *Chinese Thought and Institutions*, Chicago, pp. 31-71.

—— (1958), Review of Wittfogel, K. A. (1957), *ASR*, XXIII, 446-448.

EICHHORN, W. (1954), "Description of the Rebellion of Sun En and Earlier Taoist Rebellions," *Mitteilungen des Instituts für Orientforschung*, II.

EIICHI, K. (1960), "The New Confucianism and Taoism in China and Japan from the Fourth to the Thirteenth Centuries A.D.," *Journal of World History*, V, 801-829.

EISENSTADT, S. N. (1958), "The Study of Oriental Despotism as Systems of Total Power" (review of Wittfogel, K. A., 1957), *JAS*, XVII, 435-447.

ESCARRA, J. (1933), "Law, Chinese," in *Encyclopedia of the Social Sciences*, vol. IX, pp. 249-254.

—— (1936), *Le droit chinois*, Peking.

FAIRBANK, J. K. (ed.) (1957), *Chinese Thought and Institutions*, Chicago.

—— (1958), *The United States and China*, Cambridge, Mass.

FRANKE, H. (1940), "Dschan Mong-fü: Das Leben eines chinesischen Staatsmannes, Gelehrten und Künstlers unter der Mongolenherrschaft," *Sinica*, XV, 25-46.

—— (1949), *Geld und Wirtschaft in China unter der Mongolenherrschaft*, Leipzig.

—— (1951), "Neue Arbeiten zur Soziologie Chinas," *Saeculum*, II, 215-306.

—— (1953[a]), "Zur Grundsteuer in China während der Ming Dynastie (1368–1644)," *Zeitschrift für vergleichende Rechtswissenschaft*, LVI, 94-103.

—— (1953[b]), "Das Begriffsfeld des Staatlichen im chinesischen Kulturbereich," *Saeculum*, IV, 231-239.

FRANKE, O. (1925), "Der Ursprung der chinesischen Geschichtsschreibung," *Sitz. der preussischen Akademie der Wissenschaften, Hist.-phil. Klasse*, 276-309.

—— (1930-52), *Geschichte des chinesischen Reiches*, Berlin.

—— (1931), "Staatssozialistische Versuche im alten und mittelalterlichen China," *Sitz. der preussischen Akademie der Wissenschaften, Hist.-phil. Klasse*, 218-242.

—— (1932), "Der Bericht Wang An Shih's von 1058 über Reform des Beamtentums," *ibid.*, 264-312.

—— (1933[a]), "Das Konfuzianische System und die chinesische Krisis der Gegenwart," *Forschungen und Fortschritte*, IX.

—— (1933[b]), "Die angebliche Bekehrung chinesischer Kaiser zu einer fremden Religion," *ibid.*, 333-334.

—— (1937), "Zur Beurteilung des chinesischen Lehenswesens," *Sitz. der preussischen Akademie der Wissenschaften, Hist.-phil. Klasse*, 359-377.

—— (1945), *Aus Kultur und Geschichte Chinas; Vorträge und Abhandlungen aus den Jahren 1902–1942*, Peking.

—— (1946), Yu Ch'ien, *Monumenta Serica*, XI, 87-122.

FRANKE, W. (1956), Der gegenwärtige Stand der Forschung zur Geschichte Chinas im 15ten und 16ten Jahrhundert, *Saeculum*, VII, 413-442.

FRISCH, H. (1927), *Die lezten Jahre der Sung*, Berlin.

GALE, E. M. (1929), "Historical Evidences Relating to Early Chinese Public Finance," *Proceedings of the Pacific Coast Branch, American Historical Association*, pp. 48-62.

—— (1930), "Public Administration of Salt in China: A Historical Survey," *Annals of the Academy of Political and Social Sciences*, CLII, 241-251.

—— (1931), *Discourses on Salt and Iron: A Debate on State Control of Commerce and Industry in Ancient China*, Leiden.

GALT, H. S. (1951), *A History of Chinese Educational Institutions*, London.

GERNET, J. (1956), *Les aspects économiques du Bouddhisme*, Saigon.

—— (1958), *La vente en Chine d'après les contrats de Touen-Houang (IXième–Xième siècles)*, Leiden.

GLASENAPP, H. V. (1953), "Der Buddhismus in der Krise der Gegenwart," *Saeculum*, IV, 250-266.

—— (1940), "A Note on the Ta Ming Shih-lu," *TP*, XXXVI, 81-85.

GOODRICH, L. C. (1953), *The Literary Inquisition of Ch'ien-Lung*, Baltimore.

GRIMM, T. (1960), *Erziehung und Politik im Konfuzianischen China der Ming-Zeit (1368–1644)*, Wiesbaden.

GROOT, J. J. M. DE (1903), *Sectarianism and Religious Persecution in China*, Amsterdam.

HAENISCH, E. (1940), *Steuergerechtsame der chinesischen Klöster unter der Mongolenherrschaft*, Leipzig.

—— (1944), *Die Ehreninschrift für den Rebellengeneral Ts'ui Lih im Licht der konfuzianischen Moral, eine Episode aus dem 13ten Jahrhundert*, Berlin.

—— (1951), *Politische Systeme und Kämpfe im alten China*, Berlin.

—— (1952[a]), *Fürst und Volk, Soldat und Beamter in Staatsnot*, Munich.

—— (1952[b]), "Han Yü's Einspruch gegen die Prüfungssperre im Jahre 803, ein Kapitel aus der T'ang Zeit," *ZDMG*, CII, 280-300.

HALL, J. W. (1959), "The Confucian Teacher in Tokugawa Japan," in Nivison, D. S., and Wright, A. F. (eds.), *Confucianism in Action*, Stanford, Calif., pp. 268-301.

HALOUN, G. (1949-52), "The Liang-Chou Rebellion (184–221 A.D.)," *Asia Major*, I–II, 119-132.

HAMILTION, C. H. (1951), "Buddhism," in MacNair, H. F. (ed.), *China*, Berkeley, Calif., pp. 290-301.

HAN, Y. S. (1946), "The Chinese Civil Service Yesterday and Today," *Pacific Historical Review*, XV, 158–170.

HO, K. L. A. (1952), "The Grand Council in the Ch'ing Dynasty," *FEQ*, XI, 167-182.

HO, P. T. (1959), "Aspects of Social Mobility in China, 1368–1911," *Comparative Studies in Society and History*, I, 330-359.

HODOUS, L. (1951), "Folk Religion," in MacNair, H. F. (ed.), *China*, Berkeley, Calif., pp. 231-245.

HOLZMAN, D. (1957), "Les débuts du système médiéval de choix et de classement des fonctionnaires," in *Mélanges de l'institut des hautes études chinoises*, Paris, pp. 387-414.

HOU, J. C. (1956), "Frontier Horse Markets in the Ming Dynasty," in Zen, E. T., and De Francis, J. (eds.), *Chinese Social History*, Washington, D.C., pp. 309-333.

HSIA, N. (1956), "The Land Tax in the Yangtse Provinces before and after the Taiping Rebellion," *ibid.*, pp. 361-363.

HSIEH, P. C. (1925), *The Government of China (1644–1911)*, Baltimore.

HSÜ, L. T. (1956), "Social Relief during the Sung Dynasty," in Zen, E. T., and De Francis, J. (eds.), *Chinese Social History*, Washington, D.C., pp. 207-217.

HU, C. T. (1955), "The Yellow-River Administration in the Ching Dynasty," *FEQ*, XIV, 505-515.

HU, S. (1932), "The Development of Zen Buddhism in China," *Chinese Social and Political Science Review*, XV.

HUCKER, C. O. (1950), "The Chinese Censorate of the Ming Dynasty (Including an Analysis of Its Activities during the Decade 1424–1434)," (mimeo), University of Chicago thesis.

——— (1951), "The Traditional Chinese Censorate and the New Peking Regime," *American Political Science Review*, XV, 1040-1053.

——— (1958), "Governmental Organization of the Ming Dynasty," *HJAS*, XXI, 1-67.

——— (1959[a]), "Confucianism and the Chinese Censorial System," in Nivison, L. D., and Wright, A. F. (eds.), *Confucianism in Action*, Stanford, Calif., pp. 182-208.

——— (1959[b]), "Statecraft and Censorship in Ming China," in conference on Political Power in Traditional China (mimeo), Laconia, N.H.

HUGHES, E. R. (1932), "Political Idealists and Political Realists of China in the Fourth and Third centuries B.C.," *North China Branch, Royal Asiatic Society*, LXIII, 46-65.

HULSEWÉ, A. F. P. (1955), *Remnants of Han Law*, Vol. I (introductory studies and an annotated translation of ch. 22 and 23 of the *History of the Former Han Dynasty*), Leiden.

HUNG, W. (1957), "A Bibliographical Controversy at the T'ang Court (719 A.D.)," *HJAS*, XX, 74-135.

KAIZUKA, S. (1959), "Confucianism in Ancient Japan," *Journal of World History*, V, 41-58.

KALTENMARK, M. (1959[a]), "Le Confucianisme," in *Aspects de la Chine*, pp. 146-151.

——— (1959[b]), "Le Taoisme," *ibid.*, pp. 151-160.

KRACKE, E. A. (1953), *Civil Service in Early Sung China (960–1067)*, Cambridge, Mass.

——— (1955), "Sung Society; Change within Tradition," *FEQ*, XIV, 479-489.

——— (1957), "Religion, Family, and Individual in the Chinese Examination System," in Fairbank, J. K. (ed.), *Chinese Thought and Institutions*, Chicago, pp. 251-268.

KROKER, E. J. (1935), "Die Legitimation der Macht im chinesischen Altertum," *Sinologica*, III, 129-144.

LATTIMORE, O. (1951), *Inner Asian Frontiers of China*, New York.

LEE, S. C. (1954), "Administration and Bureaucracy: The Power Structure in Chinese Society," in *Transactions of the Second World Congress of Sociology*, London, pp. 3-16.

LEVENSON, J. R. (1953), " 'History' and 'Value': The Tensions of Intellectual Choice in Modern China," in Wright, A. F. (ed.), *Studies in Chinese Thought*, Chicago, pp. 146-194.

——— (1958), *Confucian China and Its Modern Fate*, London.

——— (1959), "The Suggestiveness of Vestiges: Confucianism and Monarchy at the Last," in Nivison, D. S., and Wright, A. F. (eds.), *Confucianism in Action*, Stanford, Calif., pp. 244-267.

LEVY, H. S. (1956), "Yellow Turban Religion and Rebellion at the End of Han," *JAOS*, LXXVI, 214-227.

——— (1959), "How a Prince Became Emperor: The Accession of Hsüan Tsung (713–755)," *Sinologica*, VI, 101-119.

LEVY, M. (1955), "Contrasting Factors in the Modernization of China and Japan," in Kuznets, S. S., et al. (eds.), *Economic Growth*, Durham, N.C., pp. 493-537.

LI, C. N. (1956), "Price Control and Paper Currency in Ming," in Zen, E. T., and De Francis, J. (eds.), *Chinese Social History*, Washington, D.C., pp. 281-299.

LI, H. (1936), *Les censeurs sous la dynastie Mandchoue (1644–1911) in Chine*, Paris.

LIANG, F. C. (1956[a]), "The 'Ten-Parts' Tax System of Ming," in Zen, E. T., and De Francis, J. (eds.), *Chinese Social History*, Washington, D.C., pp. 271-281.

——— (1956[b]), "Local Tax Collectors in the Ming Dynasty," *ibid.*, pp. 249-271.

LIEBENTHAL, W. (1952), "Was ist chinesischer Buddhismus?" *Études Asiatiques*, VI, 116-129.

——— (1954), "On Trends in Chinese Thought," in *Silver Jubilee Volume of the*

Zinbun-Kagaku-Kenyusyo-Kyoto University, Kyoto.

LIU, H. C. W. (1959), "An Analysis of Chinese Clan Rules: Confucian Theories in Action," in Nivison, D. S., and Wright, A. F. (eds.), *Confucianism in Action,* Stanford, Calif., pp. 63-96.

LIU, J. T. C. (1957), "An Early Sung Reformer—Fou Chung-Yen," in Fairbank, J. K. (ed.), *Chinese Thought and Institutions,* Chicago, pp. 105-132.

—— (1959[a]), *Reform in Sung China: Wang An-shih (1021–1086) and His New Policies,* Cambridge, Mass.

—— (1959[b]), "Some Classifications of Bureaucrats in Chinese Historiography," in Nivison, D. S., and Wright, A. F. (eds.), *Confucianism in Action,* Stanford, Calif., pp. 165-181.

—— (1959[c]), "Eleventh-Century Chinese Bureaucrats: Some historical Classifications and Behavioral Types," *Administrative Science Quarterly,* IV, 207-226.

LO, P. L. (1955), "The Emergence of China as a Sea Power during the Late Sung and Early Yüan Periods," *FEQ,* XIV, 389-505.

MACNAIR, H. F. (ed.) (1951), *China,* Berkeley, Calif.

MARSH, R. M. (1960), "Bureaucratic Constraints on Nepotism in the Ch'ing Period," *JAS,* XIX, 117-135.

MARTIN, I. (1949), Review of Bünger, K., 1946, *JAOS,* LXIX, 154-157.

MARTIN, W. A. P. (1893), *The Chinese, Their Education, Philosophy, and Letters,* New York.

MASPERO, H. (1938), "Les régimes fonciers en Chine," *Recueils de la société Jean Bodin,* III, 303-314.

—— (1950[a]), *Études historiques,* Paris.

—— (1950[b]), *Les religions chinoises,* Paris.

—— (1950[c]), *Le Taoisme,* Paris.

MEADOWS, T. T. (1856), *The Chinese and Their Rebellions,* London.

MICHAEL, F. H. (1942), *Frontier and Bureaucracy: The Origin of Manchu Rule in China,* Baltimore.

—— (1946), "Chinese Military Tradition," *Far Eastern Survey,* XV, 65-87.

—— (1951), "From the Fall of T'ang to the Fall of Ch'ing (906–1912)," in MacNair, H. F. (ed.), *China,* Berkeley, Calif., pp. 89-112.

—— (1955), "State and Society in Nineteenth Century China," *World Politics,* VII, 419-434.

—— (1955-56), "The Fall of China," *ibid.,* VIII, 296-306.

MIYAKAWA, H. (1955), "An Outline of the Naito Hypothesis and Its Effects on Japanese Studies of China," *FEQ,* XIV, 533-552.

—— (1960), "The Confucianization of South China," in Wright, A. F. (ed.), *The Confucian Persuasion,* Stanford, Calif., pp. 21-47.

MURAMUTSU, Y. (1960), "Some Themes in Chinese Rebel Ideologies," *ibid.,* pp. 241-268.

MURPHEY, R. (1954), "The City as a Center of Change: Western Europe and China," *Annals of the Association of American Geographers,* XLIV, 349-362.

NICOLAS-VANDIER, N. (1959[a]), "Les échanges entre le Bouddhisme et le Taoïsme des Han aux T'ang," in *Aspects de la Chine,* pp. 166-171.

—— (1959[b]), "Le Néo-Confucianisme," *ibid.,* pp. 175-180.

NIVISON, D. S. (1953), "The Problem of 'Knowledge' and 'Action' in Chinese Thought since Wang Yang-ming," in Wright, A. F. (ed.), *Studies in Chinese Thought,* Chicago, pp. 112-145.

—— (1959), "Ho-shen and His Accusers: Ideology and Political Behavior in the Eighteenth Century," *ibid.,* pp. 209-243.

—— and WRIGHT, A. F. (eds.) (1959), *Confucianism in Action,* Stanford, Calif.

PARSONS, J. B. (1957), "The Culmination of a Chinese Peasant Rebellion," *JAS,* XVI, 387-401.

PULLEYBLANK, E. G. (1954), "China," in Sinor, D. (ed.), *Orientalism and History,* Cambridge, pp. 57-81.

——— (1955), *The Background of the Rebellion of An Lu-shan*, London.

——— (1958), Review of K. A. Wittfogel,
Oriental Despotism, BSOAS, XXI, 657-660.

——— (1960), "Neo-Confucianism and Neo-
Legalism in T'ang Intellectual Life, 755–
805," in Wright, A. F. (ed.), *The Confucian
Persuasion*, Stanford, Calif., pp. 77-115.

RATCHNEVSKY, P. (1937), *Un code des Yüan*,
Paris.

REISCHAUER, E. O. (1955), *Ennin's Travels
in T'ang China*, New York.

RIASANOVSKY, V. A. (1937), "Mongol Law
and Chinese Law in the Yüan Dynasty," *Chinese Social and Political Science Review*,
XX, 266-289.

RIDEOUT, J. K. (1949), *Politics in Medieval
China*, Canberra.

——— (1949-52), "The Rise of the Eunuchs
during the T'ang Dynasty," *Asia Major*, I,
53-72; III, 42-58.

RIEGER, M. (1937), "Zur Finanz- und Agrar-
geschichte der Ming Dynastie," *Sinica*, XII,
130-144, 235-252.

SCHURMANN, H. F. (1956[a]), "Traditional
Property Concepts in China," *FEQ*, XV,
507-516.

——— (1956[b]), *Economic Structure of the
Yüan Dynasty* (translation of ch. 93 and 94
of the *Yüan shih*), Cambridge, Mass.

——— (1957), "On Social Themes in Sung
Tales," *HJAS*, XX, 239-262.

SCHWARTZ, B. (1959), "Some Polarities in
Confucian Thought," in Nivison, S. D., and
Wright, A. F. (eds.), *Confucianism in Action*,
Stanford, Calif., pp. 50-62.

SEUBERLICH, W. (1952), "Kaisertreue oder
Auflehnung? Eine Episode der Ming Zeit,"
ZDMG, CII, 304-314.

SHIH, V. Y. C. (1956), "Some Chinese Rebel
Ideologies," *TP*, XLIV, 150-227.

SHIVELY, D. H. (1959), "Motoda Eifu: Confucian Lecturer to the Meiji Emperor," in
Nivison, S. D., and Wright, A. F. (eds.), *Confucianism in Action*, Stanford, Calif., pp.
302-334.

SHRYOCK, J. K. (1951), "Confucianism," in

MacNair, H. F. (ed.), *China*, Berkeley, Calif.,
pp. 245-254.

SIAO, K. F. (1939), *Exposé historique et
analytique de la théorie des cinq pouvoirs
en Chine*, Brussels.

SJÖQUIST, K. O. (1938), *Das Fêng-Chien
Wesen (der chinesische Feudalismus) nach
Abhandlungen aus verschiedenen Dynastien*,
Berlin.

SOLOMON, B. (1955), *Han Yü's Shun-tsung
shih-lu: The Veritable Record of the T'ang
Emperor Shun-tsung*, Cambridge, Mass.

SPRENKEL, B. O. VAN DER (1952), "High
Officials of the Ming," *BSOAS*, XIV, 87-114.

——— (1956), Review of Franke, O. (1930-
52), *BSOAS*, XVIII, 312-322.

——— (1958), *The Chinese Civil Service:
The 19th Century*, Canberra.

SPRENKEL, S. VAN DER (1956), "A Sociological Analysis of Chinese Legal Institutions
with Special Reference to the Ch'ing Period"
(mimeo), University of London thesis.

STANGE, H. O. H. (1934), *Leben, Persönlich-
keit, und Werk Wang Mang's*, Berlin.

——— (1939), *Die Monographie über
Wang-Mang*, Leipzig.

——— (1950), "Geschichte Chinas vom
Urbeginn bis auf zur Gegenwart," in Waldschmidt, E., *et al.*, *Geschichte Asiens*, Munich, pp. 363-542.

——— (1951), Review of Eberhard, W.
(1948[d]), *HZ*, CLXXII, 615-618.

SWANN, N. L. (1950), *Food and Money in
Ancient China: The Earliest Economic History of China to A.D. 25*, Princeton, N.J.

TAYLOR, G. E. (1933), "The Taiping Rebellion: Its Economic Background and Social
Theory," *Chinese Social and Political Science Review*, XVI, 545-614.

TÊNG, S. Y. (1951), "From the Fall of Chou
to the Fall of T'ang (*ca.* 221 B.C.–906 A.D.*),"*
in MacNeir, H. F. (ed.), *China*, Berkeley,
Calif., pp. 72-89.

THEUNISSEN, P. (1938), *Su Ts'in und die
Politik der Längs- und Quer-Achse (Tsung-
Heng-Schule) im chinesischen Altertum*,
Breslau.

TSUKAMOTO, Z. (1930), "Chinese Buddhism in the Middle Period of the T'ang Dynasty, with Special Reference to Fa-Chao and the Doctrine of the Pure Lord," *Memoir of Tōhō Bunka Gakun Kyōto Kenkyvjo*, vol. IV, Kyōto.

—— (1960), "The Early Stages in the Introduction of Buddhism into China (up to the Fifth Century A.D.)," *Journal of World History*, V, 546-572.

TWITCHETT, D. (1956[a]), Review of Yoshi-yuki, S., *Studies in the History of Chinese Land Tenure Systems* (Tokyo, 1954), *BSOAS*, XVIII, 388-389.

—— (1956[b]), "The Government of T'ang in the Early Eighth Century" (review of Pulleyblank, E. G., 1955), *BSOAS*, XVIII, 322-330.

—— (1956[c]), "Monastic Estates in T'ang China," *Asia Major*, V, 123-146.

—— (1957[a]), "The Fragment of the T'ang Ordinances of the Department Water-ways Discovered at Tun-huang," *Asia Major*, VII, 23-80.

—— (1957[b]), "The Monasteries and China's Economy in Medieval Times," *BSOAS*, XIX, 527-549.

—— (1957[c]), "Recent Work on Medieval Chinese Social History by Sudō Yoshi-yuki," *Journal of the Economic and Social History of the Orient*, I, 145-148.

—— (1958), Reviews of Hulsewé, A. F. P. (1955), Balázs, E. (1954[c]), Schurmann, H. F. (1956[b]), *BSOAS*, XXI, 651-656.

—— (1959), *"The Fan Clan's Charitable Estate (1050–1760),"* in Nivison, D. S., and Wright, A. F. (eds.), *Confucianism in Action*, Stanford, Calif., pp. 97-133.

WANG, K. (1956), "The System of Equal Land Allotments in Medieval Times," in Zen, E. T., and De Francis, J. (eds.), *Chinese Social History*, Washington, D.C., pp. 57-185.

WANG, Y. C. (1936), "The Rise of Land Tax and the Fall of Dynasties in Chinese History," *Pacific Affairs*, IX, 201-220.

—— (1949), "An Outline of the Central Government of the Former Han Dynasty," *HJAS*, XII, 134-185.

WANG, Y. T. (1953), "Slaves and Other Comparable Social Groups, during the Northern Dynasties (386–618)," *HJAS*, XVI, 293-364.

WEBER, M. (1922), *Gesammelte Aufsätze zur Religionssoziologie*, Tübingen, vol. I.

WILBUR, C. M. (1943), "Industrial Slavery in China during the Former Han Dynasty (206 B.C.–25 A.D.)," *Journal of Economic History*, III, 56-69.

WILHELM, H. (1935-36), "Der Prozess der A Yün," *Monumenta Serica*, I, 338-351.

WILHELM, H. (1951), "The Po-Hsüeh Hung-ju Examination of 1679," *JAOS*, LXXI, 60-66.

WILLIAMSON, H. R. (1937), *Wang An Shih: A Chinese Statesman and Educationalist of the Sung Dynasty*, London.

WITTFOGEL, K. A. (1935), "The Foundations and Stages of Chinese Economic History," *Zeitschrift für Sozialforschung*, IV, 26-60.

—— (1938), "Die Theorie der oriental-ischen Gesellschaft," *ibid.*, VII, 90-122.

—— (1950), Review of Eberhard, W. (1948[d]), *Artibus Asiae*, XIII, 103-106.

—— (1951), "Chinese Society and the Dynasties of Conquest," in MacNair, H. F. (ed.), *China*, Berkeley, Calif., pp. 112-127.

—— (1957), *Oriental Despotism: A Comparative Study of Total Power*, New Haven.

——, and FÊNG, C. S. (1949), *History of Chinese Society (907–1125)*, Philadelphia.

WRIGHT, A. F. (1948), *The Pioneer Mission-ary Fo-tu-teng*, *HJAS*, XI.

—— (1951), "Fu I and the Rejection of Buddhism," *Journal of the History of Ideas*, XII, 33-47.

—— (ed.) (1953), *Studies in Chinese Thought*, Chicago.

—— (1957[a]), "The Formation of Sui Ideology (581–604)," in Fairbank, J. K. (ed.), *Chinese Thought and Institutions*, Chicago, pp. 71-106.

—— (1957[b]), "Buddhism and Chinese Culture: Phases of Interaction," *JAS*, XVII, 17-43.

—— (1959), *Buddhism in Chinese History*, Stanford, Calif.

—— (ed.) (1960), *The Confucian Persuasion*, Stanford, Calif.

WRIGHT, M. C. (1957), *The Last Stand of Chinese Conservatism (The T'ung-chih Restoration 1862–1874)*, Stanford, Calif.

YANG, C. I. (1956[a]), "Evolution of the Status of 'Dependents,'" in Zen, E. T., and De Francis, J. (eds), *Chinese Social History*, Washington, D.C., pp. 142-157.

—— (1956[b]), "Lower Castes in the T'ang Dynasty," *ibid.*, pp. 185-192.

YANG, C. K. (1957), "The Functional Relationship between Confucian Thought and Chinese Religion," in Fairbank, J. K. (ed.), *Chinese Thought and Institutions*, Chicago, pp. 269-291.

—— (1959), "Some Characteristics of Chinese Bureaucratic Behavior," in Nivision, D. S., and Wright, A. F. (eds.), *Confucianism in Action*, Stanford, Calif., pp. 134-164.

YANG, L. S. (1946), "Notes on the Economic History of the Chin Dynasty," *HJAS*, IX, 107-185.

—— (1952), *Money and Credit in China*, Cambridge, Mass.

—— (1955), "Schedules of Work and Rest in Imperial China," *HJAS*, XVIII, 301-326.

—— (1957[a]), "The Concept of 'Pao' as a Basis for Social Relations in China," in Fairbank, J. K. (ed.), *Chinese Thought and Institutions*, Chicago, pp. 291-310.

—— (1957[b]), "Die Organisation der chinesischen offiziellen Geschichtsschreibung; Prinzipien und Methoden der offiziellen Geschichtswerke von der T'ang bis zur Ming Dynastie," *Saeculum*, VIII, 196-209.

—— (1957[c]), "Economic Justification for Spending: An Uncommon Idea in Traditional China," *HJAS*, XX, 36-53.

—— (1950), "Buddhist Monasteries and Four Money Raising Institutions in Chinese History," *HJAS*, XIII, 174-191.

ZEN, E. T., and DE FRANCIS, J. (eds.) (1956), *Chinese Social History*, Washington, D.C.

J. India

DAS, S. K. (1925), *Economic History of Ancient India*, Calcutta.

DIKSHITAR, V. R. R. (1923-29), *Hindu Administrative Institutions*, Madras.

DUNBAR, G. (1937), *Geschichte Indiens von den ältesten Zeiten bis zur Gegenwart*, Munich.

—— (1951), *India and the Passing of the Empire*, London.

GHOSHAL, U. N. (1929), *Contributions to the History of the Hindu Revenue System*, Calcutta.

HILLEBRANDT, A. (1916), "Zum altindischen Königrecht," *ZDMG*, LXX, 41-48.

—— (1923), *Altindische Politik*, Jena.

INGALLS, D. H. H. (1954), "Authority and Law in Ancient India," supplement, *JAOS*, LXXIV, 34-45.

JAGASWAL, K. P. (1943), *Hindu Polity*, Calcutta.

MAJUMDAR, R. C. (1922), *Corporate Life in Ancient India*, Calcutta.

——, et al. (1948), *An Advanced History of India*, London.

MOOKERJI, A. (1920), *Local Government in Ancient India*, Oxford.

MOOKERJI, R. K. (1919), *Local Government in Ancient India*, Oxford.

NARENDA, N. (1921), *Aspects of Ancient Indian Polity and Law*, Oxford.

PRANANATHA, V. (1929), *A Study in the Economic Conditions of Ancient India*, London.

PRASAD, B. (1928), *The State in Ancient India: A Study in the Structure and Practical Working of Political Institutions in North India in Ancient Times*, London.

SARKAR, B. N. (1922), *The Political Institutions and Theories of the Hindus: A Study in Comparative Politics*, Leipzig.

SATRI, K. A. N. (1912), *The Theory of Pre-Muslim Indian Polity*, Madras.

SINHA, H. N. (1938), *Sovereignty in Ancient Indian Polity*, London.

K. Maurya, Gupta, and Mogul India

1. MAURYA

BARUA, B. M. (1934), *Inscriptions of Aśoka*, Calcutta.

—— (1946), *Aśoka and His Inscriptions*, Calcutta.

BHANDARKAR, D. R. (1932), *Aśoka*, Calcutta.

BHANDARKAR, R. G. (1920), *A Peep into the Early History of India: From the Foundation of the Maurya Dynasty to the Downfall of the Gupta Dynasty*, Bombay.

BHARGAVA, P. L. (1935), *Chandragupta Maurya*, Lucknow.

KERN, F. (1956), *Aśoka, Kaiser und Missioner*, Berne.

MEHTA, R. N. (1939), *Pre-Buddhist India*, Bombay.

MOOKERJI, R. K. (1928), *Aśoka*, London.

—— (1943), *Chandragupta Maurya and His Times*, Madras.

VALLÉE POUSSIN, L. DE LA (1930), *L'Inde aux temps des Mauryas*, Paris.

2. GUPTA

BANERJI, R. D. (1933), *The Age of the Imperial Guptas*, Benares.

MOOKERJI, R. K. (1948), *The Gupta Empire*, Bombay.

MUNSHI, K. M. (1941), "Golden Age of the Imperial Guptas," *Bharatiya Vidya*, III, 113-125.

SHEMBAMEKAR, K. M. (1953), *The Glamour about the Guptas*, Bombay.

TRIPATHI, R. S. (1940), "Religious Toleration under the Imperial Guptas," *Indian Historical Quarterly*, XV, 1-12.

3. MOGUL

AZIZ, A. (1942), *The Imperial Treasury of the Indian Moghuls*, Lahore.

DHARMA, B. (1952), "The Raushania Movement and the Mughals," *Islamic Culture*, XXVI, 57-68.

GRENARD, F. (1931), *Baber: First of the Moguls*, London.

KHAN, S. A. (1931), "Bombay in the Reign of Aurangzeb," *Islamic Culture*, V, 251-281; 372-406.

LYBYER, A. H. (1913), "The Government of the Mogul Empire," in *The Government of the Ottoman Empire*, Cambridge, Mass., Appendix IV.

MALLESON, G. B. (1908), *Akbar and the Rise of the Mughal Empire*, Oxford.

MORELAND, W. H. (1920), *India at the Death of Akbar*, London.

—— (1923), *From Akbar to Aurangzeb*, London.

—— (1929), *The Agrarian System in Moslem India*, Cambridge.

OWEN, S. J. (1912), *The Fall of the Mogul Empire*, London.

PRASAD, I. (1955), *The Life and Times of Humayun*, Calcutta.

SARKAR, J. (1920), *Mughal Administration*, Calcutta.

—— (1954), *A Short History of Aurangzeb (1618–1707)*, Calcutta.

SMITH, V. A. (1919), *Akbar*, Oxford.

VARMA, R. C. (1952), "The Tribal Policy of the Mughals (Akbar to Aurangzeb)," *Islamic Culture*, XXVI, 13-34.

L. The Byzantine Empire

ABEL, F. M. (1955), "Fondations byzantines et waqfs arabes," *Revue internationale des droits de l'antiquité*, II, 394-395.

ANDRÉADÈS, A. (1911), "Les finances byzantines," *Revue des sciences politiques*, XXVI, 620-630.

—— (1921[a]), "La vénalité des offices, est-elle d'origine byzantine?," *Revue historique de droit français et étranger*, XLV, 232-241.

—— (1921[b]), "Le montant du budget de l'empire byzantin," *Revue des études greques*, XXXIV, 20-56.

—— (1924), "De la monnaie et de la puissance d'achat des métaux précieux dans l'empire byzantin," *Byzantion*, I, 75-115.

—— (1926), "Le recrutement des fonctionnaires et les universités dans l'empire byzantin," in *Mélanges de droit romain dédiés a Georges Cornil*, Paris, pp. 17-40.

—— (1934), "Byzance, paradis des monopoles et des privilèges," *Byzantion*, IX, 171-181.

—— (1935), "Floraison et décadence de la petite propriété dans l'empire byzantin," in *Mélanges Ernest Mehain*, Paris, pp. 261-266.

ANGELOV, D. (1945-46), *Die Rolle des Byzantischen Kaisers in der Rechtssprechung*, Sofia.

ASHBURNER, W. (1910-12), "The Farmer's Law," *Journal of Hellenic Studies*, XXX, 85-108; XXXII, 68-83.

BACH, E. (1942), "Les lois agraires byzantines du XIème siècle," *Classica et Mediaevalia*, V, 70-91.

BARKER, E. (ed.) (1957), *Social and Political Thought in Byzantium from Justinian I to the Last Palaeologus*, Oxford.

BAYNES, N. H. (1926), *The Byzantine Empire*, New York and London.

—— (1929), *Constantine the Great and the Christian Church*, London.

—— (1952), "The Emperor Heraclius and the Military Theme System," *English Historical Review*, LXVII, 380-381.

—— (1955), *Byzantine Studies and Other Essays*, London.

——, and MOSS, H. ST.L. B. (eds.) (1948), *Byzantium: An Introduction to East Roman Civilization*, Oxford.

BECK, H. G. (1955), "Der Byzantinische 'Ministerpräsident,'" *BZ*, XLVIII, 309-338.

—— (1956), *Vademecum des Byzantinischen Aristokraten*, Graz.

BELL, H. I. (1917), "The Byzantine Servile State in Egypt," *Journal of Egyptian Archaeology*, IV, 86-106.

BENESEVIC, V. N. (1926-28), "Die byzantinischen Ranglisten nach dem Kletorologion Philotei und nach den Jerusalemer Handschriften," *Byzantinisch-neugriechische Jahrbücher*, V, 97-167; VI, 143-145.

BERCHEM, D. VAN (1952), *L'armée de Dioclétien et la réforme constantinienne*, Paris.

BERKHOF, H. (1947), *Kirche und Kaiser*, Zurich.

BEYER, W. C. (1959), "The Civil Service of the Ancient World," *Public Administration Review*, XIX, 243-249.

BOAK, A. E. R. (1919), "Imperial Coronation Ceremonies of the Fifth and Sixth Centuries," *Harvard Studies in Classical Philology*, XXX, 37-49.

—— (1929), "The Book of the Prefect," *Journal of Economic and Business History*, I, 597-619.

——, and DUNLAP, J. (1924), *Two Studies in Later Roman and Byzantine Administration*, New York.

BORSARI, S. (1954), "L'amministrazione del tema di Sicilia," *Revista storica italiana*, LXVI, 143-151.

BRATIANU, G. I. (1930), "La question l'approvisionnement de Constantinople à l'époque byzantine et ottomane," *Byzantion*, V, 83-107.

—— (1933), "Servage de la plèbe et régime fiscal—essai d'histoire comparée roumaine, slave et byzantine," *Annales*, V, 445-462.

——— (1934[a]), "Une expérience d'économie dirigée: Le monopole du blé à Byzance au XIième siècle," *Byzantion*, IX, 643-662.

——— (1934[b]), *Privilèges et franchises municipales dans l'empire byzantin*, Paris.

——— (1937), "Empire et 'démocratie' à Byzance," *BZ*, XXXVII, 86-111.

——— (1938), *Etudes byzantines d'histoire économique et sociale*, Paris.

——— (1948[a]), "Assemblées d'états en Europe orientale," in *Actes du sixième congrès international d'études byzantines*, Paris, vol. I, pp. 40-49.

——— (1948[b]), 'Démocratie dans le lexique byzantin à l'époque des paléologues," in *Mémorial L. Petit*, Bucharest, pp. 32-40.

BRÉHIER, L. (1899), *Le schisme oriental du XIième siècle*, Paris.

——— (1904), *La querelle des images, VIIIième–IXième siècles*, Paris.

——— (1917), "La transformation de l'empire byzantin sous les Héraclides," *Journal des savants*, XV, 401-415.

——— (1924), *Les populations rurales au IXième siècle*, Byzantion, I, 177-190.

——— (1927-29), "Notes sur l'enseignement supérieur à Constantinople," *Byzantion*, III, 72-94; IV, 13-28.

——— (1937), Review of Grabar, A., *L'empereur dans l'art byzantin* (Paris, 1936), *Journal des savants*, XXXV, pp. 62-74.

——— (1938), "Iconoclasme," in Fliche, A., and Martin, V. (eds.), *Histoire de l'Église*, vol. V, pp. 431-470.

——— (1945), Review of Diehl, C., *et al.* (1945), *Journal des savants*, XLIII, 128-133.

——— (1946), "L'investiture des patriarches de Constantinople au moyen-âge," in *Miscellanea G. Mercati*, Rome, vol. III, p. 123.

——— (1947), *Vie et mort de Byzance*, Paris.

——— (1948[a]), "Priest and King," in *Mémorial L. Petit*, Bucharest, pp. 41-45.

——— (1948[b]), "Le recruitement des patriarches de Constantinople pendant la période byzantine," in *Actes du sixième congrès international d'études byzantines*, Paris, vol. I, pp. 221-227.

——— (1949[a]), "Les empereurs byzantins dans leur vie privée," *RH*, CLXXXVIII, 193-217.

——— (1949[b]), *Les institutions de l'Empire byzantin*, Paris.

——— (1950), *La civilisation byzantine*, Paris.

BRIGHTMAN, F. E. (1901), "Byzantine Imperial Coronations," *Journal of Theological Studies*, II, 359.

BUCKLER, G. (1929), *Anna Comnena: A Study*, Oxford.

BURY, J. B. (1889), *A History of the Later Roman Empire from Arcadius to Irene (395–800)*, London.

——— (1910), *The Constitution of the Later Roman Empire*, Cambridge.

CAMPENHAUSEN, H. V. (1951), "Die Entstehung der Byzantinischen und abendländischen Staatsanschauung des Mittelalters," *Theologische Literaturzeitung*, LXXVI, 203-208.

CASSIMATIS, G. (1939), "La politique sociale dans les novelles de Léon le Sage," *Studi bizantini e neoellenici*, V, 539.

CHARANIS, P. (1940-41[a]), "Coronation and Its Constitutional Significance in the Later Roman Empire," *Byzantion*, XV, 49-66.

——— (1940-41[b]), "Internal Strife at Byzantium in the Fourteenth Century," *Byzantion*, XV, 208-230.

——— (1944), "The Phonikon and Other Byzantine Taxes," *Speculum*, V, 19.

——— (1944-45), "On the Social Structure of the Later Roman Empire," *Byzantion*, XVII, 39-57.

——— (1948), "The Monastic Properties and the State in the Byzantine Empire," *Dumbarton Oaks Papers*, IV, 53-118.

——— (1951[a]), "On the Social Structure and Economic Organization of the Byzantine Empire in the Thirteenth Century and Later," *Byzantinoslavica*, XII, 94-153.

——— (1951[b]), "The Aristocracy of Byzantion in the Thirteenth Century," in *Studies in Roman Economic and Social History in Honor of A. C. Johnson*, Princeton, N.J., pp. 336-356.

——— (1953[a]), "Economic Factors in the

Decline of the Byzantine Empire," *Journal of Economic History*, XIII, 412-425.

—— (1953[b]), "A Note on the Population and Cities of the Byzantine Empire in the Thirteenth Century," in *Joshua Starr Memorial Volume*, New York, pp. 135-148.

—— (1957), Review of Ostrogorsky, G. (1956[b]), *Speculum*, XXXII, 596-597.

CLARKE, W. K. L. (1913), *St. Basil the Great: A Study in Monasticism*, Cambridge.

COLLINET, P. (1912-52), *Etudes historiques sur le droit de Justinien*, Paris.

—— (1936), "La politique de Justinien à l'égard des colons, *Studi bizantini e neoellenici*, V, 610-611.

—— (1947), *La nature des actions, des interdits et des exceptions dans l'oeuvre de Justinien*, Paris.

CONSTANTINESCU, N. A. (1924), "Réforme sociale ou réforme fiscale?" *Bulletin de l'académie roumaine, section historique*, XI, 95-96.

—— (1949), "Assemblées d'états en Europe orientale," in *Actes du septième congrès international d'études byzantines*, Brussels, pp. 40-49.

COURTOIS, C. (1949), "Exconsul-Observations sur l'histoire du consulat à l'époque byzantine," *Byzantion*, XIX, 37-58.

DANSTRUP, J. (1946[a]), "Indirect Taxation at Byzantium," *Classica et Mediaevalia*, VIII, 139-168.

—— (1946[b]), "The State and Landed Property in Byzantium to 1250," *ibid.*, 22-267.

DARKO, E. (1946-48), "Le rôle des peuples nomades cavaliers dans la transformation de l'empire romain aux premiers siècles du moyen âge," *Byzantion*, XVIII, 85-97.

DARKO, J. (1939), "La militarizazione dell impero byzantino," *Studi bizantini e neoellenici*, V, 88-99.

DELAHAYE, H. (1948), "Byzantine Monasticism," in Baynes, N. H., and Moss, H. St.L. B. (eds.), *Byzantium: An Introduction to East Roman Civilization*, Oxford, pp. 136-166.

DEMOUGEOT, E. (1946), "La théorie du pouvoir impérial au début du cinquième siècle," in *Mélanges de la société toulousaine d'études classiques*, I, 191-206.

DENDIAS, M. (1939), "Études sur le gouvernement et l'administration en Byzance," in *Actes du cinqième congrès international d'études byzantines*, Rome, pp. 122-145.

DIEHL, C. (1888), *Études sur l'administration byzantine dans l'exarchat de Ravenne (568–751)*, Paris.

—— (1905), "L'origine du régime des thèmes dans l'empire byzantin," *Études byzantines*, pp. 276-292.

—— (1906-08), *Figures byzantines*, Paris.

—— (1924), "Le sénat et le peuple byzantin aux VIIième et VIIIième siècles," *Byzantion*, I, 201-213.

—— (1927), "The Government and Administration of the Byzantine Empire," in *The Cambridge Mediaeval History*, vol. IV, ch. 23.

—— (1929), *La société byzantine à l'époque des Comnènes*, Paris.

—— (1930), *Histoire de l'empire byzantin*, Paris.

—— (1943), *Les grands problèmes de l'histoire byzantine*, Paris.

—— (1957), *Byzantium—Greatness and Decline*, New Brunswick, N.J.

——, and MARÇAIS, G. (1936), *Le monde oriental de 395 à 1081*, Paris.

——, et al. (1945), *L'Europe orientale de 1081 à 1453*, Paris.

DIETRICH, K. (1918), *Hellenism in Asia Minor*, New York.

DÖLGER, F. (1927), *Beiträge zur Geschichte der Byzantinischen Finanzverwaltung, besonders des 10 und 11 Jahrhunderts*, Leipzig.

—— (1933), "Die Frage des Grundeigentums in Byzanz," *Bulletin of the International Committee of Historical Sciences*, V, 5-15.

—— (1939), Die Kaiserkunde der Byzantiner als Ausdruck ihrer politischen Anschauungen, *HZ*, CLIX, 229-250.

—— (1953), *Byzanz und die Europäische Staatenwelt*, Speyer.

—— (1956), "Finanzgeschichtliches aus

der byzantinischen Kaiserkanzlei des 11 Jahrhundert," *Sitz. der Bayrischen Akademie der Wissenschaften, Phil.-hist. Klasse,* I.

DOWNEY, G. (1951), "The Economic Crisis at Antioch under Julian the Apostate," in *Studies in Roman Economic and Social History in Honor of A. C. Johnson,* Princeton, N.J., pp. 312-321.

DVORNIK, F. (1946), "The Circus Parties in Byzantium, Their Evolution and Their Suppression," *Byzantina-Metabyzantina,* I, 119-133.

—— (1948), *The Photian Schism, History and Legend,* Cambridge.

DYAKONOV, A. P. (1945), "The Byzantine Demes and Factions in the Fifth to the Seventh Centuries," *Vizantiysky Sbornik,* I, 144-227.

ENSSLIN, W. (1939), "Das Gottesgnadentum des autokratischen Kaisertums der frühbyzantinischen Zeit," *Studi bizantini e neoellenici,* V, 154-166.

—— (1940), "Der Kaiser und die Staatskirche in der frühbyzantinischen Zeit," in *Actes du sixième congrès international d'études byzantines,* Paris, pp. 11-13.

—— (1946), *Zur Frage der ersten Kaiserkrönung durch den Patriarchen und zur Bedeutung dieses Aktes im Wahlzeremoniell,* Würzburg.

—— (1948), "The Emperor and the Imperial Administration," in Baynes, N. H., and Moss, H. St.L. B. (eds.), *Byzantium: An Introduction to East Roman Civilization,* Oxford, pp. 268-358.

FRESHFIELD, E. H. (1932), *Roman Law in the Later Roman Empire,* Cambridge.

FUCHS, F. (1926), *Die höheren Schulen von Konstantinopel im Mittelalter,* Leipzig and Berlin.

GELZER, H. (1899), *Die Genesis der byzantinischen Themenverfassung,* Leipzig.

—— (1907), "Das Verhältnis von Staat und Kirche in Byzanz," in *Ausgewählte Kleine Schriften,* Leipzig, pp. 57-141.

GOUBERT, P. (1946), "L'administration de l'Espagne byzantine," *REB,* IV, 70-110.

GRABAR, A. (1936), *L'empereur dans l'art byzantin,* Paris.

GRÉGOIRE, H. (1927-28[a]), Review of Ostrogorsky, G. (1929[b]), *Byzantion,* IV, 765-771.

—— (1927-28[b]), Review of Fuchs, F. (1926), *ibid.,* 771-778.

—— (1946), "Le peuple de Constantinople, ou les Bleus et les Verts," *Comptes rendus de l'académie des inscriptions et belles lettres,* pp. 568-578.

—— (1948), "The Byzantine Church," in Baynes, N. H., and Moss, H. St.L. B. (eds.), *Byzantium: An Introduction to East Roman Civilization,* Oxford, pp. 93-143.

GREN, E. (1941), *Kleinasien und der Ostbalkan in der wirtschaftlichen Entwicklung der römischen Kaiserzeit,* Uppsala.

GRIERSON, P. (1954), "The Debasement of the Bezant in the Eleventh Century," *BZ,* XLVII, 379-394.

GROSSE, R. (1920), *Römische Militärgeschichte von Galerius bis zum Beginn der byzantinischen Themenverfassung,* Berlin.

GRUMEL, V. (1949), "La profession médicale à Byzance," *REB,* VII, 42-76.

GUILLAND, R. (1943), "Les eunuques dans l'empire byzantin: Étude de titulature et de prosopographie byzantine," *REB,* I, 197-238.

—— (1944-45), "Fonctions et dignités des eunuques," *REB,* II, 185-225; III, 179-214.

—— (1946[a]), "La collation et la perte ou déchéance des titres nobiliaires à Byzance," *REB,* IV, 24-69.

—— (1946[b]), "Études sur l'histoire administrative de Byzance," *Byzantina-Metabyzantina,* I, 165-179.

—— (1947[a]), "Le droit divin á Byzance," *Études orientales et slaves,* XLII, 142-168.

—— (1947[b]), "Études sur l'histoire administrative de l'empereur byzantin: Le Césarat," *Orientalia Christiana Periodica,* XIII, 168-194.

—— (1947-48), "La noblesse de race à Byzance," *Byzantinoslavica,* IX, 307-314.

—— (1949), "Études sur l'histoire administrative de l'empire byzantin: Le Grand Connétable," *Byzantion*, XIX, 99-111.

—— (1950[a]), "Contribution a l'histoire administrative de l'empire byzantin; Le Drongaire et le Grand Drongaire de la Veille," *BZ*, XLIII, 340-365.

—— (1950[b]), "Études de titulature et de prosopographie byzantines: Le Protostrator," *REB*, VII, 156-179.

—— (1950[c]), "Études sur l'histoire administrative à Byzance: Le Domestique des Scholes," *REB*, VIII, 5-63.

—— (1951), "Études de titulature et de prosopographie byzantines: Les chefs de la marine byzantine: Drongaire de la Flotte, Grand Drongaire de la Flotte, Duc de la Flotte, Mégaduc," *BZ*, XLIV, 212-240.

—— (1953[a]), "Vénalité et favoritisme à Byzance," *REB*, X, 35-46.

—— (1953[b]), "Études sur l'histoire administrative de l'empire byzantin: Le Stratopédarque et le Grand Stratopédarque, *BZ*, XLVI, 63-90.

—— (1953[c]), "La noblesse byzantine à la haute époque," *Hellenika*, IV, 255-266.

—— (1953-55), "La politique sociale des empereurs byzantins de 867 à 1081," (mimeo), *Les cours de Sorbonne*, Paris.

—— (1954), "Sur les dignitaires du Palais et sur les dignités de la Grande Église, du Pseudo-Codinos: ch. 1-4, 8-13," *Byzantinoslavica*, XV, 214-229.

HADJINICOLAOU-MARAVA, A. (1950), *Recherches sur la vie des esclaves dans le monde byzantin*, Athens.

HARTMANN, L. M. (1889), *Untersuchungen zur Geschichte der byzantinischen Verwaltung in Italien (540–750)*, Leipzig.

HEYD, W. (1923), *Histoire du commerce du Levant*, Leipzig, 2 vols.

HUSSEY, J. M. (1937), *Church and Learning in the Byzantine Empire (867–1185)*, London.

—— (1950), "The Byzantine Empire in the Eleventh Century: Some Different Interpretations," *Transactions of the Royal Historical Society*, XXXII, 71-85.

—— (1957), *The Byzantine World*, London.

IORGA, N. (1940[a]), "La vie de province dans l'empire byzantin," *Etudes byzantines*, II, 145-172.

—— (1940[b]), "Le village byzantin," *ibid.*, 371-412.

JANSSENS, Y. (1936), "Les Bleus et les Verts sous Maurice, Phocas et Héraclius," *Byzantion*, XI, 499-536.

JENKINS, R. J. H. (1953), *The Byzantine Empire on the Eve of the Crusades*, London.

JOHNSON, A. C., and WEST, L. C. (1944), *Currency in Roman and Byzantine Egypt*, Princeton, N.J.

JUGIE, M. (1941), *Le schisme byzantin: Aperçu historique et doctrinal*, Paris.

KANTOROWICZ, E. H. (1956), " 'Feudalism' in the Byzantine Empire," in Coulborn, R. (ed.), *Feudalism in History*, Princeton, N.J., pp. 151-166.

KARAYANOPULUS, J. (1956), "Die Kollektive Steuerverantwortung in der frühbyzantinischen Zeit," *VSWG*, XLIII, 289-322.

KATZ, S. (1938), "Some Aspects of Economic Life in the Byzantine Empire," *Pacific Historical Review*, VII, 27-39.

KOLIAS, G. (1939), *Ämter- und Würdenkauf im Früh- und Mittelbyzantinischen Reich*, Athens.

LANDER, G. B. (1940), "Origin and Significance of Byzantine Iconoclastic Controversy," *Medieval Studies*, II, 127-150.

LAURENT, V. (1956), "Une famille turque au service de Byzance: Les Mélikes," *BZ*, XLIX, 349-368.

LEICHT, P. S. (1937), *Corporazioni romane e arti medievali*, Turin.

LEMERLE, P. (1948), "Le juge général des Grecs et la réforme judiciaire d'Andronic III," in *Mémorial L. Petit*, Bucharest, pp. 292-316.

—— (1949), "Recherches sur les institutions judiciaires à l'époque des paléologues," *Annuaire de l'institut de philologie et d'histoire orientale et slave*, IX, 369-384.

—— (1950), Review of Bréhier, L. (1947-50), *Journal des savants*, pp. 130-138.

—— (1958), "Esquisse pour une histoire agraire de Byzance: Les sources et les problèmes," *RH, CCXIX,* 32-74, 254-284; CCXX, 43-94.

LEVCHENKO, M. V. (1946), Matériaux pour l'histoire interne de l'empire romain d'orient aux cinqième et sixième siècles," in Gregoire, H. (ed.), *Les études byzantines en Russie soviétique,* Brussels, pp. 12-95.

LIPCHITZ, E. (1946), "La paysannerie byzantine et la colonisation slave," *ibid.,* pp. 96-143.

LOPES, G. (1933), *Le corporazioni byzantini,* Rome.

LOPEZ, R. S. (1945), "Silk Industry in the Byzantine Empire," *Speculum,* XX, 1-42.

—— (1951[a]), "The Dollar of the Middle Ages," *Journal of Economic History,* XI, 209-234.

—— (1951[b]), "La crise du besant au dixième siècle et la date du Livre du Préfet," *Annuaire de l'institut de philologie et d'histoire orientale et slave,* X, 403-418.

LOT, F. (1927), *La fin du monde antique et le début du moyen âge,* Paris.

MALAFOSSE, J. DE (1949), *Les lois agraires à l'èpoque byzantine: Tradition et exégèse,* Toulouse.

MANOJLOVIC, M. (1936), "Le peuple de Constantinople," *Byzantion,* II, 617-716.

MARICQ, A. (1949), "La durée du régime des partis populaires à Constantinople," *Bulletin de la classe des lettres de l'académie royale de Belgique,* XXV, 63-74.

MICKWITZ, G. (1936[a]), *Die Kartelfunktionen der Zünfte und ihre Bedeutung bei der Entstehung des Zahlwesens,* Helsingfors.

—— (1936[b]), "Die Organisationsformen zweier Byzantinischen Gewerbe im X Jahrhundert," *BZ,* XXXVI, 63-76.

—— (1936[c]), "Byzance et l'occident médiéval," *Annales,* VIII, 21-28.

MILLET, G. (1925), "L'origine du Logothéte Général, chef de l'administration financière à Byzance," in *Mélanges F. Lot,* Paris, pp. 563-573.

MITARD, M. (1930), "Le pouvoir impérial du temps de Léon VI," in *Mélanges C. Diehl,* Paris, vol. I, pp. 217-223.

MORAVCSIK, G., and JENKINS, R. J. H. (1949), *Constantine Porphyrogenitus: De Administrando Imperio,* Budapest.

MUTAVCIEV, P. (1940), "Le problème de la féodalité à Byzance," in *Actes du sixième congrès international d'études byzantine,* Paris, pp. 43-44.

NEUMANN, C. (1894), *Die Weltstellung des Byzantinischen Reiches vor den Kreuzzügen,* Leipzig.

OECONOMOS, L. (1918), *La vie religieuse dans l'empire byzantin au temps des Comnènes et des Anges,* Paris.

OHNSORGE, W. (1952), "Drei Deperdita der byzantinischen Kaiserkanzlei und die Frankenadresse im Zeremonien-buch des Konstantinos Porphyrogenitos," *BZ,* XLV, 320-340.

—— (1954), "Die Legation des Kaisers Basileios II an Heinrich II," *Historisches Jahrbuch,* LXXIII, 61-73.

OSTROGORSKY, G. (1927), "Die ländliche Steuergemeinde des byzantinischen Reiches im 10 Jahrhundert," *VSWG,* XX, 1-108.

—— (1929[a]), "Die wirtschaftlichen und sozialen Entwicklungsgrundlagen des byzantinischen Reiches," *VSWG,* XXII, 9, 129-143.

—— (1929[b]), *Studien zur Geschichte des byzantinischen Bilderstreites,* Breslau.

—— (1930[a]), "Über die vermeintliche Reformtätigkeit der Isaurier," *BZ,* XXX, 394-400.

—— (1930[b]), "Les débuts de la querelle des images," in *Mélanges C. Diehl,* Paris, vol. I, pp. 235-255.

—— (1931), "Das Steuersystem im byzantinischen Altertum und Mittelalter," *Byzantion,* VI, 229-240.

—— (1932), "Löhne und Preise in Byzanz," *BZ,* XXXII, 293-333.

—— (1936), "Die Entwicklung der Kaideridee im Spiegel der Byzantinischen Krönungsordnung," *Studi bizantini e neoellenici,* V, 299.

—— (1940), "Geschichte und Entwicklung der Byzantinischen Krönungsordnung," in

Actes du sixième congrès international d'étu-des byzantines, Paris, p. 14.

―――― (1941), "Die Perioden der Byzantinischen Geschichte," *HZ,* CLXIII, 229-254.

―――― (1942), "Agrarian Conditions in the Byzantine Empire in the Middle Ages," in Clapham, J. H., and Power, E. (eds.), *Cambridge Economic History,* vol. I, pp. 194-223.

―――― (1947), "The Peasant's Pre-emption Right," *Journal of Roman Studies,* XXXVII, 117-126.

―――― (1949), "Le grand domaine dans l'empire byzantin," *Recueils de la société Jean Bodin,* IV, 35-50.

―――― (1951), "Urum-Despotes: Die Anfange der Despotenwürde in Byzanz," *BZ,* XLIV, 448-460.

―――― (1952), "La pronoia: Contribution à l'étude de la féodalité a Byzance et chez les slaves du sud," *Byzantion,* XXII, 437-518.

―――― (1954), *Pour l'histoire de la féodalité byzantine,* Brussels.

―――― (1956[a]), *History of the Byzantine State,* Oxford.

―――― (1956[b]), "Staat und Gesellschaft der frühbyzantinischen Zeit," in Valjavec, F. (ed.), *Historia Mundi,* Berne, vol. IV, pp. 556-569.

―――― (1956[c]), *Quelques problèmes d'histoire de la paysannerie byzantine,* Brussels.

―――― (1959), "Paysannerie et grands domaines dans l'empire byzantin," *Recueils de la société Jean Bodin,* II, 123-133.

PALANQUE, J. R. (1933), *Essai sur la préfecture du prétoire du Bas-Empire,* Paris.

PARGOWE, J. (1905), *L'église byzantine de 527 à 847,* Paris.

PRINGSHEIM, F. (1950), "Justinian's Prohibition of Commentaries to the Digest," *Revue internationale des droits de l'antiquité,* V, 383-416.

RAMOS, A. J. (1952), "Un curioso cargo en la burocratia bisantina el Questo," *Revista de estudios politicos,* XLII, 107-129.

ROUILLARD, G. (1928), *L'administration civile de l'Egypte byzantine,* Paris.

―――― (1930), *Un grand bénéficiaire sous*

Alexis Comnène: Leon Képhalis, BZ, XXX, 444-450.

―――― (1940), "La politique agraire et la politique fiscale des comnènes et des anges," in *Actes du sixième congrès international d'études byzantines,* Paris, pp. 44-45.

―――― (1953), *La vie rurale dans l'empire byzantin,* Paris.

RUNCIMAN, S. (1929), *The Emperor Romanus Lecapenus and His Reign,* Cambridge.

―――― (1933), *Byzantine Civilization,* London.

―――― (1952), "Byzantine Trade and Industry," in Clapham, J. H., and E. Power. (eds.), *Cambridge Economic History of Europe,* vol. II, pp. 86-118.

―――― (1955), *The Eastern Schism,* Oxford.

SCHULZ, F. (1953), *History of Roman Legal Science,* Oxford.

SEGRÈ, A. (1940), "On the Date and Circumstances of the Prefect's Letter: P. OXY, 2106," *Journal of Egyptian Archaeology,* XXVI, 114-115.

―――― (1940-41), "Inflation and Its Implication in Early Byzantine Times," *Byzantion,* XV, 249-280.

―――― (1942-43), "Essays on Byzantine Economic History," *Byzantion,* XVI, 393-445.

―――― (1945), "Studies in Byzantine Economy," *Traditio,* III, 101-129.

―――― (1947), "The Byzantine Colonate," *Traditio,* V, 103-133.

SERISKI, P. M. (1941), *Poenae in iure byzantino ecclesiastico ab initiis ad saeculum XI (1054),* Rome.

SESTON, W. (1940), "Les origines de la capitation sous le Bas-Empire," in *Actes du sixième congrès international d'études byzantines,* Paris, pp. 29-30.

―――― (1948), "Le but de la rèforme agraire et de l'organisation des castes dans le Bas-Empire," *ibid.,* vol. I.

SETTON, K. M. (1953), "On the Importance of Land Tenure and Agrarian Taxation in the Byzantine Empire, from the Fourth Century to the Fourth Crusade," *American Journal of Philology,* LXXIV, 225-259.

SEUDIAS, M. (1939), "Études sur le gouvernement et l'administration à Byzance," in *Actes du cinquième congrès international d'études byzantines*, Rome.

ŠEVČENKO, I. (1949), "Léon Bardales et les juges généraux," *Byzantion*, XIX, 256-259.

—— (1952), "An Important Contribution to the Social History of Late Byzantium," in *Annals of the Ukrainian Academy of Arts and Science in the U.S.*, pp. 448-459.

SICKEL, W. (1898), "Das byzantinische Krönungsrecht bis zum 10 Jahrhundert," *BZ*, VII, 511-557.

SINOGOWITZ, B. (1953[a]), "Die byzantische Rechtgeschichte im Spiegel der Neuerscheinungen," *Saeculum*, IV, 313-333.

—— (1953[b]), "Die Begriffe Reich, Macht und Herrschaft im Byzantinischen Kulturbereich," *Saeculum*, IV, 450-455.

STADTMÜLLER, G. (1937), "Oströmische Bauern und Wehrpolitik," *Neue Jahrbücher für deutsche Wissenschaft*, XIII, 421-438.

STEIN, E. (1919), *Studien zur Geschichte des byzantinischen Reiches*, Stuttgart.

—— (1920), "Ein Kapitel vom persischen und vom byzantinischen Staat," *Byzantinisch-neugriechische Jahrbucher*, I, 50-89.

—— (1923-25), Review of Andréadès, A. (1921[b]), *BZ*, XXIV, 377-387.

—— (1924), "Untersuchungen zur spätbyzantinischen Verfassungs- und Wirtschaftsgeschichte," *Mitteilungen zur Osmanischen Geschichte* II, 1-59, 248-256.

—— (1928[a]), "Von Altertum zum Mittelalter: Zur Geschichte der byzantinischen Finanzverwaltung," *VSWG*, XXI, 158-170.

—— (1928[b]), *Geschichte des spätrömischen Reiches*, Vienna.

—— (1930), "L'administration de l'Egypte byzantine, *Gnomon*, VI, 401-407.

—— (1940), "La disparition du Sénat de Rome," in *Actes du sixième congrès international d'études byzantines*, Paris, pp. 24-25.

—— (1949), *Histoire du Bas-Empire: Vol. II, De la disparition de l'empire d'occident à la mort de Justinien (476-565)*, Paris.

—— (1954), "Introduction à l'histoire et aux institutions byzantines," *Traditio*, LXXIV, 95-168.

STÖCKLE, A. (1911), *Spätrömische und byzantinische Zünfte*, Leipzig.

SVORONOS, N. G. (1951), "Le serment de fidélité a l'empereur byzantin et sa signification constitutionelle," *REB*, IX, 106-142.

TANNER, J. R., *et al.* (eds.) (1936), *Cambridge Medieval History: Vol. IV, The Eastern Roman Empire*.

TREITINGER, O. (1958), *Die oströmische Kaiser- und Reichsidee nach ihrer Gestaltung im höfischen Zeremoniell: Vom oströmischen Staats und Reichsgedanken*, Darmstadt.

VASILIEV, A. A. (1933), "On the Question of Byzantine Feudalism," *Byzantion*, VIII, 584-604.

—— (1936), "Justinian's Digest," *Studi bizantini e neoellenici*, V, 711-734.

—— (1937), Review of Diehl, C., and Marçais, G. (1936), *Byzantinisch-neugriechische Jahrbücher*, XIII, 114-119.

—— (1952), *History of the Byzantine Empire, 324–1453*, Madison, Wis.

XANALATOS, D. A. (1937), *Beiträge zur Wirtschafts- und Sozialgeschichte Makedoniens im Mittelalter*, Munich.

ZACHARIA VON LINGENTHAL, C. E. (1892), *Geschichte des griechisch-römischen Rechtes*, Berlin.

ZAKYTHINOS, D. A. (1947-48), "Crise monétaire et crise économique à Byzance du XIIIième au XVIème siècle," *L'hellénisme contemporain*, I, 162-192; II, 150-167.

—— (1948), "Processus de féodalisation," *ibid.*, II, 499-534.

—— (1950), "Étatisme byzantin et expérience hellénistique," *Annuaire de l'institut de philologie et d'histoire orientales et slaves*, X, 667-680.

ZIEGLER, A. W. (1953), "Die byzantinische Religionspolitik und der sog. Caesaropapismus," in *Festschrift F. P. Diels*, Munich, pp. 81-97.

M. Islam

ABDURRAZIQ, A. (1933-34), "L'Islam et les bases du pouvoir," *Revue des études islamiques*, III, 353-391; IV, 163-222.

BECKER, C. H. (1924-32), *Islamstudien: Vom Werden und Wesen der Islamischen Welt*, Leipzig, 2 vols.

BEHRNANER, W. (1860-61), *Mémoire sur les institutions de police chez les arabes, les persans et les turcs*, JA, XV, 461-508, XVI, 114-190, 347-392; XVII, 5-76.

BIRGE, J. K. (1937), *The Beklashi Order of Dervishes*, London.

BROCKELMANN, C. (1943), *Geschichte der islamischen Völker und Staaten*, Munich and Berlin.

BUSSI, E. (1949), "Gli libri di diritto musulmano," in *Actes du septième congrès international d'études byzantines*, Brussels, vol. I, pp. 339-340.

GABRIELLI, F. (1950), "Studi di storia musulmana," *Rivista storica italiana*, LXII, 99-110.

GRUNEBAUM, G. E. VON (1946), *Medieval Islam: A Study in Cultural Orientation*, Chicago.

—— (ed.) (1954), *Studies in Islamic Cultural History*, American Anthropologist Memoir 76.

—— (1955[a]), *Islam: Essays in the Nature and Growth of a Cultural Tradition*, London.

—— (ed.) (1955[b]), *Unity and Variety in Muslim Civilization*, Chicago.

HEYD, W. (1923), *Histoire du commerce du Levant au moyen-âge*, Leipzig, 2 vols.

HODGSON, M. G. S. (1955), *The Order of Assassins*, The Hague.

—— (1960), "The Unity of Later Islamic History," *Journal of World History*, V, 879-914.

KRUSE, H. (1954), "Die Begründung der islamischen Völkerrechtslehre: Muhammed a-Saibani," *Saeculum*, V, 221-241.

LEVY, R. (1957), *The Social Structure of Islam*, Cambridge.

LEWIS, B. (1937), "The Islamic Guilds," *Economic History Review*, VIII, 20-37.

—— (1950), *The Arabs in History*, London.

—— (1954), "Islam," in Sinor, D. (ed.), *Orientalism and History*, Cambridge, pp. 16-33.

—— (1955), "The Concept of an Islamic Republic," *Die Welt des Islams*, IV, 1-10.

MASSÉ, H. (1957), *L'Islam*, Paris.

MASSIGNON, M. (1920), "Le corps de métier et la cité musulmane," *Revue internationale de sociologie*, XXVIII, 473.

ROSENTHAL, E. I. J. (1958), *Political Thought in Medieval Islam*, Cambridge.

SCHACHT, J. (1950), *The Origins of Muhammadan Jurisprudence*, Oxford.

SHERWANI, H. K. (1953), "The Genesis and Progress of Muslim Socio-Political Thought," *Islamic Culture*, XXVII, 135-148.

TAESCHNER, F. (1934), "Die islamischen Futuwwabünde," *ZDMG*, LXXXVII, 6-49.

TYAN, E. (1938-43), *Histoire de l'organisation judiciaire en pays d'Islam*, Paris.

VATIKIOTIS, P. J. (1954[a]), "A Reconstruction of the Fatimid Theory of the State: The Apocalyptic Nature of the Fatimid State," *Islamic Culture*, XXVIII, 399-409.

—— (1954[b]), "The Syncretic Origins of the Fatimid Da'wa," *ibid.*, 475-491.

WIET, G. (1937), *L'Egypte arabe de la conquête à la conquête ottomane (642–1517)*, Paris.

N. Abbassids and Saffawids

1. ABBASSIDS

AMEDROZ, H. F. (1913), "Abbassid Administration in Its Decay," *JRAS*, 823-842.

ARNOLD, T. W. (1924), *The Caliphate*, Oxford.

BRUNSCHVIG, R. (1955), "Considerations sociologiques sur le droit musulman ancien," *Studia Islamica*, III, 61-74.

CAHEN, C. (1953), "L'évolution de l'Iqta du IX au XIII siècle," *Annales*, VIII, 25-52.

—— (1954), "Fiscalité, proprieté, antagonisme sociaux en Haute-Mésopotamie an temps des premiers Abbasides," *Arabica*, I, 136-152.

—— (1955[a]), "The Body Politic," in Grunebaum, E. von (ed.), *Unity and Variety in Muslim Civilization*, Chicago, pp. 132-166.

—— (1955[b]), "L'histoire économique et sociale de l'orient musulman médiéval," *Studia Islamica*, III, 93-116.

—— (1957[a]), "Leçons d'histoire musulmane (VIIIième–XIième siècle)" (mimeo), *Les cours de Sorbonne*, Paris.

—— (1957[b]), "Les facteurs économiques et sociaux dans l'ankyklose culturelle de l'Islam," in Brunschwig, R., and Grunebaum, G. E. von (eds.), "Classicisme et declin culturel dans l'histoire de l'Islam," in *Actes du symposium international d'histoire de la civilisation musulmane*, Paris, pp. 195-217.

—— (1959), "Mouvements populaires et autonomisme urbain dans l'Asie musulmane du moyen-âge," *Arabica*, V, 225-250; VI, 25-56, 233-265.

CANARD, M. (1946-47), "L'impérialisme des Fatimides et leur propaganda," *Annales de l'institut d'études orientales*, VI, 156-193.

DENNETT, D. C., JR. (1939), "Marwin ibn Muhammad: The Passing of the Umayyad Caliphate," in *Summary of Theses of the Harvard Graduate School*, pp. 103-105.

—— (1950), *Conversion and the Poll Tax in Early Islam*, Cambridge, Mass.

EHRENKREUZ, A. S. (1959), Studies in the Monetary History of the Near East in the Middle Ages, *Journal of the Economic and Social History of the Orient*, II, 128-161.

GARDET, L. (1954), *La cité musulmane: Vie sociale et politique*, Paris.

GAUDEFROY-DEMOMBYNES, M. (1946), *Les institutions musulmanes*, Paris.

GOITEIN, S. D. (1942), *The Origins of the Vezirate and Its True Character*, Hyderabad.

—— (1949), "A Turning Point in the History of the Muslim State (à propos of Ibn al-Mugaffa's Kitab as-Sahaba)," *Islamic Culture*, XXIII, 120-135.

GRUNEBAUM, G. E. VON (1955), "Die islamische Stadt," *Saeculum*, VI, 138-154.

HOEUERBACH, W. (1950), "Zur Heeresverwaltung der Abbassiden," *Der Islam*, XXIX, 257-290.

KHADURI, M. (1947), "Nature of the Islamic State," *Islamic Culture*, XXI, 327-331.

LEWIS, B. (1937), "The Islamic Guilds," *Economic History Review*, VIII, 20-37.

—— (1940), *The Origins of Isma'ilism*, Cambridge.

—— (1950), *The Arabs in History*, London.

—— (1953), "Some Observations on the Significance of Heresy in the History of Islam," *Studia Islamica*, I, 43-64.

LICHTENSTADTER, I. (1949), "From Particularism to Unity: Race, Nationality and Minorities in Early Islamic Empire," *Islamic Culture*, XXIII, 251-280.

LOKKEGAARD, F. (1950), *Islamic Taxation in the Classic Period with Special Reference to Circumstances in Iraq*, Copenhagen.

LOTZ, W. (1937), *Staatsfinanzen in den ersten Jahrhunderten des Khalifenreichs*, Munich.

MEZ, A. (1937), *Renaissance of Islam*, London.

MUIR, W. (1924), *The Caliphate: Its Rise, Decline and Fall*, Edinburgh.

NIEUWENHUIJZE, C. A. O. VAN (1959), "The Ummah—An Analytic Approach," *Studia Islamica*, X, 5-22.

SAMADI, S. B. (1955[a]), "Some Aspects of the Theory of the State and Administration under the Abbasids," *Islamic Culture*, XXIX, 120-150.

—— (1955[b]), "Social and Economic Aspects of Life under the Abbassid Hegemony at Baghdad," *ibid.*, 237-245.

SCHACHT, J. (1950), *The Origins of Muhammadan Jurisprudence*, Oxford.

—— (1955), "The Law," in Grunebaum, G. E. von (ed.), *Unity and Variety in Muslim Civilization*, Chicago, pp. 65-86.

SPULER, B. (1954), "Iran and Islam," in Grunebaum, G. E. von (ed.), *Studies in Islamic Cultural History*, American Anthropologist Memoir 76, pp. 47-56.

—— (1955), "Iran: The Persistent Heritage," in Grunebaum, G. E. von (ed.), *Unity and Variety in Muslim Civilization*, Chicago, pp. 167-182.

TRITTON, A. S. (1930), *The Caliphs and Their Non-Muslim Subjects*, London.

2. SAFFAWIDS

HINZ, W. (1936), *Irans Aufstieg zum Nationalstaat im 15ten Jahrhundert*, Berlin.

LAMBTON, A. K. S. (1953), *Landlord and Peasant in Persia*, Oxford.

—— (1954), *Islamic Society in Persia*, London.

—— (1955), "Quis custodiet custodes? Some Reflections on the Persian Theory of Government," *Studia Islamica*, V, 125-148; VI, 125-146.

LOCKHART, L. (1958), *The Fall of the Safavi Dynasty*, Cambridge.

MINORSKY, V. (ed.) (1943), *Tadhkirat al-Mulūk*, London.

—— (1955), "Iran: Opposition, Martyrdom and Revolt," in Grunebaum, E. G. von (ed.), *Unity and Variety in Muslim Civilization*, Chicago, pp. 183-206.

ROEMER, H. R. (1953), "Die Safawiden," *Saeculum*, IV, 27-44.

SAVORY, R. M. (1960), The Principal Offices of the Safawid State during the Reign of Isma'il I, *BSOAS*, XXIII, 91-105

SYKES, P. M. (1930), *A History of Persia*, London.

O. The Ottoman Empire

ALDERSON, A. D. (1956), *The Structure of the Ottoman Dynasty*, Oxford.

ARNAKIS, G. G. (1953), "Futtuwa Traditions in the Ottoman Empire: Akhis, Bektrashi Dervishes and Craftsmen," *Journal of Near Eastern Studies*, XII, 232-247.

CAHEN, C. (1951), "Notes pour l'histoire des turcomans d'Asie Mineure au XIIIième siècle," *JA*, CCXXXIX, 335-355.

DAVISON, R. H. (1946), "Reform in the Ottoman Empire (1856–1876)," in *Summary of Theses of Harvard Graduate School*, pp. 155-158.

FISHER, S. N. (1941), "Civil Strife in the Ottoman Empire, 1481–1503," *Journal of Modern History*, VIII, 449-466.

GIBB, H. A. R., and BOWEN, H. (1950), *Islamic Society and the West*, London, Vol. I, Part 1.

—— (1957), *ibid.*, Part 2.

GIESE, F. G. (1926), "Das Seniorat im osmanischen Herscherhause," *Mitteilungen zur Osmanischen Geschichte*, II, 1-59, 248-256.

GLADDEN, E. N. (1937), "Administration of the Ottoman Empire under Suleiman," *Public Administration*, XV, 187-193.

HODGSON, M. G. S. (1960), "The Unity of Later Islamic History," *Journal of World History*, V, 879-914.

INALCIK, H. (1954), "Ottoman Methods of Conquest," *Studia Islamica*, II, 103-129.

KISSLING, H. J. (1953), "Aus der Geschichte des Chalvetijje-Ordens," *ZDMG*, CIII, 233-289.

―――― (1954), "The Sociological and Educational Role of the Dervish Orders in the Ottoman Empire," in Grunebaum, G. E. von (ed.), *Studies in Islamic Cultural History*, American Anthropologist Memoir 76, pp. 23-35.

KÖPRÜLÜ, M. J. (1926), *Les origines du Bektachisme: Essai sur le développement historique de l'hétérodoxie musulmane en Asie Mineure*, Paris.

―――― (1935), *Les origines de l'empire ottomane*, Paris.

LEWIS, B. (1958), "Some Reflections on the Decline of the Ottoman Empire," *Studia Islamica*, IX, 111-127.

LÜTFÜ, J. (1939), "Les problèmes fonciers dans l'empire ottomane au temps de sa fondation," *Annales*, XI, 233-237.

LYBYER, A. (1913), *The Government of the Ottoman Empire in the Time of Suleiman the Magnificent*, Cambridge, Mass.

MILLER, B. (1941), *The Palace School of Muhammad the Conqueror*, Cambridge, Mass.

PARRY, V. J. (1957), "The Ottoman Empire (1481–1520)," in Potter, G. R. (ed.), *New Cambridge Modern History*, vol. I, ch. 14.

―――― (1958), "The Ottoman Empire (1520–1566)," in Elton, G. R. (ed.), *ibid.*, vol. II, ch. 17.

SAYAR, I. M. (1951), "The Empire of the Saljuqids of Asia Minor," *Journal of Near Eastern Studies*, X, 268-280.

STAVRIANOS, L. S. (1957[a]), *The Balkans since 1433*, New York.

―――― (1957[b]), *The Ottoman Empire: Was It the Sick Man of Europe?* New York.

STOIANOVICH, T. (1960), "The Conquering Balkan Orthodox Merchant," *Journal of Economic History*, XX, 234-313.

STRIPLING, G. W. F. (1942), *The Ottoman Turks and the Arabs, 1511–1574*, Urbana, Ill.

WITTEK, P. (1928), "Türkentum und Islam," *Archiv für Sozialwissenschaft und Sozialpolitik*, LIX, 489-525.

―――― (1936), *Deux chapitres de l'histoire des turcs de Roum*, Brussels.

―――― (1938), *The Rise of the Ottoman Empire*, London.

―――― (1952), "Le rôle des tribus turques dans l'Empire ottomane," in *Mélanges Géorges Smets*, Brussels, pp. 665-676.

WRIGHT, W. L., JR. (1935), *Ottoman Statecraft*, Princeton, N.J.

P. Moslem Spain

CASTEJON, C. R. (1948), *Los juristas hispano-musulmanes*, Madrid.

DOZY, R. (1932), *Histoire des musulmanes d'Espagne*, Leiden.

GONZALEZ PALENCIA, A. (1923), *El califato occidental*, Madrid.

―――― (1929), *Historia de la España musulmana*, Barcelona.

HOLE, E. C. (1958), *Andalus: Spain under the Muslims*, London.

IRVING, T. B. (1954), "Falcon of Spain: A Study of Eighth Century Spain," *Orientalia* (Lahore), VI, 158.

LEVI-PROVENÇAL, E. (1932), *L'Espagne musulmane au Xième siècle: Institutions et vie social*, Paris.

―――― (1950-53), *Histoire de l'Espagne musulmane*, Paris.

MAHMOUD, M. (1948), *Essai sur la chute du califat umayyade de Cordove en 1009*, Cairo.

SANCHEZ-ALBORNOZ, C. (1932), "L'Espagne et l'Islam," *RH*, CLXIX, 327-339.

―――― (1946), *La España musulmana*, Buenos Aires.

SCOTT, S. (1904), *History of the Moorish Empire in Europe*, Philadelphia.

SHERWANI, H. K. (1930), "Incursions of the Muslims into France, Piedmont and Switzerland (from the Evacuation of Narbonne in 759 up to the Colonization of Provence in 889)," *Islamic Culture*, IV, 588-624.

WATTS, H. E. (1893), *Spain, Being a Summary of Spanish History from the Moorish Conquest to the Fall of Granada*, London.

Q. The Roman Empire
(ESPECIALLY FIRST TO FOURTH CENTURIES)

ALFÖLDI, A., (1952), *A Conflict of Ideas in the Later Roman Empire: The Clash between the Senate and Valentine I*, Oxford.

—— (1956), "Römische Kaiserzeit," in Valjavec, F. (ed.), *Historia Mundi*, Berne, vol. IV, pp. 190-297.

BANG, M. (1906), *Die Germanen im römischen Dienst bis zum Regierungsantritt Constantins*, Berlin.

BARKER, E. (1947), "The Conception of Empire," in Baily, C. (ed.), *The Legacy of Rome*, Oxford, pp. 45-90.

BAYNES, N. H. (1943), "The Decline of the Roman Power in Western Europe: Some Modern Explanations," *Journal of Roman Studies*, XXXIII, 29-35.

BEYER, W. C. (1959), "The Civil Service of the Ancient World," *Public Administration Review*, XIX, 243-249.

BOAK, A. E. R. (1950), "The Role of Policy in the Fall of the Roman Empire," *Michigan Alumnus Quarterly Review*, LVI, 291-294.

—— (1955[a]), *History of Rome to 565 A.D.*, New York.

—— (1955[b]), *Manpower Shortage and the Fall of the Roman Empire in the West*, Ann Arbor, Mich.

BOISSIER, G. (1875), *L'opposition sous les Césars*, Paris.

BURN, A. R. (1952), *The Government of the Roman Empire from Augustus to the Antonines*, London.

CANTARELLI, L. (1926-27), "Per l'amministrazione e la storia dell'Egitto romano," *Aegyptus*, VII, 282-285; VIII, 89-97.

CHARLESWORTH, M. P. (1936), "The Flavian Dynasty," in *The Cambridge Ancient History*, vol. XI, pp. 1-45.

DE LAET, S. J. (1949), *Aspects de la vie sociale et économique sous Auguste et Tibère*, Brussels.

DE REGIBUS, L. (1925), "Decio e la crisi dell'imperio Romano nel III secolo," *Didaskaleion*, III, 1-11.

ENSSLIN, W. (1956), "The Senate and the Army," in *The Cambridge Ancient History*, vol. XII, pp. 57-67.

GLOVER, T. R. (1919), *The Conflict of Religions in the Early Roman Empire*, London.

HEICHELHEIM, F. M. (1956), "Romische Sozial- und Wirtschaftsgeschichte," in Valjavec F. (ed.), *Historia Mundi*, Berne, vol. IV, pp. 397-488.

HENDERSON, B. W. (1908), *Civil War and Rebellion in the Roman Empire*, London.

HIRSCHFELD, O. (1877), *Untersuchungen auf dem Gebiete der Romischen Verwaltungsgeschichte*, Berlin.

HOMO, L. (1950), *Les institutions politiques romaines: De la cité a l'état*, Paris.

JONES, A. H. M. (1949), "The Civil Service (Clerical and Sub-clerical Grades)," *Journal of Roman Studies*, XXXIX, 38-53.

—— (1950), "The Aerarium and the Fiscus," *ibid.*, XI, 22-29.

—— (1954), "Imperial and Senatorial Jurisdiction in the Early Principate," *Historia*, III, 464-488.

—— (1955), "The Decline and Fall of the Roman Empire," *History*, XL, 209-226.

KRAEMER, C. J. (1953), "The Historical Pattern," in *The Age of Diocletian—A Sym-*

posium, The Metropolitan Museum of Art, New York, pp. 1-9.

LAST, H. (1936[a]), "The Principate and the Administration," in *The Cambridge Ancient History*, vol. XI, pp. 393-432.

—— (1936[b]), "Rome and the Empire," *ibid.*, pp. 435-477.

LONGDEN, R. P. (1936[a]), "Nerva and Trajan," *ibid.*, pp. 188-223.

—— (1936[b]), "The Wars of Trajan," *ibid.*, pp. 223-251.

MATTINGLY, H. (1957), *Roman Imperial Civilization*, London.

MILLER, S. N. (1956), "The Army and the Imperial House," in *The Cambridge Ancient History*, vol. XII, pp. 19-35.

MOMIGLIANO, A. (1934), *Claudius the Emperor and His Achievement*, Oxford.

PFLAUM, H. G. (1950), *Les procurateurs équèstres sous le haut empire romain*, Paris.

SCHILLER, A. A. (1949[a]), "Bureaucracy and the Roman Law," *Seminar*, VII, 26-48.

—— (1949[b]), "The Jurists and the Prefects of Rome," *Revue internationale des droits de l'antiquité*, II, 319-359.

—— (1953), "Factors in the Development of the Late Classic Law," *Seminar*, XI, 1-11.

SCHULTZ, F. (1946), *History of Roman Legal Science*, Oxford.

STUART-JONES, H. (1947), "Administration," in Baily, C. (ed.), *The Legacy of Rome*, Oxford, pp. 91-140.

STAUB, A. (1939), *Vom Herrscherideal der Spätantike: Forschungen zur Kirchen—und Geistesgeschichte*, Stuttgart.

STEIN, A. (1927), *Der Römische Ritterstand*, Munich.

SYME, R. (1939), *The Roman Revolution*, Oxford.

VINOGRADOFF, P. (1911), "Social and Economic Conditions of the Roman Empire in the Fourth Century," in *The Cambridge Ancient History*, vol. I, ch. 18.

WALTHER, W. (1942), "Bauertum und römisches Wesen," *Neue Jahrbücher für Antike und Deutsche Bildung*, V, 293-303.

WEBER, W. (1936[a]), "Hadrian," in *The Cambridge Ancient History*, vol. XI, pp. 294-325.

—— (1936[b]), "The Antonines," *ibid.*, pp. 325-391.

WESTERMAN, W. L. (1955), *The Slave Systems in Greek and Roman Antiquity*, Philadelphia.

R. The Spanish-American Empire

ALTAMIRA, R. (1936), "La legislación indiana como elemento de la historia de las ideas coloniales españolas," *Revista de historia de América*, I, 1-24.

—— (1939), "La décentralisation législative dans le régime colonial espagnol (XVIième—XVIIIième siècles)," *Bulletin du comité international des sciences historiques*, XI, 165-190.

—— (1940-45), "Los cedularios como fuente historica de la legislación indiana," *Revista de historia de América*, X, 5-87; XIX, 61-129.

—— (1947-48), "Estudios sobre las fuentes de conocimiento del derecho indiano," *ibid.*, XXIV, 313-341; XXV, 69-134.

BAGU, S. (1949), *Economia de la sociedad colonial*, Buenos Aires.

BARBER, R. K. (1932), *Indian Labor in the Spanish Colonies*, Albuquerque, N.M.

BELAUNDE GUINASSI, M. (1945), *La encomienda en el Peru*, Lima.

BENEYTO, P. J. (1955), "Tradicion, ideologia y sociedad en la institucionalisacion de la independencia," *Revista de estudios políticos*, LXXXIII, 149-171.

BORAH, W. (1941), "The Collection of Tithes in the Bishopric of Oaxaca in the Sixteenth Century," *HAHR*, XXI, 386-409.

—— (1943), *Silk Raising in Colonial Mexico*, Berkeley, Calif.

—— (1949), "Tithe Collection in the Bishopric of Oaxaca (1601–1867)," *HAHR*, XXIX, 498-517.

—— (1951), *New Spain's Century of Depression*, Berkeley, Calif.

—— (1954), *Early Colonial Trade between Mexico and Peru*, Berkeley, Calif.

—— (1956), "Representative Institutions in the Spanish Empire in the Sixteenth Century—The New World," *The Americas*, XII, 246-257.

——, and COOK, S. F. (1958), *Price Trends of Some Basic Commodities in Central Mexico (1531–1570)*, Berkeley, Calif.

BROWN, V. L. (1925), "Anglo-Spanish Relations in America in the Closing Years of the Colonial Era," *HAHR*, V, 327-483.

—— (1926), "The South Sea Company and Contraband Trade," *American Historical Review*, XXX, 662-678.

—— (1928), "Contraband Trade: A Factor in the Decline of Spanish Empire in America," *HAHR*, VIII, 178-189.

CARANDE, R. (1952), "Der Wanderhirt und die überseeische Ausbreitung Spaniens," *Saeculum*, III, 373-387.

CARDOS, J. M. (1955), "La política economica indiana de los Cortes de Castilla," *Revista de estudios políticos*, LXXXII, 173-192.

CARNEY, J. J., JR. (1939), "Early Spanish Imperialism," *HAHR*, XIX, 138-185.

CASTAÑEDA, C. E. (1929), "The Corregidor in Spanish Colonial Administration," *HAHR*, IX, 446-470.

—— (1955), "Spanish Medieval Institutions and Overseas Administration: The Prevalance of Medieval Concepts," *The Americas*, XI.

CASTRO, R. B. (1959), "El desarrollo de la población hispano-americana (1492–1950)," *Journal of World History*, V, 325-343.

CHAMBERLAIN, R. S. (1943), "The Corregidor in Castile," *HAHR*, XXIII, 222-257.

CHAPMAN, C. E. (1942), "Spanish Consulados," in Curtio-Wilgus, A. C. (ed.), *Hispanic American Essays*, Chapel Hill, N.C., pp. 78-84.

CHAUNU, P. (1956), "Pour une histoire économique de l'Amérique espagnole coloniale," *RH*, CCXVI, 209-218.

CHEVALIER, F. (1944), "Les municipalités indiennes en Nouvelle Espagne (1520–1860)," *Anuario de historio del derecho español*, XV, 352-386.

—— (1952), *La formation des grands domaines au Mexique: Terre et société aux 16ième et 17ième siècles*, Paris.

CHRISTELOW, A. (1942), *Contraband Trade between Jamaica and the Spanish Main, and the Free Port Act of 1766*, HAHR, XXII, 309-343.

—— (1947), "Great Britain and the Trades from Cadiz and Lisbon to Spanish America and Brazil, 1759–1783," *HAHR*, XXVII, 2-29.

CORBITT, D. C. (1939), " 'Mercedes' and 'Realengos': A Survey of the Public Land System in Cuba," *HAHR*, XIX, 262-285.

CUNNINGHAM, C. H. (1919), *The Audiencia in the Spanish Colonies as Illustrated by the Audiencia of Manila (1583–1800)*, Berkeley, Calif.

DESDEVISES DU DEZERT, G. (1914), "L'inquisition aux Indes espagnoles à la fin du XVIIIième siècle," *Revue hispanique*, XXX, 1-118.

—— (1917), *L'église espagnole des Indes à la fin du XVIIIième siècles*, Paris.

DIEGO Y CARRA, P. V. (1953), "Bartolomé de las Casas y las controversias teologico-juridicas de India," *Boletín de la real academia de historia*, CXXXII, 231-268.

DURAND, J. (1953), *La transformación social del conquistador*, Mexico City.

DUSENBERRY, W. H. (1947), "Woolen Manufacture in Sixteenth Century New Spain," *The Americas*, IV, 223-234.

FISHER, L. E. (1926), *Viceregal Administration in the Spanish-American Colonies*, Berkeley, Calif.

—— (1929), *The Intendant System in Spanish America*, Berkeley, Calif.

—— (1936), "Colonial Government," in Curtis Wilgus, A. (ed.), *Colonial Hispanic America*, Washington, D.C., ch. VII.

FRIEDE, J. (1952), "Las casas y el movimiento indigenista en España y América en la primera mitad del siglo XVII," *Revista de historia de América*, XXXIV, 339-411.

GALLO, A. G. (1942), "Los orígenes de la administración territorial de las Indias," *Anuario de historia del derecho español*, XIX, 16-17.

——— (1944), *Los orígenes de la administración governmental de la Indias*, Madrid.

——— (1951[a]), "Los encomienderos indios," *Revista de estudios políticos*, LV, 144-161.

——— (1951[b]), "El derecho indiano y la independencia de América," *ibid.*, LX, 157-180.

——— (1952), "Los virreinatos americanos bajo los Reyes Católicos," *ibid.*, LXV, 189-210.

——— (1953), "El desarrollo de la historiografía jurídica indiana," *ibid.*, LXX, 163-185.

GARCIA, J. A. (1900), *La ciudad indiana*, Buenos Aires.

GIBSON, C. (1953), "Rotation of Alcaldes in the Indian Cabildo of Mexico City," *HAHR*, XXXIII, 212-224.

——— (1955), "The Transformation of the Indian Community in New Spain (1500–1800)," *Journal of World History*, II, 581-608.

GOMENSORO, J. (1945), "Proceso social y economico del Uruguay," *Revista de América*, IV, 207-210.

GONGORA, M. (1951), *El estado en el derecho indiano: Epoca de Fundación (1492–1570)*, Santiago de Chile.

GRAY, W. H. (1948), "Early Trade Relations between the United States and Venezuela," *Estudios de historia del instituto panamericano de geografía e historia*, I, 87-107.

GRIFFIN, C. C. (1949), "Economic and Social Aspects of the Era of Spanish American Independence," *HAHR*, XXIX, 170-188.

——— (1951), "Unidad y variedad en la historia americana, *Estudios de historia del instituto panamericano de geografía e historia*," IV, 97-123.

GUTHRIE, C. L. (1939), "Colonial Economy: Trade, Industry, and Labor in Seventeenth Century Mexico City," *Revista de historia de América*, VII, 103-134.

HAMILTON, E. J. (1929[a]), "Imports of American Gold and Silver into Spain, (1503-1660)," *Quarterly Journal of Economics*, XLIII, 436-499.

——— (1929[b]), "American Treasure and the Rise of Capitalism (1500–1700)," *Economica*, IX, 338-357.

——— (1934), *"American Treasure and the Price of Revolution in Spain (1501–1650),"* Cambridge, Mass.

——— (1944), "Monetary Problems in Spain and Spanish America (1751–1800)," *Journal of Economic History*, IV, 21-48.

HANKE, L. (1935), *The First Social Experiments in America: A Study in the Development of Spanish Indian Policy in the Sixteenth Century*, Cambridge, Mass.

——— (1936[a]), "Theoretical Aspects of the Spanish Discovery, Exploration and Administration of America," in *Summary of Theses of Harvard Graduate School*, pp. 195-196.

——— (1936[b]), "The 'Requerimiento' and Its Interpreters," *Revista de historia de América*, I, 25-34.

——— (1937), "Pope Paul III and the American Indians," *Harvard Theological Review*, XXX, 65-102.

——— (1949), *The Spanish Struggle for Justice in the Conquest of America*, Philadelphia.

——— (1951), *Bartolomé de Las Casas, an Interpretation of his Life and Writings*, The Hague.

——— (1952), *Bartolomé de Las Casas, Bookman, Scholar and Propagandist*, Philadelphia.

——— (1956), *The Imperial City of Potosí*, The Hague.

HARING, C. H. (1914–1915), "American Gold and Silver Production in the First Half of the Sixteenth Century," *Quarterly Journal of Economics*, XXIX, 433-474.

—— (1918), "The Early Spanish Colonial Exchequer," *American Historical Review,* XXIII, 779-796.

—— (1922), "Ledgers of the Royal Treasurers in Spanish America in the Sixteenth Century," *HAHR,* II, 173-187.

—— (1927), "The Genesis of Royal Government in the Spanish Indies," *HAHR,* VII, 141-191.

—— (1947), *The Spanish Empire in America,* New York.

HERNÁNDEZ Y SANCHEZ-BARBA, M. (1954), "La población hispanoamericana y su distribución social en el siglo XVIII," *Revista de estudios políticos,* LXXVIII, 111-142.

—— (1955), "La participación del Estado en la estructuración de los grupos humanos en Hispanoamérica durante el siglo XVI," *ibid.,* LXXXIV, 193-227.

HOWE, W. (1949), *The Mining Guild of New Spain and Its Tribunal General (1770–1821),* Cambridge, Mass.

HUMPHREYS, R. A. (1952), *Liberation in South America (1806–27): The Career of James Paroissien,* London.

JANE, C. (1929), *Liberty and Despotism in South America,* Oxford.

KONETZKE, R. (1943), *Das Spanische Weltreich,* Munich.

—— (1946), "El mestizaje y su importancia en el desarrollo de la población hispano-americana durante le época colonial," *Revista de Indias,* XXIII, XXIV.

—— (1949[a]), "La esclavitud de los indios como elemento en la estructuración social de Hispanoamérica," in *Estudios de historia social de España,* Madrid, vol. I.

—— (1949[b]), "Las ordenanzas de gremios como documentos de la historia social de Hispanoamérica durante la época colonial," *ibid.,* vol. I, pp. 483-523.

—— (1951[a]), "Estado y sociedad en India," *Estudios Americanos,* X.

—— (1951[b]), "La formación de la nobleza en India," *ibid.,* 329-357.

—— (1952), "Die Entstehung des Adels in Hispano-Amerika während der Kolonialzeit," *VSWG,* XXXIX, 215-250.

—— (1953), *Formación social de Hispano América (1493–1592),* Madrid.

—— (1954), Review of Góngora, M. (1949), *HZ,* CLXXVII, 640-641.

—— (1961), "Staat und Gesellschaft in Hispanoamerika am Vorabend der Unabhangigkeit," *Saeculum,* XII, pp. 158-169.

LANNING, J. T. (1940), *Academic Culture in the Spanish Colonies,* New York.

LEA, H. C. (1908), *The Inquisition in the Spanish Dependencies,* New York.

LEONARD, I. A. (1942), *Best Sellers of the Lima Book Trade, 1583, HAHR,* XXII, 5-33.

LEVENE, R. (1927-28), *Investigaciones acerca de la historia económica del Virreinato de la Plata,* La Plata, 2 vols.

—— (1953), "Nuevas investigaciones históricas sobre el régimen político y jurídico de España en indias hasta la recopilación de leyes de 1680," *Journal of World History,* I, 463-490.

MADARIAGA, S. (1947), *The Fall of the Spanish American Empire,* London.

MANCHESTER, A. K. (1931), "The Rise of the Brazilian Aristocracy," *HAHR,* XI, 145-168.

MARSHALL, C. E. (1939), "The Birth of the Mestizo in New Spain," *HAHR,* XIX, 161-184.

MIRANDA, J. (1941-42), "La función economica del encomiendero en los orígenes del regimen colonial de Neuva España," *Anales del instituto nacional de antropología e historia,* II, 421-462.

—— (1944), "Notas sobre la introducción de la mesta en la Nueva España," *Revista de historia de América,* XVII, 1-26.

—— (1951), "La tasación de las cargas indígenas de la Nueva España durante el siglo XVI, excluyendo el tributo," *Revista de historia de América,* XXXV, 77-96.

—— (1952[a]), *Las ideas y las instituciones políticas mexicanas,* Mexico City.

—— (1952[b]), *El tributo indígeno en la Nueva España durante el siglo XVI,* Mexico City.

MOORE, J. P. (1954), *The Cabildo in Peru under the Habsburgs: A Study in the Origins and Powers of the Town-Council in the Vice-Royalty of Peru (1530–1700)*, Durham, N.C.

MÖRNER, M. (1953), *The Political and Economic Activities of the Jesuits in the La Plate Region: The Habsburg Era*, Stockholm.

MOSES, B. (1908), *South America on the Eve of Emancipation*, New York.

—— (1919), *Spain's Declining Power in South America (1730–1806)*, Berkeley, Calif.

—— (1926), *The Intellectual Background of the Revolution in South America*, New York.

OTS CAPDEQUI, J. M. (1932), "Apuntes para la historia del municipio hispanoamericano del período colonial," *Anuario de historia del derecho español*, I, 93-157.

—— (1934[a]), "Las instituciones económicas hispanoamericanas del periodo colonial, *ibid.*, XI, 211-282.

—— (1934[b]), *Instituciones sociales de la América española en el período colonial*, La Plata.

—— (1939), "Algunas consideraciones en torno a la política económica y fiscal del estado español en las Indias," *Revista de las Indias*, II, 172-181.

—— (1940), *Estudios de historia del derecho español en las Indias*, Bogota.

—— (1941), *El estado españo en las Indias*, Mexico City.

—— (1945), "Del absolutismo de los Austrias al despotismo de los Borbones," *Revista de América*, IV, 211-217.

—— (1946[a]), *Nuevos aspectos del siglo XVIII español en América*, Bogota.

—— (1946[b]), *El régimen de la tierra en la América española durante el período colonial*, Ciudad Trujillo.

—— (1951), "Interpretación institucional de la colonización española en América," *Estudios de historia del instituto panamericano de geografía e historia*, IV, 287-314.

PALM, E. W. (1951), "Los orígenes del urbanismo imperial en América," *ibid.*, II, 239-260.

PARANHOS, A. (1948), "Evolucão economica do Brasil," *ibid.*, I, 249-345.

PARES, R. (1936), *War and Trade in the West Indies (1739–1763)*, New York.

PARRA, C. (1933), *Filosofía universitaria venezolana (1788–1821)*, Caracas.

PARRY, J. H. (1940), *The Spanish Theory of Empire in the Sixteenth Century*, Cambridge.

—— (1948), *The Audiencia of New Galicia in the Sixteenth Century: A Study in Spanish Colonial Government*, Cambridge.

—— (1953), *The Sale of Public Offices in the Spanish Indies under the Hapsburgs*, Berkeley, Calif.

—— (1957), "The Development of the American Communities—Latin-America," in Lindsay, J. O. (ed.), *New Cambridge Modern History*, vol. VII, pp. 487-499.

PHELAN, J. L. (1959), "Free versus Compulsory Labor: Mexico and the Philippines (1540–1640)," *Comparative Studies in Society and History*, I, 189-201.

—— (1960), "Authority and Flexibility in the Spanish Imperial Bureaucracy," *Administrative Science Quarterly*, V, 47-66.

PIERSON, W. W. (1922), "Some Reflections on the Cabildo as an Institution," *HAHR*, V, 573-596.

—— (1941), "La intendencia de Venezuela en el régimen colonial," *Boletin de la academia nacional de la historia*, XXIV, 259-275.

—— (1942), "The Foundation and Early History of the Venezuelan Intendencia," in Curtis Wilgus, A. (ed.), *Hispanic American Essays*, Chapel Hill, N.C., pp. 99-114.

PRIESTLEY, H. I. (1916), *José de Galvez, Visitor-General of New Spain (1765–1771)*, Berkeley, Calif.

—— (1918), "The Old University of Mexico," *University of California Chronicle*, XXI, No. 4.

RIPPY, J. F. (1948), "The Dawn of Manufacturing in Venezuela," *Estudios de historia del instituto panamericano de geografía e historia*, I, 71-87.

ROSCHER, W. (1944), *The Spanish Colonial System*, Cambridge.

SAYOUS, A. E. (1928-29), "Partnerships in the Trade between Spain and America and also in the Spanish Colonies in the Sixteenth Century," *Journal of Economic and Business History*, I, 282-301.

—— (1930), "Les changes de l'Espagne sur l'Amérique au XVIIième siècle," *Revue d'économie politique*, XLI, 1417-1443.

—— (1934), "Les débuts du commerce de l'Espagne avec l'Amérique (1503–1518)," *RH*, CLXXIV, 185-215.

SCHÄFER, E. (1935-47), *El consejo real y supremo de las Indias*, Seville.

SERVICE, E. R. (1951), "The Encomienda in Paraguay," *HAHR*, XXXI, 230-252.

SIMPSON, L. B. (1934), *Studies in the Administration of the Indians of New Spain: I. The Laws of Burgos, 1512; II. The Civil Congregation*, Berkeley, Calif.

—— (1938), *ibid., III. The Repartimiento System of Native Labor in New Spain and Guatemala*.

—— (1940), *ibid., IV. The Emancipation of the Indian Slaves and the Resettlement of the Freedmen (1548–1555)*.

—— (1950), *The Encomienda in New Spain: The Beginning of Spanish Mexico*, Berkeley, Calif.

SPELL, J. R. (1935), "Rousseau in Spanish America," *HAHR*, XV, 260-267.

STAUPER, F. M. (1927), "Church and State in Peru," *HAHR*, VII, 410-437.

THOMAS, A. B. (1956), *Latin America: A History*, New York.

VAZQUES, C. A. (1945), "La universidad de los criollos," *Revista mexicana de sociología*, VII.

VIDA VICEUS, J. (1957), *Historia social y económica de España y América*, Barcelona.

VILLABOLOS, N. M. (1951), *Política indigena en los orígenes de la sociedad chilena*, Santiago de Chile.

VILLARÁN, M. V. (1938), *La universidad de San Marcos de Lima: Los orígines (1548–1577)*, Lima.

VIÑAS Y MEY, C., and PAZ, R. (1949-51), *Relaciones de los pueblos de España ordenadas por Felipe II*, Madrid.

VIRGILIO, C. F. (1948), "Sistema tributario do Brazil durante lo periodo colonial," *Estudios de historia del instituto panamericano de geografía e historia*, I, 229-242.

WHITAKER, A. P. (ed.) (1942), *Latin America and the Enlightment*, New York.

—— (1955), "La historia intelectual de Hispanoamérica en el siglo XVIII," *Revista de historia de América*, XL, 553-573.

WOLFF, I. (1956), "Chilenische Opposition gegen die Wirtschaftspolitik des Vicekönigreichs Peru (1778–1810)," *VSWG*, XLIII, 146-168.

ZAVALA, S. (1935[a]), *La encomienda indiana*, Madrid.

—— (1935[b]), *Las instituciones jurídicas en la conquista de América*, Madrid.

—— (1936), "Los trobajadores autillaros en el siglo XVI en el siglo XVII," *Revista de historia de América*, I, 31-69; II, 60-89.

—— (1943), *New Viewpoints on the Spanish Colonization of America*, Philadelphia.

—— (1944), *Ensayos sobre la colonización española en América*, Buenos Aires.

—— (1945), *Contribución a la historia de las instituciones coloniales de Guatemala*, Mexico City.

—— (1947[a]), *La filosofía política en la conquista de América*, Mexico City.

—— (1947[b]), "Apuntes históricos sobre la meneda del Paraguay," *El trimestre económico*, XIII, 126-143.

—— (1949), "De encomiendes y propiedad territorial en algunas regiones de la América española," in *Estudios indianos*, Madrid.

—— (1951), "Formación de la historia americana," *Estudios de historia del instituto panamericano del geografía e historia*, IV, 125-163.

S. Absolutist Europe

BARKER, E. (1945), *The Development of Public Services in Western Europe (1660–1930)*, New York.

BELOFF, M. (1954), *The Age of Absolutism*, London.

BRAUDEL, F., and SPOONER, F. C. (1955), "Les métaux monétaires et l'économie du XVIième siècle," in *Relazioni del congresso internazionale di scienze storiche*, Rome, vol. IV, pp. 233-264.

CLARK, G. (1929-59), *The Seventeenth Century*, Oxford.

—— (1957), *Early Modern Europe (from about 1450 to about 1720)*, London.

COBBAN, A. (1957), "The Enlightenment," in Lindsay, J. O. (ed.), *New Cambridge Modern History*, vol. VII, ch. V.

COLEMAN, D. C. (1957), "Eli Heckscher and the Idea of Mercantilism," *Scandinavian Economic History Review*, V, 3-22.

COSTS, A. W. (1958), "In the Defense of Heckscher and the Idea of Mercantilism," *Scandinavian Economic History Review*, VI, 175-187.

DHONDT, J. (1948), Review of Lousse, E. (1943), *Revue belge de philologie et d'histoire*, XXVI, 284-292.

GOODWIN, A. (ed.) (1953), *The European Mobility in the Eighteenth Century*, London.

GREAVES, R. W. (1957), "Religion," in Lindsay, J. O. (ed.), *New Cambridge Modern History*, vol. VII, pp. 113-140.

HARTUNG, F. (1937), "Die geschichtliche Bedeutung des aufgeklärten Despotismus in Preussen und in den deutschen Kleinstaaten," *Bulletin of the International Committee of Historical Sciences*, IX, 3-21.

—— (1957), *Enlightened Despotism*, London.

——, and MOUSNIER, R. (1955), "Quelques problèmes concernant la monarchie absolue," in *Relazioni del comitato internazionale di scienze storiche*, Rome, vol. IV, pp. 2-55.

HATTON, R. M. (1957), "Scandinavia and the Baltic," in Lindsay, J. O. (ed.), *New Cambridge Modern History*, vol. VII, pp. 339-364.

HAUSER, H. (1940), "La prépondérance espagnole (1559–1660)," in *Peuples et Civilisations*, Paris, vol. IX.

——, and RENAUDET, A. (1938), "Les débuts de l'âge moderne: La renaissance et la réforme," *ibid.*, vol. VIII.

HEATON, H. (1937), "Heckscher on Mercantilism," *Journal of Political Economy*, XLV, 370-393.

HECKSCHER, E. F. (1932), *Der Merkantilism*, Jena.

HELLER, H. (1934), *Staatslehre*, Leiden.

HINTZE, O. (1930), "Typologie der ständischen Verfassung des Abendlandes," *HZ*, CXLI, 229-248.

—— (1931), "Weltegeschichtliche Bedingungen der Repräsentativverfassung," *HZ*, CXLIII, 1-47.

—— (1942), "Der Commissarius und seine Bedeutung in der allgemeinen Verfassungsgeschichte," in *Staat und Verfassung*, Leipzig, pp. 232-264.

JEDIN, H. (1955), "Zur Entwicklung des Kirchenbegriffs im 16ten Jahrhundert," in *Relazioni del congresso internazionale di scienze storiche*, Rome, vol. IV, pp. 59-74.

KELLENBENZ, H. (1957), "Die Unternehmerische Betätigung der Verschiedene Stände während des Übergangs zur Neuzeit," *VSWG*, XLIV, 1-25.

KIERNAN, V. G. (1957), "Foreign Mercenaries and Absolute Monarchy," *Past and Present*, XI, 66-86.

LABROUSSE, E. (1955), "Voies nouvelles vers une histoire de la bourgeoisie occidentale au XVIIIième et XIXième siècles," in *Relazioni del congresso internazionale di scienze storiche*, Rome, vol. IV, pp. 365-396.

——, and MOUSNIER, R. (1955), *Le XVIIIième siècle: Révolution intellectuelle technique et politique (1715–1815)*, Paris.

LEFÈBVRE, G. (1949), "La despotisme éclairé," *Annales de l'histoire de la Révolution française*, CXIV, 97-115.

LEONARD, E. J. (1955), "La notion et le fait de l'église dans la réforme protestante," in *Relazioni del congresso internazionale di scienze storiche*, Rome, vol. IV, pp. 75-110.

LEULLIOT, P. (1955), "Les industries textiles: Problèmes généraux et orientation des récherches," *ibid.*, pp. 285-294.

LHÉRITIER, M. (1923), "Le rôle historique du despotisme éclairé, particulièrement au 18ième siècle," *Bulletin of the International Committee of Historical Sciences*, I, 601-612.

—— (1937), "Rapport général: L'oeuvre des despotes éclairés," *ibid.*, IX, 205-225.

LINDSAY, J. O. (1957[a]), "The Social Classes and the Foundations of the States," in Lindsay, J. O. (ed.), *The New Cambridge Modern History*, vol. V, VII, pp. 50-66.

—— (1957[b]), "Monarchy and Administration, European Practice," *ibid.*, pp. 141-160.

LOTZ, W. (1935), "Studien über Steuerverpachtung," *Sitz. der Bayerischen Akademie der Wissenschaften, Phil.-hist. Abteilung*, 1-33.

LOUSSE, E. (1937), "La formation des ordres dans la société médiévale," in "L'organisation corporative du moyen-âge à la fin de l'ancien régime," in *Études présentées à la Commission internationale pour l'histoire des assemblées d'états*, Louvain, vol. II, pp. 61-90.

—— (1943), *La société d'ancien régime, organisation et représentation corporatives*, Louvain.

MEUVRET, J. (1955), "L'agriculture en Europe au XVIIième et XVIIIième siècles," in *Relazioni del congresso internazionale di scienze storiche*, Rome, vol. IV, pp. 139-168.

MOMMSEN, W. (1938), "Zur Beurteilung des Absolutismus," *HZ*, CLVIII, 52-77.

MORAZÉ, C. (1948), "Finances et despotisme: Essai sur les despotes éclairés," *Annales*, XX, 279-296.

MURET, P. (1942), "La prépondérance anglaise (1715-1763)," in *Peuples et Civilisations*, Paris, vol. XI.

ORCIBAL, J. (1955), "L'idée d'église chez les catholiques du XVIIIième siècle," in *Relazioni del congresso internazionale di scienze storiche*, Rome, vol. IV, pp. 111-135.

PIRENNE, H., *et al.* (1931), "La fin du moyen-âge," in *Peuples et Civilisations*, Paris, vol. VII.

REDLICH, F. (1953), "European Aristocracy and Economic Development," *Explorations in Entrepreneurial History*, VI, 78-92.

ROBERTS, M. (1956), *The Military Revolution (1560-1660)*, Belfast.

SAGNAC, P. (1941), "La fin de l'ancien régime et la révoläion américaine," *Peuples et Civilisations*, Paris, vol. XII.

——, and SAINT-LÉGER, A. DE (1949), "Louis XIV (1661-1715)," *ibid.*, vol. X.

SCHNEE, H. (1952), "Die Hoffinanz und der moderne Staat," *Saeculum*, III, 132-160.

SKALWEIT, S. (1957), "Das Herrscherbild des 17ten Jahrhundert," *HZ*, CLXXXIV, 65-80.

SLICKER VAN BATH, B. H. (1955), "Agriculture in the Low Countries," in *Relazioni del congresso internazionale di scienze storiche*, Rome, vol. IV, pp. 169-204.

STONE, L. (1957), "The Nobility in Business (1540-1640)," *Explorations in Entrepreneurial History*, X, 54-62.

SWART, K. W. (1949), *Sale of Offices in the Seventeenth Century*, The Hague.

TREUE, W. (1957), "Das Verhältniss von Fürst, Staat und Unternehmer in der Zeit des Merkantilismus," *VSWG*, XLIV, 26-56.

VIDALENE, J. (1955), "La métallurgie et les industries secondaires en Europe occidentale et centrale au XVIIIième siècle," in *Relazioni del congresso internazionale di scienze storiche*, Rome, vol. IV, 295-303.

VINER, J. (1948), "Power versus Plenty as Objectives of Foreign Policy in the Seventeenth and Eighteenth Centuries," *World Politics*, I, 1-29.

WILSON, C. H. (1957), "The Growth of Overseas Commerce and European Manufacture," in Lindsay, J. O. (ed.), *New Cambridge Modern History*, vol. VII, pp. 27-49.

—— (1958), *Mercantilism*, London.

WITTRAM, R. (1948), "Formen und Wandlungen des europäischen Absolutismus," in *Glaube und Geschichte, Festschrift für F. Gogarten zum 13/1/1947*, Giessen, pp. 278-299.

T. Austria
(ESPECIALLY EIGHTEENTH CENTURY)

BENEDIKT, E. (1936), *Kaiser Joseph II*, Vienna.

BLUM, J. (1948), *Noble Landowners and Agriculturers in Austria (1815–1848)*, Baltimore.

FRANZ, G. (1955), *Liberalismus*, Munich.

GOOCH, G. P. (1951), *Maria Teresa and Other Studies*, London.

GROSS, L. (1924-25), "Der Kampf zwischen Reichskanzlei und österreichischer Hofkanzlei um die Führung der auswärtigen Geschichte," *Historische Vierteljahrschrift*, XXII, 279-312.

HANTSCH, H. (1951-53), *Die Geschichte Österreichs*, Graz.

HINTZE, O. (1901), "Der österreichische und der preussische Beamtenstaat im 17ten und 18ten Jahrhundert," *HZ*, LXXXVI, 402-444.

JELUSIC, K. (1936), "La noblesse autrichienne," *Annales*, VIII, 355-365.

MACARTNEY, C. A. (1957), "The Habsburg Dominions," in Lindsay, J. O. (ed.), *New Cambridge Modern History*, vol. VII, pp. 391-415.

MÜLLER, P. (1937), "Der aufgeklärte Absolutismus in Österreich," *Bulletin of the International Committee of Historical Sciences*, IX, 22-37.

PETERKA, O. (1937), "Das Zeitalter des aufgeklärten Absolutismus als rechtgeschichtliche Epoche Böhmens," *ibid.*, 135-146.

SCHASCHING, S. T. (1954), *Staatsbildung und Finanzentwicklung: Ein beitrag zur Geschichte des Östreichischen Staatskredites in der 2 Hälfte des 18 Jahrhundert*, Innsbruck.

SCHENK, H. G. (1953), "Austria," in Goodwin, A. (ed.), *The European Nobility in the Eighteenth Century*, London, pp. 102-117.

SCHWARTZ, H. F. (1943), *The Imperial Privy Council in the Seventeenth Century*, Cambridge, Mass.

VALJAVEC, F. (1945), *Der Josephinismus: Zur geistigen Entwicklung Österreichs im 18 und 19 Jahrhundert*, Munich.

U. Spain
(ESPECIALLY SIXTEENTH AND EIGHTEENTH CENTURIES)

ALCÁZAR, C. (1933), "Los hechos del despotismo ilustrado en España," *Bulletin of the International Committee of Historical Sciences*, V, 737-751.

DESDEVISES DU DEZERT, G. (1925), "La société espagnole au XVIIIième siècle," *Revue hispanique*, LXV, 225-321; LXVI, 321-654.

—— (1927), "Les institutions de l'Espagne," *Revue hispanique*, LXX, 1-554.

HAMILTON, E. J. (1932), "En période de révolution économique: La monnaie en Castille (1501–1650)," *Annales*, IV, 140-149, 242-256.

—— (1943), "Money and Economic Recovery in Spain under the First Bourbon," *Journal of Modern History*, XV, 192-206.

—— (1954), "The Decline of Spain," in Carus-Wilson, E. H. (ed.), *Essays in Economic History*, London, pp. 215-226.

KONETZKE, R. (1953), "Entrepreneurial Activities of Spanish and Portuguese Noblemen in Medieval Times," *Explorations in Entrepreneurial History*, VI, 115-121.

KÖNIGSBERGER, H. G. (1951), *The Government of Sicily under Philip II of Spain: A Study in the Practice of Empire*, London.

ORTIZ, A. D. (1955), *La sociedad española en el siglo XVIII*, Madrid.

PINTA LLORENTE, M. DE LA (1953), "El sentido de la cultura española en el siglo XVIII e intelectuales de la época," *Revista de estudios políticos*, LXVIII, 79-114.

SARRAILH, J. (1951), *La vie religieuse en Espagne à la fin du XVIIIième siècle*, Oxford.

—— (1954), *L'Espagne éclairée de la seconde moitié du XVIIIième siècle*, Paris.

—— (1955), "La crise spirituelle et économique de l'Espagne à la fin du 18ième siècle," *Journal of Modern History*, XXVII, 1-13.

SUÁREZ, F. (1950), *La crisis política del antiguo régimen en España*, Madrid.

TREVOR-DAVIES, R. (1939), *The Golden Century of Spain*, London.

—— (1957), *Spain in Decline (1621–1700)*, London.

V. *Sweden*
(ESPECIALLY SEVENTEENTH AND EIGHTEENTH CENTURIES)

ANDERSSON, I. (1956), *A History of Sweden*, London.

GOHLIN, P. (1953), "Entrepreneurial Activities of the Swedish Aristocracy," *Explorations in Entrepreneurial History*, VI, 43-63.

HATTON, R. M. (1957), "Scandinavia and the Baltic," in Lindsay, J. O. (ed.), *New Cambridge Modern History*, vol. VII, pp. 339-364.

ROBERTS, M. (1953), "Sweden," in Goodwin, A. (ed.), *The European Nobility in the Eighteenth Century*, London, pp. 136-153.

—— (1953-58), *Gustavus Adolphus*, London.

—— (1956), *The Military Revolution in Sweden (1560–1660)*, Belfast.

STAVENOW, L. (1933), "Der aufgeklärte Absolutismus des 18ten Jahrhunderts in Schweden," *Bulletin of the International Committee of Historical Sciences*, V, 762-772.

W. *Russia*
(ESPECIALLY SEVENTEENTH AND EIGHTEENTH CENTURIES)

BAIN, R. N. (1909), "Russia under Anne and Elizabeth," in *The Cambridge Modern History*, vol. VI, pp. 301-328.

BELOFF, M. (1953), "Russia," in Goodwin, A. (ed.), *The European Nobility in the Eighteenth Century*, London, pp. 172-189.

BRUNNER, O. (1953), "Europäisches und Russisches Bürgertum," *VSWG*, XL, 1-27.

ECK, A. (1959), "L'asservissement du paysan russe," in *Recueils de la société Jean Bodin*, II, 243-264.

FLORINSKY, M. T. (1953), *Russia: A History and an Interpretation*, New York.

LEROY-BEAULIEU, A. (1894), *The Empire of the Tsars*, New York.

LYASHCHENKO, P. I. (1949), *History of the National Economy of Russia to the 1917 Revolution*, New York.

MIRSKY, D. S. (1942), *Russia: A Social History*, London.

NOLDE, B. (1952-53), *La formation de l'empire russe*, Paris.

PARES, B. (1958), *A History of Russia*, London.

PORTAL, R. (1949), "Manufactures et classes sociales en Russie au XVIIIième siècle," *RH*, CCI, 161-185; CCII, 1-23.

—— (1950), *L'Oural au XVIIIième siècle*, Paris.

—— (1953), "La Russie industrielle à la veille de l'émancipation des serfs," *Études d'histoire moderne et contemporaine*, V, 147-183.

ROBINSON, G. T. (1949), *Rural Russia under the Old Regime*, New York.

ROSSOVSKY, H. (1953), "The Serf Entrepreneur in Russia," *Explorations in Entrepreneurial History*, VI, 207-239.

SACKE, G. (1932), "Katharina II im Kampf um Thron und Selbstherrschaft," *Archiv für Kulturgeschichte*, XXIII, 191-216.

——— (1938[a]), "Adel und Bürgertum in der Regierungszeit Katharinas II von Russland," *Revue belge de philologie et d'histoire*, XVII, 815-852.

——— (1938[b]), "Adel und Bürgertum in der gesetzgebenden Kommission Katharinas II von Russland," *Jahrbücher für Geschichte Osteuropas*, III, 408-417.

——— (1940), "Die Gesetzgebende Kommission Katharinas II," *Jahrbucher für Geschichte Europas*, II.

SUMNER, B. H. (1947), "Peter the Great," *History*, XXXII, 39-50.

——— (1949), *A Short History of Russia*, New York.

SZEFTEL, M. (1956), "Aspects of Feudalism in Russian History," in Coulborn, R. (ed.), *Feudalism in History*, Princeton, N.J., pp. 167-184.

VERNADSKII, G. (1954), *A History of Russia*, New Haven.

YOUNG, I. (1957), "Russia," in Lindsay, J. O. (ed.), *New Cambridge Modern History*, vol. VII, pp. 318-338.

X. Prussia

(ESPECIALLY SEVENTEENTH AND EIGHTEENTH CENTURIES)

BREYSIG, K. (1892), "Der brandenburgische Staatsanhalt in der zweiten Hälfte des 17ten Jahrhunderts," *Jahrbuch für Gesetzgebung, Verwaltung und Volkswirtschaft im Deutschen Reich*, XVI, 1-42, 449-526.

BRUFORD, W. H. (1935), *Germany in the Eighteenth Century*, Cambridge.

——— (1957), "The Organization and Rise of Prussia," in Lindsay, J. O. (ed.), *New Cambridge Modern History*, vol. VII, pp. 292-317.

CARSTEN, F. L. (1950), "The Great Elector and the Foundation of the Hohenzollern Despotism," *English Historical Review*, LXV, 175-203.

——— (1954), *The Origins of Prussia*, Oxford.

——— (1955), "Prussian Despotism at Its Height," *History*, XL, 42-67.

——— (1959), *Princes and Parliaments in Germany from the Fifteenth Century to the Eighteenth Century*, Oxford.

CRAIG, G. A. (1955), *The Politics of the Prussian Army (1640–1945)*, Oxford.

DORN, W. (1931), "The Prussian Bureaucracy in the Eighteenth Century," *Political Science Quarterly*, XLVI, 403-423.

DORWART, R. A. (1953), *The Administrative Reforms of Frederick William I of Prussia*, Cambridge, Mass.

FAY, S. B. (1946), *The Hohenzollern Household and Administration in the Sixteenth Century*, Northampton, Mass.

HARTUNG, F. (1941), *Studien zur Geschichte der Preussischen Verwaltung I: Vom 16ten Jahrhundert zum Zusammenbruch des alten Staates in Jahre 1806*, Berlin.

——— (1943), *ibid., II: Der Oberpräsident*, Berlin.

HINTZE, O. (1896[a]), "Die ständischen Elemente in dem Regierungssystem Friedrich des Grossen," *Forschungen zur brandenburgischen und preussischen Geschichte*, IX.

——— (1896[b]), "Preussische Reformbestrebungen vor 1806," *HZ*, LXXVI, 413-443.

——— (1898), "Zur Agrarpolitik Friedrichs des Grossen," *Forschungen zur brandenburgischen und preussischen Geschichte*, X, 275-309.

——— (1900), "Staat und Gesellschaft unter dem ersten König von Preussen," *Gesammelte Abhandlungen*, Leipzig, vol. III, pp. 347-452.

——— (1901), "Der österreichische und der preussische Beamtenstaat im 17ten und 18ten Jahrhundert," *HZ*, LXXXVI, 402-444.

——— (1902), "Staatenbildung und Verfassungsentwicklung," *HZ*, LXXXVIII, 1-21.

——— (1903), "Geist und Epochen der preussischen Geschichte," *Hohenzollern-Jahrbuch*, VII, 76-90.

——— (1906), *Staatsverfassung und Heeresverfassung*, Dresden.

——— (1907), "Die Entstehung der modernen Staatsministerien," *HZ*, XCIII, 53-111.

——— (1914), "Die Hohenzollern und der Adel," *HZ*, CXII, 494-524.

——— (1915), *Die Hohenzollern und ihr Werk*, Berlin.

——— (1931[a]), "Wesen und Wandlungen des modernen Staates," *Sitz. der preussischen Akademie der Wissenschaften, Phil.-hist. Klasse*, 790-810.

——— (1931[b]), "Kalvinismus und Staatsräson in Brandenburg zu Beginn des 17ten Jahrhunderts," *HZ*, CXLIV, 229-286.

——— (1932), "Die Entstehung des modernen Staatslebens," *Sitz. der preussischen Akademie der Wissenschaften, Phil.-hist. Klasse*, 925-931.

——— (1942), "Der Commissarius und seine Bedeutung in der allgemeinen Verfassungsgeschichte," in *Staat und Verfassung*, Leipzig, pp. 232-264.

——— (1943[a]), "Der preussische Staatsminister im 19ten Jahrhundert," in *Gesammelte Abhandlungen*, Leipzig, vol. III, 563-652.

——— (1943[b]), "Das preussische Militär und der Beamtenstaat im 18ten Jahrhundert," *ibid.*, vol. II, pp. 453-63.

——— (1943[c]), "Hof und Landesverwaltung in der Mark Brandenburg unter Joachim II," *ibid.*, pp. 53-63.

——— (1944), "Die Entstehung des modernen Staatslebens," *Forschungen und Fortschritte*, XX, 46-47.

HIRSCH, F. (1908), "Der Versuch einer Finanzreform in Brandenburg in den Jahren 1651–55," in *Festschrift F. G. Schmoller*, pp. 23-48.

KELLENBENZ, H. G. (1953), "German Aristocratic Enterpreneurship: Economic Activities of the Holstein Nobility in the Sixteenth and Seventeenth Centuries," *Explorations in Entrepreneurial History*, VI, 103-115.

KINGSLEY, D. (1935), "Central Administration in Brandenburg Prussia: Its Character and Development before Frederick the Great," in *Summary of Theses of Harvard Graduate School*, pp. 148-151.

KOCH, W. (1926), "Hof und Regierungsverfassung König Friedrich I von Preussen (1697–1710)," *Untersuchungen zur deutschen Staats- und Rechtsgeschichte*, CXXXVI, Heft 136.

ROSENBERG, H. (1943-44), "The Rise of the Junkers in Brandenburg Prussia (1410–1653)," *American Historical Review*, XLIX, 1-23, 221-243.

——— (1958), *Bureaucracy, Aristocracy and Autocracy: The Prussian Experience (1660–1815)*, Cambridge, Mass.

SCHMOLLER, G. VON (1870), "Der preussische Beamtenstand unter Friedrich Wilhelm," *Preussische Jahrbücher*, XXV, 148-172.

——— (1898), *Umrisse und Untersuchungen zur Verfassungs-und Wirtschaftsgeschichte besonders des Preussischen Staates im 17ten und 18ten Jahrhundert*, Leipzig, especially pp. 106-246, 289-313.

——— (1910), *The Mercantile System and Its Historical Significance*, London.

——— (1921), *Preussische Verfassungs-, Vervaltungs-, und Finanzgeschichte*, Berlin.

SCHROTTER, R. VON (1914), "Das preussische Offizierkorps unter dem ersten König von Preussen," *Forschungen zur brandenburgischen und preussischen Geschichte*, XXVII, 97-167.

Y. France
(ESPECIALLY SEVENTEENTH AND EIGHTEENTH CENTURIES)

ANTOINE, M. (1951), "Les comités de ministres sous le règne de Louis XIV," *Revue historique de droit français et étranger,* XXIX, 193-230.

ARDASCHEFF, P. (1909), *Les intendants de province sous Louis XVI,* Paris.

ARTZ, F. B. (1937), "Les débuts de l'éducation technique en France (1500–1700)," *Revue d'histoire moderne,* XII, 469-519.

BAMFORD, P. W. (1957), "Entrepreneurship in Seventeenth and Eighteenth Century France," *Explorations in Entrepreneurial History,* IX, 204-213.

BARBER, E. G. (1955), *The Bourgeoisie in Eighteenth Century France,* Princeton, N.J.

BLOCH, M. (1922), *Les caractères originaux: La ville et la campagne au XVIIième siècle,* Paris.

—— (1930), "La lutte pour l'individualisme agraire dans la France du XVIIIième siècle," *Annales,* II, 329-383, 511-551.

—— (1936), "Sur le passé de la noblesse française," *Annales,* VIII, 366-378.

BOUTERON, M. (1937), "La fonctionnement du conseil du roi Louis XVI, expliqué par l'un de ses sécretaires," *Revue d'histoire moderne,* XII, 325-337.

CARRÉ, H. (1890), "La noblesse de robe au temps de Louis XV," *Bulletin de la faculté des lettres de Poitiers,* pp. 344-355, 385-394.

—— (1920), *La noblesse de France et l'opinion publique au XVIIIième siècle,* Paris.

CHENON, E. (1929), *Histoire générale du droit français,* Paris.

COBBAN, A. (1950), "The 'Parlements' of France in the Eighteenth Century," *History,* XXXV, 64-80.

—— (1957[a]), "The Enlightenment," in Lindsay, J. O. (ed.), *New Cambridge Modern History,* vol. VII, ch. V.

—— (1957[b]), "The Decline of Divine-Right Monarchy in France," *ibid.,* ch. X.

COLE, C. W. (1939), *Colbert and a Century of French Mercantilism,* New York.

—— (1943), *French Mercantilism (1683–1700),* New York.

COORNAERT, E. (1941), *Les corporations en France avant 1789,* Paris.

—— (1952), "L'état et les villes à la fin du moyen-âge: La politique d'Anvers," *RH,* CCVII, 185-210.

D'AVENEL, G. (1901), *La noblesse française sous Richelieu,* Paris.

DOUCET, R. (1948), *Les institutions de la France au XVIième siècle,* Paris.

DUPONT-FERRIER, G. (1902), *Les officiers royaux des bailliages et sénéchaussées et les institutions monarchiques locales,* Paris.

—— (1932), "Les institutions de la France sous le règne de Charles V," *Journal des savants,* pp. 385-400, 433-445.

DUR, P. (1945), "The Right of Taxation in the Political Theory of the French Religious Wars," *Journal of Modern History,* XVII, 289-303.

EGRET, J. (1952), "L'aristocratie parlementaire française à la fin de l'Ancien Régime," *RH,* CCVIII, 1-15.

—— (1955), "Les origines de la Révolution en Bretagne (1788–1789)," *RH,* CCXIII, 189-215.

FORD, F. L. (1953), *Robe and Sword,* Cambridge, Mass.

FRÉVILLE, H. (1937), "Notes sur les subdélégués généraux et subdélégués de l'intendance de Bretagne au XVIIIième siècle," *Revue d'histoire moderne,* XII, 408-448.

GIRARDET, R. (1953), *La société militaire dans la France contemporaine (1815–1939),* Paris.

GIRAUD, M., (1952), "Crise de conscience et d'autorité a la fin du règne de Louis XIV," *Annales,* XXIV, 172-190, 293-302.

GÖHRING, M. (1938), *Amterkauflichkeit im Ancien Régime,* Berlin.

—— (1947), *Weg und Sieg der Modernen Staatsidee in Frankreich*, Tübingen.

GOUBERT, P. (1953), Review of Swart, K. W. (1949), *Annales*, XXV, 210-214.

—— (1956), "The French Peasantry of the Seventeenth Century: A Regional Example," *Past and Present*, X, 55-77.

GRAND, R. (1941), "Justice criminelle: Procédure et peines dans les villes aux XIIIième et XIVième siècles," *Bibliothèque de l'école de Chartes*, CII, 51-108.

GRASSBY, R. B. (1960), "Social Status and Commercial Enterprise under Louis XIV," *Economic History Review*, XIII, 19-38.

HANOTAUX, G. (1886), *Etudes historiques sur le XVIième et le XVIIième siècle en France*, Paris.

HARTLEY, T. (1933), "The Intendancy in New France," in *Summary of Theses of Harvard Graduate School*.

HAUSER, H. (1944), *La pensée et l'action économiques du Cardinal Richelieu*, Paris.

HERLANT, C. (1933), "Projets de création d'une banque royale," *Revue d'histoire moderne*, VIII, 143-160.

JEGADEN, R. (1951), "La communauté des notaires au châtelet de Paris au XVIIième siècle," *Revue historique de droit français et étranger*, XXIX, 352-382.

KING, E. (1949), *Science and Rationalism in the Government of Louis XIV (1661–1633)*, Baltimore.

KÖNIGSBERGER, H. G. (1955), "The Organisation of Revolutionary Parties in France and the Netherlands during the Sixteenth Century," *Journal of Modern History*, XXVII, 335-351.

KOSSMAN, E. H. (1954), *La Fronde*, Leiden.

LEFÈBVRE, G. (1929), "La place de la Révolution dans l'histoire agraire de la France," *Annales*, I, 506-519.

LEONARD, E. (1948), "La question sociale dans l'armée française au XVIIIième siècle," *Annales*, XX, 135-149.

LÉVY-BRUHL, H. (1933), "La noblesse de France et le commerce à la fin de l'ancien régime," *Revue d'histoire moderne*, VIII, 209-235.

LOUGH, J. (1954), *An Introduction to Seventeenth Century France*, London.

—— (1960), *An Introduction to Eighteenth Century France*, London.

MATHIEZ, A. (1925), "Un club révolutionnaire inconnu: Le club de la Réunion," *RH*, CXLVIII, 63-72.

MEUVRET, J. (1947), "Circulation monétaire et utilisation économique de la monnaie dans la France du XVIième et du XVIIIième siècles," *Études d'histoire moderne et contemporaine*, I, 14-28.

MOUSNIER, R. (1938), "La vénalité des charges au XVIIième siècle: Les offices de la famille normande D'Amfreville," *RH*, CLXXXIII, 10-27.

—— (1947), "Le conseil du roi de la mort de Henri V au gouvernement personnel de Louis XIV," *Études d'histoire modern et contemporaine*, I, 29-67.

—— (1948), *La vénalité des offices sous Henri IV et Louis XIII*, Rouen.

—— (1951), "L'évolution des finances publiques en France et en Angleterre pendant les guerres de la ligue d'Augsburg et de la succession d'Espagne," *RH*, CCV, 1-23.

—— (1955), "L'opposition politique bourgeoise à la fin du XVIième siècle et au début du XVIIIième siècle," *RH*, CCXIII, 1-20.

—— (1958), "Recherches sur les soulèvements populaires en France avans la Fronde," *Revue d'histoire moderne et contemporaine*, V, 81-113.

NORMAND, C. (1908), *La bourgeoisie française au XVIIIième siècle*, Paris.

NÜRNBERGER, R. (1949), *Die Politisierung des französischen Protestantismus*, Tübingen.

OLIVIER-MARTIN, F. (1933), "Les pratiques traditionnelles de la royauté française et le despotisme éclairé," *Bulletin of the International Committee of Historical Sciences*, V, 701-713.

—— (1937), "Le déclin et la suppression des corps en France au XVIIIième siècle," in

Lousse, E. (ed.), *L'organisation corporative du moyen-âge à la fin de l'ancien régime*, Louvain, pp. 151-163.

PAGÈS, G. (1928), *La monarchie de l'Ancien Régime en France*, Paris.

—— (1932[a]), "La vénalité des offices dans l'ancienne France," *RH*, CLXIX, 477-495.

—— (1932[b]), "Essai sur l'évolution des institutions administratives en France," *Revue d'histoire moderne*, VII, 8-57, 113-137.

—— (1937), "Le conseil du roi sous Louis XIII, *ibid.*, XII, 293-324.

—— (1938), "Le conseil du roi et la vénalité des charges pendant les premières années du ministère de Richelieu," *RH*, CLXXXII, 245-282.

PRESTWICH, M. (1957), "The Making of Absolute Monarchy (1559–1683)," in Wallace-Hadrill, J. M., and McManner, J. (eds.), *France: Government and Society*, London, pp. 105-133.

RÉBILLON, A. (1928), "Les états de Bretagne et les progrès de l'autonomie provinciale au XVIIIième siècle," *RH*, CLIX, 261.

REINHARD, M. (1956), "Élite et noblesse dans la seconde moitié du XVIIIième siècle," *Revue d'histoire moderne et contemporaine*, III, 5-37.

RICOMMARD, J. (1937), "Les subdélégues des intendants jusqu' à leur érection en titre d'office," *Revue d'histoire moderne*, XII, 338-407.

—— (1948), "La suppression et la liquidation des offices des subdélégués," *Revue historique de droit français et étranger*, XXVI, 36-95.

RUSSEL, J. (1954), "The Third Estate in the Estates General of Pontoise, 1561," *Speculum*, XXIX, 460-476.

SAGNAC, P. (1945), *La société et la monarchie absolue (1661–1715)*, Paris, especially pp. 59-63.

—— (1946), *La révolution des idées et des moeurs et le déclin de l'ancien régime (1715–1788)*, Paris.

—— (1951), *La composition des Etats généraux et de l'Assemblée nationale (1789)*, *RH*, CCVI, 8-28.

SCLECHTER, E. (1951), "La monnaie en France au 16ième siècle: Droit public, droit privé," *Revue historique de droit français et étranger*, XXIX, 500-521.

SÉRIEUX, P. (1938), "Le parlemente de Paris et la surveillance des maisons d'aliénés et de correctionnaires aux XVIIième et XVIIIième siècles," *ibid.*, XVII, 404-459.

SIX, G. (1929), "Fallait-il quatre quartiers de noblesse pour être officier à la fin de l'Ancien Régime?" *Revue d'histoire moderne*, IV, 47-56.

STRAYER, J. R., and TAYLOR, C. H. (1939), *Studies in Early French Taxation*, Cambridge, Mass.

SWART, K. W. (1949), *Sale of Offices in the Seventeenth Century*, The Hague.

VAISSIÈRE, P. DE (1903), *Gentilshommes compagnards de l'ancienne France*, Paris.

VIARD, P. P. (1927), "La dime en France au XVIIIième siècle," *RH*, CLVI, 241.

ZELLER, G. (1933), "La monarchie d'ancien régime et les frontières naturelles," *Revue d'histoire moderne*, VIII, 305-333.

—— (1939), "Gouverneurs de province au XVIième siècle," *RH*, CLXXXL, 225.

—— (1944), "De quelques institutions mal connues du XVIième siècle," *RH*, CXCIV, 193-289.

—— (1947), "L'administration monarchique avant les intendants; parlements et gouverneurs," *RH*, CXVII, 180-215.

—— (1948), *Les institutions de la France au XVIième siècle*, Paris.

—— (1952), "La vie économique de l'Europe au XVIième siècle," (mimeo.), in *Les cours de Sorbonne*, Paris.

Z. England

ASHLEY, M. (1952), *England in the Seventeenth Century*, London.

ASHTON, T. S. (1955[a]), "Le développment de l'industrie et du commerce anglais au XVIIIième siècle," in *Relazioni del congresso internazionale di scienze storiche*, Rome, vol. IV, pp. 275-284.

——— (1955[b]), *An Economic History of England in the Eighteenth Century*, London.

AYLMER, G. E. (1961), *The King's Servants: The Civil Service of Charles I*, London.

BELOFF, M. (1938), *Public Order and Popular Disturbances, 1660–1714*, Oxford.

BLACK, J. B. (1936), *Reign of Elizabeth*, Oxford.

BRIGGS, A. (1956), "Middle-Class Consciousness in English Politics (1780–1846)," *Past and Present*, IX, 65-74.

BROCK, W. R. (1957), "Monarchy and Administration, the English Inspiration," in Lindsay, J. O. (ed.), *The New Cambridge Modern History*, vol. VII, pp. 160-163.

BROWNING, A. (1935), *The Age of Elizabeth*, London.

——— (1948), "Parties and Party Organisation in the Reign of Charles II," *Transactions of the Royal Historical Society*, XXX, 21-37.

BURRAGE, C. (1912), *Early English Dissenters in the Light of Recent Research (1550–1641)*, Cambridge.

BUTTERFIELD, H. (1950), *George III, Lord North and the People*, London.

CAMPBELL, M. L. (1945), *The English Yeoman under Elizabeth and the Early Stuarts*, London.

CHRISTIE, J. R. (1956), "Economical Reform and 'The Influence of the Crown' (1770)," *Cambridge Historical Journal*, XII, 144-154.

CLAPHAM, J. H. (1947), *The Bank of England: A History*, Cambridge.

CLARK, G. (1955), *The Later Stuarts (1660–1714)*, Oxford.

DALE, R. W. (1907), *History of English Congregationalism*, London.

DAVIES, R. W. (1937), *The Early Stuarts (1603–1660)*, Oxford.

——— (1955), *The Restoration of Charles II (1658–1660)*, Oxford.

DES LONGRAIS, F. J. (1956), "Le droit criminel anglais au moyen âge," *Revue historique de droit français et étranger*, XXXIV, 391-435.

ELTON, G. R. (1953), *The Tudor Revolution in Government*, London.

EYCK, E. (1950), *Pitt versus Fox, Father and Son*, London.

FEILING, K. (1924), *A History of the Tory Party (1640–1714)*, Oxford.

FISHER, F. J. (1954), "Commercial Trends and Policy in Sixteenth-Century England," in Carus-Wilson, E. M. (ed.), *Essays in Economic History*, London, pp. 152-172.

FRANK, J. (1955), *The Levellers*, Cambridge, Mass.

GARDINER, S. R. (1884), *History of England (1603–1642)*, London.

——— (1894-97), *History of the Great Civil War (1643–1649)*, London.

——— (1897-1901), *History of the Commonwealth and Protectorate (1649–1660)*, London.

HABAKKUK, H. J. (1953), "Economic Functions of English Landowners in the Seventeenth and Eighteenth Centuries," *Explorations in Entrepreneurial History*, VI, 92-103.

HALLER, W. (1955), *Liberty and Reformation in the Puritan Revolution*, New York.

HARRISON, D. (1953), *Tudor England*, London.

HILL, C. (1955), *The English Revolution*, London.

HOLDSWORTH, W. (1938), *History of English Law*, London.

HOSKINS, W. G. (1955), "English Agriculture in the Seventeenth and Eighteenth Centuries," in *Relazioni del congresso inter-*

nazionale di scienze storiche, Rome, vol. IV, pp. 205-226.

HUGHES, E. (1952), *North County Life in the Eighteenth Century: The North-East (1700–1750)*, Oxford.

JORDAN, W. K. (1932), *The Development of Religious Toleration in England to the Death of Queen Elizabeth*, London.

KEMP, B. (1957), *King and Commons (1660–1832)*, London.

LIPSON, E. (1929-30), "England in the Age of Mercantilism," *Journal of Economic and Business History*, II.

——— (1943), *The Economic History of England: The Age of Mercantilism*, London.

MACKIE, J. D. (1952), *The Earlier Tudors*, Oxford.

MANNING, B. (1956), "The Nobles, the People and the Constitution," *Past and Present*, IX, 42-64.

MATHEW, D. (1948), *The Social Structure in Caroline England*, Oxford.

MITCHELL, W. M. (1957), *Rise of the Revolutionary Party in the English House of Commons, 1603–1629*, Oxford.

MORTON, A. L., and TATE, G. (1956), *The British Labour Movement (1770–1920)*, London.

MOUSNIER, R. (1951), "L'évolution des finances publiques en France et en Angleterre pendant les guerres de la ligue d'Augsbourg et de la succession d'Espagne," *RH*, CCV, 1-23.

NAMIER, L. B. (1929), *The Structure of Politics at the Accession of George III*, London.

——— (1930), *England in the Age of the American Revolution*, London.

——— (1952), *Monarchy and the Party System*, Oxford.

NEALE, J. E. (1949), *The Elizabethan House of Commons*, London.

——— (1953), *Elizabeth I and Her Parliaments (1559–1581)*, London.

NEF, J. U. (1940), *Industry and Government in France and England (1540–1640)*, Philadelphia.

NOTESTEIN, W. (1954), *The English People on the Eve of Colonization (1603–1630)*, New York.

OGG, D. (1934), *England in the Reign of Charles II*, Oxford.

——— (1955), *England in the Reign of James II and William III*, London.

OTWAY-RUTHVEN, J. (1936), "The King's Secretary in the Fifteenth Century," *Transactions of the Royal Historical Society*, XIX, 81-100.

PARES, R. (1953), *King George III and the Politicians*, Oxford.

——— (1957), *Limited Monarchy in Great Britain in the Eighteenth Century*, London.

PICKTHORN, K. W. M. (1949), *Early Tudor Government*, Cambridge.

PLUMB, J. H. (1950), *England in the Eighteenth Century*, London.

POLLARD, A. F. (1926), *Factors in Modern History*, New York.

POSTAN, M. M. (1930), "Private Financial Instruments in Medieval England," *VSWG*, XXIII, 26-75.

RICHARDS, R. D. (1929), *The Early History of Banking in England*, London.

RICHARDSON, W. C. (1952), *Tudor Chamber Administration (1485–1547)*, Baton Rouge.

ROWSE, A. L. (1951), *The England of Elizabeth*, London.

RUPP, E. G. (1947), *Studies in the Making of the English Protestant Tradition*, Cambridge.

SCHENK, W. (1948), *The Concern for Social Justice in the Puritan Revolution*, London.

STONE, L. (1947), "State Control in Sixteenth Century England," *Economic History Review*, XVII, 103-120.

SYKES, N. (1934), *Church and State in the Eighteenth Century*, Cambridge.

TAWNEY, R. H. (1912), *The Agrarian Problem in the Sixteenth Century*, London and New York.

——— (1926), *Religion and the Rise of Capitalism*, New York.

——— (1954), "The Rise of the Gentry

(1558–1640)," in Carus-Wilson, E. M. (ed.), *Essays in Economic History*, London, pp. 173-214.

THOMPSON, M. A. (1938), *A Constitutional History of England (1642 to 1801)*, London.

TREVELYAN, G. M. (1930-34), *England under Queen Anne*, London.

—— (1944), *English Social History*, London.

TREVOR-ROPER, H. R. (1953), *The Gentry (1540–1640)*, London.

VINCENT, V. A. L. (1950), *The State and School Education (1648–60) in England and Wales*, London.

WALCOTT, R. (1956), *English Politics in the Early Eighteenth Century*, Oxford.

WEDGWOOD, C. V. (1955), *The Great Rebellion: The King's Peace (1637–1641)*, London.

WENHAM, R. B. (1956), "The Tudor Revolution in Government," *English History Review*, LXXI, 92-95.

WHITLEY, W. T. (1923), *A History of British Baptists*, London.

WILLIAMS, B. (1939), *The Whig Supremacy (1714–60)*, Oxford.

WILLIAMS, C. H. (1935), *The Making of the Tudor Despotism*, Toronto.

WILLIAMS, O. C. (1955), *The Clerical Organization of the House of Commons (1661–1850)*, Oxford.

WILLIAMSON, J. A. (1953), *The Tudor Age*, London.

ZAGORIN, P. (1954), *A History of Political Thought in the English Revolution*, London.

ZEEVELD, W. G. (1948), *Foundations of Tudor Policy*, Cambridge, Mass.

DATE DUE

FACULTY

MAY 1 4 '76

DEC 1 6 1998

GAYLORD

PRINTED IN U.S.A.